WEBSTER'S DICTIONARY

W9-BNF-386

Printed in USA

Staff

Vicki Nichols
Kathleen Flickinger
Cindy Carter
Marsha Tischner

Rules of Spelling

(1.) The most common way to form the plural of a noun is to add an *s*.
(example: *girl, girls; town, towns; hall, halls*).

(2.) The plural of nouns which end in *y* following a consonant are formed by dropping the *y* and adding *ies*.
(example: *country, countries; baby, babies; family, families*).

(3.) The pluarl of nouns which end in *y* following a vowel are formed by adding an *s*.
(example: *toy, toys; boy, boys; attorney, attorneys*).

In this quick reference dictionary, a double dash (--) indicates a hyphenated word, and a single dash (-) indicates syllabication.

Each entry is bold type followed by the part of speech in *italics*. Sub-entries are indicated in bold type after the main definition.

A, a The first letter of the English alphabet; the highest grade, meaning excellent or best.

aard-vark n.

A burrowing African animal, which resembles the anteater and feeds on ants and termites.

ab-a-ca n. A plant from the Philippines whose leafstalks are the source of Manila hemp.

a-back adv. Unexpectedly; by surprise; startled.

ab-a-cus n. A frame holding parallel rods with beads, used for manual computation, especially by the Chinese.

a-baft adv. On or toward the stern, aft, or hind part of a ship.

a-ban-don v. To yield utterly; to desert; to forsake; to withdraw protection, support, or help. **abandoned** adj., **abandonment** n., **abandonedly** adv.

a-base v. To lower in rank, prestige, position, or estimation; to cast down, to humble.

a-base-ment n. A state of depression, degradation, or humiliation.

a-bash v. To embarrass; to disconcert; to make ashamed or uneasy.

a-bate v. To deduct; to make less; to reduce in quantity, value, force, or intensity. **-er** n., **abatable**, **abated** adj.

ab-be n. A French title given to a priest.

ab-bey n. An abbey church, a monastery, or convent.

ab-bre-vi-ate v. To make briefer; to abridge; to shorten; to reduce to a briefer form, as a word or phrase.

ab-bre-vi-a-tion n. A shortened form of a word or phrase, used to represent the full form. **-or** n., **-ory** adj.

ab-di-cate v. To relinquish power or responsibility formally. **abdication** n.

ab-do-men n. That part of the human body that lies between the thorax and the pelvis. **abdominal** adj., **-ally** adv.

ab-duct v. To carry away wrongfully, as by force or fraud; to kidnap; to draw aside or away. **-or**, **abduction** n.

a-beam adv. At right angles to the keel of a ship.

a-bed adv. In bed; on a bed; to bed.

ab-er-rant adj. Straying from the right way or usual course. **aberrantly** adv.

a-bet v. To incite, encourage, or assist.

ab-hor v. To dislike intensely; to loathe. **abhorrer**, **abhorrence** n.

a-bide v. To tolerate; to bear; to remain; to last; to conform to; to comply with.

a-bil-i-ty n. State of being able; possession of qualities necessary; competence; skill.

ab-ject adj. Sunk to a low condition; groveling; mean; despicable. **abjection**, **abjectness** n.

ab-jure v. To renounce solemnly or on oath; to repudiate; to forswear. **-er** n.

a-blaze adv. On fire; brilliantly lighted up; very excited; angry.

a-ble adj. Having sufficient ability; capable or talented. **-ness** n., **-y** adv.

ab-ne-gate v. To deny; to refuse or renounce; to relinquish or surrender.

ab-nor-mal adj. Not normal; irregular; unnatural. **-ity** n., **abnormally** adv.

a-board adv. On board a ship or other vehicle.

a-bode n. A dwelling place; home.

a-bol-ish v. To put an end to; to annul. **abolisher**, **-ment** n., **abolishable** adj.

a-bom-i-na-ble adj. Detestable; loathsome. **-bly** adv., **abominableness** n.

a-bort v. To terminate or cause to terminate an operation or procedure before completion.

a-bor-tion n. Induced termination of pregnancy before the fetus can survive; something malformed.

a-bound v. To have plenty; to exist in large numbers.

a-bout adv. Approximately; on every side, here and there.

a-bove adv. Higher or greater than; in or at a higher place.

a-brade v. To wear or rub off; to grate off; abrasive, scouring.

ab-re-ac-tion n. To eliminate a bad experience by reliving it.

a-breast adv. or adj. Side by side.

a-bridge v. To make smaller, fewer, or shorter while maintaining essential contents. **abridger** n., **abridgable**, **abridgeable** adj.

a-broad adv. Widely; in many places; outside one's country; at large.

ab-ro-gate v. To cancel; to put an end to; to repeal. **abrogation** n., **abrogable**, **abrogative** adj.

ab-rupt adj. Happening or coming suddenly with no warning. **abruptness** n., **abruptly** adv.

ab-scess n. An infected place in the body which becomes sore and swollen and contains pus. **abscessed** adj.

ab-scind v. To cut off; to sever; to pare away; to separate.

ab-scond v. To remove oneself, as to flee from justice. **absconder** n.

ab-sence n. Being absent, not present; inattention.

ab-sent adj. Not present; away; lacking; nonexistent. **absently** adv.

ab-so-lute adj. Unconditional; without restraint; perfect. **absoluteness** n., **absolutely** adv.

ab-solve v. To set free or release from duties, guilt, or penalty. **absolver** n., **absolvable** adj.

ab-sorb v. To take in; to take up the full attention; to engage one's whole attention. **absorbability** n., **absorbable** adj.

ab-sorp-tion n. The act of giving full attention or having great interest.

ab-stain v. To refrain from doing something. **abstainer** n.

ab-ste-mi-ous adj. Showing moderation in the use of drink and food.

abstemiousness *n.*, **abstemiously** *adv.*

ab-sten-tion *n.* The act of holding off from using or doing something.

ab-stract *v.* To remove from, reduce, or summarize. **abstractedness** *n.*

ab-struse *adj.* Hard or difficult to understand. **-ness** *n.*, **abstrusely** *adv.*

ab-surd *adj.* Contrary to reason; clearly untrue or unreasonable. **absurdity**, **absurdness** *n.*

a-bun-dance *n.* Ample supply; plenty; amount more than enough.

a-buse *v.* To use in an improper or wrong way. *n.* Improper treatment.

a-but *v.* To border; to touch at one end.

a-but-ment *n.* Support at the end of an arch or bridge.

a-bys-mal *adj.* Immeasurably deep or low.

a-byss *n.* A deep crack or gap in the earth. **abyssal** *adj.*

a-ca-cia *n.* Thorny tree or shrub of warm climates.

a-can-thus *n.* A prickly plant, native to the Mediterranean region.

a-cap-pel-la *adj.* Singing without instrumental accompaniment.

a-cat-a-lec-tic *adj.* Not stopping short; having the complete number or syllables, in a line of verse.

ac-cede *v.* To consent; to agree; to arrive at a certain condition or state.

ac-cel-er-ate *v.* To make run or work faster; to increase the speed. **-tion** *n.*

ac-cent *n.* An effort to make one syllable more prominent than the others.

ac-cept *v.* To take what is given; to believe to be true; to agree. **accepter**, **acceptor** *n.*

ac-cept-able *adj.* Satisfactory; proper; good enough. **acceptableness**, **acceptability** *n.*, **acceptably** *adv.*

ac-cep-tance *n.* Approval or belief; an accepting or being accepted.

ac-cess *n.* Admission, entrance; attack. **accessibility** *n.*, **accessible** *adj.*

ac-ces-sion *n.* In Computer Science, the act of obtaining data from storage.

ac-ces-si-ble *adj.* Easy access or approach.

ac-ces-sory *n.*, *pl.* **-les** Aiding or contributing.

ac-ci-dent *n.* A happening that is not planned or expected. **accidental** *adj.*, **accidentally** *adv.*

ac-claim *v.* To greet with strong approval or loud applause; to hail or cheer.

ac-cli-mate *v.* To get used to a different climate or new surroundings.

ac-co-lade *n.* Award; praise; ceremony used in conferring knighthood.

ac-com-mo-date *v.* To give room or lodging; to make fit; to adjust.

ac-com-mo-dat-ing *adj.* Ready to help; willing to please; obliging.

ac-com-pa-ni-ment *n.* Something that goes well with another.

ac-com-pa-nist *n.* A person who plays a musical accompaniment.

ac-com-pa-ny *v.* To be together with; to go along with.

ac-com-plice *n.* Companion who helps another break the law.

ac-com-plish *v.* To perform; to carry out; to complete; to do.
accomplisher *n.*, **accomplishable** *adj.*

ac-com-plish-ment *n.* Finish; completion.

ac-cord *n.* Harmony; agreement. *v.* To grant or award. **accordance** *n.*

ac-cord-ing-ly *adv.* In a way that is proper and fitting.

ac-cost *v.* To come close to and to speak first in an unfriendly manner.

ac-count *n.* A description; a statement of debts and credits in money transactions; a record; a report. **account** *n.*

ac-coun-tan-cy *n.* The profession of an accountant.

ac-cred-it *v.* To authorize someone; to give official power. **accreditation** *n.*

ac-crete *v.* To grow together or join. **accretive** *adj.*

ac-crue *v.* To result naturally; to increase at certain times.

ac-cu-mu-late *v.* To collect or gather over a period of time; to pile up. **-or** *n.*

ac-cu-ra-cy *n.* **-cies** Exactness; precision; the fact of being accurate or without mistakes.

ac-cu-rate *adj.* Without mistakes or errors; careful and exact; correct.

ac-curs-ed *adj.* Sure to end badly; under a curse; unpleasant or annoying; very bad. **accursedness** *n.*, **accursedly** *adv.*

ac-cu-sa-tion *n.* A charge that a person is guilty of breaking the law.

ac-cu-sa-tive *adj.* Relating to the direct object of a preposition or of a verb.

ac-cuse *v.* To find fault with; to blame; to charge someone with doing wrong or breaking the law. **accuser** *n.*

ac-custom *v.* To familiarize by habit.

ac-custom-ed *adj.* Customary; usual.

ac-e-tate *n.* Salt formed by union of acetic acid with a base, used in making rayon and plastics.

a-ce-tic acid *n.* The main ingredient of vinegar; a sour, colorless liquid that has a sharp smell.

a-cet-y-lene *n.* A highly inflammable, poisonous, colorless gas that burns brightly with a hot flame, used in blowtorches for cutting metal.

ache *v.* To give or have a dull, steady pain; to want very much; to long for.

a-chieve *v.* To set or reach by trying hard; to do; to succeed in doing; to accomplish. **achiever** *n.*

a-chieve-ment *n.* Something achieved by work, courage, or skill.

A-chil-les ten-don *n.*

The tendon that connects the heelbone and calf muscles.

achro-ma-tism *n.* A quality of giving of images practically free from extraneous colors.

ac-id *n.* A chemical compound containing hydrogen that forms a salt when combined with a base; dissolves in water, has a very sour taste, makes lit-mus paper turn red.

ac-id head *n.* A user of the drug LSD.

a-cid-i-ty *n.* Condition or quality of being acid.

acid rain *n.* Acid precipitation that falls as rain.

a-cid-u-late *v.* To become or make somewhat acid.

ack-ack *n.* Antiaircraft fire.

ac-know-ledge *v.* To admit the truth, existence or reality. -ment *n.*, -able *adj.*

ac-me *n.* The highest point of attainment; peak.

ac-ne *n.* A common inflammatory disease of young people in which pimples continue to appear on the body.

ac-o-lyte *n.* An altar boy or someone who assists a priest at Mass.

ac-o-nite *n.* A poisonous plant with flowers resembling hoods.

a-corn squash *n.* An acorn-shaped squash with yellow flesh and a ridged rind.

a-cot-y-ledon *n.* A plant as a fern or moss, which does not have seed leaves.

a-cous-tic *adj.* Having to do with sound or the sense of hearing; the sense of sound; absorbing sound. acoustical *n.*, acoustically *adv.*

a-cous-tics *n.* The scientific study of sound; total effect of sound, especially in an enclosed space. acoustician *n.*

ac-quaint *v.* To make familiar; to let know, to make aware; to inform.

ac-quaint-ance *n.* A person whom one knows but not as a close friend. acquaintanceship *n.*

ac-qui-esce *v.* To agree without arguing; to comply without protest. -ent *adj.*

ac-quire *v.* To secure control or possession; to become the owner. acquirer *n.*

ac-quire-ment *n.* The act of acquiring something, as a skill gained by learning.

ac-quir-ed im-mun-ity *n.* Immunity against diseases that one develops during a lifetime.

ac-qui-si-tion *n.* Something that is acquired; the act of acquiring.

ac-quis-i-tive *adj.* Eager to gain and possess things; greedy.

ac-quit *v.* To rule that a person accused of something is not guilty; to conduct oneself; to behave. acquittal *n.*

a-cre *n.* A measurement of land that equals 43,560 square feet.

ac-rid *adj.* Having a sharp, bitter, or irritating taste or smell. acridity, acridness *n.*, acridly *adv.*

ac-ri-mo-ni-ous *adj.* Sharp or bitter in speech or manner. acrimoniousness *n.*, acrimoniously *adv.*

ac-ro-bat *n.* One who is skilled in gymnastic feats. acrobatic *adj.*

ac-ro-pho-bi-a *n.* Unusual fear of heights.

a-cross *prep.* From side to side; to one side from the other.

a-cros-tic *n.* A series of lines or a poem in which certain letters in each line form a name or motto. -ally *adv.*

a-cryl-ic *n.* Relating to or of acrylic acid or its derivatives.

acrylic fiber *n.* A fiber which is made of chemicals, used in making fabrics.

ac-ry-lo-ni-trile *n.* A liquid organic compound used to make acrylic fibers and rubber.

act *n.* Doing something; a thing done; deed; an action; a showing of emotion which is not real or true; a law; decree; one of the main parts of a play, opera, etc. -ability *n.*, -able *adj.*

ac-tin-o-gen *n.* An element which is radioactive.

ac-tion *n.* The process of doing or acting; an effect produced by something; a lawsuit.

ac-ti-vate *v.* To put into action. -tion *n.*

ac-tive *adj.* Working; full of action; busy; lively; quick. activeness *n.*, -ly *adv.*

ac-tiv-ism *n.* A practice based on direct action to affect changes in government and social conditions.

ac-tiv-ity *n.* Being active, in motion; normal power of body or mind.

ac-tor *n.* A person who acts in movies, plays, television shows, etc.

ac-tress *n.* A female actor.

ac-tu-al *adj.* Acting or existing in fact or reality; as it really is, true, real.

ac-tu-ate *v.* To put into motion or action.

ac-u-punc-ture *n.* A traditional Chinese means of treating some illnesses or of lessening pain by putting thin needles into certain parts of the body.

a-cute *adj.* Extremely sensitive; sharp and quick, as pain; shrewd. acuteness *n.*, acutely *adv.*

ad-age *n.* A proverb; a wise or true saying.

a-da-gi-o *adj.* Term used in music to tell how fast a piece should be played.

ad-a-mant *adj.* Standing firm; not giving in easily; unyielding. adamantly *adv.*

a-dapt *v.* To fit or suit; to change oneself as to adjust to new conditions. -ness *n.*

ad-ap-ta-tion *n.* An act of changing so as to fit or become suitable.

add *v.* To join or put something with another so that there will be more; to cause an increase. add up *v.* To make sense; to be reasonable. add up to *v.* To indicate; to mean. addable, addible *adj.*

ad-dax *n.* An African antelope with spiral twisted horns.

ad-der *n.*

A common poisonous snake found in America and Europe.

ad-dict *n.* A person with a habit so strong that he cannot easily give it up. addiction *n.*, addicted *v.*

ad-di-tion *n.* An adding of numbers to find their total; the act of joining one thing to another.

additional *adj.*, **additionally** *adv.*

ad-di-tive *n.* A substance added to another in small amounts to alter it.

ad-dle *v.* To become or make confused; to spoil.

ad-duce *v.* To offer as proof or give as a reason. **adducer** *n.*, **adducible** *adj.*

ad-e-noids *n.* Lymphoid tissue growths in the upper part of the throat behind the nose; may need to be removed surgically.

a-dept *adj.* Highly skilled; expert. **adeptly** *adv.*, **adeptness** *n.*

ad-e-qua-cy *n.* The state of being good enough to fill a requirement.

ad-e-quate *adj.* Sufficient; good enough for what is needed.

ad-here *v.* To stay attached; to stick and not come loose; to stay firm.

ad-her-ent *n.* A person who follows a leader, party, or belief.

a-dieu *n.* A word for good-by.

a-di-os *interj.* Spanish for good-by.

ad-in-ter-im *adj.* In the meantime.

ad-ja-cent *adj.* Close to or nearby.

ad-ja-cent an-gles *n.* Two angles with a side in common, having the same vertex.

ad-jec-tive *n.* A word used to describe a noun or pronoun.

ad-join *v.* To be next to; to be in or nearly in contact with.

ad-journ *v.* To close a meeting or session for a time. **adjournment** *n.*

ad-junct *n.* Something less important added to something with more importance. **adjunctly** *adv.*, **adjunctive** *adj.*

ad-jure *v.* To ask urgently; to command solemnly. **adjuration** *n.*

adjust *v.* To arrange or change; to make work correctly; to regulate. **-ability** *n.*

ad-just-ment *n.* The act or process of changing; a settlement of a suit or claim.

ad-ju-tant *n.* An administrative staff officer who serves as a secretary to the commanding officer.

ad-lib *v.* To improvise; to compose or make up spontaneously.

ad-min-is-ter *v.* To direct or manage; to give or carry out instructions.

ad-min-is-tra-tion *n.* The people who manage a school, company, or organization.

ad-mi-ra-ble *adj.* Worthy of being admired or praised; excellent.

ad-mi-ral *n.* The highest rank for a naval officer; the commanding officer.

ad-mire *v.* To hold a high opinion; to regard with wonder, delight, and pleased approval.

ad-mis-si-ble *adj.* Capable of being admitted, accepted or allowed.

ad-mis-sion *n.* The right or act of being admitted; an admitting of the truth of something; a confession.

ad-mit *v.* To take or accept as being the truth; to permit or give the right to enter. **admittedly** *adv.*

ad-mit-tance *n.* Permission to enter.

ad-mit-ted-ly *adv.* One's own admission or confession.

ad-mix-ture *n.* Blend; mingling.

ad-mon-ish *v.* To warn a person to correct a fault; to criticize in a gentle way.

ad-mo-ni-tion *n.* A mild criticism or warning.

ad-o-les-cent *n.* A person in the transitional period between childhood and adulthood.

a-dopt *v.* To legally take into one's family and raise as their own. **-ion** *n.*

a-dor-a-ble *adj.* Very likable; charming. **adorably** *adv.*, **adorableness** *n.*

a-dore *v.* To love greatly; to worship or honor highly; to like very much.

a-dorn *v.* To add splendor or beauty.

ad rem *adj.* Relevant to a point at issue.

a-dre-nal gland *n.* A small endocrine gland that consist of a medulla and cortex, located near the kidney.

a-drift *adv.* Drifting; floating freely without being steered; having no clear purpose or aim.

a-droit *adj.* Skillful and clever in difficult circumstances. **adroitly** *adv.*

ad-sorb *v.* To collect and hold as molecules of gases, liquids; to become adsorbed. **adsorbable** *adj.*

ad-ulate *v.* To give greater praise or flattery than is proper or deserved. **-ion** *n.*

a-dult *n.* A man or woman who is fully grown; a mature person. *adj.* Having reached full size and strength. **-hood** *n.*

a-dul-ter-ate *v.* To make impure or of less quality by adding improper ingredients.

ad-vance *v.* To move ahead; to make or become higher; to increase in value or price.

ad-van-tage *n.* A better chance or more forcible position; a condition, thing or event that can help or benefit; the first point, after deuce scored in the game of tennis.

ad-vent *n.* A coming or arrival; the four Sundays before Christmas.

ad-verb *n.* A word used with a verb, adjective, or another adverb to tell when, where, how, what kind, or how much.

ad-verse *adj.* Opposed; not helpful; against someone or something. **adverseness** *n.*, **adversely** *adv.*

ad-ver-si-ty *n.* Bad luck or misfortune.

ad-ver-tise *v.* To draw public attention to a product you wish to sell. **-er** *n.*

ad-vice *n.* Suggestion or recommendation regarding a course of action or decision.

ad-vis-a-ble *adj.* Fit to be done or advised. **advisability**, **advisableness** *n.*

ad-vis-ed-ly *adv.* Deliberately; with consideration.

ad-viser *n.* A person who gives an opinion or advises.

ad-vo-cate *v.* To write or speak in favor of or support. **advocate** *n.*

a-e-des *n.* A mosquito that transmits yellow fever.

ae-gis *n.* Protection; support or sponsorship.

aer-ate *v.* To purify by exposing to the open air.

aer-i-al *adj.* Of or in the air; pertaining

to aircraft. *n.* An antenna for television or radio. **aerially** *adv.*

aer-ie *n.* The nest of a predatory bird, built on a cliff or other high places.

aer-o-bics *n.* Strenuous exercise that increases oxygen to the heart and lungs, therefore strengthening them.

aer-o-nau-tics *pl., n.* The science of designing and constructing aircraft.

aer-o-pause *n.* The region in the upper atmosphere where aircraft cannot fly.

aer-o-sol *n.* A liquid substance under pressure within a metal container.

aes-thet-ic *adj.* Having a love for beauty.

aes-thet-ics *n.* The study of the nature of beauty. **aesthetically** *adv.*

a-far *adv.* Far off; far away.

af-fa-ble *adj.* Good natured, easy to talk to; friendly. **affably** *adv.*

af-fair *n.* An event or happening; matters of business or public concern.

af-fect *v.* To move emotionally; to feel sympathetic or sad; to bring about a change in. **affecting, affected** *adj.*

af-fec-ta-tion *n.* Artificial behavior that is meant to impress others.

af-fec-tion *n.* A tender or fond feeling towards another.

af-fec-tion-ate *adj.* Loving and gentle.

af-fi-da-vit *n.* A written statement by a person swearing that something is the truth.

af-fil-i-ate *v.* To join in, connect, or associate with. **affiliation** *n.*

af-fin-i-ty *n.* A special attraction with kinship; a natural attraction or liking.

af-firm *v.* To declare positively and be willing to stand by the truth.

af-fix *n.* To attach; to fasten.

af-flict *v.* To cause suffering or pain; to cause mental suffering. **affliction** *n.*

af-flu-ence *n.* Wealth; riches; abundance.

af-flu-ent *adj.* Prosperous; rich; having all the wealth or money needed.

af-ford *v.* To be able to provide; to have enough money to spare.

af-fray *n.* Brawl or noisy fight.

af-front *v.* To insult one to his face; to confront.

a-flame *adj.* Burning; in flames; glowing.

a-flut-ter *adj.* Nervously excited.

a-foot *adj.* In the progress of happening; walking; on foot.

a-foul *adv.* Tangled; entangled in a collision.

a-fraid *adj.* Hesitant; filled with fear; reluctant.

a-fresh *adv.* Once more; again.

aft *adv.* At, close to, near, or toward the rear of an aircraft or stern of a ship.

af-ter *adv.* In the rear. *prep.* Following.

af-ter-ef-fect *n.* An effect coming after.

af-ter-math *n.* Consequence; result.

af-ter-thought *n.* An idea occurring later.

a-gain *adv.* Moreover; another time; once more.

a-gainst *prep.* In exchange for; in preparation for.

a-gape *adv.* With expectation; in wonder; open-mouthed.

ag-ate *n.* The type of quartz that has bands of colors.

a-ga-ve *n.* Fleshy-leaved tropical American plant.

age *n.* The length of time from beginning to a certain date; the time of life when a person has full legal rights; the age of 21. *v.* To grow or become old; to mature.

aged *adj.* Grown or become old. **agedness** *n.,* **agedly** *adv.*

age-ism *n.* Discrimination based on a person's age.

a-gen-da *n.* Program or list of things to be done.

a-gent *n.* One who acts as the representative of another; one who acts or exerts power.

ag-glor-na-men-to *n.* Bringing up to date.

ag-glom-er-ate *v.* To collect; to form into a mass. **agglomerate** *n.*

ag-glu-ti-nate *v.* To join by adhesion; to cause red blood cells to clump together.

ag-glu-ti-nin *n.* A substance that causes agglutination; a group or mass formed by the union of separate elements.

ag-gran-dize *v.* To enlarge, to extend; to increase. **aggrandizement** *n.*

ag-gra-vate *v.* To annoy; to make worse.

ag-gre-gate *adj.* To gather together into a mass or whole. **aggregate** *adj.*

ag-gres-sion *n.* Hostile action or behavior; an unprovoked assault.

ag-gres-sive *adj.* Offensive; distressing; pushy; afflicting. **aggressiveness** *n.*

a-ghast *adj.* Appalled; struck with amazement.

ag-ile *adj.* Marked by the ability to move quickly and easily; nimble. **agility** *n.*

ag-itate *v.* To disturb; to upset; to stir or move with violence; to try to arouse the public interest. **-ion, -or** *n.*

ag-nos-tic *n.* One who doubts that there is a God or life hereafter. **-ism** *n.*

a-go *adj. & adv.* In the past; gone by.

a-gog *adj.* Excited; eagerly expectant.

ag-o-nize *v.* To afflict with great anguish or to suffer. **agonized, agonizing** *adj.*

ag-o-ny *n., pl.* **-nies** Intense mental distress or physical pain; anguish.

ag-o-ra-pho-bi-a *n.* Fear of open spaces.

a-gree *v.* To give assent; to consent; to share an understanding or opinion; to be beneficial or suitable; to correspond.

a-gree-a-ble *adj.* Pleasant; pleasing; willing; ready to consent. **agreeableness** *n.,* **agreeably** *adv.*

a-gree-ment *n.* Harmony; concord.

ag-ri-cul-ture *n.* Raising of livestock; farming and cultivating the crops.

a-ground *adv. & adj.* Stranded; on the ground; to run ashore; beached.

a-gue *n.* Fever accompanied by chills or shivering and sweating. **aguish** *adj.*

a-head *adv.* Before; in advance; to or at the front of something.

a-hoy *interj.* A nautical call or greeting.

aid *v.* To give help or assistance. **-er** *n.*

AIDS *n.* Disease that destroys the body's immunological system; Acquired Immune Deficiency Syndrome.

ail *v.* To feel sick; to make ill or uneasy.

ai-lan-thus *n.* A tree with numerous pointed leaves.

ai-ler-on *v.* Movable control flap on the trailing edge of an airplane wing.

ail-ment *n.* A mild illness.

aim *v.* To direct a weapon; to direct purpose. *n.* Intention.

aim-less *adj.* Lacking of purpose.

ain't *contr.* Am not, are not, is not, has not, or have not.

a-l-o-li *n.* Rich garlic flavored mayonnaise.

air *n.* An odorless, tasteless, colorless, gaseous mixture; primarily composed of nitrogen (78%) and oxygen (21%); the sky; a breeze. **on the air** Broadcast.

air-craft *n.* A machine that flies, such as a helicopter, airplane, or glider.

air-craft car-ri-er *n.* A large ship which carries airplanes on which they can be landed and launched.

air-crew *n.* A crew that mans an airplane.

air-dry *v.* To dry by exposing to the air.

air-field *n.* Paved runways at an airport; landing strip.

air-flow *n.*

The motion of air around a body as relative to the surface of a body immersed in it.

air-foil *n.* Part of an airplane which controls stability, lift, thrust, etc.

air-frame *n.* The structure of a rocket or airplane without an engine.

air-freight *n.* Freight that is transported from one location to another by air.

air gun *n.* Gun which is operated by compressed air.

air-hole *n.* A hole that is used to discharge or admit air into an area.

air-ing *n.* Exposing something in the open air.

air lane *n.* The regular route of travel for airplanes.

air letter *n.* A letter that is transmitted by means of an aircraft.

air-lift *n.* System of transporting supplies or troops by air when ground routes are blocked.

air-line *n.* An air transportation company or system.

air-lin-er *n.* A large passenger airline.

air lock *n.* Airtight compartment between regions of unequal pressure.

air-mail & air mail *n.* Mail sent by means of air.

air-man *n.* A person enlisted in the air force.

air-man-ship *n.* The skill in navigating or piloting an airplane.

air-plane *n.* A vehicle capable of flight, heavier than air, and propelled by jet engines or propellers.

air pocket *n.* A condition in the atmosphere that can cause an airplane to loose altitude quickly.

air-port *n.* A terminal station for passengers where aircraft take off and land.

air raid *n.* Bombing attack by military aircraft.

air-ship *n.* Dirigible; a self-propelled lighter-than-air aircraft.

air-y *adj.* Open to the air; breezy; light as air; graceful or delicate. **airiness** *n.*, **airily** *adv.*

aisle *n.* Passageway between rows of seats, as in a church, auditorium, or airplane. **aisled** *adj.*

a-jar *adv. & adj.* Partially opened.

a-kim-bo *adj. & adv.* Bent; with a crook.

a-kin *adj.* Related, as in family; similar in quality or character.

al-a-bas-ter *n.* A dense, translucent, tinted or white, fine-grained gypsum. **alabastrine** *adj.*

a la carte *n.* Separate price for each item on the menu.

a-lack *interj.* An exclamation expressive of sorrow.

a-lac-ri-ty *n.* Readiness; cheerfulness; eagerness; briskness.

a la mode *n.* Served with ice cream, as pie; fashionable.

a-larm-ist *n.* Someone who needlessly alarms others. **alarmism** *n.*

a-las *interj.* Expressive of anxiety or regret.

a-late *or* **alated** *adj.* Winged; having wings. **alation** *n.*

alb *n.* White linen robe worn by clergy during Mass.

al-ba-core *n.* Large marine fish; major source of canned tuna.

al-ba-tross *n.* Large, web-footed, long-winged sea bird.

al-be-it *conj.* Although; even though.

al-bi-no *n.* An animal or person with an abnormal whiteness of the skin and hair and pink colored eyes.

al-bu-men *n.* White of an egg.

al-bu-min *n.* Several proteins found in the white of eggs, blood serum, milk, and plant and animal tissue.

al-bu-min-ous *adj.* Relating to, having the properties of or containing albumen.

al-caz-ar *n.* A Spanish fortress or palace.

al-che-my *n.* Traditional chemical philosophy concerned primarily with changing base metals into gold.

al-co-hol *n.* Intoxicating liquor containing alcohol; ethanol; a series of related organic compounds.

al-cove *n.* Recess or partly enclosed extension of a room.

al-de-hyde *n.* Any of a class of highly reactive chemical compounds obtained by oxidation of alcohols.

al-der *n.* Tree of the birch family, grows in marshy soil.

al-der-man *n.* Member of a municipal legislative body.

ale *n.* Beverage similar to, but more bitter than beer, made from malt by fermentation.

a-lem-bic *n.* A glass or metal vessel formerly used in distillation.

a-lert *adj.* Vigilant; brisk; watchful; active. *n.* A signal by siren of air attack. **alertly** *adv.*, **alertness** *n.*

al-fres-co *adv. & adj.* In the fresh air; outside.

al-gae *pl., n.* Various primitive, chiefly aquatic, one-celled or multicellular plants, as the seaweed.

al-ge-bra *n.* Generalization of math in which symbols represent members of a specified set of numbers and are related by operations that hold for all numbers in the set. **algebraic**, **algebraically** *adv.*, **algebraist** *n.*

a-li-as *n., pl.* **aliases** Assumed name. *adv.* Otherwise known as.

al-ien-a-ble *adj.* Able to be transferred to the ownership of another. **-bility** *n.*

al-ien-ate *v.* To cause to become indifferent or unfriendly. **alienation** *n.*

al-ien-ist *n.* A psychiatrist accepted by a court as an expert on mental stability.

a-lign *v.* To arrange in a line; to take one side of an argument or cause. **aline** *v.*

a-lign-ment *or* **alinement** *n.* Arrange or position in a straight line.

a-like *adj.* Similar, having close resemblance. *adv.* In the same manner, way, or degree.

al-i-ment *n.* Nourishment; food. **alimentation** *n.*, **alimental** *adj.*

al-i-men-ta-ry *adj.* Pertaining to nutrition or food.

al-i-men-ta-ry canal *n.* The tube of the digestive system from the mouth to the anus, including the pharynx, esophagus, stomach, and intestines.

al-i-men-ta-tion *n.* The process or act of affording nutriment. **-tive** *adj.*

a-live *adj.* Living; having life; in existence or effect; full of life. **-ness** *n.*

a-li-yah *n.* Immigration of Jewish people to Israel.

a-liz-a-rin *n.* A red-orange compound used in dyes.

al-ka-line *adj.* Of, relating to, or containing an alkali. **alkalinity** *n.*

al-ka-lin-ize *adj.* To make alkaline.

al-ka-loid *n.* Any of various nitrogen containing organic bases obtained from plants. **alkaloidal** *adj.*

al-ka-lo-sis *n.* Unusually high alkali content in the blood and tissues.

all *adj.* Total extent or total entity; being a whole number, amount, or quantity.

al-lay *v.* To relieve; to lessen; to calm; to pacify. **allayer** *n.*

al-le-ga-tion *n.* The act or result of alleging.

al-lege *v.* To affirm; to assert to be true; to declare without proof.

al-le-giance *n.* Loyalty to one's nation, cause, or sovereign; obligations of a vassal to an overlord. **allegiant** *adj.*

al-le-gret-to *adv., Mus.* Slower than al-

legro but faster than andante.

al-lele *n.* Any of a group of possible mutational forms of a gene.

al-ler-gen *n.* Substance which causes an allergy. **allergenic** *adj.*

al-ler-gist *n.* A doctor specializing in allergies.

al-ler-gy *n.* **-gies** Pathological or abnormal reaction to environmental substances, as foods, dust, pollens, or microorganisms. **allergic** *adj.*

al-le-vi-ate *v.* To make more bearable. **alleviation**, **alleviator** *n.*

al-lit-er-ate *v.* To arrange or form words beginning with the same sound. **-or** *n.*

al-lit-er-a-tion *n.* Occurrence of two or more words having the same initial sound. **alliterative** *adj.*

al-lo-cate *v.* To assign; to allot.

al-lot *v.* To distribute or set aside as a share of something. **-ment** *n.*

al-low *v.* To make a provision for, to permit; to permit to have; to admit; to concede **allowable** *adj.*, **allowably** *adv.*

al-low-ance *n.* The act of allowing something, a regular amount of money, food, etc.; a price discount.

al-loy *v.* Something that has been added to; item reduced purity or value.

al-lude *n.* To refer to something indirectly. **allusion** *n.*, **allusive** *adj.*

al-lure *v.* To entice; to tempt. *n.* Attraction; charm; enticement. **allurement**, **allurer** *n.*, **alluringly** *adv.*

al-lu-sion *n.* The act of referring to something indirectly; an hint.

al-lu-vi-um *n.* Sediment deposited by flowing water as in a river bed. **alluvial** *adj.*

al-mond *n.* An oval, edible nut with a soft, light-brown shell; tree bearing such nuts.

al-most *adv.* Not quite; slightly short of.

alms *pl., n.* Goods or money given to the poor in charity.

alms-house *n.* A poorhouse.

a-lo-ha *interj.* Hawaiian expression of greeting or farewell.

a-loof *adj.* Indifferent; distant.

a-loud *adv.* Orally; audibly.

al-pha-bet *n.* The letters of a language, arranged in an order fixed by custom.

al-pha-bet-i-cal *adj.* Arranged in the traditional order of the letters of a language. **alphabetically** *adv.*

al-pha-bet-ize *v.* To arrange in alphabetical order.

al-pha de-cay *n.* Decay of an atomic nucleus as it emits an alpha particle.

al-read-y *adv.* By this or a specified time.

al-so *adv.* Likewise; besides; in addition.

al-tar *n.* An elevated structure before which religious ceremonies may be held or sacrifices offered.

al-ter *v.* To make change or become different; to modify; to castrate or spay, as an animal. **-ability**, **alteration** *n.*

al-ter-a-tive *adj.* Tending to alter or produce alterations.

al-ter-ca-tion *n.* Noisy and heated quarrel.

al-ter e-go *v.* An intimate friend; another

aspect of oneself.

al-ter-nate v. To happen or follow in turn; to occur in successive turns. n. Substitute. **alternately** adv.

al-ter-nat-ing cur-rent n. Electric current that reverses direction at regular intervals.

al-ter-na-tive n. A choice between two or more possibilities; one of the possibilities to be chosen. **-ly** adv.

al-ter-na-tive adj. Allowing a choice.

al-ter-na-tor n. Electric generator producing alternating current.

al-though conj. Even though.

al-tim-e-ter n. Instrument for measuring and indicating altitude.

al-ti-tude n. The height of a thing above a reference level; above the earth's surface; above sea level.

al-to-geth-er adv. Entirely; with all included or counted.

al-tru-ism n. Selfless concern for the welfare of others. **altruist** n., **altruistic** adj., **altruistically** adv.

al-um n. Any one of several similar double sulfates.

a-lu-mi-na n. Any of several forms of aluminum oxide.

a-lu-mi-num n. A silvery-white, ductile metallic element used to form many hard, light, corrosion resistant alloys.

a-lum-na n., pl. **-nae** Female graduate or former student of a school, college, or university.

al-ways adv. Continuously; forever; on every occasion; at all times.

am n. First person, singular, present tense of be.

a-mal-gam n. An alloy of mercury with other metals, as with tin or silver; a blend of diverse elements.

a-mal-ga-mate v. To mix so as to make a unified whole; to blend. **amalgamation, amalgamator** n.

a-man-dine adj. Made or garnished with almonds.

am-a-ranth n. Various weedy plants with greenish or purplish flowers; an imaginary flower that never fades.

am-a-ryl-lis n. A bulbous plant with large, lily-like, reddish or white flowers.

am-a-teur n. One who engages in an activity as a pastime rather than as a profession; one who lacks expertise. **amateurish** adj., **amateurism** n.

am-a-to-ry adj. Of or expressive of sexual love.

a-maze v. To astound; to affect with surprise or wonder. **amazingly** adv., **amazedness, -ment** n., **amazing** adj.

am-bass-a-dor n. Official representative of the highest rank, accredited by one government to another.

am-ber-gris n. A waxy, grayish substance produced by sperm whales, and used in making perfumes.

am-bi-ance n. Environment; atmosphere.

am-bi-dex-trous adj. Able to use both hands with equal facility.

am-bi-ent adj. Surrounding.

am-big-u-ous adj. Doubtful; uncertain.

ambiguousness n., **ambiguously** adv.

am-bi-tion n. Strong desire to achieve; will to succeed; the goal or object desired.

am-bi-tious adj. Challenging. **ambitiousness** n., **ambitiously** adv.

am-biv-a-lence n. Existence of mutually different feelings about a person or thing.

am-ble v. To move at a leisurely pace.

am-bu-lance n. Vehicle equipped to transport the injured or sick.

am-bu-la-to-ry adj. Moving about; movable; of or to do with walking.

am-bus-cade n. Ambush.

am-bush n. Surprise attack made from a hidden position. **ambush** v., **ambusher, ambushment** n.

A-me-ba also **Amoeba** n

Single-celled semi-fluid living animal

a-me-lio-rate v. To become or make better. **ameliorator, amelioration** n., **ameliorative** adj.

a-men interj. Used at the end of a prayer to express solemn approval.

a-me-na-ble adj. Responsive; tractable; accountable. **amenableness, amenability** n.

a-mend v. To correct; to improve; to rectify. **amendable** adj., **amender** n.

a-mend-ment n. Correction, reformation or improvement; the parliamentary procedure where such alteration is made.

a-mends pl., n. Compensation for insult or injury.

a-men-i-ty n., pl. **-ties** Agreeableness; means of comfort or convenience.

a-merce v. To punish. **amercment** n.

am-e-thyst n. Violet or purple form of transparent corundum or quartz, used as a gemstone. **amethystine** adj.

a-mi-a-ble adj. Friendly and pleasant. **amiableness, amiability** n., **-ly** adv.

am-i-ca-ble adj. Harmonious; friendly. **amicability, amicableness** n., **-ly** adv.

a-mid prep. In the middle of; surrounded by.

a-mid-ships adv. Halfway between the bow and the stern.

a-midst prep. In the middle of; surrounded by; during.

a-mi-go n. A friend.

am-i-ty n. Relationships that are friendly, as between two states.

am-me-ter n. A tool measuring electric current.

am-mo n. Ammunition.

am-mo-nia n. Colorless, pungent gas.

am-mo-ni-um hy-drox-ide n. A colorless, basic aqueous solution of ammonia.

am-ne-sia n. The loss of memory. **-iac** n.

am-nes-ty n., pl. **-ties** Pardon for political offenders.

a-moe-ba n., pl. **-bas** or **-bae** Various minute one-celled organisms having an indefinite, changeable form.

a-mong prep. In or through the midst of; between one another.

a·mon·til·la·do *n., pl.* **-dos** A pale, dry sherry.

a·mor·al *adj.* Neither moral nor immoral. **amorality** *n.,* **amorally** *adv.*

am·o·rous *adj.* Inclined to or indicative of sexual love. **amorousness** *n.*

a·mor·phous *adj.* Lacking definite form; shapeless; general; vague.

am·or·tize *v.* To liquidate a loan by installment payments; a loan. **-tion** *n.*

a·mount *n.* Aggregate, sum or total quantity. *v.* To be equivalent.

a·mour *n.* A forbidden love affair.

a·mour—pro·pre *n.* Self-respect.

am·per·age *n.* Strength of an electric current, expressed in amperes.

am·pere *n.* Unit of electric current equal to a flow of one amp per second.

am·per·sand *n.* The character or sign that represents and (&).

am·phet·a·mine *n.* Colorless volatile liquid; a drug.

amphi *prefix.* Around, on both sides, all around on all sides.

am·phib·i·an *n.* An organism, as a frog or toad, developing from an aquatic state into an air-breathing state; aircraft that can take off and land on land or water; a vehicle that can take off or land on land or water.

am·phi·the·a·ter *n.* A round or oval building having tiers of seats rising around an arena.

am·ple *adj.* Sufficient; abundant; large. **ampleness** *n.,* **amply** *adv.*

am·pli·tude *n.* Maximum value of a periodically varying quantity; greatness of size; fullness.

am·pli·tude mod·u·la·tion *n.* The encoding of a carrier wave by variation of its amplitude in accordance with a signal.

am·pul *or* **am·pule** *n.* A small, sealed vial containing a hypodermic injection solution.

am·pu·tate *v.* To cut off; to remove, as a limb from one's body. **amputation** *n.*

am·pu·tee *n.* A person who has had one or more limbs amputated.

a·muck *adv.* In an uncontrolled manner; a murderous frenzy; out of control.

am·u·let *n.* A charm worn as protection against evil or injury.

a·muse *v.* To entertain in an agreeable, pleasing way. **-ment** *n.,* **amusable** *adj.*

an *adj.* One; one sort of; each; form of "a" used before words beginning with a vowel or with an unpronounced "h" as an elephant or honor.

an·a·dem *n.* A wreath for the head.

a·nae·mi·a *n.* Variant of anemia.

an·aes·the·sia *n.* Variant of anesthesia.

an·a·gram *n.* Word formed by transposing the letters of another word. **anagrammatical, anagrammatic** *adj.*

a·nal *adj.* Of or relating to the anus.

anal *abbr.* Analogous; analogy; analysis; analytic.

an·al·ge·sia *n.* Inability to feel pain while awake. **analgesic** *adj. & n.*

an·a·log com·put·er *n.* A computer where numerical data are represented by measurable quantities as lengths, electrical signals, or voltage.

a·nal·o·gous *adj.* Similar; corresponding in certain ways. **analogously** *adv.*

an·a·logue *n.* Something that bears resemblance to something else.

a·nal·o·gy *n., pl.* **-gies** Connection between things that are otherwise dissimilar; a conclusion or opinion that if two things are alike in some respects they must be alike in others.

a·nal·y·sis *n.* Breaking up or separation of something into its parts so as to examine them and see how they fit together; result.

an·a·lyst *n.* A person who analyzes or who is skilled in analysis.

an·a·lyze *v.* To make an analysis of.

an·a·pest *n.* Metrical foot make up of two short syllables followed by one long one. **anapestic** *adj.*

an·ar·chic *adj.* Of, like, or promoting confusion or disorder.

an·ar·chism *n.* Belief that all forms of government act in an unfair way against the liberty of a person and should be done away with.

an·ar·chy *n.* Lack of political authority, disorder and confusion; the absence of any purpose or standard.

a·nas·to·mo·sis *n.* Connection or union of branches, as of rivers, leaf veins, or blood vessels. **anastomotic** *adj.*

a·nas·tro·phe *n.* Changing the normal syntactic order of words.

a·nath·e·ma *n.* Curse; ban; or excommunication. **anathematize** *v.*

a·nat·o·mize *v.* To examine in great detail; to analyze; in biology, to dissect. **anatomization** *n.*

a·nat·o·my *n., pl.* **-mies** Structure of an organ or organism; a detailed analysis. **anatomical, anatomic** *adj.*

an·ces·try *n., pl.* **-tries** Line of descent; lineage ancestors collectively.

an·ces·tor *n.* A person who comes before one in a family line; someone earlier than a grandparent; forefather. **ancestral** *adj.*

an·chor *n.*

Heavy metal device lowered into the water by a chain to keep a ship from drifting. *v.* To attach or fix firmly.

an·chor·age *n.* A place for anchoring a ship; a strong support that keeps something steady.

an·cho·rite *n.* A religious hermit.

anchor man *n.* The main member of a team of newscasters.

an·cho·vy *n.*

A very small fish of the herring family; usually salted, canned in oil, and used for making sauces and relishes.

an·cient *adj.* Anything belonging to the

early history of people; very old.
ancientness n., **anciently** adv.
and conj. Together with; along with; as well as; added to; as a result; plus; also.

an-dan-te adv., Mus. Rather slow in tempo. **andante** adj.

an-dan-ti-no adj., Mus. Slightly faster in tempo than andante.

and-i-ron n. Heavy metal support for logs or wood in a fireplace.

andr n. The male sex; masculine.

an-dro-gen n. Hormone that develops and maintains masculine characteristics. **androgenic** adj.

an-drog-y-nous adj. Having the characteristics or nature of both male and female; having both staminate and pistillate flowers in the same cluster with the male flowers uppermost. **androgynal**, **androgyny** n.

an-droid n. In science fiction; a synthetic man made to look like a human being.

an-ec-dote n. Short account of a story of some happening or about some person. **anecdotal, -tic** adj., **anecdotist** n.

an-echo-ic adj. Neither having or producing echoes.

a-ne-mi-a n. The condition in which a person's blood does not have enough red corpuscles or hemoglobin and, therefore, does not carry a normal amount of oxygen.

a-ne-mic adj. Of or having anemia.

an-e-mom-e-ter n. Instrument for measuring wind force and speed.

a-nem-o-ne n. A plant with purple, white, or red cup-shaped flowers.

a-nent prep. Regarding; concerning.

an-es-the-sia n. Condition in which one has no feeling of heat, touch, or pain in all or part of the body.

an-es-the-tize v. To bring on unconsciousness by giving anesthetics; to remove the capacity to feel pain in a localized area.

a-new adv. Again; once more; in a new way.

an-gel n. An immortal being attendant upon God; a very kind and lovable person; a helping or guiding spirit.

an-gel-i-ca n. A plant with aromatic seed, used as flavoring.

an-ger n. Feeling of extreme hostility; rage; wanting to fight back.

an-gi-na n. A disease marked by painful choking spasms and attacks of suffocation pain. **anginous, anginose** adj., **anginal** adj.

angina pec-to-ris n. Severe pain in the chest, associated with feelings of apprehension and suffocation.

an-gle v.

A shape made by two straight lines meeting in a point or two surfaces meeting along a line.

an-gle-worm n. Earthworm, used as fishing bait.

an-gli-cize v. To make English in form, idiom, or character. **anglicization** n.

an-gling n. The act of fishing with a hook and line.

an-go-ra n. The long silky hair of the Angora rabbit or Angora goat; yarn or fabric made from the hair of an Angora goat or rabbit.

an-gry adj. Feeling or showing anger; having a menacing aspect; inflamed. **angrily** adv.

an-guish n. Great suffering, from worry, grief, or pain; agony.

an-gu-lar adj. Having angles or sharp corners; measured by an angle or degrees of an arc; gaunt, bony, lean. **angularity** n., **angularly** adv.

an-hy-dride n. Chemical compound formed from another by removing the water.

an-hy-drous adj. Does not contain any water.

an-i-line n. Colorless, oily, poisonous liquid, used to make rubber, dyes, resins, pharmaceuticals, and varnishes.

an-i-mad-vert v. To comment with disapproval. **animadversion** n.

an-i-mal n. Any being other than a human being; any four-footed creature; beast. **animalize** v.

an-i-mal-cule n. Microscopic or minute animal.

an-i-mate v. To give liveliness, life or spirit to; to cause to act; to inspire. **animatedly** adv., **animation** n.

a-ni-ma-to adv., Mus. In a lively or animated manner; used as a direction. **animato** adj.

an-i-ma-tor n. One who animates, such as an artist or technician who produces an animation, such as a cartoon.

an-i-mism n. A belief in primitive tribes that natural objects and forces have souls. **animist** n., **animistic** adj.

an-i-mos-i-ty n., pl. **-ties** Hostility; bitterness; hatred.

an-i-mus n. Feeling of animosity.

an-i-on n. An ion with a negative charge that is attracted to an anode; electrolysis.

an-ise n. A plant with yellowish-white flower clusters and licorice-flavored seeds; aniseed.

an-i-seed n. Seed used for flavoring and in medicine.

an-i-sette n. Anise-flavored liqueur.

an-kle n. Joint that connects the foot with the leg; slender section of the leg immediately above this joint.

an-klet n. A short sock, an ornament worn around the ankle.

ann abbr. Annals; annual; annuity.

an-nals pl., n. Descriptive record; history. **annalist** n.

an-neal v. To heat and then cool glass slowly to make it less brittle.

an-nex v. To add or join a smaller thing to a larger one. **annexation** n.

an-ni-hi-late v. To destroy completely; totally. **annihilate, annihilation** n.

an-ni-ver-sa-ry n., pl. **-ries** The date on which something happened at an earlier time; this event celebrated on this date each year.

an-no-tate v. To use notes to give one's opinions. annotation, annotator n., annotative adj.

an-nounce v. To proclaim; to give notice. announcement n.

an-noy v. To bother; to irritate; to make slightly angry. -ing adj., -ingly adv.

an-noy-ance n. A nuisance; irritation; act of annoying.

an-nu-al adj. Recurring or done at the same time each year; a yearly publication, as a yearbook. annually adv.

an-nu-i-tant n. Person who receives an annuity.

an-nu-i-ty n., pl. -ties Annual payment of an income or allowance.

an-nul v. To cancel a marriage or a law; to do away with; to put an end to. annullable adj., annulment n.

an-nu-lar adj. Shaped like or forming a ring. annularity n., annularly adv.

an-nun-ci-ate v. To proclaim; to announce.

an-nun-ci-a-tion n. An announcement; the act of announcing.

an-ode n. Positively charged electrode. anodic adj., anodically adv.

an-o-dize v. To coat a metallic surface by electrolysis with a protective oxide.

a-noint v. To apply oil in a religious ceremony. anointer, anointment n.

a-nomaly n., pl. -lies Anything irregular or abnormal. anomalistic, -lous adj.

a-non adv. Soon; in a short period of time.

a-non-y-mous adj. An unknown or withheld name, agency. anonymity, anonymousness n., anonymously adv.

an-oth-er adj. Additional; one more different, but of the same character.

ans abbr. Answer.

an-swer n. A written or spoken reply, as to a question; a result or solution, as to a problem. v. To respond correctly; to be responsible for. answerable adj.

ant n.

A small insect, usually without wings; which lives in or on the ground, or in wood in large colonies.

ant abbr. Antenna; antonym.

ant-ac-id n. A substance which neutralizes or weakens acids.

an-tag-o-nism n. Hostility; condition of being against; the feeling of unfriendliness toward.

an-tag-o-nize v. To arouse hostility; to make an enemy of someone.

Ant-arc-tic n. Large area of land completely covered with ice; the South Pole.

ant-eat-er n. Animal with a long snout and a long, sticky tongue, feeding mainly on ants.

an-te-ce-dent adj. One event that precedes another; previous.

an-te-date v. To precede in time; to give an earlier date than the actual date.

an-te-lope n. A slender, long-horned, swift-running, hoofed mammal.

an-te me-rid-i-em n. Time before noon, abbreviated as "A.M.".

an-ten-na n., pl. -nae Slender feelers on the head of an insect, lobster, crab, etc.; wire or set of wires used in radio and television to send and receive signals.

an-te-pe-nult n. The third syllable from the end of a word. -timate adj. & n.

an-te-ri-or adj. Toward or at the front; coming before; earlier.

an-te-room n. Waiting room; a room leading to a larger more, important room.

an-them n. Hymn of praise or loyalty; an official song of a country, school, etc.

an-ther n. The part of the flower where the pollen is located at the end of a stamen.

an-thol-o-gy n. A collection of stories, poems, or other writings.

an-thra-cite n. Coal with a high carbon content and low volatile matter; hard coal. anthracitic adj.

an-thrax n. The infectious, usually fatal disease found in animals such as cattle and sheep; disease that can be transmitted to man.

an-thro-po-cen-tric adj. To interpret reality in terms of human experience and values.

an-thro-poid n. Gorillas or chimpanzees resembling man.

an-thro-pol-o-gy n. The science that studies the origin, culture, and development of man. anthropologic, anthropological adj., -ally adv., anthropologist n.

an-thro-po-mor-phism n. The ascribing of human motivation and human characteristics to something that is not human. anthropomorphic adj.

an-ti n. One who opposes a group, policy, practice, or proposal.

an-ti-anx-i-ety adj. Preventing or relieving anxiety.

an-ti-bal-lis-tic missile n. A missile designed to destroy a ballistic missile.

an-ti-bi-ot-ic n. A substance, as streptomycin or penicillin, that is produced by organisms, as fungi and bacteria, effective in the destruction of microorganisms and used widely to prevent or treat diseases.

an-ti-bod-y n. Proteins generated in the blood that react to foreign proteins or carbohydrates of certain types, neutralizing them and producing immunity against certain microorganisms or their toxins.

an-tic n. Mischievous caper or act.

An-ti-christ n. A great enemy of Christ. Antichristian adj.

an-tic-i-pate v. To look forward; to act in advance of; to foresee. anticipation, anticipator n., anticipatory adj.

an-ti-cli-max n. A letdown or decline; a commonplace conclusion; a series of on which metal is formed.

anx-i-e-ty *n.* A state of uncertainty; disturbance of the mind regarding uncertain events.

anx-ious *adj.* Troubled in mind or worried about some uncertain matter or event. **-ness** *n.*, **anxiously** *adv.*

any *adj.* One; no matter which; some; every; and quantity or part.

any-body *pron.*, *pl.* **-bodies** Anyone; any person.

any-how *adv.* By any means; in any why; whatever.

any-more *adv.* At present and from now on.

any-one *pron.* Any person; anybody.

any-place *adv.* Anywhere.

any-thing *pron.* Any occurrence, object or matter.

any-time *adv.* At any time whatever.

any-way *adv.* Nevertheless; anyhow; in any manner; carelessly.

any-where *adv.* In, at, or to any place; to any degree or extent.

a-or-ta *n.*, *pl.* **-tas** *or* **-tae** The main artery that carries blood away from the heart; distributes blood to all of the body except the lungs. **aortal, -ic** *adj.*

a-pace *adv.* Rapid in pace; quickly.

a-part *adv.* Separate or at a distance; in pieces; to pieces; to set aside.

a-part-heid *n.* In the Republic of South Africa, an official policy of political, social, and economic discrimination and segregation against nonwhites.

a-part-ment *n.* A suite or room in a building equipped for individual living.

ap-a-thy *n.* The lack of emotions or feelings. **apathetic** *adj.*, **apathetically** *adv.*

ap-a-tite *n.* Mineral used as a source of phosphorus compounds.

ape *n.* A large mammal such as a gorilla, chimpanzee, or monkey; a very clumsy, coarse person. **aped** *v.*

a-pe-ri-tif *n.* A drink of alcoholic liquor consumed before a meal.

ap-er-ture *n.* An opening.

a-pex *n.*, *pl.* **apexes** *or* **apices** The highest point; tip; top.

a-pha-sia *n.* Any partial or total loss of the ability to express ideas, resulting from brain damage. **aphasiac** *n.*, **aphasic** *adj. & n.*

aphe-lion *n.* The point in an orbit farthest from the sun.

aphid *n.* Small insects that suck sap from plants.

aph-o-rism *n.* Brief statement of truth or principal. **aphorist** *n.*, **aphoristically** *adv.*, **aphoristic** *adj.*

apho-tic *adj.* Without light.

aph-ro-dis-i-ac *adj.* Increasing or arousing the sexual desire or potency.

a-pi-ary *n.* Place where bees are kept and raised for their honey.

a-piece *adv.* For or to each one.

a-plomb *n.* Assurance; poise; self-confidence.

apo- *pref.* Lack of; separation of; being away from.

a-poc-ry-phal *adj.* False; of questionable significant events or happenings.

anticlimactic *adj.*, **-cally** *adv.*

an-ti-dote *n.* A substance that counteracts an injury or poison. **-al** *adj.*

an-ti-gen *n.* Substance, when introduced into the body, stimulates the production of antibodies. **antigenic** *adj.*, **antigenically** *adv.*, **antigenicity** *n.*

an-ti-his-ta-mine *n.* A drug used to relieve the symptoms of allergies and colds by interfering with the production of histamines. **antihistaminic** *adj.*

an-ti-log-a-rithm *n.* The number corresponding to a given logarithm.

an-ti-mat-ter *n.* A form of matter that is composed of antiparticles.

an-ti-mo-ni-al *adj.* Containing or of antimony.

an-ti-mo-ny *n.* Silver-white metallic element used in chemistry, medicine, and alloys, etc.

an-tin-o-my *n.* An opposition or contradiction.

an-ti-par-ti-cle *n.* Identically matched atomic particles, but with exactly opposite electrically charged magnetic properties and spin.

an-tip-a-thy *n.*, *pl.* **-thies** Feeling of repugnance or opposition. **antipathetic, -al** *adj.*, **-ally** *adv.*

an-ti-per-spi-rant *n.* Substance applied to the underarm to reduce excessive perspiration.

an-tiph-o-ny *n.* One that echoes or answers another; responsive chanting or singing.

an-ti-pode *n.* A direct opposite.

an-ti-pro-ton *n.* The antiparticle of a proton.

an-tique *adj.* Belonging to or of ancient times. *n.* An object that is over 100 years old. **antique** *v.*

an-ti--Sem-ite *n.* A person hostile toward Jews. **anti-Semitic** *adj.*, **-Semitism** *n.*

an-ti-sep-sis *n.* Condition of being free from pathogenic bacteria and the method of obtaining this condition.

an-ti-sep-tic *adj.* Pertaining or capable of producing antisepsis; thoroughly clean. **antiseptically** *adv.*

an-ti-so-cial *adj.* Unsociable; opposed to society.

an-tith-e-sis *n.*, *pl.* **-e -ses** Direct opposition or contrast. **antithetical, antithetic** *adj.*

an-ti-trust *adj.* Having to do with the regulation of trusts, monopolies, and cartels.

ant-ler *n.*

One of a pair of bony growths on the head of a member of the deer family. **-ed** *adj.*

an-to-nym *n.* A word opposite in meaning to another word.

an-uria *n.* The inability to urinate.

a-nus *n.* The lower opening of the alimentary canal.

an-vil *n.* A heavy block of steel or iron

authenticity. **apocryphally** *adv.*

ap-o-gee *n.* The point most distant from earth in the moon's orbit.

a-pol-o-get-ic *adj.* Making an expression of apology. **apological**, **-ally** *adv.*

a-pol-o-gize *v.* To make an apology.**-er** *n.*

a-pol-o-gy *n., pl.* **-gies** A statement expressing regret for an action or fault; a formal justification or defense.

ap-o-plex-y *n.* Sudden loss of muscular control, consciousness, and sensation resulting from a rupture or blockage of the blood vessel in the brain.

a-pos-ta-sy *n., pl.* **-sies** Desertion of one's political party, religious faith, or cause.

a-pos-tate *n.* One who forsakes his faith or principles.

apos-te-ri-o-ri *adj., L.* Inductive; reasoning from facts to principles or from effect to cause.

a-pos-tro-phe *n.* The mark (') used to indicate the removal of letters or figures, the plural of letters or figures, and the possessive case; the act of turning away; addressing the usually absent person or a usually personified thing rhetorically.

a-pos-tro-phize *v.* To make use of apostrophe.

a-poth-e-car-ies' **mea-sure** *pl., n.* A measurement used mainly by pharmacists; a measurement of capacity.

a-poth-e-car-y *n., pl.* **-caries** A person who prepares drugs for medical uses.

apo-the-ci-um *n.* A single-celled structure in many lichens and fungi that consists of a cupped body bearing asci on the exposed flat or concave surface.

ap-o-thegm *n.* A short, essential, and instructive formulation or saying. **apothegmatical**, **apothegmatic** *adj.*

apo-the-o-sis *n.* The perfect way to explain or define something or someone.

ap-pall *v.* To overcome by shock or dismay; to weaken; to fail; to become pale.

ap-pa-ra-tchik *n.* A member of the Communist party.

ap-pa-ra-tus *n., pl.* **-tuses** Appliance or an instrument designed and used for a specific operation.

ap-par-ent *adj.* Clear and opened to the eye and mind; open to view, visible. **apparently** *adv.*, **apparentness** *n.*

ap-par-ent time *n.* Time of day so indicated by a sundial or the sun.

ap-pa-ri-tion *n.* An unusual or unexpected appearance; the act of being visible; a ghostly figure. **-al** *adj.*

ap-par-i-tor *n.* An official person sent to carry out the order of a judge, court, or magistrate.

ap-peal *n.* Power to arouse a sympathetic response; an earnest plea.

ap-pear *v.* To come into existence; to come into public view; to come formally before an authorized person.

ap-pease *v.* To give peace; to cause to stop or subside; to calm; to pacify. **appeasable** *adj.*, **appeasement** *n.*

ap-pel-late *adj.* Having the power to

hear and review the decisions of the lower courts.

ap-pel-la-tion *n.* Identifying by a name or title.

ap-pel-la-tive *adj.* Having to do with the giving of names; relating to or of a common noun. **-tive** *n.*, **-ly** *adv.*

ap-pend *v.* To add an appendix or supplement, as to a book; to attach.

ap-pen-dec-to-my *n.* The surgical removal of the appendix.

ap-pen-dix *n. Med.*

Ascending
colon

Cecum

Appendix

medical term that refers to a small hollow blind process or the vermiform appendix.

ap-per-cep-tion *n.* The mental understanding of something perceived in terms of previous experience. **apperceptively** *adv.*, **apperceptive** *adj.*

ap-per-tain *v.* To belong to or connect with, as a rightful part.

ap-petite *n.* The craving or desire for food. **appetitive** *adj.*

ap-plaud *v.* To express or show approval by clapping the hands. **-able** *adj.*

ap-plause *n.* The expression of public approval. **applausive** *adj.*

ap-pli-ance *n.* A piece of equipment or device designed for a particular use.

ap-pli-ca-ble *adj.* Appropriate; suitable; capable of being applied. **-bility** *n.*

ap-pli-cant *n.* A person who applies for a job or position.

ap-plies *adj.* Putting something to practical use to solve definite problems.

ap-point *v.* To arrange something; to fix or set officially. **-able** *adj.*, **-er** *n.*

ap-por-tion *v.* To divide and share according to a plan. **apportionment** *n.*

ap-pose *v.* To apply one thing to another; to put before. **apposable** *adj.*

ap-po-site *adj.* Highly appropriate or pertinent. **-ness** *n.*, **appositely** *adv.*

ap-po-si-tion *n.* A grammatical construction where a noun or noun phrase is followed by another; the explanatory equivalent. **appositional** *adj.*

ap-prais-al *n.* The evaluation of property by an authorized person.

ap-praise *v.* To estimate the value, worth, or status of a particular item. **-ment**, **appraiser** *n.*, **appraising** *adj.*

ap-pre-cia-ble *adj.* Capable of being measured or perceived, noticed, or estimated. **appreciably** *adv.*

ap-pre-ci-ate *v.* To recognize the worth, quality, or significance.

ap-pre-ci-a-tion *n.* The expression of admiration, gratitude, or approval; increase in value. **ap-pre-cia-tive** *adj.*

ap-pre-hend *v.* To anticipate with anxiety, dread or fear; to recognize the meaning of; to grasp; to understand.

ap-pre-hen-si-ble *adj.* Capable of being apprehended.

ap-pre-hen-sion *n.* The act of or comprehending power to comprehend; suspicion or fear of future events.

ap-pre-hen-sive *adj.* Viewing the future with anxiety or fear. -ly *adv.*

ap-pressed *adj.* Pressed close to or lying flat against.

ap-prise *v.* To inform; to give notice.

ap-proach *v.* To come near to or draw closer; to be close in appearance. *n.* Access to or reaching something.

ap-pro-ba-tion *n.* A formal approval.

ap-pro-pri-ate *v.* To take possession of; to take without permission. *adj.* Suitable for a use or occasion; fitting. appropriately *adv.*, -or, -ness *n.*

ap-pro-pri-a-tion *n.* Money set apart for a particular use; the act or instance of appropriating.

ap-prov-al *n.* The act of approving; subject to acceptance or refusal.

ap-prove *v.* To regard or express a favorable opinion; to give formal or official approval. approvingly *adv.*

ap-prox-i-mate *adj.* Located close together; almost accurate or exact.

ap-pur-te-nance *n.* Something that belongs with another more important thing; an accessory that is passed along with.

ap-pur-te-nant *adj.* Constitutes a legal attachment.

aprax-ia *n.* Inability to execute complex coordinate movement. apraxic *adj.*

apri-o-ri *adj.* Based on theory rather than personal experience; deductive.

ap-ro-pos *adv.* At a good time; by the way.

apse *n.* A semicircular or polygonal projection of a building or church.

ap-si-dal *adj.* Relating to an apse.

apt *adj.* Unusually qualified or fitting; appropriate; having a tendency; suitable; quick to understand.

ap-ti-tude *n.* A natural talent or ability; quickness in learning

aqua *n.*, *pl.* **aquae**, **aquas** Water; aquamarine.

aqua-lunger *n.* A scuba diver.

aqua-naut *n.* A scuba diver who lives inside and outside of an underwater shelter for an extended period of time.

aqua pura *n.* Very pure water.

aqua regia *n.* Mixture of hydrochloric and nitric acids that dissolves platinum or gold.

a-quat-ic *adj.* Anything occurring on or in the water.

aqua-vitae *n.* A very strong liquor; alcohol.

aq-ue-duct *n.* A conduit for carrying a large quantity of flowing water; a bridge-like structure supporting a canal over a river.

aq-ue-ous *adj.* Like or resembling water; dissolved in water; watery.

aqueous humor *n.* The clear fluid in the chamber of the eye between the cornea and lens.

aq-ui-cul-ture or **aqua-cul-ture** *n.* The cultivation of produce in natural water; hydroponics. **aquicultural** *adj.*

aq-ui-fer *n.* The layer of underground gravel, sand, or rocks where water collects.

aq-ui-line *adj.* Resembling or related to an eagle; hooked or curved like the beak on an eagle.

a-quiv-er *adj.*, *Slang* Trembling or quivering.

ar-a-besque *n.* An intricate style or design of interwoven leaves, flowers, and geometric forms.

ar-a-ble *adj.* Land that is suitable for cultivation by plowing.

a-rach-nid *n.* Arthropods that are mostly air-breathing, having four pairs of legs but no antennae; an insect as a spider. arachnidan *n.*, arachnid *adj.*

ara-ne-id *n.* A breed of spider.

ar-ba-lest *n.* Military weapon from medieval times with a steel bow, used to throw balls and stones arbalester *n.*

ar-bi-ter *n.* A person chosen to decide a dispute, having absolute power of determining and judging.

ar-bi-tra-ble *adj.* Subject to arbitration.

ar-bit-ra-ment *adj.* The settling of a dispute; the power or right of deciding.

ar-bi-trar-y *adj.* Something based on whim or impulse. -ily *adv.*, -iness *n.*

ar-bi-tra-tor *n.* A person chosen to settle a dispute or controversy between parties.

ar-bor *n.* A garden shelter that is shady and covered with or made of climbing plants. arborous *adj.*

ar-bo-re-al *adj.* Resembling or related to a tree; living in trees. arboreally *adv.*

ar-bo-re-tum *n.* A place for studying and exhibiting trees, shrubs, and plants cultivated for educational and for scientific purposes.

ar-bo-ri-cul-ture *n.* The ornamental cultivation of shrubs and trees. arboriculturist *n.*

ar-bor-ist *n.* A specialist in the maintenance and care of trees.

ar-bo-ri-za-tion *n.* The formation of an arrangement or figure of a bush or shrub.

ar-bo-rize *v.* To branch repeatedly and freely.

ar-bo-vi-rus *n.* Various viruses transmitted by arthropods, including the causative agents for yellow fever and encephalitis.

ar-bu-tus *n.* A fragrant pinkish flower that blossoms early in the spring.

arc *n.* Something that is curved or arched; the luminous discharge of electric current across a gap of two electrodes.

ar-cade *n.* An arched covered passageway supported by columns; a long arched gallery or building.

ar-cad-ed *adj.* Furnished with arcades or arches.

ar-ca-dia *n.* The ancient Greek area usually chosen as background for poetry; region of simple quiet and pleasure.

arch n.

A structure that spans over an open area and gives support.

ar-chae-ol-o-gy n. Scientific study of ancient times and ancient peoples. **archaeological** adj., **archaeologist** n.

ar-cha-ic adj. Something that belongs to an earlier time; characteristic of an earlier language; now used only in special cases.

ar-cha-ism n. Something that is outdated or old fashioned, as an expression or word. **archaistic** adj., **archaist** n.

arch-an-gel n. The highest in order of angels. **archangelic** adj.

arch-di-o-cese n. The territory or district of an archbishop. **archdiocesan** adj.

arch-en-e-my n. One who is a chief enemy.

ar-cher-y n. The practice or art of shooting with a bow and arrow. **archer** n.

ar-che-spore n. A single cell or group of cells from which a mother spore is formed.

ar-che-type n. An original from which other things are patterned.

arch-fiend n. A chief or principal friend; a person of great wickedness, especially Satan.

ar-chi-tect n. A person who may design and or supervise the construction of large structures.

ar-chi-tec-ton-ic adj. To resemble architecture in organization or structure. **architectonically** adv.

ar-chi-tec-ture n. The art or science of designing and building structures; a method or style of construction or building. **architectural** adj.

ar-chi-trave n. In classical architecture, a horizontal piece supported by the columns of a building.

ar-chives pl., n. Public documents or records; the place where archives are kept. **archival** adj., **archivist** n.

arch-way n. A passage or way under an arch; an arch over a passage.

arc lamp n. Electric lamp which produces light as when a current passes between two incandescent electrodes.

arc-tic adj. Extremely cold or frigid; relating to the territory north of the Arctic Circle.

-ard or **-art** suff. A person who is characterized by performing something excessively.

ar-dor n. Extreme warmth or passion; emotion; intense heat.

ar-du-ous adj. Taking much effort to bring forth; difficult. **arduously** adv.

are v. First, second, and third person plural and second person singular of the verb "to be".

ar-e-a n. A flat or level piece of ground.

area-way n. A sunken area in a basement that offers access, light and air.

a-re-ca n. Tall palm of southeast Asia that has white flowers and red or orange egg-shaped nuts.

a-re-na n. Enclosed area for public entertainment, such as football games, concerts, etc.

a-re-na the-ater n. A theater with the stage located in the center and the audience seated around the stage.

aren't contr. Are not.

ar-gen-tite n. A lustrous ore.

ar-gil-la-ceous adj. Resembling or containing clay.

ar-go-sy n., pl. **-sies** A fleet of ships; a large merchant ship.

ar-got n. A secret, specialized vocabulary.

ar-gu-able adj. Open to argument.

ar-gue v. To debate, to offer reason for or against a subject; to dispute, argue, or quarrel; to persuade or influence.

ar-gu-men-ta-tion n. The process or art of arguing; debating.

ar-gu-men-ta-tive adj. Given to argument.

ar-gyle or **argyll** n. A pattern knitted with varicolored, diamond-shaped designs.

a-ri-a n. A vocal piece with accompaniment sung in solo; part of an opera.

ar-id adj. Insufficient rain; dry; lacking in interest or feeling; dull. **aridity** n.

a-right adv. Correctly; rightly.

a-rise v. To come from a source; to come to attention.

aris-ta n., pl. **-tae** or **-tas** Bristle-like appendage or structure.

ar-is-toc-ra-cy n. A government by the best individuals or by a small privileged class; a class or group viewed as superior; the hereditary privileged ruling nobility or class.

a-rith-me-tic adj. Branch of math that deals with addition, subtraction, multiplication, division. **arithmetical** adj., **arithmetically** adv.

a-rith-met-ic mean n. The number received by dividing the sum of a set of quantities by the number of quantities in the set.

a-rith-met-ic pro-gres-sion n. A progression in which the difference between any term and the one before or after is constant, as 2,4,6,8, etc.

-ar-i-um suff. The place or thing connected to or relating with.

arm n. The part between the shoulder and the wrist; upper limb of the human body. v. To furnish with protection against danger. **armer** n.

ar-ma-da n. A fleet of warships; a large force of moving things.

ar-ma-dil-lo n. A burrowing nocturnal animal with an armor-like covering of jointed, bony plates.

ar-ma-ment n. Military supplies and weapons; the process of preparing for battle.

ar-ma-ture n. The main moving part of an electric device or machine; a piece of soft iron that connects the poles of a magnet.

arm-chair *n.* A chair with armrests or supports.
adj. Remote from the direct dealing with problems.

arm-ed for-ces *n.* The combined air, military, and naval forces of a nation.

arm-ful *n., pl.* **armfuls** *or* **armsful** As much as the arm can hold.

arm-hole *n.* The opening in a garment for the arm.

ar-mi-stice *n.* The temporary suspension of combat by mutual agreement; truce.

arm-let *n.* A band worn on the upper arm.

ar-moire *n.* A large wardrobe or cupboard.

ar-mor *n.* Covering used in combat to protect the body, made from a heavy metal. **armor** *v.,* **armored** *adj.*

ar-mor-er *n.* A person who makes armor; one who assembles, repairs, and tests firearms.

ar-mory *n., pl.* **-mories** The supply of arms for attack or defense; the place where military equipment is stored.

arm-pit *n.* The hollow area under the arm where it joins the shoulder.

arm-rest *n.* The support for the arm, as on a chair.

ar-my *n., pl.* **-mies** A group of persons organized for a country's protection; the land forces of a country.

ar-my-worm *n.* Moth whose larvae travels in multitudes from one area to another destroying grain and grass.

ar-ni-ca *n.* Plant of the genus Arnica with yellow flowers from which a form of a tincture, as a liniment, is made.

a-ro-ma *n.* A distinctive fragrance or pleasant odor. **-tical,** aromatic *adj.*

a-round *adv.* To or on all sides; in succession or rotation; from one place to another; in a circle or circular movement.

arouse *v.* To wake up from a sleep; to stir; to excite. **arousal** *n.*

ar-peg-gi-o *n.* Tones of a chord produced in succession and not simultaneously.

arr *abbr.* Arranged; arrival; arrive.

ar-rack *n.* An alcoholic beverage distilled from the juices of the coconut palm, from the Far or Near East.

ar-raign *v.* To called before a court to answer a charge or indictment; to accuse of imperfection, inadequacy, or of wrong doing. **arraignment** *n.*

ar-range *v.* To put in correct order or proper sequence; to prepare for something; to take steps to organize something; to bring about an understanding or an agreement; to prepare or change a musical composition for instruments or voices other than those that is was written for.

ar-range-ment *n.* The state or being arranged; something made by arranging things or parts together.

ar-rant *adj.* Extreme; being notoriously without moderation. **arranty** *adv.*

ar-ras *n.* A screen or wall hanging of tapestry.

ar-ray *v.* To place or set in order; to draw up; to decorate or dress in an impressive attire. **arrayer** *n.*

ar-rears *n., pl.* The state of being behind something, as an obligation, payment, etc.; an unfinished duty.

ar-rear-age *n.* The condition of having something unpaid or overdue.

ar-rest *n.* To stop or to bring an end to; to capture; to seize; to hold in custody by the authority of law. **arrester, arrestor, arrestment** *n.*

arrest-ee *n.* A person under arrest.

ar-rest-ing *adj.* Very impressive or striking; catching the attention. **-ly** *adv.*

ar-rhyth-mia *n.* The alteration in rhythm of the heartbeat, either in force or time.

ar-rhyth-mic *adj.* Lacking regularity or rhythm.

ar-riv-al *n.* The act of arriving.

ar-ri-ve *v.* To reach or get to a destination.

ar-ro-gance *n.* An overbearing manner, intolerable presumption; an insolent pride. **arrogant, arrogantly** *adv.*

ar-row *n.* A weapon shot from a bow; a sign or mark to show direction.

ar-row-head *n.* The striking end of an arrow, usually shaped like a wedge. **arrowheaded** *adj.*

ar-row-root *n.* A starch-yielding plant of tropical America.

ar-row-wood *n.* Shrubs with tough pliant shoots that were formerly used in making arrowheads.

ar-rowy *adj.* To move swiftly; something that resembles an arrow.

ar-se-nal *n.* A collection of weapons; a place where arms and military equipment are manufactured or stored.

ar-se-nic *n.* A solid, poisonous element, steel-gray in color, used to make insecticide or weed killer. **arsenic, arsenical** *adj.*

ar-son *n.* The fraudulent burning of property. **arsonist** *n.,* **arsonous** *adj.*

art *n.* A human skill of expression of other objects by painting, drawing, sculpture, etc.; a branch of learning.

ar-te-ri-ole *n.* One of the small terminal twigs of an artery that ends in capillaries.

ar-ter-y *n., pl.* **-teries** A blood vessel that carries blood from the heart to the other parts of the body; a major means for transportation. **arterial** *adj.*

ar-te-sian well *n.*

A well that produces water without a pump.

art form *n.* The recognized form of an artistic expression.

art-ful *adj.* Showing or performed with skill or art. artfully *adv.*, artfulness *n.*

art glass *n.* Glass designed for decorative purposes; novelty glassware.

ar-thral-gia *n.* Pain that occurs in one or more joints. arthralgic *adj.*

ar-thritic *n.* A person who has arthritis. *adj.* Affected with arthritis; showing effects associated with aging.

ar-thri-tis *n.* Inflammation of joints due to infectious or metabolic causes.

ar-thro-pod *n.* An animal with jointed limbs and segmented body, as a spider. arthropodal, arthropodan, arthropodous *adj.*

ar-ti-choke *n.* A plant with a thistle-like head, which can be cooked and eaten as a vegetable.

ar-ti-cle *n.* A term or clause in a contract; a paragraph or section; a condition or rule; an object, item or commodity.

ar-tic-u-lar *adj.* Related to or of a joint.

ar-tic-u-late *adj.* Able to express oneself clearly, effectively, or readily; speaking in distinct words, or syllables. -ness, articulator *n.*, articulately *adv.*

ar-ti-fact *n.* Something made by man showing human modification or workmanship.

ar-ti-fice *n.* An artful or clever skill; ingenuity.

ar-ti-fi-cial *adj.* Not genuine; made by man; not found in nature. artificially *adv.*

ar-til-lery *n.* Weapons, especially cannons; troops that are trained in the use of guns and other means of defense.

ar-ti-san *n.* A mechanic or a craftsman.

art-ist *n.* A person who practices the fine arts of painting, sculpture, etc.

ar-tiste *n.* One who is an expert in the theatrical profession.

ar-tis-tic *adj.* Relating to the characteristic of an artist or art. artistically *adv.*

art-ist-ry *n.* The artistic ability, or quality of workmanship or effect.

art-less *adj.* Lacking knowledge, art, or skill; crude; natural; simple. artlessly *adv.*, artlessness *n.*

art-mobile *n.* A trailer that carries an art collection for exhibition on road tours.

art-work *n.* The artistic work of an artist.

as *adv.* In the manner like; of the same degree or amount; similar to.

as-bes-tos *n.* A noncombustible, fibrous, mineral form of magnesium silicate that is used especially in fireproofing. asbestine *adj.*

as-cend *v.* To rise up from a lower level; to climb; to mount; to walk up. ascendible, ascendable *adj.*

as-cen-dant *or* ascsendent *adj.* Rising; moving up.

as-cent *n.* A way up; a slope; the act of rising.

as-cer-tain *v.* To find out for certain; to make sure. -ment *n.*, -able *adj.*

as-cet-icism *n.* The practice of strict self-denial through personal and spiritual discipline.

as-cot *n.* A scarf or broad tie that is placed under the chin.

as-cribe *v.* To assign or attribute to something. ascribable, ascription *v.*

a-sex-u-al *adj.* Lacking sexual reproductive organs; without sex. asexuality *n.*

asg *abbr.* Assigned, assignment.

ash *n.* A type of tree with a hard, tough elastic wood; the grayish dust remaining after something has burned.

a-shamed *adj.* Feeling guilt, disgrace, or shame; feeling unworthy or inferior. ashamedly *adv.*

a-shore *adv.* On or to the shore.

aside *adv.* Out of the way; to a side.

ask *v.* To request; to require or seek information. asker *n.*

askance *adv.* With a side glance; with suspicion or distrust.

askew *adv. or adj.* Out of line, not straight.

a-slant *adv.* In a slanting direction.

a-sleep *adv.* In a state of sleep; lacking sensation; numb; not alert.

a-slope *adv.* In a slanting or sloping position or direction.

a-so-cial *adj.* Selfish, not social.

as-par-a-gus *n.* A vegetable with tender shoots, very succulent when cooked.

as-pect *n.* The situation, position, view, or appearance of something.

as-peri-ty *n., pl.* -ties Roughness in manner.

as-persion *v.* False charges or slander; defamation; maligning.

as-phyx-i-ate *v.* To suffocate, to prevent from breathing. asphyxiation *n.*

as-pic *n.* A savory jelly made from fish, meat, or vegetable juices.

as-pi-rate *v.* To give pronunciation with a full breathing sound; to draw out using suction. aspiration *n.*

as-pire *v.* To desire with ambition; to strive toward something that is higher. aspiringly *adv.*, aspirer *n.*

as-pi-rin *n.* Medication used for the relief of pain and fever.

ass *n.* A hoofed animal; a donkey; a stupid or foolish person.

as-sail *v.* To attack violently with words or blows. assailant *n.*

as-sault *n.* A very violent physical or verbal attack on a person. assaulter *n.*

as-say *n.* To evaluate or to assess; to try; to attempt. assayer *n.*

as-sem-blage *n.* A collection of things or people; artistic composition made from junk, scraps; and miscellaneous materials.

as-sem-ble *v.* To put together the parts of something; to come together as a group. assembly *n.*

as-sent *v.* To agree on something. -er *n.*

as-sert *v.* To declare or state positively, to maintain; to defend.

as-sess *v.* To fix or assign a value to something. assessor *n.*

as-sess-ment *n.* The official determination of value for tax purposes.

as-set *n.* A valuable quality or possession; all of the property of a business or a person that can be used to cover liabilities.

as-sev-er-ate v. To state positively, firmly, and seriously. asseveration n.

as-sign v. To designate as to duty; to give or allot; to attribute. assignable adj.

as-sign-ment n. A given amount of work or task to undertake; a post, position, or office to which one is assigned.

as-sim-i-late v. To take in, to understand; to make similar; to digest or to absorb into the system.
assimilator, assimilation n.

as-sist v. To give support, to aid, to give help. assistance, assistant n.

as-size n. A fixed or customary standard.

as-so-ci-ate v. To connect or join together. n. A partner, colleague, or companion.

as-so-ci-a-tion n. An organized body of people having a common interest; a society. associational adj.

as-so-nance n. The repetition of sound in words or syllables.

as-sort v. To distribute into groups of a classification or kind. assorter n., assortative adj.

as-sort-ed adj. Made up of different or various kinds.

as-suage v. To quiet, pacify; to put an end to by satisfying. assuagement n.

as-sua-sive adj. Having a smooth, pleasant effect or quality.

as-sume v. To take upon oneself to complete a job or duty; to take responsibility for; to take for granted.
assumable adj., assumably adv.

as-sump-tion n. An idea or statement believed to be true without proof.

as-sure v. To give the feeling of confidence; to make sure or certain.

as-sured adj. Satisfied as to the truth or certainty. assuredly adv.

as-ter n.

A plant having white, bluish, purple, or pink daisy-like flowers.

as-ter-isk n. The character (*) used to indicate letters omitted or as a reference to a footnote.

a-stern adv. & adj. Toward the rear or back of an aircraft or ship.

as though conj. As if.

astig-ma-tism n. A defect of the lens of an eye resulting in blurred or imperfect images.

as to prep. With reference to or regard to; concerning; according to.

as-ton-ish v. To strike with sudden fear, wonder, or surprise.

as-tound v. To fill with wonder and bewilderment. -ing adj. -ingly adv.

as-tra-khan n. The curly fur from a young lamb of the southeast U.S.S.R.

as-tral adj. Resembling, or related to the stars.

a-stray adv. Away from a desirable or proper path or development.

as-trin-gent adj. Able to draw together or to constricting tissue. astringency n.

as-trol-o-gy n. The study of the supposed influences of the planets and stars and their movements and positions on human affairs. -ical adj., -er n.

as-tro-naut n. A person who travels in a spacecraft beyond the earth's atmosphere.

as-tro-nau-tics n. The technology and science of the construction and operation of a spacecraft.
astronautical adj. astronautically adv.

as-tron-o-my n. The science of the celestial bodies and their motion, magnitudes, and constitution -er n.

as-tro-phys-ics n. Branch of astronomy dealing with the chemical and physical constitution of the celestial bodies.
astrophysical adj., astrophysicist n.

as-tute adj. Sharp in discernment; very shrewd. astutely adv., astuteness n.

a-sun-der adv. Separate into parts or positions apart from each other.

a-sym-metric adj. Something that is not symmetrical. asymmetry n.

at prep. To indicate presence, occurrence, or condition; used as a function word to indicate a certain time.

at-a-vism n. The reappearance a hereditary characteristic that skipped several generations. atavistic adj.

atax-ia n. Any nervous disorder with an inability to coordinate voluntary muscular movements. ataxic adj.

at-el-ier n. An artist's workshop.

a-the-ism n. The disbelief that God exists.

athe-ist n. A person who does not believe in God. -ic, atheistical adj.

a-thirst adj. Having a strong, eager desire for something.

ath-lete n. A person who participates in sports, as football, basketball, soccer, etc.

ath-let-ic adj. Relating to athletes; physically strong and active.

a-thwart adv. Opposition to the expected or right; from one side to another.

a-tilt adj. & adv. Inclined upward or tilted in some way.

at-las n. A collection or book of maps.

at-mos-phere n. A gaseous mass that surrounds a celestial body, as the earth; a predominant mood or feeling.

at-oll n. An island of coral that encircles a lagoon either partially or completely.

at-om n.

A tiny particle, the smallest unit of an element.

at-om-ic en-er-gy n. Energy that is released by changes in the nucleus of an atom.

a-ton-al adj. Marked by the deliberate avoidance of a traditional key or tonal center.

a-tone v. To give satisfaction; to make amends.

atop adj. On the top of something.

atri-um n. One of the heart chambers; the main hall of a Roman house.

a-tro-cious adj. Exceedingly cruel or evil.

a-troc-i-ty n., pl. -ties The condition of being atrocious; an atrocious act.

at-tach v. To bring together; to fasten or become fastened; to bind by personal attachments. **attachable** adj.

at-tain v. To arrive at or reach a goal. **attainability** n., -**able** adj. -**ness** n.

at-taint v. To disgrace or stain; to achieve or obtain by effort.

at-tar n. The fragrant oil from flowers.

at-tempt v. To make an effort to do something. **attempt** n.

at-tend v. To be present; to take charge of or to look after.

at-ten-tion n. Observation, notice, or mental concentration. **attentive** adj., **attentively** adv., **attentiveness** n.

at-ten-u-ate v. To lessen the force, amount or value; to become thin; to weaken. **attenuation** n.

at-test v. To give testimony or to sign one's name as a witness. **attestation** n.

at-ti-tude n. A mental position; the feeling one has for oneself.

at-tor-ney n., pl. -**neys** A person with legal training who is appointed by another to transact business for him.

at-tract v. To draw by appeal; to cause to draw near by appealing qualities.

at-trib-ute v. To explain by showing a cause. n. A characteristic of a thing or person. **attributable** adj.

at-tune v. To bring something into harmony; to put in tune; to adjust.

a-typ-i-cal adj. Not confirming to the typical type. **atypically** adv.

au cou-rant adj. Fully familiar or informed.

auc-tion n. A public sale of merchandise to the highest bidder. **auctioneer** n.

auc-to-ri-al adj. Having to do with an author.

au-da-cious adj. Bold, daring, or fearless; insolent. -**ly** adv., -**ity** n.

au-di-ble adj. Capable of being heard.

au-di-o adj. Of or relating to sound or its high-fidelity reproduction.

au-dit n. Verification or examination of financial accounts or records.

au-di-to-ry adj. Related to the organs or sense of hearing.

aught n. Zero (0).

aug-ment v. To add to or increase; to enlarge. **augmentation, augmenter** n., **augmentative, augmentable** adj.

au-ra n., pl. -**ras**, -**rae** An emanation said to come from a person's or an animal's body.

au-ral adj. Relating to the ear or the sense of hearing. **aurally** adv.

au-re-ate adj. Of a brilliant golden color.

au-re-ole n. A halo.

au re-voir interj. Used in expressing farewell to someone.

au-ri-cle n. The two upper chambers of the heart.

au-ric-u-lar adj. Dealing with the sense of hearing or of being in the shape of the ear.

aus-tere adj. Stern in manner and appearance. **austerity** n.

au-then-tic adj. Real; genuine; worthy of acceptance.

au-then-ti-cate v. To prove something is true or genuine. **authentication, authenticity, authenticator** n.

author n. A person who writes an original literary work. **author** v.

au-thor-i-ty n., pl. -**ties** A group or person with power; a government; an expert.

au-thor-ize v. To give authority, to approve, to justify.

au-to-bahn n. Highway in Germany.

au-to-bi-og-ra-phy n., pl. -**phies** The life story of a person, written by that person. **autobiographer** n.

au-toch-tho-nous adj. Native to an area.

au-toc-ra-cy n. Government by one person who has unlimited power. **autocrat** n., **autocratic** adj.

au-to-di-dact n. A person who has taught himself. **autodidactic** adj.

au-to-graph n. A handwritten signature.

au-to-in-tox-i-ca-tion n. Self-poisoning caused by metabolic wastes of other toxins in the body.

au-to-mate v. To operate by automation; To convert something to automation.

au-to-mat-ic adj. Operating with very little control; self-regulating.

au-ton-o-my n. Independence; self-government.

au-to-ma-tion n. The equipment and techniques used to acquire automation.

au-to-nom-ic adj. Pertaining to the autonomic system of the nervous system.

au-to-nom-ic ner-vous sys-tem n. The part of the body's nervous system which is regulated involuntarily.

au-top-sy n., pl. -**sies** Postmortem examination; the examination of a body after death to find the cause of death.

au-to-stra-da n. An expressway in Italy.

aux-il-ia-ry adj. Providing help or assistance to someone; giving support.

aux-il-ia-ry verb n. Verbs that accompany a main verb and express the mood, voice, or tense.

auxin n. The hormone in a plant that stimulates growth.

a-vail v. To be of advantage or use; to use. n. The advantage toward attaining a purpose or goal.

a-vail-able adj. Ready or present for immediate use. -**ness** adj., -**ly** adv.

av-a-lanche n. A large amount of rock or snow that slides down a mountainside.

a-vant--garde n. The people who apply and invent new ideas and styles in a certain field.

av-a-rice n. One's desire to have wealth and riches.

a-vast interj., Naut. A command to stop or cease.

a-venge v. To take revenge for something. **avenger** *n*.

a-ver *v.* To be firm and to state positively. **averment** *n*.

av-er-age *n.* Something that is typical or usual, not being exceptional; common.

a-verse *adj.* Having a feeling of distaste or repugnance. **-ness** *n.*, **aversely** *adv.*

a-vert *v.* To prevent or keep from happening; to turn aside or away from.

a-vi-ary *n.* A place where birds are kept.

a-vi-a-tion *n.* The operation of planes and other aircraft.

a-vi-a-tor *n.* Pilot of an aircraft.

av-id *adj.* Greedy; eager; enthusiastic.

av-o-ca-do *n*.

The pear-shaped edible fruit from the avocado tree, having a large seed and yellowish-green pulp.

av-o-ca-tion *n.* A pleasurable activity that is in addition to the regular work a person must do; a hobby.

a-void *v.* To stay away from; to shun; to prevent or keep from happening. **avoidable** *adj.*, **avoidably** *adv.*

a-vouch *v.* To assert; to guarantee.

a-vow *v.* To state openly on a subject.

a-wait *v.* To wait for something.

a-wake *v.* To wake up; to be alert or watchful.

a-ware *adj.* Being conscious or mindful of something. **awareness** *n.*

a-way *adv.* At a distance; apart from.

awe *n.* A feeling of wonder mixed with reverence. **awe** *v.*

a-wea-ry *adj.* Tired.

aw-ful *adj.* Very unpleasant or dreadful.

a-while *adv.* For a short time.

a-whirl *adj.* To spin around.

awk-ward *adj.* Not graceful; clumsy. **awkwardly** *adv.*, **awkwardness** *n.*

a-wry *adv.* In a twisted or turned position.

ax *or* **axe** *n.* Tool used to split wood.

ax-i-om *n.* Statement recognized as being true; something assumed to be true without proof. **-atic** *adj.*, **-cally** *adv.*

ax-is *n.*, *pl.* **axes**

The line around an object or body that rotates or may be thought to rotate.

ax-le *n.* A spindle or shaft around which a wheel or pair of wheels revolve.

a-yah *n.* A native nursemaid or maid in India.

a-zo-ic *adj.* Time period which occured before life first appeared on the earth.

AZT *abbr.* Azidothymidine; a drug that improves the symptoms of AIDS; (Acquired Immune Deficiency Syndrome), allowing a longer and better life. Approved early 1987 by the Federal Government for prescription use.

az-ure *n.* The blue color of the sky.

B, b The second letter of the English alphabet; a student's grade rating of good, but not excellent.

bab-ble *v.* To reveal secrets; to chatter senselessly; to talk foolishly.

babe *n.* A very young child or infant.

ba-bel *n.* Babbling noise of many people talking at the same time.

ba-boon *n.* A species of the monkey family with a large body and big canine teeth.

ba-by *n.*, *pl.* **babies** A young child; infant. **babyish** *adj.*

bac-ca-lau-re-ate *n* A degree given by universities and colleges.

bach-e-lor *n.* An unmarried male; the first degree one can receive from a four year university.

ba-cil-lus *n.*, *pl.* **bacilli** A rod-like microscopic organism which can cause certain diseases.

back *n.* The rear part of the human body from the neck to the end of the spine, also the rear part of an animal.

back-ache *n.* A pain in the back.

back-bite *v.* To gossip or speak in a nasty way about a person who is not present.

back-board *n.* A board that gives support when placed under or behind something.

back-bone *n.* The spinal column or spine of the vertebrates; the strongest support, or strength.

back-drop *n.* A curtain or scene behind the back of a stage set.

back-er *n.* One who gives support to a cause.

back-field *n.* Football players who are positioned behind the line of scrimmage.

back-fire *n.* Premature explosion of unburned exhaust gases or ignited fuel of an internal-combustion engine.

back-gam-mon *n.* A game played by two people wherein each player tries to move his counters on the board, at the same time trying to block his opponent.

back-ground *n.* The area or surface behind which objects are represented; conditions leading up to a happening; the collection of a person's complete experience.

back-hand *n.* A stroke in the game of tennis, made with the back of the hand facing outward. **backhand** *v.*, **backhanded** *adj.*

back-ing *n.* Support or aid; a supply in reserve.

back-lash *n* A violent backward movement or reaction.

back-log *n.* An accumulation of unfinished work; a reserve supply.

back-pack *n.* A piece of equipment used to carry items on the back, mounted on a lightweight frame, and constructed of nylon or canvas.

back-pedal *v.* To move backward or retreat.

back-rest *n.* A support given to the back.

back room *n.* A room in the rear of a building for inconspicuous group meetings.

back-saw *n.* Saw with metal ribs on its back side.

back-seat *n.* The seat in the back of an auto-mobile, etc.; an inferior position.

back-side *n.* The buttocks.

back-slide *v.* To lapse back into a less desirable condition, as in a religious practice. **backsliding** *v.*, **backslider** *n.*

back-spin *n.* A spin which rotates in the reverse direction.

back-stage *n.* The area behind the performing area in a theatre.

back-stop *n.* Something that prevents a ball from being hit out of play.

back-stretch *n.* The opposite of the homestretch on a racecourse.

back-stroke *n.* A swimming stroke performed while on the back.

back-swept *adj.* Slanting or swept backward.

back-talk *n.* A smart or insolent reply.

back-track *v.* To reverse a policy; to retrace previous steps. **backtracking** *v.*

back-up *n.* One that serves as an alternative or substitute.

back-ward *adv.* Toward the back; to or at the back. **backwardness** *n.*, **backwards** *adv.*

back-wash *n.* A backward flow of water.

back-wa-ter *n.* A body of water turned back by an obstruction.

back-woods *n., pl.* A sparsely populated, heavily wooded area. **backwoodsman** *n.*

ba-con *n.* Side and back of a pig, salted and smoked.

bac-ter-ia *pl., n.* The plural of bacterium.

bac-te-ri-cide *n.* A substance that kills bacteria.

bac-te-ri-ol-o-gy *n.* Scientific study of bacteria.

bac-te-ri-um *n., pl.* **-ria** Any of various forms of numerous unicellular micro organisms that cause disease. **bacterial** *adj.*

bad *adj.* Naughty or disobedient; unfavorable; inferior; poor; spoiled; invalid. **badly** *adv.*

badger *n.*

A sturdy burrowing mammal. *v.* To harass or trouble persistently.

bad-lands *pl., n.* Area with sparse life, peaks, and eroded ridges.

bad-min-ton *n.* A court game played with long-handled rackets and a shuttlecock.

baf-fle *v.* To puzzle; to perplex. *n.* A device that checks or regulates the flow of gas, sound, or liquids etc. **baffled, baffling** *v.*

bag *n.* A flexible container used for holding, storing, or carrying something. **bag** *v.* **bagful** *n.*, **baggy** *adj.*

ba-gasse *n.* Plant residue.

ba-gel *n.* A hard, glazed, round roll with a chewy texture and a hole in the middle.

bag-gage *n.* The personal belongings of a traveler.

bag-gy *adj.* Loose. **baggily** *adv.*

bag-man *n.* A person who collects illicit payments for another.

bag-pipe *n.* A wind instrument with a leather bag and melody pipes. **bagpiper** *n.*

ba-guette *n.* A gem in the shape of a long, narrow rectangle.

bag-wig *n.* An 18th century wig with the hair in the back contained in a small silk bag.

bag-worm *n.* A type of moth larva that lives in a silk case covered with plant debris, very destructive to evergreens.

bail *n.* The security or money given to guarantee the appearance of a person for trial. *v.* To remove water from a boat by dipping and emptying the water overboard. **bailor, bailer** *n.*

bail-iff *n.* The officer who guards prisoners and keeps order in a courtroom.

bail-i-wick *n.* The office or district of a bailiff.

bails-man *n.* The person who puts up the bail for another.

bait *v.* To lure; to entice. *n.* Food that is used to catch or trap an animal.

baize *n.* A coarse woolen or cotton cloth.

bake *v.* To cook in an oven; to harden or dry. **baking, baked** *v.*, **baker** *n.*

baker's dozen *n.* Thirteen.

bak-ing pow-der *n.* A leavening agent used in baking consisting of carbonate, an acid substance, and flour or starch.

bak-ing soda *n.* Sodium bicarbonate.

bak-sheesh *n.* A tip or gratuity.

bal-a-lai-ka *n.* A three-stringed musical instrument.

bal-ance *n.* Device for determining the weight of something; the agreement of totals in the debit and credit of an account.

bal-co-ny *n., pl.* **-nies** Gallery or platform projecting from the wall of a building.

bald *adj.* Lacking hair on the head.

bal-der-dash *n.* Nonsense.

bale *n.* A large, bound package or bundle.

ba-leen *n.* A whalebone.

balk *v.* To refuse to go on; to stop short of something. *n.* A rafter or crossbeam extending from wall to wall. **balking** *v.*, **balky** *adj.*

ball *n.* A round body or mass; a pitched baseball that is delivered outside of the strike zone.

bal-lad *n.* A narrative story or poem of folk origin; a romantic song.

bal·last *n.* Heavy material placed in a vehicle to give stability and weight.

ball bear·ing *n.* A bearing that reduces friction by separating the stationary parts from the moving ones.

bal·le·ri·na *n.* A female ballet dancer in a company.

bal·let *n.* An artistic expression of dance by choreographic design.

bal·lis·tic missile *n.* A projectile that is self-powered, is guided during ascent, and has a free fall trajectory at descent.

bal·loon *n.* A bag inflated with gas lighter than air which allows it to float in the atmosphere, used as a child's toy.

bal·lot *n.* A slip of paper used in secret voting. *v.* To vote by ballot.

ball·park *n.* A stadium where ball games are played.

ball·point *n.* A pen that has a small self-inking writing point.

bal·ly·hoo *n.* Exaggerated advertising.

balm *n.* A fragrant ointment that soothes, comforts, and heals.

ba·lo·ney *n., Slang* Nonsense.

bal·sa *n.* American tree that is very light in weight.

bal·sam *n.* A fragrant ointment from different trees; a plant cultivated for its colorful flowers.

bal·us·ter *n.* The upright post that supports a handrail.

bam·boo *n.* Tropical, tall grass with hollow, pointed stems.

bam·boo·zle *v.* To trick or deceive. bamboozled, bamboozling *v.*

ban *v.* To prohibit; to forbid. banning, banned *v.*

ba·nal *adj.* Trite; lacking freshness.

ba·nan·a *n.* The crescent-shaped usually yellow, edible fruit of a tropical plant.

band *n.* A strip used to trim, finish, encircle, or bind; the range of a radio wave length; a group of musicians who join together to play their instruments.

band·age *n.* A strip of cloth used to protect an injury. bandage *v.*

ban·dan·na *n.* A brightly colored cotton or silk handkerchief.

ban·deau *n.* A narrow band worn in the hair; a narrow brassiere.

ban·dit *n., pl.* bandits, banditti A gangster or robber. banditry *n.*

ban·do·leer *n.* A belt worn over the shoulder with pockets for cartridges.

ban·dy *adv.* Bent; crooked; curved outward.

bane *n.* A cause of destruction. -ful *adj.*

bang *n.* A sudden loud noise; short hair cut across the forehead. *v.* To move or hit with a loud noise.

ban·gle *n.* A bracelet worn around the wrist or ankle.

ban·ish *v.* To leave; to drive away. banished, banishing *v.*, -er, -ment *n.*

ban·jo *n.* A stringed instrument similar to a guitar. banjoist *n.*

bank *n.* A slope of land adjoining water; an establishment that performs financial transactions. bankable *adj.*

bank·rupt *n., pl.* -cies One who is legally insolvent and whose remaining property is divided among creditors. bankrupt *v.*, bankruptcy *n.*

ban·ner *n.* A piece of cloth, such as a flag, that is used as a standard by a commander or monarch.

ban·nock *n.* Unleavened or flat cake made from barley or oatmeal.

banns *pl., n.* The announcement of a forthcoming marriage.

ban·quet *n.* An elaborate dinner or feast.

ban·yan *n.* A tree from the tropics whose aerial roots grow downward to form additional roots.

bap·tism *n.* A Christian sacrament of spiritual rebirth through the application of water. baptismal *adj.*

bap·tize *v.* To immerse in water during baptism. baptized, -ing *v.*, baptizer *n.*

bar *n.* A rigid piece of material used as a support; a counter where a person can receive drinks. *v.* To prohibit or exclude.

barb *n.* A sharp projection that extends backward making it difficult to remove. barbed *adj.*

bar·bar·i·an *n.* A person or culture thought to be primitive and therefore inferior. barbarous, barbaric *adj.*

bar·be·cue *n.* An outdoor fireplace or pit for roasting meat. barbecue *v.*

bar·bell *n.* A bar with weights at both ends, used for exercise.

bar·ber *n.* A person whose business is cutting and dressing hair and shaving and trimming beards.

bar·ber·shop *n.* The place of business where hair is cut.

bard *n.* A poet. bardic *adj.*

bare *adj.* Exposed to view; without coloring. bare *v.*, bareness *n.*

bare·back *adv. & adj.* Riding a horse without a saddle.

bare·ly *adv.* Sparsely; by a very little amount.

barf *v. Slang* To vomit.

bar·gain *n.* A contract or agreement on the purchase or sale of an item; a purchase made at a favorable or good price. bargainer *n.*

barge *n.* A flat-bottomed boat. *v.* To intrude abruptly.

bar·i·tone *n.* A male voice in the range between tenor and bass.

bark *n.* The outer covering of a tree; the abrupt, harsh sound made by a dog. barker *n.*

bar·ley *n.* A type of grain used for food and for making whiskey and beer.

bar mitz·vah *n.* A Jewish boy who, having reached the age of 13, assumes the moral and religious duties of an adult.

barn *n.* A farm building used to shelter animals and to store farm equipment and products.

bar·na·cle *n.* A fish with a hard shell that remains attached to an underwater surface.

ba·rom·et·er *n.* An instrument that records the weight and pressure of the atmosphere.

bar-on *n.* The lowest rank of nobility in Great Britain. **-ness** *n.*, **baronial** *adj.*

ba-roque *adj.* An artistic style characterized by elaborate and ornate forms.

bar-rack *n.* A building for housing soldiers.

bar-ra-cu-da *n., pl.* **-da, -das** A fish with a large, narrow body, found in the Atlantic Ocean.

bar-rage *n.* A concentrated outpouring or discharge of missiles from small arms.

bar-ra-try *n.* The unlawful breach of duty by a ship's crew that results in injury to the ship's owner.

bar-rel *n.* Wooden container with round, flat ends of equal size and sides that bulge.

bar-ren *adj.* Lacking vegetation; sterile.

bar-rette *n.* A clasp or small bar used to hold hair in place.

bar-ri-cade *n.* Barrier.

bar-ri-er *n.* A structure that restricts or bars entrance.

bar-room *n.* A building or room where a person can purchase alcoholic beverages sold at a counter.

bar-row *n.* A rectangular, flat frame with handles; a wheelbarrow.

bar-tend-er *n.* A person who serves alcoholic drinks and other refreshments at a bar.

bar-ter *v.* To trade something for something else without the exchange of money. **-ing** bartered *v.*, **barterer** *n.*

ba-salt *n.* A greenish-black volcanic rock.

base *n.* The fundamental part; the lowest part; the bottom. **base** *v.*

base-ball *n.* A game played with a ball and bat; the ball used in a baseball game.

base-board *n.* A molding that covers the area where the wall meets the floor.

base-ment *n.* The foundation of a building or home.

bash *v.* To smash with a heavy blow; *Slang* A party. **bashed, bashing** *v.*

bash-ful *adj.* Socially shy. **bashfully** *adv.*

ba-sic *adj.* Forming the basis; fundamental. **basically** *adv.*

BASIC *n.* A common computer programming language.

bas-il *n.* An herb used as seasoning in cooking.

bas-o-lisk *n.* A tropical American lizard.

ba-sin *n.* A sink; a washbowl; a round open container used for washing; an area that has been drained by a river system.

ba-sis *n., pl.* **bases** The main part; foundation.

bask *v.* To relax in the warmth of the sun. **basking, basked** *v.*

bas-ket *n.* An object made of woven material, as straw, cane, or other flexible items. **basketry** *n.*

bas-ket-ball *n.* A game played on a court with two teams; each team trying to throw the ball through the basketball hoop at the opponents' end of the

bas-ket-ball *n.* A game played on a court with two teams; each team trying to throw the ball through the basketball hoop at the opponents' end of the court.

bass *n., pl.* **basses**

A fresh water fish, one of the perch family.

bas-si-net *n.* A basket on legs used as an infant's crib.

bas-soon *n.* A woodwind instrument with a low-pitched sound.

bas-tard *n.* An illegitimate child. *Slang* A disagreeable, nasty, or mean person. **bastardize** *v.*

baste *v.* To run a loose stitch to hold a piece of material in place for a short time. **-ed, -ing** *v.*

bat *n.*
A wooden stick made from strong wood; a nocturnal flying mammal. **bat** *v.*, **batter** *n.*

bath *n., pl.* **-baths** The act of washing the body.

bathe *v.* To take a bath. **bathing** *v.*

bat-mitz-vah *n.* A Jewish girl who having reached the age of thirteen, assumes the moral and religious duties of an adult.

bat-ter *v.* To beat or strike continuously; to assault. *n.* A cricket or baseball player at bat. **battering, battered** *v.*

bat-tery *n.* A group of heavy guns.

bat-tle *n.* A struggle; combat between opposing forces. *v.* To engage in a war or battle. **battled, battling** *v.*

bawd *n.* A prostitute. **bawdy** *adj.*

bawl *v.* To cry very loudly.

bay *n.* The inlet of a body of water; a main division or compartment.

bay-berry *n.* Evergreen shrub used for decorations and making candles.

bay-o-net *n.* A spear-like weapon.

ba-zaar *n.* A fair where a variety of items are sold as a money-making project for charity, clubs, churches, or other such organizations.

ba-zooka *n.* Weapon for firing rockets.

be *v.* To occupy a position; to exist; used with the present participle of a verb to show action; used as a prefix to construct compound words, as behind, before, because, etc.

beach *n.* Pebbly or sandy shore of a lake, ocean, sea, or river.

bea-con *n.* A coastal guiding or signaling device.

bead *n.* A small round piece of material with a hole for threading. **beading** *n.*

beak *n.* The bill of a bird. **beaked** *adj.*

beak-er *n.* Large, widemouthed cup for drinking; a cylindrical, glass laboratory vessel with a lip for pouring.

beam *n.* Large, oblong piece of wood or metal used in construction. *v.* To shine.

bean *n.* An edible seed or seed pod.

bear *n., pl.* **bears**

A carnivorous mammal. *v.* To endure; to carry; to support. **bearable,** *adj.*

beard *n.* Hair growing on the chin and cheeks. **bearded, beardless** *adj.*

beast *n.* A four-legged animal. **-ly** *adj.*

beat *v.* To strike repeatedly; to defeat. *adj.* Exhausted, very tired. **beaten** *adj.*, **beat, beater** *n.*

be-a-tif-ic *adj.* Giving or showing extreme bliss or joy.

be-at-i-tude *n.* The highest form of happiness; heavenly bliss.

beau *n.* Sweetheart; dandy.

beau-ty *n.* Quality that is pleasing to the eye. **beautiful** *adj.*, **beautifully,** *adv.*

be-bop *n.* Slang Jazz music.

be-calm *v.* To make quiet. **becalming** *v.*

be-cause *conj.* For a reason; since.

beck *n.* A summons; a call.

be-come *v.* To come, to be, or to grow. **becoming** *adj.*

bed *n.* Furniture for sleeping; a piece of planted or cultivated ground. **-ding** *n.*

be-dazzle *v.* To confuse with bright lights. **bedazzling, bedazzled** *v.*

bed-bug *n.* A wingless insect that sucks blood and infests human homes, especially beds.

bed-fast *adj.* Confined to a bed; bedridden.

bed-lam *n.* A state or situation of confusion.

be-drag-gled *adj.* Limp and wet; soiled as though pulled through mud.

bee *n.* A hairy-bodied insect characterized by structures for gathering pollen and nectar from flowers.

beech *n.* A tree of light-colored bark, with edible nuts.

beef *n., pl.* **beefs, beeves** A cow, steer, or bull that has been fattened for consumption. **beefy** *adj.*

beer *n.* An alcoholic beverage.

bees-wax *n.* The wax from bees that is used for their honeycombs.

beet *n.* The root from a cultivated plant that can be used as a vegetable or a source of sugar.

bee-tle *n.* An insect with modified, horny front wings, which cover the membranous back wings when it is not in flight.

be-fit *v.* To be suitable. **befitting** *adj.*

be-fore *adv.* Earlier; previously. *prep.* In front of.

be-friend *v.* To be a friend to someone.

beg *v.* To make a living by asking for charity. **beggar** *n.*, **beggarly** *adj.*

be-gan *v.* The past tense of begin.

be-get *v.* To cause or produce.

be-gin *v.* To start; to come into being; to commence. **beginner, beginning** *n.*

be-gone *v.*, *interj.* Go away; depart.

be-go-nia *n.* A tropical plant with waxy flowers and showy leaves.

be-grime *v.* To soiled with grime.

be-grudge *v.* To envy someone's possessions or enjoyment.

be-guile *v.* To deceive; to delight; to charm. **beguiled** *v.*

be-gun *v.* The past participle of begin.

be-half *n.* The support or interest of another person.

be-have *v.* To function in a certain manner; to conduct oneself in a proper manner. **behaving** *v.*, **behavior,** *n.*

be-head *v.* To remove the head from the body; to decapitate.

be-held *v.* Past participle of behold.

be-hind *adv.* To or at the back; late or slow in arriving.

be-hold *v.* To look at; to see.

be-hoove *v.* To benefit or give advantage.

beige *n. or adj.* A light brownish, grey color.

being *n.* One's existence.

be-la-bor *v.* To work on or to discuss beyond the point where it is necessary; to carry to absurd lengths.

be-lat-ed *adj.* Tardy; late. **belatedly** *adv.*

bel can-to *n.* Operatic singing with rich lyricism and brilliant vocal means.

belch *v.* To expel stomach gas through the mouth.

bel-fry *n., pl.* **belfries** The tower that contains the bell of a church.

be-lief *n.* Something that is trusted or believed.

be-lieve *v.* To accept as true or real; to hold onto religious beliefs. **believable** *adj.*, **believer** *n.*

be-lit-tle *v.* To think or speak in a slighting manner of someone or something. **belittled, belittling** *v.*

bell *n.* A metal instrument that gives a metallic sound when struck.

bel-la-don-na *n.* A poisonous plant with black berries; a medicine extracted from the belladonna plant.

bell--bot-toms *pl., n.* Pants with legs that flare at the bottom.

belles--let-tres *pl., n.* Literature that is regarded not for its value, but for its artistic quality.

bel-lig-er-ent *adj.* Hostile and inclined to be aggressive. **belligerence** *n.*, **belligerent** *n.*

bel-low *v.* To make a deep, powerful roar like a bull. **bellowed, bellowing** *v.*

bel-lows *n.* An instrument that produces air in a chamber and expels it through a short tube.

bel-ly *n., pl.* **bellies** The abdomen or the stomach.

be-long *v.*, *pl.* **belongings** *n.* To be a part of. **belonging** *n.*

be-loved *adj.* To be dearly loved.

be-low *adv.* At a lower level or place. *prep.* To be inferior to.

belt *n.* A band worn around the waist; a zone or region that is distinctive in a special way.

belt-way *n.* A highway that encircles an urban area.

be-muse *v.* To bewilder or confuse; to

be lost in thought.

bemusing v., **bemused** adj.

bench n. A long seat for more than two people; the seat of the judge in a court of law.

bend v. To arch; to change the direct course; to deflect. -ing v., **bender** n.

beneath adv. To or in a lower position; below; underneath.

ben-e-dict n. A previously confirmed bachelor who was recently married.

ben-e-dic-tion n. A blessing given at the end of a religious service.

ben-e-fac-tion n. A charitable donation; a gift. **benefactor** n.

ben-e-fice n. Fixed capital assets of a church that provide a living.

be-nef-i-cence n. The quality of being kind or charitable.

ben-e-fi-cial adj. Advantageous; helpful. **beneficially** adv.

ben-e-fit n. Aid; help; an act of kindness; a social event or entertainment to raise money for a person or cause.

be-nev-o-lence n. The inclination to be charitable. **benevolent** adj.

be-night-ed adj. Overtaken by night.

be-nign adj., pl. -ities. Having a gentle and kind disposition; gracious; not malignant. **benignly** adv.

ben-i-son n. A blessing; benediction.

bent adj. Curved, not straight. n. A fixed determination; purpose.

be-numb v. To dull; to make numb.

be-queath v. To give or leave to someone by will; to hand down. -al n.

be-quest n. Something that is bequeathed.

be-rate v. To scold severely.

be-reave v. To deprive; to suffer the loss of a loved one.

bereft adj., **bereavement** n.

be-ret n. A round, woolen cap that has no brim.

berg n. A large mass of ice; iceberg.

ber-i-ber-i n. Nervous disorder from the deficiency of vitamin B producing partial paralysis of the extremities.

berry n., pl. **berries** An edible fruit, such as a strawberry or blackberry.

ber-serk adj. Destructively violent.

berth n. Space at a wharf for a ship or boat to dock; a built-in bunk or bed on a train or ship.

ber-yl n. A mineral composed of silicon, oxygen, and beryllium that is the major source of beryllium.

be-ryl-li-um n. A corrosion-resistant, rigid, light-weight metallic element.

be-seech v. To ask or request earnestly.

be-side prep. At the side of; next to.

be-siege v. To surround with troops; to harass with requests.

be-sit v. To surround on all sides.

be-smear v. To soil; to smear.

be-som n. A broom made of twigs that are attached to a handle, used to sweep floors.

be-spat-ter v. To splash; to soil.

be-speak v. To indicate; to speak.

best adj. Exceeding all others in quality or excellence; most suitable, desirable, or useful.

bes-tial adj., pl. -ities Of or relating to an animal; brutish. -ly adv., **bestiality** n.

bes-ti-ar-y n. A medieval collection of fables about imaginary and real animals, each with a moral.

be-stir v. To rouse into action.

best man n. The attendant of a bridegroom at a wedding.

be-stow v. To present or to give honor.

be-stride v. To step over or to straddle.

bet n. An amount risked on a stake or wager.

be-take v. To cause oneself to make one's way; move or to go.

beta particle n. High-speed positron or electron coming from an atomic nucleus that is undergoing radioactive decay.

be-ta-tron n. Accelerator in which electrons are propelled by the inductive action of a rapidly varying magnetic field.

be-think v. To remember or to remind oneself.

be-tide v. To happen to; to take place.

be-to-ken v. To show by a visible sign.

be-tray v. To be disloyal or unfaithful; to indicate; to deceive. **betrayal** n.

be-troth v. To promise to take or give in marriage. **betrothal** n.

be-trothed n. A person to whom one is engaged to marry.

bet-ter adj. More suitable, useful, desirable, or higher in quality. v. To improve oneself. **betterment** n.

be-tween prep. The position or time that separates; in the middle or shared by two.

be-twixt prep. Not knowing which way one should go; between.

bev-el n. The angle at which one surface meets another when they are not at right angles.

bev-er-age n. A refreshing liquid for drinking other than water.

bev-y n., pl. -bevies A collection or group; a flock of birds.

be-wail v. To express regret or sorrow.

be-ware v. To be cautious; to be on guard.

be-wil-der v. To confuse; to perplex or puzzle. **bewilderment** n.

be-witch v. To fascinate or captivate completely. **-ery** n., **bewitchment** v.

bey n. The Turkish title of respect and honor.

be-yond prep. Outside the reach or scope of; something past or to the far side.

bez-el n. A flange or groove that holds the beveled edge of an object such as a gem in a ring mounting.

be-zique n. A card game that uses a deck of 64 cards, similar to pinochle.

bi pref. Two; occurring two times; used when constructing nouns.

bi-a-ly n. A baked roll with onions on the top.

bi-an-nu-al adj. Taking place twice a year; semiannual. **biannually** adv.

bi-as n. A line cut diagonally across the

grain of fabric; prejudice. v. To be or
to show prejudice.

bib n. A cloth that is tied under the chin
of small children to protect their
clothing.

Bi-ble n. The holy book of Christianity,
containing the Old and New Testa-
ments. **Biblical** adj., **Biblically** adv.

bib-li-og-ra-phy n., pl. -phies A list of
work by a publisher or writer; a list of
sources of information. -her n.

bib-u-lous adj. Inclined to drink, of or
related to drinking.

bi-cen-ten-ni-al adj. Happening once
every 200 years. n. Anniversary or
celebration of 200 years.

bi-ceps n.

Large muscle in the
front of the upper
arm and at the back
of the thigh.
bicipital adj.

bick-er v. To quarrel or argue. **bicker** n.

bi-con-cave adj. Bowing in on two sides.

bi-cul-tur-al adj. Having or containing
two distinct cultures.

bi-cus-pid n. A tooth with two roots.

bi-cy-cle n. A two-wheeled vehicle
propelled by pedals. **bicyclist** n.

bid v. To request something; to offer to
pay a certain price. n. One's intention
in a card game. **bidder** n.

bid-dy n. A young chicken; hen. Slang A
fussy woman.

bide v. To remain; to wait.

bi-det n. A basin for bathing the genital
and anal areas.

bi-en-ni-al adj. Occurring every two
years; lasting for only two years.
biennially adv.

bier n. A stand on which a coffin is
placed before burial.

bi-fo-cal adj. Having two different focal
lengths.

bifocals pl., n. Lenses used to correct
both close and distant vision.

bi-fur-cate v. To divide into two parts.

big adj. Very large in dimensions, intensity, and extent; grown-up;
bountiful. **bigness** n.

big-a-my n., pl. **bigamies** The act of
marrying one person while still
married to another. **bigamist** n.

big head adj. A conceited person.
bigheadedness n.

big--hearted adj. Being generous and
kind.

bighorn n A sheep from the mountainous western part of North
America.

bight n. The slack in a rope; a bend in
the shoreline.

big-ot n., pl. -ries A person who is
fanatically devoted to one group,
religion, politics, or race.
bigoted adj., **bigotry** n.

big-wig n. A person of authority.

bike n. A bicycle. **bike** v., **biker** n.

bi-ki-ni n. A scanty, two-piece bathing
suit.

bi-lat-er-al adj. Having or relating to
two sides.

bile n. A brownish-yellow alkaline liquid
that is secreted by the liver.
billary adj.

bilge n. Lowest inside part of the hull of
a ship.

bi-lin-gual adj. Able to speak two languages with equal ability.

bil-ious adj. Undergoing gastric distress
from a sluggish gallbladder or liver.

bilk v. To cheat or swindle.

bill n. Itemized list of fees for services
rendered; a document presented containing a formal statement of a case
complaint or petition; the beak of a
bird. **bill** v., **biller** n.

bill-board n. A place for displaying
advertise-ments.

bill-fold n. Pocket-sized wallet for holding money and personal information.

bil-liards n. Game played on a table with
cushioned edges.

bil-lion n. A thousand million.

bil-lion-aire n. A person whose wealth
equals at least one billion dollars.

bill of lading n. A form issued by the
carrier for promise of delivery of merchandise listed.

Bill of Rights n. The first ten amendments to the United States Constitution.

bil-low n. Large swell of water or
smoke; wave. **billowy** adj.

bil-ly club n. A short wooden club used
for protection or defense.

billy goat n. A male goat.

bi-met-al-lism n. The use of two metals,
gold and silver, as legal tenders.

bi-month-ly adj., pl. -lies Occurring
every two months.

bin n. An enclosed place for storage.

bi-na-ry adj. Made of two different
components or parts.

bind v. To hold with a belt or rope; to
bandage; to fasten and enclose pages
of a book between covers. **binding** n.

bind-er n. A notebook for holding
paper; payment or written statement
legally binding an agreement.

bind-er-y n., pl. -eries The place where
books are taken to be bound.

binge n. Uncontrollable selfindulgence; a
spree.

bin-go n. A game of chance in which a
person places markers on numbered
cards in accordance with numbers
drawn by a caller.

bin-na-cle n. A place where a ship's
compass is contained.

bin-oc-u-lar n. A device designed for
both eyes to bring objects far away
into focus.

bi-o-chem-is-try n. Chemistry of substances and biological processes.

bi-o-de-grad-a-ble adj. Decomposable
by natural processes.

bi-o-feed-back n. The technique of controlling involuntary bodily functions.

bi-o-haz-ard n. Biological material that
threatens humans and or their environment if infective.

biological warfare *n.* Warfare that uses organic biocides or diseaseproducing microorganisms to destroy crops, livestock, or human life.

bi-ol-o-gy *n.* Science of living organisms and the study of their structure, reproduction, and growth. **biological** *adj.*, **biologist** *n.*

bi-o-med-i-cine *n.* Medicine that has to do with human response to environmental stress.

bi-on-ics *n.* Application of biological principles to the study and design of engineering systems, as electronic systems.

bi-o-phys-ics *n.* The physics of living organisms.

bi-op-sy *n., pl.* **biopsies** The examination for the detection of a disease in tissues removed from a living organism.

bi-ot-ic *adj.* Related to specific life conditions or to life itself.

bi-o-tin *n.* Part of the vitamin B complex found in liver, milk, yeast, and egg yolk.

bi-par-ti-san *adj.* Support by two political parties. **bipartisanship** *n.*

bi-plane *n.* A glider or airplane with wings on two levels.

bi-polar *adj.* Having or related to two poles; concerning the earth's North and South Poles.

bi-racial *adj.* Composed of or for members of two races.

birch *n.* A tree providing hard, closegrained wood.

bird *n.* A warm-blooded, egg-laying animal whose body is covered by feathers.

bird-brain *n., Slang* A person who acts in a silly fashion.

bird-ie *n.* A stroke under par in the game of golf; a shuttlecock.

bi-ret-ta *n.* Cap worn by Roman Catholic clergy, square in shape.

birl-ing *n.* A game of skill in which two lumberjacks try to balance on a floating log while spinning the log with their feet.

birth *n.* The beginning of existence. *v.* To bring forth a baby from the womb.

birth con-trol *n.* A technique used to control or prevent the number of children born by lessening the chances of conception.

birth-day *n.* The day a person is born and the anniversary of that day.

birth-mark *n.* A blemish or mark on the skin present at birth.

birth-place *n.* The place of birth.

birth-rate *n.* The ratio of the number of births to a given population over a specified period of time.

birth-right *n.* Privilege granted by virtue of birth especially to the first-born.

birth-stone *n.* A gemstone that represents the month a person was born in.

bis *adv.* Again; encore.

bis-cuit *n.* Small piece of bread made with baking soda or baking powder; a cookie.

bi-sect *v.* To divide or cut into two equal parts. **bisection** *n.*

bi-sex-u-al *adj.* Sexually relating to both sexes.

bish-op *n.* A Christian clergyman with high rank. **bishopric** *n.*

bis-muth *n.* A white, crystalline metallic element.

bi-son *n.*

A large buffalo of northwestern America, with a dark-brown coat and short, curved horns.

bisque *n.* A creamy soup made from fish or vegetables; unglazed clay.

bis-sex-tile *adj.* Related to the extra day occurring in a leap year.

bis-tro *n., pl.* **bistros** A bar or small nightclub.

bit *n.* A tiny piece or amount of something; a tool designed for boring or drilling especially, drilling for oil; in computer science, either of two characters, as the binary digits zero and one, of a language that has only two characters; a unit of information; storage capacity, as of a computer memory.

bitch *n.* A female dog; a spiteful woman. *v.* To complain.

bite *v.* To cut, tear, or crush with the teeth. **bite** *n.,* **bitingly** *adv.*

bit-stock *n.* A brace that secures a drilling bit.

bit-ter *adj.* Having a sharp, unpleasant taste. **bitterly** *adv.,* **bitterness** *n.*

bit-ter-sweet *n.* A woody vine whose root, when chewed, has first a bitter, then a sweet taste.

bi-tu-mi-nous coal *n.* Coal that contains a high ratio of bituminous material and burns with a smoky flame.

bi-valve *n.* A mollusk that has a hinged two-part shell, a clam or oyster.

biv-ou-ac *n.* A temporary military camp in the open air.

bi-week-ly *n.* Occurring every two weeks.

bi-year-ly *n.* Occurring every two years.

bi-zarre *adj.* Extremely strange or odd.

blab *v.* To reveal a secret by indiscreetly talking; to gossip.

blab-ber *v.* To chatter; to blab. **blabber** *n.*

blab-ber-mouth *n., Slang* A person who gossips.

black *adj.* Very dark in color; depressing; cheerless; darkness, the absence of light. **blackness** *n.,* **blackly** *adv.*

black--and--blue *adj.* Discolored skin caused by bruising.

black-ball *n.* A vote that prevents a person's admission to an organization or club.

black belt *n.* The rank of expert in karate.

black-berry *n., pl.* **berries** A thorny plant with black edible berries that have small seeds.

black-bird n. A small bird, the males of the species having mostly all black feathers.

black-board n. Hard, slate-like board written on with chalk.

black box n. The container that protects the tape recordings of airline pilots from water and fire, normally recoverable in the event of an accident.

black eye n. A bruise or discoloration around the eye.

black-head n. A small mass of dirt that clogs the pore of the skin.

black-jack n. A card game in which each player tries to accumulate cards with points higher than that of the dealer, but not more than 21 points.

black-light n. Ultraviolet or invisible infrared light.

black magic n. Witchcraft.

black-mail n. The threat of exposing a past discreditable act or crime; money paid to avoid exposure. **blackmailer** n.

black market n. The illegal buying or selling of merchandise or items.

black-out n. The temporary loss of electrical power. v. To conceal lights that might be seen by enemy aircraft.

black sheep n. A person who is considered a loser by a respectable family.

black-smith n. A person who shapes iron with heat and a hammer.

black-top n. Asphalt, used to pave or surface roads.

black widow n. A spider that is extremely poisonous.

blad-der n. The expandable sac in the pelvis that holds urine.

blade n. The cutting part of a knife; the leaf of a plant or a piece of grass.

blame v. To hold someone guilty for something; to find fault. **blameless** n.

blanch v. To remove the color from something, as to bleach; to pour scalding hot water over fresh vegetables.

bland adj. Lacking taste or style. **blandly** adv., **blandness** n.

blan-dish v. To coax by flattery.

blank adj. Having no markings or writing; empty; confused. **blankly** adv., **blankness** n.

blank check n. Carte blanche; freedom of action.

blan-ket n. A woven covering used on a bed.

blank verse n. A poem of lines that have rhythm but do not rhyme.

blare v. To make or cause a loud sound.

blar-ney n. Talk that is deceptive or nonsense.

blast n. A strong gust of air; the sound produced when a horn is blown. **blasted** adj.

blast-off n. The launching of a space ship.

bla-tant adj. Unpleasant; offensively loud; shameless. **blatancy** n.

blath-er v. To talk, but not making sense.

blaze n. A bright burst of fire; a sudden outburst of anger; a trail marker; a white mark on an animal's face.

bla-zon v. To make known. **blazoner** n.

bldg abbr. Building.

bleach v. To remove the color from a fabric; to become white.

bleach-ers pl., n. Seating for spectators in a stadium.

bleak adj. Discouraging and depressing; barren; cold; harsh. **bleakness** n., **bleakly** adv.

bleat n. The cry of a sheep or goat.

bleed v. To lose blood, as from an injury; to extort money; to mix or allow dyes to run together.

bleed-ing heart n. A plant with pink flowers; a person who feels very sympathetic toward the underprivileged.

bleep n. A signal with a quick, loud sound.

blem-ish n. A flaw or defect.

blend v. To mix together smoothly, to obtain a new substance. **blender** n.

bless v. To honor or praise; to confer prosperity or well-being.

bless-ed adj. Holy; enjoying happiness.

bless-ing n. A short prayer before a meal.

blight n. A disease of plants that can cause complete destruction.

blimp n. A large aircraft with a nonrigid gas-filled hull.

blind adj. Not having eyesight; something that is not based on facts. n. A shelter that conceals hunters.

blind date n. A date between two strangers that has been arranged by a third party.

blind-ers pl., n. Flaps that are attached to the bridle of a horse, restricting side vision.

blind-fold v. To cover the eyes with a cloth; to block the vision. **blindfolded** adj.

blink v. To squint; to open and close the eyes quickly; to take a quick glance.

blink-er n. A signaling light that displays a message; a light on a car used to indicate turns.

blintz n. A very thin pancake rolled and stuffed with cottage cheese or other fillings.

blip v. To remove; erase sounds from a recording. n. The brief interruption as the result of blipping.

bliss n. To have great happiness or joy. **blissful** adj., **blissfully** adv.

blis-ter n. The swelling of a thin layer of skin that contains a watery liquid.

blithe adj. Carefree or casual. **blithery** adv., **blitheness** n.

blitz n. A sudden attack; an intensive and forceful campaign.

bliz-zard n. A severe winter storm characterized by wind and snow.

blk abbr. Black, block.

bloat v. To swell or puff out.

blob n. A small shapeless mass.

bloc n. A united group formed for a common action or purpose.

block n. A solid piece of matter; the act of obstructing or hindering something. **blockage** n., **blocker** n.

block-ade n. The closure of an area. **blockader** n., **blockade** v.

blond adj. A golden or flaxen color. **blondish** adj.

blonde adj. A woman or girl with blond hair.

blood n. The red fluid circulated by the heart throughout the body that carries oxygen and nutrients to all parts of the body.

blood bank n. A place where blood is processed, typed, and stored for future needs.

blood count n. The determination of the number of white and red corpuscles in a specific amount of blood.

blood-cur-dling adj. Terrifying; horrifying.

blood-hound n. A breed of dogs with a very keen sense of smell.

blood-let-ting n. The act of bleeding a vein as part of medical therapy.

blood-mobile n. A portable blood bank that visits different locations, drawing and collecting blood from donors.

blood poisoning n. The invasion of the blood by toxin produced by bacteria; septicemia.

blood-shot adj. Redness; irritation especially of the eyes.

blood-stream n. The circulation of blood in the vascular system.

blood-sucker n. An animal that sucks blood.

blood vessel n. Any canal in which blood circulates, such as a vein, artery, or capillary.

blood-y adj. Stained with blood; having the characteristics of containing blood. **bloodiness** n., **bloodied** adj.

bloom v. To bear flowers; fo flourish; to have a healthy look. **blooming** adj.

bloom-ers n., pl. Loose trousers that are gathered at the knee or just below.

bloop-er n. An embarrassing blunder made in public.

blos-som n. A flower or a group of flowers of a plant that bears fruit. v. To flourish; to grow.

blot n. A spot or stain. v. To dry with an absorbent material.

blotch n. An area of a person's skin that is discolored. **blotch** v., **blotchily** adj.

blouse n. A loosely fitting shirt or top.

blow v. To move or be in motion because of a current of air. n. A sudden hit with a hand or fist. **blower** n.

blow—by—blow adj. Minutely detailed in description.

blow dry v. To dry one's hair with a hand-held hair dryer.

blow-hole n. A hole in the ice that enables aquatic mammals to come up and breathe; the nostril of a whale and other cetaceans.

blow-out n. The sudden deflation of a tire that occurs while driving.

blow-torch n. A hand-held tool that generates a flame hot enough to melt soft metals.

blow-up n. An enlargement; a photograph; an explosion of a violent temper.

blubber n. The fat removed from whales and other marine mammals. **blubbery** adj.

blue n. A color the same as the color of a clear sky; the hue that is between violet and green.

blue baby n. An infant with a bluish colored skin, caused by inadequate oxygen in the blood.

blue-fish n. A game fish of the tropical waters of the Atlantic and Indian Oceans.

blue-grass n. Folk music of the southern United States, played on guitars and banjos.

blue jay n. A bird having mostly blue colored feathers.

blue-nose n. A person who advocates a rigorous moral code.

blue-print n. A reproduction of technical drawings or plans, using white lines on a blue background.

blue ribbon n. The award given for placing first in a contest.

blues pl., n. A style of jazz from American Negro songs; a state of depression.

blue spruce n. An evergreen tree from the Rocky Mountains.

bluff v. To deceive or mislead; to intimidate by showing more confidence than the facts can support. n. A steep and ridged cliff.

blun-der n. An error or mistake caused by ignorance. v. To move clumsily. **blunderer** n.

blun-der-buss n. A short gun with a flared muzzle.

blunt adj. Frank and abrupt; a dull end or edge. **bluntly** adv.

blur v. To smudge or smear; to become hazy.

blurt v. To speak impulsively.

blush v. To be embarrassed from modesty or humiliation and to turn red in the face; to feel ashamed. n. Make-up used to give color to the cheekbones. -**ful** adj., **blushingly** adv.

blus-ter n. A violent and noisy wind in a storm. **bluster** v., **blusterer** n.

blvd abbr. Boulevard

bo-a n.

A large nonvenomous snake of the Boidea family which coils around prey and crushes it.

boar n.

A male pig; wild pig.

board n. A flat piece of sawed lumber; a flat area on which games are played. v. To receive lodging, meals or both, usually for pay; to enter a ship, train, or plane. **boarder** n.

board-walk *n.* A wooden walkway along a beach.

boast *v.* To brag about one's own accomplishments. **-er** *n.*, **boastful** *adj.*

boat *n.* A small open craft or ship.

boat-swain *n.* Warrant or petty officer in charge of the rigging, anchors, and crew of a ship.

bob *v.* To cause to move up and down in a quick, jerky movement.

bob-bin *n.* A spool that holds thread in a sewing machine.

bob-by *n.* An English police officer.

bob-by socks *pl.*, *n.* An ankle sock, usually worn by teenaged girls.

bob-cat *n.* A wildcat of North America, with reddish-brown fur, small ears, and a short tail.

bob-o-link *n.* An American song bird, the male has black, yellowish and white feathers.

bob-sled *n.* Racing sled which has steering controls on the front runners.

bode *v.* To foretell by omen or sign.

bod-ice *n.* The piece of a dress that extends from the shoulder to the waist.

bod-kin *n.* A small instrument with a sharp point for making holes in fabric.

body-n *n.* The main part of something; the physical part of a person. **bodily** *adv.*

bod-y build-ing *n.* The development and toning of the body through diet and exercise.

body-guard *n.* A person hired to protect another person.

body-surf *v.* To ride on a wave without a surfboard. **bodysurfer** *n.*

bo-gey *n.* In golf, one stroke over par for a hole.

bog-gle *v.* To pull away from with astonishment.

bo-gus *adj.* Something that is counterfeit; worthless in value.

bo-he-mi-an *n.* A person whose life-style is unconventional.

boil *v.* To raise the temperature of water or other liquid until it bubbles; to evaporate; reduce in size by boiling. *n.* A very painful, pus-filled swollen area of the skin caused by bacteria in the skin.

boil-er *n.* A vessel that contains water and is heated for power.

bois-ter-ous *adj.* Violent, rough and stormy; undisciplined. **boisterously** *adv.*

bold *adj.* Courageous; showing courage; distinct and clear. **boldly** *adv.*, **boldness** *n.*

bold-face *n.* A style of printing type with heavy thick lines.

bole *n.* A tree trunk.

bo-le-ro *n.* A short jacket without sleeves, worn open in the front.

boll *n.* A rounded capsule that contains seeds, as from the cotton plant.

boll wee-vil *n.* A small beetle whose larvae damage cotton bolls.

bo-lo-gna *n.* A seasoned, smoked sausage.

bol-ster *n.* A long, round pillow.

bolt *n.* A threaded metal pin designed with a head at one end and a removable nut at the other; a thunderbolt; a large roll of material. *v.* To run or move suddenly.

bomb *n.* A weapon that is detonated upon impact releasing destructive material as gas or smoke. *Slang* A complete and total failure.

bom-bard *v.* To attack repeatedly with missiles or bombs. **bombarder** *n.*, **bombardment** *n.*

bom-bast *n.* Very ornate speech. **bombastic** *adj.*

bom-ba-zine *n.* Silk or cotton fabric woven with diagonal ribbing.

bombed *adj.*, *Slang* Drunk.

bomber *n.* A military aircraft that carries and drops bombs.

bo-na fide *adj.* Performed in good faith; genuine; authentic.

bo-nan-za *n.* A profitable pocket or vein of ore; great prosperity.

bon-bon *n.* Chocolate or fondant candy with a creamy, fruity, or nutty center.

bond *n.* Something that fastens or binds together; a duty or binding agreement; an insurance agreement in which the agency guarantees to pay the employer in the event an employee is accused of causing financial loss. **bonded** *adj.*

bond-age *n.* Slavery; servitude.

bond ser-vant *n.* One who agrees to work without pay.

bonds-man *n.* One who agrees to provide bond for someone else.

bone *n.*

The calcified connecting tissue of the skeleton. **bone** *v.*

bone--dry *adj.* Completely without water.

bone-head *n.*, *Slang* A stupid person. **boneheaded** *adj.*

bon-er *n.*, *Slang* A mistake or blunder.

bon-fire *n.* An open outdoor fire.

bo-ni-to *n.* A game fish related to the tuna.

bon-kers *adj.*, *Slang* Acting in a crazy fashion.

bon-net *n.* A woman's hat that ties under the chin.

bon-ny *adj.* Attractive or pleasing; pretty.

bon-sai *n.* A small ornamental shrub grown in a shallow pot.

bo-nus *n.*, *pl.* **-nuses** Something that is given over and above what is expected.

bon voyage *n.* A farewell wish for a traveler to have a pleasant and safe journey.

boo *n.* Verbal expression showing disapproval or contempt.

boo--boo *n.*, *Slang* A mistake, blunder, or minor injury.

boog-ie *v.*, *Slang* To dance especially to rock and roll music.

book *n.* A group of pages fastened along the left side and bound between a protective cover; literary work that is written or printed.

book-ie *n.*, *Slang* A bookmaker.

book-ing *n.* A scheduled engagement.

book-keep-ing *n.* The business of recording the accounts and transactions of a business. **bookkeeper** *n.*

boom *n.* A deep, resonant sound; a long pole extending to the top of a derrick giving support to guide lifted objects. *v.* To cause to flourish or grow swiftly.

boo-mer-ang *n.* A curved, flat missile that can be thrown so that it returns to the thrower.

boon *n.* Something that is pleasant or beneficial; a blessing; favor.

boon-docks *pl., n. Slang* Back country.

boon-dog-gle *n.* A useless activity; a waste of time.

boor *n.* A person with clumsy manners and little refinement; rude person.

boost *v.* To increase; to raise or lift by pushing up from below. *n.* An increase in something.

boost-er *n.* A promoter; a supplementary or additional dose of vaccine.

boot *n.* A protective covering for the foot; any protective sheath or covering. In computer science, to load a computer with an operating system or other software.

boo-tee *n.* A soft, knitted sock for a baby.

booth *n.* A small enclosed compartment or area; display area at trade shows for displaying merchandise for sale; an area in a restaurant with a table and benches.

boot-leg *v., Slang.* To sell, make, or transport liquor illegally.

booze *n., Slang.* An alcoholic drink.

bo-rax *n.* A crystalline compound used in manufacturing detergents and phar-maceuticals.

bor-der *n.* A surrounding margin or edge; a political or geographic boundary.

bor-der-land *n.* Land near or on a border; an indeterminate situation.

bor-derline *n.* A line or mark indicating a border.

bore *v.* To make a hole through or in something using a drill; to become tired, repetitious, or dull. **boredom** *n.*

bo-re-al *adj.* Located in or of the north.

bo-ric acid *n.* A colorless or white mixture that is used as a preservative and as a weak antiseptic.

born *adj.* Brought into life or being; having an innate talent.

born-again *adj.* Having accepted Jesus Christ as a person's personal savior.

bo-ron *n.* A soft, brown nonmetallic element used in nuclear reactor control elements, abrasives, and flares.

bor-ough *n.* A self-governing incorporated town, found in some United States cities; an incorporated British town that sends one or more representatives to Parliament.

bor-row *v.* To receive money with the intentions of returning it; to use another idea as one's own.

borscht *n.* Hot or cold beet soup.

BOS *abbr.* Basic Operating System; the program that handles the routine functions of computer operations, such as accessing the disk drive, displaying information on the screen, handling input and output, etc.

bos-ky *adj.* Thickly covered with trees or shrubs; related to a wooded area.

bos-om *n.* The female's breasts; the human chest; the heart or center of something.

boss *n.* An employer or supervisor for whom one works. *v.* To command; to supervise. **bossiness** *n.*, **bossy** *adj.*

bot-a-ny *n.* The science of plants. **botanical** *adj.*, **botanist** *n.*

botch *v.* To ruin something by clumsiness; to repair clumsily. **botcher** *n.*

both *adj.* Two in conjunction with one another.

both-er *v.* To pester, harass, or irritate; to be concerned about something. **bothersome** *adj.*

bot-tle *n.* A receptacle, usually made of glass, with a narrow neck and a top that can be capped or corked; formula or milk that is fed to a baby.

bot-tle-neck *n.* A narrow, obstructed passage, highway, road, etc.; a hindrance to progress or production.

bot-tom *n.* The lowest or deepest part of anything; the base; underside; the last; the land below a body of water. *Informal* The buttocks. **bottomless** *adj.*

bottom line *n.* The end result; lowest line of a financial statement, showing net loss or gain.

bot-u-lism *n.* Food poisoning, often fatal, caused by bacteria that grows in improperly prepared food.

bouf-fant *adj.* Full; puffed out.

bough *n.* The large branch of a tree.

bouil-lon *n.* A clear broth made from meat.

boul-der *n.* A large round rock.

boul-e-vard *n.* A broad city street lined with trees.

bounce *v.* To rebound or cause to rebound; to leap or spring suddenly; to be returned by a bank as being worthless or having no value.

bounc-er *n.* A person who removes disorderly people from a public place.

bounc-ing *adj.* Healthy; vigorous; robust; lively and spirited.

bound *n.* A leap or bounce. *v.* To limit; to be tied.

bound-a-ry *n., pl.* **-ries** A limit or border.

bound-en *adj.* Under an obligation or agreement.

bound-er *n.* A vulgar person.

bound-less *adj.* Without limits. **boundlessly** *adv.*

boun-te-ous *adj.* Plentiful or generous; giving freely. **bounteously** *adv.*, **bounteousness** *n.*

boun-ti-ful *adj.* Abundant; plentiful. **bountifully** *adv.*

bounty *n.* Generosity; an inducement or reward given for the return of something; a good harvest.

bou-quet *n.* A group of cut flowers; the aroma of wine.

bour-bon *n.* Whiskey distilled from fermented corn mash.

bour-geois *pl.*, *n.* A member of the middle class. **bourgeois** *adj.*

bout *n.* A contest or match; the length of time spent in a certain way.

bou-tique *n.* A small retail shop that sells specialized gifts, accessories, and fashionable clothes.

bou-ton-niere *n.* A flower worn in the buttonhole of a man's jacket.

bo-vine *adj.* Of or relating to an ox or cow.

bow *n.* The front section of a boat or ship; bending of the head or waist to express a greeting or courtesy; a weapon made from a curved stave and strung taut to launch arrows; a rod strung with horsehair, used for playing stringed instruments.

bowd-ler-ize *v.* To expurgate. **bowdlerization** *n.*

bow-el *n.* The digestive tract located below the stomach; the intestines.

bow-ie knife *n.* A single-edged thick-bladed hunting knife.

bowl *n.* A hemispherical container for food or liquids; a bowl-shaped part, as of a spoon or ladle; a bowl-shaped stadium. *v.* To participate in the game of bowling.

bow-leg *n.* An outward curvature of the leg at the knee.

bowl-er *n.* A person that bowls.

bowl-ing *n.* A game in which a person rolls a ball down a wooden alley in order to knock down a triangular group of ten wooden bowling pins.

bowling alley *n.* A building containing alleys for the game of bowling.

bowl over *v.* To astound; to be astounded.

bow-sprit *n.* A spar that projects forward from the stem of a ship.

box *n.* A small container or chest, usually with a lid; a special area in a theater that holds a small group of people; a shrub or evergreen with leaves and hard wood that is yellow in color. *v.* to fight with the fists.

box-car *n.* An enclosed railway car used for the transportation of freight.

box-er *n.* A person who boxes professionally; a German breed of dog with short hair, brownish coat, and a square nose or muzzle.

box-ing *n.* A sport in which two opponents hit each other using padded gloves on their hands, forming fists.

box office *n.* An office where theatre tickets are purchased.

boy *n.* A male youth or child. **boyhood** *n.*

boy-cott *v.* To abstain from dealing with, buying, or using as a means of protest.

bra *n.* Brassiere.

brace *n.* A device that supports or steadies something. **brace** *v.*

brace-let *n.* An ornamental band for the wrist.

brack-en *n.* A large species of fern with tough stems and finely divided fronds.

brack-et *n.* A support attached to a vertical surface that projects in order to hold a shelf or other weight. *v.* To enclose a word in brackets ( ).

brack-ish *adj.* Containing salt; distasteful.

bract *n.* A leaf-like plant below a flower cluster or flower.

brad *n.* A nail that tapers to a small head.

brag *v.* To assert or talk boastfully.

brag-ga-do-ci-o *n.*, *pl.* A cockiness or arrogant manner; empty bragging.

brag-gart *n.* A person who brags.

braid *v.* To interweave three or more strands of something; to plait.

braille *n.* A system of printing for the blind, consisting of six dots, two across and four directly under the first two. Numbers and letters are represented by raising certain dots in each group of six.

brain *n.* The large mass of nerve tissue enclosed in the cranium, responsible for the interpretation of sensory impulses, control of the body, and coordination; the center of thought and emotion in the body. **braininess** *n.*, **brainless** *adj.*, **brainlessness** *n.*

braise *v.* To cook by first browning in a small amount of fat, adding a liquid such as water, and then simmering in a covered container.

brake *n.* A device designed to stop or slow the motion of a vehicle or machine. **brake** *v.*

brake fluid *n.* The liquid contained in hydraulic brake cylinders.

bram-ble *n.* A prickly shrub or plant such as the raspberry or blackberry bush.

bran *n.* The husk of cereal grains that is separated from the flour.

branch *n.* An extension from the main trunk of a tree. *v.* To divide into different subdivisions.

bran-dish *v.* To wave or flourish a weapon.

brand name *n.* A company's trademark.

brand-new *adj.* Unused and new.

bran-dy *n.*, *pl.* **-dies** An alcoholic liquor distilled from fermented fruit juices or wine. **brandied** *adj.*, **brandy** *v.*

brash *adj.* Hasty, rash, and unthinking; insolent; impudent.

brass *n.* An alloy of zinc, copper and other metals in lesser amounts. *Slang.* A high-ranking officer in the military.

bras-siere *n.* A woman's undergarment with cups to support the breasts.

brass tacks *pl.*, *n.* The details of immediate, practical importance.

brat *n.* An ill-mannered child.

brat-wurst *n.* A fresh pork sausage.

braun-schwei-ger *n.* Smoked liverwurst.

bra-va-do *n.* A false showing of bravery.

brave *adj.* Having or displaying courage. *n.* An American Indian warrior.

brav-er-y *n.* The quality of or state of being brave.

bra-vo *Interj.* Expressing approval.

brawl *n.* A noisy argument or fight.

brawn *n.* Well-developed and solid

muscles. **brawniness** n., **brawny** adj.

bray v. To make a loud cry like a donkey.

braze v. To solder using a nonferrous alloy that melts at a lower temperature than that of the metals being joined together.

bra-zen adj. Made of brass; shameless or impudent.

bra-zier n. A person who works with brass; a metal pan that holds burning charcoal or coals.

breach n. Ruptured, broken, or torn condition or area; a break in friendly relations. v. To break the law or obligation.

breach of promise n. The violation of a promise.

bread n. A leavened food made from a flour or meal mixture and baked. *Slang* Money. v. To cover with bread crumbs before cooking.

bread-fruit n. A tropical tree with lobed leaves and edible fruit.

bread-stuff n. Bread; a cereal product; meal, grain, or flour.

breadth n. The distance or measurement from side to side; width.

bread-win-ner n. The one whose pay supports a household.

break v. To separate into parts with violence or suddenness; to collapse or give way; to change suddenly. *Informal* A stroke of good luck.

break-age n. Things that are broken.

break-down n. Failure to function.

break-er n. A wave that breaks into foam.

break-fast n. The first meal of the day.

breast n. The milk-producing glandular organs on a woman's chest; the area of the body from the neck to the abdomen.

breast-bone n. The sternum.

breast-plate n. A metal plate worn on the chest for protection.

breath n. The air inhaled and exhaled in breathing; a very slight whisper, fragrance, or breeze.

breathe v. To draw air into and expel from the lungs; to take a short rest.

breather n. A small opening in an otherwise air-tight enclosure; one that breathes.

breath-tak-ing adj. Astonishing; awesome. **breathtakingly** adv.

breech n., pl. -es The buttocks; the hind end of the body; the part of a gun or firearm located at the rear of the bore. *plural* Trousers that fit tightly around the knees.

breed v. The genetic strain of domestic animals, developed and maintained by mankind. **breeding** n.

breeze n. A slight gentle wind; something that is accomplished with very little effort. **breezy** adj.

breve n. The curved mark over a vowel to indicate a short or unstressed syllable.

bre-vi-ar-y n. A book that contains prayers and psalms for the canonical hours.

brev-i-ty n., pl. -ties A brief duration; conciseness.

brew v. To make beer from malt and hops by boiling, infusion, and germentation. **brewer** n.

brew-er-y n. A building or plant where beer or ale is brewed.

bribe v. To influence or induce by giving a token or anything of value for a service. **bribe** n.

brib-ery n. The practice of giving or receiving a bribe.

bric-a-brac n. A collection of small objects.

brick n. A molded block of baked clay, usually rectangular in shape.

brick-bat n. A piece of a brick used as a weapon when thrown as a missile.

brick-lay-er n. A person who lays bricks as a profession.

bri-dal adj. Relating to a bride or a nuptial ceremony.

bride n. A women just married or about to be married.

bride-groom n. A man just married or about to be married.

brides-maid n. A woman who attends a bride at her wedding.

bridge n. A structure that provides passage over a depression or obstacle; a card game for four players.

bridge-work n. The construction of dental work.

bri-dle n. A harness used to restrain or guide a horse. **bridler** n.

brief n. A concise, formal statement of a client's case. adj. Short in duration. v. To summarize or inform in a short statement. **-ly** adv., **briefness** n.

brief-case n. A small, flat, flexible case for holding and carrying papers or books.

bri-er n. A woody, thorny, or prickly plant.

brig n. A prison on a ship; a twin-masted, square-rigged sailing ship.

bri-gade n. A military unit organized for a specific purpose.

brig-and n. A person who lives as a robber; bandit.

bright adj. Brilliant in color; vivid; shining and emitting or reflecting light; happy; cheerful; lovely. **brightness** n.

bril-liant adj. Very bright and shiny; sparkling; radiant; extraordinarily intelligent.

brim n. The edge or rim of a cup.

brim-ful adj. Completely full.

brim-stone n. Sulfur.

brin-dle adj. Having dark streaks or flecks on a gray or tawny background.

brine n. Water saturated with salt; the water contained in the oceans and seas.

bring v. To carry with oneself to a certain place; to cause, act, or move in a special direction.

brink n. The upper edge or margin of a very steep slope.

bri-oche n. A roll made from flour, eggs, butter, and yeast.

bri-quette *n.* A small brick-shaped piece of charcoal.

brisk *adj.* Moving or acting quickly; being sharp in tone or manner; energetic, invigorating or fresh. **briskly** *adv.,* **briskness** *n.*

bris-ket *n.* The meat from the lower chest or breast of an animal.

bris-ling *n.* A small fish that is processed like a sardine.

bris-tle *n.* Short, stiff, coarse hair. *v.* To react in angry defiance. **bristly** *adj.*

britch-es *pl., n.* Trousers; breeches.

brit-tle *adj.* Very easy to break; fragile. **brittleness** *n.*

bro *abbr.* Brother.

broach *n.* A tapered and serrated tool used for enlarging and shaping a hole.

broad *adj.* Covering a wide area; from side to side; clear; bright. **broadly** *adv.*

broad-cast *v.* To transmit a program by television; to make widely known. **broadcaster** *n.*

broad-cloth *n.* A textured woolen cloth with a lustrous finish.

broad-en *v.* To become or make broad or broader.

broad-loom *adj.* Woven on a wide loom. *n.* Carpet woven in this manner.

broad-mind-ed *adj.* Tolerant of varied views; liberal. **broadmindedness** *n.*

broad-side *n.* The side of a ship that is above the water line; a sheet of paper printed on both sides and then folded.

bro-cade *n.* A silk fabric with raised patterns in silver and gold.

broc-co-li *n.* A green vegetable from the cauliflower family, eaten before the small buds open.

bro-chure *n.* A booklet or pamphlet.

bro-gan *n.* A sturdy oxford shoe.

brogue *n.* A strong regional accent.

broil *v.* To cook by exposure to direct radiant heat.

broil-er *n.* A device, usually a part of a stove, that is used for broiling meat; a young chicken.

broke *adj.* Penniless; completely without money.

bro-ken *adj.* Separated violently into parts.

bro-ken-hearted *adj.* Overcome by despair or grief.

bro-ken home *n.* A family situation in which the parents are not living together.

bro-ker *n.* A person who acts as a negotiating agent for contracts, sales, or purchases in return for payment.

bro-ker-age *n.* The establishment of a broker.

bro-mide *n.* A compound of bromine with other elements; a sedative; a commonplace idea or notion. **bromidic** *adj.*

bro-mine *n.* A nonmetallic element of a deep red, toxic liquid that gives off a disagreeable odor.

bron-chi-al *adj.* Pertaining to the bronchi or their extensions. **bronchially** *adv.*

bron-chus *n.* Either of two main branches of the trachea that lead directly to the lungs.

bron-co *n.* A wild horse of western North America.

bron-to-saur *n.* A very large dinosaur.

bronze *n.* An alloy of tin, copper, and zinc; moderate olive brown to yellow in color. **bronze** *v.,* **bronze** *adj.*

Bronze Age *n.* Human culture between the Iron Age and the Stone Age.

brooch *n.* A large decorative pin.

brood *n.* The young of an animal ; a family of young. *v.* To produce by incubation; to hatch; to think about at length.

brood-er *n.* An enclosed heated area for raising young chickens.

brook *n.* A small fresh-water stream that contains many rocks.

broom *n.* A long-handled implement used for sweeping; a shrub with small leaves and yellow flowers.

bros *abbr.* Brothers.

broth *n.* The liquid in which fish, meat, or vegetables have been cooked; also called stock.

broth-el *n.* A house of prostitution; a whorehouse.

broth-er *n.* A male who shares the same parents as another person. **brotherly** *adj.,* **brotherliness** *n.*

brother-hood *n.* The state of being brothers; one that is related to another for a particular purpose.

brother-in-law *n.* The brother of one's spouse; the husband of one's sister; the husband of one's spouse's sister.

broug-ham *n.* A vehicle without a cover over the driver's seat.

brought *v.* The past tense of bring.

brow *n.* The ridge above the eye where the eyebrow grows.

brow-beat *v.* To bully; dominate; intimidate.

brown *n.* A color between yellow and red; a dark or tanned complexion.

brown bag-ging *n.* The practice of bringing one's lunch to work.

brown bread *n.* Bread made from whole wheat flour.

brown-le *n.* A good-natured elf believed to perform helpful services; a square, chewy piece of chocolate cake.

brown-out *n.* An interruption of electrical power.

brown sugar *n.* Sugar with crystals covered by a film or refined dark syrup.

browse *v.* To look over something in a leisurely and casual way.

bruise *n.* An injury that ruptures small blood vessels and discolors the skin without breaking it.

brunch *n.* A combination of a late breakfast and an early lunch.

bru-net *or* **bru-nette** *n.* A person with dark brown hair.

brunt *n.* The principal shock, or force.

bru-tal *adj.* Very harsh or cruel treatment. **brutality** *n.,* **brutally** *adv.,* **brutalize** *v.*

brute *n.* A person characterized by

physical power rather than intelligence; a person who behaves like an animal. **brutish** *adj.*

bub-ble *n.* A small round object, usually hollow; a small body of gas contained in a liquid. *v.* To produce bubbles.

bubble gum *n.* A chewing gum that can be blown into bubbles.

bub-bly *adj.* Something full of bubbles. *Slang* Champagne.

bu-bo *n.* Inflammatory swelling of the lymphatic glands, especially in the area of the groin or armpits.

bu-bon-ic plague *n.* The contagious and normally fatal disease that is transmitted by fleas from infected rats, characterized by fever, diarrhea, chills, and vomiting.

buck *n.* The adult male deer; the lowest grade in the military category. *v.* To throw a rider; to oppose the system. *Slang* A dollar.

buck-board *n.* An open carriage with four wheels and a seat attached to a flexible board.

buck-et *n.* A vessel used to carry liquids or solids; a pail.

buck-et seat *n.* A separate seat with a rounded or molded back.

buck-eye *n.* A tree with flower clusters and glossy brown nuts.

buck-le *v.* To warp, crumple, or bend under pressure. *n.* Metal clasp for fastening one end to another.

buck-ram *n.* A coarse, stiff fabric that is sized with glue and used for interlinings in garments and in bookbindings.

buck-shot *n.* A coarse lead shot for shotgun shells.

buck-tooth *n.* A large, prominently projecting front tooth. **-ed** *adj.*

buck-wheat *n.* A plant with small edible seeds that are often ground into flour and used as a cereal grain.

bud *n.* Something that has not developed completely; a small structure that contains flowers or leaves that have not developed.

bud-dy *n.* A good companion, partner, or friend.

budge *v.* To give way to; to cause to move slightly.

bud-get *n.* The total amount of money allocated for a certain purpose.

buff *n.* A leather made mostly from skins of buffalo, elk, or oxen, having the color of light to moderate yellow.

buf-fa-lo *n.* A wild ox with heavy forequarters, short horns, and a large muscular hump. *v.* To bewilder, to intimidate.

buff-er *n.* A tool used to polish or shine; in computer science, a part of the memory used to hold information temporarily while data transfers from one place to another. *v.* To lessen, absorb, or protect against the shock of an impact.

buf-fet *n.* A meal placed on a side table so that people may serve themselves; a side table for serving food. *v.* To strike sharply with the hand.

buf-foon *n.* A clown; a stupid person; an uneducated person.

bug *n.* Any small insect; a concealed listening device. *v.* To bother or annoy.

bug-gy *n.* A small carriage pulled behind a horse.

bu-gle *n.* A brass instrument without keys or valves. **bugle** *v.,* **bugler** *n.*

build *v.* To erect by uniting materials into a composite whole; to fashion or create; to develop or add to. *n.* The form or structure of a person.

build-ing *n.* A roofed and walled structure for permanent use.

built--in *adj.* Containing something within a structure.

bulb *n.* A rounded underground plant such as a tulip that lies dormant in the winter and blooms in the spring; an incandescent light for electric lamps. **bulbous** *adj* Resembling a bulb in shape.

bulge *n.* A swelling of the surface caused by pressure from within. **bulgy** *adj.*

bulk *n.* A large mass; anything that has great size, volume, or units. **bulky** *adj.*

bulk-age *n.* A substance that increases the bulk of material in the intestine, therefore stimulating peristalsis.

bulk-head *n.* The partition that divides a ship into compartments; a retaining wall along a waterfront.

bull *n.* The adult male in cattle and other large mammals. *Slang* Nonsense talk.

bull *abbr.* Bulletin.

bull-dog *n.* A short-haired dog with a stocky build and an undershot lower jaw.

bull-doze *v.* To move or dig up with a bulldozer. *Slang* To bully.

bull-dozer *n.* A tractor-like machine with a large metal blade in front for moving earth and rocks.

bul-let *n.* A cylindrical projectile that is fired from a gun.

bul-le-tin *n.* A broadcasted statement of public interest; a public notice.

bull-fight *n.* A Spanish or Mexican spectacle in which men known as matadors engage in fighting bulls.

bull-head-ed *adj.* Headstrong and stubborn.

bul-lion *n.* Refined gold or silver in the uncoined state.

bull-ish *adj.* Tending to cause or hopeful of rising prices, as in the stock market.

bull-pen *n.* The area where pitchers warm up during a baseball game.

bull's eye *n.* The center of a target.

bull snake *n.* The center of a target.

bull-ter-ri-er *n.* A breed of dog crossed between a terrier and a bulldog.

bul-ly *n., pl.* **-ies** A person who is mean or cruel to weaker people.

bul-rush *n.* Tall grass as found in a marsh.

bul-wark *n.* A strong protection or support.

bum *n.* One who begs from others; one who spends time unemployed. *v.* To loaf.

bum-mer *Slang* Depressing.

bum-ble-bee *n.*

A large hairy bee.

bump *v.* To collide with, knock, or strike something. *n.* A swelling or lump on a person's body.

bump-er *n.* A device on the front of vehicles that absorbs shock and prevents damage.

bump-kin *n.* An awkward, stupid, or unsophisticated country person.

bump-tious *adj.* Crudely self-assertive and forward; pushy.

bun *n.* Any of a variety of plain or sweet small breads; tightly rolled hair that resembles a bun.

bunch *n.* A cluster or group of items that are the same.

bun-co *n.* A game of confidence; a swindling scheme.

bun-dle *n.* Anything wrapped or held together. *Slang* A large amount of money. bundler *n.*

bundle up. *v.* To dress warmly, usually using many layers of clothing.

bun-gle *v.* To work or act awkwardly or clumsily. bungler *n.*

bun-ion *n.* An inflamed, painful swelling of the first joint of the big toe.

bunk *n.* A narrow bed that is built in; one of a tier of berths on a ship.

bun-ker *n.* A tank for storing fuel on a ship; an embankment or a sand trap creating a hazard on a golf course.

bun-kum *n.* Meaningless talk.

bun-ny *n., pl.* **-nies** A small rabbit.

Bun-sen burner *n.* An adjustable gas-burning laboratory burner.

bunt *v.* To tap a pitched ball with a half swing. *n.* The center of a square sail.

bunt-ing *n.* A hooded blanket for a baby.

buoy *n.* A floating object to mark a channel or danger. *v.* To stay afloat.

buoy-an-cy *n.* The tendency of an object or body to remain afloat in liquid or to rise in gas or air.

bur. *abbr.* Bureau.

bur-den *n.* Something that is hard to bear; a duty or responsibility; a ship's capacity for carrying cargo.

bur-dock *n.* A coarse plant with purplish flowers.

bu-reau *n., pl.* **bureaus, bureaux.** A low chest for storing clothes; a branch of the government or a subdivision of a department.

bu-reauc-ra-cy *n., pl.* **-cies.** A body of nonelected officials in a government; the administration of a government through bureaus.

burg *n.* A town or city.

bur-geon *v.* To put forth new life as in leaves, buds, etc.

burg-er *n., Slang* A hamburger.

bur-glar *n.* A person who steals personal items from another person's home.

bur-glar-ize *v.* To commit burglary.

bur-glar-proof *adj.* Protected and secure against burglary.

bur-gla-ry *n.* The breaking and entering of a private home with the intent to steal.

bur-i-al *n.* The process or act of burying.

burl *n.* A woody, often flat and hard, hemispherical growth on a tree.

bur-lap *n.* A coarse cloth woven from hemp or jute.

bur-lesque *n.* Theatrical entertainment with comedy and mocking imitations.

bur-ly *adj.* Very heavy and strong.

burn *v.* To be destroyed by fire; to consume fuel and give off heat. *n.* An injury produced by fire, heat, or steam; the firing of a rocket engine in space.

burn-er *n.* The part of a fuel-burning device where the fire is contained.

bur-nish *v.* To make shiny by rubbing; to polish.

burnt *adj.* Affected by burning.

burp *n.* A belch.

bur-ro *n.* A small donkey.

bur-row *n.* A tunnel dug in the ground by an animal.

bur-sar *n.* The person or official in charge of monies at a college.

bur-si-tis *n.* An inflammation of the small sac between a tendon and the knee, elbow, or shoulder joints.

burst *adj.* To explode or experience a sudden outbreak; to very suddenly become visible or audible. *n.* A sudden explosion or outburst.

bus *n., pl.* **busses** A large passenger vehicle. bus *v.*

bus *abbr.* Business.

bus boy *n.* A waiter's assistant; one who removes dirty dishes from a table and he resets it.

bus-by *n.* A fur hat that is worn in certain regiments of the British Army.

bush *n.* A low plant with branches near the ground; a dense tuft or growth; land that is covered intensely with undergrowth.

bushed *adj., Slang* Extremely exhausted; tired.

bush-el *n.* A unit of dry measurement which equals four pecks or 2,150.42 cubic inches; a container that holds a bushel.

bush-mas-ter *n.* The largest New World venomous snake.

bush-whack *v.* To travel through thick woods by cutting bushes and small trees; to ambush. bushwacker *n.*

busi-ness *n.* A person's professional dealings or occupation; an industrial or commercial establishment.

bus-kin *n.* A boot that reaches halfway to the knee; tragedy as that of an ancient Greek drama.

bus-man's holiday *n.* Vacation or holiday where a person follows the same practice of his usual occupation.

bust *n.* A sculpture that resembles the upper part of a human body; the breasts of a women. *v.* To break or burst; to become short of money.

bus-tle *n.* A padding that gives extra bulk to the back of a woman's skirt.

bus·y *adj.* Full of activity; engaged in work. **busily** *adv.*, **-ness** *n.*

busy-body *n.* An inquisitive person who interferes with someone else's business.

but *conj.* On the contrary to; other than; if not; except for the fact.

bu·tane *n.* A gas produced from petroleum, used as a fuel refrigerant and aerosol propellant.

butch·er *n.* One who slaughters animals and dresses them for food.

but·ler *n.* A male servant of a household.

butt *n.* The object of ridicule; the thick large or blunt end of something. *v.* To hit with horns or the head; to be joined at the end.

but·ter *n.* A yellow substance churned from milk.

but·ter·fat *n.* The natural fat from milk that floats to the top of unpasteurized milk.

but·ter·fin·gers *n.* An awkward, clumsy person.

but·ter·fly *n.*, *pl.* **-flies** A narrow-bodied insect with four broad, colorful wings.

but·ter·milk *n.* The liquid that remains after butter has been churned from milk.

but·tocks *pl.*, *n.* The two round fleshy parts of the rump.

but·ton *n.* A small disk that interlocks with a buttonhole to close a piece of garment.

but·ton·hole *n.* The slit through which a button is inserted to close a piece of garment.

but·tress *n.* A support made of brick or stone.

bux·om *adj.* Lively; happy. **buxomness** *n.*

buy *v.* To purchase in exchange for money. *n.* Anything that is bought.

buy·er *v.* A person who buys from a store or an individual.

buzz *v.* To make a low vibrating sound, as a bee.

buz·zard *n.* A broad-winged vulture from the same family as the hawk.

buzz·er *n.* An electrical signaling device that makes a buzzing sound.

by *prep.* Up to and beyond; to go past; not later than; next to; according to.

bye *n.* A position in which a contestant has no opponent after pairs are drawn for a tournament, and, therefore, advances to the next round.

bye-bye *Slang* Farewell.

by-gone *adj.* Gone by; past.

by-law *n.* A rule or law governing internal affairs of a group or organization.

by--product *n.* Material that is left over when something is manufactured but also has a market value of its own.

byte *n.* In computer science, a sequence of adjacent binary digits operated on as a unit.

by-word *n.* A well-known proverb.

C, c The third letter of the English alphabet; the Roman numeral for 100.

cab *n.* A taxicab; the compartment where a person sits to drive a large truck or machinery.

ca·bal *n.* A group that conspires against a government or other public institution.

ca·ban·a *n.* A small building or shelter on the beach or at the side of a pool.

cab·a·ret *n.* A restaurant that provides dancing and live entertainment.

cab·bage *n.*

A plant with large, edible green leaves, eaten as a vegetable.

cab·in *n.* A small, roughly-built house, especially one made from logs; the living quarters on a ship; the area of an airplane for the passengers and crew members.

ca·ble *n.* A heavy rope made from fiber or steel; a bound group of insulated conductors.

ca·boo·dle *n.*, *Slang* The entire unit, amount, or collection.

ca·boose *n.* The last car of a train, that contains the eating and sleeping quarters for the crew.

ca·ca·o *n.* Any tree of the chocolate family; the dried seed of the cacao tree from which chocolate and cocoa are made.

cach·a·lot *n.* A sperm whale.

cache *n.* A safe place to hide and conceal goods.

ca·chet *n.* A mark of distinction or authenticity.

ca·coph·o·ny *n.* A harsh and disagreeable sound. **cacophonous** *adj.*

cac·tus *n.*, *pl.* **-es, -ti** A leafless plant with a thick, prickly surface, which grows primarily in hot and dry regions.

ca·dav·er *n.* The body of a person who has died; pale and gaunt.

ca·dence *n.* A rhythmic movement or flow.

ca·den·za *n.* An elaborate ornamental section for a soloist near the end of a concerto.

ca·det *n.* A student in training at a naval or military academy. **cadetship** *n.*

cadge *v.* To beg or to receive by begging; to mooch. **cadger** *n.*

cad·re *n.* The group of trained personnel that forms the heart of an organization.

ca·du·ce·us *n.* The symbol of the medical profession, a winged staff entwined with two serpents entwined around it.

cae·su·ra *n.* A pause or break in a line of verse or poetry.

caf·feine *n.* A stimulant found in coffee, tea, and dark colas.

caf·tan *n.* A loose-fitting, full-length garment worn in the Near East.

cage *n.* A box-like structure enclosed with bars or grating for the confinement of animals.

ca-gey *adj.* Shrewd, wary, or cautious.

ca-hoot *n.* A questionable relationship with an associate.

cais-son *n.* A waterproof structure that is used for construction work underwater.

ca-jole *v.* To wheedle or coax someone into doing something.

cake *n.* A sweet food made from flour, eggs, and shortening. **cake** *v.*

cal-a-bash *n.* A large hard-shelled gourd that can be used as a utensil.

cal-a-boose *n., Slang* A jail.

cal-a-mine *n.* A pink powder of zinc oxide and ferric oxide mixed with mineral oils to form a lotion for skin irritations such as poison ivy.

ca-lam-i-ty *n., pl.* **-ies** Misfortune or great distress. **-tous** *adj.,* **-ly** *adv.*

cal-ci-fy *v.* To become or make chalky or stony. **calcification** *n.*

cal-cine *v.* To heat to a high temperature without melting, but causing loss of moisture and reduction. **calcination** *n.*

cal-ci-um *n.* The alkaline element that is found in teeth and bones; the element symbolized by Ca.

cal-cu-late *v.* To figure by a mathematical process, to evaluate; to estimate. **calculable** *adj.,* **calculably** *adv.*

cal-cu-lat-ed *adj.* Worked out beforehand with careful estimation. **calculatedly** *adv.*

cal-cu-lat-ing *adj.* Shrewd consideration of self-interest.

cal-cu-la-tor *n.* A machine with a keyboard for automatic mathematical operation.

cal-cu-lus *n., pl.* **-es** A stone in the gallbladder or kidneys; the mathematics of integral and differential calculus.

cal-dron *n.* A large boiler or kettle.

cal-en-dar *n.* A system for showing time divisions by years, months, weeks, and days; the twelve months in a year.

cal-en-der *n.* A machine that makes paper and cloth smooth and glossy.

cal-ends *n.* The first day of the new moon.

cal-i-ber *n.* The inner diameter of a tube or gun; the quality or worth of something.

cal-i-co *n.* Cotton fabric with figured patterns.

cal-i-per *n.* An instrument with two curved, hinged legs, used to measure inner and outer dimensions.

ca-liph *n.* A religious and secular head in Islam. **caliphate** *n.*

cal-is-then-ics *n.* Exercises that develop muscular tone and promote good physical condition.

call *v.* To call out to someone; to name or designate; to telephone; to pay a short visit; to demand payment.

cal-la *or* **cal-la lilly** *n.* A family of white and yellow flowers enclosing a clublike flower stalk.

cal-lig-ra-phy *n.* The art of writing with a pen using different slants and positions.

call-ing *n.* The occupation or profession of a person.

cal-li-ope *n.* A keyboard musical instrument that is fitted with steam whistles.

cal-lous *adj.* Having calluses; to be without emotional feelings. **callously** *adv.,* **callousness** *n.*

cal-lus *n., pl.* **-luses** A thickening of the horny layer of the skin.

calm *adj.* Absence of motion; having little or no wind, storms, or rough water.

cal-o-mel *n.* A white, tasteless compound used as a purgative.

cal-o-rie *n., pl.* **-ries** A measurement of the amount of heat or energy produced by food. **caloric** *adj.*

cal-u-met *n.* A pipe used by the North American Indians during ceremonies; also known as a peace pipe.

ca-lum-ni-ate *v., pl.* **-nies** To slander; to malign.

cal-um-ny *n., pl.* **-ies** A statement that is malicious, false, and damaging to someone's reputation.

ca-lyp-so *n., pl.* **calypsos** Improvised ballad of the West Indies with lyrics on topical or humorous subjects.

ca-lyx *n., pl.* **calyxes, calyces** The outer cover of a flower.

cam *n.* A curved wheel used to produce a reciprocating motion.

ca-ma-ra-de-rie *n* Good will among friends.

cam-ber *n.* A slight curve upward in the middle.

cam-bric *n.* A cotton fabric or white linen.

came *n.* A grooved lead bar that is used to hold together the panes of glass in latticework or stained-glass windows. *v.* Past tense of to come.

cam-el *n.*

An animal used in desert regions, having either one or two humps on its back.

ca-mel-lia *n.* A shrub with shiny green leaves and various colored flowers.

ca-mel-o-pard *n.* A giraffe.

cam-er-a *n.* An apparatus for taking photographs in a lightproof enclosure with an aperture and shuttered lens through which the image is focused and recorded on photosensitive film.

cam-i-sole *n.* A woman's short, sleeveless undergarment.

cam-ou-flage *v.* To disguise by creating the effect of being part of the natural surroundings.

cam-paign *n.* An organized operation designed to bring about a particular political, commercial, or social goal.

cam-pa-ni-le *n., pl.* **-iles** A free-standing bell tower that is associated with a church.

camp-er *n.* A person who camps in makeshift shelters for recreation; a vehicle specially equipped for casual travel and camping.

cam-phor *n.* A crystalline compound used as an insect repellent.

camp-site *n.* The area used for camping.

cam-pus *n.* The buildings and grounds of a college, school, or university.

cam-shaft *n.* The shaft of an engine that is fitted with cams.

ca-nal *n.* A man-made water channel for irrigating land.

ca-nal-ize *v.* To convert into canals; to make new canals.

ca-nar-y *n., pl.* **-ies** A green or yellow songbird which is popular as a caged bird.

can-cel *v.* To invalidate or annul; to cross out; to neutralize.

can-cer *n.* A malignant tumor that invades healthy tissue and spreads to other areas; the disease marked by such tumors. **cancerous** *adj.*

can-de-la-bra *n., pl.* **candelabrum** A decorative candlestick with several branching arms for candles.

can-did *adj.* Free from bias, malice, or prejudice; honest and sincere.

can-di-date *n., pl.* A person who is aspires to or is nominated or qualified for a membership, award, or office. **candidacy**, **candidature** *n.*

can-dor *n.* Straightforwardness; frankness of expression.

ca-nine *adj.* Relating to or resembling a dog; of the dog family.

can-ker *n.* An ulcerated sore in the mouth.

canned *adj.* Preserved and sealed under pressure.

can-ner-y *n., pl.* **-ies** A company that processes canned meat, vegetables, and other foods.

can-ni-bal *n.* Any animal who survives by eating one of its own kind; a person who survives by eating the flesh of human beings. **cannibalism** *n.,* **cannibalization** *n.,* **cannibalistic** *adj.*

can-ni-bal-ize *v.* To remove parts from a plane for use as replacements in another plane.

can-ny *adj.* Thrifty; careful; cautious; shrewd.

ca-noe *n.*

A lightweight, slender boat with pointed ends which moves by paddling. **canoe** *v.,* **canoeist** *n.*

can-on *n.* The laws established by a church council; a priest serving in a collegiate church or cathedral. **canonical** *adj.*

can-on-ize *v.* To officially declare a deceased person a saint. **canonization** *n.*

can-o-py *n., pl.* **-ies** A cloth covering used as an ornamental structure over a bed; the supporting surface of a parachute; the transparent cover over the cockpit of an airplane.

cant *n.* The external angle of a building.

v. To throw off by tilting

can-ta-bi-le *n.* A lyrical, flowing style of music.

can-ta-loupe *n.* A sweet-tasting, orange-colored muskmelon.

can-tan-ker-ous *adj.* Bad-tempered and argumentative. **cantakerously** *adv.*

can-ta-ta *n.* A drama that is sung but not acted.

can-ter *n.* An easy lope just a little slower than a gallop, but faster than a trot.

can-ti-cle *n.* A hymn or chant sung in church.

can-ti-lev-er *n.* A long structure, such as a beam, supported only at one end.

can-ton *n.* A small area of a country divided into parts. **cantonal** *adj.*

can-ton-ment *n.* One or more temporary billets for troops.

can-tor *n.* The chief singer in a synagogue.

can-vas *n.* A heavy fabric used in making tents and sails for boats; a piece of canvas that is used for oil paintings.

can-vass *v.* To travel through a region to solicit opinions or votes; to take a poll or survey. **canvasser** *n.*

can-yon *n.* A deep and narrow gorge with steep sides.

ca-pa-ble *adj.* Having the ability to perform in an efficient way; qualified. **capability**, *n.,* **capably** *adv.*

ca-pa-cious *adj.* Having a lot of room or space.

ca-pac-i-tance *n.* The property of a body or circuit which allows it to store an electrical charge. **capacitive** *adj.*

ca-pac-i-tor *n.* The circuit element composed of metallic plates that are separated by a dielectric and are used to store a charge temporarily.

ca-pac-i-ty *n., pl.* **-ies** The ability to contain, receive, or absorb; having the aptitude or ability to do something.

ca-par-i-son *n.* An ornamental covering for a horse, saddle, or harness.

cap-il-lary *n., pl.* **-ies** Any of the small vessels that connect the veins and arteries. *adj.* Having a hair-like bore; very fine or small in size.

cap-i-tal-ism *n.* The economic system in which the means of distribution and production are privately owned and operated for private profit.

capitalist *n.* A person who invests in a business. **capitalistic** *adj.*

cap-i-ta-tion *n.* A census or tax of equal amount for each person.

ca-pit-u-late *v.* To surrender under terms of an agreement. **-tor** *n.,* **-tory** *adj.*

ca-price *n.* A sudden change of action or mind without adequate reason; a whim. **capricious** *adj.,* **-ness** *n.*

cap-size *v.* To overturn in a boat.

cap-stan *n., Naut.* A drum-like apparatus rotated to hoist weights by winding in a cable on a ship or boat.

cap-su-lated *adj.* Formed or in a capsule-like state. **capsulation** *n.*

cap-sule *n.* A small gelatinous case for a dose of oral medicine; a fatty sac that surrounds an organ of the body, as the kidney, and protects it; a summary in a brief form. **capsular** *adj.*

cap-tion *n.* A subtitle; a description of an illustration or picture.

cap-tious *adj.* Deceptive; critical.

cap-ti-vate *v.* To hold the attention, fascinate, or charm a person or group of people. **captivation** *n.,* **captivator** *n.*

cap-tive *n.* A person being held as a prisoner.

cap-ture *v.* To take something or someone by force. **capturer** *n.*

car *n.* An automobile; an enclosed vehicle, as a railroad car.

ca-rafe *n.* A glass bottle for serving wine or water.

car-a-mel *n.* A chewy substance primarily composed of sugar, butter, and milk.

car-a-mel-ize *v.* To make into caramel.

car-at *n.* The unit of weight for gems that equals 200 milligrams.

car-a-way *n.* An aromatic seed used in cooking.

car-bide *n.* A carbon compound with a more electropositive element.

car-bine *n.* A short-barreled rifle, light in weight.

car-bo-hy-drate *n.* A group of compounds, including starches, celluloses, and sugars that contain carbon, hydrogen, and oxygen.

car-bon *n.* A nonmetallic element that occurs as a powdery noncrystalline solid; the element symbolized by C. **carbonization** *n.,* **carbonize** *v.*

car-bon-ate *v.* To add or charge with carbon dioxide gas, as in a beverage. **carbonation** *n.*

car-bon copy *n.* The copy of an original made with carbon paper. *Slang* An exact copy.

car-bon di-ox-ide *n.* An odorless, colorless, nonflammable gas, removed from the atmosphere by the photosynthesis of plants and returned by the respiration of animals.

car-bon mon-ox-ide *n.* An odorless, colorless gas that is formed by the incomplete oxidation of carbon, burns with a blue flame, an is highly poisonous when inhaled.

car-bon tet-ra-chlo-ride *n.* A nonflammable, colorless, poisonous liquid used as a cleaning fluid and in fire extinguishers.

car-bun-cle *n.* An infection of the skin and deeper tissue which is red, inflamed, full of pus, and painful.

car-bu-re-tor *n.* The device in gasoline engines that mixes vapor, fuel, and air for efficient combustion.

car-cass *n.* The dead body of an animal; something that no longer has life.

car-ci-no-ma *n.* A malignant tumor; cancer. **carcinomatous** *adj.*

car-di-ac *adj.* Relating to the heart.

car-di-ac mas-sage *n.* A procedure performed by a physician to restore proper circulation and respiration for someone in distress.

car-di-gan *n.* A sweater with an opening down the front.

car-di-o-gram *n.* The curve recorded by a cardiograph and is used in the diagnosis of heart defects.

car-di-ol-o-gy *n.* The study of the heart, its diseases, and treatments. **-ist** *n.*

car-di-o-pul-mo-nary *adj.* Relating to the heart and lungs.

car-di-o-pul-mo-nary re-sus-ci-ta-tion *n.* A procedure used to restore breathing after cardiac arrest by using mouth-to-mouth resuscitation.

car-di-o-vas-cu-lar *adj.* Involving and relating to the heart and the blood vessels.

care *n.* A feeling of concern, anxiety, or worry; guardianship or custody. *v.* To show interest or regard.

ca-reen *v.* To lurch or twist from one side to another while moving rapidly.

ca-reer *n.* The profession or occupation a person takes in life. **career** *n.*

care-ful *adj.* Exercising care; cautious; watchful.

ca-ress *v.* To gently show affection by touching or stroking. **caress** *n.*

car-go *n.* Freight; the goods and merchandise carried on a ship, plane, or other vehicle.

car-i-bou *n.*

A large antlered deer of northern North America.

car-il-lon *n.* A set of tuned bells in a tower, that are usually played by a keyboard.

car-mine *n.* A vivid red color; crimson; deep purplish red.

car-nage *n.* A bloody slaughter; war; massacre.

car-nal *adj.* Relating to sensual desires. **carnality** *n.,* **carnally** *adv.*

car-na-tion *n.* A fragrant perennial flower in a variety of colors.

car-nel-ian *n.* A clear red chalcedony that is used as a gem.

car-ni-vore *n.* A flesh-eating animal. **carnivorous** *adj.,* **carnivorously** *adv.*

car-ol *n* A song to celebrate joy or praise. **caroler** *n.,* **carol** *v.*

ca-rouse *v.* To be rowdy and to be in a drunken state. **carouser** *n.*

car-pal *adj.* Pertaining to the wrist and the bones in the wrist.

car-pel *n., Bot.* A seed vessel or pistil.

car-pen-ter *n.* A person who builds and repairs wooden structures. **-ry** *n.*

car-pet bag *n.* An old-fashioned traveling bag made from carpet.

car-rot *n.* An orange vegetable that is a root.

car-rou-sel *n.* A merry-go-round.

cart *n.* A two-wheeled vehicle for moving heavy goods; a small lightweight vehicle that can be moved around by hand.

car·tel *n.* A group of independent companies that have organized to control prices, production, etc.

car·ti·lage *n.* A tough, elastic substance of connective tissue attached to the surface of bones near the joints. **cartilaginous** *adj.*

car·tog·ra·phy *n.* The art of developing charts and maps. **cartographer** *n.*, **cartographic** *adj.*

car·ton *n.* A container made from cardboard.

carve *v.* To slice meat or poultry; to cut into something; to create, as sculpture.

cary·at·id *n.* A supporting column sculptured in the form of a female figure.

cas·cade *n.* A waterfall that flows over steep rocks.

cas·ing *n.* A protective covering or container; the framework of a window or door.

ca·sein *n.* A dairy protein that is used in foods and in manufacturing adhesives and plastics.

cash·ew *n.* A tropical American tree that produces an edible nut that can be eaten raw or roasted.

cash·ier *n.* An employee who handles cash as part of his job description; an officer in a bank in charge of receiving or distributing money.

cash·mere *n.* The wool from the Kashmir goat; the yarn made from this wool.

ca·si·no *n.*, *pl.* **-nos** A public establishment open especially for gambling.

cask *n.* A large wooden vessel or barrel; the quantity that a cask will hold.

cas·ket *n.* A coffin; a small chest or box.

cas·que *n.* A helmet. **casqued** *adj.*

cas·se·role *n.* A dish in which the food is baked and also served; food cooked and served in this manner.

cas·sette *n.* A cartridge of magnetic tape used in tape recorders to play and record.

cas·sock *n.* A close-fitting garment worn by members of the clergy.

cast *v.* To hurl or throw with force; to direct or turn; to shed; to give a certain part or role; to deposit or give a vote on something; to make or throw, as with a fishing line. *Naut.* To fall off, to veer; to be shipwrecked or marooned at sea. *n.* A dressing made from plaster of paris used on a broken bone.

cas·ta·net *n.*, *pl.* **-nets** An instrument made from a pair of ivory or hardwood shells, held in the palm of the hand and clapped together with the fingers.

cast·a·way *adj.* Throw away. *n.* One who is shipwrecked or discarded.

caste *n.* A social separation based on a profession, hereditary, or financial hierarchy.

cas·tel·lat·ed *adj.* Adorned by battlements and turrets.

cast·er *n.* A small set of swiveling rollers that are fastened under pieces of furniture and the like.

cas·ti·gate *v.* To punish or criticize severely. **castigation, castigator** *n.*

cast·ing *n.* The act of one that casts.

cas·tle *n.* A fort or fortified dwelling for nobility; any large house or place of refuge; a stronghold.

cast-off *adj.* Discarded; thrown away.

castor oil *n.* An oil from the seeds of a tropical plant used as a cathartic and lubricant.

cas·trate *v.* To remove the testicles; to remove the ovaries; to spay. **-tion** *n.*

ca·su·al *adj.* Informal; occurring by chance. **casually** *adv.*, **casualness** *n.*

ca·su·al·ty *n.*, *pl.* **-ies** One who is injured or killed in an accident. *Milit.* A soldier who is killed, wounded, taken prisoner by the enemy, or missing in action.

cat *n.* A small domesticated animal, a pet; any of the animals in the cat family, such as the lion, lynx, tiger, etc.

cat·a·clysm *n.* A sudden and violent disaster. **cataclysmic, cataclysmal** *adj.*

cat·a·combs *n.* An underground passage with small rooms for coffins.

cat·a·falque *n.* The structure that supports a coffin during a state funeral.

cat·a·lep·sy *n.* A condition in which there is a rigidity of the muscles, causing the patient to remain in a fixed position or posture.

cat·a·log *or* **cat·a·logue** *n.* A publication containing a list of names, objects, etc.

cat·a·lyst *n.*, *Chem.* Any substance that alters and decreases the time it takes a chemical reaction to occur.

cat·a·ma·ran *n.* A boat with twin hulls.

cat·a·pult *n.* An ancient military device for throwing arrows or stones; a device for launching aircraft from the deck of a ship.

cat·a·ract *n.* A large waterfall or downpour. *Pathol.* A disease of the lens of the eye, causing total or partial blindness.

ca·tarrh *n.*, *Pathol.* Inflammation of the nose and throat. **catarrhal** *adj.*

ca·tas·tro·phe *n.* A terrible and sudden disaster. **catastrophic** *adj.*

catch *v.* To take; to seize or capture; to reach in time; to intercept; to become entangled or fastened. **catch** *n.*

catch-all *n.* A container or bag for odds and ends.

catch·er *n.* A person who catches a ball.

cat·e·gor·i·cal *adj.* Absolute; certain; related to or included in a category without qualification. **-ly** *adv.*

cat·e·go·rize *v.* To place in categories.

cat·e·go·ry *n.*, *pl.* **-ries** A general group to which something belongs.

ca·ter *v.* To provide a food service; to bring directly to a location. **caterer** *n.*

cat·er·pil·lar *n.* The very fuzzy, wormlike, brightly-colored spiny larva of a moth or butterfly.

cat·er·waul *n.* The harsh cry made by cats at mating time. **caterwaul** *v.*

ca·the·dral *n.* A large and important church, containing the seat of a bishop.

cath·e·ter *n.*, *Med.* A thin, flexible tube

that is inserted into body cavities for drainage and to draw urine from the bladder. **catheterize** v.

cath-ode n. The negatively charged electrode which receives positively charged ions during electrolysis.

cath-ode ray tube n. The vacuum tube on which images are found, used in a computer screen.

cat-i-on n. A positively charged ion that is attracted in electrolytes to a negative electrode. **cationic** adj.

cat-nap n. A short nap. **catnap** v.

CAT scan n. A cross-sectional picture produced by a scanner, used to x-ray the body by using computerized axial tomography.

cat-tail n. A long marsh plant that has minute brown flowers and long leaves, used in making chair seats and in dried flower arrangements.

cat-tle n., pl. Farm animals raised for meat and dairy products.

cat-ty--cor-nered adj. Not straight; sitting at an angle.

cau-cus n. A meeting of a political party to make policy decisions and to select candidates.

cau-li-flow-er n. A vegetable related to broccoli and cabbage.

caulk v. To seal seams and edges against leakage of water and air. **caulker** n.

cause v. To produce a result, consequence, or effect. n. A goal, principle; a reason; motive. **causer** n.

cau-se-rie n. A short informal conversation or chat.

cause-way n. A paved highway through a marsh tract; raised road over water.

cau-ter-ize v. To sear or burn with a hot instrument. **cauterization** n.

cau-ter-y n. A very hot instrument used to destroy tissue that does not seem normal.

cau-tion n. A warning careful planning.

cau-tious adj. Very careful.

cav-al-cade n. A group of horse-drawn carriages or riders, forming a procession.

cav-a-lier n. A very gallant gentleman; a knight.

cav-al-ry n., pl. -ies Army troops trained to fight on horseback or in armored vehicles. **cavalryman** n.

cave n. An underground tomb or chamber with an opening at the ground surface.

ca-ve-at n. A formal legal notice to stop the proceedings until both sides have a hearing; a warning or caution.

cav-ern n. A very large underground cave. **cavernous** adj.

cav-i-ar or **cav-i-are** n. The eggs of large fish, eaten as an appetizer.

cav-i-ty n., pl -ies A decayed place in a tooth; a hollow or hole.

cease v. To come to an end or put an end to; to stop.

cease-fire v. To stop fighting, usually as a result of a truce.

cease-less adj. Endless. **ceaselessly** adv.

ce-cum or **cae-cum** n., Anat. The pouch where the large intestine begins.

ce-dar n. An evergreen tree with fragrant, reddish wood.

ce-dil-la n. A diacritical mark placed under the letter c in the French vocabulary to indicate a modification or alteration of the usual phonetic sound.

ceil-ing n. The overhead covering of a room; the maximum limit to something; the maximum height for visibility under specified conditions for aircraft.

cel-e-brate v. To observe with ceremonies, rejoicing, or festivity. **celebration** n.

cel-eb-ri-ty n., pl. -ies A famous person.

cel-er-y n. A green vegetable with an edible stalk.

ce-les-ta n. A musical instrument which produces bell-like tones when the keyboard and metal plates are struck by hammers.

ce-les-tial adj. Heavenly; spiritual.

cel-i-bate n. A person who remains unmarried because of religious vows; one who is sexually abstinent. **celibacy** n., **celibate** adj.

cell n.

A typical cell

The smallest unit of any organism that is capable of independent function, is composed of a small mass of cytoplasm, usually encloses a central nucleus, and is surrounded by a membrane or a rigid cell wall; a cavity of an ovary or pericarp that is seed-bearing. Electr. The part of a battery that generates the electricity; in computer science, the location in memory that holds a single unit of information; a byte. A prison; a small room.

cel-lar n. An underground area, beneath a building, used for storage.

cel-lo n. A base instrument of the violin family. **cellist** n.

cel-lo-phane n. A transparent paper-like material made from treated cellulose that has been processed in thin, clear strips.

cel-lu-lar adj. Consisting of cells.

cel-lu-lite n. A fatty deposit or area under the skin.

cel-lu-lose n. A carbohydrate that is insoluble in ordinary solvents and forms the fundamental material for the structure of plants.

ce-ment n. A construction material made up of powdered, calcined rock and clay materials which when added with water, set up as a hard, solid mass.

cem-e-ter-y n., pl. -ies The place for burying the dead.

cen-ser *n.* A vessel or container for burning incense.

cen-sor *n.* A person who examines films and printed materials to determine what might be objectionable. **-ship** *n.*

cen-sure *n.* An expression of criticism and/or disapproval.

cen-sus *n.* An official count of the population.

cent *n.* One; one hundredth of a dollar.

cen-te-nar-i-an *n.* A person who has reached the age of 100 or more.

cen-ter *n.* The place of equal distance from all sides; the heart; in sports, a person who holds the middle position, as in the forward line.

cen-ti-pede *n.* A flat arthropod with numerous body segments and legs.

cen-tral *adj.* In, near, or at the center; of primary importance. **-ly** *adv.*, **-lze** *v.*

cen-tral ner-vous sys-tem *n.* The nervous system that consists of the spinal cord and the brain.

cen-trif-u-gal *adj.* Moving or directing away from a center location.

cen-tu-ry *n., pl.* **-ies** A period consisting of 100 years.

ce-ram-ic *adj.* Of or relating to a brittle material made by firing a nonmetallic mineral, such as clay. **ceramics** *n.*

ce-re-al *n.* An edible grain eaten as a breakfast food.

cer-e-bel-lum *n., pl.* **-bellums** The part of the brain responsible for the coordination of voluntary muscular movements.

cer-e-bral hem-or-rhage *n.* The rupture of an artery in the brain, which allows blood to escape.

cer-e-bral pal-sy *n.* A variety of chronic conditions in which brain damage, usually occurring at birth, impairs motor function and control.

cer-e-brum *n., pl.* **-brums** *or* **-bra** The brain structure that is divided into two cerebral hemisphere's and occupies most of the cranial cavity.

cer-e-mo-ni-al *adj.* Mark by or relating to a ceremony. **ceremonially** *adv.*

cer-e-mo-ny *n., pl.* **-ies** A ritual or formal act performed in a certain manner.

ce-rise *n.* The color of deep purplish red.

cer-tain *adj., pl.* **-ties** Being very sure of something; without any doubt; inevitable; not mentioned but assumed. **certainly** *adv.*

cer-tif-i-cate *n.* A document stating the truth or accuracy of something; a document that certifies fulfillment of duties or requirements, as of a course of study.

cer-ti-fi-ca-tion *n.* A certified statement.

cer-ti-fy *v.* To testify in writing that something is true or a fact.

cer-vi-cal *adj.* Relating to the neck of the cervix.

ce-si-um *n.* An electrometal, white in color, from the alkali group, used in photoelectric cells.

ces-sa-tion *n.* The act of stopping or ceasing.

ces-sion *n.* The act of giving up territory or rights to another.

chafe *v.* To become sore by rubbing; to irritate.

cha-grin *n.* A feeling of distress caused by disappointment, failure, or humiliation.

chain *n.* A connection of several links; anything that confines or restrains. **chain gang** Prisoners that are chained together. **chain reaction** Series of events that directly affect one another.

chair *n.* A seat with four legs and a back, intended for one person; a seat of office; the chairman. *Slang* Electric chair. **chair lift** A chair suspended from cables that is used to carry people and snow equipment up or down the ski slopes.

chair-man *n., pl.* **-men** The person presiding over a committee, board, or other meeting.

chaise *n.* A one-horse vehicle for two people.

cha-let *n.* A cottage that has a gently sloping and overhanging roof.

chal-ice *n.* A drinking goblet or cup.

chalk *n.* A soft mineral made from fossil seashells, used for marking on a surface, such as a slate board. **chalky** *adj.*

chalk-board *n.* A blackboard made from slate.

chal-lah *or* **cha-lah** A loaf of braided bread made with extra eggs, traditionally eaten by Jews on holidays and the Sabbath.

chal-lenge *n.* A demand for a contest; a protest. *v.* To call into question.

chal-lis *n.* A lightweight printed cloth in rayon, cotton, or wool.

cham-ber *n.* A bedroom in a large home; a judge's office; a meeting place or hall for a legislative body; the compartment of a gun that holds the charge.

cham-ber-lain *n.* The high-ranking person or official of a royal court.

cham-ber-maid *n.* A maid who takes care of bedrooms at a hotel.

cham-pagne *n.* A white sparkling wine.

cham-pi-on *n.* The holder of first place in a contest; one who defends another person.

cham-pi-on-ship *n.* The competition that determines a winner.

chance *n.* The random existence of something happening; a gamble or a risk.

chan-cel *n.* The area of a church that contains the altar and choir.

chan-cel-lor *n.* The chief director or minister of state in certain countries in Europe. **chancellorship** *n.*

chan-cer-y *n.* The office for the safekeeping of official records.

chan-cre *n.* A lesion that is the first indication of syphilis.

chan-croid *n.* A sore or lesion in the genital area that is similar to a chancre, but does not involve syphilis.

chanc-y *adj.* Risky; dangerous.

chan-de-lier *n.* A light fixture with many branches for lights that is suspended from the ceiling.

chan-dler n. A person who makes and sells candles. **chandlery** n.

change v. To become or make different; to alter; to put with another; to use to take the place of another; to freshen a bed by putting clean coverings on. n. Coins; money given back when the payment exceeds the bill. **changeable** adj., **changeably** adv.

chan-nel n. The deepest part of a stream, river, or harbor; the course that anything moves through or past; a groove.

chant n. A melody in which all words are sung on the same note. v. To celebrate with a song. **chanter** n.

cha-os n. Total disorder. **chaotic** adj., **chaotically** adv.

chap n., Slang A fellow; a man. v. To dry and split open from the cold and wind.

chap-el n. A place to worship, usually contained in a church.

chap-er-on or **chap-er-one** n. An older woman who supervises younger people. **chaperone** v.

chap-lain n. A clergyman who conducts religious services for a group.

chap-let n. A garland for the head; a string of beads.

chap-ter n. One division of a book; a branch of a fraternity, religious order, or society.

char-ac-ter n. A quality or trait that distinguishes an individual or group; a person that is portrayed in a play; a distinctive quality or trait. adj. Distinctive; peculiar.

cha-rades pl. n. A game in which the syllables of words are acted out by each player.

chard n. On edible white beet with large, succulent leaves.

charge v. To give responsibility; to ask a price; to accuse; to impute something to; to command; to record a debt owed. n. Management; custody; supervision; an expense or price. Slang A thrill. **chargeable** adj.

charg-er n. An apparatus for recharging a battery.

char-i-ot n. An ancient horse-drawn vehicle used to fight battles. **-eer** n.

char-i-ty n. Money or help given to aid the needy; an organization, fund, or institution whose purpose is to aid those in need.

cha-ri-va-ri n. A mock serenade to newlyweds, performed with horns, tin pans, etc.

char-la-tan n. One who falsely claims to possess knowledge or a skill he does not have. **charlatanism** n.

charm n. The ability to delight or please; a small ornament that has a special meaning, usually worn on a bracelet.

char-nel n. A special room or building that contains the bones or bodies of the dead.

chart n. A map, graph, or table that gives information in a form that is easy to read.

char-ter n. An official document that grants certain privileges and rights. v. To lease or hire a vehicle or aircraft.

char-treuse n. A light yellowish green.

char-y adj. Wary; cautious; not wasting time, resources, or money. **charily** adv., **chariness** n.

chase v. To follow quickly; to pursue; to run after. **chase**, **chaser** n.

chasm n. A very deep crack in the earth's surface.

chas-sis n. The rectangular framework that supports the body and engine of a motor vehicle.

chaste adj. Morally pure; modest; not guilty of participating in sexual intercourse.

chas-tise v. To severely reprimand; to punish by beating. **chastisement** n.

chas-u-ble n. The vestment without sleeves worn over the alb by a priest when celebrating Mass.

chat v. To converse in a friendly manner.

chat-tel n. An item of movable personal property.

chauf-feur n. A person who is hired to drive an automobile for another person.

chau-vin-ism n. The unreasonable belief in the superiority of one's own group. **chauvinist** n., **chauvinistic** adj.

cheap adj. Inexpensive; low in cost; of poor quality. **cheaply** adv., **-ness** n.

cheapen v. To lessen the value; to make cheap.

cheat v. To deprive of by deceit; to break the rules. **cheater** n.

check v. To control or restrain; to examine for correctness or condition.

cheek n. The fleshy part of the face just below the eye and above and to the side of the mouth.

cheer v. To give courage to; to instill with courage or hope.

cheer-ful adj. Having good spirits.

cheese n. A food made from the curd of milk that is seasoned and aged.

cheese-cloth n. A loosely-woven cotton gauze.

chee-tah n. A swift-running, long-legged African wildcat.

chef n. A male cook who manages a kitchen; the head cook.

che-la n. The pincer-like claw of an arachnid.

chem-i-cal adj. Of or related to chemistry. **chemically** adv.

che-mise n. A woman's loose undergarment which resembles a slip; a loose-fitting dress that hangs straight down from the shoulders.

chem-ist n. A person who is versed in chemistry.

chem-is-try n. The scientific study of the composition, structure, and properties of substances and their reactions.

che-mo-ther-a-py n. The treatment of a disease, such as cancer, with chemicals. **chemotherapeutic** adj.

che-nille n. A fuzzy, soft cord used to make rugs, bedspreads, and other fabrics.

cher-ish v. To treat with love; to hold dear.

che-root n. A cigar that is cut off square at both ends.

cher-ry n., pl. **-ies** A fruit tree bearing a small, round, deep, or purplish red fruit with a small, hard stone.

cher-ub n., pl. **-cherubs** A beautiful young child; a representation of an angel resembling a child with a rosy face and wings.

chess n. A game played on a chessboard by two people, each of whom has sixteen pieces and tries to checkmate his opponent's king in order to win the game.

chest n. The part of the upper body that is enclosed by the thorax; the ribs; a box usually having a hinged lid, used for storage.

ches-ter-field n. An overcoat with concealed buttons and a velvet collar.

chest-nut n. A tree bearing edible reddish-brown nuts; a nut from a chestnut tree.

chew v. To crush or grind with the teeth; to masticate. n. The act of chewing. **chewer** n., **chewy** adj.

chi-a-ro-scu-ro n. The distribution of shade and light in a picture.

chick n.

A young chicken or bird. Slang A young woman.

chick-en n. A domestic fowl; the edible meat of a chicken. Slang Cowardly; afraid; losing one's nerve.

chick-en feed n. Food for chickens. Slang Very little money.

chick-en--heart-ed adj. Timid or cowardly.

chic-le n. The milky juice of a tropical tree; the principal ingredient of chewing gum.

chic-o-ry n., pl. **-ies** An herb with blue flowers used in salads, the dried, roasted roots of which are used as a coffee substitute.

chide v. To scold or find fault. **chider** n.

chief n. The person of highest rank. **chiefly** adv., **-or** adj.

chief-tain n. The head of a group, clan, or tribe.

chif-fon n. A sheer fabric made from rayon or silk. adj. In cooking, having a fluffy texture.

chif-fo-nier n. A tall chest of drawers with a mirror at the top.

chig-ger n. A mite that attaches itself to the skin and causes intense itching.

chi-gnon n. A roll of hair worn at the back of the neck.

chil-blain n. An inflammation of the hands and feet caused by exposure to cold.

child n., pl. **children** A young person of either sex; adolescent; a person between infancy and youth. **childish** adj.

child abuse n. Sexual or physical maltreatment of a child by a guardian, parent, or other adult.

child-birth n. The act of giving birth.

child-hood n. The time or period of being a child.

child-like adj. Characteristic of a child.

chil-l or **chile** or **chil-li** n. A hot pepper; a sauce made of meet and chili or chili powder.

chill v. To be cold, often with shivering; to reduce to a lower temperature. n. A feeling of cold.

chi-me-ra n. An absurd fantasy; an imaginary monster with a goat's body, a lion's head, and a serpent's tail.

chim-ney n. A flue for smoke to escape, as from a fireplace.

chin n. The lower part of the face. v. To lift oneself up while grasping an overhead bar until the chin is level with the bar.

chine n. The spine or backbone of animals.

chink n. A narrow crack.

chintz n. A printed cotton fabric which is glazed.

chintz-y adj. Cheap.

chip n. A small piece that has been broken or cut from another source; a disk used in the game of poker; in Computer Science, an integrated circuit engraved on a silicone substrate.

chip-munk n.

A striped rodent of the squirrel family.

chi-ro-prac-tic n. A method of therapy in which the body is manipulated to adjust the spine. **chiropractor** n.

chirp n. The high-pitched sound made by a cricket or a small bird. **chirp** v.

chis-el n. A tool with a sharp edge which is used to shape and cut metal, wood, or stone.

chit n. A voucher indicating the amount owed for food or drink; a lively girl.

chit-chat n. Casual conversation or small talk.

chi-tin n. The substance that forms the hard outer cover of insects.

chit-ter-lings pl., n. The small intestines of a pig, used as food.

chiv-al-ry n., pl. **-ies** The brave and courteous qualities of an ideal knight.

chive n. An herb used as flavoring in cooking.

chlo-ride n. A compound of chlorine with a double positive element.

chlo-rine n. A greenish-yellow compound used to purify water, bleach, and disinfectant.

chlo-ro-phyll n. The green pigment that is found in photosynthetic organisms.

chock n. A wedge or block placed under a wheel to prevent motion. **chock** v.

choc-o-late n. A preparation of ground and roasted cacao nuts that is usually sweetened; a candy or beverage made from chocolate. **chocolaty** adj.

choice n. To select or choose; the opportunity, right, or power to choose.

choir n. An organized group of singers that usually perform in a church.

chok-er n. A necklace that fits tightly around the neck.

cho-les-ter-ol n. A fatty crystalline substance that is derived from bile and is present in most gallstones, the brain, and blood cells.

choose v. To select or pick out; to prefer; to make a choice. **chosen** adj., **choosy** or **choosey** adj.

chop v. To cut by making a sharp downward stroke; to cut into bits or small pieces.

chop-per n., Slang A helicopter.

chop-pers pl., n., Slang False teeth.

chop-py adj. Rough; irregular; jerky.

cho-ral adj. Pertaining to, written for, or sung by a choir or chorus.

chore n. A daily task; a task that becomes unpleasant or burdensome.

cho-re-a n. An acute nervous disease especially of children, marked by irregular and uncontrollable movement of muscles.

cho-re-og-ra-phy n. The creation of a dance routine. **choreograph** v., **choreographer** n., **choreographic** adj.

chor-is-ter n. A choirboy or a member of a choir.

chor-tle v. To chuckle with glee, especially in triumph or joy. **chortle**, **chortler** n.

cho-rus n., pl. -ses A group of people who sing together; repeated verses of a song.

cho-sen adj. Selected or preferred above all.

Christ n. Jesus; The Messiah; God's son who died to save Christians from sin.

chris-ten v. To baptize; to give a Christian name at baptism; to use for the first time. **christening** n.

chro-mat-ic adj. Relating to color.

chro-mo-some n. One of several small bodies in the nucleus of a cell, containing genes responsible for the determination and transmission of hereditary characteristics.

chron-ic adj. Frequently recurring; continuing for long periods of time.

chron-i-cle n. A record of events written in the order in which they occurred. **chronicle** v., **chronicler** n.

chrys-a-lis n., pl.-ses The enclosed pupa from which a moth or butterfly develops.

chry-san-the-mum n. A cultivated plant having large, showy flowers.

chuck-le v. To laugh quietly with satisfaction. **chuckler** n.

chum n. A close friend or pal.

chunk n. A thick piece of anything; a large quantity of something; a lump.

church n. A building for Christian worship; a congregation of public Christian worship.

churl n. A rude or rustic person. **churlish** adj., **churlishness** n.

chut-ney n. An agreeable condiment of fruit, spices, and herbs.

ci-der n. The juice from apples.

ci-gar n. Rolled tobacco leaves used for smoking.

cig-a-rette n. or **cig-a-ret** A small amount of tobacco rolled in thin paper for smoking.

cinch n. The strap for holding a saddle. Slang Something easy to do.

cin-cho-na n. A tree in South America whose bark yields quinine.

cinc-ture n. A belt or cord to put around the waist. v. To encircle or surround with a cincture.

cin-der n. A piece of something that is partially burned. **cindery** adj.

cin-e-ma n., pl. -mas A motion picture; a motion picture theatre; the business of making a motion picture.

cin-e-mat-o-graph n. A movie projector or camera.

cin-e-ma-tog-ra-phy n. The art of photographing a motion picture.

cin-na-bar n. A mineral which is the principal source of mercury.

ci-pher n. The symbol for the absence of quantity; O; secret writing that has a prearranged key or scheme.

cir-cuit n. The closed path through which an electric current flows.

cir-cuit court n. The lowest court of record, located in various counties or districts over which its jurisdiction extends.

cir-cu-lar adj. Moving in a circle or round-like fashion; relating to something in a circle; having free motion, as the air.

cir-cu-late v. To pass from place to place or person to person; to distribute in a wide area. **circulation**, **circulator** n., **circulatory** adj.

cir-cum-cise v. To remove the foreskin on the male penis. **circumcision** n.

cir-cum-fer-ence n. The perimeter or boundary of a circle. **circumferential** adj.

cir-cum-flex n. A mark indicating the quality or sound of vowels as they appear in words.

cir-cum-scribe v. To confine something within drawn boundaries; to surround.

cir-cum-stance n. A fact or condition that must be considered when making a decision.

cir-cum-stan-tial adj. Incidental; not essential; dependent on circumstances.

cir-cum-stan-ti-ate adj. Providing support or circumstantial evidence.

cir-cum-vent v. To outwit or gain advantage; to avoid or go around. **circumvention** n., **circumventive** adj.

cir-rho-sis n. A liver disease that is ultimately fatal. **cirrhotic** adj.

cir-rus n., pl. -cirri A high altitude, white, wispy cloud.

cis-tern n. A man-made tank or artificial reservoir for holding rain water.

cit-a-del n. A fortress commanding a city; a stronghold.

ci-ta-tion n. An official summons from a court; a quotation used in literary or legal material; an honor.

cite v. To bring forward as proof; to summon to action; to rouse.

cit-i-zen n. A resident of a town or city; a native or naturalized person entitled to protection from a government.

citric acid n. A colorless acid found in lime, lemon, and other juices.

cit-ron n. A fruit resembling a lemon, but less acidic and larger in size.

cit-rus n., pl. **citrus, citruses** Any of a variety of trees bearing fruit with thick skins, as limes, oranges, lemons, and grapefruits.

cit-y n. A place larger than a town.

civ-et n. A cat-like mammal that secretes a musky fluid from the genital glands, which is used in perfumery.

civ-ic adj. Relating to or of a citizen, city, or citizenship.

civ-il adj. Relating to citizens; relating to the legal proceedings concerned with the rights of private individuals.

ci-vil-ian n. A person not serving in the military, as a firefighter, or as a policeman.

civ-i-li-za-tion n. A high level of social, cultural, and political development.

civ-il rights pl., n. Rights guaranteed to citizens; the rights provided by the 13th and 14th amendments of the United States Constitution.

claim v. To ask for one's due; to hold something to be true.

claim, claimant n.

clair-voy-ance n. The ability to visualize in the mind distant objects or objects hidden from the senses. **clairvoyant** n.

clam-ber v. To climb by using both the hands and feet. **clamberer** n.

clam-my adj. Damp, cold, and sticky.

clam-or n. A loud noise or outcry; a vehement protest or demand. **clamourous** adj., **clamorously** adv.

clan n. A large group of people who are related to one another by a common ancestor. **-nish** adj., **clansman** n.

clan-des-tine adj. Kept or done in secrecy for a purpose.

clang v. To cause or make a loud, ringing, metallic sound.

clan-gor n. A loud series of clangs.

clap v. To applaud; to strike the hands together with an explosive sound.

clap-per n. The part of a bell that hits against the side.

clar-i-fy v. To become or make clearer.

clar-i-net n. A woodwind instrument with a single reed. **clarinetist** n.

clar-i-ty n. The state or quality of being clear.

clash v. To bring or strike together; to collide; to conflict.

clasp n. A hook to hold parts of objects together; a grasp or grip of the hands.

clas-sic adj. Belonging in a certain category of excellence; having a lasting artistic worth.

clas-si-fy v. To arrange or assign items, people, etc., into the same class or category. **classification** n.

clat-ter v. To make or to cause a rattling sound. **clatter** n.

claus-tro-pho-bia n. A fear of small or enclosed places.

clav-i-cle n. The bone that connects the breastbone and the shoulder blade.

cla-vier n. An instrument with a keyboard, such as the harpsichord.

clean adj. Free from impurities, dirt, or contamination; neat in habits.

clear adj. Free from precipitation and clouds; able to hear, see, or think easily; free from doubt or confusion.

cleat n. A metal projection that provides support, grips, or prevents slipping.

cleav-er n. A knife used by butchers.

clef n. A symbol indicating which pitch each line and space represents on a musical staff.

clem-ent adj. Merciful; mild.

cler-gy n. The group of men and women who are ordained as religious leaders and servants of God.

clerk n. A worker in an office who keeps accounts, records, and correspondence up to date; a person who works in the sales department of a store.

clev-er adj. Mentally quick; showing dexterity and skill.

cleverly adv., **cleverness** n.

cli-ent n. A person who secures the professional services of another.

cli-en-tele n. A collection of patients, customers, or clients.

cliff n. A high, steep edge or face of a rock.

cli-mac-ter-ic n. A time in life when physiological changes.

cli-mate n. The weather conditions of a certain region generalized or averaged over a period of years; the prevailing atmosphere. **climatic** adj.

cli-max n. The point of greatest intensity and fullest suspense; the culmination.

climb v. To move to a higher or lower location; to advance in rank or status. **climbable** adj., **climber** n.

clinch v. To secure; to fasten; to settle definitively. **clinch** n.

cling v. To hold fast to; to grasp or stick; to hold on and resist emotional separation. **clinger** n.

clin-ic n. A medical establishment connected with a hospital; a center that offers instruction or counseling.

clink v. To cause a light ringing sound.

clip v. To cut off; to curtail; to cut short.

clique n. A small and exclusive group of people.

clob-ber v., Slang To hit repeatedly and violently.

cloche n. A bell-shaped, close-fitting hat.

clock n. An instrument that measures time. v. To time with a clock, stopwatch, etc.

clod n. A large piece or lump of earth; a stupid, ignorant person.

clog v. To choke up. n. A shoe with a wooden sole.

clone n. An identical reproduction grown from a single cell of the original. **clone** v.

close adj. Near, as in time, space, or

relationship; nearly even, as in competition; fitting tightly. v. To shut.

clos-et n. A small cabinet, compartment, or room for storage. **closet** v.

clot n. A thick or solid mass, as of blood.

clothe v. To provide clothes; to cover with clothes; to wrap.

clo-ture n. A parliamentary action that calls for an immediate vote.

clout n. A heavy blow with the hand. *Slang* The amount of influence or pull a person may have. **clout** v.

clo-ver n. A plant that has a dense flower and trifoliolate leaves.

cloy v. To make one sick or disgusted with too much sweetness.

clum-sy adj. Lacking coordination, grace, or dexterity; not tactful or skillful. **clumsily** adv., **clumsiness** n.

clus-ter n. A bunch; a group.

clut-ter n. A confused mass of disorder.

co-ad-ju-tor n. An assistant.

co-ag-u-lant n. A substance that causes coagulation.

co-ag-u-late v. To clot. **coagulation** n.

coal n. A mineral widely used as a natural fuel; an ember.

co-a-lesce v. To come together or to grow as one.

co-ali-tion n. A temporary alliance.

coarse adj. Lacks refinement; of inferior or low quality; having large particles; harsh. **coarseness** n.

coax v. To persuade by tact, gentleness, or flattery. **coaxingly** adv.

co-ax-i-al adj. Having common coincident axes.

cob n. A male swan; a corncob; a thickset horse that has short legs.

co-balt n. A hard, lustrous metallic element that resembles iron and nickel.

cob-ble v. To make or repair shoes; to make or put together roughly.

CO-BOL n. In Computer Science, computer programming that is simple and based on English.

coc-cyx n. The small bone at the bottom of the spinal column.

coch-i-neal n. A brilliant scarlet dye prepared from the dried, pulverized bodies of certain female insects of tropical America.

coch-le-a n. The spiral tube of the inner ear, forming an essential part for hearing.

cock-ade n. A knot of ribbon or something similar worn on a hat as a badge.

cock-le n. European bivalve mollusk of the edible species, having ridged, somewhat heart-shaped shells.

co-co n. The fruit obtained from the coconut palm.

co-coa n. The powder from the roasted husked seed kernels of the cocoa.

co-coon n. The protective fiber or silk pupal case that is spun by insect larvae.

cod-dle v. To cook just below the boiling point; to simmer.

code n. A system of set rules; a set of secret words, numbers, or letters used as a means of communication; in Computer Science, the method of representing information or data by using a set sequence of characters, symbols, or words. **code** v.

co-dex n. An ancient manuscript of the classics or Scriptures.

co-ed-u-ca-tion n. An educational system for both men and women at the same institution. **coeducational** adj.

co-erce v. To restrain or dominate with force; to compel by law, authority, fear, or force.

co-e-val adj. Of the same time period.

co-ex-ist v. To exist at the same time or together; the ability to live peaceably with others in spite of differences.

cof-fee n. A beverage prepared from ground beans of the coffee tree.

cof-fer n. A strongbox or chest made for valuables.

cof-fin n. A box in which a corpse is buried.

cog n. A tooth or one of series of a teeth on the rim of wheel in a machine or a mechanical device.

co-gent adj. Compelling; forceful; convincing.

cog-i-tate v. To think carefully about or to ponder. **cogitation** n.

co-gnac n. A fine brandy made in France.

cog-nate adj. From a common ancestor; identical or similar in nature; related.

cog-ni-zance n. Perception of fact; awareness; recognition; observation.

cog-no-men n., pl. **cognomens** A person's surname; nickname.

co-hab-it v. To live together as husband and wife.

co-here v. To stick or hold together.

co-hort n. A group of people who are united in one effort; an accomplice.

coif n. A close-fitting hat that is worn under a nun's veil.

coil n. A series of connecting rings. v. To wind in spirals.

coin n. A flat, rounded piece of metal used as money. v. To invent or make a new phrase or word.

co-in-cide v. To happen at the same time; to agree exactly.

co-in-ci-dence n. Two events happening at the same time by accident but appearing to have some connection.

co-i-tus n. Physical union of male and female sexual organs; sexual intercourse.

cole n. A plant such as the cabbage or a vegetable of the same family.

col-ic n. A sharp pain in the abdomen caused by muscular cramps or spasms, occurring most often in very young babies.

col-i-se-um n. A large amphitheater used for sporting games.

col-lab-o-rate v. To cooperate or work with another person. **collaboration**, **collaborator** n.

col-lapse v. To fall; to give way; to fold and assume a smaller size; to lose all or part of the air in a lung.

col-lar n. The upper part of a garment

that encircles the neck and is often folded over.

col·lar·bone *n., Anat.* The clavicle, located near the neck.

col·late *v.* To compare in a critical fashion; to assemble in correct sequence or order.

col·lat·er·al *adj.* Serving to support; guaranteed by stocks, property, bonds, etc.

col·league *n.* Someone who works in the same profession or official body.

col·lect *v.* To gather or assemble; to gather donations or payments. **collectible, collection** *n.*

col·lide *v.* To come together with a direct impact; to clash; to come into conflict.

col·lo·cate *v.* To compare facts and arrange in correct order.

col·lo·di·on *n.* A highly flammable spray solution used to protect wounds and used for photographic plates.

col·loid *n.* A glue-like substance, such as gelatin, that cannot pass through animal membranes.

col·lo·quy *n., pl.* **-quies** A formal conversation or conference.

col·lu·sion *n.* A secret agreement between two or more people for an illegal purpose.

col·o·ny *n., pl* **-ies** A group of emigrants living in a new land away from, but under the control of, the parent country; a group of insects, as ants.

col·o·phon *n.* The inscription at the end of a book that gives the publication facts.

col·or·a·tion *n.* The arrangement of different colors or shades.

co·los·sal *adj.* Very large or gigantic in degree or size.

col·umn *n.* A decorative and/or supporting pillar used in construction; a vertical division of typed or printed lines on paper. **columnar** *adj.*

co·ma *n.* A deep sleep or unconsciousness caused by an illness or injury.

co·ma·tose *adj.* Unconscious.

com·bine *v.* To unite; to merge. *n.* A farm machine that harvest by cutting, threshing, and cleaning the grain.

com·bus·tion *n.* The chemical change that occurs rapidly and produces heat and light; a burning. **combustive** *adj.*

come *v.* To arrive; to approach; to reach a certain position, state, or result; to appear; to come into view.

com·e·dy *n., pl.* **-ies** A humorous, entertaining performance with a happy ending; a real-life comical situation.

co·mes·ti·ble *n.* Something that is fit to eat. *adj.* Fit to eat.

com·et *n.* A celestial body that moves in an orbit around the sun, consisting of a solid head that is surrounded by a bright cloud with a long, vaporous tail.

com·ic *adj.* Characteristic of comedy. *n.* A comedian. Comics Comic strips.

com·i·cal *adj.* Amusing; humorous.

com·ma *n.* The punctuation mark (,) used to indicate separation of ideas or a series in a sentence.

com·mand *v.* To rule; to give orders; to dominate. *n.* In computer science, the instruction given that specifies an operation to be performed.

com·mand·ing *adj.* Dominating by size or position.

com·mem·o·rate *v.* To honor the memory of; to create a memorial to. **commemoration, commemorator** *n.*

com·mence *v.* To begin; to start.

com·mence·ment *n.* A graduation ceremony.

com·mend *v.* To give praise; to applaud. **commendable** *adj.*, **commendation** *n.*

com·men·su·rate *adj.* Equal in duration, extent, or size. **commensuration** *n.*

com·ment *n.* A statement of criticism, analysis, or observation.

com·merce *n.* The exchanging of products or materials; buying and selling.

com·mer·cial *adj.* Of or relating to a product; supported by advertising. *n.* An advertisement on radio or television.

com·mis·er·ate *v.* To display or feel sympathy for someone.

com·mis·sar *n.* An official of the Communist Party whose duties include enforcement of party loyalty and political indoctrination.

com·mis·sar·y *n., pl.* **-ies** A store that sells food and supplies on a military base.

com·mit·tee *n.* A group of persons appointed or elected to perform a particular task or function. **committeeman, committeewoman** *n.*

com·mode *n.* A movable washstand with storage underneath; a toilet; a low chest of drawers or bureau.

com·mo·di·ous *adj.* Roomy; spacious.

com·mon *adj.* Having to do with, belonging to, or used by an entire community or public; vulgar; unrefined.

com·mon de·nom·i·na·tor *n.* A number that can be evenly divided by all the denominators of a set of fractions.

com·mon frac·tion *n.* A fraction with both the denominator and numerator being whole numbers.

com·mon law *n.* The unwritten system of law that is based on judicial decisions, customs, and usages.

com·mon·weal·th *n.* The common good of the whole group of people.

com·mu·ni·ca·ble *adj.* Capable of being transmitted, as with a disease. **communicability** *n.*

com·mu·ni·cate *v.* To make known; to cause others to partake or share something.

com·mu·ni·ca·tion *n.* The act of transmitting ideas through writing or speech; the means to transmit messages between person or places.

com·mun·ion *n.* The mutual sharing of feelings and thoughts; a religious fellowship between members of a church.

com·mu·nism *n.* A system of government

in which goods and production are commonly owned; the theory of social change and struggle toward communism through revolution.

com-mu-ni-ty *n.*, *pl.* -ies A group of people living in the same area and under the same government; a class or group having common interests and likes.

com-mute *v.* To travel a long distance to one's job each day; to exchange or to substitute.

com-muter *n.* One who travels a long distance on a regular basis.

com-pact *adj.* Packed together or solidly united; firmly and closely united.

com-pac-tor *n.* A device for compressing trash into a small mass for disposal.

com-pan-ion *n.* An associate; a person employed to accompany or assist another; one hired to travel or live with another. **companionship** *n.*

com-pan-ion-a-ble *adj.* Friendly; sociable. **companionably** *adv.*

com-pan-ion-way *n.*, *Naut.* A stairway leading from a ship's deck to the cabin below.

com-pa-ra-ble *adj.* Capable of comparison; worthy of comparison; similar. **comparability** *n.*, **comparably** *adv.*, **comparative** *adj.*

com-pare *v.* To speak of or represent as similar or equal to; to note the similarities or likenesses of.

com-par-i-son *n.* Likeness; similarity. *Gram.* Modification of an verb or adjective that indicates the positive, comparative, or superlative degree.

com-part-ment *n.* One of the sections into which an enclosed area is divided.

com-pass *n.* An instrument used to determine geographic direction; an enclosed area or space.

com-pas-sion *n.* Sympathy for someone who is suffering or distressed in some way. **compassionate** *adj.*

com-pat-i-ble *adj.* Able to function, exist, or live together harmoniously. **compatibility** *n.*, **compatibly** *adv.*

com-pa-tri-ot *n.* A person of the same country.

com-peer *n.* A person that is a peer or equal.

com-pel *v.* To urge or force action.

com-pen-dium *n.*, *pl.* -diums A short summary.

com-pen-sate *v.* To make up for; to make amends; to pay; to neutralize or counterbalance. **compensation** *n.*, **compensatory** *adj.*

com-pete *v.* To contend with others; to engage in a contest or competition.

com-pe-tent *adj.* Having sufficient ability; being capable. **competence**, **competency** *n.*

com-pe-ti-tion *n.* The act of rivalry or competing; a trial of skill or ability; a contest between teams or individuals.

com-pet-i-tor *n.* One who competes against another.

com-pile *v.* To put together material gathered from a number of sources; in Computer Science, to convert our language into machine language.

compilation *n.*, **compiler** *n.*

com-plai-sance *n.* The willingness to please, to oblige. **complaisant** *adj.*

com-ple-ment *n.* Something that perfects, completes, or adds to. -**ary** *adj.*

com-plete *adj.* Having all the necessary parts; whole; concluded. **completion** *n.*

com-plex *adj.* Consisting of various intricate parts. **complexity** *n.*, **complexly** *adv.*

com-plex-ion *n.* The natural color and texture of the skin. **complexioned** *adj.*

com-pli-ance *n.* The act of agreeing passively to a request, rule, or demand; the tendency to yield to others. **compliant** *adj.*, **compliancy** *n.*

com-pli-cate *v.* To make or become involved or complex.

com-plic-i-ty *n.* An involvement or association with a crime.

com-pli-ment *n.* An expression of praise or admiration.

com-pli-men-ta-ry *adj.* Conveying a compliment.

com-ply *v.* To agree, to consent to, or obey a command or wish. **complier** *n.*

com-po-nent *n.* A constituent part.

com-port *v.* To behave or conduct oneself in a certain way.

com-pose *v.* To make up from elements or parts; to produce or create a song; to arrange, as to typeset. **composer** *n.*

com-posed *adj.* Calm.

com-pos-ite *adj.* Made up from separate elements or parts; combined or compounded. *Bot.* Characteristic of a plant with densely clustered flowers.

com-po-si-tion *n.* The act of putting together artistic or literary work; a short essay written for an assignment in school. **compositional** *adj.*

com-post *n.* A fertilizing mixture that consists of decomposed vegetable matter.

com-po-sure *n.* Tranquillity; calm self-possession.

com-pote *n.* Fruit that is preserved or stewed in syrup; a dish used for holding fruit, candy, etc.

com-pre-hend *v.* To perceive, to grasp mentally, or to understand fully; to comprise; to include.

com-pre-hen-si-ble *adj.* Capable of being understood. **comprehensibility** *n.*, **comprehensibly** *adv.*

com-pre-hen-sive *adj.* Large in content or scope.

com-press *v.* To press together into a smaller space; to condense.

com-prise *v.* To consist of; to be made up of. **comprisable** *adj.*

com-pro-mise *n.* The process of settling or the settlement of differences between opposing sides.

comp-trol-ler *n.* A person appointed to examine and verify accounts.

com-pul-sion *n.* The act or state of being compelled; an irresistible urge or impulse to act irrationally.

compulsive *adj.*

com-pute v. To ascertain or determine by the use of mathematics; to determine something by the use of a computer. computability, comutation n., computable adj.

com-puter n. A person who computes; a high speed, electronic machine which performs logical calculations, processes, stores, and retrieves programmed information.

com-puter lan-guage n. The various codes and information that are used to give data and instructions to computers.

con v. To study carefully. Slang To swindle or trick.

con-cat-e-nate v. To join, connect, or link together. concatenate adj., concatenation n.

con-cave adj. Hollowed and curved inward. concavely adv., concave n.

con-ceal v. To keep from disclosure, sight, or knowledge; to hide. concealable adj., concealment n.

con-cede v. To grant or yield to a right or privilege; to acknowledge as true. conceder n., conceded adj.

con-ceive v. To become pregnant; to create a mental image. conceivability n., conceivable adj., conceivably adv.

con-cen-trate v. To give intense thought to; to draw to a common point; to intensify by removing certain elements; to become compact. concentrative adj., concentrator n.

con-cen-tra-tion n. The state of being concentrated or the act of concentrating; the process or act of giving complete attention to a certain problem or task.

con-cen-tra-tion camp n. An enclosed camp for the confinement of political dissidents, aliens, or prisoners of war.

con-cept n. A generalized idea formed from particular occurrences or instances; an opinion. conceptual adj.

con-cep-tion n. The union of sperm and egg; a mental thought or plan.

con-cern n. Something to consider; sincere interest; something that affects one's business or affairs. v. To be interested in; to be involved with. concerned adj.

con-cert n. A musical performance for a group of people; agreement in purpose, action, or feeling. v. To act or plan together. concerted adj.

con-cer-to n., pl. -tos, -ti A composition that features one or more solo instruments.

con-ces-sion n. The act of conceding; something that has been conceded; a tract of land that is granted by a government for a particular use.

con-ces-sion-aire n. The operator or holder of a concession.

conch n. A tropical marine mollusk having a large spiral shell and flesh that is edible.

con-chol-o-gy n. The study of mollusks and shells. conchological adj.,

conchologist n.

con-cil-i-ate v. To win over or to gain a friendship. conciliation, conciliator n., conciliatory adj.

con-cise adj. Short and to the point.

con-clave n. A private or secret meeting; the private meeting of the Roman Catholic cardinals to elect a new pope.

con-clude v. To close or bring to an end; to bring about an agreement; to arrive at a decision; to resolve. conclusion n.

con-clu-sive adj. Putting an end to any questions or doubt.

con-coct v. To make by combining ingredients; to devise or to plan. concoction n.

con-com-i-tant adj. Accompanying. concomitance n., concomitantly adv.

con-cord n. Accord; harmony; friendly and peaceful relationships.

con-cor-dance n. A condition of concord or agreement; the alphabetical index of major words used by an author, listed in the order of use in a book.

con-cor-dant adj. Exist in agreement; harmonious. concordantly adv.

con-course n. A large, open space for the assembling or passage of crowds.

con-cres-cence n. Increase by the addition of particles; growing together.

con-crete adj. Pertaining to a specific instance or thing; naming a specific class of things. n. A construction material made from sand, gravel, and cement. v. To bring together in one body or mass. concretely adv., concreteness n.

con-cu-bine n. A woman living with a man and not being legally married to him. concubinage n.

con-cu-pis-cence n. A strong sexual desire; lust. concupiscent adj.

con-cur v. To agree or express approval; to cooperate; to happen at the same time; to coincide. concurrence n.

con-cur-rent adj. Referring to an event that happens at the same time as another; acting together.

con-cus-sion n. A sudden and violent jolt; a violent injury to an organ, especially the brain. concussive adj.

con-demn v. To find to be wrong; to show the guilt; to announce judgment upon; to officially declare unfit for use. condemnable, condemnatory adj., condemnation, condemner n.

con-dense v. To make more concentrated or compact; to change something from a liquid state to a solid state or from a gaseous to a liquid state. condensation, condenser n., condensible adj.

con-di-ment n. A relish, spice, or sauce used to season food.

con-di-tion n. The mode or state of existence of a thing or person; a circumstance that is found to be necessary to the occurrence of another; a provision in a contract or will that leaves room for modification or changes at a future date. Slang A sickness or ailment. condition v.

con-di-tion-al adj. Tentative; depending

on a condition; implying or expressing a condition. *Gram.* A mood, clause, tense, or condition. conditionality *n.*, conditionally *adv.*

con-di-tioned *adj.* Prepared for a certain process or action by past experience.

con-di-tion-er *n.* An application that improves the usability of a substance.

con-do *n.*, *Slang* Condominium.

con-dom *n.* A thin rubber sheath used to cover the penis, serving as an antivenereal or contraceptive purpose during sexual intercourse.

con-do-min-i-um *n.* A joint ownership; an apartment in which all units are owned separately; a building in which the units are owned by each tenant.

con-done *n.* To overlook; to forgive; to disregard. condoner *n.*

con-dor *v.* One of the largest flying birds, with a bare head and a white downy neck.

con-du-cive *adj.* Contributing towards or promotion; helpful. conduce *v.*

con-duct *v.* To lead and direct a performance of a band or orchestra; to guide or show the way; to lead; to direct or control the course of; to transmit heat, electricity, or sound. *n.* Behavior. conductibility *n.*, conduction *n.*, conductible *adj.*

con-duc-tor *n.* A person who conducts a musical ensemble; one who is in charge of a railroad or streetcar. *Phys.* Any substance that conducts light, electricity, heat, or sound.

con-duit *n.* A pipe used to pass electric wires or cable through; a channel or pipe that water passes through.

cone *n.* A solid body that is tapered evenly to a point from a base that is circular; a wafer that is cone-shaped and used for holding ice cream.

con-fab-u-late *v.* To chat or speak informally. confabulation, confabulator *n.*, confabulatory *adj.*

con-fec-tion-er-y *n.* Candy and sweets as a whole; a store that sells candy and sweets. confection *n.*

con-fed-er-a-cy *n.*, *pl.* -ies The union of eleven southern states that seceded from the United States during the Civil War of 1861-1865 and established the Confederate Sate of America.

con-fed-er-ate *n.* An ally or friend; a person who supports the Confederacy. confederate *v.*

con-fer *v.* To consult with another; to hold a conference; to give or grant. conferment, conferral, conferrer *n.*, conferrable *adj.*

con-fer-ence *n.* A formal meeting for discussion; a league of churches, schools, or athletic teams.

con-fess *v.* To disclose or admit to a crime, fault, sin, or guilt; to tell a priest or God of one's sins. confessedly *adv.*

con-fes-sion *n.* The act of confessing.

con-fes-sion-al *n.* The small enclosure where a priest hears confessions.

con-fet-ti *pl.*, *n.* Small pieces of paper thrown during a happy occasion.

con-fide *v.* To entrust a secret to another. confider *n.*, confiding *adj.*, confidingly *adv.*

con-fi-dence *n.* A feeling of selfassurance; a feeling of trust in a person; reliance; good faith. confident *adj.*

con-fi-den-tial *adj.* Hold as a secret; having another's entrusted confidence. confidentiality *n.*, confidentially *adv.*

con-fig-u-ra-tion *n.* An arrangement of pats or things; the arrangement of elements. configurationally *adv.*

con-fine *v.* To keep within a certain boundary or limit. confines, confinement, confiner *n.*

con-firm *v.* To establish or support the truth of something; to make stronger; to ratify and bind by a formal approval. confirmable, confirmatory *adj.*

con-fir-ma-tion *n.* The act of confirming to show proof; a religious rite that admits a person to full membership in a church.

con-fis-cate *v.* To seize for public use; to officially seize. confiscation, confiscator *n.*

con-flate *v.* To combine two different ideas into a whole. conflation *n.*

con-flict *n.* A battle; clash; a disagreement of ideas, or interests. conflict *v.*, conflictive *adj.*

con-flu-ence *n.* The flowing together of two streams or rivers; the point where the two join. confluent *adj.* & *n.*, confluently *adv.*

con-form *v.* To be similar in form or character; to adhere to prevailing customs or modes. conformable *adj.*, conformably *adv.*

con-for-ma-tion *n.* The manner in which something is shaped, structured, or arranged.

con-found *v.* To amaze, confuse, or perplex; to confuse one thing for another.

con-front *v.* To put or stand face to face with defiance. confrontation *n.*, confrontational *adj.*

con-fuse *v.* To mislead or bewilder; to jumble or mix up. confusedness *n.*, confusingly *adv.*

con-fu-sion *n.* The state of being confused.

con-fute *v.* To prove to be invalid or false. confutable *adj.*, confutation *n.*

con-geal *v.* To jell; to solidify; to change from a liquid to a solid form.

con-gen-ial *adj.* Having similar character habits, or tastes; sociable; friendly. congeniality *n.*, congenially *adv.*

con-gen-i-tal *adj.* Existing from the time of birth, but not from heredity.

con-gest *v.* To enlarge with an excessive accumulation of blood; to clog. congestion *n.*, congestive *adj.*

con-glom-er-ate *n.* A business consisting of many different companies; gravel that is embedded in cement material.

con-grat-u-late *v.* To acknowledge an achievement with praise.

congratulator *n.*, congratulatory *adj.*

con-grat-u-la-tions *pl.*, *n.* The expression of or the act of congratulating.

con-gre-gate *v.* To assemble together in a crowd. congregator *n.*

con-gre-ga-tion *n.* A group of people meeting together for worship.

Con-gress *n.* The United States legislative body, consisting of the Senate and the House of Representatives.

con-gru-ent *adj.* Agreeing to conform; in mathematics, having exactly the same size and shape.

con-ic *or* con-i-cal *adj.* Related to and shaped like a cone.

conj *abbr.* Conjunction.

con-jec-ture *n.* A guess or conclusion based on incomplete evidence. conjecturable *adj.*, conjecture *v.*

con-join *v.* To unite; join to together.

con-ju-gal *adj.* Pertaining to the relationship or marriage of husband and wife.

con-ju-gate *adj.* To change the form of a verb; to join in pairs. conjugately *adv.*, conjugative *adj.*, conjugator *n.*

con-junct *adj.* Combined; joined together.

con-junc-tion *n.* The act of joining; the state of being joined. *Gram.* A word used to join or connect other words, phrases, sentences, or clauses.

con-junc-ti-va *n.*, *pl.* -vas, -vae The membrane lining of the eyelids. conjunctival *adj.*

con-junc-tive *adj.* Connective; joining. *Gram.* Serving as a conjunction.

con-junc-ti-vi-tis *n.*, *Pathol.* Inflammation of the membrane that lines the eyelids.

con-jure *v.* To bring into the mind; to appeal or call on solemnly; to practice magic.

con-nect *v.* To join; to unite; to associate, as to relate. connectedly *adv.*, connector, connecter *n.*

con-nec-tion *n.* An association of one person or thing to another; a union, link, or bond; an influential group of friends or associates.

con-nec-tive *adj.* Capable of connecting; tending to connect. *n.* Something that connects as a word. connectivity *n.*

con-nive *v.* To ignore a known wrong, therefore implying sanction; to conspire; to cooperate in secret.

con-nois-seur *n.* A person whose expertise in an area of art or taste allows him to be a judge; an expert. connoisseurship *n.*

con-no-ta-tion *n.* The associative meaning of a word in addition to the literal meaning. connotative *adj.*

con-note *v.* To imply along with the literal meaning.

con-nu-bi-al *adj.* Having to do with marriage or the state of marriage. connubiality *n.*, connubially *adv.*

con-quer *v.* To subdue; to win; to overcome by physical force.

con-quis-ta-dor *n.*, *pl.* -dors A Spanish conquer + or of the sixteenth century.

con-san-guin-e-ous *adj.* Having the same

blood; descended from the same ancestor. consanguineously *adv.*

con-science *n.* The ability to recognize right and wrong regarding one's own behavior.

con-sci-en-tious *adj.* Honest; scrupulous; careful.

con-scious *adj.* Aware on one's own existence and environment; aware of facts or objects.

con-script *n.* One who is drafted or forced to enroll for a service or a job.

con-se-crate *v.* To declare something to be holy; to dedicate to sacred uses. consecration, consecrator *n.*

con-sec-u-tive *adj.* Following in uninterrupted succession. consecutively *adv.*, consecutiveness *n.*

con-sen-sus *n.* A general agreement; a collective opinion.

con-sent *v.* To agree; an acceptance. consenter *n.*

con-se-quence *n.* The natural result from a preceding condition or action; the effect.

con-se-quent *adj.* Following as a natural result or effect. consequently *adv.*

con-se-quen-tial *adj.* Having or showing self-importance. consequentially *adv.*

con-serv-a-tive *adj.* Opposed to change; desiring the preservation of the existing order of things; moderate; cautious; wanting to conserve. conservatively *adv.*, conservativeness *n.*

con-ser-va-to-ry *n.*, *pl.* -ries A school of dramatic art or music; a greenhouse.

con-serve *v.* To save something from decay, loss, or depletion; to maintain; to preserve fruits with sugar. *n.* A mixture of several fruits cooked together with sugar and sometimes raisins or nuts. conservable *adj.*, conserver *n.*

con-sid-er *v.* To seriously think about; to examine mentally; to believe or hold as an opinion; to deliberate.

con-sid-er-a-ble *adj.* Large in amount or extent; important; worthy of consideration. considerably *adv.*

con-sid-er-a-tion *n.* The taking into account of circumstance before forming an opinion; care and thought; a kind or thoughtful treatment or feeling. considering *prep.*

con-sign *v.* To commit to the care of another; to deliver or forward, as merchandise; to put aside, as for specific use. consignee *n.*, consignable *adj.*, consignor, consignment *n.*

con-sist *v.* To be made up of.

con-sis-ten-cy *n.*, *pl.* -cies Agreement or compatibility among ideas, events, or successive acts; the degree of texture, viscosity, or density. consistent *adj.*

con-sis-to-ry *n.*, *pl.* -ries In the Roman Catholic Church, the assembly of all cardinals with the pope presiding over them.

con-sole *v.* To give comfort to someone. consolable *adj.*, consolation *n.*, consolingly *adv.*

con-sol-i-date *v.* To combine in one or to form a union of; to form a compact mass. **consolidation, consolidator** *n.*

con-so-nant *n.* A sound produced by complete or partial blockage of the air from the mouth, as the sound of b, f, k, s, t; the letter of the alphabet that represents such a sound. *adj.* In agreement. **consonantal** *adj.*, **consonantly** *adv.*

con-sort *n.* A spouse; companion or partner. *v.* To unite or keep in company.

con-sor-ti-um *n., pl.* **-tia** *n.* An association with banks or corporations that require vast resources.

con-spic-u-ous *adj.* Noticeable. **conspicuously** *adv.*, **conspicuousness** *n.*

con-spir-a-cy *n., pl.* **-ies** A plan or act of two or more persons to do an evil act.

con-spire *v.* To plan a wrongful act in secret; to work or act together. **conspirator** *n.*

con-sta-ble *n.* A peace officer.

con-stant *adj.* Faithful; unchanging; steady in action, purpose, and affection. *Math* A quantity that remains the same throughout a given problem. **constancy** *n.*, **constantly** *adv.*

con-ster-na-tion *n.* Sudden confusion or amazement.

con-sti-pa-tion *n.* A condition of the bowels characterized by difficult or infrequent evacuation. **constipate** *v.*

con-stit-u-en-cy *n., pl.* **-cies** A group of voters that is represented by an elected legislator.

con-stit-u-ent *adj.* Having the power to elect a representative. *n.* A necessary element or part.

con-sti-tu-tion *n.* The fundamental laws that govern a nation; structure or composition. **constitutional** *adj.*, **constitutionality** *n.*

con-strain *v.* To restrain by physical or moral means. **constrained** *adj.*

con-straint *n.* The threat or use of force; confinement; restriction.

con-strict *v.* To squeeze, compress, or contract. **constriction** *n.*, **constrictive** *adj.*, **constrictively** *adv.*

con-struct *v.* To create, make, or build. **constructor, constructer** *n.*

con-struc-tive *adj.* Useful; helpful; building, advancing, or improving; resulting in a positive conclusion. **constructively** *adv.*, **constructiveness** *n.*

con-strue *v.* To interpret; to translate; to analyze grammatical structure.

con-sul-ate *n.* The official premises occupied by a consul.

con-sult *v.* To seek advice or information from; to compare views. **consultant, consultation** *n.*

con-sume *v.* To ingest; to eat or drink; to destroy completely; to absorb; to engross. **consumable** *adj. & n.*

con-sum-er *n.* A person who buys services or goods.

con-sum-mate *v.* To conclude; to make a marriage complete by the initial act of sexual intercourse.

con-sump-tion *n.* Fulfillment; the act of consuming; the quantity consumed; tuberculosis.

con-sump-tive *adj.* Tending to destroy or waste away; affected with or pertaining to pulmonary tuberculosis. **consumptively** *adv.*, **consumptiveness** *n.*

con-ta-gion *n.* The transmitting of a disease by contact. **contagious** *adj.*, **contagiously** *adv.*, **contagiousness** *n.*

con-tain *v.* To include or enclose; to restrain or hold back. **containable** *adj.*, **containment** *n.*

con-tain-er *v.* Something that holds or carries, as a box or can.

con-tain-er ship *n.* A ship that is designed to carry containerized cargo.

con-tam-i-nate *v.* To pollute or make inferior by adding undesireable elements; to taint; to infect; to make dirty or to soil. **contamination** *n.*

con-temn *v.* To scorn or despise.

con-tem-plate *v.* To look over; to ponder; to consider thoughtfully. **contemplation** *n.*, **contemplative** *adj.*

con-tem-po-ra-ne-ous *adj.* Occurring or living at the same time; contemporary.

con-tempt *n.* The act of viewing something as mean, vile, or worthless scorn; legally, the willful disrespect or disregard of authority.

con-temp-tu-ous *adj.* Feeling or showing contempt. **contemptuously** *adv.*

con-tend *v.* To dispute; to fight; to debate; to argue. **contender** *n.*

con-tent *n.* Something contained within; the subject matter of a book or document; the proportion of a specified part. *adj.* Satisfied. **contentment** *n.*, **contentedly** *adv.*, **contented** *adj.*

con-ten-tion *n.* Competition; rivalry; controversy; argument. **contentious** *adj.*, **contentiously** *adv.*

con-test *n.* A competition; strife; conflict. *v.* To challenge. **contestable** *adj.*, **contestant, contester** *n.*

con-text *n.* A sentence, phrase, or passage so closely connected to a word or words that it affects their meaning; the environment in which an event occurs.

con-ti-nent *n.* One of the seven large masses of the earth: Asia, Africa, Australia, Europe, North America, South America and Antarctica.

con-ti-nen-tal *adj.* Of or characteristic of a continent.

con-ti-nen-tal di-vide *n.* A divide separating rivers or streams that flow to opposite sides of a continent.

con-ti-nu-i-ty *n., pl.* **-ties** The quality of being continuous.

con-tin-u-ous *adj.* Uninterrupted. **continuously** *adv.*, **continuousness** *n.*

con-tort *v.* To severely twist out of shape.

con-tor-tion-ist *n.* An acrobat who exhibits unnatural body positions.

con-tour *n.* The outline of a body, figure, or mass.

con-tra-band *n.* Illegal or prohibited traffic; smuggled goods.

con-tra-bass *n.* A double bass, also called a contrabassoon.

con-tra-cep-tion *n.* The voluntary prevention of impregation.

con-tract *n.* A formal agreement between two or more parties to perform the duties as stated.

con-trac-tion *n.* The act of contracting; a shortening of a word by omitting a letter or letters and replacing them with an apostrophe (').

con-trac-tile *adj.* Having the power to contract.

con-tra-dict *v.* To express the opposite side or idea; to be inconsistent. contradictable, contradictory *adj.*, contradicter, contradictor *n.*

con-tral-to *n.*, *pl.* -tos The lowest female singing voice.

con-trap-tion *n.* A gadget.

con-tra-puntal *adj.* Relating to counterpoint. contrapuntally *adv.*

con-trar-y *adj.* Unfavorable; incompatible with another. contrarily *adv.*, contrariness *n.*

con-trast *v.* To note the differences between two or more people, things, etc. contrastable *adj.*

con-tra-vene *v.* To be contrary; to violate; to oppose; to go against.

con-trib-ute *v.* To give something to someone; to submit for publication. contribution *n.*, contributive, contributory *adj.*, contributively *adv.*

con-trite *adj.* Grieving for sin or shortcoming. contritely *adv.*, contrition *n.*

con-trol *v.* To have the authority or ability to regulate, direct, or dominate a situation. controllable *adj.*

con-trol-ler *n.* The chief accounting officer of a business, also called the comptroller.

con-tro-ver-sy *n.* A dispute; a debate; a quarrel. controversial *adj.*

con-tro-vert *v.* To contradict; to deny.

con-tu-me-ly *n.*, *pl* -lies Rude treatment.

co-nun-drum *n.* A riddle with an answer that involves a pun; a question or problem with only a surmise for an answer.

con-va-lesce *v.* To grow strong after a long illness. convalescence *n.*, convalescent *adj.*

con-vec-tion *n.* The transfer of heat by the movement of air, gas, or heated liquid between areas of unequal density. convectional *adj.*

con-vene *v.* To meet or assemble formally. convenable *adj.*, convener *n.*

con-ven-ience *n.* The quality of being convenient or suitable.

con-vent *n.* A local house or community of a religious order, especially for nuns.

con-ven-ti-cle *n.* A secret meeting for religious study or worship.

con-ven-tion-al *adj.* Commonplace, ordinary.

con-verge *v.* To come to a common point. convergence *n.*, convergent *adj.*

con-ver-sa-tion *n.* An informal talk.

converse *v.* To involve oneself in conversation with another.

con-ver-sion *n.* The act or state of changing to adopt new opinions or beliefs; a formal acceptance of a different religion. conversional *adj.*

con-vex *adj.* Curved outward like the outer surface of a ball. convexity *n.*

con-vey *v.* To transport; to pass information on to someone else; to conduct.

con-vey-ance *n.* The action of conveying; the legal transfer of property or the document effecting it.

con-vict *v.* To prove someone guilty. *n.* A prisoner.

con-vic-tion *n.* The act of being convicted.

con-vince *v.* To cause to believe without doubt. convincingly *adv.*

con-vo-ca-tion *n.* A formal or ceremonial assembly or meeting.

con-voke *v.* To call together for a formal meeting.

con-voy *n.* A group of cars, trucks, etc., traveling together. *v.* To escort or guide.

con-vulse *v.* To move or shake violently. convulsive *adj.*, convulsively *adv.*

con-vul-sion *n.* A violent involuntary muscular contraction.

cool *adj.* Without warmth; indifferent or unenthusiastic. *Slang* First-rate; composure.

cool-ant *n.* The cooling agent that circulates through a machine.

coon *n.*, *Informal* A raccoon.

coop *n.* A cage or enclosed area to contain animals, as chickens.

co-op *n.* A cooperative.

co-op-er-ate *v.* To work together toward a common cause. cooperation, -or *n.*

co-op-er-a-tive *adj.* Willing to cooperate with others. cooperatively *adv.*, cooperativeness *n.*

co-opt *v.* To elect or choose as a new member.

cop *n.*, *Informal* A police officer.

cope *v.* To strive; to struggle or contend with something. *n.* The long cape worn by a priest on special ceremonial occasions.

cop-ier *n.* A machine that makes copies of original material.

co-pi-lot *n.* The assistant pilot on an aircraft.

co-pi-ous *n.* Large in quantity; abundant.

cop-out *n.*, *Slang* A way to avoid responsibility.

cop-per *n.* A metallic element that is a good conductor of electricity and heat, reddish-brown in color.

cop-ra *n.* Dried coconut meat that yields coconut oil.

copse *n.* A thicket made up of trees or small bushes.

cop-ter *n.*, *Slang* A helicopter.

cop-u-la *n.*, *Gram.* A word or words which connect a subject and predicate.

cop-u-late *v.* To have sexual intercourse.

copy *v.*, *pl.* -ies To reproduce an original. *n.* A single printed text. copyist *n.*

coq au vin *n.* Chicken cooked in wine.

co-quette *n.* A woman who flirts.

cor-al *n.* The stony skeleton of a small sea creature, often used for jewelry.

cord *n.* A string or twine.

cor-dial *adj.* Warm-hearted and sincere.

n. A liqueur. **cordiality** *n.*,
cordially *adv.*

cord-ite *n.* A smokeless gunpowder.

cor-du-roy *n.* A durable cotton fabric which has a ribbed pile.

co-re-spon-dent *n.* A person charged with having committed adultery with the defendant in a divorce case.

cor-ne-a *n.* The transparent membrane of the eyeball. **corneal** *adj.*

cor-net *n.* A three valved, brass musical instrument. **cornetist** *n.*

corn-meal *n.* Meal made from corn.

corn-row *v.* To braid the hair in rows very close to the head.

corn-stalk *n.* A stalk of corn.

cor-nu-co-pi-a *n.* A curved goat's horn overflowing with flowers, fruit, and corn to signify prosperity.

corn-y *adj.*, *Slang* Trite or mawkishly old-fashioned.

co-rol-la *n.* The petals of a flower.

cor-ol-lary *n.*, *pl.* **-ies** Something that naturally or incidentally follows or accompanies.

cor-o-nar-y *adj.* Of or relating to the two arteries that supply blood to the heart muscles. **coronary** *n.*

cor-o-nary throm-bo-sis *n.* A blockage of the coronary artery of the heart.

cor-po-rate *adj.* Combined into one joint body; relating to a corporation.

cor-po-ra-tion *n.* A group of merchants united in a trade guild; any group or persons that act as one.

cor-po-re-al *adj.* Of a physical nature.

corpse *n.* A dead body.

cor-pu-lence *n.* The excessive accumulation of body fat; obesity.

cor-pus-cle *n.* A minute particle or living cell, especially as one in the blood.

cor-pus de-lic-ti *n.* The essential evidence pertaining to a crime.

cor-rect *v.* To make free from fault or mistakes. **correctable,** *adj.*

cor-rel-a-tive *adj.* Having a mutual relation.

cor-ri-gen-dum *n.*, *pl.* **-da** An error in print that is accompanied by its correction.

cor-ri-gi-ble *adj.* Able to correct; capable of being corrected.

cor-rob-o-rate *v.* To support a position or statement with evidence.
corroboration *n.*, **corroborative** *adj.*

cor-rode *v.* To eat away through chemical action. **corrodible** *adj.*,
corrosion *n.*, **corrosive** *adj.* & *n.*

cor-rupt *adj.* Dishonest; evil. *v.* To become or make corrupt. **corrupter** *n.*

cor-sage *n.* A small bouquet of flowers worn on a woman's shoulder or wrist.

cor-sair *n.* A pirate; a fast moving vessel.

cor-tege *n.* A ceremonial procession; a funeral procession.

cor-tex *n.*, *pl.* **-tices** The external layer of an organ, especially the gray matter that covers the brain; the bark of trees and the rinds of fruits.

cor-ti-sone *n.* A hormone produced by the adrenal cortex, used in the treatment of rheumatoid arthritis.

co-run-dum *n.* An aluminum oxide used as an abrasive.

cor-us-cate *v.* To sparkle. **coruscation** *n.*

co-ry-za *n.* An acute inflammation of the upper respiratory system.

co-sign *v.* To sign a document jointly.

co-sig-na-to-ry *n.*, *pl.* **-ies** One who jointly cosigns a document.

cos-met-ic *n.* A preparation designed to beautify the face. **cosmetically** *adv.*

cos-me-tol-o-gy *n.* The study of cosmetics and their use. **cosmetologist** *n.*

cos-mog-o-ny *n.* The creation of the universe.

cos-mo-naut *n.* A Soviet astronaut.

cos-mo-pol-i-tan *adj.* Being at home anywhere in the world.

cos-mop-o-lite *n.* A cosmopolitan person.

cos-mos *n.* An orderly and harmoniously systematic universe.

cos-set *v.* To pamper; pet.

cost *n.* The amount paid or charged for a purchase. **cost** *v.*, **costly** *adj.*

cos-tive *adj.* Affected with or causing constipation.

cot *n.* A small, often collapsible bed.

cot-tage *n.* A small house, usually for vacation use.

cough *v.* To suddenly expel air from the lungs with an explosive noise.

could *v.* Past tense of can.

could-n't *contr.* Could not.

cou-lomb *n.* The unit of quantity used to measure electricity; the amount conveyed by one amphere in one second.

coun-cil *n.* A group of people assembled for consultation or discussion; an official legislative or advisory body.
councilman, councilor *n.*

coun-sel *n.* Advice given through consultation; a lawyer engaged in the management or trial of a court case.

coun-sel-or *n.* One who gives advice; a lawyer.

coun-te-nance *n.* The face as an indication of mood or character; bearing or expression that would suggest approval or sanction.

coun-ter-act *v.* To oppose and, by contrary action, make ineffective.

coun-ter-bal-ance *n.* A force or influence that balances another; a weight that balances another. **counterbalance** *v.*

coun-ter-claim *n.* A contrary claim made to offset another.

coun-ter-cul-ture *n.* A culture with values opposite those of traditional society.

coun-ter-es-pi-o-nage *n.* Espionage aimed at discovering and thwarting enemy espionage.

coun-ter-ir-ri-tant *n.* An irritation that diverts attention from another.

coun-ter-of-fen-sive *n.* A military offensive designed to thwart an enemy attack.

coun-terpane *n.* A covering.

coun-terpart *n.* One that matches or complements another.

coun-ter-plea *n.* A plea made in answer to a previous plea.

coun·ter·pro·duc·tive *adj.* Tending to hinder rather than aid in the attainment of a goal.

coun·ter·ten·or *n.* An adult tenor with a very high range, higher than that of the average tenor.

coun·ter·vail *v.* To counteract.

count·less *adj.* Too many or too numerous to be counted.

coun·tri·fied *adj.* Of or relating to country life; rural; unsophisticated.

coun·try *n., pl.* **-ies** A given area or region; the land of one's birth, residence, or citizenship; a state, nation, or its territory.

coup *n.* A brilliant, sudden move that is usually highly successful.

cou·ple *n.* A pair; something that joins two things together; a few. *v.* To join in marriage or sexual union.

cou·plet *n.* Two rhyming lines of poetry in succession.

cour·age *n.* Mental or moral strength to face danger without fear. **courageous** *adj.*, **courageously** *adv.*

cou·ri·er *n.* A messenger; a person who carries contraband for another.

course *n.* The act of moving in a path from one point to another.

cour·te·ous *adj.* Marked by respect for and consideration of others.

cour·te·san *n.* A prostitute one who associates with or caters to high-ranking or wealthy men.

cour·te·sy *n., pl.* **-ies** Courteous behavior; general allowance despite facts.

court·house *n.* A building for holding courts of law.

court·i·er *n.* One in attendance at a royal court.

cov·e·nant *n.* A formal, binding agreement; a promise or pledge.

cov·et *v.* To wish for enviously; to crave possession of that which belongs to someone else.

cov·ey *n.* A small group of birds, especially quail or partridges.

cow·ard *n.* One who shows great fear or timidity. **cowardice** *n.*

cox·comb *n.* A conceited foolish person.

cox·swain *n.* One who steers a boat or racing shell.

coy *adj.* Quieting or shy, or to pretending to be so. **coyness** *n.*

coz·en *v.* To swindle, cheat, deceive, win over, or induce to do something by coaxing or trickery. **cozener** *n.*

co·zy *adj.* Comfortable and warm; snug. *n.* A cover placed over a teapot to retain the warmth. **cozily** *adv.*

crack *v.* To make a loud explosive sound; to break, snap, or split apart. *Slang* A highly dangerous and addictive form of cocaine.

crag *n.* A steep, jagged rock or cliff. **cragged, craggy** *adj.*

cra·ni·um *n., pl.* **crania** The skull, especially the part in which the brain is enclosed. **cranial** *adj.*

crank·y *adj.* Grouchy, irritable.

cran·ny *n., pl.* **-ies** A small break or crevice; an obscure nook or corner.

craps *v.* A gambling game played with two dice.

crash *v.* To break violently or noisily; to damage in landing, usually an airplane; to collapse suddenly, usually a business.

crass *adj.* Insensitive and unrefined.

cra·vat *n.* A necktie.

crave *v.* To desire intensely.

cra·ven *adj.* Completely lacking courage.

crav·ing *n.* An intense longing or desire.

craw *n.* The crop of a bird; the stomach of a lower animal.

craw·fish *n.* A crayfish.

crawl *v.* To move slowly by dragging the body along the ground in a prone position; to move on hands and knees; to progress slowly.

creak *v.* A squeaking or grating noise. **creaky** *adj.*, **creakily** *adv.*

crease *n.* A line or mark made by folding and pressing a pliable substance. **crease** *v.*

cre·ate *v.* To bring something into existence; to give rise to.

cre·a·tion *n.* The act of creating; something that is created; the universe.

cre·a·tive *adj.* Marked by the ability to create; inventive; imaginative. **creatively** *adv.*, **creativeness** *n.*

cre·a·tor *n.* One that creates. **The Creator.** God.

crea·ture *n.* Something created; a living being.

cre·dence *n.* Belief.

cre·den·za *n.* A buffet or sideboard, usually without legs.

cred·i·ble *adj.* Offering reasonable grounds for belief. **credibility** *n.*

cred·u·lous *adj.* Gullible; ready to believe on slight or uncertain evidence. **credulously** *adv.*

creed *n.* A brief authoritative statement of religious belief.

creek *n.* A narrow stream. **up the creek** In a difficult or perplexing situation.

creel *n.* A wicker basket for holding fish.

creep *v.* To advance at a slow pace; to go timidly or cautiously.

cre·mate *v.* To reduce to ashes by burning.

cre·o·sote *n.* An oily liquid mixture obtained by distilling coal tar, used especially as a wood preservative.

crept *v.* The past tense of creep.

cre·pus·cu·lar *adj.* Of, resembling, or relating to twilight.

cre·scen·do *adv.* In music, gradually increasing in loudness.

cres·cent *n.* The shape of the moon in its first and fourth quarters, defined with a convex and a concave edge.

cress *n.* Any of numerous plants with sharp-tasting edible leaves.

cre·tin *n.* One afflicted with cretinism; a person with marked mental deficiency.

cre·tin·ism *n.* A condition marked by physical stunting and mental deficiency.

cre·tonne *n.* A strong cotton or linen cloth, used especially for curtains and upholstery.

cre-vasse *n.* A deep crack or crevice.

crev-ice *n.* A narrow crack.

crew-el *n.* Slackly twisted worsted yarn, used in embroidery.

cri-er *n.* One who calls out public notices.

crime *n.* An act or the commission of an act that is forbidden by law.

crimp *v.* To cause to become bent or crinkled; to pinch in or together.

crim-son *n.* A deep purplish color. *v.* To make or become crimson.

cringe *v.* To shrink or recoil in fear.

crin-kle *v.* To wrinkle. **crinkly** *adj.*

crin-o-line *n.* An open-weave fabric used for lining and stiffening garments.

cri-sis *n., pl.* **crises** An unstable or uncertain time or state of affairs.

crisp *adj.* Easily broken; brittle; brisk or cold; sharp; clear. *v.* To make or become crisp. **crisply** *adv.*, **crispness** *n.*

cri-te-ri-on *n., pl.* **criteria** A standard by which something can be judged.

crit-ic *n.* A person who is critical; a person who examines a subject and expresses an opinion as to its value.

crit-i-cal *adj.* Very important, as a critical decision; tending to criticize harshly. **critically** *adv.*

crit-i-cism *n.* The act of criticizing, usually in a severe or negative fashion.

crit-i-cize *v.* To be a critic; to find fault with; to judge critically; to blame.

croak *n.* A hoarse, raspy cry such as that made by a frog. *v.* To utter a croak. *Slang* To die.

cro-chet *n.* The needlework achieved by looping thread with a hooked needle.

crock *n.* An earthenware pot or jar most often used for cooking or storing food.

croc-o-dile *n.*

Any of various large, thick-skinned, long-bodied reptiles of tropical and subtropical regions.

croc-o-dile tears *n., pl.* Insincere grief.

cro-cus *n., pl.* **crocuses** A plant having solitary, long-tubed flowers and slender, linear leaves.

crone *n.* A witch-like, withered old woman.

cro-ny *n., pl.* **-ies** A close friend.

crook *n.* A bent or hooked implement; a bend or curve; a person given to dishonest acts. *v.* To bend or curve.

croon *v.* To sing in a gentle, low voice; to make a continued moaning sound. **croon** *n.*

crop *n.* A plant which is grown and then harvested for use or for sale; a riding whip. *v.* To cut off short; to appear unexpectedly.

cro-quet *n.* An outdoor game played by driving wooden balls through hoops with long-handled mallets.

cro-quette *n.* A small patty or roll of minced food that is breaded and deep fried.

cross *n.*

A structure consisting of an upright post and a crossbar, used especially by the Romans for execution, such as the cross on which Jesus was crucified; something that tries one's virtue or patience; a medal with the shape of the cross, such as the one used as a Christian emblem; a mark formed by the intersection of two lines. *v.* In biology, to interbreed a plant or an animal with one of a different kind; to go over; to intersect; to turn against; to go against. *adj.* Ill-tempered.

cross-bar *n.* A horizontal bar or line.

crotch *n.* The angle formed by the junction of two parts, such as legs or branches. **crotched** *adj.*

crotch-et *n.* A peculiar opinion or preference.

crouch *v.* To bend at the knees and lower the body close to the ground.

croup *n.* A spasmodic laryngitis, especially of children, marked by a loud, harsh cough and difficulty in breathing. **croupy** *adj.*

crou-pi-er *n.* One who collects and pays bets at a gambling table.

crou-ton *n.* A small piece of toasted or fried bread.

crow *n.* A large, black bird.

crowd *n.* A large group of people gathered together. *v.* To assemble in large numbers; to press close.

CRT *abbr.* Cathode Ray Tube.

cru-cial *adj.* Extremely important; critical.

cru-ci-ble *n.* A vessel used for melting and calcining materials at high temperatures; a hard test of someone.

cru-ci-fy *v.* To put to death by nailing to a cross; to treat cruelly; to torment.

crude *adj.* Unrefined; lacking refinement or tact; haphazardly made. *n.* Unrefined petroleum. **-ly** *adv.*, **-ness** *n.*

cruel *adj.* Inflicting suffering; causing pain. **cruelly** *adv.*, **cruelty** *n.*

cru-et *n.* A small glass bottle normally used as a container for oil or vinegar.

crumb *n.* A small fragment of material, particularly bread.

crum-ble *v.* To break into small pieces.

crum-ple *v.* To bend or crush out of shape; to cause to collapse; to be crumpled.

crunch *v.* To chew with a crackling noise; to run, walk, etc., with a crushing noise. **crunch** *n.*

crush *v.* To squeeze or force by pressure so as to damage or injure; to reduce to particles by pounding or grinding; to put down or suppress. **-able** *adj.*, **-er** *n.*

crus-ta-cean *n.* Any one of a large class of aquatic arthropods, including lobsters and crabs, with a segmented body and paired, jointed limbs.

crux *n.* An essential or vital moment; a

main or central feature.

cry *v.* To shed tears; to call out loudly; to utter a characteristic call or sound; to proclaim publicly. **cry** *n.*

crypt *n.* An underground chamber or vault primarily used to bury the dead.

cryp-tic *adj.* Intended to be obscure; serving to conceal.

cryp-tog-ra-phy *n.* The writing and deciphering of messages in secret code. **cryptographer** *n.*

crys-tal *n.* Quartz that is transparent or nearly transparent; a body that is formed by the solidification of a chemical element; a clear, high-quality glass. **crystalline** *adj.*

crys-tal-lize *v.* To cause to form crystals or assume crystalline form; to cause to take a definite form; to coat with crystals, especially sugar crystals.

cub *n.* The young of the lion, wolf, or bear; an awkward child or youth.

cub-by-hole *n.* A small enclosed area.

cube *n.* A regular solid with six equal squares, having all its angles right angles. **cube** *v.*

cube root *n.* A number whose cube is a given number.

cubic *adj.* Having the shape of a cube; having three dimensions; having the volume of a cube with the edges of a specified unit.

cu-bi-cle *n.* A small partitioned area.

cub-ism *n.* An art style that portrays the subject matter with geometric forms.

cu-bit *n.* An ancient unit of measurement that equals approximately eighteen to twenty inches.

cuffs *n.* Handcuffs.

cui-rass *n.* A piece of armor for the breast and back, used for protection.

cui-sine *n.* A style of cooking and preparing food; the food prepared.

cu-li-nar-y *adj.* Relating to cooking.

cull *v.* To select the best from a group. **culler** *n.*

cul-mi-nate *v.* To reach or rise to the highest point. **culmination** *n.*

cu-lotte *n.* A woman's full pants made to look like a skirt.

cul-pa-ble *adj.* Meriting blame.

cul-prit *n.* A person guilty of a crime.

cult *n.* A group or system of religious worship. **cultic** *adj.*, **cultist** *n.*

cul-ti-vate *v.* To improve land for planting by fertilizing and plowing; to improve by study; to encourage. **cultivatable** *adj.*, **cultivator** *n.*

cul-vert *n.* A drain that runs under a road or railroad.

cum-ber-some *adj.* Clumsy; unwieldy.

cum-mer-bund *n.* A wide sash worn by men in formal attire.

cu-mu-lus *n.*, *pl.* **cumuli** A white, fluffy cloud with a rounded top and a flat base.

cu-ne-i-form *n.* Wedge-shaped characters used in ancient Babylonian, Assyrian, and Sumerian writing.

cun-ning *adj.* Crafty; sly. **cunningly** *adv.*

cup *n.* A small, open container with a handle, used for drinking; a measure of capacity that equals 1/2 pint, 8 ounces, or 16 tablespoons.

cu-pid-i-ty *n.* An excessive desire for material gain.

cu-po-la *n.* A rounded roof; a small vaulted structure that usually rises above a roof.

cur *n.* A mongrel; a dog of mixed breeds.

cu-rate *n.* A member of the clergy that assists the priest.

cu-ra-tor *n.* A person in charge of a museum.

curd *n.* The coagulated portion of milk used for making cheese.

cure *n.* Recovery from a sickness; a medical treatment; the process of preserving food with the use of salt, smoke, or aging.

cu-ret-tage *n.* Surgical cleaning and scraping.

cu-ri-o *n.* An unusual or rare object.

cu-ri-ous *adj.* Questioning; inquisitive; eager for information. **curiosity** *n.*, **curiously** *adv.*

curl *v.* To twist into curves; shape like a coil. *n.* A ringlet of hair. **curler**, **curliness** *n.*, **curly** *adj.*

cur-mudg-eon *n.* An ill-tempered person.

cur-rant *n.* A small seedless raisin.

cur-ren-cy *n.*, *pl.* **-cies** Money in circulation.

cur-rent *adj.* Belonging or occurring in the present time. *n.* Water or air that has a steady flow in a definite direction. **currently** *adv.*

cur-ric-u-lum *n.*, *pl.* **-la**, **-lums** The courses offered in a school.

cur-ry *v.* To groom a horse with a brush. *n.* A pungent spice used in cooking.

cur-ry-comb *n.* A special comb used to curry a horse.

curse *n.* A prayer or wish for harm to come to someone or something.

cursor *n.* In computer science, the flashing square, underline, or other indicator on the CRT screen of a computer that shows where the next character will be deleted or inserted.

cur-sive *n.* A flowing writing in which the letters are joined together. **-ly** *adv.*

curt *adj.* Abrupt; rude. **curtly** *adv.*, **curtness** *n.*

cur-tail *v.* To shorten. **curtailment** *n.*

cur-tain *n.* A piece of material that covers a window and can be either drawn to the sides or raised.

curt-sy *n.*, *pl.* **-sies** A respectful gesture made by bending the knees and lowering the body.

cush-ion *n.* A pillow with a soft filling. *v.* To absorb the shock or effect.

cus-pid *n.* A pointed canine tooth.

cus-pi-dor *n.* A spittoon.

cuss *v.* To use profanity.

cus-tard *n.* A mixture of milk, eggs, sugar, and flavoring that is baked.

cus-to-di-an *n.* One who has the custody or care of something or someone.

cus-to-dy *n.*, *pl.* **-dies** The act of guarding; the care and protection of a minor.

cus-tom *n.* An accepted practice of a

community or people; the usual manner of doing something. **customs** The tax one must pay on imported goods.

cus-tom--built *adj.* Built to one's special order.

cus-tom-er *n.* A person with whom a merchant or business person must deal, usually on a regular basis.

cut *v.* To penetrate with a sharp edge, as with a knife; to omit or leave something out; to reap or harvest crops in the fields. *Slang* To cut class; to share in the profits. **cut** *n.*

cut back *v.* To reduce; to prune.

cute *adj.* Attractive in a delightful way.

cut-lass *or* **cut-las** *n.* A thick, short, curved sword.

cut-lery *n.* Cutting instruments used at the dinner table and used to prepare food for cooking.

cut--rate *adj.* Offering merchandise at a lower than normal price.

cut-ter *n., Naut.* A fast-sailing vessel with a single mast.

cut-throat *n.* A murderer; a thug.

cut up *v.* To act foolishly; to behave like a clown; to cut into pieces.

cy-a-nide *n., Chem.* A compound of cyanogen with a metallic element; a poison.

cyc-la-men *n.* A plant with red, white, or pink flowers.

cy-cle *n.* A recurring time in which an event occurs repeatedly; a bicycle or motorcycle. **cyclical** *adj.,* **cyclically** *adv.*

cy-clist *n.* A person who rides a cycle.

cy-clone *n.* A storm with wind rotating about a low pressure center, accompanied by destructive weather. **cyclonic** *adj.*

cy-clo-tron *n.* Machine that obtains high-energy electrified particles by whirling at a high speed in a strong magnetic field.

cyl-in-der *n.*

A long, round body that is either hollow or solid. **cylindrical** *adj.*

cyn-ic *n.* One who believes that all people have selfish motives. **cynical** *adj.,* **cynicism** *n.*

cy-no-sure *n.* A person or object that attracts admiration and interest.

cy-press *n.* An evergreen tree that grows in a warm climate and bears small scale-like needles.

cyst *n.* An abnormal sac or vesicle which may collect and retain fluid. **cystic** *adj.*

cyst-ic fi-bro-sis *n.* A congenital disease, usually developing in childhood and resulting in disorders of the lungs and pancreas.

cys-ti-tis *n.* An inflammation of the bladder.

cy-tol-ogy *n.* The scientific study of cell formation, function, and structure. **cytological, cytologic** *adj.,* **cytologist** *n.*

czar *n.* An emperor or king or one of the former emperors or kings of Russia.

D, d The fourth letter of the English alphabet; the Roman numeral for 500.

dab *v.* To touch quickly with light, short strokes.

dab-ble *v.* To play in a liquid, as water, with the hands; to work in or play with in a minor way. **dabbler** *n.*

dad *n., Informal* Father.

dad-dy *n., pl.* **-dies** *Informal* Father.

dad-dy--long-legs *n.* An insect with very long legs and a rounded body that resembles a spider.

daf-fo-dil *n.* A bulbous plant with solitary yellow flowers.

daft *adj.* Insane; crazy; foolish. **daftly** *adv.,* **daftness** *n.*

dag-ger *n.* A pointed, short-edged weapon which is used for stabbing.

da-querre-o-type *n.* A very early photographic process which used silver-coated metallic plates that were sensitive to light.

dahl-ia *n.* A perennial plant having tuberous roots and showy purple, red, yellow, or white flowers.

dai-ly *adj., pl.* **-lies** To occur, appear, or happen every day of the week. *n.* A newspaper which is published daily.

dai-ly dou-ble *n.* A bet that is won by picking the winners of two specified races occurring on the same day.

dain-ty *adj., pl.* **-ties** Having or showing refined taste; delicately beautiful. **daintily** *adv.,* **daintiness** *n.*

dai-qui-ri *n.* A cocktail made with rum and lime juice.

dair-y *n., pl.* **-ies** A commercial establishment which processes milk for resale. **dairymaid, dairyman** *n.*

dai-sy *n., pl.*-**ies** A plant having flowers with yellow disks and white rays.

dale *n.* A small valley.

dal-ly *v.* To waste time; to dawdle; to flirt. **dallier, dalliance** *n.*

dam *n.* A barrier constructed for controlling or raising the level of water; female animal who has had offspring.

dam-age *n.* An injury to person or property; in law, the compensation given for loss or injury. **damageable** *adj.,* **damagingly** *adv.*

dam-ask *n.* An elaborately patterned, reversible fabric, originally made of silk.

damn *v.* To swear or curse at; to pronounce as bad, worthless, or a failure. **damnation, damnableness** *n.*

damp *adj.* Between dry and wet; of or relating to poisonous gas or foul air found in a mine. **dampish** *adj.,* **damply** *adv.*

dam-sel *n.* A maiden; a young unmarried woman.

dam-son *n.* The tree that produces an oval purple plum of the same name.

dance *v.* To move rhythmically to music using improvised or planned steps and gestures. **dance, dancer** *n.*

dan-dle *v.* To move a child or infant up and down on the knees or in the arms with a gentle movement. **dandler** *n.*

dan-ger *n.* An exposure to injury, evil, or loss.

dan·ger·ous *adj.* Unsafe.
dangerously *adv.*, dangerousness *n.*

dan·gle *v.* To hang loosely and swing to and fro; to have an unclear grammatical relation in a sentence.

dank *adj.* Uncomfortably damp; wet and cold. dankly *adv.*, dankness *n.*

dan·seuse *n.*, *pl.* -seuses A female ballet dancer.

dap·per *adj.* Stylishly dressed.

dap·ple *v.* To make variegated or spotted in color.

dare *v.* To have the boldness or courage to undertake an adventure; to challenge a person as to show proof of courage. dare *n.*, daring *adj.*,

dare-devil *n.* A person who is bold or reckless. daredevilry, daredeviltry *n.*

dark *adj.* Dim; to have little or no light; to be difficult to comprehend; of a deep shade of color, as black or almost black. in the dark To do in secret; to be in a state of ignorance.

dark·en *v.* To become or make dark or darker. darkish *adj.*, darkly *adv.*

dar·ling *n.* A favorite person; someone who is very dear; a person tenderly loved. darlingly *adv.*, darlingness *n.*

darn *v.* To mend a hole by filling the gap with interlacing stitches. darner *n.*

dart *n.* A pointed missile either shot or thrown. darts *pl.* The game of throwing darts at a usually round target.

dash *v.* To break or shatter with a striking violent blow; to move quickly; to rush; to finish or perform a duty in haste. dash, dasher *n.*

das·tard *n.* A coward; a sneak.
dastardliness *n.*, dastardly *adj.*

da·ta *pl.*, *n.* The figures or facts from which conclusions may be drawn.

da·ta bank *n.* In computer science, the location in a computer where information is stored.

da·ta pro·cess·ing *n.* In computer science, the business of handling and storing information using computers and other available machines.

date *n.* A particular point in time; a day, month, or year; the exact time at which something happens; a social engagement; a person's partner on such an occasion. date *v.*

da·tum *n.*, *pl.* -ta A single piece of information.

daub *v.* To coat or smear with grease, plaster, or an adhesive substance.

daugh·ter *n.* The female offspring of a man or woman; a female descendant.
daughter–in–law *n.* One's son's wife.

daunt *v.* To intimidate or discourage.

dav·it *n.* A small crane on the side of a ship, for lifting its boats.

daw·dle *v.* To waste; to take more time than is needed. dawdler *n.*

dawn *n.* The beginning of a new day; to begin to understand, expand, or develop. dawning *n.*

day *n.* The period of time that falls between dawn and nightfall; the time that is represented by one rotation of the earth upon its axis, twenty-four hours; the large portion of a day spent in a particular way.

day·light sav·ings time *n.* The period of the year, beginning in the spring, when clocks are moved ahead by one hour.

daze *v.* To bewilder or stun with a heavy blow or shock. dazedly *adv.*

dea·con *n.* The clergyman who ranks immediately below a priest.
deaconess, deaconry, deaconship *n.*

dead *adj.* Without life; no longer in existence or use; dormant; quiet; in law, no longer in force.

dead-beat *n.*, *Slang* A person who avoids paying his debts.

dead-end *n.* A point from which one cannot progress; a street having no outlet.

dead-eye *n.* A sharpshooter.

dead heat *n.* A contest where two or more entrants finish at the same time.

dead-line *n.* A time limit when something must be finished.

dead-ly *adj.* Very dangerous; likely to cause death.

dead pan *adj.*, *Slang* Having no expression on one's face.

dead reck·on·ing *n.*, *Naut.* A method of computing a vessel's position by compass and log without the use of astronomical observation.

deaf *adj.* Totally or partially unable to hear; refusing or unwilling to listen.

deal *v.* To distribute or pass out playing cards; to be occupied or concerned with a certain matter; to discuss, consider, or take affirmative action. *n.* An indefinite amount; a business transaction. dealer *n.*

deal·er·ship *n.* A franchise to sell a certain item in a specified area, as a car dealer.

deal·ing *n.*, *Slang* Involved in the buying and selling of illegal drugs.

dean *n.* The head administrator of a college, high school, or university.
deanship *n.*

dear *adj.* Greatly cherished; loved.
dearly *adv.*, dearness *n.*

death *n.* Termination; the permanent cessation of all vital functions.

death-bed *n.* The bed on which a person dies; the last hours.

death-blow *n.* An event or blow that is fatal.

death-cup *n.* A poisonous mushroom.

death-less *adj.* Immortal; not subject to death.

death-ly *adj.* Fatal; causing death.

death rate *n.* Ratio of deaths to the population of a certain area.

death-trap *n.* An unsafe structure.

death-watch *n.* A vigil kept on a person who is dying.

de·ba·cle *n.* A sudden downfall, failure, or collapse.

de·bark *v.* To disembark.

de·base *v.* To lower in character or value; demean. debasement *n.*

de·bate *v.* To discuss or argue opposing points; to consider; to deliberate.
debatable *adj.*, debatably *adv.*

de-bauch v. To lead away from morals; to corrupt. debauchery, -ment n.

de-ben-ture n. A voucher given as an acknowledgment of debt.

de-bil-i-tate v. To make feeble or weak. debilitation n., debilitative adj.

deb-it n. A debt or item recorded in an account v. To enter a debt in a ledger.

de-brief v. To interrogate or question in order to obtain information.

de-bris n. Scattered or discarded remains or waste.

debt n. That which someone owes, as money, services, or goods; an obligation to pay or render something to another.

debt-or n. A person owing a debt to another.

de-bug v. To find and remove a concealed electronic listening device; in computer science, to remove errors in a computer program.

de-bunk v., Informal To expose false pretensions.

de-but n. A first public appearance; the formal introduction to society; the beginning of a new career. debut v.

deb-u-tante n. A young woman making her debut in society.

dec-ade n. A period of ten years; a set or group of ten.

de-ca-dence n. A process of decay or deterioration; a period or condition of decline, as in morals. decadent adj., decadently adv.

de-caf-fein-at-ed adj. Having the caffeine removed.

dec-a-gon n., Geom.

A polygon with ten sides and ten angles. decagonal adj., decagonally adv.

dec-a-gram or del-a-gram n. In the metric system, a measure of weight equal to 10 grams.

de-cal n. A design or picture transferred by decalcomania.

de-cal-co-ma-ni-a n. The process of transferring pictures or designs printed on special paper to glass, wood, and other materials.

dec-a-li-ter or dek-a-li-ter n. In the metric system, a measure of capacity equal to 10 liters.

dec-a-logue or dec-a-log n. The Ten Commandments.

dec-a-me-ter or dek-a-me-ter n. In the metric system, a measure of length equal to 10 meters.

de-camp v. To break camp; to leave or depart suddenly.

de-cant v. To pour off liquid without disturbing the sediments; to pour from one container to another. decantation n.

de-cant-er n. A decorative stoppered bottle for serving wine or other liquids.

de-cap-i-tate v. To cut off the head; to behead. decapitation, decapitator n.

de-cath-lon n. An athletic event with ten different track and field events in all of which each contestant participates.

de-cay v. To decline in quantity or quality; to rot. Phys. To diminish or disintegrate by radioactive decomposition.

de-cease v. To die. decedent n., deceased adj.

de-ceit n. Deception; the quality of being deceptive; falseness. deceitful adj., deceitfully adv.

de-ceive v. To mislead by falsehood; to lead into error; to delude. deceivable adj., deceiver n.

de-cel-er-ate v. To decrease in velocity. deceleration, decelerator n.

de-cen-ni-al adj. Happening once every 10 years; continuing for ten years. decennially adv.

de-cent adj. Adequate; satisfactory; kind; generous; characterized by propriety of conduct, speech, or dress; respectable. Informal Properly or adequately clothed. decently adv., decentness n.

de-cep-tion n. The act of deceiving; the fact or state of being deceived; anything which deceives or deludes.

de-cep-tive adj. Having the tendency or power to deceive. deceptively adv., deceptiveness n.

de-ci-are n. In the metric system, one tenth of an are.

de-ci-bel n. A measurement of sound; one tenth of a bel.

de-cide v. To settle; to determine, as a controversy or contest; to determine the conclusion or issue of; to make up one's mind. decider n.

de-cid-ed adj. Definite or unquestionable; exhibiting determination. decidedly adv., decidedness n.

de-cid-u-ous adj., Biol. Shedding or falling off at maturity or at a certain season, such as fruit, leaves, petals, antlers, or snake skins.

dec-i-gram n. In the metric system, the tenth part of a gram.

dec-i-li-ter n. In the metric system, the tenth part of a liter.

de-cil-lion n. The cardinal number written as one followed by thirty-three zeros; a thousand nonillions. decillionth adj. & n.

dec-i-mal n. A proper fraction based on the number 10 and indicated by the use of a decimal point; every decimal place indicating a multiple of a power of 10; a number with a decimal point; a decimal fraction or one of its digits.

de-c-i-mal point n. A period placed to the left of a decimal fraction.

dec-i-mate v. To destroy or kill a large proportion of something; to select by lot and kill one out of every ten.

dec-i-meter n. In the metric system, the tenth part of a meter.

de-ci-sion n. The act of deciding; a judgment or conclusion reached by deciding; in boxing, a victory decided when there has not been a knockout.

de-ci-sive adj. Ending uncertainty or dispute; conclusive; characterized by firmness; unquestionable; unmistakable. **decisively** adv.

dec-i-stere n. In the metric system, a cubic decimeter, or the tenth part of a stere.

de-claim v. To speak or deliver loudly and rhetorically; to give a formal speech; to attack verbally. **declamation** n., **declamatory** adj.

de-clas-si-fy v. To remove the security classification of a document.

de-clen-sion n. A descent; a sloping downward; a decline; a deviation, as from a belief. Gram. The inflection of nouns, pronouns, and adjectives according to case, number, and gender.

dec-li-na-tion n. The act of bending downward or inclining; deviation, as in conduct or direction; the angle formed between the direction of a compass needle and the true north; a polite refusal.

de-cline v. To reject or refuse something; to grow frail gradually, as in health.

de-cliv-i-ty n., pl. **-ties** A steep downward slope or surface. **declivitous**, **declivous** adj.

de-coct v. To extract by boiling; to condense. **decoction** n.

de-code v. To convert from a coded message into plain language. **decoder** n.

de-com-pose v. To decay; to separate into constituent parts. **-able** adj., **decomposer**, **decomposition** n.

de-com-press v. To relieve of pressure; to bring a person back to normal air pressure, as divers or caisson workers.

de-con-ges-tant n. An agent that relieves congestion.

de-con-tam-i-nate v. To make free of contamination by destroying or neutralizing poisonous chemicals, radioactivity, or other harmful elements. **-tion**, **decontaminator** n.

de-con-trol v. To free from the control of, especially from governmental control.

de-cor n. The style of decorating a room, office, or home.

dec-o-rate v. To adorn or furnish with fashionable or beautiful things; to confer a decoration or medal upon.

dec-o-ra-tion n. The process, art, or act of decorating; a thing or group of things which decorate; an emblem, badge, medal, or award.

dec-o-ra-tive adj. Suitable for decoration; ornamental. **decoratively** adv., **decorativeness** n.

dec-o-rous adj. Marked by decorum; seemly; proper. **decorously** adv., **decorousness** n.

de-co-rum n. Proper behavior; good or fitting conduct.

de-crease v. To grow or cause to grow gradually less or smaller; to diminish. n. The process or act of decreasing or the resulting state; a decline.

de-cree n. An authoritative and formal order or decision; a judicial judgment.

dec-re-ment n. The process or act of decreasing; the amount lost by gradual waste or diminution. **decremental** adj.

de-crep-it adj. Broken down or worn out by old age or excessive use. **decrepitly** adv., **decrepitude** n.

de-cre-scen-do n., pl. **-dos** Mus. A gradual decrease in force or loudness. **decrescendo** adj. & adv.

de-crim-i-nal-ize v. To remove the criminal classification of; to no longer prohibit.

de-cry v. To disparage or condemn openly; to denounce. **decrier** n.

ded-i-cate v. To set apart, as for sacred uses; to set apart for special use, duty, or purpose.

de-duce v. To derive a conclusion by reasoning. **deducible** adj.

de-duct v. To subtract or take away from.

de-duc-tion n. The act of deducing or subtracting; an amount that is or may be deducted; the process or act of deducting. **-tive** adj., **deductively** adv.

deed n. Anything performed or done; a notable achievement or feat.

deem v. To judge or consider.

deep-en v. To become or make deep or deeper.

deep-freeze v. To quick-freeze. Slang An appliance for storing frozen foods.

deep-six v., Slang To throw overboard; to get rid of; to toss out.

deer n., pl. deer

A hoofed ruminant mammal having deciduous antlers, usually in the male only, as the elk, moose, and reindeer.

deer fly n. Any of the various bloodsucking flies.

deer-skin n. A deer's hide or the leather made from it.

de-es-ca-late v. To decrease or be decreased gradually, as in intensity, scope, or effect.

de-face v. To spoil or mar the appearance or surface of something.

de fac-to adj. Really or actually exercising authority.

de-fal-cate v. To embezzle; to misuse funds. **defalcation** n.

de-fame v. To slander or libel. **defamation**, **defamatory** adj., **-er** n.

de-fault v. To neglect to fulfill an obligation or requirement.

de-feat v. To win a victory; to beat; to prevent the successful outcome of.

def-e-cate v. To discharge feces from the bowels. **defecation**, **defecator** n.

de-fend v. Protect.

de-fend-ant n. The person charged in a criminal or civil lawsuit.

de-fense n. The action of defending.

de-fer v. To delay or postpone.

de-fi-ance n. The instance or act of defying; a challenge. **defiant** adj., **-ly** adv.

de-fi-cient adj. Lacking in a necessary

element.

def·i·cit *n.* Deficiency in amount.

de·flect *v.* To turn aside; to swerve from a course. **deflectable**, **deflective** *adj.*, **deflection**, **deflector** *n.*

de·fog *v.* To remove fog from, as from the inside of an automobile.

de·fo·li·ant *n.* A chemical sprayed or dusted on plants or trees to cause the leaves to drop off. **defoliate** *v.*

de·for·est *v.* To clear of forests or trees.

de·fraud *v.* To cheat; to swindle. **-er** *n.*

de·fray *v.* To provide for or to make payment on something.

de·frost *v.* To cause to thaw out; to remove the ice or frost from. **-er** *n.*

deft *adj.* Skillful and neat in one's actions. **deftly** *adv.*, **deftness** *n.*

de·funct *adj.* Dead; deceased. **defunctive** *adj.*, **defunctness** *n.*

de·fuse *v.* To remove the detonator or fuse from; to remove or make less dangerous, tense, or hostile.

de·fy *v.*, *pl.* **-fies** To confront or resist boldly and openly; to challenge someone to do something or not do something; to dare. **defier** *n.*

de·gauss *v.* To neutralize the magnetic field of something.

de·grade *v.* To reduce in rank, status, or grade; to demote.

de·hu·man·ize *v.* To deprive of human qualities, especially to make mechanical and routine.

de·hu·mid·i·fy *v.* To remove the moisture from. **dehumidifier** *n.*

de·hy·drate *v.* To cause to lose moisture or water. **dehydration** *n.*

de·ice *v.* To rid of or keep free of ice.

de·i·fy *v.* To glorify or idealize; to raise in high regard; to worship as a god.

deign *v.* To think it barely worthy of one's dignity; to condescend.

de·ject *v.* To lower the spirits; to dishearten. **-ion**, **-edness** *n.*, **dejectedly** *adv.*

de·jec·tion *n.* The state or condition of being dejected; depression; melancholy.

de ju·re *adv.*, *L.* By right; legally or rightfully.

deka- *or* **deca-** *combining form* In the metric system, ten times a specified unit.

dek·are *or* **dec·are** *n.* In the metric system, a thousand square meters or 10 ares.

dek·a·stere *or* **dec·a·stere** *n.* In the metric system, a measure of volume equal to 10 steres.

deke *v.*, *Slang* In hockey, to outmaneuver an opponent by faking a shot or movement.

de·lay *v.* To put off until a later time; to defer; to cause to be late or detained.

de·lec·ta·ble *adj.* Giving great pleasure; delightful; savory; delicious.

de·lec·ta·tion *n.* Enjoyment or pleasure.

del·e·ga·tion *n.* The act of delegating or the state of being delegated; a person or group of people appointed to represent others.

de·lete *v.* To cancel; to take out. **-ion** *n.*

del·e·te·ri·ous *adj.* Causing moral or physical injury; harmful. **deleteriousness** *n.*

deleteriously *adv.*, **deleteriousness** *n.*

de·li *n.*, *Slang* A delicatessen.

de·lib·er·ate *v.* To say or do something intentionally; to plan in advance.

del·i·ca·cy *n.*, *pl.* **-cies** A select or choice food; the quality or state of being delicate.

de·li·cious *adj.* Extremely enjoyable and pleasant to the taste.

deliciously *adv.*, **deliciousness** *n.*

de·light *n.* A great joy or pleasure. *v.* To give or take great pleasure; to rejoice; to gratify or please highly.

delighted *adj.*, **delightedly** *adv.*

de·lim·it *v.* To give or prescribe the limits of.

de·lin·e·ate *v.* To represent by a drawing; to draw or trace the outline of something; to sketch; to represent in gestures or words. **delineation** *n.*

de·lin·quent *adj.* Neglecting to do what is required by obligation or law; falling behind in a payment.

del·i·quesce *v.*, *Chem.* To become liquid by absorbing atmospheric moisture; to melt. **deliquescent** *adj.*

de·lir·i·um *n.* A temporary or sporadic mental disturbance associated with fever, shock, or intoxication and marked by excitement.

de·lir·i·um tre·mens *n.* Acute delirium resulting from chronic and excessive use of alcohol.

del·ta ray *n.* An electron ejected from matter ionizing radiation.

de·lude *v.* To mislead the mind or judgment; to deceive; to cause to be deceived.

del·uge *v.* To flood with water; to overwhelm; to destroy. *n.* A great flood.

de·lu·sion *n.* A false, fixed belief held in spite of contrary evidence.

delusional, **delusive** *adj.*

de luxe *or* **de·luxe** *adj.* High elegance or luxury.

delve *v.* To search for information with careful investigation.

de·mag·net·ize *v.* To remove the magnetic properties of. **-ation** *n.*

dem·a·gogue *n.* A person who leads the populace by appealing to emotions and prejudices.

de·mar·cate *v.* To set boundaries or limits; to separate or limit. **-tion** *n.*

de·mean *v.* To behave or conduct oneself in a particular manner; to degrade; to humble oneself or another.

de·mean·or *n.* A person's conduct toward others; a person's general behavior.

de·ment·ed *adj.* Insane.

de·men·tia *n.* An irreversible deterioration of intellectual faculties.

de·mer·it *n.* A fault; a defect; a mark against one's record, especially for bad conduct in school.

de·mesne *n.* A manor house with the adjoining lands; a domain; a region; in law, lands held in one's own power.

dem·i·john *n.* A large, narrow-necked

bottle usually enclosed in wicker.

de-mil-i-ta-rize v. To remove the military characteristics from. -ation n.

dem-i-mon-daine n. A woman who belongs to the demimonde.

dem-i-monde n. A class of women who are supported by wealthy protectors or lovers.

de-mise n. Death; in law, a transfer of an estate by lease or will.

dem-i-tasse n. A small cup of very strong coffee; the name of the cup used to hold this beverage.

dem-o n., pl. -os *Slang* A demonstration to show product use and purpose.

de-mo-bi-lize v. To disband; to release from the military service.

de-moc-ra-cy n., pl. -cies A form of government exercised either directly by the people or through their elected representatives; rule by the majority; the practice of legal, political, or social equality.

de-mog-ra-phy n. Study of the characteristics of human population, such as growth, size, and vital statistics.

de-mol-ish v. To tear down; to raze.

dem-o-li-tion n. The process of demolishing, especially destruction with explosives.

de-mon-e-tize v. To deprive the currency of its standard value; to withdraw currency from use. demonetization n.

de-mo-ni-ac adj. Like or befitting a demon; to be influenced or possessed by or as by demons; of, resembling, or suggestive of a demon.

de-mon-ol-o-gy n. The belief or study in demons.

de-mon-stra-ble adj. Obvious or apparent. demonstrability n., -ably adv.

dem-on-strate v. To show or prove by reasoning or evidence; to make a public protest. -tion, demonstrator n.

de-mor-al-ize v. To undermine the morale or confidence of someone; to degrade; to corrupt. -ation, -er n.

de-mote v. To reduce in rank, grade, or position. demotion n.

de-mul-cent n. A soothing substance. demulcent adj.

de-mur v. To take issue; to object. -ral n.

de-mure adj. Reserved and modest; coy. demurely adv.

de-mur-rer n. In law, a plea to dismiss a lawsuit on the grounds that the plaintiff's statements are insufficient to prove claim.

de-na-ture v. To change the nature or natural qualities of, especially to make unfit for consumption. denaturant, denaturation n.

den-drite n., *Physiol.* The branching process of a nerve cell which conducts impulses toward the cell body. dendritic adj., dendritically adv.

den-drol-ogy n. The botanical study of trees.

den-gue n., *Pathol.* An infectious tropical disease transmitted by mosquitoes, characterized by severe joint pains and fever.

de-ni-al n. A refusal to comply with a request; refusal to acknowledge the truth of a statement; abstinence; self-denial.

den-i-grate v. To slander; to defame.

den-im n. A strong, twilled cotton used for jeans, overalls, and work clothes.

de-nom-i-nate v. To give a name to; to designate.

de-nom-i-na-tion n. The name of a group or classificatio

de-nom-i-na-tor n. In mathematics, the term for the bottom half of a fraction, which indicates the number of equal parts into which the unit is divided; a common characteristic or trait.

de-no-ta-tion n. The meaning of, or the object or objects designated by a word; an indication, as a sign.

de-note v. To make known; to point out; to indicate; to signify; to designate; to mean, said of symbols or words. denotable, denotative adj.

de-noue-ment n. The final solution of a novel, play, or plot.

de-nounce v. To attack or condemn openly and vehemently; to accuse formally; to announce the ending of something in a formal way. -er n.

dense adj. Compact; thick; close; slow to understand; stupid. -ly adv., -ness n.

den-si-ty n., pl. -ties The state or quality of being dense or close in parts; the quantity or amount of something per unit measure, area, volume, or length.

den-tal adj. Pertaining to the teeth; of or pertaining to dentistry.

den-tal hy-gien-ist n. A licensed dental professional who provides preventive dental care, as cleaning and instruction on how to care for teeth at home.

den-ti-frice n. A preparation in powder or paste form for cleaning the teeth.

den-tine or **den-tin** n. The hard, calcified part of the tooth beneath the enamel, containing the pulp chamber and root canals.

den-tist n. A licensed person whose profession is the diagnosis, treatment, and prevention of diseases of the gums and teeth. dentistry n.

den-ti-tion n. The kind, number, and arrangement of teeth, as in humans and other animals; the process of cutting teeth.

de-nude v. To remove all covering; to be or cause to be naked. *Geol.* To come into view by erosion. denudation n.

de-nun-ci-a-tion n. Open disapproval of a person or action; an accusation; warning or threat.

de-ny v. To declare untrue; to refuse to acknowledge or recognize; to withhold; to refuse to grant. **to deny oneself** To refuse oneself something desired; self-denial.

de-o-dor-ant n. A product designed to prevent, mask, or destroy unpleasant odors.

de-o-dor-ize v. To destroy, modify, or disguise the odor of. deodorization, deodorizer n.

de-ox-i-dize v. To remove the oxygen from; to reduce from the state of an oxide. deoxidization, deoxidizer n.

de-ox-y-ri-bo-nu-cle-ic acid n. A nucleic acid which forms a principal constituent of the genes and is known to play a role of importance in the genetic action of the chromosomes, also known as DNA.

de-part v. To leave; to go away; to deviate.

de-part-ment n. The distinct division or part of something, as in a business, college, or store. Informal An area of special activity or knowledge. -al adj.

de-part-men-tal-ize v. To divide into organized departments. -ation n.

de-part-ment store n. A large retail store selling various types of merchandise and services.

de-par-ture n. The act of taking leave or going away; a divergence; a deviation.

de-pend v. To rely on; to trust with responsibilities; to be determined or conditioned.

de-pend-a-ble adj. Capable of being depended upon; trustworthy. dependability, -ness n., -y adv.

de-pend-ence or **de-pend-ance** n. The quality or state of being dependent; trust or reliance; the state of being contingent on or determined by something else.

de-pend-en-cy or **de-pend-an-cy** n., pl. -cies The state of being dependent; a territory separate from but still subject to another state, territory, or country.

de-pict v. To represent in a sculpture or a picture; to describe or represent in words. depiction n.

dep-i-late v. To remove the hair from. depilation, depilator n.

de-pil-a-to-ry n., pl. -ries A chemical which removes hair, usually in cream or liquid form.

de-plete v. To exhaust, empty, or use up a supply of something. depletion n.

de-plor-a-ble adj. Grievous; lamentable; very bad; wretched. deplorably adv.

de-plore v. To have, show, or feel great disapproval of something.

de-ploy v. To spread out; to place or position according to plans. -ment n.

de-po-lit-i-cize v. To remove the political status or aspect from.

de-po-nent n. A person who testifies under oath giving sworn testimony, especially in writing.

de-pop-u-late v. To quickly remove or lower the population greatly, as by massacre or disease. depopulation n.

de-port v. To banish or expel someone from a country; to behave in a specified manner. -ation, deportee n.

de-port-ment n. One's conduct; behavior.

de-pose v. To remove from a powerful position or office; in law, to declare or give testimony under oath. deposable adj., deposal n.

de-pos-it v. To put, place, or set something down; to entrust money to a bank; to put down in the form of a layer, as silt; to give as security or partial payment. deposit, depositor n.

dep-o-si-tion n. The act of deposing, as from an office; that which is deposited; in law, written testimony given under oath.

de-pos-i-to-ry n., pl. -ries A place where anything is deposited for safekeeping.

de-prave v. To render bad or worse; in morals, to corrupt or pervert. depraved adj., depravity n.

dep-re-cate v. To express regret for or disapproval of; to belittle. deprecatingly adv., -ion, deprecator n.

de-pre-ci-ate v. To lessen in value or price. depreciator n., depreciative, depreciatory adj.

de-pre-ci-a-tion n. A loss in efficiency or value resulting from age or usage; the decline in the purchasing value of money.

de-press v. To make gloomy; to lower the spirits of; to lessen in energy or vigor; to press down; to lower; to diminish in value or price. -or n.

de-pres-sant adj. Acting to lower the nervous or functional activities. n. A sedative; a depressant agent.

de-pres-sed adj. Dejected; sad; low in spirits; lower than, even with, or below the surface; reduced in amount, value, or power.

de-pres-sion n. The state of being or the act of depressing; a severe decline in business, accompanied by increasing unemployment and falling prices. Psych. A condition of deep dejection characterized by lack of response to stimulation and withdrawal.

de-pres-sive adj. Tending to depress; related to psychological depression.

de-prive v. To take something away from; to keep from using, acquiring, or enjoying. deprivable adj.

dep-u-ta-tion n. A person or persons who are acting for another or others; the act of deputing or the state of being deputed.

de-pute v. To appoint as a deputy, an agent, or other figure of authority; to delegate; to transfer.

dep-u-tize v. To act as a deputy; to appoint as a deputy.

dep-u-ty n., pl. -ties The person designated or authorized to act for in the absence of, or to assist another, generally a sheriff; a member of a legislative body in certain countries.

de-rail v. To run off the rails; to cause a train to run off the rails. derailment n.

de-range v. To disturb the arrangement or normal order of; to unbalance the reason; to make insane. -ment n.

der-by n., pl. -bies An annual horse race especially for 3-year-olds; a race open to all contestants; a stiff hat made from felt with a round crown and a narrow, curved brim.

de-reg-u-late v. To decontrol or remove from regulation or control. -ion n.

der-e-lict adj. Neglectful of obligations; remiss. n. Abandoned or deserted, as a ship at sea; a vagrant; a social outcast.

der-e-lic-tion *n.* Voluntary neglect, as of responsibility; the fact or state of being abandoned.

de-ride *v.* To ridicule; to treat with scornful mirth. **derider, derision** *n.,* **deridingly** *adv.,* **derisive** *adj.*

de ri-gueur *adj.* Prescribed or required by manners, custom, or fashion.

der-i-va-tion *n.* The act of or process of deriving; the process used to form new words by the addition of affixes to roots, stems, or words.

de-riv-a-tive *adj.* Of or relating to something derived.

de-rive *v.* To receive or obtain from a source. *Chem.* To produce a compound from other substances by chemical reaction.

der-mal *or* **der-mic** *adj.* Relating to or of the skin.

der-ma-ti-tis *n., Pathol.* An inflammation of the skin.

der-ma-tol-o-gy *n.* The medical study of the skin and the diseases related it.

der-o-gate *v.* To take or cause to take away from; to distract; to cause to become inferior. **derogation** *n.*

de-rog-a-tory *adj.* Having the effect of belittling; lessening. **derogatorily** *adv.*

der-ri-ere *n.* The buttocks.

der-ring-do *n.* A courageous or daring action or spirit.

der-rin-ger *n.* A short-barreled, large-bored, pocket-sized pistol.

des-cant *v.* To play or sing a varied melody.

de-scend *v.* To move from a higher to a lower level; to pass through inheritance; to come from a particular family. *Astron.* Moving toward the horizon.

de-scen-dent *n.* One who descends from another individual; an offspring.

de-scen-dant *or* **de-scen-dent** *adj.* Proceeding downward; descending from an ancestor.

de-scent *n.* A slope; lowering or decline, as in level or status.

de-scribe *v.* To explain in written or spoken words; to draw or trace the figure of. **describable** *adj.,* **describer** *n.*

de-scrip-tion *n.* The technique or act of describing; an account or statement that describes. **descriptive** *adj.*

de-scry *v.* To catch sight of; to discover by observation. **descrier** *n.*

des-e-crate *v.* To violate something sacred, turning it into something common or profane. **desecration** *n.*

de-seg-re-gate *v.* To remove or eliminate racial segregation in. **desegregation** *n.*

de-sen-si-tize *v.* To make less sensitive; to eliminate the sensitivity of an individual, tissue, or organ, as to an allergen. **desensitizer, desensitization** *n.*

des-ert *v.* To abandon or forsake.

de-ser-tion *n.* The act of deserting or leaving; in law, the willful abandonment of one's spouse, children, or both.

de-serve *v.* To be worthy of or entitled to.

de-served *adj.* Merited; earned. **deserving** *adj.,* **deservingly** *adv.*

des-ic-cant *n.* A silica gel used to absorb moisture; any material used to absorb moisture.

des-ic-cate *v.* To preserve by drying, such as food; dehydrate. **desiccation** *n.,* **desiccative** *adj.*

de-sid-er-a-tum *n., pl.* **-ta** A desired and necessary thing.

de-sign *v.* To draw and sketch preliminary outlines; to invent or create in the mind; to have as an intention or goal. *n.* An artistic or decorative piece of work; a project; a plan; a well thoughtout intention. **designedly** *adv.,* **designer** *n.*

des-ig-nate *v.* To assign a name or title to; to point out; to specify; to appoint or select, as to an office. **designate** *adj.,* **designation** *n.*

de-sign-ing *adj.* Of or relating to the art or act of making designs; scheming or plotting; crafty. **designingly** *adv.*

de-sir-a-ble *adj.* Pleasing, attractive, or valuable; worthy of desire. **desirability, desirableness** *n.*

de-sire *v.* To long for; to wish; to crave; to request or ask for; to have sexual appetite.

de-sir-ous *adj.* Having a craving or strong desire.

de-sist *v.* To stop doing something; to cease from an action.

desk *n.*

A table or piece of furniture usually with drawers or compartments and a top for writing; a stand or table to hold reading materials; a department in a newspaper office, as the copy desk.

des-o-late *adj.* Made unfit for habitation; useless; forlorn; forsaken. **desolately** *adv.*

des-o-la-tion *n.* A wasteland; the condition of being ruined or deserted; loneliness.

de-spair *v.* To lose or give up hope; to abandon all purpose. **despair** *n.,* **despairing** *adj.,* **despairingly** *adv.*

des-per-a-do *n., pl.* **-does** *or* **-dos** A dangerous, desperate, or violent criminal.

des-per-ate *adj.* Rash, violent, reckless, and without care, as from despair; intense; overpowering.

des-per-a-tion *n.* The state of being desperate.

des-pi-ca-ble *adj.* Deserving scorn or contempt; despicably *adv.*

de-spise *v.* To regard with contempt; to regard as worthless. **despiser** *n.*

de-spite *prep.* Notwithstanding; in spite of.

de-spoil *v.* To rob; to strip of property or possessions by force. **despoiler, despoilment, despoliation** *n.*

de-spond v. To lose hope, courage, or spirit. **despondently** adv.

de-spon-den-cy n. A dejection of spirits from loss of courage or hope. **despondent** adj.

des-pot n. An absolute ruler; a tyrant. **despotic** adj., **despotism** n.

des-sert n. A serving of sweet food, as pastry, ice cream, or fruit, as the last course of a meal.

des-ti-na-tion n. The point or place to which something or someone is directed; the purpose or end for which something is created or intended.

des-tine v. To be determined in advance; to design or appoint a distinct purpose. **destined** adj.

des-ti-ny n., pl. **-nies** The inevitable loss or fate to which a person or thing is destined; fate; a predetermined course of events.

des-ti-tute adj. Utterly impoverished; not having; extremely poor. **destitution** n.

de-stroy v. To ruin; to tear down; to demolish; to kill; to make useless or ineffective.

de-stroy-er n. One that destroys. Milit. A small maneuverable warship.

de-struct n., Aeros. The deliberate destruction of a defective or dangerous missile or rocket after launch.

de-struc-ti-ble adj. Capable of being destroyed. **destructibility** n.

de-struc-tion n. The state of or the act of being destroyed. **destructive** adj., **destructively** adv., **destructiveness** n.

des-ue-tude n. A condition or state of disuse.

de-sul-fur-ize v. To remove sulfur from. **desulfurizer, desulfurizationer** n.

des-ul-to-ry adj. Something that occurs by chance; lacking continuity; aimless.

de-tach v. To unfasten, disconnect, or separate; to extricate oneself; to withdraw.

de-tached adj. Separate; apart.

de-tach-ment n. The process of separating. Milit. A shipment of military equipment or personnel from a larger unit for special duty.

de-tail n. A part or item considered separately. Milit. Military personnel selected for a particular duty.

de-tain v. To stop; to keep from proceeding; to delay.

de-tect v. To find out or perceive; to expose or uncover, as a crime. **detectable, adj., detection, detector** n.

de-tec-tive n. A person whose work is to investigate crimes, discover evidence, and capture criminals.

de-tent n. A pawl.

de-ten-tion n. The act of or state of being detained; in law, a time or period of temporary custody which precedes disposition by a court.

de-ter v. To prevent or discourage someone from acting by arousing fear, uncertainty, intimidation, or other strong emotion. **determent** n.

de-ter-gent n. A cleansing agent which is chemically different from soap.

detergency, detergence n.

de-te-ri-o-rate v. To worsen; to depreciate. **deterioration** n., **deteriorative** adj.

de-ter-mi-nate adj. Definitely fixed or limited; conclusive. Bot. The terminating in a bud or flower, as each axis of an inflorescence. **determinately** adv., **determinateness** n.

de-ter-mine v. To settle or decide conclusively or authoritatively; to limit to extent or scope; to fix or ascertain; to give direction or purpose to; in law, to come to an end. **determinable** adj., **determinably** adv., **determination** n.

de-ter-mined adj. Showing or having a fixed purpose; resolute; firm. **determinedly** adv.

de-ter-rent n. Something which deters. adj. Serving to deter. **deterrently** adv.

de-test v. To dislike strongly. **detestable** adj., **detestation** n.

de-throne v. To remove from the throne, to depose, as a king.

det-o-nate v. To explode suddenly and violently. **detonation** n.

det-o-na-tor n. The device, such as a fuse or percussion cap, used to detonate an explosive.

de-tour n. A road used temporarily instead of a main road; a deviation from a direct route or course of action.

de-tox-i-fy v. To free oneself from dependence on drugs or alcohol. **detoxification** n.

de-tract v. To take away from; to diminish; to divert. **detraction** n., **detractor** n., **detractive** adj.

de-train v. To leave or cause to leave a railroad train. **detrainment** n.

det-ri-ment n. Damage; injury; loss; something which causes damage, injury, or loss. **detrimental** adj., **detrimentally** adv.

de-tri-tus n. Loose fragments or particles formed by erosion, glacial action, and other forces; debris.

deuce n. Two; a playing card or the side of a die with two spots or figures; in tennis, a tie in which each side has 40 points. Informal The devil, bad luck, or a mild oath.

deu-te-ri-um n. The isotope of hydrogen which contains one more neutron in its nucleus than hydrogen does.

deut-sche mark n. The standard monetary unit of East and West Germany, equivalent to 100 pfennigs.

de-val-u-ate v. To reduce or lessen the value of. **devaluation** n.

dev-as-tate v. To destroy; to ruin; to overwhelm; to overpower.

de-vel-op v. To bring out or expand the potentialities.

de-vi-ant adj. Anything which deviates from a norm, especially from an accepted standard. **deviance, deviant** n.

de-vi-ate v. To turn away from a specified prescribed behavior or course. **deviation** n.

de-vice n. Something constructed and used for a specific purpose, as a machine; a crafty or evil scheme or plan; an ornamental design; a motto or an emblem.

dev-il *or* **Devil** *n.* The spirit of evil, the ruler of Hell; Satan; a wicked or malevolent person; a daring, clever, and energetic person; a printer's apprentice, also called a printer's devil. **the devil to pay** Trouble to be expected as a consequence of something.

dev-il-fish *n.*, *pl.* **-fishes** Any of the large cephalopods, as the octopus.

dev-il-ish *adj.* To resemble or have the characteristics of a devil. *Informal* Extreme.

dev-il's ad-vo-cate *n.* One who argues about something with which he or she may not disagree, as for the sake of argument.

dev-il-try *n.*, *pl.* **-tries** Malicious mischief; cruelty or wickedness.

de-vi-ous *adj.* Leading away from the straight, regular, or direct course; rambling; straying from the proper way. *Slang* Underhanded. **deviously** *adv.*, **deviousness** *n.*

de-vise *v.* To form in the mind; to contrive; to plan; to invent; in law, to transmit or give by will. *n.* The act of bequeathing lands; a clause in a will conveying real estate.

de-vi-see *n.* In law, the person to whom a devise is made.

de-vi-sor *n.* In law, the person who devises property.

de-vi-tal-ize *v.* To make weak; to destroy the vitality. **devitalization** *n.*

de-void *adj.* Empty; utterly lacking; without.

de-voir *n.* The act or expression of courtesy or respect; duty or responsibility.

de-volve *v.* To pass duty or authority on to a successor.

de-vote *v.* To apply time or oneself completely to some activity, purpose, or cause. **devotement** *n.*

de-vot-ed *adj.* Feeling or showing devotion; set apart, as by a vow; consecrated. **devotedly** *adv.*,

dev-o-tee *n.* An enthusiastic supporter; one who is deeply devoted to anything; one marked by religious ardor.

de-vo-tion *n.* A strong attachment or affection, as to a person or cause; zeal or ardor in the performance of religious duties or acts; the state or act of being devoted. **devotional** *adj.*, **devotionally** *adv.*

de-vour *v.* To destroy or waste; to eat up greedily; to engulf. **devourer** *n.*

de-vout *adj.* Extremely and earnestly religious; showing sincerity; displaying piety or reverence. **devoutly** *adv.*, **devoutness** *n.*

dew *n.* Moisture condensed from the atmosphere in minute drops onto cool surfaces; something which is refreshing or pure.

dew-ber-ry *n.* The fruit of many species of trailing blackberries; the plant which bears such fruit.

dew-claw *n.* A rudimentary toe in some

dogs and other mammals.

dew-lap *n.* The loose skin under the throat and neck of cattle and certain dogs.

dew point *n.* The temperature at which condensation of vapor occurs.

dex-ter-i-ty *n.* Proficiency or skill in using the hands or body; cleverness.

dex-ter-ous *or* **dex-trous** *adj.* Skillful or adroit in the use of the hands, body, or mind. **dexterously** *adv.*

dex-trose *n.* Sugar found in animal and plant tissue and derived synthetically from starches.

di-a-be-tes *n.*, *Pathol.* A metabolic disorder characterized by deficient insulin secretion, leading to excess sugar in the urine and blood, extreme hunger, and thirst.

di-a-bet-ic *adj.*, *Med.* Pertaining to, or affected with diabetes. **diabetic** *n.*

di-a-bol-ic *or* **di-a-bol-i-cal** *adj.* Wicked; proceeding from the devil; satanic or infernal. **diabolically** *adv.*, **-ness** *n.*

di-a-crit-ic *n.* A mark near or through a phonetic character or combination of characters, to indicate a special phonetic value or to distinguish words otherwise graphically identical. **diacritical, diacritic** *adj.*

di-a-dem *n.* A crown or headband worn to symbolize or indicate royalty or honor.

di-aer-e-sis *n.* Variation of dieresis.

di-ag-no-sis *n.*, *pl.* **-ses** An analysis and examination to identify a disease; the result of diagnosis. **diagnose** *v.*, **diagnostic** *adj.*, **diagnostician** *n.*

di-ag-o-nal *adj.* In mathematics, joining two opposite corners of a polygon which are not adjacent. *n.* A diagonal or slanting plane or line.

di-a-gram *n.* A sketch, plan, drawing, or outline designed to demonstrate or clarify the similarity among parts of a whole or to illustrate how something works. **diagram** *v.*, **diagrammatic**, **diagrammatical** *adj.*, **-ly** *adv.*

di-a-lec-tic *n.* The act or practice of argument or exposition in which the conflict between contradictory facts or ideas is resolved.
dialectical, dialectic *adj.*

di-a-logue *or* **dialog** *n.* A conversation involving two or more persons; a conversational passage in a literary work.

di-al-y-sis *n.*, *pl.* **-ses** The separation of substances in solution, which is accomplished by passing them through membranes or filters. **kidney dialysis** A form of *dialysis* used to cleanse the blood of impurities and wastes when the kidneys are unable to perform this function.

di-am-e-ter *n.* In mathematics, a straight line which passes through the center of a circle or sphere and stops at the circumference or surface; a measurement of that distance.

di-a-met-ri-cal *or* **diametric** *adj.* Along or relating to a diameter; exactly opposite; contrary. **diametrically** *adv.*

di-a-mond *n., pl.* -s A very hard, highly refractive, colorless, or white crystalline of carbon used as a gem; a playing card with a red, lozenge-shaped figure; a precious gem; in baseball, the shape of a baseball field.

dia-mond an-ni-ver-sa-ry *n.* The 60th or 75th anniversary.

di-a-pa-son *n.* The full range of a voice or an instrument; in a pipe organ, either of two principal stops which form the tonal basis for the entire scale.

di-a-per *n.* A folded piece of soft, absorbent material placed between a baby's legs and fastened at the waist. *v.* To put a diaper on.

di-aph-a-nous *adj.* Of such fine texture as to be transparent or translucent; delicate. **diaphanously** *adv.*

di-ar-rhe-a *or* **di-ar-rhoe-a** *n., Pathol.* A disorder of the intestines causing excessively frequent, loose bowel movements.

di-a-ry *n., pl.* -ries A daily record, especially a personal record of one's activities, experiences, or observations; a journal; a book for keeping such records. **diarist** *n.*

di-as-to-le *n., Physiol.* The normal rhythmic dilatation and relaxation of the heart cavities during which they fill with blood. **diastolic** *adj.*

di-as-tro-phism *n., Geol.* Any of the processes through which the earth's crust, as mountains and continents, are formed.

di-a-ther-my *n., pl.* -mies *Med.* The generation of heat in the body tissues by high-frequency electromagnetic waves.

di-a-tom *n.* Any of various tiny planktonic algae whose walls contain silica.

di-a-tom-ic *adj.* Having two atoms in a molecule.

di-a-ton-ic *adj., Mus.* Relating to a standard major or minor scale of eight tones without the chromatic intervals.

di-a-tribe *n.* A bitter, often malicious criticism or denunciation.

dib-ble *n.* A gardener's pointed tool used to make holes in soil, especially for planting bulbs or seedlings. **dibble** *v.*

dice *pl., n.*

Two or more small cubes of wood, bone, or ivory having the sides marked with dots from one to six; a game of chance. *v.* To gamble with dice; to cut food into small cubes.

di-chot-o-my *n., pl.* -mies A division into two mutually exclusive subclasses. *Bot.* The branching of something in which each successive axis forks into two equally developed branches.

di-chro-mate *n., Chem.* A chemical compound with two chromium atoms per anion.

di-chro-mat-ic *adj., Zool.* Having two color phases within the species apart

from the changes due to age or sex. *Pathol.* Having the ability to see only two of the three primary colors.

dick-er *v.* To haggle or work towards a deal or bargain.

dick-ey *or* **dick-ie** *or* **dick-y** *n., pl.* -eys *or* -ies A woman's blouse front worn under a jacket or low-necked dress; the detachable shirtfront for a man; a small bird.

di-cot-y-le-don *n.* A plant which has two seed leaves. **dicotyledonous** *adj.*

dic-tate *v.* To read or speak aloud for another to record or transcribe; to give commands, terms, rules, or other orders with authority. *n.* A directive or guiding principle. **dictation** *n.*

dic-ta-ting ma-chine *n.* A phonographic machine which records and reproduces speech, as for dictation.

dic-ta-tor *n.* A person having absolute authority and supreme governmental powers; one who dictates.

dic-ta-to-ri-al *adj.* Tending to dictate; relating to or characteristic of a dictator. **dictatorially** *adv.*

dic-tion *n.* The selection and arrangement of words in speaking and writing; the manner of uttering speech sounds.

dic-tion-ar-y *n., pl.* -ies A reference book containing alphabetically arranged words together with their definitions and usages.

dic-tum *n., pl.* -ta *or* -tums An authoritative or positive utterance; a pronouncement; a saying that is popular.

did *v.* Past tense of do.

di-dac-tic *or* **didactical** *adj.* Being inclined to teach or moralize excessively. **didactically** *adv.,* **didacticism** *n.*

did-dle *v.* To cheat; to swindle; to waste valuable time.

did-n't *contr.* Did not.

di-do *n., pl.* -dos *or* -does *Informal* A mischievous caper; an antic.

die *v.* To expire; to stop living; to cease to exist; to fade away; to cease operation or functioning, as an engine. to **die hard** To resist defeat or death to the end. to **die off** To be removed one after another by death.

die cast-ing *n.* The process of giving an alloy or metal a desired shape; the act of cutting, stamping, or shaping with or as with a die.

diel-drin *n.* A highly toxic and persistent chemical which is used as an insecticide.

di-e-lec-tric *n., Elect.* A nonconductor of electricity.

di-er-e-sis *n., pl.* -ses The mark over a vowel indicating that it is to be pronounced in a separate syllable.

die-sel *n.* A diesel engine or a vehicle driven by a diesel engine.

die-sink-er *n.* A person who engraves metal dies.

di-et *n.* A regulated selection of food and drink, especially one followed for medical or hygienic reasons; something that is taken or provided regularly; an assembly or legislature.

di-e-tet-ics *pl., n.* The study of diet and or the regulations of a diet.
dietetical, dietetic *adj.,*
dietetically *adv.,* **dietitian, -ian** *n.*

di-eth-yl-stil-bes-trol *n.* A synthetic estrogen used especially to treat menstrual disorders.

dif-fer *v.* To have different opinions; to disagree.

dif-fer-ence *n.* The quality, state, or degree of being different or unlike; a controversy or cause for a disagreement; in mathematics, the amount by which a number or quantity is less or greater than another.

dif-fer-ent *adj.* Not the same; separate; other; marked by a difference; unlike; differing from the ordinary.
differently *adv.,* **differentness** *n.*

dif-fer-en-tia *n., pl.* **-tiae** A specific difference; something that distinguishes a species from others of the same genus.

dif-fer-en-tial *adj.* Relating to or showing a difference or differences. *n.* The amount or degree to which similar things differ.

dif-fer-en-tial cal-eu-lus *n.* In mathematics, the difference or variation of a function with respect to changes in independent variables.

dif-fer-en-tial gear *n., Mech.* A coupling consisting of a train of gears used to connect two or more shafts to allow different rates of wheel rotation, as on curves.

dif-fer-en-ti-ate *v.* To show, state, or distinguish the difference; to become or make different. **differentiation** *n.*

dif-fi-cult *adj.* Hard to do, deal with, or accomplish; hard to please.

dif-fi-cul-ty *n., pl.* **-ties** The quality or state of being difficult; something that requires great effort; conflicts or problems.

dif-fi-dent *adj.* Lacking confidence in oneself; timid. **diffidence** *n.,*
diffidently *adv.*

dif-frac-tion *n., Phys.* A modification of light rays, especially a beam of light as it passes an aperture or obstacle.

dif-fuse *v.* To pour out and spread freely in all directions; to scatter. **diffusion** *n.*

dig *v.* To turn up, break up, or remove the earth with a shovel; to discover or learn by investigation or research. *Slang* To understand, like, appreciate or enjoy. *Informal* To work intensively.

di-gest *v.* To change ingested food into usable form; to mentally assimilate; to endure; to tolerate patiently; to decompose or soften with moisture or heat. **digestibility** *n.,*
digestible, digestive *adj.*

di-gest-ion *n.* The chemical and muscular action of transforming food into an assimilable state.

dig-it *n.* A number 1 to 9 and usually 0; A toe or finger.

dig-i-tal *adj.* Pertaining to or like the fingers or digits; expressed in digits, especially for computer use; reading in digits, as a clock.

dig-i-tal com-put-er *n.* In computer science, a computer using data that is represented as digits to perform operations.

dig-i-tal-is *n.* The foxglove plant; a drug prepared from dried leaves of foxglove, used as a heart stimulant.

dig-ni-fied *adj.* Showing or possessing dignity; poised.

dig-ni-fy *v.* To give dignity or distinction to something.

dig-ni-tary *n., pl.* **-ies** A person of high rank, notability, and influence.

dig-ni-ty *n., pl.* **-ties** The quality or state of being excellent; the quality of being poised or formally reserved in appearance and demeanor; a high rank, office, or title.

di-graph *n.* A pair of letters, as the ea in seat or oa in boat, that represents a single sound. **digraphic** *adj.*

di-gress *v.* To turn away or aside from the main subject in a discourse; to wander. **digression** *n.,* **digressive** *adj.,*
digressively *adv.*

dik-dik *n.* A very small African antelope.

dike *n.* An embankment made of earth, built to hold and control flood waters, also known as a levee.

di-lap-i-dat-ed *adj.* Being in a state of decay or disrepair. **dilapidation** *n.*

di-late *v.* To become or make enlarged; to expand. **dilatable** *adj.,* **dilation,**
dilator *n.*

di-la-to-ry *adj.* Tending to cause decay; characterized by delay; slow; tardy.
dilatorily *adv.*

di-lem-ma *n.* A predicament requiring a choice between equally undesirable alternatives.

dil-et-tante *n., pl.* **-tantes** *or* **-tanti** One who has an amateurish and superficial interest in something.

dil-i-gent *adj.* Showing painstaking effort and application in whatever is undertaken; industrious. **diligence** *n.,*
diligently *adv.*

dill *n.* An aromatic herb with aromatic leaves and seeds used as seasoning.

dil-ly *n., pl.* **-lies** *Slang* Someone or something that is extraordinary.

dil-ly--dal-ly *v.* To waste time with indecision or hesitation.

di-lute *v.* To weaken, thin, or reduce the concentration of by adding a liquid.

dime *n.* A United States coin worth ten cents or one tenth of a dollar.

di-men-sion *n.* A measurable extent, as length, thickness, or breadth. **dimensions** *pl.* The magnitude or scope of something. **dimensional** *adj.,*
dimensionality *n.*

di-min-ish *v.* To become or make smaller or less; to reduce in power, rank, or authority; to decrease; to taper. **diminishable** *adj.,*
diminishment, diminution *n.*

dim-in-ished *adj.* Reduced; lessened.

di-min-u-en-do *adv.* Gradually lessening

in volume. **diminuendo** *adj. & n.*

di-min-u-tive *adj.* Very small; tiny.

dim-i-ty *n., pl.* **-ies** A sheer cotton fabric woven with cords, stripes, or checks.

dim-mer *n.* A rheostat used to reduce the intensity of an electric light.

dim-ple *n.* A slight depression in the surface of the skin, especially one made visible in the cheek by smiling; a slight surface depression. **dimple** *v.*

dim-wit *n., Slang* A simpleminded or stupid person. **dimwitted** *adj.*, **dimwittedly** *adv.*, **dimwittedness** *n.*

din *n.* A loud, confused, harsh noise.

dine *v.* To eat dinner.

di-nette *n.* A small room or alcove which is used as a dining room.

din-ghy *n., pl.* **-ghies** A small rowboat; an inflatable rubber raft.

din-ky *adj., Informal* Insignificant or small.

din-ner *n.* The last meal of the day, taken usually between the hours of 5:00 and 7:00 P.M.; a banquet or formal meal.

din-ner-ware *n.* The tableware used in serving a meal.

di-no-saur *n., Paleon.*

A group of extinct reptiles from the Mesozoic period, some of which were the largest land animals known to exist.

dint *n.* Means; force; effort. *v.* To drive with force.

di-o-cese *n.* The territory under the jurisdiction of a bishop. **diocesan** *adj. & n.*

di-ode *n.* An electron tube which permits electrons to pass in only one direction, used as a rectifier.

di-o-ra-ma *n.* A miniature scene in three dimensions.

diph-the-ri-a *n., Pathol.* An acute contagious disease caused by bacillus and characterized by formation of a false membrane in the throat and other air passages by weakness and by fever.

diph-thong *n., Phon.* A blend of a single speech sound which begins with one vowel sound and moves to another in the same syllable, as oi in oil, oi in coil or oy in toy.

di-plo-ma *n.* A document issued by a college, school, or university testifying that a student has earned a degree or completed a course of study.

di-plo-ma-cy *n., pl.* **-cies** The art or practice of conducting international negotiations; skill and tact in dealing with people.

dip-lo-mat *n.* A person employed in diplomacy. **diplomatic** *adj.*

dip-per *n.* One that dips; a container for dipping; a long-handled cup for dipping water. *Astron.* The Big Dipper and the Little Dipper, two northern constellations.

dip-so-ma-ni-a *n.* An insatiable craving for alcohol. **dipsomaniac** *n. & adj.*

dip-ter-ous *adj.* Pertaining to or of animals having a single pair of wings such as the fly, gnat, and mosquito.

dip-tych *n.* A pair of painted or carved panels which are hinged together.

dir *abbr.* Director.

dire *adj.* Dreadful or terrible in consequence. **direly, direfully** *adv.*

di-rect *v.* To control or regulate the affairs of; to command or order; to direct or tell someone the way.

di-rect cur-rent *n.* An electrical current which flows in only one direction.

di-rec-tion *n.* The act of directing; an order or command; the path or line along which something points, travels, or lies. **directional** *adj.*

di-rec-tive *n.* A regulation or order from someone with authority.

di-rect-ly *adv.* Immediately; at once; in a direct manner or line; doing without an agent, medium, or go-between.

di-rec-tor *n.* A person who manages or directs; one of a group of persons who supervises the affairs of an institute, corporation or business.

di-rec-to-ry *n., pl.* **-ries** A book listing data, alphabetically or classified, containing the names and addresses of a specific group, persons, organizations, inhabitants, or businesses.

dirge *n.* A slow mournful song; a funeral hymn.

dir-i-gi-ble *n.* A lighter-than-air plane which may be steered by means of its own motive power.

dirk *n.* A dagger.

dirn-dl *n.* A lady's full-skirted dress with a gathered waistband.

dis-a-ble *v.* To make powerless or to incapacitate; to disqualify legally.

dis-a-buse *v.* To free from delusion, misunderstanding, or misconception.

dis-ad-van-tage *n.* A circumstance that is unfavorable; loss or damage; detriment. **disadvantage** *v.*

dis-af-fect *v.* To weaken or destroy the affection or loyalty of. **disaffection** *n.*, **disaffectedly** *adv.*, **disaffected** *adj.*

dis-a-gree *v.* To vary in opinion; to differ; to argue; to quarrel; to be unfavorable or unacceptable.

dis-a-gree-able *adj.* Offensive or unpleasant. **disagreeably** *adv.*

dis-al-low *v.* To refuse to allow; to reject as invalid or untrue. **disallowance** *n.*

dis-ap-pear *v.* To vanish; to drop from sight. **disappearance** *n.*

dis-ap-point *v.* To fail to satisfy the desires, hopes, or expectations of.

dis-ap-pro-ba-tion *n.* Disapproval; condemnation.

dis-ap-prove *v.* To refuse to approve; to reject; to condemn. **disapproval** *n.*

dis-arm *v.* To make harmless; to deprive or take away the weapons or any means of attack or defense. **disarmament** *n.*

dis-ar-range *v.* To disturb the order of something. **disarrangement** *n.*

dis-ar-ray n. A state of confusion or disorder; an upset or turmoil.

dis-as-sem-ble v. To take apart.

dis-as-so-ci-ate v. To break away from or to detach oneself from an association.

dis-as-ter n. An event that causes great ruin or distress; a sudden and crushing misfortune. **disastrous** adj., **disastrously** adv.

dis-a-vow v. To disclaim or deny any responsibility for or knowledge of.

dis-band v. To disperse; to break up.

dis-bar v. In law, to be expelled officially from the legal profession.

dis-be-lieve v. To refuse to believe in something. **disbelief, disbeliever** n.

dis-burse v. To pay out. **disbursement, disbursal, disburser** n.

disc or **disk** n., Informal A phonograph record.

dis-cern v. To detect visually; to detect with senses other than that of vision; to comprehend mentally; to perceive as separate and distinct. **discerner, discernment** n., **discernible** adj.

dis-ci-ple n. One who accepts and assists in spreading the doctrines of another. **Disciple** One of Christ's followers.

dis-ci-pline n. Training which corrects, molds, or perfects the mental faculties or moral character; behavior which results from such training.

dis-claim v. To disavow any claim to or association with. **disclaimer** n.

dis-close v. To make known; to bring into view. **disclosure** n.

dis-co n., pl. **-cos** A discotheque.

dis-color v. To alter or change the color of. **discoloration** n.

dis-com-fit v. To defeat in battle; to make upset or uneasy. **discomfiture** n.

dis-com-fort n. Physical or mental uneasiness; pain; an inconvenience. v. To make uncomfortable.

dis-com-mode v. To inconvenience.

dis-com-pose v. To disrupt the composure or serenity of; to unsettle; to destroy the order of. **discomposure** n.

dis-con-cert v. To upset; to discompose; to perturb. **disconcertingly** adv.

dis-con-nect v. To sever or break the connection of or between.

dis-con-nect-ed adj. Not connected.

dis-con-so-late adj. Without consolation; dejected; cheerless; sorrowful. **disconsolately** adv.

dis-con-tent n. Lack of contentment; dissatisfaction. v. To make unhappy. **discontent** n., **discontented** adj.

dis-con-tin-ue v. To come or bring to an end; to break the continuity of; to interrupt; to stop trying, taking, or using. **discontinuance, discontinuation** n.

dis-cord n. Lacking accord or harmony; a harsh combination of musical sounds. **discordant** adj.

dis-co-theque n. A nightclub where music is provided for dancing.

dis-coun-te-nance v. To look upon with disfavor; to make uneasy.

dis-cour-age v. To deprive or be deprived of enthusiasm or courage; to hinder by disfavoring.

discouragement n., **discouragingly** adv.

dis-course n. A conversation; a formal and lengthy discussion of a subject. v. To write or converse extensively. **discourser** n.

dis-cour-te-ous adj. Lacking consideration or courteous manners. **discourteously** adv., **discourtesy** n.

dis-cov-er v. To make known or visible; to observe or learn of for the first time. **discoverable** adj., **discoverer, discovery** n.

dis-cred-it v. To mar the reputation of or disgrace someone or something; to injure the reputation of. n. Loss of credit or reputation; doubt; disbelief. **discreditable** adj., **discreditably** adv.

dis-creet adj. Tactful; careful of appearances; modest. **discreetly** adv., **discreetness** n.

dis-crep-an-cy n., pl. **-cies** A difference in facts; an instance of being discrepant. **discrepant** adj.

dis-crete adj. Separate; made up of distinct parts.

dis-cre-tion n. The quality or act of being discreet; the ability to make responsible choices; power to decide; the result of separating or distinguishing.

dis-cur-sive adj. Covering a wide field of subjects in a quick manner; rambling from subject to subject. **discursively** adv., **discursiveness** n.

dis-cuss v. To investigate by argument or debate; to consider or examine something through discourse. **discussible** adj., **discussion** n.

dis-cus-sant n. A participant in a discussion.

dis-dain v. To treat contemptuously; to look on with scorn. **disdainfully** adv.

dis-ease n. A condition of the living animal, plant body, or one of its parts which impairs normal functioning; a condition of ill health. **diseased** adj.

dis-em-bark v. To go or put ashore from a ship; unload.

dis-em-body v. To release or free the soul or physical existence.

dis-em-bow-el v. To remove the bowels or entrails; to eviscerate. **disembowelment** n.

dis-en-chant v. To free from false beliefs or enchantment. **disenchantingly** adv., **disenchanting** adj.

dis-en-cum-ber v. To relieve of hardships; to free from encumbrance; unburden.

dis-en-fran-chise v. To disfranchise. **disenfranchisement** n.

dis-en-gage v. To free from something that holds or otherwise engages; to set free. **disengagement** n.

dis-en-tan-gle v. To relieve of entanglement, confusion, etc. **disentanglement** n.

dis-es-teem v. To regard with little esteem. n. Lack of esteem.

dis-fa-vor n. Disapproval; the state of being disliked. **disfavor** v.

dis-fig-ure v. To mar, deface, or deform the appearance of something or someone. **disfigurement** n.

dis-fran-chise v. To deprive of a legal right or privilege, especially the right to vote. **disfranchisement** n.

dis-grace n. The state of having lost grace, favor, respect, or honor; something that disgraces.

dis-grun-tle v. To make dissatisfied or discontented.

dis-guise v. To alter the customary appearance or character of in order to prevent recognition.

dis-gust v. To affect with nausea, repugnance, or aversion; to cause one to become impatient or lose attention.

dis-ha-bille n. The state of being carelessly dressed; undress.

dis-har-mo-ny n. Lack of harmony or agreement; discord.

dish-cloth n. A cloth used for washing dishes; also called a dishrag.

dis-heart-en v. To cause to lose spirit or courage; to discourage, demoralize, or dispirit.

di-shev-el v. To mess up or disarrange; to throw into disorder or disarray.

dis-hon-est adj. Lack of honesty; arising from or showing fraud or falseness. **dishonesty** n., **dishonestly** adv.

dis-hon-or n. The deprivation of honor; disgrace; the state of one who has lost honor; a cause of disgrace.

dish-rag n. A dishcloth.

dish-wash-er n. A person or a machine which washes dishes.

dis-il-lu-sion v. To deprive of illusion; to disenchant.

dis-in-cline v. To make or to be unwilling; to be or cause to be not interested.

dis-in-fect v. To cleanse and make free from infection, especially by destroying harmful microorganisms; to sterilize. **disinfection** n.

dis-in-gen-u-ous adj. Lacking frankness, sincerity, or simplicity; crafty; not straightforward.

dis-in-her-it v. To deliberately deprive of inheritance; to depose of previously held privileges.

dis-in-te-grate v. To break or reduce into separate elements, parts, or small particles; to destroy the unity or integrity of; to explode; to undergo a change in structure, as an atomic nucleus. **disintegration, disintegrator** n.

dis-in-ter v. To exhume or dig up something buried; to bring to light, disclose, uncover, or expose.

dis-in-ter-est-ed adj. The state of being unbiased, impartial, unselfish, or not interested; free from selfish motive or interest. **disinterest** n., **disinterestedly** adv.

dis-join v. To end the joining of; to become detached; to disconnect.

disk or **disc** n. A thin, flat, circular object; in computer science, a round, flat plate coated with a magnetic substance on which data for a computer is stored; a fairly flat, circular, metal object used to break up soil; the imple-

ment employing such tools.

disk op-er-at-ing sys-tem n. In computer science, the software which controls the disk drives and disk accessing; abbreviated as DOS.

disk pack n. In computer science, a computer storage device which has several magnetic disks to use and store as a unit.

dis-like v. To regard with aversion or disapproval. n. Distaste.

dis-lo-cate v. To put out of place or proper position. Med. To displace a bone from a socket or joint.

dis-lodge v. To remove or drive out from a dwelling or position; to force out of a settled position.

dis-loy-al adj. Not loyal; untrue to personal obligations or duty. **disloyally** adv., **disloyalty** n.

dis-mal adj. Causing gloom or depression; depressing; lacking in interest or merit. **dismally** adv., **dismalness** n.

dis-man-tle v. To strip of dress or covering or to strip of furniture and equipment; to take apart. **dismantlement** n.

dis-may v. To deprive or be deprived of courage or resolution through the pressure of sudden fear or anxiety. **dismay** n., **dismayingly** adv.

dis-mem-ber v. To cut, pull off or disjoin the limbs, members, or parts of.

dis-miss v. To discharge or allow to leave; to remove from position or service; to bar from attention or serious consideration; in law, to disallow or reject any further judicial consideration on a claim or action. **dismissal** n., **dismissible** adj.

dis-mount v. To get down from; to remove from a seat, setting, or support; to take apart; to disassemble.

dis-o-bey v. To refuse or fail to obey; to be disobedient. **disobedient** adj., **disobediently** adv.

dis-o-blige v. To act contrary to the wishes of; to neglect or refuse to act in accordance with the wishes of; to offend; to inconvenience. **disobligingly** adv.

dis-or-der n. Breach of peace or public order; lack of good order; an abnormal physical or mental condition; an ailment. v. To disturb the order of; to disturb the normal or regular functions of. **disorderly** adj., **disorderliness** n.

dis-or-gan-ize v. To destroy or break up the organization, unity, or structure of. **disorganization** n.

dis-own v. To refuse to acknowledge or claim as one's own.

dis-pa-rate adj. Altogether dissimilar; unequal. **disparately** adv., **disparateness** n.

dis-pas-sion-ate adj. Free from bias or passion. **dispassionately** adv.

dis-patch or **des-patch** v. To send off to a particular destination or on specific business; to dispose of quickly; to kill summarily. n. The act of dispatching; a message sent with speed; a message; a news story sent to a newspaper.

dis·pel v. To drive off or away.

dis·pense v. To give out; to distribute; to administer; to let go or exempt. **dispense with** To get rid of; to forgo.

dis·perse v. To break up or scatter in various directions; to spread or distribute from a common source; to distribute. **dispersible** adj., **dispersion**, **dispersal** n.

di·spir·it v. To deprive of or be deprived of spirit; to discourage or be discouraged. **dispiritedly** adv.

dis·place v. To change the position of; to take the place of; to discharge from an office; to cause a physical displacement of. **displacement** n.

dis·play v. To put forth or spread; to put in view; to show off. n. The act of displaying; in computer science, a device which gives information in a visual form such as on a cathode-ray tube (computer screen or CRT).

dis·please v. To cause the disapproval or annoyance of; to cause displeasure. **displeasingly** adv., **displeasure** n.

dis·pose v. To put in place; to finally settle or come to terms. **dispose of** To get rid of; to attend to or settle; to transfer or part with, as by selling. **disposable** adj.

dis·pos·sess v. To deprive of possession or ownership of land, possessions, or property. **dispossession** n.

dis·pro·por·tion n. Lack of proportion, symmetry or proper relation. **disproportion** v., **disproportional**, **disproportionate** adj., **disproportionately** adv.

dis·prove v. Prove to be false or erroneous. **disproof** n., **disprovable** adj.

dis·pu·ta·tion n. The act of disputing; a debate.

dis·pute v. To debate or argue; to question the validity of; to strive against or to resist. n. A verbal controversy; a quarrel. **disputable** adj., **disputably** adv., **disputant**, **disputer** n.

dis·qual·i·fy v. To deprive of the required properties or conditions; to deprive of a power or privilege; to make ineligible for a prize or further competition. **disqualification** n.

dis·quiet v. To take away the tranquillity of; to trouble. **disquieting** adj., **disquietingly** adv.

dis·qui·si·tion n. A formal inquiry into or discussion of a subject.

dis·re·gard v. To ignore; to neglect; to pay no attention to; to treat without proper attention. **disregard** n., **disregardful** adj.

dis·re·pair n. The state of being in need of repair, usually due to neglect.

dis·re·pute n. A state of being held in low esteem; loss of a good reputation; disgrace. **disreputable** adj.

dis·re·spect n. Lack of respect or reverence. **disrespect** v., **disrespectful** adj., **disrespectfully** adv.

dis·robe v. To undress.

dis·rupt v. To throw into disorder or confusion; upset; to cause to break down. **disruption** n., **disruptive** adj.

dis·sat·is·fy v. To fail to satisfy; to disappoint. **dissatisfaction** n., **dissatisfied** adj.

dis·sect v. To cut into pieces; to expose the parts of something, such as an animal, for examination; to analyze in detail. **dissector** n.

dis·sem·ble v. To conceal or hide the actual nature of; to put on a false appearance; to conceal facts. **dissembler** n.

dis·sem·i·nate v. To scatter or spread, as if by sowing, over a wide area. **dissemination**, **disseminator** n.

dis·sen·sion n. Difference of opinion; discord; strife.

dis·sent v. To differ in opinion or thought. n. Difference of opinion; refusal to go along with an established church.

dis·ser·ta·tion n. A formal written discourse or treaties, especially one submitted for a doctorate.

dis·serv·ice n. An ill turn; an ill service, injury, or harm.

dis·sev·er v. To sever; to divide; to separate **disseverance**, **disseverment** n.

dis·si·dent adj. Strong and open difference with an opinion or group. **dissident**, **dissidence** n.

dis·sim·i·lar adj. Different; not the same; unlike. **dissimilarity** n.

dis·si·mil·i·tude n. Lack of resemblance; unlikeness.

dis·sim·u·late v. To conceal under a false appearance; to dissemble.

dis·si·pate v. To disperse or drive away; to squander or waste; to separate into parts and scatter or vanish; to become dispersed; to lose irreversibly.

dis·so·ci·ate v. To break from the association with another. **dissociation** n.

dis·so·lute adj. Loose in morals; lacking moral restraint. **dissolutely** adv., **dissoluteness** n.

dis·so·lu·tion n. The act or process of changing from a solid to a fluid form; the separation of body and soul; death.

dis·solve v. To pass into solution, such as dissolving sugar in water; to overcome, as by emotion; to fade away; to become decomposed; to terminate. **dissolvable** adj.

dis·so·nance n., Mus. Lack of agreement; a conflict. Mus. A harsh or disagreeable combination of sounds; discord. **dissonant** adj., **dissonantly** adv.

dis·suade v. To alter the course of action; to turn from something by persuasion or advice. **dissuader**, **dissuasion** n., **dissuasive** adj.

dis·taff n. A staff rotation for holding the flax, tow, or wool in spinning; the female side of a family; women in general.

dis·tal n. Relatively remote from the point of attachment or origin.

dis·tance n. Separation in time or space;

the degree of separation between two points; the space that separates any two specified points in time; the quality or state of being distant; aloofness. *v.* To put space between; to keep at a distance.

dis-tant *adj.* Apart or separate by a specified amount of time or space; situated at a great distance; coming from, going to, or located at a distance; remotely related.
distantly *adv.*, distantness *n.*

dis-taste *v.* To feel aversion to; to have an offensive taste; dislike.
distastefully *adv.*, distastefulness *n.*

dis-tend *v.* To expand from internal pressure. distensible *adj.*, distention, distension *n.*

dis-till *v.* To extract by distillation; to give off in drops. distiller, distillery *n.*

dis-til-late *n.* The condensed substance separated by distillation.

dis-tinct *adj.* Distinguished from all others; clearly seen; unquestionable.
distinctly *adv.*, distinctness *n.*

dis-tinc-tion *n.* The act of distinguishing; a difference; a special honor or recognition.

dis-tinc-tive *adj.* Serving to give style or distinction to. distinctiveness *n.*

dis-tin-guish *v.* To recognize as being different; to discriminate; to make something different or noticeable.
distinguishable, distinguished *adj.*, distinguishably *adv.*

dis-tort *v.* To twist or bend out of shape; to twist the true meaning of; to give a misleading account of. distortion *n.*

dis-tract *v.* To draw or divert one's attention away from something; to cause one to feel conflicting emotions.
distraction *n.*

dis-trait *adj.* Absent-minded.

dis-traught *adj.* Deeply agitated with doubt or anxiety; crazed.

dis-tress *v.* To cause suffering of mind or body. *n.* Pain or suffering; severe physical or mental strain; a very painful situation; a state of danger or desperate need. distressingly *adv.*

dis-trib-ute *v.* To divide among many; to deliver or give out; to classify.
distribution *n.*, distributive *adj.*

dis-trib-u-tor *n.* A person that distributes, such as a wholesaler; a device which directs electrical current to the spark plugs of a gasoline engine.

dis-trict *n.* An administrative or political section of a territory; a distinctive area. district *v.*

dis-trict at-tor-ney *n.* The public prosecuting officer of a judicial district.

dis-trust *n.* Suspicion; doubt. *v.* To doubt; to suspect. distrustful *adj.*, distrustfully *adv.*

dis-turb *v.* To destroy the tranquillity or composure of; to unsettle mentally or emotionally; to interrupt or interfere with; to bother. disturbance, disturber *n.*

dis-u-nite *v.* To divide or separate.

dis-u-ni-ty *n.* Discord; unrest.

dis-use *n.* The state of not using; out of use.

ditch *n.* A trench in the earth. *v.* To dig a ditch in; to surround with a ditch. *Slang* To discard; to get rid of something; to land a disabled aircraft on water.

ditch dig-ger *n.* One that digs ditches.

dith-er *n.* A state of nervousness or indecision; commotion.

dit-to *n.*, *pl.* -tos An exact copy; the same as stated before. ditto mark The pair of marks (" ") used to substitute the word *ditto. adv.* As before.

dit-ty *n.*, *pl.* -ties A short, simple song.

dit-ty bag *n.* A small bag used by sailors to hold small articles, such as thread, buttons, and other small personal effects.

di-u-ret-ic *adj.* Tending to cause an increase in the flow of urine. *n.* A drug given to increase the amount of urine produced.

di-ur-nal *adj.* Having a daily cycle or recurring every day; of, relating to, or occurring in the daytime; opening in the daytime and closing at night.
diurnally *adv.*

di-va *n.*, *pl.* -vas or -ve A prima donna; a female opera star.

di-van *n.* A long, backless and armless sofa or couch.

dive *v.* To plunge into water headfirst; to plunge downward at a sharp angle; to submerge; to rush headlong. *n.* The act or an instance of diving; a submerging of a submarine; a sharp decline. *Slang* A disreputable bar; in boxing, a faked knockout; in football, an offensive play in which the ball carrier plunges into the line for short yardage. diver *n.*

dive--bomb *v.* To bomb something from an airplane by making a steep dive toward the target and releasing the bomb. dive-bomber *n.*

div-er *n.* A person who dives; a person who stays underwater for prolonged periods by having air supplied either from the surface or from compressed air tanks.

di-verge *v.*

To move or extend in different directions from a common point; (diverging rays of light); to differ in opinion or manner. divergent *adj.*

di-vers *adj.* Various; several.

di-verse *adj.* Unlike in characteristics; having various forms or qualities.
diversely *adv.*, diverseness *n.*

di-ver-si-fy *v.* To give variety to something; to engage in varied operations; to distribute over a wide range of types or classes. diversification *n.*

di-ver-sion *n.* The act of diverting from a

course, activity or use; something that diverts or amuses. **diversionary** *adj.*

di-ver-si-ty *n., pl.* **-ties** A difference; variety; unlikeness.

di-vert *v.* To turn from a set course; to give pleasure by distracting the attention from something that is burdensome or oppressive. **diversionary** *adj.*, **diversion, diversity** *n.*

di-vest *v.* To undress or strip, especially of clothing or equipment; to deprive or dispossess of property, authority, or title; to take away from a person. **divestment** *n.*

di-ves-ti-ture *n.* The act of divesting; the compulsory transfer of title or disposal of interests upon government order.

di-vide *v.* To separate into parts, areas, or groups; to separate into pieces or portions and give out in shares; to cause to be apart; in mathematics, to perform mathematical division on a number. An act of dividing; a dividing ridge between drainage areas.

div-i-dend *n.* An individual share of something distributed; a bonus; a number to be divided; a sum or fund to be divided and distributed.

di-vine *adj.* Of, relating to, preceding from, or pertaining to God. *Informal* Extremely pleasing. *n.* A clergyman or theologian. *v.* To foretell. **divineness** *n.,* **divinely** *adv.*

di-vi-sion *n.* Separation; something which divides, separates, or marks off; the act, process, or instance of separating or keeping apart; the condition or an instance of being divided in opinion; in mathematics, the process of discovering how many times one quantity is contained in another. *Milit.* A self-sufficient tactical unit capable of independent action. **divisional** *adj.*

di-vi-sive *adj.* Tending to create dissension or disunity. **divisiveness** *n.*

di-vi-sor *n* In mathematics, the number by which a dividend is to be divided.

di-vorce *n.* The legal dissolution of a marriage; the complete separation of things. **divorce** *v.,* **divorcee** *n.*

div-ot *n.* A square of turf or sod; a piece of turf torn up by a golf club while making a shot.

di-vulge *v.* To reveal or make known; to disclose; to reveal a secret.

dix-ie-land *n.* Distinctly American jazz music, usually played by a small band and characterized by ensemble and solo improvisation.

diz-zy *adj.* Having a whirling sensation in the head with loss of proper balance; mentally confused; caused by or marked by giddiness; extremely rapid. **dizzily** *adv.,* **dizzy** *v.*

do *v.* To bring to pass; to bring about; to perform or execute; to put forth; to exert; to bring to an end. *n.* A festive get-together; a command to do something. *Mus.* The first tone of a scale. **do away with** To destroy; to kill. **do in** To tire completely; to kill. **do up** To

adorn or dress lavishly; to wrap and tie.

do-cent *n.* A teacher at a college or university; a guide or lecturer in a museum.

doc-ile *adj.* Easily led, taught, or managed. **docility** *n.*

dock *n.* A landing slip or pier for ships or boats; a loading area for trucks or trains; an enclosure where the defendant sits or stands in a criminal trail. *Bot.* A weedy plant with small flower clusters. *v.* To haul or guide into a dock; to become docked. *Aeros.* To connect, as in two or more spacecrafts.

dock-age *n.* A charge for the use of a dock; docking facilities.

dock-et *n.* A brief written summary of a document; an agenda; an identifying statement about a document placed on its cover.

dock-yard *n.* A shipyard; a place where ships are repaired or built.

doc-tor *n.* A person trained and licensed to practice medicine, such as a physician, surgeon, dentist, or veterinarian; a person holding the highest degree offered by a university. *v.* To restore to good condition; to practice medicine; to administer medical treatment; to tamper with; to alter for a desired end. **doctoral** *adj.*

doc-tor-ate *n.* The degree, status, or title of a doctor.

doc-trine *n.* Something taught as a body of principles; a statement of fundamental government policy especially in international relations. **doctrinal** *adj.*

doc-u-ment *n.* An official paper utilized as the basis, proof, or support of something. *v.* To furnish documentary evidence of; to prove with, support by, or provide by documents. **documentation** *n.*

doc-u-men-ta-ry *adj.* Relating to or based on documents; an artistic way of presenting facts. **documentary** *n.*

dod-der *v.* To tremble, shake, or totter from weakness or age. *n., Bot.* A parasitic, twining vine.

dodge *v.* To avoid by moving suddenly; to evade a responsibility by trickery or deceit; to shift suddenly. **dodge** *n.*

doe *n., pl.* **does** *or* **doe** A mature female deer; any of various mammals, as the hare or kangaroo.

does-n't *contr.* Does not.

dog-ged *adj.* Stubbornly determined; obstinate **doggedly** *adv.,* **doggedness** *n.*

dog-ma *n.* A rigidly held doctrine proclaimed to be true by a religious group; a principle or idea considered to be the absolute truth.

dog-mat-ic *adj.* Marked by an authoritative assertion of unproved or unprovable principles. **dogmatically** *adv.*

dog paddle *n.* A beginner's swimming stroke in which the arms and legs move up and down. **dog-paddle** *v.*

do-jo *n.* A school of instruction in the Japanese martial arts.

dol-drums *pl., n.* A period of listlessness or despondency. *Naut.* The ocean region near the equator where there is very little wind.

dole-ful *adj.* Filled with grief or sadness. **dolefully** *adv.,* **dolefulness** *n.*

dol-lar *n.* A coin, note, or token representing one dollar; the standard monetary unit of the U.S.

dol-lop *n.* A lump or blob of a semiliquid substance; an indefinite amount or form.

dol-ly *n., pl.* **-lies** A doll; a low, flat frame on wheels or rollers used to move heavy loads; a wheeled apparatus for moving a motion picture or television camera toward or away from the action.

dol-men *n.* A prehistoric monument made up of a huge stone set on upright stone.

do-lor-ous *adj.* Marked by grief or pain; sad; mournful. **dolorously** *adv.,* **dolorousness** *n.*

dol-phin *n.*

Any of various small cetaceans with the snout in the shape of a beak and the neck vertebrae partially fused.

dolt *n.* A stupid person.

do-main *n.* A territory under one government; a field of activity or interest.

dome *n.* A roof resembling a hemisphere; something suggesting a dome.

do-mes-tic *adj.* Of or relating to the home, household or family life. **domestically** *adv.,* **domesticity** *n.*

dom-i-cile *n.* A dwelling place, house, or home. **domicile** *v.,* **domiciliary** *adj.*

dom-i-nant *adj.* Having the most control or influence; most overwhelming; in genetics, producing a typical effect even when paired with an unlike gene for the same characteristic. **dominance** *n.,* **dominantly** *adv.*

dom-i-nate *v.* To rule or control; to exert the supreme determining or guiding influence on; to occupy the most prominent position in or over. **domination, dominator** *n.*

dom-i-no the-o-ry *n.* The theory that if a certain event occurs, a series of similar events will follow.

don *v.* To put something on; to dress.

done *adj.* Completely finished or through; doomed to failure, defeat, or death; cooked adequately.

do-nee *n.* A recipient of a gift.

done for *adj.* Mortally stricken; doomed; left with no opportunity for recovery; ruined.

don-key *n., pl.* **-keys** The domesticated ass. *Informal* A stubborn person.

do-nor *n.* One who gives, donates, or contributes.

don't *contr.* Do not.

dor-mant *adj.* Asleep; a state of inactivity or rest. **dormancy** *n.*

dor-sal *adj., Anat.* Of, relating to, or situated on or near the back.

do-ry *n., pl.* **-ries** A small flat-bottomed boat with high, flaring sides and a sharp bow.

DOS *abbr.* Disk operating system.

dose *n.* The measured quantity of a therapeutic agent to be taken at one time or at stated intervals. *Med.* The prescribed amount of radiation to which a certain part of the body is exposed. **dosage** *n.,* **dose** *v.*

dos-si-er *n.* A complete file of documents or papers giving detailed information about a person or affair.

dote *v.* To show excessive affection or fondness; to exhibit mental decline, especially as a result of senility.

dou-ble *adj.* Twice as much; composed of two like parts; designed for two.

dou-ble-cross *v., Slang* To betray.

dou-ble joint-ed *adj.* Having unusually flexible joints which allow connected parts to bend at abnormal angles.

doubt *v.* To be uncertain or mistrustful about something; to distrust. **doubt, doubter** *n.*

dough-ty *adj.* Marked by valor; brave.

dour *adj.* Stern and forbidding; morose and ill-tempered.

douse *v.* To plunge into liquid; to throw water on; to drench; to extinguish.

dove *n.* Any of numerous pigeons; a gentle, innocent person. **dovish** *adj.*

dow-a-ger *n.* A widow holding a title or property from her dead husband; a dignified, elderly woman.

dow-dy *adj.* Not neat or tidy; oldfashioned. **dowdier, dowdiest** *adj.*

dow-el *n.* A round wooden pin which fits tightly into an adjacent hole to fasten together the two pieces.

dow-er *n.* The part of a deceased man's estate that is given to his widow by law. *v.* To provide with a dower.

down *adv.* Toward or in a lower physical condition; from a higher to a lower position; the direction that is opposite of up.

down-er *n., Slang* A depressant or sedative drug; a barbiturate; something that is depressing.

down-ward *or* **down-wards** *adv.* From a higher to a lower place.

down-wind *adv. & adj.* In the direction toward which the wind blows.

dowse *v.* To search for with a divining rod to find underground water or minerals. **dowser** *n.*

dox-ol-o-gy *n., pl.* **-gies** A hymn or verse in praise of God.

doz-en *n.* Twelve of a kind; a set of twelve things. **dozen, dozenth** *adj.*

drab *adj.* Of a light, dull brown or olive brown color; commonplace or dull. **drabness** *n.*

drach-ma *n., pl.* **-mas** *or* **-mae** A silver coin of ancient Greece.

drag *v.* To pull along or haul by force; to move with painful or undue slowness;

to bring by force; to proceed slowly; to lag behind. *Slang* To puff on a pipe, cigarette, or cigar. *n.* Something which retards motion or action; a tool used under water to detect or collect objects; something which is boring or dull. *Slang* Someone or something that is bothersome; a street; a race. **dragger** *n.*

drag-on *n.*

An mythical, giant, serpent-like, winged, fire-breathing monster.

drag-on-fly *n.*

A large insect which holds it's wings in a horizontal position and during it's naiad stage has rectal gills.

drake *n.* A male duck.
dram *n.* A small drink; a small portion.
drank *v.* Past tense of drink.
dras-tic *adj.* Acting extremely harsh or severe. **drastically** *adv.*
draught *n. & v.* A variation of draft.
draughts *pl., n.* The game of checkers, as referred to by the British.
draw-back *n.* An undesirable feature.
drawl *v.* To speak slowly with prolonged vowels.
dray *n.* A low, heavy cart without sides, used for hauling.
dread *v.* To fear greatly; to anticipate with alarm, anxiety, or reluctance. *n.* A great fear.
dread-ful *adj.* Inspiring dread; very distasteful or shocking; awful.
drea-ry *adj.* Bleak and gloomy; dull. **drearily** *adv.*, **dreariness** *n.*
dregs *pl., n.* The sediment of a liquid; the least desirable part.
drench *v.* To wet thoroughly; to throw water on. **drencher** *n.*
drew *v.* Past tense of draw.
drive *v.* To propel, push, or press onward; to repulse by authority; to force into a particular act or state.
driv-el *v.* To slobber; to talk nonsensically. **drivel** *n.*
driz-zle *n.* A fine, quiet, gentle rain.
droll *adj.* Whimsically comical.
drom-e-dar-y *n., pl.* -ies A one-humped camel, widely used in northern Africa and western Asia as a beast of burden.
drool *v.* To let saliva dribble from the mouth. *Informal* To make an exaggerated expression of desire. **drool** *n.*
droop *v.* To hang or bend downward; to become depressed. **droop, droopiness** *n.*, **droopy** *adj.*
drop-sy *n., Med.* A diseased condition in which large amounts of fluid collect in the body tissues and cavities.
dross *n.* An impurity which forms on the surface of molten metal; inferior,

trivial, or worthless matter.
drought *or* **drouth** *n.* A prolonged period of dryness; a chronic shortage of something.
drove *n.* A herd being driven in a body; a crowd. *v.* Past tense of drive.
drown *v.* To kill or die by suffocating in a liquid; to cause not to be heard by making a loud noise; to drive out.
drowse *v.* To doze. **drowse** *n.*
drows-y *adj.* Sleepy; tending to induce sleep. **drowsiness** *n.*
drub *v.* To hit with a stick; to abuse with words; to defeat decisively.
drudge *n.* A person who does tiresome or menial tasks. **drudge** *v.*, **drudgery** *n.*
drug *n.* A substance used in the treatment of disease or illness; a narcotic. *v.* To take drugs for narcotic effect; to mix or dose with drugs.

drum *n.*

A musical percussion instrument consisting of a hollow frame with a cover stretched across one or both ends, played by beating with sticks or the hands; something with the shape of a drum; a cylindrical container; a metal container holding a capacity between 12 and 110 gallons; any of various percoid fishes that make a drumming noise. *v.* To beat a drum; to tap rhythmically or incessantly; to instill by repetition; to dismiss in disgrace. **drum up** To invent or devise; to go out and actively pursue new accounts or business.
drunk-ard *adj.* A person who is intoxicated by liquor.
drupe *n.* A fruit, as the peach, usually having one large pit or seed.
dry-ad *n.* A wood nymph.
dry goods *pl., n.* Textile fabrics as distinguished from foodstuffs and hardware.
du-al *adj.* Made up or composed of two parts; having a double purpose.
du-bi-ous *adj.* Causing doubt; unsettled in judgment; reluctant to agree; question as to quality or validity; verging on impropriety. **dubiously** *adv.*
du-cal *adj.* Pertaining to a duke or dukedom.
duch-ess *n.* The wife or widow of a duke; a female holding a ducal title in her own right.

duck *n.*

Any of various swimming birds with short necks and legs; the flesh of any of these birds used as food. *Slang* A person. *v.* To lower the head and body quickly; to evade; to plunge quickly under water.
duct *n.* A bodily tube or canal, especially one carrying a secretion; a tubular passage through which something flows.

duc-tile *adj.* Capable of being drawn into a fine strand or wire; easily influenced or persuaded.

dude *n., Informal* A city person vacationing on a ranch; a man who is a fancy dresser. *Slang* A fellow.

dudg-eon *n.* A sullen, displeased, or indignant mood.

due *adj.* Owed; payable.

du-et *n.* A musical composition for two performers or musical instruments.

dul-cet *adj.* Melodious; pleasing to the ear; having an agreeable, soothing quality.

dul-ci-mer *n.* A musical stringed instrument played with two small picks or by plucking.

du-ly *adv.* In a proper or due manner.

dumb *adj.* Unable to speak; temporarily speechless. *Informal* Stupid. **dumbly** *adv.*, **dumbness** *n.*

dunce *n.* A slow-witted person.

dune *n.* A ridge or hill of sand blown or drifted by the wind.

dung *n.* The excrement of animals; manure.

dun-geon *n.* A dark, confining, underground prison chamber.

dunk *v.* To dip a piece of food into liquid before eating; to submerge someone in a playful fashion.

du-o *n., pl.* -os An instrument duet; two people in close association.

du-o-de-num *n., pl.* -dena *or* -denums The first portion of the small intestine, extending from the lower end of the stomach to the jejunum. **duodenal** *adj.*

du-plex *adj.* Double. *n.* An apartment with rooms on two adjoining floors; having two parts.

du-pli-cate *adj.* Identical with another.

du-ra-ble *adj.* Able to continue for a prolonged period of time without deterioration. **durability** *n.*

du-ra-tion *n.* The period of time during which something exists or lasts.

du-ress *n.* Constraint by fear or force; in law, coercion illegally applied; forced restraint.

dur-ing *prep.* Throughout the time of; within the time of.

dwin-dle *v.* To waste away; to become steadily less.

dying *adj.* Coming to the end of life.

dy-nam-ic *adj.* Marked by energy and productive activity or change; of or relating to energy, motion, or force.

dy-nam-ics *n., Phys.* The part of physics which deals with force, energy, and motion and the relationship between them.

dys-en-ter-y *n.* An infection of the lower intestinal tract which produces pain, fever, and severe diarrhea.

dys-lex-i-a *n.* An impairment in one's ability to read. **dyslexic** *adj.*

dys-pep-sia *n.* Indigestion. **dyspeptic** *adj.*

dys-pro-si-um *n.* A metallic element used in nuclear research, symbolized by Dy.

dys-tro-phy *n.* Atrophy of muscle tissue; any of various neuromuscular disorders, especially muscular dystrophy.

E, e The fifth letter of the English alphabet. *Mus.* The third tone in the natural scale of C.

each *adj.* Everyone of two or more considered separately. *adv.* To or for each; apiece.

each other *pron.* Each in reciprocal action or relation; one another.

ea-ger *adj.* Marked by enthusiastic interest or desire; having a great desire or wanting something. **-ly** *adv.*, **-ness** *n.*

ea-gle *n.* A large, powerful bird of prey having a powerful bill, broad strong wings, and soaring flight; a U.S. gold coin worth ten dollars; a score of two under par on a hole in golf.

eagle--eyed *adj.* Having exceptional vision.

ear *n., Anat.*

The hearing organ in vertebrates, located on either side of the head; any of various organs capable of detecting vibratory motion; the ability to hear keenly; attention or heed; something that resembles the external ear. **all ears** Listen closely. **by ear** Without reference to written music.

earl *n.* A British title for a nobleman ranking above a viscount and below a marquis. **earldom** *n.*

ear-ly *adj.* Occurring near the beginning of a period of time; a development or a series; distant in past time; before the usual or expected time; occurring in the near future. *adv.* Near the beginning of time; far back in time. **earlier, earliest** *adj.*

early bird *n.* An early riser; a person who arrives early.

earn *v.* To receive payment in return for work done or services rendered; to gain as a result of one's efforts.

ear-nest *n.* A serious mental state; payment in advance to bind an agreement; a pledge. *adj.* Characterized by an intense and serious state of mind; having serious intent. **earnestly** *adv.*, **earnestness** *n.*

earn-ings *pl., n.* Something earned, such as a salary.

earth *n.* The third planet from the sun and the planet on which there is life; the outer layer of the world; ground; soil; dirt.

ease *n.* A state of being comfortable; freedom from pain, discomfort, or care; freedom from labor or difficulty; an act of easing or a state of being eased. *v.* To free from pain or discomfort; to lessen the pressure or tension; to make less difficult; to move or pass with freedom. **at ease** Free from discomfort. *Milit.* Standing silently with the feet apart, as in a military formation. **easeful** *adj.*, **easefully** *adv.*

ea-sel *n.* A frame used by artists to support a canvas or picture.

east *n.* The direction opposite of west; the direction in which the sun rises.

-erly *adj.* & *adv.*, -ward *adj.*, -ds *adv.*

Easter *n.* A Christian festival which celebrates the resurrection of Christ.

easy *adj.* Capable of being accomplished with little difficulty; free from worry or pain; not hurried or strenuous; something readily obtainable. **easily** *adv.*, **easiness** *n.*

easy going *adj.* Taking life easy; without worry, concern, or haste.

eat *v.* To chew and swallow food; to erode; to consume with distress or agitation; to take a meal. **eat crow** To accept what one has been fighting against. **eat one's heart out** To grieve bitterly. **eat one's words** To retract what has been said. **eat out of one's hand** To accept the domination of another. **eater** *n.*

eaves *pl.*, *n.* The overhanging edge of a roof.

ebb *n.* The return of the tide towards the sea; a time of decline. *v.* To recede, as the tide does; to fall or flow back; to weaken.

ebb tide *n.* The tide while at ebb; a period of decline.

eb-o-ny *n.*, *pl.* -nies The dark, hard, colored wood from the center of the ebony tree of Asia and Africa. *adj.* Resembling ebony; black.

e-bul-lient *adj.* Filled with enthusiasm. **ebullience** *n.*, **ebulliently** *adv.*

eb-ul-li-tion *n.* The process of boiling or bubbling; a sudden release of emotion.

ec-cen-tric *adj.* Differing from an established pattern or accepted norm; deviating from a perfect circle; not located at the geometrical center. *n.* An odd or erratic person; a disk or wheel with its axis not situated in the center. **eccentrically** *adv.*, **eccentricity** *n.*

ec-cle-si-as-ti-cal *n.* A clergyman; a person officially serving a church. *adj.* Of or relating to a church.

ech-e-lon *n.* A formation, as of military aircraft or naval vessels, resembling a series of steps where each rank is positioned slightly to the right or left of the preceding one; a level of command or authority; a hierarchy.

ech-o *n.*, *pl.* -oes Repetition of a sound by reflecting sound waves from a surface; the sound produced by such a reflection; a repetition; the reflection of transmitted radar signals by an object. *v.* To repeat or be repeated by; to imitate.

ec-lec-tic *adj.* Having components from diverse sources or styles. **eclectic** *n.*

e-clipse *n.* A total or partial blocking of one celestial body by another. *v.* To fall into obscurity or decline; to cause an eclipse of.

e-clip-tic *n.*, *Astron.* The circle formed by the intersection of the plane of the earth's orbit and the celestial sphere.

e-logue *n.* A short pastoral poem in the form of a dialogue.

ec-o-cide *n.* The deliberate destruction of the natural environment, caused by pollutants.

e-col-o-gy *n.* The branch of science concerned with the interrelationship of organisms and their environments; the relationship between living organisms and their environments. **ecologic** *adj.*, **ecologically** *adv.*, **ecologist** *n.*

ec-o-nom-ic *adj.* The science relating to the development, production, and manage-ment of material wealth; relating to the necessities of life.

ec-o-nom-i-cal *adj.* Not wasteful; frugal; operating with little waste. **-ly** *adv.*

ec-o-nom-ics *pl.*, *n.* The science which treats production, distribution, and consumption of commodities. **-ist** *n.*

e-con-o-mize *v.* To manage thriftily; to use sparingly. **economizer** *n.*

e-con-o-my *n.*, *pl.* -mies Careful management of money, materials, and resources; a reduction in expenses; a system or structure for the management of resources and production of goods and services.

ec-ru *n.* A light yellowish brown, as the color of unbleached linen.

ec-sta-sy *n.*, *pl.* -sies The state of intense joy or delight. **ecstatic** *adj.*, **ecstatically** *adv.*

ec-u-men-i-cal *adj.* Worldwide or general in extent, application, or influence; promoting unity among Christian churches or religions. **ecumenically** *adv.*, **ecumenism** *n.*

ec-ze-ma *n.* A noncontagious inflammatory skin condition, marked by itching and scaly patches. **eczematous** *adj.*

ed-dy *n.*, *pl.* -dies A current, as of water, running against the direction of the main current, especially in a circular motion. **eddy** *v.*

e-del-weiss *n.* An Alpine plant having woolly leaves and small flowers.

edge *n.* The thin, sharp, cutting side of a blade; keenness; sharpness; the border where an object or area begins or ends; an advantage. *v.* To furnish with an edge or border; to sharpen; to move gradually. **on edge** Tense.

ed-i-ble *adj.* Safe or fit for consumption. **edibility**, **edible** *n.*

e-dict *n.* A public decree; an order or command officially proclaimed.

ed-i-fy *v.* To benefit and enlighten, morally or spiritually. **edification**, **edifer** *n.*

ed-it *v.* To prepare and correct for publication; to compile for an edition; to delete or change. **editor** *n.*

e-di-tion *n.* The form in which a book is published; the total number of copies printed at one time; one similar to an original version.

ed-i-to-ri-al *n.* An article in a newspaper or magazine which expresses the opinion of a publisher or editor. *adj.* Of or relating to an editor or an editor's work; being or resembling an editorial. **editorially** *adv.*

ed-u-cate *v.* To supply with training or schooling; to supervise the mental or moral growth of. **educator** n.

e-duce v. To call forth or bring out; to develop from given facts.

eel n., pl. **eel** or **eels** A snake-like marine or freshwater fish without scales or pelvic fins.

ee-rie or **ee-ry** adj. Suggesting or inspiring the supernatural or strange; spooky. **eerily** adv., **eeriness** n.

ef-face v. To remove or rub out. **effacer, effacement** n.

ef-fect n. Something produced by a cause; the power to produce a desired result; the reaction something has on an object; a technique which produces an intended impression. **take effect** To become operative. **effecter** n.

ef-fec-tive adj. Producing an expected effect or proper result. **effectiveness** n.

ef-fem-i-nate adj. Having a more woman-like quality or trait than a man. **effeminacy** n., **effeminately** adv.

ef-fer-ent adj., Physiol. Carrying away or outward from a central organ or part. **efferent** n., **efferently** adv.

ef-fete adj. Exhausted of effectiveness or force; worn-out; decadent.

ef-fi-ca-cious adj. Producing an intended effect. **efficaciously** adv.

ef-fi-cient adj. Adequate in performance with a minimum of waste or effort; giving a high ratio of output.

ef-fi-gy n., pl. **-gies** A life-size sculpture or painting representing a crude image or dummy of a hated person.

ef-flo-res-cence n. A time of flowering; a slow process of development; the highest point. **efflorescent** adj.

ef-flu-ence n. An act of flowing out; something that flows out or forth. **effluent** adj. & n.

ef-flu-vi-um n., pl. **-via** or **-viums** An unpleasant vapor from something. **effluvial** adj.

ef-fort n. Voluntary exertion of physical or mental energy; a difficult exertion; a normally earnest attempt or achievement; something done through exertion. Phys. A force applied against inertia. **effortless** adj.

ef-fron-ter-y n., pl. **-ies** Shameless boldness; impudence.

ef-ful-gent adj. Shining brilliantly; radiant. **effulgence** n.

ef-fu-sion n. An instance of pouring forth; an unrestrained outpouring of feeling. **effuse** v., **effusive** adj., **effusively** adv.

egg n. The hard-shelled reproductive cell of female animals, especially one produced by a chicken, used as food. v. To incite to action.

egg-beat-er n. A kitchen tool with rotating blades used to mix, blend, or beat food.

egg-head n., Informal An intellectual; highbrow.

egg-nog n. A drink of beaten eggs, sugar, and milk or cream, often mixed with alcohol.

egg-plant n. A widely cultivated perennial plant which yields an egg-shaped edible fruit.

egg-roll n. A thin egg-dough casing filled with minced vegetables and sometimes meat or seafood which is fried.

eg-lan-tine n. The sweetbrier, a type of rose.

e-go n. The self thinking, feeling, and acting distinct from the external world. Physiol. The conscious aspect that most directly controls behavior and is most in touch with reality.

e-go-cen-tric adj. Thinking, observing, and regarding oneself as the object of all experiences. **egocentric, egocentricity** n.

e-go-ma-ni-a n. Self obsession. **egomaniac** n., **egomaniacal** adj.

ego trip n. Slang Something which satisfies the ego.

e-gre-gious adj. Outstandingly or remarkably bad; flagrant. **-ly** adv.

e-gress n. The act of coming out; emergence; a means of departing; exit.

e-gret n.

Any of several species of white wading birds having long, drooping plumes.

E-gypt n. A country located in northeast Africa and southwest Asia. **Egyptian** adj. & n.

ei-der n. A large sea duck found in northern regions, having soft down which is used for comforters, pillows, etc.

eight n. The cardinal number which follows seven. **eighth** n., adj. & adv.

eight ball n. The black ball with the number eight in the game of pool. **behind the eight ball** Slang In a bad spot.

ei-ther pron. One or the other. conj. Used before the first of two or more alternatives linked by or. adj. One or the other of two. adv. Likewise; also.

e-jac-u-late v. To eject abruptly, as in semen; to utter suddenly and briefly; to exclaim. **ejaculation** n., **ejaculatory** adj.

e-ject v. To throw out; to expel. **ejection, ejector** n.

eke out v. To obtain with great effort.

e-lab-o-rate adj. Planned or carried out with great detail; very complex; intricate. v. To work out or complete with great detail; to give more detail. **elaborateness, -tion** n., **-ly** adv.

e-land n. A large African antelope with a tan coat and large spiral horns.

e-lapse v. To slip or glide away.

e-las-tic adj. Complying with changing circumstances; capable of easy adjustment. **elastically** adv., **elasticity** n.

e-late v. To make proud of. **elation** n.

el-bow n. A sharp turn, as in a river or road, which resembles an elbow. Anat. The outer joint of the arm between the upper arm and forearm.

elbow-room *n.* Ample room to move about; enough space for comfort.

eld-er *adj.* Older. *n.* One who is older than others; a person of great influence; an official of the church. *Bot.* A shrub bearing reddish fruit.

e-lect *v.* To choose or select by vote, as for an office; to make a choice. *adj.* Singled out on purpose; elected but not yet inaugurated. *n.* One chosen or set apart, especially for spiritual salvation.

e-lec-tric *or* **e-lec-tri-cal** *adj.* Relating to electricity. **electrically** *adv.*

e-lec-tri-cian *n.* A person whose job it is to install or maintain electric equipment.

e-lec-tric-i-ty *n., Phys., Chem.* A force that causes bodies to attract or repel each other, responsible for a natural phenomena as lightning; electric current as a power source; emotional excitement.

e-lec-tro-car-di-o-gram *n.* The record produced by an electrocardiograph machine.

e-lec-tro-car-di-o-graph *n.* An electric instrument which detects and records the heartbeat.

e-lec-tro-cute *v.* To kill or execute by the use of electric current. **electrocution** *n.*

e-lec-trode *n.* A conductor by which an electric current enters or leaves.

e-lec-tro-dy-nam-ics *n., Phys.* The study of the interactions of moving electric charges. **electrodynamic** *adj.*

e-lec-trol-y-sis *n., Chem., Phys.* A chemical decomposition by an electric current; destruction of tumors or hair roots by an electric current.

e-lec-tro-mag-net *n.* A magnet consisting of a soft iron core magnetized by an electric current passing through a wire which is coiled around the core.

e-lec-trom-e-ter *n.* An instrument for detecting or measuring electric potential or differences between two conductors.

e-lec-tro-mo-tive *adj.* Of, pertaining to, or tending to produce electric current.

e-lec-tron *n., Elect.* A subatomic particle with a negative electric charge found outside of an atoms nucleus.

e-lec-tro-stat-ic *adj.* Pertaining to static electric charges.

e-lec-tro-stat-ics *pl., n., Phys.* The physics of static electric charges.

e-lec-tro-type *n.* A duplicate metal plate made by electroplating a mold of the original plate which is used in printing. **electrotype** *v.*

el-ee-mos-y-nar-y *adj.* Of, pertaining to, or contributed as charity.

el-e-gance *n.* Refinement in appearance, movement, or manners. **elegant** *adj.*

el-e-gy *n., pl.* **-gies** A poem expressing sorrow and lamentation for one who is dead.

el-e-ment *n.* A constituent part. *Chem. & Phys.* A substance not separable into less complex substances by chemical means. **elements** *pl.* The conditions of the weather.

el-e-men-ta-ry *adj.* Fundamental, essential; referring to elementary school; introducing fundamental principles.

el-e-phant *n.*

A large mammal having a long, flexible trunk and curved tusks.

el-e-phan-ti-a-sis *n., Pathol.* The enormous enlargement of affected parts along with hardening caused by obstruction of lymphatics from parasitic worms.

el-e-vate *v.* To lift up or raise; to promote to a higher rank.

e-lev-en *n.* A cardinal number with a sum equal to ten plus one. **eleventh** *n.*

elf *n., pl.* **elves** An imaginary being with magical powers, often mischievous; a small, mischievous child. **elfish** *adj.*

e-lic-it *v.* To bring or draw out; to evoke.

e-lide *v.* To omit, especially to slur over in pronunciation, as a vowel, consonant, or syllable. **elision** *n.*

e-lim-i-nate *v.* To get rid of, remove; to leave out, to omit; to excrete, as waste. **elimination, -tor** *n.,* **-ive, -ory** *adj.*

e-lite *n.* The most skilled members of a group; a small, powerful group; a type size yielding twelve characters to the inch. **elite** *adj.*

e-lix-ir *n., Phar.* A sweetened aromatic liquid of alcohol and water, used as a vehicle for medicine; a medicine regarded as a cure-all.

elk *n., pl.* **elks** *or* **elk** The largest deer of Europe and Asia.

ell *n.* An extension of a building at right angles to the main structure.

el-lipse *n., Geom.* A closed curve, somewhat oval in shape.

el-lip-tic *or* **el-lip-ti-cal** *adj.* Of, pertaining to, or shaped like an ellipse.

elm *n.* Any of various valuable timber and shade trees with arching branches.

el-o-cu-tion *n.* The art of effective public speaking. **-ary** *adj.,* **elocutionist** *n.*

e-lope *v.* To run away, especially in order to get married, usually without parental permission. **elopement, eloper** *n.*

el-o-quent *adj.* Having the power to speak fluently and persuasively; vividly expressive. **eloquence** *n.,* **-ly** *adv.*

else *adj.* Different; other; more; additional. *adv.* In addition; besides.

else-where *adv.* To or in another place.

e-lu-ci-date *v.* To make clear, clarify; to explain. **elucidator, elucidation** *n.*

e-lude *v.* To evade or avoid; to escape understanding.

e-ma-ci-ate *v.* To become or cause to become extremely thin from the loss of appetite. **emaciation** *n.*

em-a-nate *v.* To come or give forth, as from a source. **emanation** *n.*

e-man-ci-pate *v.* To liberate; to set free

from bondage. **emancipation,**
emancipator n.

e-mas-cu-late v. To castrate; to deprive
of masculine vigor. **emasculation,**
emasculator n.

em-balm v. To treat a corpse with pre-
servatives in order to protect from
decay. **embalmer** n.

em-bank v. To support, protect, or
defend with a bank of earth or stone.
embankment n.

em-bar-go n., pl. **-goes** A prohibition or
restraint on trade, as a government
order forbidding the entry or departure of merchant vessels, for example
the oil embargo of 1973. **embargo** v.

em-bark v. To board a ship; to set out on
a venture. **embarkation** n.

em-bar-rass v. To cause to feel self-
conscious; to confuse; to burden with
financial difficulties **embarrassment** n.

em-bas-sy n., pl. **-sies** The head-quarters
of an ambassador.

em-bat-tle v. To prepare or arrange for
battle.

em-bed v. To fix or enclose tightly in a
surrounding mass.

em-bel-lish v. To adorn or make beautiful with ornamentation; to decorate;
to heighten the attractiveness by adding ornamental details. **-ment** n.

em-ber n. A small piece of glowing coal
or wood, as in a dying fire. **embers** pl.
The smoldering ashes or remains of a
fire.

em-bez-zle v. To take money or other
items fraudulently. **embezzlement** n.

em-bit-ter v. To make bitter; to create
feelings of hostility. **embitterment** n.

em-bla-zon v. To decorate in bright
colors.

em-blem n. A symbol of something; a
distinctive design. **emblematic,**
emblematical adj.

em-bod-y v. To give a bodily form to; to
personify. **embodiment** n.

em-bold-en v. To encourage; to make
bold.

em-bo-lism n., Med. The blockage of a
blood vessel, as by an air bubble or a
detached clot.

em-bon-point n. Plumpness; stoutness.

em-boss v. To shape or decorate in
relief; to represent in relief.

em-bou-chure n., Mus. The part of a
wind instrument which is applied to
the lips to produce a musical tone.

em-bow-er v. To enclose, cover, or shelter.

em-brace v. To clasp or hold in the arms;
to hug; to surround; to take in mentally or visually. n. The act of embrac-
ing; a hug.

em-bra-sure n., Arch. A flared opening
in a wall, as for a door or window.

em-bro-cate v. To moisten and rub an
injured part of the body with a liquid
medicine. **embrocation** n.

em-broi-der v. To decorate with ornamental needlework; to add fictitious
details. **embroidery** n.

em-broil v. To involve in contention or

violent actions; to throw into confusion. **embroilment** n.

em-bry-o n., pl. **-os** An organism in its
early developmental stage, before it
has a distinctive form; in the human
species, the first eight weeks of
development, especially before birth
or germination; a rudimentary stage.
embryonic adj.

em-bry-ol-o-gy n. The science concerned
with the origin, structure, and growth
of embryos. **embryological** adj.,
embryologist n.

em-cee n., Informal A master of
ceremonies.

e-mend v. To correct or remove faults.
emendation, emender n.

em-er-ald n. A bright-green, transparent
variety of beryl, used as a gemstone.

e-merge v. To rise into view; to come
into existence. **emergence** n., **-ent** adj.

e-mer-gen-cy n., pl. **-cies** A sudden and
unexpected situation requiring prompt
action.

e-mer-i-tus adj. Retired from active duty
but retaining the honorary title held
immediately before retirement.

em-er-y n. A grainy, mineral substance
having impure corundum, used for
polishing and grinding.

e-met-ic adj. A medicine used to induce
vomiting. **emetic** n.

em-i-grate v. To move from one country
or region to settle elsewhere.

e-mi-gre n. A refugee.

em-i-nent adj. High in esteem, rank, or
office; conspicuous; outstanding.
eminently adv.

eminent domain n. The right of a
government to take or control
property for public use.

e-mir n. A Moslem prince.

em-is-sar-y n., pl. **-ies** A person sent out
on a mission.

e-mit v. To send forth; to throw or give
out.

e-mol-lient n. A substance for the soothing and softening of the skin.
emollient adj.

e-mol-u-ment n. Profit; compensation, as
a salary or perquisite.

e-mote v. To show emotion, as in acting.

e-mo-tion n. A strong surge of feeling;
any of the feelings of fear, sorrow, joy,
hate, or love; a particular feeling, as
love or hate.

em-pa-thy n., Physiol. Identification with
and understanding the feelings of
another person. **empathic,**
empathic adj.

em-pen-nage n. The rear section or tail
of an aircraft.

em-per-or n. The ruler of an empire.

em-pha-sis n., pl. **-ses** Significance or
importance attached to anything.

em-phat-ic adj. Expressed or spoken
with emphasis. **emphatically** adv.

em-pire n. The territories or nations
governed by a single supreme
authority.

em-pir-i-cal or **em-pir-ic** adj. Depending
on or gained from observation or ex-

periment rather than from theory and science. **empirically** adv.

em-place-ment n. A platform for guns or military equipment.

em-ploy v. To engage the service or use of; to devote time to an activity. **employable** adj., **employer**, **-ment** n.

em-ploy-ee or **em-ploy-e** n. A person who works for another in return for salary or wages.

em-po-ri-um n., pl. **-riums** or **-ria** A large store which carries general merchandise.

em-pow-er v. To authorize; to delegate; to license.

em-press n. A woman who rules an empire; an emperor's wife or widow.

emp-ty adj. Containing nothing; vacant; lacking substance. **emptily** adv., **emptiness** n.

em-py-re-an n. Pertaining to the highest part of heaven; the sky.

e-mu n. A swift-running Australian bird which is related to the ostrich.

em-u-late v. To strive to equal, especially by imitating. **emulation** n., **emulous** adj.

e-mul-sion n., Chem. A suspended mixture of small droplets, one within the other. Photog. A light-sensitive coating on photographic paper, film, or plates. **emulsive** adj.

en-a-ble v. To supply with adequate power, knowledge, or opportunity; to give legal power to another.

en-act v. To make into law. **enactment** n.

e-nam-el n. A decorative or protective coating fused on a surface, as of pottery; a paint that dries to a hard, glossy surface; the hard outermost covering of a tooth. v. To apply, inlay, or decorate with enamel.

en-am-or v. To inflame with love; to charm.

en-camp v. To form or stay in a camp. **encampment** n.

en-cap-su-late v. To enclose or encase in a capsule. **encapsulation** n.

en-ceph-a-li-tis n., Pathol. Inflammation of the brain.

en-chain v. To put in chains.

en-chant v. To put under a spell; to bewitch; to charm; to delight greatly. **enchantment** n.

en-cir-cle v. To form a circle around; to move around. **encirclement** n.

en-clave n. A country surrounded by a foreign country; a cultural group living within a larger group.

en-close v. To surround on all sides; to put in the same envelope or package with something else. **enclosure** n.

en-co-mi-um n., pl. **-miums** or **-mia** High praise.

en-com-pass v. To surround; to form a circle; to enclose.

en-core n. An audience's demand for a repeat performance; a performance in response to an encore. v. To call for an encore.

en-coun-ter n. An unplanned or unexpected meeting or conflict. v. To come

upon unexpectedly; to confront in a hostile situation.

encounter group n. A therapy group formed to increase people's sensitivity and to reveal their feelings so that they openly relate to others.

en-cour-age v. To inspire with courage or hope. **-ment** n., encouragingly adv.

en-croach v. To intrude upon the rights or possessions of another. **encroacher**, **encroachment** n.

en-crust v. To cover with a crust; to crust. **encrustation** n.

en-cum-ber v. To hinder or burden with difficulties or obligations. **encumbrance** n.

en-cyc-li-cal n., Rom. Cath. Ch. A papal letter to the bishops of the world.

en-cy-clo-pe-di-a n. A comprehensive work with articles covering a broad range of subjects. **encyclopedic** adj.

en-cyst v. To become enclosed in a sac. **encystment** n.

end n. A part lying at a boundary; the terminal point at which something concludes; the point in time at which something ceases; a goal; a fragment; a remainder; in football, either of the players in the outermost position on the line of scrimmage. v. To come or bring to a termination; to ruin or destroy; to die.

en-dan-ger v. To expose or put into danger or imperil. **endangerment** n.

en-dan-gered adj. Threatened with extinction.

en-dear v. To make beloved or dear. **endearingly** adv.

en-dear-ment n. The state of being endeared.

en-deav-or n. An attempt to attain or do something. **endeavor** v.

en-dem-ic adj. Peculiar to a particular area or people.

en-dive n. A herb with crisp succulent leaves, used in salads; a plant related to the endive.

en-do-cri-nol-o-gy n. The area of science or study of the endocrine glands and various secretions. **endocrinologist** n.

en-dog-e-nous adj., Biol. Originating or growing from within.

en-dor-phin n. Hormones with tranquilizing and pain-killing capabilities, secreted by the brain.

en-dorse v. To write one's signature on the back of a check, so as to obtain the cash indicated on the front, or on the back of a car title, so as to show transfer of ownership. **endorsee**, **endorsement** n.

en-do-scope n., Med. An instrument used to examine a bodily canal or hollow organ. **endoscopic** adj., **endoscopy** n.

en-dow v. To supply with a permanent income or income-producing property; to bestow upon. **endowment** n.

en-dure v. To undergo; to sustain; to put up with; to tolerate; to bear. **endurable** adj.

end-wise or **end-ways** adv. On end; lengthwise.

en-e-ma *n.* The injection of a liquid into the rectum for cleansing; the liquid injected.

en-e-my *n., pl.* -mies One who seeks to inflict injury on another; a foe; a hostile force or power.

en-er-gy *n., pl.* -gies Capacity or tendency for working or acting; vigor; strength; vitality of expression. *Phys.* The capacity for doing work; usable heat or electric power.

en-er-vate *v.* To deprive of vitality or strength; to weaken. enervation *n.*

en-fee-ble *v.* To weaken; to make feeble. enfeeblement *n.*

en-fold *v.* To enclose; to wrap in layers; to embrace.

en-force *v.* To compel obedience; to impose by force or firmness. enforcer *n.* enforceable *adj.*, enforcement.

en-fran-chise *v.* To grant with civil rights, as the right to vote; to give a franchise to. enfranchisement *n.*

en-gage *v.* To employ or hire; to secure or bind, as by a contract; to pledge oneself, especially to marry; to undertake conflict; to participate. *Mech.* To interlock.

en-gen-der *v.* To give rise to; to exist; to cause.

en-gine *n.* A machine which converts energy into mechanical motion; a mechanical instrument; a locomotive.

en-gorge *v.* To swallow greedily. *Pathol.* To fill an artery with blood.

en-graft *v.*, *Bot.* To join or fasten, as if by grafting.

en-grave *v.* To carve or etch into a surface; to carve, cut, or etch into a stone, metal, or wood for printing; to print from plates made by such a process.

en-grav-ing *n.* The act or technique of one that engraves; the impression printed from an engraved plate.

en-gross *v.* To occupy the complete attention of; to copy or write in a large, clear hand. engrossingly *adv.*

en-gulf *v.* To enclose completely; to submerge; to swallow.

en-hance *v.* To make greater; to raise to a higher degree. enhancement *n.*

e-nig-ma *n.* One that baffles; anything puzzling; a riddle.

en-jamb-ment *or* **en-jambe-ment** *n.* Construction of a sentence from one line of a poem to the next, allowing related words to fall on different lines.

en-join *v.* To command to do something; to prohibit, especially by legal action. enjoiner *n.*

en-joy *v.* To feel joy or find pleasure in; to have the use or possession of. enjoyable *adj.*, enjoyably *adv.*

en-large *v.* To make larger; to speak or write in greater detail. enlargement, enlarger *n.*

en-light-en *v.* To give a broadening or revealing knowledge; to give spiritual guidance or light to. enlightenment *n.*

en-list *v.* To secure the help or active aid of. *Milit.* To sign-up for service with the armed forces. enlistment *n.*

en-liv-en *v.* To make livelier, cheerful or vigorous. enlivener *n.*

en masse *adv., Fr.* All together; grouped.

en-mesh *v.* To catch in a net; to entangle.

en-mi-ty *n., pl.* -ties Deep hatred; hostility.

en-no-ble *v.* To make noble or honorable in quality or nature; to confer the rank of nobility. ennoblement *n.*

en-nui *n.* Boredom; weariness.

e-nor-mi-ty *n., pl.* -ties Excessive wickedness; an outrageous offense or crime.

e-nor-mous *adj.* Very great in size or degree. enormously *adv.*, -ness *n.*

e-nough *adj.* Adequate to satisfy demands or needs. *adv.* To a satisfactory degree.

en-quire *v.* Variation of inquire.

en-rage *v.* To put or throw into a rage.

en-rap-ture *v.* To enter into a state of rapture; to delight.

en-rich *v.* To make rich or richer; to make more productive.

en-roll *or* **en-rol** *v.* To enter, place, or write one's name on a roll, register, or record. enrollment, enrollment *n.*

en-sconce *v.* To settle securely; to shelter.

en-sem-ble *n.* A group of complementary parts that are in harmony; a coordinated outfit of clothing; a group of people performing together; music for two or more performers.

en-shrine *v.* To place in a shrine; to hold sacred. enshrinement *n.*

en-shroud *v.* To cover with a shroud.

en-sign *n.* An identifying flag or banner, as one displayed on a ship or aircraft. *Milit.* A commissioned officer of the lowest rank in the U.S. Navy or Coast Guard.

en-si-lage *n.* The process of storing and preserving green fodder in a silo; fodder that has been stored. ensile *v.*

en-slave *v.* To make a slave of; to put in bondage. enslavement *n.*

en-snare *v.* To catch; to trap.

en-sue *v.* To follow as a consequence.

en-sure *v.* To make certain of.

en-tail *v.* To have as a necessary accompaniment or result; to restrict the inheritance of property to a certain line of heirs. entailment *n.*

en-tan-gle *v.* To tangle; to complicate; to confuse. entanglement *n.*

en-tente *n., Fr.* A mutual agreement between governments for cooperative action; the parties to an entente.

en-ter *v.* To go or come into; to penetrate; to begin; to become a member of or participant in; in law, to make a record of.

en-ter-prise *n.* A large or risky undertaking; a business organization; boldness and energy in practical affairs.

en-ter-tain *v.* To harbor or give heed to; to accommodate; receive as a guest; to amuse. entertainer, entertainment *n.*

en-thrall *v.* To fascinate; to captivate. enthrallment *n.*

en-throne *v.* To place on a throne.

en-thu-si-asm *n.* Intense feeling for a

cause; eagerness. **enthusiast** *n.*, **enthusiastic** *adj.*

en-tice *v.* To attract by arousing desire. **enticer, enticement** *n.*

en-tire *adj.* Having no part left out; whole; complete. **entirely** *adv.*

en-ti-tle *v.* To give a name to; to furnish with a right. **entitlement** *n.*

en-ti-ty *n., pl.* **-ties** The fact of real existence; something that exists alone.

en-tomb *v.* To place in a tomb. **-ment** *n.*

en-to-mol-o-gy *n.* The study of insects. **entomologist** *n.*, **entomologic** *adj.*

en-trails *pl., n.* Internal organs of man or animals.

en-trance *n.* The act of entering; the means or place of entry; the first appearance of an actor in a play.

en-trance *v.* To fascinate; enchant. **entrancement** *n.*, **entrancingly** *adv.*

en-trap *v.* To catch in a trap. **-ment** *n.*

en-treat *v.* To make an earnest request of or for.

en-trench *v.* To dig a trench, as for defense; to fix or sit firmly. **-ment** *n.*

en-tre-pre-neur *n., Fr.* A person who launches or manages a business venture. **entrepreneurial** *adj.*

en-trust *v.* To transfer to another for care or performance; to give as a trust or responsibility.

en-try *n., pl.* **-tries** An opening or place for entering; an item entered in a book, list, or register.

en-twine *v.* To twine about or together.

e-nu-mer-ate *v.* To count off one by one. **enumeration, enumerator** *n.*

e-nun-ci-ate *v.* To pronounce with clarity; to announce; proclaim. **enunciation** *n.*

en-ve-lope *n.* Something that covers or encloses; a paper case, especially for a letter, having a flap for sealing. *v.* To completely enclose.

en-ven-om *v.* To make poisonous; to embitter.

en-vi-a-ble *adj.* Highly desirable. **-ly** *adv.*

en-vi-ron-ment *n.* Surroundings; the combination of external conditions which affect the development and existence of an individual, group, or organism. **-al** *adj.*, **-ly** *adv.*

en-vi-ron-men-tal-ist *n.* A person who seeks to preserve the natural environment.

en-vi-rons *pl., n.* A surrounding region; a place; outskirts, especially of a city.

en-vis-age *v.* To have or form a mental image of.

en-voy *n.* A messenger or agent; a diplomatic representative who is dispatched on a special mission.

en-vy *n., pl.* **-vies** A feeling of discontent or resentment for someone else's possessions or advantages; any object of envy. *v.* To feel envy because of or toward. **envious** *adj.*

en-zyme *n., Biochem.* Proteins produced by living organisms that function as biochemical catalysts in animals and plants. **enzymatic** *adj.*

e-o-li-an *adj., Geol.* Caused by or transmitted by the wind.

e-on *n.* An indefinite period of time.

ep-au-let *or* **ep-au-lette** *n.* A shoulder ornament, as on a military uniform.

e-pergne *n.* An ornamental centerpiece for holding flowers or fruit, used on a dinner table.

e-phed-rine *n., Chem.* A white, odorless alkaloid used to relieve nasal congestion.

e-phem-er-al *adj.* Lasting a very short time. **ephemerally** *adv.*

ep-ic *n.* A long narrative poem celebrating the adventures and achievements of a hero. **epic** *adj.*

ep-i-cen-ter *n.* The part of the earth's surface directly above the focus of an earthquake.

ep-i-cure *n.* One having refined tastes, especially in food and wine.

ep-i-dem-ic *adj.* Breaking out suddenly and affecting many individuals at the same time in a particular area, especially true of a contagious disease; anything that is temporarily widespread, as a fad. **epidemic** *n.*

ep-i-der-mis *n., Anat.*

Epidermis

Dermis

The outer, nonvascular layer of the skin. **epidermal** *adj.*

ep-i-glot-tis *n., Anat.* The leaf-shaped, elastic cartilage that covers the base of the tongue that covers the windpipe during the act of swallowing. **epiglottal** *adj.*

ep-i-gram *n.* A clever, brief, pointed remark or observation; a terse, witty poem or saying. **epigrammatic** *adj.*

ep-i-graph *n.* An inscription on a tomb, monument, etc.; a motto or quotation placed at the beginning of a literary work.

e-pig-ra-phy *n.* The study and interpretation of inscriptions. **epigrapher** *n.*

ep-i-lep-sy *n., Pathol.* A nervous disorder marked by attacks of unconsciousness with or without convulsions. **epileptic** *n. & adj.*

ep-i-logue *or* **ep-i-log** *n.* A short speech given by an actor to the audience at the end of a play; an appended chapter placed at the end of a novel or book, etc.

ep-i-neph-rine *or* **ep-i-neph-rin** *n., Biochem.* A hormone secreted by the adrenal medulla of the adrenal glands that raises the blood pressure and quickens the pulse, used in synthesized form as a cardiovascular stimulant.

e-piph-a-ny *n.* The Christian festival held on January 6th, celebrating the manifestation of Christ to the Gentiles as represented by the Magi; also known as the Twelfth Day.

ep-i-phyte n., Bot. A plant that receives its nourishment from the air and rain while growing on another plant, as an orchid, moss, or lichen. **epiphytic** adj.

e-pis-co-pa-cy n., pl. -cies The government of a church by bishops; an episcopate.

e-pis-co-pal adj. Pertaining to or governed by bishops.

e-pis-co-pate n. The term, rank, or position of a bishop; bishops as a group.

ep-i-sode n. A section of a poem, novel, etc., that is complete in itself; an occurrence; an incident. **episodic** adj.

e-pis-tle n. A formal letter. Epistle One of the letters in the New Testament. **epistolary** adj.

ep-i-taph n. An inscription, as on a tomb or gravestone, in memory of a deceased person.

ep-i-the-li-um n., pl. -liums or -lia Biol. The thin, membranous tissue consisting of one or more layers of cells, forming the covering of the outer bodily surface and most of the internal surfaces and organs. **epithelial, epithelioid** adj.

ep-i-thet n. A term, word, or phrase used to characterize a person or thing; an abusive phrase or word.

e-pit-o-me n. A concise summary, as of a book; an extreme or typical example.

e-pit-o-mize v. To be a perfect example.

ep-och n. A point in time marking the beginning of a new era. **epochal** adj.

ep-ox-y n., pl. -ies Chem. A durable, corrosion-resistant resin used especially in surface glues and coatings.

eq-ua-ble adj. Not changing or varying; free from extremes; evenly proportioned; uniform; not easily upset.

e-qual adj. Of the same measurement, quantity, or value as another; having the same privileges or rights.

e-qual-ize v. To become or make equal or uniform equalization, equalizer n.

e-qual op-por-tu-ni-ty em-ploy-er n. An employer who does not discriminate on the basis of age, race, sex, religion, etc.

e-qua-nim-i-ty n. Composure.

e-quate v. To consider or make equal.

e-qua-tion n. The act or process of being equal; a mathematical statement expressing the equality of two quantities, usually shown as $(=)$.

e-qua-tor n. The great imaginary circle around the earth; a line lying in a plane perpendicular to the earth's polar axis. **equatorial** adj.

eq-uer-ry n., pl. -ries The officer in charge of the horses of royalty; the personal attendant to a member of the British royal family.

e-ques-tri-an adj. Pertaining or relating to horsemanship. n. The person who rides or performs on a horse. **equestrienne** n.

e-qui-an-gu-lar adj., Geom. Having all angles equal.

e-qui-dis-tant adj. Having equal distances.

e-qui-lat-er-al adj. Having all sides equal. **equilateral** n.

e-qui-lib-ri-um n., pl. -ums Phys. The state of balance between two opposing forces or influences; any state of compromise, adjustment, or balance.

e-quine adj. Pertaining to or like a horse.

e-qui-nox n. Either of the two times a year when the sun crosses the celestial equator and the days and nights are equal in time. **equinoctial** adj.

e-quip v. To furnish or fit with whatever is needed for any undertaking or purpose; to dress for a certain purpose or reason.

eq-ui-page n. A carriage that is equipped with horses and attendants.

e-quip-ment n. The state or act of being equipped; the material one is provided with for a special purpose.

eq-ui-ta-ble adj., pl. -ties Being impartial in treatment of judgment. **equitableness** n., **equitably** adv.

eq-ui-ta-tion n. The art or act of horse riding.

eq-ui-ty n., pl. -ties Fairness or impartiality; the value of property beyond a mortgage or liability; in law, justice based on the concepts of fairness and ethics.

e-quiv-a-lent adj. Being equal or virtually equal, as in effect or meaning. **equivalence, equivalency, equivalent** n., **equivalently** adv.

e-quiv-o-cal adj. Ambiguous; questionable. **equivocally** adv.

e-quiv-o-cate v. To use intentionally evasive or vague language. **equivocation, equivocator** n.

-er n., suff. A thing or person that performs the action of the root verb; a person concerned with a trade or profession, as a banker, teacher, etc.; one who lives in or comes from a certain area, as a northerner, midwesterner, etc.; used to form the comparative usage degree of adverbs and adjectives.

e-ra n. An extended period of time that is reckoned from a specific date or point in the past and used as the basis of a chronology.

e-rad-i-cate v. To destroy utterly; to remove by the roots. **eradicator, eradication** n., **eradicable** adj.

e-rase v. To remove something written. Slang To kill. **erasable** adj., **eraser, erasure** n.

er-bi-um n., Chem. A soft, metallic, silvery, rare-earth element, symbolized by Er.

ere prep., Poet. Prior to; before.

e-rect adj. In a vertical position; standing up straight. v. To construct; build. Physiol. The state of erectile tissue, as through an influx of blood.

ere-long adv., Archaic Before long.

er-e-mite n. A hermit.

erg n., Phys. A unit of work or energy.

er-go conj. & adv. Consequently; therefore.

er-gos-ter-ol n., Biochem. A steroid alcohol synthesized by yeast from sugars, converted under ultraviolet radiation to vitamin D.

er-got n. The disease of rye and other cereal plants; a drug used to contract involuntary muscles and to control hemorrhage.

er-mine n.

A weasel whose fur changes from brown to white depending on the season.

e-rode v. To wear away gradually by constant friction; to corrode; to eat away.

e-rog-e-nous adj. Responsive to sexual stimulation.

e-ro-sion n. The state or process of being eroded. **erosional** adj.

e-ro-sive adj. Eroding or tending to erode. **erosiveness** n.

e-rot-ic adj. Pertaining to or promoting sexual desire. **erotically** adv., **eroticism** n.

e-rot-ica pl., n. Art or literature with an erotic quality.

err v. To make a mistake; to sin.

er-rand n. A short trip to carry a message or to perform a specified task, usually for someone else.

er-rant adj. Wandering or traveling about in search of adventure; straying from what is proper or customary.

er-rat-ic adj. Lacking a fixed course. Med. Irregular; inconsistent. **erratically** adv.

er-ra-tum n., pl. -ta An error in writing or printing.

er-ro-ne-ous adj. To have or contain an error. **-ly** adv., **erroneousness** n.

er-ror n. Something said, believed, or done incorrectly; a mistake; the state of being wrong or mistaken; in baseball, a misplay by a team member who is not batting.

er-satz adj. A substitute that is usually inferior; artificial.

erst-while adj., Archaic Former.

er-u-dite adj. Scholarly.

er-u-di-tion n. Great learning.

e-rupt v. To burst forth violently and suddenly; to explode with steam, lava, etc., as a volcano or geyser; to break out in a skin rash or pimples.

-ery n., suff. A place of business; a business, or a place where something is performed or done: bakery; the collection of things; practice or act of something; the qualities or characteristics of something; slavery.

er-y-sip-e-las n. An acute, inflammatory, and very uncomfortable skin disease resulting from streptococcus.

e-ryth-ro-cyte n. A disk-shaped blood cell that contains hemoglobin and is responsible for the red color of blood.

es-ca-late v. To intensify, increase, or enlarge. **escalation** n.

es-ca-la-tor n. A moving stairway with steps attached to an endless belt.

es-cal-lop n. & v. Variation of scallop.

es-ca-pade n. Reckless or playful behavior; a prankish trick.

es-cape v. To break free from capture, confinement, restraint, etc; to fade from the memory; to enjoy temporary freedom from unpleasant realities. **escape, escapee, escaper** n.

es-cape-ment n., Mech. A device used in timepieces to control the movement of the wheel and supply energy impulses to a pendulum or balance; a typewriter mechanism that controls the horizontal movement of the carriage.

escape velocity n., Phys. The minimum velocity that a rocket or anybody must attain to escape or overcome the gravitational field.

escape wheel n., Mech. The rotating notched wheel in an escapement.

es-cap-ism n. An escape from unpleasant realities through daydreams or other mental diversions. **escapist** n. & adj.

es-ca-role n. Endive leaves used for salads.

es-carp-ment n. A steep slope or drop; a long cliff formed by erosion.

-escense n., suff. To give off light in a certain way, as florescence.

-escent adj., suff. To give off light in a special way, as phosphorescent; beginning to be.

es-chew v. To shun or avoid. **eschewal** n.

es-cort n. A group or individual person accompanying another so as to give protection or guidance; a male who accompanies a female in public.

es-cri-toire n. A writing desk.

es-crow n. In law, a written deed, contract, or money placed in the custody of a third party until specified conditions are met.

es-cu-do n., pl. -dos The monetary unit of Portugal.

es-cutch-eon n. A shield-shaped surface with an emblem bearing a coat of arms; a protective plate, as for a keyhole.

-ese n. & adj., suff. An inhabitant or native of; in the language or style of.

e-soph-a-gus n., pl. -gi Anat. The muscular, membranous tube through which food passes on the way from the mouth to the stomach. **esophageal** adj.

es-o-ter-ic adj. Confidential; kept secret; understood or meant for only a particular and often very small group.

es-pa-drille n. A shoe with a canvas upper and a flexible sole.

es-pal-ier n. A flat framework used to train shrubs to grow a particular way.

es-pe-cial adj. Having a very special place; apart or above others; exceptional. **especially** adv.

es-pi-o-nage n. The act or practice of spying to obtain secret intelligence.

es-pla-nade n. A flat, open stretch of land along a shoreline.

es-pou-sal n. Support or adoption, as of a cause; a wedding.

es-pouse v. To make something one's own; to take as a spouse; to marry; to give in marriage.

es-pres-so *n., pl.* **-sos** A strong coffee brewed by steam pressure from darkly-roasted beans.

es-prit *n.* Spirit; wit; mental liveliness.

es-prit de corps *n., Fr.* A group's spirit of enthusiasm and devotion to the common goals of the group.

es-py *v.* To catch a quick view or sight of.

-esque *adj., suff.* Resembling.

es-quire *n.* The title of courtesy or respect; sometimes written as Esq. behind a man's last name.

-ess *n., suff.* Female.

es-say *n.* A short composition that deals with a single topic and expresses the author's viewpoint on a subject; an effort or attempt.
essayer, essayist *n.*, essay *v.*

es-sence *n.* The real nature in which something consists; the most important element; an immaterial spirit; being.

es-sen-tial *adj.* Necessary; indispensable; containing, or being an essence.
essential, essentially *adv.*
essentiality, essentialness *n.*,

-est *adj. & adv., suff.* Used to form the superlative degree of adverbs and adjectives.

es-tab-lish *v.* To make permanent, stable, or secure; to install; to create or find; to cause to be accepted or recognized; to prove.

es-tab-lish-ment *n.* The state of being established; a place of business or residence; those collectively who occupy positions of influence and status in a society.

es-tate *n.* A usually large or extensive piece of land containing a large house; in law, the nature, degree, and extent of ownership or use of property.

es-teem *v.* To regard with respect.

es-ter *n., Chem.* Any of a class of organic compounds formed by the reaction of an acid with an alcohol.

es-thet-ic *adj.* Variation of aesthetic.

es-ti-ma-ble *adj.* Worthy of respect or admiration. **-ness** *n.*, estimably *adv.*

es-ti-mate *v.* To form or give an approximate opinion or calculation. *n.* A preliminary opinion or statement of the approximate cost for certain work.

es-ti-val *adj.* Pertaining to or of summer.

es-ti-vate *v.* To pass the summer in a state of dormancy.

es-trange *v.* To arouse hated or indifference where there had been love and caring; to disassociate or remove oneself. estrangement *n.*

es-tro-gen *n., Biochem.* Any of various steroid hormones that regulate female reproductive functions and secondary sex characteristics. estrogenic *adj.*

es-tu-ar-y *n., pl.* **-ies** The wide mouth of a river where the current meets the sea and is influenced by tides.

etch *v.* To engrave or cut into the surface by the action of acid; to sketch or outline by scratching lines with a pointed instrument. etcher *n.*

e-ter-nal *adj.* Existing without beginning or end; unending; meant to last indefinitely. eternal, eternality, eternalness *n.*, eternally *adv.*

e-ter-ni-ty *n., pl.* **-ties** Existence without beginning or end; forever; the immeasurable extent of time; the endless time after a person dies.

eth-ane *n., Chem.* An odorless, colorless, gaseous hydrocarbon from the methane series that is contained in crude petroleum and in illuminating gas.

eth-a-nol *n., Chem.* The alcohol obtained after the distillation of certain fermented sugars or starches; the intoxicant in liquors, wines, and beers; alcohol.

e-ther *n., Chem.* A highly flammable liquid compound with a characteristic odor, used as a solvent and an anesthetic; the clear upper regions of space.

e-the-re-al *adj.* Very airy and light; highly refined; delicate; heavenly. ethereally *adv.*, etherealy *adv.*

eth-ic *n., pl.* **-ics** The system of moral values; the principle of right or good conduct.

eth-i-cal *adj.* Relating to or of ethics; conforming to right principles of conduct as accepted by a specific profession, as medicine. ethically *adv.*

eth-nic *adj.* Relating to or of a national, cultural, or racial group. ethnicity *n.*

eth-nog-ra-phy *n., pl.* **-phies** The branch of anthropology dealing with the classification and description of primitive human cultures.

eth-nol-o-gy *n., pl.* **-gies** The branch of anthropology that is concerned with the study of ethnic and racial groups, their cultures, origins, and distribution.

eth-yl *n., Chem.* An organic radical occurring in ether and alcohol; a univalent hydrocarbon radical; any gasoline that is treated with tetraethyl lead to reduce engine knock. **-ic** *adj.*

eth-yl-ene *n., Chem.* A colorless, flammable gas refined from natural gas and petroleum and used as a fuel.

ethylene glycol *n., Chem.* A colorless, syrupy alcohol used as an antifreeze, solvent, and lubricant.

ethyl ether *n., Chem.* Ether.

e-ti-ol-o-gy *n.* The science and study of causes or origins. *Med.* The theory of the cause of a particular disease.
etiologic, etiological *adj.*,
etiologically *adv.*, etiologist *n.*

et-i-quette *n.* The prescribed rules, forms and practices, established for behavior in polite society or in official or professional life.

-ette *n., suff.* Small; female.

et-y-mol-o-gy *n., pl.* **-gies** The history of a word as shown by breaking it down into basic parts, tracing it back to the earliest known form, and indicating its changes in form and meaning; the branch of linguistics that deals with

etymologies. etymological,
etymologic adj., etymologist n.

et-y-mon n., pl. -mons or -ma The earlier form of a word in the same language or in the ancestral language.

eu-ca-lyp-tus n., pl. -tuses or -ti A large, native Australian tree with very aromatic leaves that yield an oil used medicinally.

eu-chre n. A card game for two to four players played with 32 cards in which the winning side must take three of five tricks. Informal To trick or cheat.

eu-gen-ics n. The science of improving the physical and mental qualities of human beings through genetics.
eugenic adj., eugenicist n.

eu-lo-gize v. To write or deliver a eulogy for. eulogist, eulogizer n.

eu-lo-gy n., pl. -gies A speech that honors a person or thing, usually delivered at a funeral; high praise. eulogistic adj., eulogistic adj., eulogistically adv.

eu-nuch n. A castrated man.

eu-phe-mism n. A substitution for a word or expression that is thought to be too strong, blunt, or painful for another person. euphemistic adj., euphemistically adv.

eu-pho-ny n., pl. -nies The agreeable sound of spoken words.
euphonious adj., euphoniously adv.

eu-pho-ri-a n. A very strong feeling of elation or well-being. euphoric adj.

eu-re-ka interj. An expression of triumph or achievement.

eu-ro-pi-um n., Chem. A soft, silvery-white, rare-earth element used in nuclear research, symbolized by Eu.

eu-sta-chian tube n., Anat. The passage between the middle ear and the pharynx that equalizes the air pressure between the tympanic cavity and the atmosphere.

eu-tha-na-sia n. The act or practice of putting to death painlessly a person suffering from an incurable disease; also called mercy killing.

eu-then-ics n. The study of improving the physical and mental qualities of human beings by controlling the environmental factors. euthenist n.

e-vac-u-ate v. To leave a threatened area, town, building, etc.; to empty; to remove the contents. Physiol. To discharge or eject, as from the bowels.
evacuation, evacuator n.

e-vac-u-ee n. A person who is evacuated from a hazardous place.

e-vade v. To baffle; to elude; to get away from by using cleverness or tricks.

e-val-u-ate v. To examine carefully; to determine the value of; to appraise.
evaluation, evaluator n.

ev-a-nesce v. To disappear; to fade away.

ev-a-nes-cent adj. Vanishing or passing quickly; fleeting. evanescence n., evanescently adv.

e-van-gel-i-cal or e-van-gel-ic adj. Relating to the Christian gospel, especially the four Gospels of the New Testament; maintaining the doctrine that the Bible is the only rule of faith.
evangelicalism n., evangelically adv.

e-van-gel-ism n. The zealous preaching and spreading of the gospel.

e-van-gel-ize v. To preach the gospel; to convert to Christianity. -ation n.

e-vap-o-rate v. To convert into vapor; to remove the liquid or moisture from fruit, milk, etc., so as to concentrate or dry it. evaporative adj., evaporator n.

e-va-sion n. The act or means of evading.

e-va-sive adj. Being intentionally vague; equivocal. -ly adv., evasiveness n.

eve n. The evening before a special day or holiday; the period immediately preceding some event; evening.

e-ven adj. Having a flat, smooth, and level surface; having no irregularities; smooth; on the same line or plane; equally matched; not owing or having anything owed to one; exactly divisible by 2; opposed to odd. to break even Informal To end with neither profit or loss, as in business. to get even One's full measure of revenge.
evenly adv., evenness n.

e-ven-hand-ed adj. Fair; impartial.
evenhandedly adv., evenhandedness n.

eve-ning n. The time between sunset and bedtime.

eve-ning dress n. Formal attire for evening.

eve-ning prim-rose n. A biennial herb with conspicuous yellow flowers that open in the evening.

evening star n. The brightest planet visible in the west just after sunset, especially Venus.

e-ven-song n. An evening prayer.

e-vent n. A significant occurrence; something that takes place; the actual or possible set of circumstances; a real or contingent situation; the final outcome; one of the parts of a sports program. eventful adj.
eventfully adv., eventfulness n.

e-ven-tide n. Evening.

e-ven-tu-al adj. Happening or expected to happen in due course of time.
eventually adv.

e-ven-tu-al-i-ty n., pl. -ties A likely or possible occurrence; the conceivable outcome.

e-ven-tu-ate v. To result ultimately; to come out eventually.

ev-er adv. At any time; on any occasion; by any possible chance or conceivable way; at all times; throughout the entire course of time.

ev-er-glade n. A tract of low, swampy land.

ev-er-green adj. A tree that has green foliage throughout the year.

ev-er-last-ing adj. Lasting or existing forever; eternal. n. One of several plants, chiefly of the aster family, whose flowers keep their form and color when dried. everlastingly adv.

ev-er-more adv., Poet. For and at all time to come; always.

e-vert v. To turn inside out or outward.

ev-er-y adj. Without exceptions; the utmost; all possible. **every now and then** From time to time; occasionally. **every other** Each alternate. **every which way** *Informal* In every way or direction and with very little order.

ev-er-y-bod-y *pron.* Every person.

ev-er-y-day *adj.* Happening every day; daily; suitable for ordinary days.

ev-er-y-one *pron.* Everybody; every person.

ev-er-y-place *adv.* Everywhere.

ev-er-y-thing *pron.* All things; whatever exists; whatever is needed, relevant, or important; the essential thing; the only thing that really matters.

ev-er-y-where *adv.* In, at, or to everyplace.

e-vict *v.* To put out or expel a tenant by legal process. **evictor, eviction** *n.*

ev-i-dence *n.* Signs or facts on which a conclusion can be based. *v.* To indicate clearly. **in evidence** Clearly present; evident.

ev-i-dent *adj.* Easily understood or seen; obvious. **evidently** *adv.*

e-vil *adj.* Morally bad or wrong; causing injury or any other undesirable result; marked by misfortune or distress; low in public esteem. **The Evil One** Satan.

e-vil-do-er *n.* A person who does evil to another. **evildoing** *n.*

e-vil-mind-ed *adj.* Obsessed with vicious or evil thoughts or intentions. **evil-mindedly** *adv.,* **evil-mindedness** *n.*

e-vince *v.* To demonstrate or indicate clearly; to give an outward sign of having a quality or feeling.

e-vis-cer-ate *v.* To remove the vital part of something; to remove the entrails. **evisceration** *n.*

e-voke *v.* To call or summon forth; to draw forth or produce a reaction; to summon up the spirits by or as by incantations. **evocation** *n.,* **evocative** *adj.,* **evocatively** *adv.*

ev-o-lu-tion *n.* The gradual process of development or change. *Biol.* The theory that all forms of life originated by descent from earlier forms. **-ary** *adj.,* **evolutionism, evolutionist** *n.*

e-volve *v.* To develop or change gradually. *Biol.* To be developed by evolutionary processes; to develop or work out. **evolvement** *n.*

ewe *n.* A female sheep.

ew-er *n.*

A large, wide-mouthed pitcher or jug.

ex *n.* The letter x. *Slang* A former spouse.

ex- *pref.* Out of; former.

ex *abbr.* Example; exchange.

ex-ac-er-bate *v.* To make more severe or worse; to aggravate. **exacerbation** *n.*

ex-act *adj.* Perfectly complete and clear in every detail; accurate in every detail with something taken as a model; similar. *v.* To be extremely careful about accuracy and detail; to force un-

justly for the payment of something; to insist upon as a strict right or obligation; to call for or require. **exaction, exactness** *n.,* **exactly** *adv.*

ex-act-ing *adj.* Making severe demands; rigorous; involving constant attention, hard work, etc. **exactingly** *adv.,* **exactingness** *n.*

ex-act-i-tude *n.* The quality of being exact.

ex-ag-ger-ate *v.* To look upon or to represent something as being greater than it really is; to make greater in intensity or size than would be normal or expected. **exaggerated, -tive** *adj.,* **exaggeration, exaggerator** *n.*

ex-alt *v.* To raise in character, honor, rank, etc.; to praise or glorify; to increase the intensity of. **exalted** *adj.,* **exaltedly** *adv.,* **exalter, exaltation** *n.*

ex-am *n., Slang* An examination.

ex-am-i-na-tion *n.* A test of skill or knowledge; the act of examining or the state of being examined; medical testing and scrutiny. **-al** *adj.*

ex-am-ine *v.* To observe or inspect; to test by questions or exercises, as to fitness or qualification. **examinee, examiner** *n.*

ex-am-ple *n.* One that is representative as a sample; one worthy of imitation; an object or instance of punishment, reprimand, etc.; a previous instance or case that is identical with or similar to something that is under consideration; a problem or exercise in algebra, arithmetic, etc. **to set an example** To act in such a way as to arouse others to imitation.

ex-as-per-ate *v.* To make frustrated or angry; to irritate. **exasperatingly** *adv.,* **exasperation** *n.*

ex-ca-vate *v.* To dig a hole or cavity; to form or make a tunnel, hole, etc., by digging, scooping, or hollowing out; to remove or uncover by digging; to unearth. **excavation, excavator** *n.*

ex-ceed *v.* To surpass in quality or quantity; to go beyond the limit. **exceeding** *adj.*

ex-ceed-ing-ly *adv.* Greater than; to an extraordinary degree or extreme.

ex-cel *v.* To surpass or to do better than others.

ex-cel-lence *n.* The state or quality of being superior or excellent; a superior trait or quality.

Ex-cel-len-cy *n., pl.* **-cies** An honorary title or form of address for high officials, as bishops or ambassadors.

ex-cel-lent *adj.* The best quality; exceptionally good. **excellently** *adv.*

ex-cel-si-or *n.* Long, firm wood shavings used in packing to protect delicate materials. *adj.* Upward; higher.

ex-cept *prep.* With the omission or exclusion of; aside from; not including; leaving out.

ex-cept-ing *prep.* With the exception that.

ex-cep-tion *n.* The act of or state of being excepted; something that is excluded from or does not conform to a general class, rule, or principle; criticism or objection.

ex-cep-tion-a-ble *adj.* Open to objection or exception. **exceptionability** *n.*, **exceptionably** *adv.*

ex-cep-tion-al *adj.* Being an exception to the rule; well above average. **exceptionally** *adv.*

ex-cerpt *n.* A passage from a book, speech, etc. *v.* To select and cite.

ex-cess *n.* The amount or condition of going beyond what is necessary, usual, or proper; overindulgence, as in drink or food.

ex-ces-sive *adj.* Exceeding what is usual, necessary, or proper; extreme. **excessively** *adv.*, **excessiveness** *n.*

ex-change *v.* To give in return for something else; to trade; to return as unsatisfactory and get a replacement. *n.* The substitution of one thing for another; a place where brokers meet to buy, sell, or trade; the mutual receiving and giving of equal sums or money. **exchangeable** *adj.*

ex-cheq-uer *n.* The treasury of a nation or organization; financial resources; funds. *Slang* One's total financial resources.

ex-cise *n.* The indirect or internal tax on the production, consumption, or sale of a commodity, such as liquor or tobacco, that is produced, sold, and used or transported within a country.

ex-cise *v.* To remove surgically. **excision** *n.*

ex-cit-a-ble *adj.* To be easily excited. **-ly** *adv.*, **excitability, excitableness** *n.*

ex-cite *v.* To stir up strong feeling, action, or emotion; to stimulate the emotions of; to bring about; to induce. **-ation, -ment** *n.*, **-edly, excitingly** *adv.*

ex-claim *v.* To cry out abruptly; to utter suddenly, as from emotion.

ex-cla-ma-tion *n.* An abrupt or sudden forceful utterance. **exclamatory** *adj.*

exclamation point *n.* A punctuation mark (!) used after an interjection or exclamation.

ex-clude *v.* To keep out; to omit from consideration; to put out. **exclusion** *n.*

ex-clu-sive *adj.* Intended for the sole use and purpose of a single individual or group; intended for or possessed by a single source; having no duplicate; the only one; complete. **exclusively** *adv.*, **exclusiveness, exclusivity** *n.*

ex-com-mu-ni-cate *v.* To deprive the right of church membership. **excommunication** *n.*

ex-co-ri-ate *v.* To tear the skin or wear off; to censure harshly. **excoriation** *n.*

ex-cre-ment *n.* Bodily waste, especially feces. **excremental** *adj.*

ex-cre-ta *pl., n.* Excretions from the body such as sweat, urine, etc.

ex-crete *v.* To throw off or eliminate waste matter by normal discharge from the body. **excretion** *n.*, **excretory** *adj.*

ex-cru-ci-at-ing *adj.* Intensely painful; agonizing. **excruciatingly** *adv.*

ex-cul-pate *v.* To free from wrong doing; to prove innocent of guilt. **exculpation** *n.*, **exculpatory** *adj.*

ex-cur-sion *n.* A short trip, usually made for pleasure; a trip available at a special reduced fare. *Phys.* The oscillating movement between two points; also, half of this total distance. **excursionist** *n.*

ex-cur-sive *adj.* To go in one direction and then another; rambling; digressive.

ex-cuse *v.* To ask forgiveness or pardon for oneself; to grant pardon or forgiveness; to overlook or accept; to apologize for; to justify; to allow one to leave; to release. *n.* A reason, justification, or explanation. **poor excuse** *Informal* An inferior example for something. **-able** *adj.*, **excusably** *adv.*

exec *abbr.* Executive; executor.

ex-e-cra-ble *adj.* Extremely bad; detestable; revolting. **execrableness** *n.*, **execrably** *adv.*

ex-e-crate *v.* To detest; to feel or express detestation for; to abhor. **execration, execrator** *n.*

ex-e-cute *v.* To carry out; to put into effect; to validate, as by signing; to carry out what has been called for in a will; to put to death by the legal authority.

ex-e-cu-tion *n.* The act of executing a job or task; a putting to death as a result of a legal decision, as the death penalty.

ex-e-cu-tion-er *n.* A person who puts others to death; a person who carries out a legal execution.

ex-ec-u-tive *n.* A manager or administrator in an organization; the branch of the government responsible for activating or putting the laws of a country into effect and for carrying out plans or policies. **executively** *adv.*

executive Council *n.* The cabinet of a provincial government in Canada.

ex-ec-u-tor *n.* The person appointed to carry out the reading and execution of a will. **executorial** *adj.*

ex-e-ge-sis *n., pl.* **-ses** An interpretation or explanation of a text. **exegetic** *adj.*, **exegetically** *adv.*

ex-em-plar *n.* Something that serves as a worthy model or imitation; a typical example.

ex-em-pla-ry *adj.* Serving as a model; worthy of imitation; commendable.

ex-em-pli-fy *v.* To show by giving examples; to be an example of. **exemplification** *n.*

ex-empt *v.* To free or excuse from an obligation or duty to which others are subject. **exempt** *adj.*, **exemption** *n.*

ex-er-cise *n.* The act of performing drills; the act of training or developing oneself; something that is done to maintain or increase a skill, such as practice on the piano. **exercises** *pl.* A ceremony, etc., such as a graduation. **exercise** *v.*, **exerciser** *n.*

ex-ert *v.* To put into action, as influence

or force; to put oneself through a strenuous effort. **exertion** n.

ex-hale v. To breathe out; the opposite of inhale; to breathe forth or give off, as air, vapor, or aroma.

ex-haust v. To make extremely tired; to drain oneself of resources, strength, etc. n. The escape or discharge of waste gases, working fluid, etc.; the waste gases, etc. that escape; the device through which waste gases are released or expelled. **exhaustible** adj., **exhaustion** n.

ex-haus-tive adj. Tending to exhaust or that which exhausts. **exhaustively** adv.

ex-hib-it v. To display, as to put up for public view; to bring documents or evidence into a court of law. **exhibition, exhibitor** n.

ex-hi-bi-tion-ism n. The practice of deliberately drawing undue attention to oneself. **-ist** n., **exhibitionistic** adj.

ex-hil-a-rate v. To elate, make cheerful, or refresh. **-tion** n., **-tive** adj.

ex-hort v. To urge by earnest appeal or argument; to advise or recommend strongly. **exhortation** n.

ex-hume v. To dig up and remove from a grave; to disinter. **exhumation** n.

ex-i-gen-cy n., pl. **-cies** The quality or state of being exigent. usually pl. A pressing need or necessity.
exigence n., **exigent** adj.

ex-ig-u-ous adj. Extremely small. **-ity** n.

ex-ile n. The separation by necessity or choice from one's native country or home; banishment; one who has left or been driven from his or her country. v. To banish or expel from one's native country or home.

ex-ist v. To have actual being or reality; to live.

ex-is-tence n. The fact or state of existing, living, or occurring; the manner of existing. **existent** adj.

ex-is-ten-tial adj. Based on experience; of or relating to existentialism. **existentially** adv.

ex-is-ten-tial-ism n. A philosophy that stresses the active role of the will rather than of reason in facing problems posed by a hostile universe. **existentialist** n.

ex-it n. A way or passage out; the act of going away or out; the departure from a stage, as in a play. **exit** v.

ex-o-bi-ol-o-gy n. The search for and study of extraterrestrial life. **exobiologist** n.

ex-o-dus n. A going forth; a departure of large numbers of people, as that of Moses and the Israelites as described in Exodus, the second book of the Old Testament.

ex officio adj. & adv., L. By virtue of or because of office or position.

ex-og-e-nous n., Biol. That which is derived from external causes.

ex-on-er-ate v. To free or clear one from accusation or blame; to relieve or free from responsibility. **exoneration** n.

ex-or-bi-tant adj. Beyond usual and proper limits, as in price or demand. **exorbitance** n., **exorbitantly** adv.

ex-or-cise v. To cast out or expel an evil spirit by prayers or incantations; to free from an evil spirit. **exorciser, exorcism, exorcist** n.

ex-o-sphere n., Meteor. The region of the earth's atmosphere starting about 400 miles up.

ex-o-ther-mic or **ex-o-ther-mal** adj. Releasing rather than absorbing heat.

ex-ot-ic adj. Belonging by nature or origin to another part of the world; foreign; strangely different and fascinating. **exotically** adv.

ex-pand v. To increase the scope, range, volume, or size; to open up or spread out; to develop more fully in form or details. **expandable** adj., **expander** n.

ex-panse n. A wide, open stretch.

ex-pan-sion n. The act of or state of being expanded; the amount of increase in range, size, or volume.

ex-pan-sive adj. Capable of expanding or inclined to expand; characterized by expansion; broad and extensive; open and generous; outgoing.
expansively adv., **expansiveness** n.

ex par-te adj. & adv. In law, giving only one side or point of view.

ex-pa-ti-ate v. To elaborate; to talk or write at length. **expatiation** n.

ex-pa-tri-ate v. To leave one's country and reside in another; to send into exile; to banish.
expatrite, expatriation n.

ex-pect v. To look forward to something as probable or certain; to look for as proper, right, or necessary. Slang To presume or suppose.

ex-pec-tan-cy n., pl. **-cies** The action or state of expecting; expectation; an object or amount of expectation.

ex-pec-tant adj. Expecting; pregnant. **expectantly** adv.

ex-pec-ta-tion n. The state or act of expecting; something that is expected and looked forward to. **expectations** pl. Something expected in the future.

ex-pec-to-rant adj. Promoting the discharge by spitting of the mucus from the respiratory tract. n. Any medicine that is used to promote expectoration.

ex-pec-to-rate v. To spit. **expectoration** n.

ex-pe-di-en-cy n., pl. **-cies** The state or quality of being expedient.

ex-pe-di-ent adj. Promoting narrow or selfish interests; pertaining to or prompted by interest rather than by what is right. **expediently** adv.

ex-pe-dite v. To speed up the progress or process of something; to do with quick efficiency. **expediter, expeditor** n.

ex-pe-di-tion n. A journey of some length for a definite purpose; the person or group and equipment that engage in such a journey; promptness.

ex-pe-di-tion-ar-y adj. Relating to or being an expedition; sent on military service abroad.

ex-pe-di-tious adj. Quick; speedy.
expeditiously adv., **expeditiousness** n.

ex-pel v. To drive or force out, as to dismiss from a school. **expellable** adj., **expeller, expulsion** n.

ex-pend v. To consume; to pay out or use up.

ex-pend-a-ble adj. Available for spending. Milit. Equipment or supplies that can be sacrificed. **expendability** n.

ex-pen-di-ture n. An amount spent; the act or process of expending.

ex-pense n. The outlay or consumption of money; the amount of money required to buy or do something. **expenses** pl. The funds that have been allotted or spent to cover incidental costs; the charges incurred by an employee while at or pertaining to work. Informal The reimbursement for such charges incurred.

ex-pen-sive adj. Costing a lot of money; high-priced. **-ly** adv., **-ness** n.

ex-pe-ri-ence n. The actual participation in something or the direct contact with; the knowledge or skill acquired from actual participation or training in an activity or event; one's total judgments or reactions based on one's past. **experience** v.

ex-pe-ri-enced adj. To be knowledgeable through actual practices, etc.

ex-per-i-ment n. The act or test performed to demonstrate or illustrate a truth; the conducting of such operations. **-al** adj., **experimentally** adv., **experimentation, experimenter** n.

ex-pert n. A person having great knowledge, experience, or skill in a certain field. adj. Skilled as the result of training or experience. **expertly** adv., **expertness** n.

ex-per-tise n. A specialized knowledge, ability, or skill in a particular area.

ex-pi-ate v. To atone for; to make amends for. **expiation, expiator** n., **expiatory** adj.

ex-pi-ra-tion n. The emission of breath; the act of breathing out.

ex-pire v. To come to an end; to breathe out, as from the mouth; to exhale. **expiration** n.

ex-plain v. To make understandable; to clarify; to give reasons for; to account for; to give an explanation for. **explainable, explanatory** adj., **explainer, explanation** n.

ex-ple-tive n. An exclamation, often profane. adj. A word added merely to fill out a sentence.

ex-pli-ca-ble adj. Capable of explanation.

ex-pli-cate v. To clear up the meaning of. **-tion, explicator** n., **explicative** adj.

ex-plic-it adj. Plainly expressed; specific; unreserved in expression; straightforward. **explicitly** adv., **explicitness** n.

ex-plode v. To cause to burst or blow up violently with a loud noise; to increase rapidly without control; to show to be false.

ex-ploit n. A deed or act that is notable. v. To use to the best advantage of; to make use of in a selfish or unethical way. **exploitable, exploitative** adj., **exploitation, exploiter** n.

ex-plore v. To examine and investigate in a systematic way; to travel through unfamiliar territory. **exploration, explorer** n., **exploratory** adj.

ex-plo-sion n. A sudden, violent release of energy; the sudden, violent outbreak of personal feelings.

ex-plo-sive adj. Marked by or pertaining to an explosion. n. A chemical preparation that explodes. **explosively** adv., **explosiveness** n.

ex-po-nent n. A person who represents or speaks for a cause or group; in mathematics, a number or symbol that indicates the number of times an expression is used as a factor. **exponential** adj., **exponentially** adv.

ex-port v. To carry or send merchandise or raw materials to other countries for resale or trade. n. A commodity exported. **exportable** adj., **exportation, exporter** n.

ex-pose v. To lay open, as to criticism or ridicule; to lay bare and uncovered; to reveal the identity of someone; to deprive of the necessities of heat, shelter, and protection. Photog. To admit light to a sensitized film or plate. **exposer** n.

ex-po-si-tion n. A statement of intent or meaning; a detailed presentation of subject matter; a commentary or interpretation; a large public exhibition. **expositor** n., **expository** adj.

ex post facto adj., L. After the fact and retroactive.

ex-pos-tu-late v. To reason earnstly with someone about the inadvisability of his or her actions in an effort to correct or dissuade that person. **-tion, -or** n., **expostulatory** adj.

ex-po-sure n. The act or state of being exposed; an indication of which way something faces. Photog. The act of exposing a sensitive plate or film; the time required for the film or plate to be exposed.

ex-pound v. To give a detailed statement of something; to explain the meaning at length. **expounder** n.

ex-press v. To formulate in words; to verbalize; to state; to comunicate through some medium other than words or signs; to squeeze or press out, as juice from fruit; to send goods, etc., by a fast or rapid means of delivery. adj. Explicit; precise. **expressly** adv.

ex-pres-sion n. Communication of opinion, thought, or feeling; the outward indication or manifestation of a condition, feeling, or quality; a particular phrase or word from a certain region of the country; a facial aspect or look that conveys a feeling; in mathematics, a symbol, sign, or set of that indicates something.

ex-pres-sion-ism n. An early 20th Century movement in the fine arts that emphasizes subjective expression of the artist's inner experiences rather than realistic representation.

expressionistic *adj.*, **expressionist** *n.*

ex-pres-sive *adj.* Of or characterized by expression; serving to indicate or express; full of expression.

expressively *adv.*, **expressiveness** *n.*

ex-press-ly *adv.* Plainly; in direct terms.

ex-press-way *n.* A multilane highway designed for rapid travel.

ex-pro-pri-ate *v.* To transfer or take property from the owner for public use; to deprive a person of property or ownership. **expropriation, -or** *n.*

ex-pul-sion *n.* The act of expelling or the state of being expelled.

ex-punge *v.* To delete or remove; to erase. **expunger** *n.*

ex-pur-gate *v.* To remove obscene or objectionable material from a play, book, etc., before it is available to the public. **expurgation, expurgator** *n.*

ex-qui-site *adj.* Delicately or intricately beautiful in design or craftsmanship; highly sensitive; keen or acute, as in pain or pleasure.

exquisitely *adv.*, **exquisiteness** *n.*

ex-tant *adj.* Still in existence; not lost or destroyed; surviving.

ex-tem-po-ra-ne-ous *adj.* Acting or performing with little or no advance preparation; spoken with regard to content, but not memorized or read word for word. **extemporaneously** *adv.*

ex-tem-po-re *adj.* Extemporaneously.

ex-tem-po-rize *v.* To make, do, or perform with little or no advance preparation; to improvise to meet circumstances. **-ation, extemporizer** *n.*

ex-tend *v.* To stretch or open to full length; to make longer, broader, or wider; to continue; to prolong; to put forth or hold out, as the hand; to exert to full capacity; to offer something. **extendible** *adj.*

ex-tend-ed *adj.* Pulled or extended out; stretched out.

ex-tend-er *n.* A substance added to another to dilute, modify, or adulterate.

ex-ten-sion *n.* The act or state of being extended; an agreement with a creditor that allows a debtor further time to pay a debt. *Phys.* The property of matter by virtue of which it occupies space. **extensional** *adj.*

ex-ten-sive *adj.* Widespread; far-reaching; having a wide range; broad in scope. **-ly** *adv.*, **extensiveness** *n.*

ex-tent *n.* The degree, dimension, or limit to which anything is extended; the area over which something extends; the size.

ex-ten-u-ate *v.* To minimize the seriousness of something as a crime or fault. **extenuation** *n.*, **extenuating** *adj.*

ex-te-ri-or *adj.* Pertaining to or of the outside; the external layer.

ex-ter-mi-nate *v.* To annihilate; to destroy completely. **extermination, exterminator** *n.*

ex-tern *or* **externe** *n.* A person that is associated with but not officially residing in a hospital or an institution.

ex-ter-nal *adj.* For, of, or on the outside; acting from the outside; pertaining to foreign countries; outside; exterior. **externals** *pl.* Outward or superficial circumstances. **externally** *adv.*

ex-tinct *adj.* Inactive; no longer existing; extinguished. **extinction** *n.*

ex-tin-guish *v.* To put an end to; to put out; to make extinct.

extinguishable *adj.*, **extinguisher** *n.*

ex-tir-pate *v.* To pull up by the roots; to destroy wholly, completely. **-tion, extirpator** *n.*, **extirpative** *adj.*

ex-tol *also* **ex-toll** *v.* To praise highly. **extoller, extolment** *n.*

ex-tort *v.* To obtain money from a person by threat, oppression, or abuse of authority. **extortion, extortionist** *n.*, **extortionate** *adj.*

ex-tra *adj.* Over and above what is normal, required, or expected. *n.* An extra edition of a newspaper that covers news of special importance; a performer hired for a small part in a movie.

ex-trac-tion *n.* The process or act of extracting; person's origin or ancestry.

ex-tra-cur-ric-u-lar *adj.* Pertaining to or of activities not directly a part of the curriculum of a school or college.

ex-tra-dite *v.* To obtain or surrender by extradition. **extraditable** *adj.*

ex-tra-di-tion *n.* The legal surrender of an alleged criminal to the jurisdiction of another country, government, or state for trial.

ex-tra-dos *n.*, *pl.* **-dos** *or* **-doses** The exterior or upper curve of an arch.

ex-tra-ga-lac-tic *adj.* Coming from beyond the galaxy; situated beyond the galaxy.

ex-tra-mar-i-tal *adj.* Adulterous.

ex-tra-mu-ral *adj.* Taking place outside of an educational building or institution; involving teams from different schools.

ex-tra-ne-ous *adj.* Coming from without; foreign; not vital or essential. **extraneously** *adv.*

ex-tra-or-di-nar-y *adj.* Beyond what is usual or common; remarkable. **extraordinarily** *adv.*

ex-tra-sen-so-ry *adj.* Beyond the range of normal sensory perception.

ex-tra-ter-res-tri-al *adj.* Occurring or originating outside the earth or its atmosphere. **extraterrestrial** *n.*

ex-tra-ter-ri-to-ri-al *adj.* Pertaining to or of extraterritoriality; situated outside of the territorial limits.

ex-tra-ter-ri-to-ri-al-i-ty *n.* An exemption from local legal jurisdiction, as that extended to foreign diplomats.

ex-trav-a-gant *adj.* Overly lavish in expenditure; wasteful; exceeding reasonable limits; immoderate; unrestrained. **extravagance** *n.*, **-ly** *adv.*

ex-trav-a-gan-za *n.* A lavish, spectacular, showy entertainment.

ex-tra-ve-hic-u-lar *adj.* Occurring or done outside a vehicle, especially a spacecraft in flight.

ex-treme *adj.* Greatly exceeding; going far beyond the bounds of moderation; exceeding what is considered moderate, usual, or reasonable; final; last.

ex-trem-ist *n.* A person who advocates or resorts to extreme measures or holds extreme views. **extremism** *n.*

ex-trem-i-ty *n., pl.* **-ties** The utmost or farthest point; the greatest degree of distress or peril; an extreme measure; an appendage or limb of the body; a hand or foot.

ex-tri-cate *v.* To free from hindrance, entanglement, or difficulties; to disengage. **extrication** *n.*

ex-trin-sic *adj.* Not inherent; outside the nature of something; from the outside; external. **extrinsically** *adv.*

ex-tro-vert *or* **extravert** *n., Psychol.* A person who is more interested in people and things outside himself than in his own private feelings and thoughts. **extroversion** *n.*

ex-trude *v.* To push or thrust out; to shape by forcing through dies under pressure; to project or protrude. **extrusion** *n.*, **extrusive** *adj.*

ex-u-ber-ant *adj.* Full of high spirits, vitality, vigor, and joy; plentiful; abundant. **exuberance** *n.*, **exuberantly** *adv.*

ex-ude *v.* To give off; to ooze or trickle forth, as sweat. **exudation** *n.*, **exudate** *n.*

ex-ult *v.* To be jubilant; to rejoice greatly. **exultant** *adj.*, **exultation** *n.*

ex-ur-bi-a *n.* The often well-to-do residential area outside the suburbs of a large city. **exurbanite** *n.*

eye *n.* An organ of sight consisting of the cornea, iris, pupil, retina, and lens; a look; gaze; the ability to judge, perceive, or discriminate. **eye of the storm** *Meteor.* The central area of a hurricane or cyclone. **eye of the wind** *Naut.* The direction from which the wind blows. **to catch one's eye** To get someone's attention. **see eye to eye** to be in complete agreement.

eye-ball *n.* The ball of the eye, enclosed by the socket and eyelids and connected at the rear to the optic nerve.

eye-ful *n., pl.* **-fuls** A satisfying or complete view.

eye-lash *n.* The stiff curved hairs growing from the edge of the eyelids.

eye-let *n.* A small perforation or hole for a hook or cord to fit through in closing a fastening; the metal ring reinforcing an eyelet.

eye-sight *n.* The faculty or power of sight; the range of vision.

eye-strain *n.* Fatigue or discomfort of the eyes, caused by excessive or improper use and marked by symptoms such as pain and headache.

eye-tooth *n., pl.* **teeth**

One of the canine teeth of the upper jaw.

F, f The sixth letter of the English alphabet; in music, the fourth tone in the scale of C major; a failing grade.

fa-ble *n.* A brief, fictitious story embodying a moral and using persons, animals, or inanimate objects as characters; a falsehood; a lie. **fabulist**, **fabler** *n.*, **fabled** *adj.*

fab-ric *n.* A cloth produced by knitting, weaving, or spinning fibers; a structure or framework, as the social fabric.

fab-ri-cate *v.* To make or manufacture; to build; to construct by combining or assembling parts; to make up in order to deceive; to invent, as a lie or story. **fabricated** *v.*, **fabrication**, **fabricator** *n.*

fab-u-lous *adj.* Past the limits of belief; incredible. **fabulously** *adv.*

fa-cade *n., Arch.* The face or front of a building; an artificial or false appearance.

fac-et *n.* One of the flat, polished surfaces cut upon a gemstone; the small, smooth surface on a bone or tooth; a phase, aspect, or side of a person or subject. **faceted** *or* **facetted** *adj.*

fa-ce-ti-ae *n.* Humorous or witty writings or remarks.

fa-ce-tious *adj.* Given to or marked by playful jocularity; humorous. **facetiously** *adv.*, **facetiousness** *n.*

face value *n.* The apparent value of something; the value printed on the face of a bill or bond.

fa-cial *adj.* Near, of, or for the face; a massage or other cosmetic treatment for the face. **facially** *adv.*

fac-ile *adj.* Requiring little effort; easily achieved or performed; arrived at without due care, effort, or examination; superficial. **-ly** *adv.*, **facileness** *n.*

fa-cil-i-tate *v.* To make easier or less difficult. **facilitating**, **facilitated** *v.*, **facilitation**, **facilitator** *n.*

fa-cil-i-ty *n., pl.* **-ies** Ease in performance, moving, or doing something; something that makes an operation or action easier.

fac-ing *n.* The lining or covering sewn to a garment; any outer protective or decorative layer applied to a surface.

fac-sim-i-le *n.* An exact copy, as of a document; the method of transmitting drawings, messages, or such by an electronic method.

fact *n.* Something that actually occurred or exists; something that has real and demonstrable existence; actuality.

fac-tion *n.* A group or party within a government that is often self-seeking and usually in opposition to a larger group; discord. **-al** *adv.*, **-alism** *n.*

fac-tious *adj.* Given to dissension; creating friction; divisive. **factiously** *adv.*

fac-ti-tious *adj.* Produced artificially; lacking authenticity or genuineness. **factitiously** *adv.*, **factitiousness** *n.*

fac-to-ry *n., pl.* **-ies** An establishment where goods are manufactured; a plant.

fac-to-tum *n.* An employee who performs all types of work.

fac-tu-al *adj.* Containing or consisting of facts, literal and exact. **factually** *adv.*,

fac-ture *n.* The process, manner or act of construction; making.

fac-ul-ty *n., pl.* **-ies** A natural ability or power; the inherent powers or capabilities of the body or mind; the complete teaching staff of a school or any other educational institution.

fad *n.* A temporary fashion adopted with wide enthusiasm. **faddish** *adj.*,

fade *v.* To lose brightness, brilliance, or loudness gradually; to vanish slowly; to lose freshness, vigor, or youth; to disappear gradually. **faded, fading** *v.*

fa-ience *n.* Earthenware that is decorated with a colorful opaque glaze.

fail-ing *n.* A minor fault; a defect.

faille *n.* A ribbed material of cotton, silk, or rayon.

fail-ure *n.* The fact or state of failing; a breaking down in health, action, strength, or efficiency; a situation in which a business becomes insolvent or bankrupt; in school, a failing grade.

faint *adj.* Having little strength or vigor; feeble; lacking brightness or clarity; dim. *n.* A sudden, temporary loss of consciousness; a swoon. **faintly** *adv.*, **faintness** *n.*

fair *adj.* Visually light in coloring; pleasing to the eye; beautiful; impartial; free from blemish or imperfection; moderately large or good; not stormy; without precipitation.

fair-y *n., pl.* **-ies** A tiny imaginary being, capable of working good or ill. *Slang* A male homosexual.

fair-y-land *n.* Any delightful, enchanting place; the land of the fairies.

faith *n.* A belief in the value, truth, or trustworthiness of someone or something; belief and trust in God, the Scriptures, or other religious writings; a system of religious beliefs.

faith-ful *adj.* True and trustworthy in the performance of duty, the fulfillment of promises or obligations, etc. **faithfully** *adv.*, **faithfulness** *n.*

faith-less *adj.* Not being true to one's obligations or duties; lacking a religious faith; unworthy of belief or trust. **faithlessly** *adv.*, **faithlessness** *n.*

fake *adj.* Having a false or misleading appearance; not genuine.

fall *v.* To drop down from a higher place or position due to the removal of support or loss of hold or attachment.

fal-la-cious *adj.* Containing or based on fundamental errors in reasoning; deceptive. **-ness** *n.* **-ly** *adv.*

fal-la-cy *n., pl.* **-ies** A deception; an error.

fall-back *n.* A place or position to which one can retreat.

fall guy *n. Slang* A person left to receive the blame or penalties; scapegoat.

fal-li-ble *adj.* Capable of making an error; liable to be deceived or misled; apt to be erroneous. **fallibility** *n.*, **fallibly** *adv.*

fall-ing—out *n.* A fight, disagreement, or quarrel.

fall—off *n.* A decrease in something.

fal-lo-pi-an tube *n.* One of a pair of long, slender ducts serving as a passage for the ovum from the ovary to the uterus.

fal-low *n.* Ground that has been plowed but left unseeded during the growing season. **fallowness** *n.*

fal-low *adj.* Light yellowish-brown in color.

false *adj.* Contrary to truth or fact; incorrect; deliberately untrue or deceptive; treacherous; unfaithful; not natural or real; artificial; in music, an incorrect pitch. **falsely** *adv.*, **falseness, falsity** *n.*

false face *n.* A mask used for a disguise at Halloween.

false-hood *n.* The act of lying; an intentional untruth.

false ribs *pl., n.* Ribs that are not united directly with the sternum. In man there are five on each side.

fal-set-to *n.* A high singing voice, usually male, that is artificially high. **falsetto** *adv.*

fal-si-fy *v.* To give an untruthful account of; to misrepresent; to alter or tamper with in order to deceive; to forge. **falsified** *v.*, **falsification, falsifier** *n.*

fal-ter *v.* To be uncertain or hesitant in action or voice; to waver; to move with unsteadiness. **-ing** *adj.*

fame *n.* Public esteem; a good reputation. **famed** *adj.*

fa-mil-iar *adj.* Being well-acquainted with; common; having good and complete knowledge of something; unconstrained or informal. **-ly** *adv.*

fa-mil-i-ar-i-ty *n., pl.* **-ties** An acquaintance with or the knowledge of something; an established friendship; an undue liberty or informality.

fa-mil-iar-ize *v.* To make oneself or someone familiar with something. **-ing, familiarized** *v.*, **familiarization** *n.*

fam-i-ly *n., pl.* **-ies** Parents and their children; a group of people connected by blood or marriage and sharing common ancestry; the members of a household; a group or class of like things; in science, a taxonomic category higher than a genus and below an order. **family** *adj.*

family name *n.* A surname or last name.

family tree *n.* A genealogical diagram showing family descent; the ancestors and descendants of a family.

fam-ine *n.* A widespread scarcity of food; a drastic shortage of or scarcity of anything; severe hunger; starvation.

fam-ish *v.* To starve or cause to starve. **famished** *adj.*

fa-mous *adj.* Well-known; renowned. *Slang* admirable. **-ly** *adv.*, **-ness** *n.*

fa-nat-ic *n.* One who is moved by a frenzy of enthusiasm or zeal. **-al** *adj.*, **fanatically** *adv.*, **fanaticism** *n.*

fan-ci-er *n.* A person having a special enthusiasm for or interest in something.

fan-ci-ful *adj.* Existing or produced only

in the fancy; indulging in fancies; exhibiting invention or whimsy in design.
fancifully adv., **fancifulness** n.

fan-dan-go n. A Spanish or Spanish-American dance in triple time; the music for this dance.

fan-fare n. A short, loud trumpet flourish; a spectacular public display.

fang n.

A long, pointed tooth or tusk an animal uses to seize or tear at its prey; one of the hollow, grooved teeth with which a poisonous snake injects its venom. **fanged** adj.

fan-jet n. An aircraft with turbojet engines.

fan-ny n., pl. -ies Slang The buttocks.

fan mail n. Mail received by a public figure from admirers.

fan-ta-sia n. A composition structured according to the composer's fancy and not observing any strict musical form.

fan-ta-size v. To create mental fantasies; to imagine or indulge in fantasies. **fantasizing, fantasized** v.

fan-tas-tic adj. Existing only in the fancy; unreal; wildly fanciful or exaggerated; impulsive or capricious; coming from the imagination or fancy. Slang Superb. **fantastically** adv.

fan-ta-sy n., pl. -ies A creative imagination; a creation of the fancy; an unreal or odd mental image; a whimsical or odd notion; a highly or ingeniously imaginative creation; in psychology, the sequence of pleasant mental images fulfilling a wish.

fare v. To be in a specific state; to turn out. n. A fee paid for hired transportation; food or a variety of foods.

fare--thee--well n. The most extreme degree; perfection.

fare-well n. Good-by; a departure. adj. Closing; parting.

far--fetched adj. Neither natural nor obvious; highly improbable.

far--flung adj. Widely distributed over a great distance.

fa-ri-na n. A fine meal obtained chiefly from nuts, cereals, potatoes, or Indian corn, used as a breakfast food or in puddings.

far-i-na-ceous adj. Made from, rich in, or composed of starch; mealy.

far--off adj. Distant; remote.

far--out adj., Slang Very unconventional.

far-ra-go n., pl. goes A confused mixture.

far--reach-ing adj. Having a wide range, effect, or influence.

far-row n. A litter of pigs.

far--see-ing adj. Having foresight; prudent; wise; having the ability to see distant objects clearly.

far--sight-ed adj. Able to see things at a distance more clearly than things nearby; wise. -ly adv., -ness n.

far-ther adv. To or at a more distant point. adj. More remote or distant.

far-ther-most adj. Most distant; farthest.

far-thest adj. To or at the greatest distance.

far-thing n. Something of little worth; a former British coin worth 1/4 of a penny.

fas-ci-nate v. To attract irresistibly, as by beauty or other qualities; to captivate; to hold motionless; to spellbind. **fascinating** adj., **fascinatingly** adv., **fascination, fascinator** n.

fast-en v. To join something else; to connect; to securely fix something; to shut or close; to focus steadily. **fastener** n.

fas-tid-i-ous adj. Exceedingly delicate or refined; hard to please in matters of taste. **fastidiously** adv., -ness n.

fast--track adj. High-powered and aggressive.

fat-al adj. Causing death; deadly; bringing ruin or disaster; destructive; decisively important; fateful; brought about by fate; destined; inevitable. **fatally** adv.

fa-tal-ism n. The belief that events or things are predetermined by fate and cannot be altered. **fatalist** n., **fatalistic** adj., **fatalistically** adv.

fa-tal-i-ty n., pl. -ies A death caused by a disaster or accident; the capability of causing death or disaster; the quality or state of being subject to or determined by fate.

fate n. The force or power held to predetermine events; fortune; inevitability; the final result or outcome; unfortunate destiny; **fated** adj.

fate-ful adj. Determining destiny; governed by fate; bringing death or disaster. **fatefully** adv., **fatefulness** n.

fa-ther n. The male parent; any male forefather; ancestor; a male who establishes or founds something. Father A priest; one of the early Christian writers who formulated doctrines and codified observances. **fatherhood, fatherliness** n., **fatherly** adj.

fa-ther--in--law n. The father of one's spouse.

fath-om-less adj. Too deep to measure; too difficult to understand.

fa-tigue n. The state or condition of extreme tiredness or weariness from prolonged physical or mental exertion. **fatigues** Military clothes for heavy work and field duty. v. To become or make tired. **fatiguing, fatigued** v.

fat-ten v. To make or become fat; to increase the amount of something. **fattening, fattened** v.

fat-ty adj. Greasy; oily; having an excess of fat.

fa-tu-i-ty n. Stupidity; foolishness.

fat-u-ous adj. Silly and foolish in a self-satisfied way. -ly adv., **fatuousness** n.

fau-cet n. A fixture with an adjustable valve used to draw liquids from a pipe or cask.

fault n. An impairment or defect; a weakness; a minor offense or mistake.

fau-na n., pl. **faunas** or **faunae** Animals living within a given area or environment. **faunal** *adj.*

fau-vism *n.* An art movement noted for the use of very flamboyant colors and bold, often distorted forms.

faux pas *n.* A false step; a social blunder.

fa-vor *n.* A helpful or considerate act; the attitude of friendliness or approbation; the condition of being held in the regard; approval or support. **favorer** *n.*, **favoringly** *adv.*

fa-vor-a-ble *adj.* Beneficial; antageous; building up hope or confidence; approving; promising. **-ness** *n.*, **-ly** *adv.*

fa-vor-ite *n.* Anything regarded with special favor or preferred above all others; in sports, the contestant considered to be the most likely winner.

fa-vor-it-ism *n.* Preferential treatment; a display of often unjust partiality.

fa-vour *n.* & *v.* British variety of favor.

fawn *n.* A young deer less than a year old; a light yellowish-brown color. **fawningly** *adv.*

fay *n.* A fairy or elf.

faze *v.* To worry; to disconcert. **fazed, fazing** *v.*

fe-al-ty *n.*, *pl.* **-ies** The obligation of allegiance owed to a feudal lord by his vassal or tenant; faithfulness; loyalty.

fear *n.* The agitated feeling caused by the anticipation or the realization of danger; an uneasy feeling that something may happen contrary to one's hopes; a feeling of deep, reverential awe and dread. *v.* To be apprehensive; to suspect. **fearfulness** *n.*

fear-ful *adj.*, **fearfully** *adv.*

fear-less *adj.* Without fear; brave; courageous. **-ness** *n.*, **-ly** *adv.*

fear-some *adj.* Causing fear; timid. **fearsomely** *adv.*, **fearsomeness** *n.*

fea-si-ble *adj.* Capable of being put into effect or accomplished; practical. **feasibility** *n.*, **feasibly** *adv.*

feast *n.* A delicious meal; a banquet; a day or days of celebration set aside for a religious purpose or in honor of some person, event, or thing. *v.* To provide with pleasure. **-ing** *v.*, **-er** *n.*

feat *n.* A notable act or achievement.

feather bed *n.* A mattress stuffed with feathers; a bed with a feather mattress.

feather-edge *n.* A very thin, fragile edge.

feather-stitch *n.* An embroidery stitch that resembles a feather, accomplished by taking one or more short stitches alternately on either side of a straight line.

fea-ture *n.* The appearance or shape of the face; the main presentation at a movie theater; a special article in a magazine or newspaper that is given special prominence. **feature** *v.*

feb-ri-fuge *n.* A medicine used to reduce fever.

feb-rile *adj.* Feverish.

fe-ces *pl.* *n.* Waste that is excreted from the bowels; excrement. **fecal** *adj.*

feck-less *adj.* Ineffective; weak; careless and irresponsible. **fecklessly** *adv.*

fe-cund *adj.* Fruitful; productive. **-ity** *n.*

fe-cun-date *v.* To make fertile.

fecundating, -ed *v.*, **fecundation** *n.*

fed *v.* Past tense of feed.

fed *abbr.* Federal, federated.

fed-er-al *adj.* Of, relating to, or formed by an agreement between two or more states or groups in which each retains certain controlling powers while being united under a central authority; of or pertaining to the United States central government. **Federal** Pertaining to or of the central government of Canada; of or supporting the Union in the American Civil War. **federally** *adv.*

fed-er-al-ism *n.* The organization or system of a federal government; the advocacy or support of this system.

fed-er-a-l-ize *v.* To join or unite in a federal union; to bring under the control of the federal government.

-ing, federalized *v.*, **federalization** *n.*

fed-er-ate *v.* To unite in a federal union or alliance. **federating, federated** *v.*

fe-do-ra *n.* A soft hat with a low crown creased lengthwise and a brim that can be turned up or down.

fed up *adj.* Extremely annoyed or disgusted.

fee *n.* A fixed charge, compensation, or payment for something; a charge for professional services; an inherited estate in land.

fee-ble *adj.* Very weak; lacking in strength; ineffective. **-ness** *n.*, **-ly** *adv.*

feeble minded *adj.* Mentally deficient; intellectually subnormal. **-ness** *n.*

feed *v.* To supply with food; to provide as food; to consume food.

feel *v.* To examine, explore, or perceive through the sense of touch; to perceive as a physical sensation; to believe; to consider; to be aware of; to be emotionally affected by; to think; to suppose; to judge; to experience the full force or impact of; to produce a sensory impression of being soft, hard, hot or cold; to produce an indicated overall condition, impression, or reaction. **feeling** *v.*

feet *n.* The plural of foot.

feign *v.* To make a false show of; to dream up a false story and tell it as the truth; to fabricate; to imitate so as to deceive. **feigned** *adj.*

feint *n.* A deceptive or misleading movement intended to draw defensive action away from the real target.

fe-lic-i-tate *v.* To congratulate.

felicitated, felicitating *v.*, **felicitation** *n.*

fe-lic-i-tous *adj.* Most appropriate; well chosen; pertinent or effective in manner or style. **felicitously** *adv.*

fe-lic-i-ty *n.*, *pl.* **-ies** Happiness; bliss; an instance or source of happiness; an agreeably pertinent or effective style.

fe-line *adj.* Of or relating to cats, including wild and domestic cats; resembling a cat, as in stealth or agility.

felinity, feline *n.*, **felinely** *adv.*

fell *v.* Past tense of fall; to strike or cause to fall down; to finish a seam with a flat, smooth strip made by joining edges, then folding under and stitching flat. *n.* Timber cut down during one season; an animal's hide; pelt. *adj.* Cruel and fierce; lethal.

fel-lah *n., pl.* **fellahin** *or* **fellaheen** An Arab peasant or laborer.

fel-low *n.* A boy or man; an associate, comrade; the counterpart; one of a pair. *Informal* A boyfriend.

fel-low-ship *n.* A friendly relationship; the condition or fact of having common interests, ideals, or experiences; the status of being a fellow at a college or university, also the financial grant made to a fellow.

fel-ly *n., pl.* **-ies**

The rim of a wooden wheel, into which spokes are inserted.

fel-on *n.* A person who has committed a felony; an inflammation in the terminal joint or at the cuticle of a finger or toe.

fel-o-ny *n., pl.* **-ies** A serious crime, such as rape, murder, or burglary, punishable by a severe sentence. **felonious** *adj.*, **-ly** *adv.*, **feloniousness** *n.*

felt *v.* Past tense of feel. *n.* An unwoven fabric made from pressed animal fibers, as wool or fur; a piece of fabric or material made of felt.

fe-male *n.* The sex that produces ova or bears young; a plant with a pistil but no stamen, which is capable of being fertilized and producing fruit. *adj.* Of or relating to the sex that produces ova or bears young; suitable to this sex having a bore, slot, or hollow part designed to receive a projecting part, as a plug or prong.

fem-i-nine *adj.* Pertaining to or of the female sex; female; characterized by qualities generally attributed to women; lacking in manly qualities. *Gram.* Applicable to females only or to persons or things classified as female. **femininely** *adv.*, **feminineness, femininity** *n.*

fem-i-nism *n.* The movement advocating the granting of the same social, political, and economic rights to women as the ones granted to men. **feminist** *n.*, **feministic** *adj.*

femme fa-tale *n., pl.* **femmes fatales** A seductive or charming woman.

fe-mur *n., pl.* **femurs** *or* **femora** The bone extending from the pelvis to the knee. **femoral** *adj.*

fen *n.* A low, marshy land; a bog.

fend *v.* To ward off or to keep off; to offer resistance. **fending, fended** *v.*

fend-er *n.* The protective device over the wheel of a car or other vehicle; a metal guard set in front of an open fireplace; the projection on the front of a locomotive or streetcar, designed to push obstructions from the tracks, also known as cow-catcher.

fen-es-tra-tion *n.* The design and position of doors and windows in a building.

fen-nel *n.* A tall herb from the parsley family which produces an edible stalk and aromatic seeds used as a flavoring.

fe-ral *adj.* Not tame nor domesticated; returned to a wild state; existing in a untamed state.

fer--de--lance *n.* A large, venomous snake of tropical America, with gray and brown markings.

fer-ment *n.* Any substance or agent producing fermentation, as yeast, mold, or enzyme; excitement; unrest; agitation. **fermentability, fermenter** *n.*, **fermentable** *adj.*

fer-men-ta-tion *n.* The decomposition of complex organic compounds into simpler substances; the conversion of glucose into ethyl alcohol through the action of zymase; great agitation; commotion.

fer-mi-um *n.* A metallic radioactive element, symbolized by Fm.

fern *n.* Any of a number of flowerless, seedless plants, having fronds with divided leaflets and reproducing by spores. **ferny** *adj.*

fe-ro-cious *adj.* Extremely savage, fierce, cruel, or bloodthirsty. *Slang* Very intense. **ferociously** *adv.*, **ferociousness, ferocity** *n.*

fer-ret *n.* A small, red-eyed polecat of Europe, often domesticated and trained to hunt rodents or rabbits. *v.* To search out by careful investigation; to drive out of hiding. **ferreter** *n.*, **ferrety** *adj.*

fer-ric *adj.* Pertaining to or containing iron.

fer-ric ox-ide *n.* A dark compound that occurs as hematite ore and rust.

fer-ro-mag-net-ic *adj.* Relating to or being typical of substances, as iron and nickel, that are readily magnetized. **ferromagnetism** *n.*

fer-rous *adj.* Pertaining to or containing iron.

fer-rule *n.* A cap or ring used near or at the end of a stick, as a walking cane, to reinforce it or prevent splitting.

fer-ry *n., pl.* **-ies** A boat or other craft used to transport people, vehicles, and other things across a body of water.

fer-ry-boat *n.* A boat used to transport passengers or goods.

fer-tile *adj., Biol.* Having the ability to reproduce; rich in material required to maintain plant growth. **fertility, fertileness** *n.*

fer-til-ize *v.* To make fertile; to cause to be productive or fruitful; to begin the biological reproduction by supplying with sperm or pollen; to make fertile by spreading or adding fertilizer. **fertilized, fertilizing** *v.*, **fertilizable** *adj.*, **fertilization** *n.*

fer-til-iz-er *n.* A material that fertilizes, such as nitrates or manure which enriches soil.

fer-ule *n.* A flat stick sometimes used to punish children. **ferule** *v.*

fer-vent *adj.* Passionate; ardent; very hot.

fervency, ferventness n., fervently adv.

fer-vid adj. Fervent to an extreme degree; impassioned; very hot; burning. **fervidly** adv., **fervidness** n.

fer-vor n. Great emotional warmth or intensity.

fes-cue n. A type of tough grass, often used as pasturage.

fes-tal adj. Pertaining to or typical of a festival, holiday, or feast.

fes-ter v. To develop or generate pus; to be a constant source of irritation or resentment.

fes-ti-val n. A particular holiday or celebration; a regularly occurring occasion.

fes-tive adj. Relating to or suitable for a feast or other celebration. **festively** adv., **festiveness** n.

fes-tiv-i-ty n., pl. **-ies** A festival; gladness and rejoicing.

fet-a n. A white Greek cheese made of goat's or ewe's milk and preserved in brine.

fe-tal adj. Relating to or like a fetus.

fe-tal po-si-tion n. The bodily position of a fetus with the spine curved, the head bowed forward, and the arms and legs drawn in toward the chest.

fetch v. To go after and return with; to draw forth; to elicit; to bring as a price; to sell for. **fetching**, **fetched** v., **fetcher** n.

fete n. A festival or feast; a very elaborate outdoor celebration. **fete** v.

fet-id adj. Having a foul odor; stinking. **fetidly** adv., **fetidness** n.

fet-ish n. An object that is regarded as having magical powers; something that one is devoted to excessively or irrationally. Psychiatry A nonsexual object that arouses or gratifies sexual desires. **fetishistic** adj., **fetishist** n.

fet-lock n. A tuft of hair that grows just above the hoof at the back of the leg of a horse.

fe-tol-o-gy n. The medical study of a fetus. **fetologist** n.

fe-tuc-ci-ne n. Narrow strips of pasta.

fe-tus n. The individual unborn organism carried within the womb from the time major features appear; especially in humans, the unborn young after the eighth week of development.

feud n. A bitter quarrel between two families, usually lasting over a long period of time.

feu-dal adj. Relating to or characteristic of feudalism. **-ize** v., **feudally** adv.

feu-dal-ism n. The political, social, and economic organization produced by the feudal system. **feudalist** n., **feudalistic** adj.

feu-da-to-ry n., pl. **-ies** One holding a feudal fee. adj. Owing feudal homage or allegiance.

fe-ver n. Abnormally high body temperature and rapid pulse; a craze; a heightened emotion or activity. **-ish** adj., **feverishly** adv., **feverishness** n.

fever blister n. A cold sore.

few adj. Small in number; not many. n. A select or limited group.

fey adj. Seemingly spellbound; having clairvoyance; acting as if under a spell.

fez n. A red felt, black-tasseled hat worn by Egyptian men.

fi-an-ce n. A man to whom a woman is engaged to be married.

fi-an-cee n. A woman to whom a man is engaged to be married.

fi-as-co n., pl. **fiascoes** A complete or total failure.

fi-at n. A positive and authoritative order or decree.

fib n. A trivial lie. **fib** v., **fibber** n.

fi-ber n. A fine, long, continuous piece of natural or synthetic material made from a filament of asbestos, spun glass, textile, or fabric; internal strength; character. **fibrous** adj.

fi-ber-glass n. A flexible, nonflammable material of spun glass used for textiles, insulation, and other purposes.

fi-ber op-tics pl., n. Light optics transmitted through very fine, flexible glass rods by internal reflection.

fiber optic adj.

fi-ber-scope n. The flexible fiber optic instrument used to view otherwise inaccessible objects.

fib-ril-la-tion n., Pathol. The rapid and uncoordinated contraction of the muscle fibers of the heart.

fi-brin n., Biochem. An insoluble protein that promotes the clotting of blood. **fibrinous** adj.

fi-brin-o-gen n., Biochem. A complex blood plasma protein that is converted to fibrin during the process of blood clotting.

fi-broid adj. Made up or resembling fibrous tissue.

fib-u-la n. Anat.

Fibula

The outer and smaller bone of the lower limb or hind leg, in humans located between the knee and ankle.

-fic adj., suffix Making; causing; rendering.

-fication n., suffix Making; production.

fi-chu n. A lightweight triangular scarf, worn about the neck and fastened loosely in front.

fick-le adj. Inconstant in purpose or feeling; changeable. **fickleness** n.

fic-tion n. Something that is created or imaginary; a literary work that is produced by the imagination and not based on fact. **fictional** adj.

fic-ti-tious adj. Nonexistent; imaginary; not genuine; false; not real. **fictitiously** adv., **fictitiousness** n.

fid-dle n. A violin. v. To play the violin; to fidget or make nervous or restless movements; to spend time in a careless way. Naut. A rack used at the table to prevent things from sliding off. **fit as a fiddle** To enjoy good or perfect health. **to play second fiddle**

To be put into a position subordinate to that of another.

fiddling, fiddled v., **fiddler** n.

fiddler crab n. A small burrowing crab found mostly off the Atlantic coast of the United States, the male being much larger than the female.

fi-del-i-ty n., pl. **-ies** Faithfulness or loyalty to obligations, vows, or duties. **Elect.** The degree to which a phonograph, tape recorder, or other electronic equipment receives and transmits input signals without distortion.

fidg-et v. To move nervously or restlessly. **fidgets** pl, n. The condition of being nervous or restless. **fidgeter, fidgetiness** n., **fidgety** adj.

fie interj. An expression of disgust or impatience in response to an unpleasant surprise.

fief n. A feudal estate in land.

field mag-net n. A magnet providing the magnetic field in a generator or electric motor.

fierce adj. Savage and violent in nature. **Slang** Very difficult or disagreeable. **fiercely** adv., **fierceness** n.

fier-y adj. Containing or composed of fire; brightly glowing; blazing; hot and inflamed; full of spirit or intense with emotion. **fieriness** n.

fi-es-ta n. A religious holiday or festival.

fife n. A small, shrill-toned instrument similar to a flute.

fif-teen n. The cardinal number equal to 14 + 1. **fifteen** adj., **-th** n., adj. & adv.

fifth n. The ordinal of five; one of five equal parts. **Mus.** The space between a tone and another tone five steps from it. **fifth** adj. & adv.

Fifth Amendment n. An amendment to the United States Constitution, ratified in 1791, guaranteeing due process of law and that no person "shall be forced to testify against himself".

fifth wheel n. A superfluous thing or person.

fif-ty n. The cardinal number equal to 5 X 10. **fiftieth** n., adj. & adv., **fifty** adj.

fifty-fifty adj., **Slang** Divided into two equal portions or parts.

fig n. A tree or shrub bearing a sweet, pear-shaped, edible fruit; the fruit of the fig tree.

fight v. To struggle against; to quarrel; to argue; to make one's way by struggling; to participate in wrestling or boxing until a final decision is reached. n. A physical battle; struggle; strife; conflict; combat. **fighting** v.

fight-er n. A person who fights. **Milit.** A fast, highly maneuverable airplane used in combat.

fig-ment n. An invention or fabrication.

fig-ure n. A symbol or character that represents a number; anything other than a letter; the visible form, silhouette, shape, or line of something; the human form or body; an individual, especially a prominent one;

the impression or appearance that a person makes; a design or pattern, as in a fabric; a figure of speech; a series of movements, as in a dance. **fig-ures** pl. In mathematics, calculations; an amount shown in numbers. v. To represent; to depict; to compute.

figured, figuring v.

fig-ure eight n. A skating maneuver shaped like an 8; anything shaped like the number 8.

fig-ure-head n. A person with nominal leadership but no real power; a carved figure on a ship's prow.

fig-ure of speech n. An expression, as a metaphor or hyperbole, where words are used in a more forceful, dramatic, or illuminating way.

fig-u-rine n. A small sculptured or molded figure; a statuette.

fil-a-ment n. A very thing, finely spun fiber, wire, or thread; the fine wire enclosed in an electric lamp bulb which is heated electrically to incandescence. **-ary, filamentous** adj.

fil-bert n. The edible nut of the hazel tree or the tree it grows on.

filch v. To steal. **filcher** n.

file n. A device for storing papers in proper order; a collection of papers so arranged; a line of persons, animals, or things placed one behind another; a hard, steel instrument with ridged cutting surfaces, used to smooth or polish. v. To march as soldiers; to make an application, as for a job.

filing, filed v.

fi-let n. A filet of meat or fish; lace or net with a pattern of squares.

fi-let mi-gnon n. A small, tender cut of beef from the inside of the loin.

fil-i-al adj. Of or relating to a son or daughter; pertaining to the generation following the parents. **filially** adv.

fil-i-buster n. An attempt to prolong, prevent, or hinder legislative action by using delaying tactics such as long speeches. **filibuster** v., **filibusterer** n.

fil-i-gree n. Delicate, lace-like ornamental work made of silver or gold intertwisted wire. **filigree** v. & adj.

fil-ing n., often **fil-ings** Particles removed by a file.

fil-let or **fi-let** n. A narrow ribbon or band for holding the hair; a strip of boneless fish or meat. v. To slice, bone, or make into fillets.

fil-lip n. A snap of the finger that has been pressed down by the thumb and then suddenly released; something that arouses or excites. **fillip** v.

fil-ly n. A young female horse.

film n. A thin covering, layer, or membrane. **Photog.** A photosensitive strip or sheet of flexible cellulose material that is used to make photographic negatives or transparencies; the film containing the pictures projected on a large screen; the motion picture itself. v. To cover with or as if with a film; to make a movie.

film-dom n. The movie industry or business.

film-strip *n.* A strip of film containing graphic matter for still projection on a screen.

fil-ter *n.* A device, as cloth, paper, charcoal, or any other porous substance, through which a liquid or gas can be passed to separate outsuspended matter. *Photog.* A colored screen that controls the kind and intensity of light waves in an exposure. *v.* To pass liquids through a filter; to strain. **filterability** *n.,* **filterable, filtrable** *adj.*

filth *n.* Anything that is dirty or foul; something that is considered offensive. **filth-y** *adj.* Highly unpleasant; morally foul; obscene. **filthily** *adv.,* **filthiness** *n.*

fil-trate *v.* To pass or cause to pass through something. *n.* Anything which has passed through the filter. **filtrating, filtrated** *v.,* **filtration** *n.*

fin *n.*

A thin membranous extension of the body of a fish or other aquatic animal, used for swimming and balancing. *Slang* A five dollar bill.

fi-na-gle *v., Slang* To get something by trickery or deceit. **finagled** *v.,* **finagling** *adj.,* **finagler** *n.*

fi-nal *adj.* Pertaining to or coming to the end; last or terminal. **finality** *n.,* **finally** *adv.*

finals *pl., n.* Something decisively final, as the last of a series of athletic contests; the final academic examination.

fi-na-le *n.* The last part, as the final scene in a play or the last part of a musical composition.

fi-nal-ist *n.* A contestant taking part in the final round of a contest.

fi-nal-ize *v.* To put into final and complete form. **finalized, finalizing** *v.,* **finalization, finalizer** *n.*

fi-nance *n.* The science of monetary affairs. **finances** Monetary resources; funds. *v.* To supply the capital or funds for something; to sell or provide on a credit basis. **financial** *adj.,* **financially** *adv.*

fin-an-cier *n.* An expert who deals with large-scale financial affairs.

finch *n.* A small bird, as a grosbeak, canary, or goldfinch, having a short stout bill.

find *v.* To come upon unexpectedly; to achieve; to attain; to ascertain.

find-er *n.* A person who finds; the device on a camera that indicates what will be in the picture.

find-ing *n.* Something that is found or discovered. **findings** *pl., n.* Conclusions or statistics that are the result of a study, examination, or investigation.

fi-ne *n., Mus.* The end.

fine arts *pl., n.* The arts of drawing, painting, sculpture, architecture,

literature, music, and drama.

fin-er-y *n., pl.* **-ies** Elaborate jewels and clothes.

fi-nesse *n.* A highly refined skill; the skillful handling of a situation.

fin-ger-print *n.* An inked impression of the pattern formed by the ridges of the skin on the tips of each finger and thumb. **fingerprint** *v.*

fin-i-al *n.* The ornamental projection or terminating part, as on a lamp shade.

fin-ick-y *adj.* Hard to please; choosy.

fi-nis *n.* The end.

fin-ish *v.* To bring to an end; to conclude; to reach the end.

fi-nite *adj.* Having bounds or limits; of or relating to a number which can be determined, counted, or measured. **finitely** *adv.,* **finiteness** *n.*

fink *n., Slang* A person that breaks a strike; an unsavory person.

fin-nan had-die *n.* Smoked haddock.

fin-ny *adj.* Having or suggesting fins or fin-like extensions.

fir *n.* An evergreen tree with flat needles and erect cones.

fire *n.* The chemical reaction of burning, which releases heat and light. *v.* To have great enthusiasm; to ignite or cause to become ignited; to bake in a kiln; to discharge a firearm or explosive; to let a person go from a job; to dismiss. **fired, firing** *v.*

fire a-larm *n.* A safety device to signal the outbreak of a fire.

fire-arm *n.* A small weapon used for firing a missile; a pistol or rifle using an explosive charge.

fire-ball *n.* A very bright meteor; a hot, incandescent sphere of air and vaporized debris. *Slang* A remarkably energetic person or thing.

fire-brand *n.* A piece of glowing or burning wood; one who stirs up or agitates conflict or trouble.

fire-break *n.* A strip of land that is cleared to prevent a fire from spreading.

fire-brick *n.* A highly heat-resistant brick, used to line furnaces and fireplaces.

fire-bug *n.* One who enjoys setting fire to buildings or homes; a pyromaniac.

fire-damp *n.* Gas, mainly methane, occurring naturally in coal mines and forming explosive mixtures with air.

fire en-gine *n.* A large motor vehicle equipped to carry firefighters and their equipment to a fire.

fire es-cape *n.* A structure, often metal, used as an emergency exit from a building.

fire ex-tin-guish-er *n.* A portable apparatus that contains fire extinguishing chemicals, which are ejected through a short nozzle and hose.

fire fight-er *n.* A person who fights fires as an occupation.

fire-fly *n.* A beetle that flies at night, having an abdominal organ that gives off a flashing light.

fire-house *n.* The building used to house

fire fighting equipment and personnel.

fire irons *pl. n.* Equipment that includes tongs, shovel, and a poker used to tend a fire, usually in a fireplace.

fire-man *n., pl.* **-men** A person employed to prevent or extinguish fires; one who tends fires.

fire-place *n.* An open recess in which a fire is built, especially the base of a chimney that opens into a room.

fire-plug *n.* A hydrant for supplying water in the event of a fire.

fire-pow-er *n., Milit.* The capacity to deliver fire or missiles, as from a weapon, military unit, or ship.

fire-proof *adj.* Resistant to fires.

fire tow-er *n.* A forest fire lookout station.

fire-trap *n.* A building made from such construction or built in such a way that it would be hard to escape from if there were a fire.

fire wall *n.* A fireproof wall in a building used as a barrier to forestall or prevent a fire from spreading.

fire-works *pl. n.* Explosives used to generate colored lights, smoke, and noise for entertainment or celebrations.

fir-ing line *n.* In combat, the front line from which gunfire is delivered; the vulnerable front position of a pursuit or activity.

firm *adj.* Relatively solid, compact, or unyielding to pressure or touch; steadfast and constant; strong and sure. *n.* A partnership of two or more persons for conducting a business. *v.* To become or make firm or firmer.

firm-ly *adv.* Unwaveringly; resolutely. **firmness** *n.*

fir-ma-ment *n.* The expanse of the heavens; the sky.

firn *n.* Snow that is partially consolidated by thawing and freezing but has not converted to glacial ice.

first *adj.* Preceding all others in the order of numbering; taking place or acting prior to all others; earliest; ranking above all in importance or quality; foremost. *adv.* Above or before all others in time, order, rank, or importance; for the very first time. *n.* The ordinal number that matches the number 1 in a series, 1st; the transmission gear producing the lowest driving speed in an automotive vehicle. **firstly** *adv.*

first aid *n.* The emergency care given to a person before full treatment and medical care can be obtained.

First Amend-ment *n.* The amendment to the Constitution of the United States which forbids Congress to interfere with religion, free speech, free press, the right to assemble peaceably, or the right to petition the government, ratified in 1791.

first-born *adj.* First in order. *n.* The child who is born first.

first class *n.* The best quality or highest rank; a class of sealed mail that consists partly or wholly of written matter; the best or most luxurious accommodations on a plane, ship, etc.

first-de-gree burn *n.* A mild burn characterized by heat, pain, and redness of the skin surface but not exhibiting blistering or charring of tissues.

first-hand *adj.* Coming directly from the original source. **firsthand** *adv.*

first la-dy *or* **First La-dy** *n.* The wife of the President of the United States or the wife or hostess of the chief executive of a state, city, or other country.

first lieu-ten-ant *n., Milit.* A commissioned officer ranking above a 2nd lieutenant and below a captain.

first per-son *n.* A category for verbs or pronouns indicating the speaker or writer of a sentence in which they are used.

first-rate *adj.* Of the finest rank, quality, or importance. **first-rate** *adv.*

firth *n.* A narrow inlet or arm of the sea.

fis-cal *adj.* Relating to or of the finances or treasury of a nation or a branch of government; financial. **fiscally** *adv.*

fish *n., pl.* **fish** *or* **fishes**

A cold-blooded, vertebrated aquatic animal having fins, gills for breathing, and usually scales; the flesh of fish used as food. **like a fish out of water** Not at ease or comfortable. *v.* To try to catch fish; to seek or find one's way; to grope; to try and obtain something in an artful or indirect way. **fishing** *n.*

fish bowl *n.* A bowl usually made of glass, serving as a small aquarium for fish; a lack of privacy.

fish-er-man *n., pl.* **-men** A person who fishes commercially or for sport and relaxation; a commercial fishing boat.

fish-er-y *n., pl.* **-ies** The business of catching, processing, or selling fish; a fish nursery or hatchery.

fish sto-ry *n.* An extravagant, boastful story that is probably not true.

fish-tail *v.* To swing from side to side while moving forward, as the motion of the rear end of a vehicle.

fish-wife *n., pl.* **-wives** A very coarse, abusive woman.

fish-y *adj.* Resembling fish, as in taste or odor; improbable; highly suspicious. **fishily** *adv.,* **fishiness** *n.*

fis-sile *adj.* Capable of being separated or split. *Physics* Fissionable. **fissility** *n.*

fis-sion *n.* The process or act of splitting into parts. *Physics* The exploding of the nucleus of an atom that leads to the formation of more stable atoms and the release of large quantities of energy. **fissionable** *adj.*

fis-sure *n.* A narrow opening, crack, or cleft in a rock. **fissure** *v.*

fist *n.* The hand closed tightly with the fingers bent into the palm. *Slang* The hand.

fist-fight *n.* A fight between two or more people without protection for the hands.

fist-ful *n., pl.* **-fuls** A hand full.

fis-tu-la *n., pl.* **-las** *or* **-lae** *Pathol.* A duct or other passage formed by the imperfect closing of a wound or abscess and leading either to the body surface or to another hollow organ. **-ous** *adj.*

fit *v.* To be the proper size and shape; to be in good physical condition; to possess the proper qualifications; to be competent; to provide a time or place for something; to belong. *adj.* Adapted or adequate for a particular circumstance or purpose. *Med.* A convulsion; an impulsive and irregular exertion or action. **fitter, fitness** *n.*

fitch *n.* The polecat of the Old World or its fur.

fit-ful *adj.* Characterized by irregular actions; capricious; restless. **fitfully** *adv.,* **fitfulness** *n.*

fit-ing *adj.* Suitable or proper. *n.* The act of trying on clothes for alteration; a piece of equipment or an appliance used in an adjustment. **fittingly** *adv.,* **fittingness** *n.*

five *n.* The cardinal number equal to 4 + 1; any symbol of this number, as 5; anything with five units, parts, or members. **five** *adj. & pron.*

fix *v.* To make stationary, firm, or stable; to direct or hold steadily; to place or set definitely; to make rigid; to arrange or adjust; to prepare, as a meal. *n.* A position of embarrassment or difficulty. *Naut.* The position of a ship determined by observations, radio, or bearings. *Slang* The injection of a narcotic, such as heroin. **fixing, fixed** *v.*

fix-a-tion *n.* The act or state of being fixed; a strong, often unhealthy preoccupation. **fixate** *v.*

fix-ture *n.* Anything that is fixed or installed, as a part or appendage of a house; any article of personal property affixed to reality to become a part of and governed by the law of real property.

fizz *n.* A hissing or bubbling sound; effervescence; tiny gas bubbles. **fizz** *v.*

flab *n.* Excessive, loose, and flaccid body tissue. **flabby** *adj.,* **flabbiness** *n.*

flab-ber-gast *v.* To astound; to amaze. **flabbergasting, flabbergasted** *v.*

flac-cid *adj.* Lacking resilience or firmness. **flaccidity** *n.,* **flaccidly** *adv.*

flac-on *n.* A small, stoppered decorative bottle.

flag *n.* A piece of cloth, usually oblong, bearing distinctive colors and designs to designate a nation, state, city, or organization. *Bot.* Any of various iris or cattail plants with long blade-shaped leaves. *v.* To mark with or adorn with flags for identification or orna-mentation; to grow weak or tired.

flag-el-lant *n.* One who whips himself or has himself whipped by another for religious motives or for sexual excite-ment. **flagellation** *n.*

flag-on *n.* A vessel or container with a handle, spout, and hinged lid, used for holding wines or liquors.

fla-grant *adj.* Obvious; glaring; disgraceful; notorious; outrageous. **flagrance, flagrancy** *n.,* **flagrantly** *adv.*

flair *n.* An aptitude or talent for something; a dashing style.

flak *n.* Antiaircraft fire; abusive or excessive criticism.

flake *n.* A small, flat, thin piece which has split or peeled off from a surface. *Slang* Oddball; eccentric. **flake** *v.,* **flakily** *adv.,* **flakiness** *n.,* **flaky** *adj.*

flam-boy-ant *adj.* Extravagantly ornate; showy; florid; brilliant and rich in color. **flamboyance, flamboyancy** *n.,* **flamboyantly** *adv.*

flame *n.* A mass of burning vapor or gas rising from a fire, often having a bright color and forming a tongue-shaped area of light; something that resembles a flame in motion, intensity, or appearance; a bright, red-yellow color; violent and intense emotion or passion. *Slang* A sweetheart. **flaming, flamed, flame** *v.*

fla-men-co *n.* A fiery percussive dance of the Andalusian gypsies with strong and often improvised rhythms.

flame-out *n.* The combustion failure of a jet aircraft engine while in flight.

fla-min-go *n.* A large, long-necked, tropical wading bird, having very long legs, and pink or red plumage.

flam-ma-ble *adj.* Capable of catching fire and burning rapidly. **flammability, flammable** *n.*

flange *n.* A projecting rim or collar used to strengthen or guide a wheel or other object, keeping it on a fixed track. **flange** *v.*

flank *n.* The fleshy part between the ribs and the hip on either side of the body of an animal or human being; the lateral part of something. *Milit.* The right or left side of a military bastion or formation. *v.* To be stationed at the side of something. **flanker** *n.*

flan-nel *n.* A woven fabric made of wool or a wool, cotton, or synthetic blend.

flannels *pl., n.* Trousers made of flannel. **flannelly** *adj.*

flan-nel-ette *n.* Cotton flannel.

flap-per *n.* A young woman of the 1920's whose dress and behavior were considered unconventional; a young bird unable to fly.

flare *v.* To blaze up or burn with a bright light; to break out suddenly or violently, as with emotion or action; to open or spread outward. **flaring, flared** *v.,* **flare** *n.*

flash *v.* To burst forth repeatedly or suddenly into a brilliant fire or light; to occur or appear briefly or suddenly. *n.* A short and important news break or transmission. **flashed, flashing** *v.*

flash-back *n.* The interruption in the continuity of a story, motion picture, drama, or novel to give a scene that happened earlier.

flash card n. A card printed with numbers or words and displayed briefly as a learning drill.

flash flood n. A violent and sudden flood occurring after a heavy rain.

flash point n. The lowest temperature at which the vapor of a combustible liquid will ignite or burn.

flash-y adj. Showing brilliance for a moment; tastelessly showy; gaudy. flashily adv., flashiness n.

flask n. A small container made of glass and used in laboratories.

flat adj. Extending horizontally with no curvature or tilt; stretched out level, prostrate or prone; lacking flavor or zest; deflated. Mus. Below the correct pitch. n. An apartment that is entirely on one floor of a building. flat broke Having little or no money. to fall flat Falling to achieve. flatly adv., -ness n.

flat-bed n. A truck that has a shallow rear platform without sides.

flat-car n. A railroad car having no roof or sides.

flat-foot n., pl. -feet A condition in which the arch of the foot is flat. Slang A police officer. flat-footed adj.

flat-out adv. In a direct way; at top speed. adj. Out-and-out.

flat-ten v. To make flat; to knock down. flattener n.

flat-ter v. To praise extravagantly, especially without sincerity; to gratify the vanity of; to portray favorably; to show as more attractive. flatterer n., flattering adj., flatteringly adv.

flat-ter-y n. Excessive, often insincere compliments.

flat-top n. A United States aircraft carrier; a short haircut having a flat crown.

flat-u-lent adj. Marked by or affected with gases generated in the intestine or stomach; pretentious without real worth or substance. flatulence n., flatulently adv.

flat-ware n. Tableware that is fairly flat and designed usually of a single piece, as plates; table utensils, as knives, forks, and spoons.

flaunt v. To display showily. flaunting v., flaunter n., flauntingly adv.

flau-tist n. A flutist.

fla-vor n. A distinctive element in the taste of something; a distinctive, characteristic quality; a flavoring. v. To impart flavor to. flavorful, flavorsome adj.

fla-vor-ing n. A substance, as an extract or something else that is used to increase the flavor.

flaw n. A defect or blemish that is often hidden and that may cause failure under stress; a weakness in character; a fault in a legal paper that may nullify it. flaw v.

flaw-less adj. Without flaws or defects; perfect. flawlessly adv., flawlessness n.

flax n. A plant with blue flowers, seeds that yield linseed oil, and slender stems from which a fine textile fiber is derived.

flax-en adj. Made of or pertaining to flax; pale yellow or golden as flax fiber.

flay v. To remove the skin of; to scold harshly.

flea n. A small, wingless, bloodsucking, parasitic jumping insect; a parasite of warm-blooded animals.

flea-bit-ten adj. Bitten or covered by fleas. Slang Shabby.

flea mar-ket n. A place where antiques and used items goods are sold.

fleck n. A tiny spot or streak; a small flake or bit. v. To mark with flecks.

fledg-ling or **fledge-ling** n. A young bird with newly acquired feathers; a person who is inexperienced; a beginner.

flee v. To run away; to move swiftly away. fleeing v., fleer n.

fleece n. A coat of wool covering a sheep; the soft wool covering a sheep. v. To shear the fleece from; to swindle; to cover with fleece. -er, fleeciness n., fleecily adv., fleecy adj.

fleet n. A number of warships operating together under the same command; a number of vehicles, as taxicabs or fishing boats, operated under one command. adj. Moving rapidly or nimbly. fleetly adv., fleetness n.

flesh n. Soft tissue of the body of a human or animal, especially skeletal muscle; the meat of animals as distinguished from fish or fowl; the pulpy substance of a fruit or vegetable; the body as opposed to the mind or soul; mankind in general; one's family. v. To arouse the hunting instinct of dogs by feeding fresh meat.

flesh and blood n. Human nature together with its weaknesses; one biologically connected to another.

flesh-ly adj. Of or pertaining to the body; sensual; worldly. fleshliness n.

flesh-pot n. A place were physical gratification is received.

flesh-y adj. Of, resembling, or suggestive of flesh; firm and pulpy; juicy as fruit. fleshiness n.

fleur-de-lis n., pl. **fleurs-de-lis**

A heraldic emblem consisting of a three-petaled iris, at one time used as the armorial emblem of French sovereigns; the emblem of Quebec Province.

flew v. Past tense of fly.

flex v. To bend the arm repeatedly; to contract a muscle. flexing, flexed v.

flex-i-ble adj. Capable of being bent or flexed; pliable; responsive to change; easily yielding. flexibility n., flexibly adv.

flex time n. A system which allows employees to set their own work schedules within a wide range of hours.

flick n. A light, quick snapping movement or the sound accompanying it. v. To strike or hit with a quick, light stroke; to cause to move with a quick movement. *Slang* A movie.

flick-er v. To burn or shine unsteadily, as a candle. n. A wavering or unsteady light; a North American woodpecker having a brownish back and a spotted breast. **flickering** n.

fli-er or **fly-er** n. One who or that which flies, especially an aviator; a daring or risky venture; a printed advertisement or handbill for mass distribution.

flight n. The act or manner of flying; a scheduled airline trip; a group that flies together; a swift or rapid passage or movement, as of time; a group of stairs leading from one floor to another; an instance of fleeing.

flight at-ten-dant n. A person employed to assist passengers on an aircraft.

flight bag n. A lightweight piece of luggage having flexible sides and outside pockets.

flight-y adj. Inclined to act in a fickle fashion; marked by irresponsible behavior, impulse, or whim; easily excited, skittish. **flightiness** n.

flim-flam n. *Slang* A swindle; trick; hoax.

flim-sy adj. Lacking in physical strength or substance; unconvincing. **flimsiness** n., **flimsily** adv.

flinch v. To wince or pull back, as from pain; to draw away. **flincher** n.

fling v. To throw or toss violently; to throw oneself completely into an activity. n. An act of casting away; a casual attempt; a period devoted to self-indulgence; unrestraint.

flint n. A hard quartz that produces a spark when struck by steel; an implement used by primitive man; an alloy which used in lighters to ignite the fuel. **flinty** adj.

flip v. To turn or throw suddenly with a jerk; to strike or snap quickly and lightly. *Slang* To go crazy; to become upset or angry; to react enthusiastically. **flip** n., **flipper** adj.

flip-pant adj. Marked by or showing disrespect, impudence, or the lack of seriousness. **flippancy** n., **-ly** adv.

flip-per n. A broad flat limb, as of a seal, adapted for swimming; a paddle-like rubber shoe used by skin divers and other swimmers.

flip side n. The reverse or opposite side.

flirt v. To make teasing romantic or sexual overtures; to act so as to attract attention; to move abruptly; to dart. n. A person who flirts; a snappy, quick, jerky movement. **flirtation**, **flirtatiousness** n., **flirtatious** adj.

flit v. To move rapidly or abruptly.

flit-ter v. To flutter. **flitter** n.

float n. An act or instance of floating; something that floats on the surface of or in a liquid.

float-ing rib n. One of the four lower ribs in the human being that are not attached to the other ribs.

flock n. A group of animals of all the same kind, especially birds, sheep, geese, etc., living, feeding or kept together; a group under the direction of a single person, especially the members of a church; a large number. v. To travel as if in a flock.

floe n. A large, flat mass of floating ice or a detached part of such a mass.

flog v. To beat hard with a whip or stick.

flood n. The great deluge depicted in the Old Testament; an overflow of water onto land that is normally dry; an overwhelming quantity. v. To overwhelm with or as if with a flood; to fill abundantly or overwhelm; to supply the carburetor of an engine with an excessive amount of fuel; in football, to send more than one pass receiver into the same defensive area.

flood-gate n. A valve for controlling the flow or depth of a large body of water.

flood-light n. An electric lamp that gives off a broad and intensely bright beam of light. **floodlight** v.

floor n. The level base of a room; the lower inside surface of a structure; a ground surface; the right, as granted under parliamentary rules, to speak to a meeting or assembly; an area dividing a building into stories. v. To cover or furnish with a floor; to knock down; to overwhelm; to puzzle; to press the accelerator of a vehicle to the floorboard.

floor ex-er-cise n. A competitive gymnastics event with tumbling maneuvers performed on a mat.

floor show n. Entertainment consisting of singing, dancing; nightclub acts.

floor-walk-er n. A department store employee who supervises the sales force and gives assistance to customers.

floo-zy n., pl. **-ies** *Slang* A sleazy, loose woman; a prostitute.

flop v. To fall down clumsily; to move about in a clumsy way. *Slang* To completely fail; to go to bed. **flop** n.

flop house n. A cheap, rundown hotel.

flop-py adj. Flexible and loose. **floppily** adv., **floppiness** n.

flop-py disk n. In computer science, a flexible plastic disk which is coated with magnetic material, used to record and store computer data.

flo-ra n., pl. **-ras** or **-rae** Plants growing in a specific region or season.

flo-ral adj. Of or pertaining to flowers.

flo-res-cence n. A state or process of blossoming. **florescent** adj.

flor-id adj. Flushed with a rosy color or redness; ornate. **-ness** n., **floridly** adv.

flo-rist n. One who grows or sells flowers and also artificial ones which are made of silk or silk-like fibers.

floss n. A loosely-twisted embroidery thread; a soft, silky fiber, such as the tassel on corn; dental floss. v. To clean between the teeth with dental floss. **flossed**, **flossing** v.

flo-ta-tion n. The act or state of floating.

flo-til-la *n.* A fleet of small vessels; a group resembling a small fleet.

flot-sam *n.* Any goods remaining afloat after a ship has sunk.

flounce *n.* A gathered piece of material attached to the upper edge of another surface, as on a curtain. *v.* To move with exaggerated tosses of the body. **flouncy** *adj.*

floun-der *v.* To struggle clumsily, as to gain footing; to act or speak in a confused way. *n.* Any of various edible marine flatfish. **-ed,** floundering *v.*

flour *n.* A soft, fine, powder-like substance obtained by grinding the meal of grain, especially wheat. *v.* To coat or sprinkle with flour. **floury** *adj.*

flour-ish *v.* To thrive; to fare well; to prosper and succeed. *n.* A decorative touch or stroke, especially in handwriting; a dramatic act or gesture; a musical fanfare, as of trumpets. **flourished,** flourishing *v.*

flout *v.* To have or show open contempt for. **floutingly** *adv.*

flow *v.* To move freely, as a fluid; to circulate, as blood; to proceed or move steadily and easily; to rise; to derive; to be abundant in something; to hang in a loose, free way. **flow** *n.*

flow chart *n.* A chart or diagram showing the sequence and progress of a series of operations on a specific project.

flow-er *n.* A cluster of petals, bright in color, near or at the tip of a seed-bearing plant; blossoms; the condition of highest development; the peak; the best example or representative of something. *v.* To produce flowers; to bloom; to develop fully.

fl oz *abbr.* Fluid ounce.

flu *n., Informal* Influenza.

flub *v.* To bungle or botch; to make a mess of. **flub** *n.*

fluc-tu-ate *v.* To shift irregularly; to change; to undulate. **fluctuation** *n.*

flue *n.* A conduit or passage through which air, gas, steam, or smoke can pass.

flu-ent *adj.* Having an understanding of a language use; flowing smoothly and naturally; flowing or capable of flowing. **fluency** *n.,* **fluently** *adv.*

fluff *n.* A ball, tuft, or light cluster of loosely gathered fibers of cotton or wool. *Slang* A mistake made by an actor or announcer in reading or announcing something. *v.* To make or become fluffy by patting with the hands. *Informal* To make an error in speaking or reading.

flu-id *n.* A substance, as water or gas, capable of flowing. *adj.* Changing readily, as a liquid. **fluidity, fluidness** *n.,* **fluidly** *adv.*

fluke *n.* A flatfish, especially a flounder; a flattened, parasitic trematode worm; the triangular head of an anchor at the end of either of its arms; a barb or point on an arrow; an unexpected piece of good luck. **fluky** *adj.*

flung *v.* Past tense of fling.

flunk *v., Slang* To fail in, as an examination or course; to give a failing grade to. **flunking, flunked** *v.*

flun-ky *or* **flun-key** *n.* A liveried servant; a person who does menial work.

flu-o-res-cence *n., Chem., Phys.* Emission of electromagnetic radiation, especially of visible light, resulting from and occurring during the absorption of radiation from another source; the radiation emitted. **fluorescence** *v.,* **fluorescent** *adj.*

fluorescent lamp *n.* A tubular electric lamp in which ultraviolet light is reradiated as visible light.

fluor-i-date *v.* To add a sodium compound to water in order to prevent tooth decay. **flouridating, flouridated** *v.,* **fluoridation** *n.*

flu-o-ride *n.* A compound of fluorine with another element or a radical.

flu-o-rine *n.* A pale yellow, corrosive, and extremely reactive gaseous element, symbolized by F.

fluor-o-scope *n.* A device for observing shadows projected upon a flourescent screen of an optically opaque object, as the human body, which may be viewed by transmission of x-rays through the object. **fluoroscope** *v.,* **fluoroscopic** *adj.,* **fluoroscopy** *n.*

flur-ry *n., pl.* **-ies** A sudden gust of wind; a brief, light fall of snow or rain, accompanied by small gusts; a sudden burst of activity or commotion.

flush *v.* To flow or rush out suddenly and abundantly; to become red in the face; to blush; to glow with a reddish color; to purify or wash out with a brief, rapid gush of water; to cause to flee from cover, as a game animal or bird. *n.* Glowing freshness or vigor; a hand in certain card games, as poker, in which all the cards are the same suit. *adj.* Having a heightened reddish color; abundant; affluent, prosperous; having surfaces that are even; arranged with adjacent sides close together; having margins aligned with no indentations; direct as a blow. *adv.* In an even position with another surface. **flushed, flushing** *v.*

flus-ter *v.* To make or become nervous or confused.

flute *n.* A high-pitched, tubular woodwind instrument equipped with finger holes and keys; a decorative groove in the shaft of a column; a small grooved pleat, as in cloth. **fluting** *n.,* **-ed** *adj.*

flut-ist *n.* A flute player.

flut-ter *v.* To flap or wave rapidly and irregularly; to fly as with a light, rapid beating of the wings; to beat erratically, as one's heart; to move about in a restless way. **flutter** *n.,* **fluttery** *adj.*

flux *n.* A flowing or discharge; a constant flow or movement; a state of constant fluctuation or change; a substance that promotes the fusing of metals and prevents oxide formation. *v.* To make fluid; to melt; to apply a flux to.

fly v.

To move through the air on wings or wing-like parts; to travel by air; to float or cause to float in the air; to escape; to flee; to pass by swiftly or quickly; to hit a fly ball. n. A folded piece of cloth that covers the fastening of a garment, especially trousers; a fly ball one has batted over the field; any of numerous winged insects, including the housefly and the tsetse; a fishing lure that resembles an insect. **fly off the handle** To react explosively.

fly·a·ble adj.

fly--by--night adj. Unstable or temporary; financially unsound.

fly-weight n. A boxer who belongs to the lightest weight class, weighing 112 pounds or less.

fly-wheel n. A rotating wheel heavy enough to regulate the speed of a machine shaft.

foal n. The young animal, as a horse, especially one under a year old. v. To give birth to a foal.

foam n. A mass of bubbles produced on the surface of a liquid by agitation; froth; a firm, spongy material used especially for insulation and upholstery. v. To cause to form foam. **foam at the mouth** To be very angry. **foaminess** n., **foamy** adj.

fob n. A chain or ribbon attached to a pocket watch and worn dangling from a pocket; an ornament or seal worn on a fob. v. To dispose of by fraud, deceit, or trickery; to put off by excuse.

focal length n. The distance to the focus from a lens surface or concave mirror.

fo·cus n., pl. **cuses** or **ci** A point in an optical system at which rays converge or from which they appear to diverge; the clarity with which an optical system delivers an image; adjustment for clarity; a center of activity or interest. v. To produce a sharp, clear image of; to adjust a lens in order to produce a clean image; to direct; to come together at a point of focus. **focal** adj., **focally** adv.

fod-der n. A coarse feed for livestock, made from chopped stalks of corn and hay.

foe n. An enemy in war; an opponent or adversary.

foe-tal adj. Variation of fetal.

foe-tus n. Variation of fetus.

fog n. A vapor mass of condensed water which lies close to the ground; a state of mental confusion or bewilderment. v. To obscure or cover with, as if with fog. **foggily** adv., **-iness** n., **foggy** adj.

fog-horn n. A horn sounded in fog to give warning.

fo-gy or **fo-gey** n. A person with old-fashioned attitudes and ideas. **-ish** adj.

foi-ble n. A minor flaw, weakness, or failing.

foil v. To prevent from being successful; to thwart. n. A very thin, flexible sheet of metal; one that serves as a contrast; a fencing sword having a light, thin, flexible blade and a blunt point. **foiled**, **foiling** v.

foist v. To pass off something as valuable or genuine.

fold v. To double or lay one part over another; to bring from an opened to a closed position; to put together and intertwine; to envelop or wrap; to blend in by gently turning one part over another. Slang To give in; to stop production; to fail in business. n. A line, layer, pleat or crease formed by folding; a folded edge; an enclosed area for domestic animals; a flock of sheep; a people united by common aims and beliefs; a church and its members. **folding**, **folded** v.

fol-de-rol n. Nonsense; a pretty but useless ornament.

fo-li-age n. The leaves of growing plants and trees; a cluster of flowers and branches.

fo-li-o n. A large sheet of paper folded once in the middle; a folder for loose papers; a book that consists of folios; a page number.

folk n., pl. **folk** or **folks** An ethnic group of people forming a nation or tribe; people of a specified group. Slang A person's parents, family, or relatives.

fol-li-cle n. A small anatomical cavity or sac.

fol-low v. To proceed or come after; to pursue; to follow the course of; to obey; to come after in time or position; to ensue; to result; to attend to closely; to understand the meaning of. **following**, **followed** v.

fol-ly n., pl. **-ies** Lack of good judgment; an instance of foolishness; an excessively costly and often unprofitable undertaking.

fo-ment v. To rouse; to incite; to treat therapeutically with moist heat. **foment**, **fomentation** n.

fond adj. Affectionate liking; cherished with great affection; deeply felt. **fondly** adv., **fondness** n.

fon-dant n. A sweet, soft preparation of sugar used in candies and icings; a candy made chiefly of fondant.

fon-dle v. To stroke, handle, or caress affectionately and tenderly. **-ed**, **-ling** v.

font n. A receptacle in a church that holds baptismal or holy water; an assortment of printing type of the same size and face.

food n. A substance consisting essentially of carbohydrates and protein used to sustain life and growth in the body of an organism; nourishment, as in solid form; something that sustains or nourishes. **food for thought** Something to think about, something to ponder.

food-stuff n. A substance having food value.

fool n. One lacking good sense or judgment; one who can easily be tricked or made to look foolish. *v.* To dupe; to act in jest; to joke. *Slang* To amuse oneself. fooling *v.*

foot *n., pl.* **feet**

The lower extremity of the vertebrate leg upon which one stands; a unit of measurement equal to 12 inches; a basic unit of verse meter that consists of a group of syllables; the end lower or opposite the head; the lowest part. *v.* To go on foot; to walk or run. *Slang* To pay the bill. on foot Walking rather than riding.

foot-bridge *n.* A bridge for pedestrians.

foot-fall *n.* A footstep; the sound of a footstep.

foot-hill *n.* A low hill at or near the foot of a mountain or a higher hill.

foot-hold *n.* A place providing support for the foot, as in climbing; a position usable as a base for advancement.

foot-ing *n.* Secure and stable position for placement of the feet; a foundation.

foot-less *adj.* Without feet.

foot-locker *n.* A small trunk for personal belongings, designed to be placed at the foot of a bed.

foot-loose *adj.* Free to move as one pleases; having no ties.

foot-note *n.* A note of reference, explanation, or comment usually below the text on a printed page; a commentary. footnote *v.*

fop *n.* A man unduly concerned with his clothes or appearance; a dandy. foppery, foppishness *n.*, foppish *adj.*

for *prep.* Used to indicate the extent of something; used to indicate the number or amount of; considering the usual characteristics of; on behalf of someone; to be in favor of. *conj.* Because; in as much as; with the purpose of.

for-ay *n.* A raid to plunder. foray *v.*

for-bade *or* **for-bad** *v.* Past tense of forbid.

for-bear *v.* To refrain from; to cease from. forbearance *n.*

for-bid *v.* To command someone not to do something; to prohibit by law; to prevent.

forbidding *adj.* Very difficult; disagreeable.

force *n.* Energy or power; strength; the use of such power.

for-ceps *n.* forceps *pl.* An instrument resembling a pair of tongs used for manipulating, grasping or extracting, especially in surgery.

forc-i-ble *adj.* Accomplished or achieved by force; marked by force. -ly *adv.*

fore *adj. & adv.* Situated in, at, or toward the front; forward. *n.* The front of something. *interj.* A cry used by a golfer to warn others that a ball is about to land in their direction.

fore--and--aft *adj.* Lying or going lengthwise on a ship; from stem to stern.

fore-arm *v.* To prepare in advance, as for a battle. *n.* The part of the arm between the elbow and the wrist.

fore-bear *or* **for-bear** *n.* An ancestor.

fore-bode *v.* To give an indication or warning in advance; to have a premonition of something evil. foreboding *n.*, forbodingly *adv.*

fore-cast *v.* To estimate or calculate in advance, especially to predict the weather. forecast, forecaster *n.*

fore-close *v.* To recall a mortgage in default and take legal possession of the mortgaged property; to exclude; to shut out. foreclosure *n.*

fore-fa-ther *n.* An ancestor.

fore-fin-ger *n.* The finger next to the thumb.

fore-foot *n.* A front foot of an animal, insect, etc.

fore-front *n.* The foremost or very front of something; the vanguard.

fore-go *v.* To go before; to precede in time, place, etc. foregoing *v.*

fore-go-ing *adj.* Before; previous.

fore-gone *adj.* Already finished or gone.

fore-ground *n.* The part of a picture or landscape represented as nearest to the viewer.

for-eign *adj.* Situated outside one's native country; belonging to; located in or concerned with a country or region other than one's own; involved with other nations; occurring in a place or body in which it is not normally located.

fore-ign-er *n.* A person from a different place or country; an alien.

fore-knowl-edge *n.* Prior knowledge of something; knowledge beforehand.

fore-lock *n.* A lock of hair growing from the front of the scalp and hanging over the forehead.

fore-man *n.* The person who oversees a group of people; the spokesperson for a jury. forewoman *n.*

fore-mast *n., Naut.* The forward mast of a sailing vessel; the mast nearest the bow of a ship.

fore-most *adj. & adv.* First in rank, position, time, or order.

fore-noon *n.* The period between sunrise and noon.

fo-ren-sic *adj.* Of, relating to, or used in courts of justice or formal debate. forensically *adv.*

fo-ren-sic med-i-cine *n.* A science dealing with the application of medicine in legal problems.

fore-or-dain *v.* Appoint or dispose of in advance; predestine.

fore-part *n.* The first or earliest part of a period of time.

fore-sail *n., Naut.* The sail carried on the foremast of a square-rigged vessel.

fore-see *v.* To know or see beforehand. foreseeable *adj.*, foreseer *n.*

fore-shad-ow *v.* To represent or warn of beforehand.

fore-shore *n.* The part of a shore uncovered at low tide.

fore-sight *n*. The act or capacity of foreseeing; the act of looking forward; concern for the future; prudence. **foresighted** *adj*., **foresightedness** *n*.

fore-skin *n*. A fold of skin that covers the glans of the penis.

for-est *n*. A large tract of land covered with trees; something resembling a forest, as in quantity or density. *v*. To cover with trees. **-ed** *adj*., **-land** *n*.

fore-stall *v*. To exclude, hinder, or prevent by prior measures.

fore-taste *v*. To sample or indicate beforehand. **foretasting**, **foretasted** *v*., **foretaste** *n*.

fore-tell *v*. To tell about in advance; to predict. **foretelling** *v*., **foreteller** *n*.

fore-thought *n*. Prior thought or planning; a plan for the future.

fore-to-ken *v*. To warn beforehand.

for-ev-er *adv*. For eternity; without end.

fore-warn *v*. To warn in advance. **-ed** *v*.

fore-word *n*. An introductory statement preceding the text of a book.

for-feit *n*. Something taken away as punishment; a penalty; something that is placed in escrow and redeemed on payment of a fine; a forfeiture.

for-gath-er *v*. To come together; to convene; to assemble. **-ing**, **-ed** *v*.

forge *n*. A furnace where metals are heated and wrought; a smithy; a workshop that produces wrought iron.

for-get *v*. To lose the memory of; to fail to become mindful or aware of at the right time. **forgetful**, **forgetable** *adj*., **forgetfully** *adv*., **forgetable** *adj*.

for-give *v*. To pardon; to give up resentment of; to cease to feel resentment against. **-ness** *n*., **-able** *adj*.

for-go *or* **fore-go** *v*. To give up or refrain from. **forgoer** *n*.

forked *adj*. Shaped like or having a fork.

for-lorn *adj*. Abandoned or left in distress; hopeless; being in a poor condition. **forlornly** *adv*., **forlornness** *n*.

form *n*. The shape or contour of something; a body of a living being; the basic nature of or particular state of something.

for-mal *adj*. Of or pertaining to the outward aspect of something; relating or concerned with the outward form of something; adhering to convention, rule, or etiquette; based on accepted conventions. **formally** *adv*.

for-mal-de-hyde *n*. A colorless, gaseous chemical used chiefly as a preservative and disinfectant in synthesizing other compounds.

for-mat *n*. A general style of a publication; the general form or layout of a publication. *v*. In computer science, to produce data in a specified form.

for-ma-tion *n*. The act or process of forming or the state of being formed; the manner in which something is formed; a given arrangement, as of troops, as a square or in a column.

for-ma-tive *adj*. Forming or having the power to form; of or pertaining to formation, growth, or development.

for-mer *adj*. Previous; preceding in place; being the first of two persons or things mentioned or referred to.

for-mer-ly *adv*. Previously.

form--fit-ting *adj*. Following closely to the contours of the body.

for-mi-da-ble *adj*. Extremely diffcult; exciting fear by reason of size or strength. **formidably** *adv*.

for-mu-la *n*., *pl*. **-las** *or* **-lae** A prescribed method of words or rules for use in a certain ceremony or procedure; a nutritious food for an infant in liquid form. *Math*. A combination or rule used to express an algebraic or symbolic form. *Chem*. A symbolic representation of the composition of a chemical compound. **formulaic** *adj*.

for-mu-late *v*. To state or express as a formula. **formulation**, **formulator** *n*., **formulating**, **formulated** *v*.

for-ni-ca-tion *n*. Voluntary sexual intercourse between two unmarried people. **fornicate** *v*., **fornicator** *n*.

for-sake *v*. To abandon or renounce; to give up. **forsaking** *v*.

for-sooth *adv*. In truth; certainly.

for-swear *v*. To renounce emphatically or upon oath; to forsake; to swear falsely; to perjure oneself. **-ing** *v*.

for-syth-i-a *n*. An Asian shrub cultivated for its early-blooming, bright, yellow flowers.

fort *n*. A fortified structure or enclosure capable of defense against an enemy; a permanent army post.

forte *n*. An activity one does with excellence; a person's strong point; the part of a sword blade between the middle and the hilt.

forth *adv*. Out into plain sight, as from seclusion; forward in order, place, or time.

forth-com-ing *adj*. Ready or about to appear or occur; readily available.

forth-right *adj*. Straightforward; direct; frank. **-ly** *adv*., **forthrightness** *n*.

forth-with *adv*. At once; promptly; immediately.

for-tis-si-mo *adv*., *Music*. Very loudly (used as a direction). **fortissimo** *adj*.

for-ti-tude *n*. Strength of mind in adversity, pain, or peril, allowing a person to withstand pain.

fort-night *n*. A period of two weeks. **fortnightly** *adj*. & *adv*.

FOR-TRAN *n*. In computer science, a programming language for problems that are expressed in algebraic terms.

for-tress *n*. A fort.

for-tu-i-tous *adj*. Occurring by chance; lucky; fortunate. **fortuitously** *adv*.

for-tu-nate *adj*. Brought about by good fortune; having good fortune.

for-tune *n*. A hypothetical force that unpredictably determines events and issues favorably and unfavorably; success that results from luck; possession of material goods; a very large amount of money.

for-tune hunt-er *n*. A person who seeks wealth through marriage.

for-ty *n., pl.* **-ies** The cardinal number equal to four times ten.
fortieth *n., adj. & adv.*,
forty *adj. & pron.*

forty winks *n., Slang* A short nap.

for-ward *adj.* At, near, or toward a place or time in advance.

fos-sil *n.* The remains of an animal or plant of a past geologic age preserved in the rocks of the earth's surface; one that is outdated.
fossilization *n.*, **fossilize** *v.*

foun-da-tion *n.* The act of founding or establishing; the basis on which anything is founded; an institution supported by an endowment; a cosmetic base for make-up.

foun-dry *n., pl.* **ries** An establishment where metal is cast.

fount *n.* A fountain; an abundant source.

four *n.* The cardinal number that equals 3 + 1; anything consisting of four units. **four** *adj. & pron.*

four-score *adj.* Being four times twenty; eighty.

four-teen *n.* The cardinal number that equals 13 + 1; anything consisting of fourteen units.
fourteen *adj. & pron.*,
fourteenth *n., adj. & adv.*

fourth *n.* The ordinal number matching the number four in a series; the fourth forward gear of a transmission in a motor vehicle. **fourth** *adj. & adv.*

four--wheel *adj.* An automotive transmission in which all four wheels are linked to the source of driving power.

fowl *n., pl.* **fowl** or **fowls** A bird used as food or hunted as game, as the duck, goose, etc.; the edible flesh of a fowl. *v.* To hunt or catch wild fowl. **fowler** *n.*

fox *n.*

A wild mammal having a pointed snout, upright ears, and a long bushy tail; the fur of a fox; a sly or crafty person. *v.* To outwit; to trick.

fox-hole *n.* A shallow pit dug by a soldier as cover against enemy fire.

fox-hound *n.* A large dog breed developed for fox hunting.

fox terrier *n.* A small dog having a wiry or smooth white coat with dark markings.

fox--trot *n.* A ballroom dance in 4/4 or 2/4 time consisting of a variety of rhythmic steps.

fox-y *adj.* Like a fox; sly or crafty; sharp *Slang* Very pretty. **foxily** *adv.*

foy-er *n.* The public lobby of a hotel, theater, etc.; an entrance hall.

fra-cas *n.* A noisy quarrel or disturbance; fight or dispute.

frac-tion *n.* A small part; a disconnected part or fragment of anything; in mathematics, an indicated quantity less than a whole number that is expressed as a decimal. *Chem.* A component of a compound separated from a substance by distilling. **fractional** *adj.*

frac-ture *n.* The act of breaking; the state of being broken. *Med.* The breaking or cracking, as in a bone.

frag-ile *adj.* Easily damaged or broken; frail; tenuous; flimsy.
fragilely *adv.*, **fragility** *n.*

frag-ment *n.* A part detached or broken; part unfinished or incomplete. *v.* To break into fragments. **fragmentation** *n.*

fra-grant *adj.* Having an agreeable, especially sweet odor. **fragrance** *n.*,
fragrantly *adv.*

frail *adj.* Delicate; weak; easily damaged.
frailly *adv.*, **frailness** *n.*

fran-chise *n.* A privilege or right granted to a person or group by a government; the constitutional right to vote; authorization to sell a manufacturer's products; the territory within which a privilege or immunity is authorized.
franchise *v.*, **franchisee, franchiser** *n.*

fran-gi-ble *adj.* Breakable. **frangibility** *n.*

frank *adj.* Sincere and straightforward.

frank-in-cense *n.* An aromatic gum resin obtained from African and Asian trees used as incense and in medicine.

fran-tic *adj.* Emotionally out of control with worry or fear.
frantically, franticly *adv.*

fra-ter-nal *adj.* Pertaining to or relating to brothers; of, pertaining to, or befitting a fraternity. *Biol.* Of or relating to a twin or twins that developed from separately fertilized ova.
fraternalism *n.*, **fraternally** *adv.*

frat-er-nize *v.* To associate with others in a friendly way; to mingle intimately with the enemy, often in violation of military law. **-ing, fraternized** *v.*

frat-ri-cide *n.* The killing of one's brother or sister; one who has killed his brother or sister. **fratricidal** *adj.*

fraud *n.* A deliberate and willful deception perpetrated for unlawful gain; a trick or swindle; an impostor; a cheat.

fraud-u-lent *adj.* Marked by or practicing fraud. **-ence** *n.*, **fraudulently** *adv.*

fraught *adj.* Full of or accompanied by something specified.

fray *n.* A brawl, or fight; a heated argument or dispute. *v.* To wear out by rubbing; to irritate one's nerves.

fraz-zle *v., Slang* To wear out; to completely fatigue. **frazzle** *n.*,

free *adj.* Not imprisoned; not under obligation; politically independent.

free-dom *n.* The condition or state of being free; political independence; possession of political rights; boldness of expression; liberty; unrestricted access or use.

freight *n.* A service of transporting commodities by air, land or water; the price paid such transportation; a train that transports goods only. *v.* To carry as cargo.

freight-er *n.* A ship used for transporting cargo.

fren-zy *n., pl.* **-ies** A state of extreme excitement or violent agitation; temporary insanity or delirium. **-ied** *adj.*

fre-quent *adj.* Happening or appearing often or time after time. *v.* To go to a place repeatedly. **frequenter, frequentness** *n.*, **frequently** *adv.*

fres-co *n., pl.* **-coes** *or* **-cos** The art of painting on moist plaster with water-based paint; a picture so painted.

fresh *adj.* Newly-made, gathered, or obtained; not spoiled, musty, or stale.

fri-a-ble *adj.* Easily crumbled or pulverized brittle. **friability, friableness** *n.*

fri-ar *n.* A member of a mendicant Roman Catholic order.

fric-as-see *n.* A dish of meat or poultry stewed in gravy. **fricassee** *v.*

fric-tion *n.* The rubbing of one surface or object against another; a conflict or clash. *Phys.* A force that retards the relative motion of two touching objects. **frictional** *adj.*

frieze *n.* A decorative horizontal band along the upper part of a wall in a room.

frig-ate *n.* A square-rigged warship of the 17th to mid 19th centuries; U.S. warship smaller than a cruiser but larger than a destroyer.

fright *n.* Sudden violent alarm or fear; a feeling of alarm. *Slang* Something very unsightly or ugly.

fright-en *v.* To fill with fear; to force by arousing fear. **-ing** *adj.*, **-ingly** *adv.*

frig-id *adj.* Very cold; lacking warmth of feeling or emotional warmth; sexually unresponsive. **-ity, -ness** *n.*, **-ly** *adv.*

frill *n.* A decorative ruffled or gathered border. *Slang* A superfluous item. **frilly** *adj.*

fringe *n.* An edging that consists of hanging threads, cords, or loops. **fringe** *v.*

frip-per-y *n., pl.* **-ies** Showy and often cheap ornamentation; a pretentious display.

friv-o-lous *adj.* Trivial; insignificant; lacking importance; not serious; silly. **frivolousness** *n.*, **frivolously** *adv.*

frizz *v.* To form into small, tight curls. **frizziness** *n.*, **frizzily** *adv.*, **frizzy** *adj.*

fro *adv.* Away from; back, as running to and fro.

frock *n.* A smock or loose-fitting robe; a robe worn by monks.

frog *n.*

Any of various small, smooth-skinned, web-footed, largely aquatic, tailless, leaping amphibians; an ornamental braid or cord; an arrangement of intersecting railroad tracks designed to permit wheels to pass over the intersection without difficulty; a perforated holder for flower stems. *Slang* Hoarseness in the throat.

frol-ic *n.* Merriness; a playful, carefree occasion. *v.* To romp about playfully; to have fun. **-ker** *n.*, **frolicsome** *adj.*

from *prep.* Starting at a particular time or place; used to indicate a specific point; used to indicate a source; used to indicate separation or removal; used to indicate differentiation, as knowing right from left.

frond *n.* A large leaf, as of a tropical fern, usually divided into smaller leaflets.

fron-tier *n.* A part of an international border or the area adjacent to it; an unexplored area of knowledge or thought. **frontiersman** *n.*

fron-tis-piece *n.* An illustration that usually precedes the title page of a book or periodical.

froth *n.* A mass of bubbles on or in a liquid, resulting from agitation or fermentation; a salivary foam, as of an animal, resulting from disease or exhaustion; anything unsubstantial or trivial. *v.* To expel froth. **frothily** *adv.*, **frothiness** *n.*, **frothy** *adj.*

frou-frou *n.* A rustling sound, as of silk; a frilly dress or decoration.

for-ward *adj.* Obstinate. **forwardness** *n.*

frown *v.* To contract the brow as in displeasure or concentration; to look on with distaste or disapproval. **frown** *n.*, **frowningly** *adv.*, **frowned, frowning** *v.*

frow-zy *or* **frow-sy** *adj.* Appearing unkempt.

fru-i-tion *n.* Achievement or accomplishment of something worked for or desired; the state of bearing fruit.

frump-y *adj.* Unfashionable; dowdy. **frump, frumpiness** *n.*

frus-trate *v.* To keep from attaining a goal or fulfilling a desire; to thwart; to prevent the fruition of; to nullify. **frustration** *n.*, **frustratingly** *adv.*, **frustrating, frustrated** *v.*

fuch-sia *n.* A chiefly tropical plant widely grown for its drooping, four-petaled flowers of purple, red, or white.

fu-gi-tive *adj.* Fleeing or having fled, as from arrest, pursuit, etc. *n.* One who flees or tries to escape.

fugue *n., Mus.* A musical composition in which the theme is elaborately repeated by different voices or instruments; a psychological disturbance in which actions are not remembered after returning to a normal state.

ful-crum *n., pl.* **-crums** *or* **-cra** The point on which a lever turns.

ful-fill *or* **ful-fil** *v.* To convert into actuality; to effect; to carry out; to satisfy. **fulfillment, fulfilment** *n.*

ful-mi-nate *v.* To condemn severely; to explode. **fulmination, fulminator** *n.*, **fulminated, fulminating** *v.*

ful-some *adj.* Offensively insincere. **fulsomely** *adv.*, **fulsomeness** *n.*

fume *n., often* **fumes** An irritating smoke, gas, or vapor. *v.* To treat with or subject to fumes; to show or feel anger or distress.

fu-mi-gate *v.* To subject to fumes in order to exterminate vermin or insects. **-ation, -tor** *n.*, **-ed, -ing** *v.*

func-tion *n.* The characteristics or proper activity of a person or thing; specific occupation, duty, or role; an official occupation, duty, or role; an official ceremony; something depending upon or varying with another; in math, a quantity whose value is dependent on the value of another. *v.* To serve or perform a function as required or expected.

fun-da-men-tal *adj.* Basic or essential; of major significance; anything serving as the primary origin; most important. **fundamental** *n.*, **fundamentally** *adv.*

fu-ner-al *n.* The service performed in conjunction with the burial or cremation of a dead person.

fun-gus *n.*, *pl.* **-gi** *or* **-guses**

Any of numerous spore-bearing plants which have no chlorophyll that include yeasts, molds, mildews, and mushrooms. **fungous, fungal** *adj.*

fu-nic-u-lar *n.* A cable railway along which cable cars are drawn up a mountain, especially one with ascending and descending cars that counterbalance one another.

fur-be-low *n.* A ruffle or frill on clothing; a piece of showy decoration or ornamentation.

fur-bish *v.* To make bright, as by rubbing; to polish; to renovate. **furbishing, furbished** *v.*

fu-ri-ous *adj.* Extremely angry; marked by rage or activity. **furiously** *adv.*

furl *v.* To roll up and secure to something, as a pole or mast; to curl or fold. **furl** *n.*

fur-nace *n.* A large enclosure designed to produce intense heat.

fur-nish *v.* To outfit or equip, as with fittings or furniture. **-er** *n.*, **furnishing** *v.*

fu-ror *n.* Violent anger; rage; great excitement; commotion; an uproar.

fur-row *n.* A long, narrow trench in the ground, made by a plow or other tool; a deep wrinkle in the skin, especially of the forehead. **furrow** *v.*

fur-tive *adj.* Done in secret; surreptitious; obtained underhandedly; stolen.

fu-ry *n.*, *pl.* **-ies** Uncontrolled anger; turbulence; an angry or spiteful woman.

fu-sil-lage *n.* The central section of an airplane, containing the wings and tail assembly.

fu-sion *n.* The act or procedure of melting together by heat; a blend produced by fusion; a nuclear reaction in which nuclei of a light element combine to form more massive nuclei, with the release of huge amounts of energy.

fus-tian *n.* A sturdy, stout cotton cloth. *adj.* Pompous, pretentious language; bombastic.

fu-tile *adj.* Ineffectual; being of no avail; without useful result; serving no useful purpose.

fuzz *n.* A mass of fine, loose particles,

G, g The seventh letter of the English alphabet. *Mus.* The fifth tone in the scale of C major. *Slang* One thousand dollars; a grand. *Physiol* A unit of force equal to that due to the earth's gravity.

gab-ar-dine *n.* A firm cotton, wool, or rayon material, having a diagonal raised weave, used for suits and coats.

gab-ble *v.* To speak rapidly or incoherently. **gabble** *n.*

gab-bro *n.* A granular igneous rock. **gabbroci, gabbroitic** *adj.*

ga-boon *n.* An African tree with reddish-brown whood and is used mainly in furniture.

gad *v.* To wander about restlessly with little or no purpose. **gadder** *n.*

gad-a-bout *n.*, *Slang* A person seeking fun.

gad-fly *n.* A fly that bites or annoys cattle and horses; an irritating, critical, but often constructively provocative person.

gadg-et *n.*, *Slang* A small device or tool used in performing miscellaneous jobs, especially in the kitchen.

gad-o-lin-i-um *n.* A metallic element, silvery-white in color, of the lanthanide series, symbolized by Gd.

gaff *n.* A sharp iron hook used for landing fish. *Naut.* A spar on the top edge of a fore-and-aft sail. *Slang* Abuse or harsh treatment.

gage *n.* Something that is given as security for an action to be performed; a pledge; anything, as a glove, thrown down as a challenge to fight.

gag-gle *n.* A flock of geese; a group; a cluster.

gai-e-ty *n.*, *pl.* **-ies** The state of being happy; cheerfulness; fun.

gai-ly *adv.* A gay or cheerful manner; showily or brightly.

gain *v.* To earn or acquire possession of something; to succeed in winning a victory; to develop an increase of; to put on weight; to secure as a profit; to improve progress; to draw nearer to.

gain-ful *adj.* Producing profits; lucrative. **gainfully** *adv.*, **gainfulness** *n.*

gain-say *v.* To deny; to contradict; dispute. **gainsayer** *n.*

gait *n.* A way or manner of moving on foot; one of the foot movements in which a horse steps or runs.

ga-la *n.* A festive celebration. **gala** *adj.*

ga-lac-tose *n.* The sugar typically occurring in lactose.

gal-ax-y *n.*, *pl.* **-ies** *Astron.* Any of the very large systems of stars, nebulae, or other celestial bodies that constitute the universe; a brilliant, distinguished group or assembly. **Galaxy** The Milky Way. **galactic** *adj.*

gale *n.*, *Meteor.* A very powerful wind stronger than a stiff breeze; an outburst, as of hilarity.

ga-le-na *n.* A metallic, dull gray mineral that is the principal ore of lead.

gall *n.*, *Physiol.* The bitter fluid secreted by the liver; bile; bitterness of feeling;

animosity; impudence; something that irritates. *v.* To injure the skin by friction; to chafe. **-ing** *adj.*, **-ingly** *adv.*

gal-lant *adj.* Dashing in appearance or dress; majestic; stately; chivalrously attentive to women; courteous. **-ly** *adv.*

gal-lant-ry *n., pl.* **-ries** Nobility and bravery; a gallant act.

gall-blad-der *or* **gall bladder** *n.*

The small sac under the right lobe of the liver that stores bile.

gal-le-on *n.* A large three-masted sailing ship.

gal-ler-y *n., pl.* **-ries** A long, narrow passageway, as a corridor, with a roofed promenade, especially an open-sided one extending along an inner or outer wall of a building; a group of spectators, as at a golf tournament; a building where statues, paintings, and other works of art are displayed; a room or building where articles are sold to the highest bidder; an underground passage in a mine. **galleried** *adj.*, **gallery** *v.*

gal-li-nule *n.* A wading bird with dark iridescent plumage.

gal-li-um *n.* A silvery metallic element used in semiconductor technology and as a component of various low-melting alloys, symbolized by Ga.

gal-li-vant *v.* To roam about in search of amusement or pleasure.

gal-lon *n.* A liquid measurement used in the U.S., equal to 4 quarts; in Great Britain, a liquid measurement which equals 4 imperial quarts; a dry measurement that equals 1/8 bushel.

gal-lop *n.* A horse's gait that is faster than a canter and characterized by regular leaps during which all four feet are off the ground at once.

gal-lows *n.* A framework of two or more upright beams and a crossbeam, used for execution by hanging.

gall-stone *n., Pathol.* A small, hard concretion of cholesterol crystals that sometimes form in the gall bladder or bile passages.

ga-lore *adj.* In great numbers; abundant; plentiful.

ga-losh *pl., n.* galoshes Waterproof overshoes which are worn in bad weather.

gal-va-nism *n.* Electricity that is produced by chemical action. *Med.* A therapeutic application of continuous electric current from voltaic cells.

gal-va-nize *v.* To stimulate or shock muscular action by an electric current; to protect iron or steel with rust resistant zinc. *Slang* To infuse with

energy. **galvanization, galvanizer** *n.*

gal-va-nom-e-ter *n., Electr.* An apparatus for detecting the presence of an electric current and for determining its strength and direction. **-metric** *adj.*

gam-bit *n.* In chess, an opening in which a piece is sacrificed for a favorable position; a maneuver that is carefully planned.

gam-ble *v.* To take a chance on an uncertain outcome as a contest or a weekly lottery number. *n.* Any risky venture. **gambler** *n.*

gam-bol *v.* To frolic, skip, or leap about in play.

gam-brel roof *Archit.* A ridged roof with the slope broken on each side, the lower slope steeper than the upper.

gam-ete *n., Biol.* Either of two mature reproductive cells, an ovum or sperm, which produce a zygote when united.

gam-in *n.* A homeless child who wanders about the streets of a town or city.

gam-ma globulin *n., Biochem.* A globulin that is present in blood plasma and contains antibodies effective against certain infectious diseases.

gamma ray *n., Phys.* Electromagnetic radiation that has energy greater than several hundred thousand electron volts.

gam-mon *n.* A cured ham; in the game of backgammon, a double victory in which a player removes all his pieces before the other player removes any.

gam-ut *n.* The whole range or extent of anything.

gam-y *adj.* Having the strong flavor of game, especially when slightly tainted; scandalous.

gan-der *n.* A male goose. *Slang* A quick glance; a look or peek.

gang *n.* A group of persons who are organized and work together or socialize regularly; a group of adolescent hoodlums or criminals. **gang up on** To attack as a group.

gan-gling *adj.* Tall and thin; lanky.

gan-gli-on *n., pl.* **-glia** *or* **-ons** *Physiol.* A collection of nerve cells located outside the spinal cord or brain. **ganglionic** *adj.*

gang-plank *n.* A temporary board or ramp used to board or leave a ship.

gan-grene *n., Pathol.* The death and decay of tissue in the body caused by a failure in the circulation of the blood supply. **gangrene** *v.*, **gangrenous** *adj.*

gan-net *n.* A large sea bird with white plumage and black wing tips, related to the pelican and heron.

gan-try *n., pl.* **-ies** *Aeros.* A bridge-like framework support, especially a movable vertical structure with platforms, that is used in assembling or servicing rockets before they are launched.

gap *n.* An opening or wide crack, as in a wall; a cleft; a deep notch or ravine in a mountain ridge, offering passage.

gape *v.* To open the mouth wide, as in

yawning; to stare in amazement with the mouth wide open; to become widely separated or open. **gaper** *n.*

ga-rage *n.* A building or structure in which motor vehicles are stored, repaired, or serviced.

gar-ble *v.* To mix up or confuse; to change or distort the meaning of with the intent to mislead or misrepresent. **garble, garbler** *n.*

gar-den *n.* A place for growing flowers, vegetables, or fruit; a piece of ground commonly used as a public resort. *v.* To work in or make into a garden. **gardener, gardening** *n.*

gar-de-nia *n.* A tropical shrub with glossy evergreen leaves and fragrant white flowers.

gar-gan-tu-an *adj.* Of enormous size; immense.

gar-gle *v.* To force air from the lungs through a liquid held in the back of the mouth and throat. **gargle** *n.*

gar-goyle *n.* A waterspout made or carved to represent a grotesque animal or human figure, projecting from a gutter to throw rain away from the side of a building.

gar-ish *adj.* Too showy and bright; gaudy. **garishly** *adv.*, **garishness** *n.*

gar-land *n.* A wreath, chain, or rope of flowers or leaves. *v.* To decorate with or form into a garland. *Naut.* A ring of rope attached to a spar to aid in hoisting or to prevent chafing.

gar-lic *n.* A plant related to the onion with a compound bulb which contains a strong odor and flavor, used as a seasoning.

gar-ment *n.* An article of clothing.

gar-ner *v.* To gather and store; to accumulate.

gar-net *n.* A dark-red silicate mineral used as a gemstone and as an abrasive.

gar-nish *v.* To add something to, as to decorate or embellish; to add decorative or flavorful touches to food or drink. **garnish** *n.*

gar-nish-ment *n.* The act of garnishing; the legal proceeding that turns property belonging to a debtor over to his creditor.

gar-ni-ture *n.* Anything that is used to garnish.

gar-ret *n.* A room in an attic.

gar-ri-son *n.* The military force that is permanently placed in a fort or town; a military post.

gar-rote *or* **gar-rotte** *n.* The former Spanish method of execution by strangulation with an iron collar tightened by a screw-like device.

gar-ru-lous *adj.* Given to continual talkativeness; chatty. **garrulity**, **garrulousness** *n.*

gar-ter *n.* A band or strap that is worn to hold a stocking in place.

gash *n.* A long, deep cut. **gash** *v.*

gas-ket *n.*, *Mech.* A rubber seal, disk, or ring used between matched machine parts or around pipe joints to prevent the escape of fluid or gas.

gas-light *n.* A light produced by burning illuminating gas.

gas mask *n.* A protective respirator which covers the face and contains a chemical air filter to protect against poisonous gases.

gas-o-hol *n.* A fuel blended from unleaded gasoline and ethanol.

gas-o-line *or* **gas-o-lene** *n.* A colorless, highly flammable mixture of liquid hydrocarbons made from crude petroleum and used as a fuel and a solvent.

gasp *v.* To inhale suddenly and sharply, as from fear or surprise; to make labored or violent attempts to breathe.

gas-tric *adj.* Of or pertaining to the stomach.

gas-tric juice *n.*, *Biochem.* The digestive fluid secreted by the stomach glands, containing several enzymes.

gas-tric ul-cer *n.*, *Pathol.* An ulcer formed on the stomach lining, often caused by excessive secretion of gastric juices.

gas-tri-tis *n.*, *Pathol.* Inflammation of the stomach lining. **gastritic** *adj.*

gas-tro-en-ter-ol-o-gy *n.* The medical study of the stomach and intestines. **gastroenterologist** *n.*

gas-tron-o-my *n.* The art of good eating. **gastronome** *n.*, **gastronomical** *adj.*

gas-tro-pod *n.* One of the large class of aquatic and terrestrial mollusks, including snails, slugs, limpets, having a single shell and a broad, muscular organ of locomotion. **-ous** *adj.*

gas-works *n.*, *pl.* **-works** An establishment where gas is manufactured.

gat *n.*, *Slang* A pistol; short for Gatling gun.

gate *n.* A movable opening in a wall or fence, commonly swinging on hinges, that closes or opens; a valve-like device for controlling the passage of gas or water through a conduit or dam; the total paid admission receipts or number in attendance at a public performance.

gate--crash-er *n.* One who gains admittance without an invitation or without paying.

gate-leg ta-ble *n.* A table with legs that swing out to support drop leaves, the legs folding against the frame when the leaves are let down.

gath-er *v.* To bring or come together into one place or group; to harvest or pick; to increase or gain; to accumulate slowly; to fold or pleat a cloth by pulling it along a thread. **gather, gathering** *n.*

gauche *adj.* Socially awkward; clumsy; boorish. **gauchely** *adv.*, **gaucheness** *n.*

gaud-y *adj.* Too highly decorated to be in good taste. **gaudiness** *n.*

gauge *or* **gage** *n.* A standard measurement, dimension, or capacity; an instrument used for measuring, testing, or registering; the distance between rails of a railroad; the diameter of the bore of a shotgun barrel. *v.* To determine the capacity, contents or volume of; to estimate; to evaluate. **gauger** *n.*

gaunt *adj.* Thin and bony; haggard; gloomy or desolate in appearance.

gaunt-let *or* **gant-let** *n.*

A challenge to fight; a glove to protect the hand; a former military punishment which forced an offender to run between two lines of men armed with clubs with which to strike him; criticism from all sides.

gauze *n.* A loosely-woven, transarent material used for surgical bandages; any thin, open-mesh material; a mist. **gauzy** *adj.*, **gauziness** *n.*

gav-el *n.* A mallet used by a presiding officer or by a person in charge to call for order or attention. **gavel** *v.*

ga-vi-al *n.* A large crocodile found in India, with long, slender jaws.

ga-votte *n.* A French dance resembling a quick-moving minuet.

gawk *v.* To gape; to stare stupidly.

gay *adj.* Merry; happy and carefree; brightly ornamental or colorful; *n.* A homosexual. **gayness** *n.*

gaze *v.* To look steadily or intently at something in admiration or wonder; to stare.

ga-zelle *n.* A small, gracefully formed antelope of northern Arabia and Africa, having curved horns and large eyes.

ga-zette *n.* A newspaper; an official publication. *v.* To publish or announce in a gazette.

gaz-et-teer *n.* A dictionary consisting of geographical facts.

gear *n., Mech.* A toothed wheel which interacts with another toothed part to transmit motion; an assembly of parts that work together for a special purpose; equipment. *v.* To regulate, match, or suit something. **gearing** *n.*

gear-shift *n., Mech.* A mechanism used for engaging or disengaging the gears in a power transmission system.

gear-wheel *or* **gear wheel** *n., Mech.* A cogwheel.

geck-o *n., pl.* **-os** *or* **-oes** Any of various small lizards of warm regions having toes with adhesive pads enabling them to climb up or down vertical surfaces.

Ge-hen-na *n.* In the New Testament, hell; a place of torment.

ge-fil-te fish *n.* Chopped fish mixed with crumbs, seasoning, and eggs, then cooked in a broth and served chilled in oval-shaped cakes or balls.

gei-sha *n., pl.* **-sha** *or* **-shas** A Japanese girl who furnishes entertainment and companionship for men.

gel *n., Chem.* A colloid that is in a more solid than liquid form. *v.* To change

into or take on the form of a gel.

gel-a-tin *or* **gel-a-tine** *n.* An almost tasteless, odorless, dried protein, soluble in water and derived from boiled animal tissues, used in making foods, drugs, and photographic film; a jelly made from gelatin. **-ous** *adj.*

geld *v.* To castrate or spay, especially a horse.

geld-ing *n.* A gelded animal.

gel-id *adj.* Very cold; frigid. **gelidity** *n.*

gem *n.* A cut and polished precious or semiprecious stone; one that is highly treasured. *v.* To set or decorate with or as with gems.

gem-ol-o-gy *or* **gem-mol-o-gy** *n.* The study of gems. **-ical** *adj.*, **-ist** *n.*

gen-darme *n., pl.* **gendarmes** An armed policeman in France.

gen-der *n., Gram.* Any of two or more categories, as feminine, masculine, and neuter, into which words are divided and which determine agreement with or selection of modifiers or grammatical forms; the quality of being of the male or female sex.

gene *n., Biol.* A functional hereditary unit which occupies a fixed location on a chromosome and controls or acts in the transmission of hereditary characteristics.

ge-ne-al-o-gy *n., pl.* **-ies** A record, table, or account showing the descent of a family, group, or person from an ancestor; the study of ancestry. **genealogical** *adj.*, **-ically** *adv.*, **-ist** *n.*

gen-er-al *adj.* Pertaining to, including, or affecting the whole or every member of a group or class; common to or typical of most; not being limited to a special class; miscellaneous; not detailed or precise. *n., Milit.* An officer in the United States Army, Air Force, or Marine Corps ranking above a colonel. **generally** *adv.*

gen-er-al as-sem-bly *n.* A legislative body. General Assembly The supreme deliberative body of the United Nations.

gen-er-al-i-ty *n., pl.* **-ies** The state or quality of being general; an inadequate, inexact or vague statement or idea.

gen-er-al-ize *v.* To draw a general conclusion from particular facts, experiences, or observations.

gen-er-al-i-za-tion *n.* Something arrived at by generalizing, such as a broad, overall statement or conclusion.

gen-er-al prac-ti-tion-er *n.* A doctor who treats a variety of medical problems rather than specializing in one.

gen-er-al-ship *n.* The office or rank of a general; leadership or management of any type.

gen-er-al staff *n., Milit.* A group of officers who assist the commander in planning and supervising military operations.

gen-er-al store *n.* A retail store selling a

large variety of merchandise but not subdivided into departments.

gen-er-ate v. To cause to be; to produce; to bring into existence, especially by a chemical or physical process. **generative** adj.

gen-er-a-tion n. A group of individuals born at about the same time; the average time interval between the birth of parents and that of their offspring. **generational** adj.

gen-er-a-tor n., Mech. A machine that changes mechanical energy into electrical energy.

ge-ner-ic adj. Relating to or indicating an entire class or group; general; pertaining to a genus or class of related things; of or relating to a class of product, or merchandise that does not bear a trademark or trade name. **generically** adv.

gen-er-ous adj. Sharing freely; abundant; overflowing. -ity n., **generously** adv.

gen-e-sis n., pl. -ses The act or state of originating. **Genesis** The first book of the Old Testament.

ge-net-ic adj. Of or pertaining to the origin or development of something; of or relating to genetics. **genetically** adv.

ge-net-ic code n., Biochem. The biochemical basis of heredity that specifies the amino acid sequence in the synthesis of proteins and on which heredity is based.

gen-ial adj. Cheerful, kind, pleasant and good-humored in disposition or manner. **geniality** n., **genially** adv.

ge-nie n. A supernatural creature, capable of taking on human form, who does one's bidding.

ge-nii n. In ancient mythology, a guardian spirit appointed to guide a person through life.

gen-i-tal adj. Of or pertaining to the reproductive organs or the process of reproduction.

gen-i-tals pl.,n. The external sexual organs. **genitalia** n.

gen-i-tive adj., Gram. Indicating origin, source, or possession. n. The genitive case. **genitival** adj.

gen-i-to-u-ri-nar-y adj., Anat. Of or pertaining to the genital and urinary organs or their functions.

gen-ius n., pl. -ses Exceptional intellectual ability or creative power; a strong, natural talent.

gen-o-cide n. The systematic extermination or destruction of a political, racial, or cultural group. **genocidal** adj.

gens n., pl. **gentes** In ancient Rome, a clan that included families of the same name that have descended through the male line.

gen-teel adj. Refined or well-bred; elegant; polite; stylish or fashionable. **genteelly** adv., **genteelness** n.

gen-tian n. An annual or perennial plant with showy blue, red, yellow, or white flowers.

gen-til-i-ty n. The quality of being gen-

teel; the members of the upper class; wellborn or well-bred persons collectively.

gen-tle adj. Not harsh, severe, rough, or loud; easily handled or managed; docile; not sudden or steep; from a good family of high social standing. Meteor. A soft, moderate breeze. v. To tame. **gently** adv., **gentleness** n.

gen-tle-folk or **gen-tle-folks** pl., n. Persons from good family backgrounds.

gen-tle-man n. A man of noble birth and social position; a courteous or polite man; used as a form of address.

gen-tle-wom-an n. A woman of noble birth and social position; a woman attendant upon a lady of rank; a well-bred or polite woman.

gen-try n. People of good family or high social standing; the aristocracy; in England, the social class that is considered the upper ranks of the middle class.

gen-u-flect v. To bend down on one knee, as in worship. **genuflection** n.

gen-u-ine adj. Real; authentic; not counterfeit or spurious; not hypocritical; sincere. **genuinely** adv., **genuineness** n.

ge-nus n., pl. **nera** Biol. A group or category of plants and animals usually including several species.

ge-o-cen-tric adj. Of or relating to the earth's center; formulated on the assumption that the earth is the center of the universe. -ally adv., -al adj.

ge-o-chem-is-try n. A branch of chemistry that deals with the chemical composition of the earth's crust. **geochemical** adj., **geochemist** n.

ge-o-des-ic dome n. A vaulted or domed structure of lightweight straight elements that form interlocking polygons.

ge-o-des-ic line n. In mathematics, the shortest line that connects two points on a given surface.

ge-od-e-sy n. The geologic science dealing with the determination of the shape, area, and curvature of the earth. **geodesist** n., **geodetic** adj.

ge-og-ra-phy n., pl. -hies The science that deals with the earth's natural climate, resources, and population.

geographer n., **geographic**, **geographical** adj., **geographically** adv.

ge-ol-o-gy n., pl. -ies The science that deals with the history, origin, and structure of the earth.

geologic, **geological** adj., **geologically** adv., **geologist** n.

ge-o-met-ric adj. According to or pertaining to the rules and principles of geometry; increasing in a geometric progression.

ge-o-met-ric pro-gres-sion n. A sequence of numbers, as 4, 8, 16, 32 where each term is the product of a constant factor and the term that precedes it.

ge-om-e-try n., pl. **ies** The branch of mathematics that deals with the measurement, properties, and relationships of lines, angles, points, surfaces and solids.

ge-o-phys-ics *pl., n.* The study of the earth as the product of complex forces that act upon it internally from outer space, with reference to exploration of the less accessible regions.

ge-o-pol-i-tics *pl., n.* The study of the influence of economic and geographical factors on the politics and policies of a nation or region. **geopolitical** *adj.*

ge-o-ther-mal *or* **ge-o-ther-mic** *adj.* Relating to the internal heat of the earth.

ge-ra-ni-um *n.* A plant having rounded leaves and clusters of pink, red, or white flowers; a plant of the genus Pelargonium, with divided leaves and purplish or pink flowers.

ger-bil *n.* An animal of the rodent family found in the desert regions of Africa and Asia Minor, having long hind legs and a long tail; a popular pet.

ger-i-at-rics *pl., n.* The medical study that deals with the structural changes, diseases, physiology, and hygiene of old age. **-ic** *adj.,* **geriatrician** *n.*

germ *n.* A small cell or organic structure from which a new organism may develop; a microorganism which causes disease. *Biol.* A reproductive cell.

ger-mane *adj.* Relevant to what is being considered or discussed.

ger-ma-ni-um *n.* A grayish-white element widely used in electronics and optics, symbolized by Ge.

germ cell *n.* An egg or sperm cell.

ger-mi-cide *n.* An agent used to destroy microorganisms or disease germs. **germicidal** *adj.*

ger-mi-nal *adj.* Of or relating to a germ or germ cell; of or in the earliest stage of development.

ger-mi-nate *v.* To begin to grow, develop, or sprout. **germination** *n.*

germ plasm *n., Biol.* The part of the protoplasm of a germ cell containing the chromosomes and genes.

ger-on-tol-gy *n.* The study of the processes and phenomena of aging. **gerontological, -ic** *adj.,* **gerontologist** *n.*

ger-ry-man-der *v.* To divide a voting area so as to advance unfairly the interests of a political party; to adjust or adapt to one's advantage.

ger-und *n., Gram.* A verb form that is used as a noun.

gest *n.* A notable deed or feat.

ge-sta-po *n.* The secret police in Germany under the Nazi regime, known for its brutality.

ges-ta-tion *n.* The carrying of a developing offspring in the uterus; pregnancy. **gestate** *v.,* **gestational** *adj.*

ges-tic-u-late *v.* To make expressive or emphatic gestures, as in speaking.

ges-ture *n.* A bodily motion, especially with the hands in speaking, to emphasize some idea or emotion. *v.* To make gestures. **gesturer** *n.*

ge-sund-heit *interj. German* A phrase used to wish good health to a person who has just sneezed.

get *v.* To come into possession of, as by receiving, winning, earning or, buying. to get ahead To attain success. to get back at To revenge oneself on. to get by To manage; to survive.

get-a-way *n.* The act of or instance of escaping by a criminal; a start, as of a race.

gew-gaw *n.* A little ornamental article of small value.

gey-ser *n.* A natural hot spring that intermittently ejects hot water and steam.

ghast-ly *adj.* Horrible; terrifying; very unpleasant or bad; ghost-like in appearance; deathly pale.

ghat *n.* A broad flight of steps that leads down to the edge of a river; a mountain pass, range, or chain.

gher-kin *n.* A very small, prickly cucumber pickled as a relish.

ghet-to *n.* A run-down section of a city in which a minority group lives because of poverty or social pressure.

ghost *n.* The spirit of a dead person which is believed to appear to or haunt living persons; a spirit; a ghostwriter; a false, faint secondary television image. **ghostly** *adj.*

ghost-writer *n.* A person hired to write for another person and to give credit for the writing to that other person.

ghoul *n.* A person who robs graves; in Moslem legend, an evil spirit which plunders graves and feeds on corpses. **-ish** *adj.,* **-ishly** *adv.,* **ghoulishness** *n.*

gi-ant *n.* A legendary man-like being of supernatural size and strength; one of great power, importance, or size. **giantess** *n.*

gib-ber *v.* To talk or chatter incoherently or unintelligibly.

gib-ber-ish *n.* Meaningless speech.

gib-bet *n.* A gallows. *v.* To execute by hanging on a gibbet.

gib-bon *n.* A slender, long-armed Asian ape.

gib-bous *adj.* The moon or a planet which is seen with more than half but not all of the apparent disk illuminated. **gibbously** *adv.,* **-ness** *n.*

gibe *v.* To ridicule or make taunting remarks. **gibe, giber** *n.*

gib-let *n., or* **giblets** The heart, liver, and gizzard of a fowl.

gid-dy *adj.* Affected by a reeling or whirling sensation; dizzy; frivolous and silly; flighty. **-ily** *adv.,* **-iness** *n.*

gift *n.* Something that is given from one person to another; a natural aptitude; a talent.

gift-ed *adj.* The state of having a special talent or ability.

gig *n.* A light, two-wheeled carriage drawn by one horse. *Naut.* A speedy, light rowboat; a spear with forks or prongs used for fishing. *Slang* A job, especially an engagement to play music. *Milit., Slang* A demerit; a punishment to military personnel.

gi-gan-tic *adj.* Of tremendous or extraordinary size; huge. **gigantically** *adv.*

gig-gle v. To laugh in high-pitched, repeated, short sounds. **giggle, giggler** n., **giggly** adj.

gig-o-lo n., A man who is supported by a woman not his wife; a man who is paid to be an escort or dancing partner.

gild v. To coat with a thin layer of gold; to brighten or adorn. **gilded** adj., **gilding, gilder** n.

gill n., Zool. The organ, as of fishes and various other aquatic invertebrates, used for taking oxygen from water. n. A liquid measure that equals 1/4 pint.

gilt adj. Covered with or of the color of gold. n. A thin layer of gold or a gold-colored substance which is applied to a surface.

gilt-edge or **gilt-edged** adj. Of the highest value or the best quality.

gim-bal n. A three ringed device that keeps an object supported on it level, as the compass of a ship.

gim-crack n. A cheap and useless object of little or no value.

gim-let n. A small, sharp tool with a bar handle and a pointed, spiral tip which is used for boring holes.

gim-mick n. A tricky feature that is obscured or misrepresented; a tricky device, especially when used dishonestly or secretly; a gadget. **gimmickry** n., **gimmicky** adj.

gin n. An aromatic, clear, alcoholic liquor distilled from grain and flavored with juniper berries; a machine used to separate seeds from cotton fibers. v. To remove the seeds from cotton with a gin.

gin-ger n. A tropical Asian plant that has a pungent aromatic root, used in medicine and cooking.

gin-ger-bread n. A dark, ginger and molasses flavored cake or cookie.

gin-ger-ly adv. Doing something very cautiously. **-iness** n., **gingerly** adj.

ging-ham n. A cotton fabric woven in solid colors and checks.

gin-gi-vi-tis n., Pathol. Inflammation of the gums.

gink-go n., pl. **-goes** or **-koes** A large Chinese shade tree cultivated in the United States, with edible fruits and nuts.

gin rum-my n. A variety of the card game rummy.

gin-seng n. A herb native to China and North America with an aromatic root believed to have medicinal properties.

gi-raffe n., pl. **-fes** or **-fe**

The tallest of all mammals, having an extremely long neck and very long legs, found in Africa.

gird v. To surround, encircle, or attach with or as if with a belt.

gird-er n. A strong, horizontal beam, as of steel or wood, which is the main support in a building.

gir-dle n. A cord or belt worn around the waist; a supporting undergarment worn by women to give support and to shape. **girdle** v.

girl n. A female child or infant; a young, unmarried woman; any woman of any age; one's sweetheart. **girlish** adj., **girlishly** adv., **girlishness** n.

girl Fri-day n. A woman employee responsible for a variety of tasks.

girl friend n. A female friend; a regular or frequent female companion of a boy or man.

girth n. The circumference or distance around something; a strap that encircles an animal's body to secure something on its back, as a saddle.

gis-mo n., Slang A part or device whose name is unknown or forgotten; a gadget.

gist n. The central or main substance, as of an argument or question.

give v. To make a present of; to bestow; to accord or yield to another; to put into the possession of another; to convey to another; to donate or contribute; to apply; to devote; to yield as to pressure; to collapse; to furnish or provide; to deliver in exchange; to pay. **give away** To hand over the bride to the bridegroom at a wedding ceremony. **give out** To collapse; to be exhausted. **give up** To surrender; to submit oneself. **giver** n.

giv-en adj. Bestowed; presented; specified or assumed.

giv-en name n. The name bestowed or given at birth or baptism.

giz-zard n. The second stomach in birds, where partly digested food is finely ground.

gla-brous adj., Biol. Having no hair or down; having a smooth surface. **glabrousness** n.

gla-cial adj. Of or pertaining to, caused by, or marked by glaciers; extremely cold. **glacially** adv.

gla-cial e-poch Geol. A portion of geological time when ice sheets covered much of the earth's surface.

gla-cier n. A large mass of compacted snow that moves slowly until it either breaks off to form icebergs or melts when it reaches warmer climates.

glad adj. Displaying, experiencing, or affording joy and pleasure; a state of being happy; being willing to help; grateful. n. Short for gladiolus.

glad-den v. To make glad.

glade n. A clearing in a forest or woods.

glad-i-a-tor n. An ancient Roman slave, captive, or paid freeman who entertained the public by fighting to the death; one who engages in an intense struggle or controversy. **gladiatorial** adj.

glad-i-o-lus ., pl. **-li** or **-luses** A plant with fleshy bulbs, sword-shaped leaves, and spikes of colorful flowers.

glad-some adj. Giving cheer; showing

joy. **gladsomely** adv., **gladsomeness** n.

glam-or-ize or **glam-our-ize** v. To make glamorous; to portray or treat in a romantic way.

glam-our or **glam-or** n. Alluring fascination or charm. **glamourous** adj.

glance v. To take a brief or quick look at something; to obliquely strike a surface at an angle and be deflected; to give a light, brief touch; to brush against.

gland n., Anat. Any of various body organs which excrete or secrete substances. **glandular** adj.

glare v. To stare fiercely or angrily; to shine intensely; to dazzle. n. An uncomfortably harsh or bright light.

glass n. A hard, amorphous, brittle, usually transparent material which hardens from the molten state, preceded by rapid cooling to prevent crystallization; any substance made of or resembling glass; a mirror, tumbler, windowpane, lens, or other material made of glass. **glasses** A pair of eyeglasses used as an aid to vision; **glassware. glass, glassy** adj.

glass blowing n. The art or process of shaping objects from molten glass by gently blowing air into them through a glass tube.

glau-co-ma n., Pathol. A disease of the eye characterized by abnormally high pressure within the eyeball and partial or complete loss of vision.

glaze n. A thin, smooth coating as on ceramics. v. To become covered with a thin glassy coating of ice; to coat or cover with a glaze; to fit with glass, as to glaze a window. **glazer** n., **glazing, glazed** v.

gleam n. A momentary ray or beam of light. v. To shine or emit light softly; to appear briefly. **gleamy** adj.

glean v. To collect or gather facts by patient effort; to collect part by part; to pick bits of a crop left by a reaper. **gleaner** n., **gleanings** pl., n.

glee n. Joy; merriment; an unaccompanied song for male voices. **gleeful** adj., **gleefully** adv.

glee club n. A singing group that is organized to sing short pieces of choral music.

glen n. A small, secluded valley.

glib adj. Spoken easily and fluently; superficial. **glibly** adv., **glibness** n.

glide v. To pass or move smoothly with little or no effort; to fly without motor power. **glidingly** adv., **gliding** v.

glid-er n. One that glides; a swing gliding in a metal frame. Aeron. An aircraft without an engine, constructed to soar on air currents.

glim-mer n. A faint suggestion; an indication; a dim unsteady light. **glimmering** v.

glimpse n. A momentary look.

glis-sade n. A gliding ballet step; a controlled slide in either a sitting or standing position, used to descend a steep, snowy, or icy incline.

glissade v., **glissader** n.

glis-san-do n., pl. -di A rapid passing from one tone to another by a continuous change of pitch.

glis-ten v. To shine softly as reflected by light. **glisten** n., -ing, **glistened** v.

glitch n. A minor mishap or malfunction. Elect. A false signal caused by an unwanted surge of power.

glit-ter n. A brilliant sparkle; small bits of light-reflecting material used for decoration. v. To sparkle with brilliance. **glittery** adj., **glittering, glittered** v.

gloat v. To express, feel, or observe with great malicious pleasure or self-satisfaction. **gloater** n., **gloating** v.

glob-al adj. Spherical; involving the whole world. **globalize** v., **globally** adv.

globe n. A spherical object; anything that is perfectly rounded; the earth; anything like a sphere, such as a fishbowl; a spherical representation of the earth, usually including geographical and political boundaries.

globe--trot-ter n. One who travels all over the world.

glob-u-lin n., Biochem. Any of a class of simple proteins found widely in blood, milk, tissue, muscle and plant seeds.

gloom n. Partial or total darkness; depression of the mind or spirits. **gloomily** adv., -iness n., **gloomy** adj.

glo-ri-fy v. To worship and give glory to; to give high praise. **glorification** n.

glo-ri-ous adj. Magnificent; resplendent; delightful; illustrious; full of glory. **gloriously** adv.

glory n., pl. -ies Distinguished praise or honor; exalted reputation; adoration and praise offered in worship; a wonderful asset; the height of one's triumph, achievement, or prosperity. v. To rejoice with jubilation.

gloss n. The sheen or luster of a polished surface; a deceptively or superficially attractive appearance; a note that explains or translates a difficult or hard to understand expression. v. To cover over by falsehood in an attempt to excuse or ignore.

glos-sa-ry n., pl. -ries A list of words and their meanings.

gloss-y adj. Having a bright sheen; lustrous; superficially attractive. n. A photo print on smooth, shiny paper. **glossily** adv., **glossiness** n.

glot-tis n., pl. -ises or -ides Anat. The opening or cleft between the vocal cords at the upper part of the larynx. **glottal** adj.

glove n. A covering for the hand with a separate section for each finger; an oversized protective covering for the hand, as that used in baseball, boxing, or hockey. **gloved** adj.

glow v. To give off heat and light, especially without a flame; to have a bright, warm, ruddy color. n. A warm feeling of emotion. **glowing** adj., **glowingly** adv.

glow-er *v.* To look sullenly or angrily at; to glare. **glower** *n.*, **gloweringly** *adv.*

glow-worm *n.* A European beetle; the luminous larva or grub-like female of an insect which displays phosphorescent light; the firefly.

glox-in-i-a *n.* A tropical South American plant with large, bell-shaped flowers.

glu-cose *n.*, *Chem.* A substance less sweet than cane sugar, found as dextrose in plants and animals and obtained by hydrolysis; a yellowish to colorless syrupy mixture of dextrose, maltose, and dextrins with a small amount of water, used especially in confectionery and baking.

glue *n.* Any of various adhesives in the form of a gelatin, made from animal substances, as bones or skins, and used to stick and hold items together. **glue** *v.*, **gluey** *adj.*

glum *adj.* Moody and silent.

glut *v.* To feed or supply beyond capacity; to provide with a supply that exceeds demand.

glu-ten *n.* A mixture of plant proteins that is used as an adhesive and as a substitute for flour. **glutenous** *adj.*

glut-ton *n.* Someone who eats immoderately; one who has a large capacity for work or punishment. **-ous** *adj.*, **gluttonously** *adv.*, **gluttony** *n.*

glyc-er-ol *n.*, *Chem.* A sweet, oily, syrupy liquid derived from fats and oils and used as a solvent, sweetener, antifreeze, and lubricant.

gly-co-side *n.*, *Chem.* Any of a group of carbohydrates which, when decomposed, produce glucose or other sugar.

gnarl *n.* A hard, protruding knot on a tree. **gnarled** *adj.*

gnash *v.* To grind or strike the teeth together, as in a rage or pain.

gnat *n.* A small, winged insect, specially one that bites or stings.

gnaw *v.* To bite or eat away with persistence; to consume or wear away.

gneiss *n.* A banded, coarse-grained rock with minerals arranged in layers.

gnome *n.* In folklore, a dwarf-like creature who lives underground and guards precious metals and treasures.

gnu *n.*, *pl.* **gnus** *or* **gnu** South African antelope with an ox-like head, curved horns, a long tail, and a mane.

go *v.* To proceed or pass along; to leave; to move away from; to follow a certain course of action; to function; to function correctly; to be in operation; to be awarded or given; to have recourse; to resort to; to pass, as of time; to be abolished or given up; to pass to someone, as by a will. *n.* An attempt; a try. **go back on** To abandon. **go for** To try; to try to obtain. **go places** To be on the road to success. **go under** To suffer destruction or defeat. **going** *v.*

go--a-head *n.* Permission; a signal to move ahead or proceed.

goal *n.* A purpose; the terminal point of a race or journey; in some games, the area, space, or object into which participants must direct play in order to score.

goal-ie *n.* A goalkeeper.

goal-keep-er *n.* The player responsible for defending the goal in hockey, soccer, and other games, preventing the ball or puck from passing over the goal for a score; a goal tender.

goat *n.* A horned, cud-chewing mammal related to the sheep; a lecherous man. *Slang* One who is a scapegoat. **goatish** *adj.*, **goatishly** *adv.*, **-ness** *n.*

goat-ee *n.* A short, pointed beard on a man's chin.

goat-skin *n.* The skin of a goat, often used for leather.

gob-ble *v.* To eat and swallow food greedily; to take greedily; to grab.

gob-ble-dy-gook *n.*, *Informal* Wordy and often unintelligible language.

gob-bler *n.* A male turkey.

go--be-tween *n.* A person who acts as an agent between two parties.

gob-let *n.* A drinking glass, typically with a base and stem.

gob-lin *n.* In folklore, an ugly, grotesque creature said to be mischievous and evil.

god *n.* Someone considered to be extremely important or valuable; an image, symbol, or statue of such a being.

God *n.* The Supreme Being; the ruler of life and the universe.

god-child *n.* A child for whom an adult serves as sponsor at baptism, circumcision, and other rites.

god-dess *n.* A female of exceptional charm, beauty, or grace.

god-father *n.* A man who sponsors a child at his or her baptism or other such ceremony.

god-head *n.* Godhood; divinity. **Godhead** The essential and divine nature of God.

god-hood *n.* The state or quality of being a god; divinity.

god-less *adj.* Not recognizing a god. **godlessness** *n.*

god-ly *adj.* Filled with love for God.

god-mother *n.* A woman who sponsors a child at his or her baptism or other such ceremony.

god-par-ent *n.* A godfather or godmother.

god-send *n.* Something received unexpectedly that is needed or wanted.

god-son *n.* A male godchild.

go--get-ter *n.* An enterprising, aggressive person.

gog-gle *n.*, *pl.* **-gles**

Spectacles or eyeglasses to protect the eyes against dust, wind, sparks, and other debris. *v.* To gaze or stare with bulging eyes.

go-ing *n.* The act of moving, leaving, or departing; the condition of roads or ground that affects walking, riding, and other movement; a condition influencing activity or progress. **goings on** Actions or behavior, used to express disapproval.

goi·ter *n.*, *Pathol.* Any abnormal enlargement of the thyroid gland, visible as a swelling in the front of the neck.

goitrous *adj.*

gold *n.* A soft, yellow, metallic element that is highly ductile and resistant to oxidation; used especially in coins and jewelry; a precious metal; a bright, vivid yellow; money; the element symbolized by Au.

gold·en an·ni·ver·sa·ry *n.* The 50th anniversary.

gold·en·rod *n.* A North American plant with small yellow flowers; the state flower of Alabama, Kentucky, and Nebraska.

gold-·filled *adj.* Made of a hard base metal over which a thick covering of gold is laid.

gold·finch *n.* A small bird, the male of which has yellow plumage with black forehead, tail, and wings.

gold·fish *n.* A reddish or brass-colored freshwater fish, cultivated as an aquarium fish.

gold mine *n.* A mine which produces gold ore; any source of great riches or profit.

gold stand·ard *n.* The monetary system based on gold of a specified weight and fineness as the unit of value and exchange.

golf *n.* A game played outdoors with a hard ball and various clubs, on a grassy course with 9 or 18 holes.

golf *v.*, **golfer** *n.*

gon·ad *n.*, *Anat.* The male or female sex gland where the reproductive cells develop; an ovary or testis.

gonadal, gonadial, gonadic *adj.*

gon·do·la *n.* A long, narrow, flat-bottomed boat propelled by a single oar and used on the canals of Venice.

gone *adj.* Past; bygone; dead; beyond hope; marked by faintness or weakness. **far gone** Exhausted; wearied; almost dead.

gon·er *n.*, *Slang* One that is near, close to death, or beyond all hope of saving.

gon·fa·lon *n.* A banner hung from a crosspiece and cut so as to end in streamers.

gong *n.* A heavy metal disk which produces a deep resonant tone when struck.

gon·o·coc·cus *n.*, *pl.* **-cocci** The bacterium which causes gonorrhea.

gonococcal, gonococcic *adj.*

gon·or·rhe·a *n.*, *Pathol.* A contagious venereal infection transmitted chiefly by sexual intercourse. **gonorrheal** *adj.*

goo·ber *n.*, *Regional* A peanut.

good *adj.* Having desirable or favorable qualities or characteristics; morally excellent; virtuous; well-behaved; tractable; proper; excellent in degree or quality; unspoiled; fresh; healthy; striking or attractive. **goods** Merchandise or wares; personal belongings; cloth; fabric. **for good** Forever; permanently. **better, best** *adj.*

good-·by or **good-·bye** *interj.* Used to express farewell. *n.* A farewell; a parting word; an expression of farewell. *adj.* Final.

good-·for-·noth·ing *n.* A person of little worth or usefulness.

good-·heart·ed *adj.* Having a kind and generous disposition. **-ness** *n.*

good-·hu·mored *adj.* Having a cheerful temper or mood; amiable.

good-humoredly *adv.*, **-humoredness** *n.*

good-·na·tured *adj.* Having an easygoing and pleasant disposition.

good-naturedly *adv.*, **-naturedness** *n.*

good-·will *n.* A desire for the well-being of others; the pleasant feeling or relationship between a business and its customers.

good·y *n.*, *pl.* **-ies** Something that is good to eat; a prissy person.

goof *n.*, *Slang* A stupid or dull-witted person; a mistake. *v.* To blunder; to make a mistake.

gook *n.*, *Slang* A slimy, sludgy, or dirty substance.

goon *n.*, *Slang* A thug or hoodlum hired to intimidate or injure someone; a person hired to break strikes; a stupid person.

goose *n.*, *pl.* **geese**

A large water bird related to swans and ducks; a female goose. *Informal* A silly person.

goose-·ber·ry *n.*, *pl.* **-ies** The edible greenish berry of a spiny shrub used for pies, jams, and other foods.

goose bumps *pl.*, *n.* A prickling sensation of the skin caused by fear or cold, also known as goose pimples and goose skin.

goose-·neck *n.* Any various devices curved like a goose's neck.

go·pher *n.* A burrowing North American rodent with large cheek pouches.

gore *v.* To stab or pierce. *n.* Blood that has been shed; a triangular or tapering piece of cloth as in a sail or skirt.

gorge *n.* A deep, narrow ravine; deep or violent disgust. *v.* To eat or devour something greedily. **gorger** *n.*

gor·geous *adj.* Beautiful; dazzling; extremely beautiful; magnificent.

gorgeously *adv.*, **gorgeousness** *n.*

go·ril·la *n.*

A large African jungle ape, having a massive, stocky body, long arms, and tusklike canine teeth.

gorse *n.* A spiny plant bearing fragrant yellow flowers.

go·ry *adj.* Covered or stained with blood; marked by much bloodshed or violence.

gos-hawk n. A large, shortwinged hawk formerly used in falconry.

gos-ling n. A young goose.

gos-pel or **Gos-pel** n. The teachings of Christ and the apostles; any information which is accepted as unquestionably true; any of the first four books of the New Testament.

gos-pel mus-ic n. American religious music based on simple folk melodies blended with rhythmic and melodic elements of spirituals and jazz.

gos-sa-mer n. The fine film or strands of a spider's web floating in the air; anything sheer, delicate, light, or flimsy. **gossamer** adj.

gos-sip n. Idle, often malicious talk; a person who spreads sensational or intimate facts. v. To spread or engage in gossip. **gossiper** n., **gossipy** adj.

gouge n. A chisel with a scoop-shaped blade used for woodcarving; a groove or hole made with or as if with a gouge v. To make a hole or groove with a gouge; to cheat, as to charge exorbitant prices. **gouger** n.

gou-lash n. A stew made from beef or veal and vegetables seasoned chiefly with paprika.

gourd n. A vine fruit related to the pumpkin, squash, and cucumber and bearing inedible fruit with a hard rind; the dried, hollowed-out shell can be used as a drinking utensil.

gour-mand n. A person who takes excessive pleasure in eating.

gour-met n. Someone who appreciates and understands fine food and drink.

gout n., Pathol. A disease caused by a defect in metabolism and characterized by painful inflammation of the joints. **gouty** adj.

gov-ern v. To guide, rule, or control by right or authority; to control or guide the action of something; to restrain. **governable** adj., **governance** n.

gov-ern-ess n. A woman employed in a private household to train and instruct children.

gov-ern-ment n. The authoritative admin-istration of public policy and affairs of a nation, state or city; the system or policy by which a political unit is governed; any governed territory, district, or area. **governmental** adj., **governmentally** adv.

gov-er-nor n. Someone who governs, as the elected chief executive of any state in the United States; an official appointed to exercise political authority over a territory. Mech. A device which will automatically controls the speed of a machine. **governorship** n.

govt abbr. Government.

gown n. A woman's dress, especially for a formal affair; any long, loose-fitting garment; a robe worn by certain officials, scholars, and clergymen.

grab v. To snatch or take suddenly; to take possession of by force or by dishonest means. Slang To capture the attention of someone or something. **grab, grabber** n., **grabby** adj.

grab bag n. A bag or container full of miscellaneous unidentified articles from which one may draw an object at random.

gra-ben n., Geol. An elongated depression in the earth, caused by the downward faulting of a portion of the earth's crust.

grace n. Seemingly effortless beauty, ease, and charm of movement, proportion, or form; a charming quality or characteristic; an extension of time that is granted after a set date, as for paying a debt.

graceful, graceless adj., **gracefully** adv., **gracefulness** n.

gra-cious adj. Marked by having or showing kindness and courtesy; full of compassion; merciful. **graciously** adv., **graciousness** n.

grack-le n. Any of various New World blackbirds having long tails and iridescent blackish plumage.

grad n., Slang A graduate.

gra-da-tion n. A gradual and orderly arrangement or progression according to quality, size, rank, or other value; the act of grading. **gradational** adj.

grade n. A step or degree in a process or series; a group or category; a level of progress in school, usually constituting a year's work; a letter or number indicating a level of achievement in school work; the degree to which something slopes, as a road, track, or other surface. Milit. Rank or rating. **grade** v.

grade school n. Elementary school, which will usually teach from kindergarten to grade 6 or grade 8.

gra-di-ent n. A slope or degree of inclination. Phys. A rate of change in variable factors, as temperature or pressure.

grad-u-al adj. Moving or changing slowly by degrees; not sleep or abrupt. **gradually** adv., **gradualness** n.

grad-u-ate v. To receive or be granted an academic diploma or degree upon completion of a course of study; to divide into categories, grades or steps. n. A person who holds an academic degree; a type container or beaker marked in units or degrees, used for measuring liquids.

grad-u-ate stu-dent A student who has received a college degree and is working toward an advanced or higher degree.

grad-u-a-tion n. The state of graduating; a commencement ceremony; issuing of diplomas or degrees.

graf-fi-to n., pl. **graf-fi-ti** An inscription or drawing made on a public wall, subway train, rock, or any other surface.

graft v. To insert a shoot from a plant into another living plant so that the two will grow together as a single plant. Surg. To transplant a piece of tissue or an organ. n. Living tissue or skin used to replace damaged or destroyed tissue or skin; the act of acquiring or getting personal profit or advantage by dishonest or unfair means through one's public position.

gra-ham n. Whole wheat flour.

grail n. The legendary cup used by Christ at the Last Supper; also called the Holy Grail.

grain n. A small, hard seed or kernel of cereal, wheat, or oats; the seeds or fruits of such plants as a group; a very small amount; a small, hard particle, as a grain of sand; the side of a piece of leather from which the hair has been removed; the characteristic markings or pattern of this side; texture; basic nature. **against the grain** Contrary to one's inclinations or temperament. **grainer** n., **grainless** adj.

grain al-co-hol n. Ethanol.

grain el-e-va-tor n. A building used to store grain.

grain-y adj. Having a granular texture; resembling the grain of wood. **graininess** n.

gram n. A metric unit of mass and weight equal to 1/1000 kilogram and nearly equal to one cubic centimeter of water at its maximum density.

gram-mar n. The study and description of the classes of words, their relations to each other, and their arrangement into sentences; the inflectional and syntactic rules of a language. **-ian** n., **grammatical** adj., **grammatically** adv.

gram-mar school n. An elementary school. Brit. A secondary or preparatory school.

gram mol-e-cule n., Chem. The quantity of a compound, expressed in grams, that is equal to the molecular weight of that compound.

gran-a-ry n., pl. **ries** A building for storing threshed grain; an area or region where grain grows in abundance.

grand adj. To be large in size, extent, or scope; magnificent; of high rank or great importance; lofty; admirable; main or principal; highly satisfactory; excellent. Slang A thousand dollars. **grandly** adv., **grandness** n.

grand-child n. The child of one's son or daughter.

grand-dad n. The father of one's mother or father.

grand-daugh-ter n. The daughter of one's son or daughter.

gran-deur n. The quality or condition of being grand; splendor; magnificence.

grand-fa-ther n. The father of one's father or mother; an ancestor. **grandfatherly** adv.

grand-fa-ther clock n. A pendulum clock enclosed in a tall narrow cabinet.

gran-dil-o-quent adj. Speaking in or characterized by a pompous or bombastic style. **grandiloquence** n.

gran-di-ose adj. Impressive and grand; pretentiously pompous; bombastic. **grandiosely** adv., **grandiosity** n.

grand mal n., Pathol. A form of epilepsy characterized by severe convulsions and loss of consciousness.

grand-moth-er n. The mother of one's father or mother; a female ancestor.

grand op-era n. A form of opera having a serious and complex plot with the complete text set to music.

grand-par-ent n. A parent of one's mother or father.

grand pi-ano n. A piano with the strings which are arranged horizontally in a curved, wooden case.

grand slam n. In bridge, the taking of all the tricks; in baseball, a home run hit with runners on first, second, and third bases.

grand-son n. A son of one's son or daughter.

grand-stand n. A raised stand of seats, usually roofed, for spectators at a racetrack or sports event.

gran-ite n. A hard, coarse-grained igneous rock composed chiefly of quartz, mica, and orthoclase, which is used for building material and in sculpture. **granitic** adj.

gran-ite-ware n. Ironware utensils coated with hard enamel.

gran-ny or **gran-nie** n. A grandmother; an old woman; a fussy person.

gra-no-la n. Rolled oats mixed with dried fruit and seeds and eaten as a snack.

grant v. To allow; to consent to; to admit something as being the truth; in law, to transfer property by a deed. n. That which is granted. **grantee**, **granter**, **grantor** n.

gran-u-lar adj. The state of being composed or seeming to be composed of containing grains or granules. **granularity** n.

gran-u-late v. To make or form into granules or crystals; to become or cause to become rough and grainy. **granulation** n.

gran-ule n. A very small grain or particle.

grape n. Any of numerous woody vines bearing clusters of smooth-skinned, juicy, edible berries, having a dark purplish blue, red, or green color, eaten raw or dried and used in making wine.

grape-fruit n. A tropical, large, round citrus fruit with a pale yellow rind and tart, juicy pulp; the tree bearing this fruit.

grape-shot n. A shot consisting of a cluster of small iron balls, formerly used to charge a cannon.

grape sug-ar n. Dextrose.

grape-vine n. A climbing vine that produces grapes; a secret or informal means of transmitting information or rumor from person to person.

graph n. A diagram representing the relationship between sets of things.

graph-ic or **graph-i-cal** adj. Describing in full detail; of or pertaining to drawings or blueprints, as in architecture.

graph-ite n. A soft black form of carbon having a metallic luster and slippery texture, used in lead pencils, lubricants, paints, and coatings. **graphitic** *adj.*

graph-ol-o-gy *n.* The study of handwriting for the purpose of analyzing a person's character or personality. **graphologist** *n.*

grap-nel *n.* A small anchor with several flukes at the end.

grap-ple *n.* An instrument with iron claws used to fasten an enemy ship alongside for boarding. *v.* To struggle or contend with; to fasten, seize or drag as with a grapple. **grappler** *n.*

grasp *v.* To seize and grip firmly; to comprehend; to understand. *n.* The power to seize and hold. **graspable** *adj.*, **grasper** *n.*

grasp-ing *adj.* Urgently desiring material possessions; greedy. **graspingly** *adv.*, **graspingness** *n.*

grass *n.* Any of numerous plants having narrow leaves and jointed stems; the ground on which grass is growing. *Slang* Marijuana. **-iness** *n.*, **grassy** *adj.*

grass-hop-per *n.*

Any of several jumping insects that has long powerful hind legs. *Slang* Any type of small, lightweight airplane which can be used for dusting crops and military observation.

grass-land *n.* Land in which grasses are the main vegetation, as a prairie.

grass-roots *pl., n.* A society of common people, thought of as having practical and highly independent views or interests. **grassroots** *adj.*

grass wi-dow *n.* A woman who is separated or divorced from her husband.

grate *v.* To reduce, shred or pulverize by rubbing against a rough or sharp surface; to make or cause to make a harsh sound. *n.* A rasping noise. **grater** *n.*, **grating** *adj.*, **gratingly** *adv.*

grate *n.* A framework or bars placed over a window or other opening; an iron frame to hold burning fuel in a fireplace or furnace.

grate-ful *adj.* The state of being thankful or appreciative for benefits or kindnesses; expressing gratitude. **gratefully** *adv.*, **gratefulness** *n.*

grat-i-fy *v.* To give pleasure or satisfaction to; to fulfill the desires of; to indulge. **gratification** *n.*

grat-ing *n.* A grate.

grat-is *adv. & adj.* Without requiring payment; free.

grat-i-tude *n.* The state of appreciation and gratefulness; thankfulness.

gra-tu-i-tous *adj.* Given or obtained without payment; unjustified; unwarranted. **-ly** *adv.*, **gratuitousness** *n.*

gra-tu-i-ty *n., pl.* **-ies** A gift, as money, given in return for a service rendered; a tip.

gra-va-men *n., pl.* **-mens** *or* **-mina** In law, the part of an accusation or charge weighing most heavily against the accused.

grave *n.* A burial place for a dead body, usually an excavation in the earth. *adj.* Very serious or important in nature; filled with danger; critical. *v.* To sculpt or carve; to engrave. *Mus.* Solemn and slow. **gravely** *adv.*, **-ness**, **-er** *n.*

grav-el *n.* Loose rock fragments often with sand. *Pathol.* The deposit of sand-like crystals that form in the kidneys; also known as kidney stones.

grave-stone *n.* A stone that marks a grave; a tombstone.

grave-yard *n.* An area set aside as a burial place; a cemetery.

grave-yard shift *n. Slang* A work shift that usually begins at midnight.

gra-vim-e-ter *n.* An implement for determining specific gravity. **gravimetry** *n.*

grav-i-tate *v.* To be drawn as if by an irresistible force; to sink or settle to a lower level.

grav-i-ta-tion *n., Physics* The force or attraction any two bodies exert towards each other. **gravitational**, **gravitative** *adj.*, **gravitationally** *adv.*

grav-i-ty *n., pl.* **-ies** The gravitational force manifested by the tendency of material bodies to fall toward the center of the earth; gravitation in general; weight; importance; seriousness.

gra-vy *n., pl.* **-ies** The juices exuded by cooking meat; a sauce made by seasoning and thickening these juices. *Slang* Money or profit which is easily acquired.

gray *or* **grey** *adj.* A neutral color between black and white; gloomy; dismal; having gray hair; characteristic of old age. **grayish** *adj.*, **grayness** *n.*

gray-beard *n., Slang* An old man.

gray-ling *n., pl.* **-ling** *or* **-lings** Any of several freshwater food and game fish with a small mouth and a large dorsal fin.

gray mat-ter *n.* The grayish-brown nerve tissue of the spinal cord and brain, consisting mainly of nerve cells and fibers; brains.

graze *v.* To feed upon growing grasses or herbage; to put livestock to feed on grass or pasturage; to brush against lightly in passing; to abrade or scrape slightly.

gra-zier *n.* One who grazes cattle.

grease *n.* Melted or soft animal fat; any thick fatty or oily substance, as a lubricant. *v.* To lubricate or coat with grease. **greasiness** *n.*, **greasy** *adj.*

grease paint *n.* Makeup used for theatre performances.

great *adj.* Very large in size or volume; prolonged in duration or extent; more than ordinary; considerable; remarkable; impressive; eminent; renowned; very good or first-rate; a generation removed from a relative. **greatly** *adv.*, **greatness** *n.*

great-aunt *n.* An aunt of either of one's parents.

great--grand-child n. A child of a grandchild.

great--grand-daugh-ter n. A daughter of a grandchild.

great--grand-fa-ther n. The father of a grandparent.

great--grand-mo-ther n. The mother of a grandparent.

great--grand-par-ent n. The father or mother of a grandparent.

great--grand-son n. The son of a grandchild.

great-heart-ed adj. Noble or generous in spirit; magnanimous. -ly adv., -ness n.

great--neph-ew n. A grandnephew.

great--niece n. A grandniece.

great seal n. The chief seal of a government.

great--un-cle n. An uncle of either of one's parents; granduncle.

grebe n. Any of various swimming and diving birds having partially webbed feet, very short tails, and a pointed bill.

greed n. Selfish desire to acquire more than one needs or deserves.

greed-y adj. Excessively eager to acquire or gain something; having an excessive appetite for drink and food; gluttonous. greedily adv., greediness n.

green adj. Of the color between yellow and blue in the spectrum; not fully matured or developed; lacking in skill or experience. n. A grassy plot or lawn, especially an area of closely mowed grass at the end of a golf fairway. greenish adj., greenness n.

green-back n. A U.S. legaltender currency note.

green bean n. A string bean; a vegetable commonly grown in private gardens.

green-er-y n., pl. -ies Green foliage or plants.

green--eyed adj. Jealous.

green-horn n. An inexperienced person; a beginner; a person who is easily fooled.

green-house n. An enclosed structure equipped with heat and moisture designed for the cultivation of plants.

green pep-per n. The unripened fruit of various pepper plants.

green-room n. The room or lounge in a theatre used by performers when they are offstage.

green thumb n. A special skill for making plants thrive.

greet v. To address someone in a friendly way; to welcome; to meet or receive in a specified manner. greeter n.

greet-ing n. A word of salutation on meeting.

gre-gar-i-ous adj. Habitually associating with others as in groups, flocks, or herds; enjoying the company of others; sociable. -ly adv., -ness n.

grem-lin n. A mischievous elf said to cause mechanical trouble in airplanes.

gre-nade n. A small explosive device detonated by a fuse and thrown by hand or projected from a rifle.

gren-a-dier n. A member of a special European corps which was formerly armed with grenades.

gren-a-dine n. A syrup made from pomegranates or red currants and used as a flavoring in mixed drinks.

grew v. Past tense of grow.

grey n., & adj. Variation of gray.

grey-hound n. One of a breed of slender, swift-running dogs with long legs.

grid n. An arrangement of regularly spaced bars; the system of intersecting parallel lines that divide maps, charts, and aerial photographs, used as a reference for locating points.

grid-dle n. A flat pan used for cooking.

grid-i-ron n. A metal framework used for broiling meat, fish, and other foods; a football field.

grief n. Deep sadness or mental distress caused by a loss, remorse, or bereavement.

griev-ance n. A real or imagined wrong which is regarded as cause for complaint or resentment; a complaint of unfair treatment.

grieve v. To cause or feel grief or sorrow.

griev-ous adj. Causing grief, sorrow, anguish, or pain; causing physical suffering. grievously adv.

grif-fin or **grif-fon** n. In Greek mythology, a fabulous beast with a lion's body, an eagle's head, and wings.

grill n. A cooking utensil made from parallel metal bars; a gridiron; food cooked on a grill; a restaurant where grilled foods are a specialty. v. To broil on a grill.

grille or **grill** n. A grating with open metalwork used as a decorative screen or room divider.

grim adj. Stern or forbidding in appearance or character; unyielding; relentless; grisly; gloomy; dismal. grimly adv., grimness n.

grim-ace n. A facial expression of pain, disgust, or disapproval. grimace v.

grime n. Dirt, especially soot clinging to or coating a surface. griminess n., grimy adj.

grin v. To smile broadly. grin n.

grind v. To reduce to fine particles; to sharpen, polish, or shape by friction; to press or rub together; to work or study hard. n. A person who works hard or who studies very hard.

grind-er n. One that grinds.

grind-ers pl., n. Slang The teeth.

grind-stone n. A flat, circular stone which revolves on an axle and is used for polishing, sharpening, or grinding.

grip n. A firm hold; a grasp; the ability to seize or maintain a hold; the mental or intellectual grasp; a suitcase. v. To grasp and keep a firm hold on; to capture the imagination or attention. gripper n., grippingly adv.

gripe v. To cause sharp pain or cramps in the bowels; to anger; to annoy; to complain.

grippe n. Influenza. grippy adj.

gris-ly adj. Ghastly; gruesome.

grist n. Grain that is to be ground; a

batch of such grain.

gris-tle *n.* Cartilage of meat. **gristly** *adj.*

grist-mill *n.* A mill for grinding grain.

grit *n.* Small, rough granules, as of sand or stone; having great courage and fortitude. *v.* To clamp the teeth together. **gritty** *adj.*

grits *pl.*, *n.* Coarsely ground hominy; coarse meal; eaten primarily in the southern states of the U.S.

griz-zle *v.* To become or cause to become gray.

grizzly bear *n.*

A large, grayish bear of western North America. **grizzlies** *pl.,n., Slang* Grizzly bears.

groan *v.* To utter a deep, prolonged sound of or as of disapproval or pain. **groan** *n.*, **groaningly** *adv.*

groat *n.* A former British coin worth four-pence; any grain without its hull; a tiny sum.

gro-cer *n.* A storekeeper who deals in foodstuffs and various household supplies.

gro-cer-y *n.*, *pl.* **-ies** A store in which foodstuffs and household staples are sold.

groceries *pl.*, *n.* The merchandise sold in a grocery.

grog *n.* Any alcoholic liquor, especially rum, mixed with water.

grog-gy *adj.* To be dazed, weak, or not fully conscious, such as from a blow or exhaustion; drunk. **groggily** *adv.*, **grogginess** *n.*

groin *n., Anat.* The crease or fold where the thigh meets the abdomen. *Archit.* The curved edge of a building formed by two intersecting vaults.

grom-met *n.* A reinforcing eyelet through which a rope, cord, or fastening may be passed. *Naut.* A ring of rope or metal used to secure the edge of a sail.

groom *n.* A male person hired to tend horses; a stableman; a bridegroom. *v.* To make neat in appearance; to prepare for a particular position, as for a political office.

grooms-man *n.*, *pl.* **-men** The best man at a wedding; any one of a bridegroom's attendants.

groove *n.* A long, narrow channel or indentation; a fixed, settled habit or routine; a rut. **groove** *v.*

groovy *adj., Slang* A state or condition of being wonderful; delightful.

grope *v.* The act of feeling about with or as with the hands, as in the dark; to look for uncertainly or blindly. **grope** *n.*, **gropingly** *adv.*

gros-beck *n.* Any of several colorful birds which are related to the finch, having a stout, short beak.

gros-grain *n.* A heavy, horizontally corded silk or rayon fabric, woven as a ribbon.

gross *adj.* Exclusive of deductions; of or relating to the total amount received; excessively large or fat; lacking refinement or delicacy; coarse; vulgar. *n.* The entire amount without deduction; an amount that equals 12 dozen or 144 items. **grossly** *adv.*, **grossness** *n.*

gross na-tion-al pro-duct *n.* The total market value of all goods and services produced by a nation in a year.

gro-tesque *adj.* Distorted, incongruous or ludicrous in appearance or style; bizarre; outlandish. **grotesque,** **grotesqueness** *n.*, **grotesquely** *adv.*

grot-to *n.*, *pl.* **-toes** *or* **-tos** A cave or cave-like structure.

grouch *n.* An habitually irritable or complaining person. **grouch** *v.*, **-ily** *adv.*, **grouchiness** *n.*, **grouchy** *adj.*

ground *n.* The surface of the earth; soil, sand, and other natural material at or near the earth's surface; the connecting of an electric current to the earth through a conductor.

grounds *n.* The land that surrounds a building; the basis for an argument, action or belief; the sediment at the bottom of a liquid, such as coffee or tea. *v.* To prevent an aircraft or pilot from flying. *Naut.* To run a boat aground.

ground *v.* Past tense of grind.

ground cov-er *n.* A low-growing plant which forms a dense, extensive growth and tends to prevent soil erosion.

ground glass *n.* Glass that has been treated so that it is not fully transparent.

ground hog *n.* A woodchuck.

ground-less *adj.* Without foundation or basis.

ground rule *n.* A basic rule; the rule in sports that modifies play on a particular field, course, or court.

ground sheet *n.* A waterproof cover to protect an area of ground, such as a baseball or football field.

ground ze-ro *n.* The point on the ground vertically beneath or above the point of detonation of an atomic bomb.

group *n.* A collection or assemblage of people, objects, or things having something in common.

grou-per *n.* A large fish related to the sea bass.

group-ie *n., Slang* A female follower of a rock group, especially when it is on tour.

group ther-a-py *n.* Psychotherapy which in-volves sessions guided by a therapist and attended by several patients who discuss their problems.

grouse *n.*, *pl.* **grouse** Any of a family of game birds characterized by mottled, brownish plumage and rounded bodies. *v.* To complain; to grumble.

grout *n.* A material used to fill cracks in masonry or spaces between tiles. **grout** *v.*, **grouter** *n.*

grove *n.* A small group of trees, lacking undergrowth.

grov-el v. To lie or crawl face downward, as in fear; to act with abject humility. groveler n., grovelingly adv.

grow v. To increase in size, develop, and reach maturity; to expand; to increase; to come into existence. to grow on To become increasingly acceptable, necessary, or pleasing to. grower n., growing v.

growl v. To utter a deep, guttural, threatening sound, as that made by a hostile or agitated animal. growling v.

grown-up n. A mature adult.

growth n. The act or process of growing; a gradual increase in size or amount. Pathol. An abnormal formation of bodily tissue, as a tumor.

grub v. To dig up by the roots; to lead a dreary existence; to drudge. n. The thick, worm-like larva of certain insects, as of the June beetle. Slang Food; to scrounge. grubbing v.

grub-by adj. Sloppy, unkempt. grubbily adv., grubbiness n.

grudge n. A feeling of ill will, rancor, or deep resentment. v. To be displeased, resentful, or envious of the possessions or good fortune of another person. grudger n., grudgingly adv.

gru-el n. A thin liquid made by boiling meal in water or milk.

gru-el-ing or gru-el-ling adj. Extremely tiring; exhausting. gruelingly adv.

grue-some adj. The state of causing horror or fright. gruesomely adv., gruesomeness n.

gruff adj. Brusque and rough in manner; harsh in sound; hoarse. gruffly adv., gruffness n.

grum-ble v. To complain in low, throaty sounds; to growl. grumble, grumbler n., grumbly adj.

grump-y adj. Irritable and moody; ill tempered. grumpily adv., -iness n.

grun-gy adj., Slang Dirty, run-down, or inferior in condition or appearance.

grunt n. The deep, guttural sound of a hog. grunt v.

gua-no n. The excrement of sea birds, used as a fertilizer.

guar-an-tee n. The promise or assurance of the durability or quality of a product; something held or given as a pledge or security. v. To assume responsibility for the default or debt of; to certify; to vouch for.

guar-an-tor n. One who gives a guarantee or guaranty.

guar-an-ty n., pl. -ies A pledge or promise to be responsible for the debt, duty, or contract of another person in case of default; something that guarantees.

guard v. To watch over or shield from danger or harm; to keep watch as to prevent escape, violence, or indiscretion. n. A defensive position, as in boxing or fencing; in football, one of two linemen on either side of the center; in basketball, one of the two players stationed near the middle of the court; a device or piece of equipment that protects against damage, loss, or harm. guarding, guarded v.

guard-rail n. The protective rail, as on a highway or any area that proposes a threat or danger.

guards-man n. A member of the U.S. National Guard.

gua-va n. A tree or shrub of the myrtle family bearing small, pear-shaped, edible, yellow-skinned fruit.

gub-ba v., Slang To tickle the neck area, especially of children and babies.

gu-ber-na-to-ri-al adj. Of or pertaining to a governor.

guern-sey n., pl. -seys A breed of brown and white dairy cattle.

guer-ril-la n. A member of an irregular military force that is capable of great speed and mobility, often operating behind enemy lines.

guess v. To make a judgment or form an opinion on uncertain or incomplete knowledge; to suppose; to believe.

guest n. A person who is the recipient of hospitality from another; a customer who pays for lodging.

guff n., Slang Nonsense or empty talk.

guf-faw n. A loud burst of laughter.

guid-ance n. The act, process, or result of guiding.

guide n. One who leads or directs another, as in a course of action; a person employed to conduct others on trips through museums and sightseeing tours. -able adj., guider n.

guide-book n. A handbook containing directions and other information for tourists and visitors.

guid-ed mis-sile n., Mil. An unmanned missile that can be controlled by radio signals while in flight.

guide-line n. Any suggestion, statement, or outline of policy or procedure.

guild n. An association of persons of the same trade or occupation.

guilt n. The condition or fact of having committed a crime or wrongdoing; the feeling of responsibility for having done something wrong.

guin-ea n. Formerly, a British gold coin worth one pound and five pence.

guin-ea fowl n. A widely domesticated bird of African origin with dark gray plumage speckled with white.

gui-tar n. A musical instrument with six strings, played by plucking or strumming.

gull n. A long-winged, web-footed sea bird, usually white and gray with a hooked upper mandible.

gull n. A gullible person; one who is easily tricked.

gul-let n., Pathol. The passage from the mouth to the stomach; esophagus; the throat; the pharynx.

gul-li-ble adj. Easily cheated or fooled. gullibility n., gullibly adv.

gul-ly n., pl. -ies A ditch or channel cut in the earth by running water.

gum-bo n. A thick soup or stew containing okra.

gum-boil n. A type of small boil or

abscess on the gum.

gump-tion *n.*, *Slang* Boldness; initiative; enterprise.

gum-shoe *n.*, *Slang* A detective.

gung ho *adj.*, *Slang* Extremely enthusiastic.

gun-pow-der *n.* An explosive powder used in blasting, fireworks, and guns.

gun-shot *n.* A shot fired from a gun.

gun-shy *adj.* Afraid of loud noises, as gunfire; wary.

gun-smith *n.* A person who makes or repairs guns.

gun-wale *or* **gun-nel** *n.* The upper edge of a ship's side.

gup-py *n.*, *pl.* **-ies**

A small, tropical freshwater fish, popular in home aquariums.

gur-gle *v.* To flow in a broken, uneven current, making low, bubbling sounds. **gurgle** *n.*, **gurglingly** *adv.*

gu-ru *n.* A spiritual teacher of Hinduism.

gus-ta-to-ry *adj.* Of or pertaining to the sense of taste or the act of tasting.

gut-less *adj.*, *Slang* Lacking courage.

guts-y *n.*, *Slang* Courageous.

gut-ter-snipe *n.* A person of the lowest class; a street urchin.

gut-tur-al *adj.* Pertaining to the throat; having a harsh, muffled, or grating quality. **guttural** *n.*, **gutturally** *adv.*

guy *n.*, *Slang* A man; a fellow.

gym *n.*, *Informal* A gymnasium.

gym-na-si-um *n.*, *pl.* **-ums** *or* **-sia** A room or building equipped for indoor sports.

gym-nas-tics *pl.*, *n.* A sport or physical exercises, especially those performed with special apparatus in a gym.

gy-ne-col-o-gy *n.* The branch of medicine dealing with the female reproductive organs, female diseases, and female organs. **gynecological,**

gyp *v.*, *Informal* To swindle, cheat, or defraud. *n.* A fraud. **gypper** *n.*

gyp-sum *n.* A mineral, hydrous calcium sulfate, used to make plaster of Paris, gypsum plaster, and plasterboard.

gy-rate *v.* To rotate or revolve around a fixed point or axis; to move or turn in a spiral motion. *adj.* Coiled or winding about. **gyrator** *n.*, **gyratory** *adj.*

gy-ro *n.* A gyroscope or gyrocompass.

gy-ro-com-pass *n.* A type of compass which has a motor-driven gyroscope so mounted that its axis of rotation maintains a constant position with reference to the true or the geographic north.

gy-ro pi-lot *n.*, *Aeron.* An automatic pilot.

gy-ro-scope *n.* A spinning wheel or disk whose spin axis maintains its angular orientation when not subjected to external torques. **gyroscopic** *adj.*

gy-ro-sta-bi-liz-er *n.* A gyroscopic instrument designed to reduce the rolling motion of ships.

H, h The eighth letter of the English alphabet.

ha-be-as cor-pus *n.* In law, a writ commanding a person to appear before a judge or court for the purpose of releasing that person from unlawful detention or restraint.

hab-er-dash-er *n.* A person who deals in men's clothing and men's furnishings.

hab-er-dash-er-y *n.*, *pl.* **-ies** The goods sold by a haberdasher.

ha-bil-i-ment *n.*, *pl.* **-ments** Clothing characteristic of an office, rank, or occasion.

hab-it *n.* Involuntary pattern of behavior acquired by frequent repetition; manner of conducting oneself; an addiction.

hab-it-a-ble *adj.* Suitable for habitation. **habitability,** **-ness** *n.*, **habitably** *adv.*

hab-i-tat *n.* The region in which an animal or plant lives or grows; the place of residence of a person or group.

hab-i-ta-tion *n.* A place of residence.

hab-it--form-ing *adj.* Producing physiological addiction.

ha-bit-u-al *adj.* Practicing by or acting according to habit; resorted to on a regular basis; regular. **habitually** *adv.*, **habitualness** *n.*

ha-ci-en-da *n.* A large estate or ranch in Spanish-speaking countries; the main building of a hacienda.

hack *v.* To cut with repeated irregular blows; to manage successfully. *n.* A tool used for hacking; a rough, dry cough; a taxi driver.

hack-le *n.* One of the long, slender, often narrow glossy feathers on the neck of a rooster; the hair on the back of the neck, especially of a dog, that rise in anger or fear.

hack-ney *n.* A horse of medium size for ordinary driving or riding; a carriage or coach available for hire. *v.* To make common or frequent use of.

hack-neyed *adj.* Trite; commonplace.

hack-saw *n.* A saw in a narrow frame for cutting metal.

had-dock *n.* A food fish that is usually smaller than the related cod and is found on both sides of the Atlantic.

had-n't *contraction* Had not.

haft *n.* A handle of a weapon or tool.

hag *n.* A malicious, ugly old woman; a witch. **haggish** *adj.*

hag-gard A worn-out, exhausted, and gaunt look, as from hunger or fatigue. **haggardly** *adv.*, **haggardness** *n.*

hag-gle *v.* To argue or bargain on price or terms. **-er** *n.*, **haggling, haggled** *v.*

hag-i-og-ra-phy *n.*, *pl.* **-phies** Biography of the lives of saints or revered persons. **hagiographer** *n.*, **hagiographic, hagiographical** *adj.*

hai-ku *n.* An unrhymed Japanese verse form with three short lines.

hail *n.* Precipitation of small, hard lumps of ice and snow; a hailstone; an exclamation, greeting, acclamation; *v.* To pour down as hail; to call loudly in greeting or welcome; to shout with enthusiasm; to signal in order to draw the attention of.

hail-stone *n.* A type of hard pellet made of frozen snow & ice.

hair *n.* One of the pigmented filaments that grow from the skin of most mammals; a covering of such structures, as on the human head and on the skin; a slender margin. **hairy** *adj.*

hair-breadth *adj.* Extremely close or narrow. *n.* An extremely small space or margin.

hair-brush *n.* A instrument used for grooming the hair.

hair-cloth *n.* A wiry, stiff fabric of horsehair.

hair--raising *adj.* Causing fear or horror.

hair-split-ing *n.* The process of making petty distinctions. **hairsplitter** *n.*

hair-spring *n.* A fine, coiled spring that regulates and controls the movement of the balance wheel in a clock or watch.

hair trig-ger *n.* A gun trigger set to react to the slightest pressure. **hair trigger** *adj.* Reacting immediately to the slightest provocation.

hake *n.* A marine food fish related to the cod.

hal-berd *n.* A medieval weapon used in the 15th and 16th centuries, having both an ax-like blade and a steel spike on the end of a long pole.

hal-cy-on *adj* Calm and tranquil; peaceful;

hale *adj.* Healthy and robust; free from defect. *v.* To compel to go. **haleness** *n.*

half *n., pl.* halves One of two equal parts into which a thing is divisible; art of a thing approximately equal to the remainder; one of a pair. *adj.* Being one of two equal parts; being partial or incomplete. **half** *adv.*

half-back *n.* In football, either of two players who, along with the fullback and quarterback, make up the backfield; a player positioned behind the front line in any of various sports.

half--caste *n.* A person having one European and one Asian parent.

half step *n., Mus.* A semitone.

half--track *n.* A vehicle propelled by continuous rear treads and front wheels.

half--wit *n.* A mentally disturbed person; a feeble-minded person. **--witted** *adj.*

hal-i-but *n.* Any of the edible flat fishes of the North Atlantic or Pacific waters.

hal-ite *n.* Large crystal or masses of salt;

hal-i-to-sis *n.* A condition or state of having bad breath.

hal-le-lu-jah *interj.* Used to express joy, praise, or jubilation. **hallelujah** *n.*

hall-mark *n.* An official mark placed on gold and silver products to attest to their purity; an indication of quality or superiority; a distinctive characteristic.

hal-low *v.* To sanctify; to make holy; to honor.

hal-lu-ci-na-tion *n.* An illusion of seeing something that is nonexistent; something one thinks is seen during a hallucination; a delusion.

hallucinate *v.,* **hallcuinational,** **hallucinative,** **adj.** **hallucinatory** *adj.*

hal-lu-ci-no-gen *n.* A drug or other agent which causes hallucination.

hallucinogenic *adj.*

ha-lo *n.* A ring of colored light surrounding the head; an aura of glory. **halo** *v.*

hal-o-gen *n.* Any of the group of nonmentallic elements including flourine, chlorine, bromine, iodine, and astatine. **halogenous** *adj.*

hal-ter *n.* A rope or strap for leading or tying an animal; a noose for hanging a person; a woman's upper garment tied behind the neck and across the back.

halve *v.* To divide into two equal parts; to lessen by half. *Informal* Share equally.

hal-yard *n.* A rope for hoisting or lowering a sail, flag, or yard.

ham *n.* The meat of a hog's thigh; the back of the knee or thigh. **ham** *v.*

ham-let *n.* A small rural village or town.

ham-mer *n.*

A hand tool with a heavy head used to drive or strike forcefully, especially nails; the part of a gun which strikes the primer or firing pin; any of the padded wooden levers which strike the strings of a piano. *v.* To strike or pound forcibly and repeatedly.

ham-mer-head *n.* A large, predatory shark of warm seas, whose eyes are set in long, fleshy projections at the sides of the head.

ham-mer-lock *n.* A hold in wrestling in which the opponent's arm is twisted upward behind his back.

ham-mer-toe *n.* A toe that is bent downward and malformed.

ham-mock *n.* A hanging bed or couch of fabric or heavy netting, suspended from supports at each end.

ham-per *v.* To interfere with movement or progress of. *n.* A large, usually covered, receptacle used to store dirty laundry.

ham-ster *n.* Any of various rodents with large cheek pouches and a short tail.

ham-string *n.* Either of two tendons located at the back of the human knee; the large tendon at the back of the hock of four-footed animals. *v.* To cripple by cutting the hamstring; to frustrate.

hand *n.* The part of the arm below the wrist, consisting of the palm, four fingers and a thumb; a unit of measure, four inches, used especially to state the height of a horse; a pointer on a dial, as of a clock, meter, or gauge; the cards dealt to or held by a player in one round of a game; a manual laborer, worker, or employee.

v. To give, offer, or transmit with the hand; direct with the hands.

hand-ball *n.* A court game in which the players bat a small rubber ball against the wall with their hands.

hand-bar-row *n.* A flat rectangular frame with handles at both ends for carrying loads.

hand-bill *n.* A hand-distributed advertisement.

hand-book *n.* A small guide or reference book giving information or instructions.

hand-car *n.* A small open four-wheeled railroad car propelled by a small motor or by hand.

hand-cuff *v.* To put handcuffs on; to make ineffective. handcuffs *pl., n.* A pair of circular metal shackles chained together that can be fastened around the wrists.

hand-gun *n.* A gun that can be held and fired with one hand.

hand-i-cap *n.* A race or contest in which advantages or penalties are given to individual contestants to equalize the odds; any disadvantage that makes achievement unusually difficult; physical disability; an obstacle. *v.* To give a handicap to.

hand-i-craft *or* **hand-craft** *n.* Skill and expertise in working with the hands; an occupation requiring manual dexterity; skilled work produced by the hands.

hand-ker-chief *n.* A type of small piece of cloth used for wiping the face or nose; a kerchief or scarf.

han-dle *v.* To touch, pick up, or hold with the hands; to represent; to trade or deal in. handler *n.*

hand-made *adj.* Made by hand or by a hand process.

hand-maid *or* **hand-maid-en** *n.* A female maid or personal servant.

hand-me-down *n.* Something, such as an article of clothing, used by a person after being outgrown or is carded by another. hand-me-down *adj.*

hand-out *n.* Free food, clothing, or cash given to the needy; a folder distributed free of charge; a flyer; a press release for publicity.

hand-pick *v.* To select with care.

hand-set *n.* A telephone receiver and transmitter combined in a single unit.

hand-shake *n.* The act of clasping hands by two people, as in greeting, agreement, or parting.

hand-some *adj.* Very good-looking or attractive; very generous, as with money. -ly *adv.*, handsomeness *n.*

hand-spring *n.* An acrobatic feat in which the body flips entirely backward or forward, while the feet pass quickly in an arc over the head.

hand-stand *n.* The feat of supporting the body on the hands with the feet balanced in the air.

hand-to-mouth *adj.* Providing or having barely enough to exist.

hand-work *n.* Work which is done by hand.

hand-writ-ing *n.* Writing performed with the hand, especially cursive; the type of writing of a person. handwriting on the wall. An omen of one's unpleasant fate.

hand-y *adj.* Easy to use or reach; helpful or useful. handily *adv.*, handiness *n.*

handy-man *n.* A person who does odd jobs.

hang *v.* To be attached to from above and unsupported from below; to fasten or be suspended so as to swing freely; to be put to death by hanging by the neck; to fasten or attach something as a picture to a wall. hangout *Slang* To spend one's time in a particular place.

han-gar *n.* A building for housing aircraft.

han-ger *n.* A device from which something may be hung or on which something hangs.

hang gli-der *n.* A device shaped like a kite from which a person hangs suspended in a harness while gliding through the air. hang gliding *n.*, hang glide *v.*

hang-man *n., pl.* -men One hired to execute people by hanging.

hang-nail *n.* The small piece of skin that hangs loose from the side or root of a fingernail.

hang-over *n.* Something remaining from what has passed; the effects of excessive alcohol intake.

hang-up *n., Slang* A psychological or emotional problem; an obstacle.

hank *n.* A loop, coil, or piece of hair, thread, or yarn.

han-ker *v.* To have a yearning or craving for something. hankerer, hankering *n.*

Ha-nuk-kah *or* **Ha-nu-kah** *n.* An eight-day Jewish holiday remembering the rededication of the Temple in Jerusalem.

hao-le *n.* A person who is not of the Hawaiian race, especially a Caucasian.

hap-haz-ard *adj.* Occurring by accident; happening by chance or at random; hit-or-miss. -ly *adv.*, haphazardness *n.*

hap-less *adj.* Unfortunate; unlucky. haplessly *adv.*, haplessness *n.*

hap-pen *v.* To occur or come to pass; to take place; to discover by chance; to turn up or appear by chance.

hap-pen-ing *n.* A spontaneous event or performance; an important event.

happen-stance *n.* An event occurring by chance.

hap-py *adj.* Enjoying contentment and well-being; glad, joyous, satisfied or pleased. happily *adv.*, happiness *n.*

hap-py-go-luck-y *adj.* Carefree and unconcerned.

ha-ra-ki-ri *n.* A Japanese suicide ritual committed by ripping open the abdomen with a knife.

ha-rangue *n.* A long, extravagant, speech; a lecture. -er *n.*

ha-rass *v.* To disturb or annoy constantly; to torment persistently.

harassment, harasser n.

har-bin-ger n. A person that initiates or pioneers a major change; something that foreshadows what is to come.

har-bor n. A place of refuge or shelter; a bay or cove; an anchorage for ships. v. To provide shelter; to entertain, as a feeling or thought. -age, -er n.

hard adj. Difficult to perform, endure, or comprehend; solid in texture or substance; resistant to cutting or penetration; containing salts which make lathering with soap difficult; high in alcoholic content. hardness n.

hard-back adj. Text bound between hard covers as opposed to paper ones.

hard--bit-ten adj. Tough or seasoned by hard experiences.

hard--boiled adj. Boiled or cooked in the shell to a hard or solid state.

hard co-py n. In computer science, the printed information or data from a computer.

hard--core or hard-core adj. Extremely graphic in presentation; obstinately resistant to change.

hard disk n. In computer science, magnetic storage consisting of a rigid disk of aluminum coated with a magnetic recording substance; contained within a removable cartridge or mounted in the hard disk of a microcomputer.

hard-en v. To make or become hard or harder; to make or become physically or mentally tough; to make or become callous or unsympathetic.

hard hat n. A protective head covering made of rigid material, worn by construction workers.

hard-head-ed adj. Having a stubborn character; obstinate. hardheadedly adv., hardheadedness n.

hard-heart-ed adj. Heartless; unfeeling. hardheartedly adv., hardheartedness n.

har-di-hood n. Resolute courage; audacious boldness; vitality; vigor.

hard-ly adj. Slang Very little; almost certainly not. adv. Forcefully; painfully; barely.

hard--nosed adj. Stubborn; hard-headed; unyielding.

hard pal-ate n. The bony forward part of the palate that forms the roof of the mouth.

hard-pan n. A layer of very hard clay-like matter or subsoil which roots cannot penetrate.

hard rock n. Rock music featuring amplified sound and modulations, and feedback.

hard-ship n. A painful, difficult condition.

hard-tack n. A hard, cracker-like biscuit made with flour and water.

hard-wood n. The wood of an angiospermous tree as opposed to that of a coniferous tree; a tree that yields hardwood.

har-dy adj. Bold and robust; able to survive very unfavorable conditions, as extreme cold; daring -iness n., -ily adv.

hare n.

Various mammals related to the rabbits but having longer ears and legs.

hare-brained adj. Foolish or silly.

hare-lip n. A congenital deformity in which the upper lip is split. -ed adj.

har-em n. The women living in a Muslim residence; the living quarters of a harem.

hark v. To listen closely. hark back To retrace one's steps; to go back to earlier times.

har-le-quin n. A jester; a clown. adj. Patterned with vividly colored diamond shapes.

har-lot n. A prostitute.

harm n. Emotional or physical damage or injury. v. To cause harm to.

harmful adj., -ly adv., harmfulness n.

harm-less adj. Without harm; not harmful.

har-mon-ic adj. Relating to musical harmony; in harmony; concordant. harmonically adv.

har-mon-i-ca n. A small, rectangular musical instrument having a series of tuned metal reeds that vibrate with the player's breath.

har-mo-ni-ous adj. Pleasing to the ear; characterized by agreement and accord; having components agreeably combined. -ly adv., harmonious n.

har-mo-ny n., pl. -ies Complete agreement, as of feeling or opinion; an agreeable combination of component parts; pleasing sounds; a combination of musical tones into chords. harmonize v., harmonizer n.

har-ness n. The working gear, other than a yoke, of a horse or other draft animal. harnesser n.

harp n. A musical instrument having a triangular upright frame with strings plucked with the fingers. v. To play a harp. harp on To write or talk about excessively. harpist n.

har-poon n. A barbed spear used in hunting whales and large fish.

harp-si-chord n. A piano-like instrument whose strings are plucked by using quills or leather points. -ist n.

har-py n., pl. -pies A vicious woman; a predatory person.

har-ri-dan n. A mean, hateful old woman.

har-ri-er n. A slender, narrow-winged hawk that preys on small animals; a hunting dog; a cross-country runner.

har-row n. A tool with sharp teeth for breaking up and smoothing soil.

har-ry v. To harass.
harsh adj. Disagreeable; extremely severe. harshly adv., harshness n.
hart n. A fully grown male deer after it has passed its fifth year.
har-um--scar-um adj. Reckless; irresponsible.
har-vest n. The process or act of gathering a crop; the season or time for gathering crops. v. To reap; to obtain as if by gathering. harvester n.
hash n. A fried or baked mixture of chopped meat and potatoes. v. To chop up into small pieces. Slang To make a mess of; to discuss at great length.
hash-ish n. The leaves and flowering tops of the hemp plant, which are chewed, drunk, or smoked for their intoxicating and narcotic effect.
hasp n. A clasp or hinged fastener that passes over a staple and is secured by a pin, bolt, or padlock.
has-sle n., Slang A type of quarrel or argument. hassle v.
has-sock n. A firm upholstered cushion used as a footstool.
haste n. Speed; swiftness of motion or action; excessive eagerness to act. make haste To hurry.
has-ten v. To act or move with haste or speed.
hast-y adj. Rapid; swift; made or done with excessive speed. -iness n.
hat n. A covering for the head with a crown and brim.
hat-box n. A container or box used for storing or carrying hats.
hatch n. A small opening or door, as in a ship's deck. v. To bring forth, as young from an egg; to devise; to contrive secretly. hatchery n.
hatch-et n. A small ax with a short handle.
hatch-way n. An opening covered by a hatch in a ship's deck.
hate v. To feel hostility or animosity toward; to dislike intensely. hatefully adv., hatefulness, hater n.
hat-ter n. A person who makes, sells, or repairs hats.
haugh-ty adj. Arrogantly proud; disdainful. -ily adv., haughtiness n.
haul v. To pull or draw with force; to move or transport, as in a truck or cart. n. The distance over which someone travels or something is transported; an amount collected at one time.
haul-age n. The process or act of hauling; a charge for hauling.
haunch n. The hip; the buttock and upper thigh of a human or animal; the loin and leg of a four-footed animal.
haunt v. To appear to or visit as a ghost or spirit; to visit frequently; to linger in the mind. haunting adj.
haut-bois or haut-boy n. An oboe.
hau-teur n. A disdainful arrogance.
have v. To hold or own, as a possession or as property. have to Need to; must. have had it Suffered or endured all

that one can tolerate.
hav-er-sack n. A bag for carrying supplies on a hike or march.
hav-oc n. Mass confusion; widespread destruction; devastation.
haw n. A hesitating sound made by a speaker who is groping for words. v. To hesitate in speaking; to falter in speaking.

hawk n.

Any of several predatory birds, with a short, hooked bill and strong claws for seizing small prey; one who advocates a war-like foreign policy; one having an aggressive attitude.
hawkish adj., -ly adv., hawkishness n.
haw-ser n. A heavy cable or rope for towing or securing a ship.
haw-thorn n. A thorny shrub or tree bearing white or pink flowers and red fruit.
hay n. Alfalfa or grass that has been cut and dried for animal food.
hay fe-ver n. An acute allergy to certain airborne pollens, marked by severe irritation of the upper respiratory tract and the eyes.
hay-fork n. A hand tool used to move hay.
hay-loft n. A upper loft in a barn or stable used to store hay.
hay-mow n. A large mound of hay stored in a loft.
hay-stack n. A pile of hay stored outdoors.
hay-wire adj., Slang Broken; emotionally out of control; crazy.
haz-ard n. A risk; chance; an accident; a anger or source of danger. v. To take a chance on; to venture. hazardous adj.
haze n. A fog-like suspension of dust, smoke, and vapor in the air; a confused or vague state of mind. v. To harass with disagreeable tasks.
ha-zel n. A small tree or shrub bearing edible brown nuts with smooth shells; a light brown or yellowish brown.
ha-zel-nut n. The edible nut of the hazel.
haz-y adj. Lacking clarity; vague. hazily adv., haziness n.
head n. The upper part of a human or animal body, containing the brain, the principal nerve centers, the eyes, ears, nose and mouth. headed adj.
head-ache n. A pain or ache in the head. Slang A bothersome problem. -y adj.
head-band n. A band of cloth worn around the head.
head-first adv. With the head in a forward position; headlong.
head-hunt-ing n. A tribal custom of decapitating slain enemies and preserving the heads as trophies.
head-ing n. A title or caption that acts as a front, beginning, or upper part of anything; the direction or course of a ship or aircraft.

head-land *n.* A high ridge or cliff projecting into the water.

head-line *n.* A title, caption, or summarizing words of a newspaper story or article printed in large type. To provide with a headline; to serve as the star performer. **headliner** *n.*

head-lock *n.* A wrestling hold in which the head of a wrestler is locked under the arm of his opponent.

head-long *adv.* Headfirst; not having deliberation. **headlong** *adj.*

head-mas-ter *n.* A school principal of a private school.

head-mis-tress *n.* A female school principal of a private school.

head-piece *n.* A helmet, cap or other covering for the head; a headset.

head-quar-ters *pl.*, *n.* The official location from which a leader directs a military unit.

head-set *n.* A pair of headphones.

head-stall *n.* The part of a bridle that goes over a horse's head.

head-stand *n.* The act of balancing the body's weight on the top of the head, with the aid of the arms.

head start *n.* An early or advance start; an advantage.

head-stone *n.* A memorial stone marker at the head of a grave, indicating a name, date of birth and date of death.

head-wat-er *n.* The source of a river or stream.

head-way *n.* Motion in a forward direction; progress toward a goal; clearance beneath an arch or ceiling.

head wind *n.* A wind blowing in the direction opposite the course of a ship or aircraft.

head-y *adj.* Tending to intoxicate; affecting the senses; headstrong. **headily** *adv.*, **headiness** *n.*

heal *v.* To restore to good health; to mend. **healable** *adj.*, **healer** *n.*

health *n.* The overall sound condition or function of a living organism at a particular time; freedom from disease or defect. **healthful** *adj.*, **healthfully** *adv.*, **healthfulness** *n.*

health-y *adj.* In a state of or having good health; characteristic of a sound condition. **-ily** *adv.*, **healthiness** *n.*

heap *n.* A haphazard assortment of things; a large number or quantity. *v.* To throw or pile into a heap.

hear *v.* To perceive by the ear; to listen with careful attention; to be informed of; to listen to officially or formally, as in a court of law. **hearer** *n.*

hear-ing *n.* One of the five senses; the range by which sound can be heard; an opportunity to be heard; in law, a preliminary examination of an accused person.

hear-ing aid *n.* An electronic device used to amplify the hearing of partially deaf persons.

heark-en *v.* To listen carefully.

hear-say *n.* Information heard from another; common talk; rumor.

hearse *n.* A vehicle for conveying a dead body to the place of burial.

heart *n.*

The hollow, primary muscular organ of vertebrates which circulates blood throughout the body; the emotional center, such as in love, hate, consideration, or compassion; the most essential part of something;

heart-ache *n.* Emotional grief; sorrow;

heart at-tack *n.* An acute malfunction or interrupted heart function.

heart-beat *n.* A pulsation of the heart, consisting of one contraction and one relaxation.

heart-break *n.* Great sorrow; deep grief. **heartbreaking** *adj.*, **-breakingly** *adv.*

heart-burn *n.* A sensation of burning in the stomach and esophagus, usually caused by excess acid in the stomach.

heart-en *v.* To give courage to.

heart-felt *adj.* Deeply felt; sincere.

hearth *n.* The floor of a fireplace, furnace; the stone that forms the front of a fireplace.

heart-land *n.* A strategically important central region, one regarded as vital to a nation's economy or defense.

heart-less *adj.* Having no sympathy; lacking compassion. **heartlessness** *n.*, **heartlessly** *adv.*

heart-rend-ing *adj.* Causing great distress, suffering emotional anguish.

heart-sick *adj.* Profoundly dejected. **heartsickness** *n.*

heart-throb *n.* One pulsation of the heart; tender emotion; a loved one.

heart--to--heart *adj.* Sincere; frank.

heart--warm-ing *adj.* A feeling of warm sympathy.

heart-wood *n.* The older, no longer active central wood of a tree.

heart-y *adj.* Marked by exuberant warmth; full of vigor; nourishing; substantial. **-ily** *adv.*, **heartiness** *n.*

heat *n.* A quality of being hot or warm; a degree of warmth; depth of feeling; a period of sexual ardor in female animals. *Slang* Pressure or stress.

heat ex-haus-tion *n.* A reaction to intense heat, a mild form of heat stroke.

heath *n.* An open tract of uncultivated wasteland covered with low-growing shrubs and plants.

hea-then *n.* A person or nation that does not recognize the God of Christianity, Judaism, or Islam; in the Old Testament, a Gentile; non-Jew. **heathenish** *adj.*, **-dom**, **heathenism** *n.*

heath-er *n.* A shrub that grows in dense masses and has small evergreen leaves and small pinkish flowers. **heather**, **heathery** *adj.*

heat stroke *n.* A state of collapse or exhaustion, accompanied by fever and marked by clammy skin, caused by excessive heat.

heave v. To raise or lift, especially forcibly; to hurl or throw. *Naut.* To push, pull, or haul, as by a rope. *Slang* To vomit. n. The act of throwing.

heaves n. A disease of horses affecting the lungs and marked by coughing and difficult breathing.

heav-en n. The sky; the region above and around the earth; the abode of God, the angels, and the blessed souls of the dead; a state or place of blissful happiness. **heavenliness** n., **heavenly** adj., **heavenward** adv. & adj.

heav-y adj. Of great weight; very thick or dense; forceful; powerful; rough and violent, as stormy weather; of great significance; grave; painful, as bad news; oppressive. **heavily** adv., **heaviness** n.

heavy-du-ty adj. Designed for hard use.

heavy-hand-ed adj. Clumsy; not tactful; oppressive. **heavy-handedly** adv., **heavy-handedness** n.

heavy-heart-ed adj. Melancholy; depressed; sad. **heavyheartedly** adv., **heavyheartedness** n.

heavy-set adj. Having a stocky build.

heavy-weight n. A person of above average weight; a competitor in the heaviest class; a boxer weighing more that 175 pounds.

heck-le v. To badger or annoy, as with questions, comments, or gibes. **-er** n.

hec-tic adj. Intensely active, rushed, or excited; marked by a persistent and fluctuating fever caused by a disease, such as tuberculosis; feverish; flushed.

he'd conj. He had; he would.

hedge n. A boundary or fence formed of shrubs or low-growing trees; a means to guard against financial loss; a deliberately ambiguous statement. **hedge** v., **hedger** n.

hedge-hog n. A small nocturnal mammal with dense, erectile spines on the back, which are presented when the animal rolls itself into a ball in self-defense; a porcupine.

hedge-hop v. To fly an aircraft close to the ground, as in spraying crops.

hedge-row n. A dense row of bushes, shrubs, or trees forming a hedge.

he-don-ism n. The doctrine devoted to the pursuit of pleasure; the philosophy that pleasure is the principal good in life. **hedonist** n., **hedonistic** adj.

heed v. To pay attention; to take notice of something. n. Attention. **-ful** adj., **heedfully** adv., **heedfulness** n.

heel n. The rounded back part of the human foot under and behind the ankle; the part of a shoe supporting or covering the heel; a lower or bottom part; the crusty ends of a loaf of bread.

heft n., *Slang* Weight; bulk. v. To gauge or estimate the weight of by lifting; to lift up.

heft-y adj. Bulky; heavy; sizable.

he-gem-o-ny n. Dominance or leadership, as of one country over another.

he-gi-ra n. A journey or departure to flee an undesirable situation.

heif-er n. A young cow, particularly one that has not produced a calf.

height n. The quality of being high; the highest or most advanced point; the distance from the base of something; the apex; the distance above a specified level; altitude; the distance from head to foot.

height-en v. To increase or become high in quantity or degree; to raise or lift.

Heim-lich ma-neu-ver n. An emergency maneuver used to dislodge food from a choking person's throat; the closed fist is placed below the rib cage and pressed inward to force air from the lungs upward.

hei-nous adj. Extremely wicked; hateful or shockingly wicked. **heinously** adv., **heinousness** n.

heir n. A person who inherits another's property or title.

heir-ess n. A female heir, especially to a large fortune.

heir-loom n. A family possession handed down from generation to generation; an article of personal property acquired by legal inheritance.

heist v., *Slang* To take from; to steal. n. A robbery.

hel-i-cal adj. Of or pertaining to the shape of a helix. **helically** adv.

hel-i-con n. A large, circular tuba that encircles the player's shoulder.

hel-i-cop-ter n.

An aircraft propelled by rotors which can take off vertically rather than needing an approach or a rolling start.

hel-i-port n. A designated area where helicopters land and take off.

he-li-um n. An extremely light, nonflammable, odorless, gaseous element, symbolized by He.

hell or **Hell** n. The abode of the dead souls condemned to eternal punishment; a place of evil, torment, or destruction; great distress; anguish; a cause of trouble or misery.

hellish adj., **hellishly** adv.

he'll contr. He will.

hel-le-bore n. A North American plant bearing white or greenish flowers and yielding a toxic alkaloid used in medicine.

hell hole n. A place of extreme wretchedness or horror.

helm n. A wheel or steering apparatus for a ship; a position or any place of control or command.

hel-met n. A protective covering for the head made of metal, leather, or plastic.

helms-man n. One who guides a ship.

hel-ot n. A serf; a slave. **helotry** n.

help v. To assist or aid. n. Assistance; relief; one that assists; one hired to help. **helper** n., **-ful** adj., **-fully** adv.

help-ing n. A single serving of food.

help-less adj. Without help; powerless; lacking strength.

Hel-sin-ki n. The capital of Finland.

hel-ter--skel-ter adv. In a confused or hurried manner; in an aimless way. adj. Rushed and confused. n. Great confusion; a tumult.

helve n. A handle on a tool such as an axe or hatchet.

hem n. A finished edge of fabric folded under and stitched. interj. A sound made as in clearing the throat, used especially to attract attention or to fill a pause in speech. v. To fold under and stitch down the edge of; to confine and surround.

he--man n. Slang A man marked by strength; a muscular man.

he-ma-tol-o-gy n. The branch of biological science that deals with blood and blood-generating organs. -ist n.

hem-i-sphere n. A half sphere that is divided by a plane passing through its center; either symmetrical half of an approximately spherical shape; the northern or southern half of the earth divided by the equator or the eastern or western half divided by a meridian. **hemispherical** adj.

hem-lock n. An evergreen tree of North America and eastern Asia, having flat needles and small cones; the wood of a hemlock; any of several poisonous herbaceous plants, having compound leaves and small whitish flowers; a poison obtained from the hemlock plant.

he-mo-glo-bin n. The respiratory pigment in the red blood cells of vertebrates containing iron and carrying oxygen to body tissues.

he-mo-phil-i-a n., Pathol. An inherited blood disease characterized by severe, protracted, sometimes spontaneous bleeding. **hemophiliac** n.

hem-or-rhage n. Bleeding, especially excessive bleeding. **hemorrhage** v.

hem-or-rhoid n., Pathol. A painful mass of dilated veins in swollen anal tissue.

hem-or-rhoids pl., n. A condition in which hemorrhoids occur.

he-mo-stat n. An agent that stops bleeding; a clamp-like instrument for preventing or reducing bleeding.

hemp n. An Asian herb; the female plant from which hashish and marijuana are produced; the tough fiber of the male plant from which coarse fabrics and rope are made. **hempen** adj.

hem-stitch n. An ornamental stitch, made by pulling out several threads and tying the remaining threads together in groups. **hemstitch** v.

hen n. A mature female bird, especially an adult female domestic fowl.

hence-forth / hence-for-ward adv. From this time on.

hench-man n. A loyal and faithful follower; one who supports a political figure chiefly for personal gain.

hen-na n. An Asian and North African ornamental tree bearing fragrant white or reddish flowers; a brownish-red dye derived from henna leaves and used as a cosmetic dye; a strong reddish brown.

hen-peck v. To domineer over one's husband by persistent nagging.

hep-a-rin n., Biochem A substance found especially in liver tissue having the power to slow or prevent blood clotting.

he-pat-ic adj. Of or like the liver.

he-pat-i-ca n. A small perennial herb having three-lobed leaves and white or lavender flowers.

hep-a-ti-tis n., Pathol. Inflammation of the liver causing jaundice.

her-ald n. A person who announces important news; one that comes before as a sign of what is to follow.

he-ral-dic adj. An official whose duty is to grant royal proclamations. v. To announce.

her-ald-ry n., pl. -ries The art or science of tracing genealogies and devising and granting coats of arms.

herb n. A soft-stemmed plant without woody tissue that usually withers and dies each year; an often pleasant-smelling plant. **herbal** adj. & n.

her-ba-ceous adj. Like, or consisting of herbs; green and leaf-like.

herb-age n. Grass or vegetation used especially for grazing; the succulent edible parts of plants.

herb-al-ist n. One who gathers, grows, and deals in herbs.

her-bar-i-um n., pl. -iums or -ia A collection of dried plant specimens that are scientifically arranged for study; a place housing a herbarium.

her-bi-cide n. A chemical agent used to kill weeds. **herbicidal** adj.

her-bi-vore n. A type of herbivorous animal.

her-biv-o-rous adj. Feeding chiefly on plant life or vegetables. -ly adv.

her-cu-le-an adj. Of unusual size, force, or difficulty; having great strength.

herd n. A number of cattle or other animals of the same kind, kept or staying together as a group; a large crowd of people. v. To bring together in a herd. **herder, herdsman** n.

here-af-ter adv. From now on; at some future time. n. Existence after death.

here-by adv. By means or by virtue of this.

he-red-i-tar-y adj. Passing or transmitted from an ancestor to a legal heir; having an inherited title or possession; transmitted or transmissible by genetic inheritance. **hereditarily** adv.

he-red-i-ty n. The genetic transmission of physical traits from parents to offspring.

here-in adv. In or into this place.

here-of adv. Relating to or in regard to this.

her-e-sy n., pl. -sies A belief in conflict with orthodox religious beliefs; any belief contrary to set doctrine.

her-e-tic *n.* A person holding opinions different from orthodox beliefs, especially religious beliefs. **heretical** *adj.*

here-to *adv.* To this matter, proposition, or thing.

here-to-fore *adv.* Up to the present time; previously.

here-un-to *adv.* Hereto; to this.

here-up-on *adv.* Immediately following or resulting from this.

here-with *adv.* Together or along with this; hereby.

her-i-ta-ble *adj.* Something capable of being inherited.

her-i-tage *n.* Property that is inherited; something handed down from past generations; a legacy.

her-maph-ro-dite *n.* A person having both male and female reproductive organs. **hermaphroditic** *adj.*

her-met-ic *or* **her-met-i-cal** *adj.* Tightly sealed against air and liquids; made impervious to outside influences. **hermetically** *adv.*

her-mit *n.* A person who lives in seclusion, often for religious reasons.

her-mit-age *n.* The dwelling place or retreat of a hermit; a secluded hideaway.

her-ni-a *n.* The protrusion of a bodily organ, as the intestine, through an abnormally weakened wall that usually surrounds it; a rupture. **hernial** *adj.*

he-ro *n., pl.* **-roes** A figure in mythology and legend renowned for exceptional courage and fortitude. **heroic** *adj.,* **heroically** *adv.*

he-ro-ic coup-let *n.* A verse consisting of two rhyming lines of iambic pentameter.

her-o-in *n.* A highly addictive narcotic derivative of morphine.

her-o-ine *n.* A woman of heroic character; the principal female character in a story or play.

her-o-ism *n.* Heroic behavior.

her-on *n.* A bird having a long slender bill, long legs, and a long neck.

her-pes *n., Pathol.* A viral infection, characterized by small blisters on the skin or mucous membranes. **-etic** *adj.*

her-pe-tol-o-gy *n.* The scientific study and treatment of reptiles and amphibians. **-ic, herpetological** *adj.,* **herpetologically** *adv.,* **herpetologist** *n.*

her-ring *n.* A valuable food fish of the North Atlantic, the young of which are prepared as sardines, the adults are pickled, salted, or smoked.

hertz *n.* A unit of frequency equaling one cycle per second.

he's *contr.* He has; he is.

hes-i-tant *adj.* Given to hesitating; lacking decisiveness. **hesitancy** *n.*

hes-i-tate *v.* To pause or to be slow before acting, speaking, or deciding; to be uncertain. **hesitatingly** *adv.,* **hesitation** *n.,* **hesitating** *v.*

het-er-o-dox *adj.* Not in accord with established beliefs or religious doctrine; holding unorthodox opinions or beliefs. **heterodoxy** *n.*

het-er-o-sex-u-al *adj.* Of or having sexual desire to the opposite sex; involving different sexes. **-ity** *n.*

hew *v.* To make or shape with or as if with an axe; to adhere strictly; to conform.

hex *n.* One held to bring bad luck; a jinx. *v.* To put under an evil spell; to bewitch.

hex-a-gon *n.* A polygon having six sides and six angles. **-al** *adj.,* **-ally** *adv.*

hex-am-e-ter *n.* A line of verse containing six metrical feet.

hey-day *n.* A time of great power, prosperity or popularity; a peak.

hi-a-tus *n.* A slight gap, break, or lapse in time from which something is missing; a break.

hi-ba-chi *n., pl.* **-chis** A deep, portable charcoal grill used for cooking food.

hi-ber-nate *v.* To pass the winter in an inactive, dormant, sleep-like state. **hibernation, hibernator** *n.*

hi-bis-cus *n.* A chiefly tropical shrub or tree, bearing large colorful flowers.

hic-cup *or* **hic-cough** *n.* An involuntary contraction of the diaphragm that occurs on inhalation and spasmadically closes the glottis, producing a short, sharp sound. **hiccup** *v.*

hick *n., Slang* A clumsy, unsophisticated country person. *adj.* Typical of hicks.

hick-o-ry *n., pl.* **-ries** A North American tree with a smooth or shaggy bark, hard edible nuts, and heavy, tough wood.

hi-dal-go *n., pl.* **-goes** A Spanish nobleman of lesser nobility.

hide *v.* To put, or keep out of sight; to keep secret; to obscure from sight; to seek shelter. *n.* The skin of an animal.

hide-bound *adj.* Obstinately narrow-minded or inflexible.

hid-e-ous *adj.* Physically repulsive; extremely ugly. **-ly** *adv.,* **-ness** *n.*

hi-er-ar-chy *n., pl.* **-chies** An authoritative body or group of things or persons arranged in successive order; a ranked series of persons or things. **-ical, -ic** *adj.,* **hierarchically** *adv.*

hi-er-o-glyph-ic *n.* A pictorial symbol representing an idea, object, or sound. **hieroglyphically** *adv.*

hi-fi *n.* High fidelity; electronic equipment, such as a phonograph, radio, or recording equipment capable of reproducing high-fidelity sound.

high *adj.* Extending upward; located at a distance above the ground; more than normal in degree or amount.

high-ball *n.* A mixed drink often served in a tall glass.

high-born *adj.* Of noble birth or ancestry.

high-boy *n.* A tall chest of drawers often in two sections with the lower one mounted on four legs.

high-bred *adj.* Highborn; descending

from superior breeding stock.

high-brow n., *Slang* One who claims to have superior knowledge or culture. **highbrow, highbrowed** adj.

high-er-up n., *Slang* A person having superior rank or status.

high-fa-lu-tin adj. Pretentious or extravagant in manner or speech.

high fash-ion n. The newest in fashion, style, or design.

high fi-del-i-ty n., *Elect.* The reproduction of sound with minimal distortion, as on records or tapes.

high--flown adj. Pretentious in language or style.

high fre-quen-cy n. A radio frequency in the band from three to thirty megacycles.

high--hand-ed adj. Overbearing and arbitrary. -**ly** adv., **highhandedness** n.

high--hat adj., *Slang* Supercilious; patronizing; snobbish; fashionable.

high jump n. A jump for height in athletics.

high-land n. Land elevated as a plateau. **highlands** pl. A hilly or mountainous region.

high-light n. A significant event or detail of special importance. v. To give emphasis to; to provide with highlights.

high--mind-ed adj. Possessing noble principles or behavior. -**mindedness** n.

high-ness n. The state of being high.

high--pres-sure adj., *Informal* Using insistent persuasive methods or tactics. v. To try to persuade by using high-pressure techniques.

high--rise n. An extremely tall building.

high--road n. A main road; a direct or guaranteed method or course.

high school n. A secondary school of grades nine through twelve or grades ten through twelve. **high schooler** n.

high seas pl., n. The open waters of an ocean or sea that are beyond the territorial jurisdiction of any one nation.

high--sound-ing adj. Pretentious or imposing in implication or sound.

high--spirited adj. Unbroken in spirit; proud.

high--stick-ing n. In hockey, an offense in which a player holds the stick above the shoulders of other players or himself.

high--strung adj. A state of being very nervous and excitable.

high tech n. An interior design that incorporates industrial materials or motifs; high technology.

high tech-nol-o-gy n. The technology that involves highly advanced or specialized systems or devices.

high--test adj. Relating to gasoline with a high octane number.

high tide n. The highest level reached by the incoming tide each day.

high--way n. A main or principal road or thoroughfare of some length which connects towns and cities and is open to the public.

high-way-man n. Formerly, a robber who waylaid travelers on highways.

hi-jack v., *Slang* To seize illegally or steal while in transit; to coerce or compel someone; to commandeer a vehicle, especially an airplane in flight.

hike v. To walk for a lengthy amount of time usually through rugged terrain or woods; to pull up clothing with a sudden motion. **hike, hiker** n.

hi-lar-i-ous adj. Boisterously happy or cheerful. **hilariously** adv., **hilarity** n.

hill n. A rounded, elevation of the earth's surface, smaller than a mountain; a pile or heap; a small pile or mound, as of soil. v. To surround or cover with hills, as potatoes. **hilliness** n., **hilly** adj.

hill-ock n. A small or low hill or mound.

hill-side n. The side or slope of a hill.

hill-top n. The summit or top of a hill.

hilt n. The handle of a dagger or sword. **to the hilt** Fully; completely; thoroughly.

him pron. The objective case of the pronoun he.

him-self pron. That identical male one; a form of the third person, singular masculine pronoun.

hind adj. Located at or toward the rear part; posterior.

hin-der v. To interfere with the progress or action of. **hinderer** n.

hind-most adj. Farthest to the rear or back.

hin-drance n. The act of hindering or state of being hindered.

hind-sight n. Comprehension or understanding of an event after it has happened.

hinge n. A jointed device which allows a part, as a door or gate, to swing or turn on another frame. v. To attach by or to equip with a hinge or hinges.

hint n. An indirect indication or suggestion. v. To make something known by a hint.

hip n. The part of the human body that projects outward below the waist and thigh; the hip joint.

hip adj., *Slang* Said to be aware of or informed about current goings on.

hip-bone n. The large, flat bone which forms a lateral half of the pelvis.

hip joint n. The joint between the hip-bone and the thighbone.

hip-pie or **hip-py** n., pl. -**ies** A young person who adopts unconventional dress and behavior along with the use of drugs to express withdrawal from middle class life and indifference to its values.

hip-po-pot-a-mus n.

A large, aquatic mammal, native to Africa, having short legs, a massive, thick-skinned hairless body, and a broad wide-mouthed muzzle.

hire v. To obtain the service of another for pay. **hirer** n.

his *adj.* The possessive case of the pronoun he.

hir-sute *adj.* Covered with hair.

his-ta-mine *n., Biochem.* A white, crystalline substance that occurs in plant and animal tissue, found to reduce blood pressure and to have a contracting action on the uterus and believed to cause allergic reactions. **-ic** *adj.*

his-tol-o-gy *n., pl.* **-ies** The study of the minute structures of animal and plant tissues as seen through a microscope. **histological** *adj.*, **histologist** *n.*

his-to-ri-an *n.* A person who specializes in the writing or study of history.

his-tor-ic *adj.* Significant or famous in history; historical.

his-tor-i-cal *adj.* Relating to or taking place in history; serving as a source of knowledge of the past; historic. **historically** *adv.*, **historicalness** *adj.*

his-to-ry *n., pl.* **-ries** Past events, especially those involving human affairs; an account or record of past events that is written in chronological order, especially those concerning a particular nation, people, activity, or knowledge; the study of the past and its significance.

his-tri-on-ics *pl., n.* Theatrical arts; feigned emotional display.

hitch *v.* To fasten or tie temporarily, with a hook or knot.

hitch-hike *v.* To travel by signaling and obtaining rides from a passing driver.

hith-er *adv.* To this place. *adj.* Situated toward this side.

hith-er-to *adv.* Up to now.

hive *n.* A natural or man-made structure serving as a habitation for honeybees; a beehive.

hives *pl., n.* Any of various allergic conditions marked by itching welts.

hoar *adj.* Having white or gray hair; grayish or white, as with frost.

hoard *n.* The accumulation of something stored away for safekeeping or future use. *v.* To amass and hide or store valuables, money. **hoarder** *n.*

hoard-frost *n.* The deposit of ice crystals that form on a cold surface exposed to moist air.

hoarse *adj.* Having a husky, gruff, or croaking voice. **-ly** *adv.*, **hoarseness** *n.*

hoars-en *v.* To become or make hoarse.

hoar-y *adj.* Ancient; aged; gray or white with age.

hoax *n.* A trick or deception. *v.* To deceive by a hoax. **hoaxer** *n.*

hob *n.* The projection at the side or interior of a fireplace used to keep things warm; an elf or hobgoblin.

hob-by *n., pl.* **-bies** An activity or interest undertaken for pleasure during one's leisure time.

hob-gob-lin *n.* An imaginary cause of terror or dread.

hob-nail *n.* A short, broad-headed nail used to stud the soles of heavy shoes against wear or slipping.

hob-nob *v.* To associate in a friendly manner; to be on familiar terms.

ho-bo *n., pl.* **ho-boes** *or* **ho-bos** A vagrant who travels aimlessly about; a tramp.

hock *n.* The joint of the hind leg of a horse, ox, or other animal which corresponds to the ankle in man.

ho-cus-po-cus *n.* Any deception or trickery, as misleading gestures; nonsense words or phrases used in conjuring or sleight of hand.

Hodg-kin's dis-ease *n., Pathol.* A disease characterized by progressive enlargement of the lymph nodes, lymphoid tissue, and spleen, generally fatal.

hoe *n.* A tool with a long handle and flat blade used for weeding, cultivating, and loosening the soil. **hoe** *v.*, **hoer** *n.*

hoe-cake *n.* A thin, flat cake made of cornmeal.

hoe-down *n., Slang* A lively country square dance; party.

hog-tie *v.* To tie together the four feet of an animal or the hands and feet of a person.

hog-wash *n.* Kitchen scraps fed to hogs; any nonsense; false or ridiculous talk or writing.

hoi pol-loi *n.* The common people; the masses.

hoist *v.* To haul or raise up. *n.* A machine used for raising large objects.

hold *v.* To take and keep as in one's hand; to grasp; to possess; to put or keep in a particular place.

hold-ing *n.* Property, as land, money, or stocks.

hold-o-ver *n.* Something that remains from an earlier time.

hold-up *n.* A robbery at gun point; a delay.

hole *n.* A cavity or opening in a solid mass or body. **hole** *v.*

hol-i-day *n.* A day set aside by law to commemorate a special person or event; a day set aside for religious observance; a day free from work; any day of rest.

ho-li-ness *n.* The state of being holy.

hol-ler *v.* To shout loudly; to yell.

hol-low *adj.* Having a cavity or space within; concaved or sunken; lacking significance or substance; not genuine; empty; meaningless. **-ly** *adv.*, **-ness** *n.*

hol-ly *n., pl.* **-ies** A tree or shrub that bears glossy spiny leaves and bright-red berries.

hol-ly-hock *n.* A tall, cultivated plant of the mallow family, widely cultivated for its tall spikes of large, variously colored flowers.

hol-mi-um *n.* A metallic element of the rare-earth group, symbolized by Ho.

hol-o-caust *n.* A widespread or total destruction, especially by fire.

hol-o-grah *n.* A handwritten document, as a letter or will, signed by the person who wrote it. **holographical** *adj.*

hol-ster *n.* A leather case designed to hold a pistol or gun. **holstered** *adj.*

ho-ly *adj.* Regarded with or characterized by divine power; sacred.

Ho-ly Land *n.* Palestine.

hom-age *n.* Great respect or honor, especially when expressed publicly.

home *n.* The place where one resides; a place of origin; one's birthplace or residence during the formative years; a place one holds dear because of personal feelings or relationships; a place of security and comfort.

home-bod-y *n., pl.* -ies One who prefers to stay at home or whose main interest centers around the home.

home-com-ing *n.* A return to one's home; a yearly celebration during which alumni return to visit their old schools.

home eco-nom-ics *n.* The principles of home management.

home-ly *adj.* Having a simple, familiar, everyday character; having plain or ugly features; unattractive. -lness *n.*

ho-me-op-a-thy *n.* A system of treating a disease with minute doses of medicines that produce the symptoms of the disease being treated. homeopath *n.*, homeopathic *adj.*

ho-me-o-sta-sis *n., Biol.* A state of equilibrium that occurs between different but related functions or elements.

home plate *n.* In baseball, the rubber slab or plate at which a batter stands.

home run *n.* In baseball, a hit that allows the batter to circle all the bases and to score.

home-sick *adj.* Longing or yearning for home and family. homesickness *n.*

home-spun *n.* Something made, woven, or spun at home; anything that is simple and plain.

home-stead *n.* A house and its land. *v.* To occupy land granted under the Homestead Act. homesteader *n.*

home-stretch *n.* The straight portion of a racecourse between the last turn and the finish line; the last or final stage of anything.

home-work *n.* Work done at home, especially school assignments.

home-y *or* **hom-y** *adj.* Suggesting the coziness, intimacy, and comforts of home. homeyness *or* hominess *n.*

hom-i-cide *n.* The killing of one person by another; a person killed by another.

hom-i-let-ic *n.* Pertaining to the nature of a sermon.

hom-i-ly *n., pl.* -ies A sermon, particularly one based on a Biblical text.

hom-i-ny *n.* Kernels of hulled and dried corn, often ground into a coarse white meal and boiled.

ho-mo-ge-ne-ous *adj.* Of the same or similar nature or kind. homogeneity, homogeneousness *n.*, -ly *adv.*

ho-mog-e-nize *v.* To process milk by breaking up fat globules and dispersing them uniformly. -ation, -er *n.*

hom-o-graph *n.* A word that is identical to another in spelling, but different from it in origin and meaning.

hom-o-nym *n.* A word that has the same sound and often the same spelling as another but a different meaning and origin.

hom-o-phone *n.* One of two or more words that have the same sound but different spelling, origin, and meaning.

Ho-mo sa-pi-ens *n.* The scientific name for the human race.

ho-mo-sex-u-al *adj.* Having sexual attraction or desire for persons of the same sex. homosexual, homosexuality *n.*

hon-cho *n., pl.* -chos The main person in charge; the boss; the manager.

hone *n.* A fine-grained stone used to sharpen cutting tools, such as knives or razors. *v.* To perfect something; to sharpen.

hon-est *adj.* Not lying, cheating, or stealing; having or giving full worth or value. honestly *adv.*, honesty *n.*

hon-ey *n., pl.* **hon-eys** A sweet, sticky substance made by bees from the nectar gathered from flowers; sweetness. *Slang* Dear; darling. -ed *or* -ied *adj.*

hon-ey-bee *n.* Any of various bees living in colonies and producing honey.

hon-ey-comb *n.* A structure consisting of a series of hexagonal cells made by bees for the storage of honey, pollen, or their eggs.

hon-ey-moon *n.* A trip taken by a newly-married couple. honeymooner *n.*

hon-ey-suck-le *n.* A shrub or vine bearing a tubular, highly fragrant flower.

honk *n.* The harsh, loud sound made by a goose; the sound made by an automobile horn. honk *v.*, honker *n.*

hon-ky--tonk *n., Slang* A cheap bar or nightclub.

hon-or *n.* High regard or respect; personal integrity; reputation; privilege; used as a title for mayors and judges. *v.* To accept something as valid.

hon-or-a-ble *adj.* Worthy of honor.

hon-or-ar-y *adj.* Relating to an office or title bestowed as an honor, without the customary powers, duties, or salaries.

hon-or-if-ic *adj.* Giving or conveying respect or honor.

hood *n.* A covering for the head and neck, often attached to a garment; the movable metal hinged cover of an automobile engine. hooded *adj.*

-hood *suff.* The quality or state of; sharing a given quality or state.

hood-lum *n.* A young, tough, wild, or destructive fellow.

hoo-doo *n.* Voodoo. *Slang* One who is thought to bring bad luck.

hood-wink *v.* To deceive; to blindfold.

hoo-ey *n., & interj., Slang* Nonsense.

hoof *n., pl.* **hooves** The horny covering of the foot in various mammals, as horses, cattle, and oxen. *Slang* To dance; to walk. on the hoof Alive; not butchered. hoofed *adj.*

hook *n.* A curved or bent piece of metal used to catch, drag, suspend, or fasten something; in golf, a stroke that sends the ball curving to the left; in boxing, to strike with a short, swinging blow; in hockey, to check illegally with the hockey stick. *Slang v.* To cause to become dependent or addicted. *Naut., Slang* An anchor. by hook or by crook

In one way or another. **hook, line, and sinker** Unreservedly; entirely. **to hookup with** To marry; to form an association.

hoo-kah *n.* A smoking pipe having a long, flexible tube that passes through a vessel of water which cools the smoke as it is drawn through.

hook-er *n., Slang* A prostitute.

hook-worm *n.* A parasitic intestinal worm with hooked mouth parts.

hook-y *n., Slang* Truant. **to play hooky** To be out of school without permission.

hoop *n.* A circular band of metal or wood used to hold staves of a cask or barrel together; in basketball, the basket.

hoop-la *n., Slang* Noise and excitement.

hoose-gow *n., Slang* A jail.

hoot *n.* The loud sound or cry of an owl. **hooter** *n.,* **hoot** *v.*

hoot *n., Slang* A very insignificant amount. **not give a hoot** Not caring.

hoot-en-an-ny *n., pl.* **-ies** An informal gathering of folk singers for a public performance.

hop *n.* A perennial herb with lobed leaves and green flowers that resemble pine cones; the dried flowers of the plant, yielding an oil used in brewing beer. *Slang* A dance; a quick trip on a plane. *v.* To move by making short leaps on one foot; to move with light springing motions.

hope *v.* To want or wish for something with a feeling of confident expectation. **to hope against hope** To continue hoping for something even when it may be in vain. **-fully** *adv.*

hope-ful *adj.* Manifesting or full of hope. *n.* A young person who shows signs of succeeding. **hope-less** *adj.*

hop-ped--up *adj., Slang* Stimulated by narcotics; drugged.

horde *adj.* A large crowd.

hore-hound *n.* A whitish, bitter, aromatic plant, whose leaves yield a bitter extract used as a flavoring in candy.

ho-ri-zon *n.* The line along which the earth and sky seem to meet; the bounds or limit of one's knowledge, experience or interest.

hor-i-zon-tal *adj.* Parallel to the horizon. **horizontal** *n.,* **horizontally** *adv.*

hor-mone *n., Physiol.* An internal secretion carried by the bloodstream to other parts of the body where it has a specific effect.

horn *n.*

A hard, bone-like, permanent projection on the heads of certain hoofed animals, as cattle, sheep, or deer; the two antlers of a deer which are shed annually. *Mus.* Any of the various brass instruments, formerly made from animal horns. **horn in** To join in a conversation or other activities without being invited. **-y** *adj.*

horn-ed toad *n.* A lizard with a flat body, a short tail, and horn-like projections on the head.

hor-net *n.* Any of various wasps which are capable inflicting a severe sting.

horn-pout *n.* A freshwater catfish with a large head and barbels for navigation.

horn-swog-gle *v.* To deceive.

hor-o-scope *n.* A chart or diagram of the relative positions of the planets and signs of the zodiac at a certain time, as that of a person's birth; used to predict the future.

hor-ri-ble *adj.* Shocking; inducing or producing horror. *Informal* Excessive; inordinate. **horribly** *adv.*

hor-rid *adj.* Horrible. **horridly** *adv.*

hor-ri-fy *v.* To cause a feeling of horror; to dismay or shock.

hor-ror *n.* The painful, strong emotion caused by extreme dread, fear, or repugnance. *Informal* Something that is disagreeable or ugly.

hors d'oeuvre *n.* An appetizer served with cocktails before dinner.

horse *n.*

A large, strong, hoofed quadruped mammal with a long mane and tail, used for riding and for pulling heavy objects; a device that generally has four legs, used for holding or supporting something; in gymnastics, a wooden, leather-covered block of wood on four legs, used for vaulting and other exercises.

horse chest-nut *n.* Any of several Eurasian trees with digitate leaves, clusters of flowers, and chestnut-like fruit.

horse-fly *n.* A large fly, the female of which sucks the blood of various mammals, such as horses and cattle.

horse-hair *n.* The hair from a horse's tail or mane; a fabric made from such hair; haircloth.

horse-hide *n.* The hide of a horse; leather made from a horse's hide. *Informal* A baseball.

horse-laugh *n.* A loud, scornful laugh.

horse-man *n.* A person who rides horseback; one who breeds or raises horses.

horse-play *n.* Rough, boisterous fun or play.

horse-pow-er *n., Mech.* A unit of power that is equal to 746 watts and nearly equivalent to the gravitational unit that equals 550 foot-pounds per second.

horse-rad-ish *n.* A tall, coarse, white-flowered herb from the mustard family; the pungent root of this plant is used as a condiment.

horse sense *n., Slang* Common sense.

horse-shoe *n.* A protective U-shaped shoe for a horse, consisting of a narrow plate of iron shaped to fit the rim of a horse's hoof. **horseshoes** A game in which the object is to encircle a stake with tossed horseshoes.

horse-shoe crab *n.* Any closely related marine arthropod with a rounded body and a stiff pointed tail.

horse-whip *n.* A whip used to control horses. *v.* To whip or flog.

hort *abbr.* Horticultural; horticulture.

hor-ti-cul-ture *n.* The art or science of raising and tending fruits, vegetables, flowers, or ornamental plants. **horticultural** *adj.*, **horticulturist** *n.*

ho-san-na *interj.* Used to praise or glorify God.

hose *n.* A sock; a stocking; a flexible tube for carrying fluids or gases under pressure. *v.* To wash; to water; to squirt with a hose.

ho-sier-y *n.* Stockings and socks.

hosp *abbr.* Hospital.

hos-pice *n.* A lodging for travelers or the needy.

hos-pi-ta-ble *adj.* Treating guests with warmth and generosity; receptive.

hos-pi-tal *n.* An institution where the injured or sick receive medical, surgical, and emergency care.

hos-pi-tal-i-ty *n.* Hospitable treatment, disposition, or reception.

hos-pi-tal-ize *v.* To place or admit in a hospital as a patient for care or treatment. **hospitalization** *n.*

host *n.* One who receives or entertains guests; one who provides a room or building for an event or function. *Biol.* A living organism, as a plant or an animal, on or in which a parasite lives.

hos-tage *n.* A person held as security that promises will be kept or terms met by a third party.

host-ess *n.* A woman who entertains socially; a woman who greets patrons at a restaurant and escorts them to their tables.

hos-tile *adj.* Of or relating to an enemy; antagonistic. **hostilely** *adv.*

hos-til-i-ty *n.*, *pl.* **-ies** A very deep-seated opposition or hatred; war.

hot *adj.* Having heat that exceeds normal body temperature; sexually excited or receptive; electrically charged, as a hot wire. *Slang* Recently and or illegally obtained.

hot air *n.*, *Slang* Idle talk.

hot cake *n.* A pancake.

hot dog *n.* A cooked frankfurter, served in a long roll. *Slang* A person who enjoys showing off.

hot-el *n.* A business that provides lodging, meals, entertainment, and other services for the public.

hot-foot *v.* To hasten.

hot-head-ed *adj.* To have a fiery temper. **hotheadedly** *adv.*, **hotheadedness** *n.*

hot-house *n.* A heated greenhouse used to raise plants.

hot line *n.* A direct telephone line that is in constant operation and ready to facilitate immediate communication.

hot plate *n.* A portable electric appliance

for heating or cooking food.

hot po-ta-to *n.* An issue or problem that involves unpleasant or dangerous consequences for anyone dealing with it.

hot rod *n.* An automobile modified or rebuilt for greater power and speed.

hot seat *n.*, *Slang* An electric chair; a position of embarrassment, anxiety, or uneasiness.

hot spring *n.* A natural spring with water temperature above 98 degrees.

hound *n.* Any of several kinds of long-eared dogs with deep voices which follow their prey by scent; a person unusually devoted to something; a fan. *v.* To pursue or drive without letting up; to nag continuously.

hour *n.* A measure of time equal to 60 minutes; one 24th of a day; the time of day or night. **hours** *pl.* A specific or certain period of time.

hour-glass *n.*

A glass instrument having two compartments from which sand, mercury, or water flows from the top compartment to the bottom.

hour-ly *adj.* Something that happens or is done every hour. **hourly** *adv.*

house *n.* A building that serves as living quarters for one or more families; home; the shelter or refuge.

how *adv.* In what manner or way; to what effect; in what condition or state; for what reason; with what meaning.

how-dy *interj.* A word used to express a greeting.

how-ev-er *adv.* In whatever way. *conj.* Nevertheless.

how-it-zer *n.* A short cannon that fires projectiles at a high trajectory.

howl *v.* To utter a loud, sustained, plaintive sound, as the wolf.

howl-er *n.* One that howls; a ridiculous or stupid blunder.

how-so-ev-er *adv.* To whatever degree or extent.

hua-ra-che *n.* A sandal with a low heel and an upper made of interwoven leather thongs.

hub *n.* The center of a wheel; the center of activity.

hub-cap *n.* The removable metal cap that covers the end of an axle, such as one used on the wheel of a motor vehicle.

huck-le-ber-ry *n.* A type of bush, related to the blueberry and bearing glossy, blackish, usually acidic berries.

hud-dle *n.* A crowd together; in football, a brief meeting of teammates to prepare for the next play. *v.* To nestle or crowd together; to confer.

hue *n.* A gradation of color running from red through yellow, green, and blue to violet; a particular color; a shade.

huff *n.* A fit of resentment or of ill temper. *v.* To exhale or breathe heavily, as from extreme exertion. **huffily** *adv.*, **huffiness** *n.*, **huffy** *adj.*

hug *v.* To embrace; to hold fast; to keep,

cling, or stay close to. -er n.

huge adj. Of great quantity, size, or extent. **hugely** adv., **hugeness** n.

hu-la n. A Hawaiian dance characterized by beautiful rhythmic movement of the hips and gestures with the hands.

hulk n. A heavy, bulky ship; the body of an old ship no longer fit for service.

hulk-ing adj. Unwieldy or awkward.

hull n. The outer cover of a fruit or seed; the framework of a boat; the external covering of a rocket, spaceship, or guided missile.

hul-la-ba-loo n. A confused noise; a great uproar.

hum v. To make a continuous low-pitched sound; to be busily active; to sing with the lips closed. **hummer** n.

hu-man adj. Of, relating to, or typical of man; having or manifesting human form or attributes. -ly adv., -ness n.

hu-mane adj. To be marked by compassion, sympathy, or consideration for other people or animals.
humanely adv., **humaneness** n.

hu-man-i-tar-i-an n. A person who is concerned for human welfare, especially through philanthropy.
humanitarian adj., **humanitarianism** n.

hu-man-i-ty n., pl. -ies The quality or state of being human; humankind.

hum-ble adj. Marked by meekness or modesty; unpretentious; lowly. v. To make humble. -ness, -er n., -ly adv.

hum-bug n. A person who passes himself off as something he is not; a fraud; a hoax.

hum-din-ger n., Slang Someone or something that is marked as superior.

hum-drum n., Slang Boring; dull.

hu-mer-us n., pl. meri The long bone of the upper arm or forelimb extending from the shoulder to the elbow.

hu-mid adj. Containing or characterized by a large amount of moisture; damp.

hu-mid-i-fy v. To make humid or more moist. **humidifier** n.

hu-mid-i-ty n. A moderate amount of wetness in the air; dampness.

hu-mi-dor n. A container used to keep cigars in which the air is kept properly humidified by a special device.

hu-mil-i-ate v. To reduce one's dignity or pride to a lower position. -ation n.

hum-ming-bird n. A very small bird with narrow wings, long primaries, a slender bill, and a very extensile tongue.

hum-mock n. A rounded knoll or hill of snow or dirt. **hummocky** adj.

hu-mor n. Something that is or has the ability to be comical or amusing. Physiol. Fluid contained in the body such as blood or lymph.
humorous adj., **humorously** adv.

hump n. The rounded lump or protuberance, as on the back of a camel. **over the hump** To be past the difficult or most critical state.

hunch n. A strong, intuitive feeling about a future event or result. v. To bend into a crooked position or posture.

hun-dred n., pl. -dreds or -dred The cardinal number equal to 10 X 10.
hundred adj. & pron.,
hundredth n., adj. & adv.

hun-ger n. A strong need or desire for food. **hungrily** adv., **hungry** adj.

hunt v. To search or look for food; to pursue with the intent of capture; to look in an attempt to find.
hunter, huntress n.

hur-dle n. A portable barrier used to jump over in a race; an obstacle one must overcome. v. To leap over.

hurl v. To throw something with great force; in baseball, to pitch.
hurl, hurler n.

hur-rah interj. Used to express approval, pleasure, or exultation. **hurrah** n. & v.

hur-ri-cane n. A tropical cyclone with winds exceeding 74 miles per hour, usually accompanied by rain, thunder, and lightning.

hur-ry v. To move or cause to move with haste. **hurriedly** adv., **hurriedness** n.

hurt v. To experience or inflict with physical pain; to cause physical or emotional harm to; to damage.

hus-band n. A man who is married.

hush v. To make or become quiet; to calm; to keep secret; to suppress. n. A silence.

hush--pup-py n., pl -ies A mixture of cornmeal that is shaped into small balls and deep fried.

husk n. The dry or membranous outer cover of certain vegetables, fruits, and seeds, often considered worthless.

husk-y adj. Having a dry cough or grating sound; burly or robust.
huskily adv., **huskiness** n.

husk-y n., pl. -ies A heavy-coated working dog of the arctic region.

hus-sy n., pl -ies A saucy or mischievous girl; a woman with doubtful morals.

hus-tle v. To urge or move hurriedly along; to work busily and quickly. Slang To make energetic efforts to solicit business or make money.
hustle, hustler n.

hut n. An often small and temporary dwelling made of simple construction; a shack.

hutch n. A compartment or chest for storage.

hy-a-cinth n. A bulbous plant that has a cluster of variously colored, highly fragrant, bell-shaped flowers.

hy-brid n. An offspring of two dissimilar plants or of two animals of different races, breeds, varieties, or species; something made up of mixed origin or makeup. **hybrid** adj.

hy-drant n. A pipe with a valve and spout which supplies water from a main source.

hy-drate n. A chemical compound formed by the union of water with another substance in definite proportions. **hydrate** v., **hydration** n.

hy-drau-lic adj. Operated, moved, or effected by the means of water; hardening or setting under water.

hy-drau-lics pl., n. The scientific study that deals with practical applications of liquids in motion.

hy-dro-gen n. A colorless, normally odorless, highly flammable gas that is the simplest and lightest of the elements, symbolized by H. -nous adj.

hy-dro-gen per-ox-ide n. A colorless, unstable, liquid compound that is used as an antiseptic solution and as a bleach.

hy-dro-pho-bi-a n. A fear of water; rabies. hydrophobic adj.

hy-dro-plane v. To skim over water with only the hull more or less touching the surface.

hy-e-na n.

Any of several strong carnivorous mammals of Africa and Asia, with coarse hair and very powerful jaws.

hy-giene n. The science of the establishment and maintenance of good health and the prevention of disease. hygienic adj., -ically adv., -ist n.

hy-men n. The thin membrane that partly closes the external vaginal orifice.

hymn n. A song of praise giving thanks to God; a song of joy. hymn v.

hype v., Slang To put on; to stimulate; to promote or publicize extravagantly.

hy-per-ten-sion n. The condition of abnormally high blood pressure. hypertensive adj. & n.

hy-phen n. A punctuation mark (-) used to show connection between two or more words. hyphen v.

hy-phen-ate v. To separate or join with a hyphen. hyphenation n.

hyp-no-sis n., pl. hypnoses A state that resembles sleep but is brought on or induced by another person whose suggestions are accepted by the subject.

hyp-not-ic adj. Inducing sleep. n. An agent, such as a drug, which induces sleep. hypnotically adv.

hyp-no-tism n. The study or act of inducing hypnosis. hypnotist n.

hyp-no-tize v. To induce hypnosis; to be dazzled by; to be overcome by suggestion.

hy-po n., pl. hypos Slang A hypodermic needle or syringe.

hy-po-chon-dri-a n. A mental depression accompanied by imaginary physical ailments. hypochondriac n.

hy-po-der-mic sy-ringe n. A syringe and hypodermic needle used for injecting a substance into one's body.

hys-ter-ec-to-my n., pl. -ies Surgery on a female which partially or completely removes the uterus.

hys-ter-ia n. A psychological condition characterized by emotional excess and or unreasonable fear.

hys-ter-ic n. A person suffering from hysteria. pl., n. A fit of uncontrollable laughter or crying; hysteria.

I, i The ninth letter of the English alphabet; the Roman numeral for one.

I pron. The person speaking or writing. n. The self; the ego.

I or i abbr. Island; isle.

i-amb or i-am-bus n. A metrical foot consisting of r short or unstressed syllable followed by an accented syllable. iambic adj. & n.

i-at-ric adj. Pertaining to medicine or a physician.

i-at-ro-gen-ic adj. Induced inadvertently by a physician or his treatment. iatrogenically adv.

ib or ibid abbr., L. Ibidem, in the same place.

i-bex n.

An Old World mountain goat with long curved horns.

i-bi-dem adv. Used in footnotes to indicate a part of literary work that was just mentioned.

i-bis n. A long-billed wading bird related to the heron and stork.

ice n. Solidly frozen water; a dessert of crushed ice which is flavored and sweetened. Informal Extreme coldness of manner. v. To change into ice; to cool or chill; to cover with icing. icily adv., iciness n., icy adj.

ice age n., Geol. A time of widespread glaciation.

ice-boat n. A vehicle with runners and usually a sail, used for sailing over ice; an icebreaker.

ice-box n. A structure designed for holding ice in which food and other perishables are stored.

ice-break-er n. A sturdy vessel for breaking a path through icebound waters; a pier or dock apron for deflecting floating ice from the base of a pier or bridge.

ice cap n. An extensive perennial covering of ice and snow that covers a large area of land.

ice hock-ey n. A version of hockey played on ice.

ice-house n. A building where ice is stored.

ice pack n. A large mass of floating, compacted ice; a folded bag filled with ice and applied to sore parts of the body.

ice water n. Water cooled by ice.

ich-thy-ol-o-gy n. The zoological study of fishes. ichthyologic, ichthyological adj., ichthyologist n.

i-ci-cle n. A hanging spike of ice formed by dripping water that freezes.

ic-ing n. A sweet preparation for coating cakes and cookies.

i-con or i-kon n. A sacred Christian pictorial representation of Jesus Christ, the Virgin Mary, or other sacred figures.

i-con-o-clast *n.* One who opposes the use of sacred images; one who attacks traditional or cherished beliefs. **iconoclasm** *n.*, **iconoclastic** *adj.*

id *n.*, *Psychol..* The unconscious part of the psyche associated with instinctual needs and drives.

I'd *contr.* I had; I should; I would.

i-de-a *n.* Something existing in the mind; conception or thought; an opinion; a plan of action.

i-de-al *n.* A concept or imagined state of perfection; highly desirable; perfect; an ultimate objective; an honorable principle or motive. *adj.* Conforming to absolute excellence. **ideally** *adv.*

i-de-al-ism *n.* The practice or tendency of seeing things in ideal form; pursuit of an ideal; a philosophical system believing that reality consists of ideas or perceptions. **-ist** *n.*, **idealistic** *adj.*

i-de-al-ize *v.* To regard or represent as ideal. **idealization** *n.*

i-dem *pron. & adj.*, *L.* The same; used to indicate a previously mentioned reference.

i-den-ti-cal *adj.* Being the same; exactly equal or much alike; designating a twin or twins developed from the same ovum. **identically** *adv.*

i-den-ti-fy *v.* To recognize the identity of; to establish as the same or similar; to equate; to associate oneself closely with an individual or group. **-iable** *adj.*

i-den-ti-ty *n.*, *pl.* **-ties** The condition or state of being a specific person or thing and recognizable as such; the condition or fact of being the same as something else.

id-e-o-gram *or* **id-e-o-graph** *n.* A pictorial symbol used in a writing system to represent an idea or thing, as Chinese characters; a graphic symbol, as $.

i-de-ol-o-gy *n.*, *pl.* **-gies** A body of ideas that influence a person, group, culture, or political party. **-ical** *adj.*

ides *pl.*, *n.* In the ancient Roman calendar, the fifteenth day of March, May, July, and October or the thirteenth day of the other months.

id-i-o-cy *n.*, *pl.* **-cies** A condition of an idiot.

id-i-om *n.* A form of expression having a meaning that is not readily understood from the meaning of its component words; the dialect of people or a region; a kind of language or vocabulary. **-atic** *adj.*, **-atically** *adv.*

id-i-o-syn-cra-sy *n.*, *pl.* **-sies** A peculiarity, as of behavior. **idiosyncratic** *adj.*, **-ally** *adv.*

id-i-ot *n.* A mentally deficient person; an extremely foolish or stupid person. **idiotic** *adj.*, **idiotically** *adv.*

i-dle *adj.* Doing nothing; inactive; moving lazily; slowly; running at a slow speed or out of gear; unemployed or inactive. **idleness** *n.*, **idler** *n.*, **idly** *adv.*

i-dol *n.* A symbol or representation of a god or deity that is worshiped; a person or thing adored.

i-dol-a-try *n.* The worship of idols; blind adoration; devotion. **-ter** *n.*, **-ous** *adj.*

i-dol-ize *v.* To admire with excessive admiration or devotion; to worship as an idol. **idolization, idolizer** *n.*

i-dyll *or* **i-dyl** *n.* A poem or prose piece about country life; a scene, event, or condition of rural simplicity; a romantic interlude. **idyllic** *adj.*, **idyllically** *adv.*

if-fy *adj.*, *Slang* Marked by unknown qualities or conditions.

ig-loo *n.* A dome-shaped Eskimo dwelling often made of blocks of snow.

ig-ne-ous *adj.*, *Geol.* Relating to fire; formed by solidification from a molten magma.

ig-nite *v.* To start or set a fire; to render luminous by heat.

ig-ni-tion *n.* An act or action of igniting; a process or means for igniting the fuel mixture in an engine.

ig-no-ble *adj.* Dishonorable in character or purpose; not of noble rank. **-ly** *adv.*

ig-no-min-i-ous *adj.* Marked by or characterized by shame or disgrace; dishonorable. **ignominy** *n.*

ig-no-ra-mus *n.* A totally ignorant person.

ig-no-rant *adj.* Lacking education or knowledge; not aware; lacking comprehension. **ignorance** *n.*

ig-nore *v.* To pay no attention to; to reject. **ignorable** *adj.*

i-gua-na *n.*

A large, dark-colored tropical American lizard.

il-e-i-tis *n.* Inflammation of the ileum.

il-e-um *n.*, *pl.* **ilea** The lower part of the small intestine between the jejunum and the large intestine.*

ill *adj.* Not healthy; sick; destructive in effect; harmful; hostile; unfriendly; not favorable; not up to standards. *adv.* In an ill manner; with difficulty; scarcely. *n.* Evil; injury or harm; something causing suffering.

I'll *contr.* I will; I shall.

ill--ad-vised *adj.* Done without careful thought or sufficient advice.

ill--bred *adj.* Ill-mannered; impolite; rude.

il-le-gal *adj.* Contrary to law or official rules. **illegality** *n.*, **llegally** *adv.*

il-leg-i-ble *adj.* Not readable; not legible. **illegibly** *adv.*, **illegibility** *n.*

il-le-git-i-mate *adj.* Against the law; unlawful; born out of wedlock. **illegitimacy** *n.*, **illegitimately** *adv.*

ill--fat-ed *adj.* Destined for misfortune; doomed; unlucky.

ill--fa-vored *adj.* Unattractive; objectionable; offensive; unpleasant.

ill--got-ten *adj.* Obtained in an illegal or dishonest way.

ill--hu-mored *adj.* Irritable; cross. **ill-humoredly** *adv.*

il·lic·it *adj.* Not permitted by custom or law; unlawful. **illicitly** *adv.*

il·lit·er·ate *adj.* Unable to read and write; uneducated. **illiteracy, -ate** *n.*

ill-man·nered *adj.* Lacking or showing a lack of good manners; rude.

ill-na·tured *adj.* Disagreeable or unpleasant disposition.

ill·ness *n.* Sickness; a state of being in poor health.

il·log·i·cal *adj.* Contrary to the principles of logic; not logical. **illogicality** *n.*, **illogically** *adv.*

ill-tem·pered *adj.* Having or showing a cross temper or disposition.

il·lu·mi·nate *v.* To give light; to make clear; to provide with understanding; to decorate with pictures or designs. **illumination, illuminator** *n.*

ill-use *v.* To treat cruelly or unjustly. *n.* Unjust treatment.

il·lu·sion *n.* A misleading perception of reality; an overly optimistic idea or belief; misconception. **-ive, -ory** *adj.*

il·lus·trate *v.* To explain or clarify, especially by the use of examples; to clarify by serving as an example; to provide a publication with explanatory features. **Illustrator** *n.*

il·lus·tra·tion *n.* The act of illustrating; an example or comparison used to illustrate.

il·lus·tra·tive *adj.* Serving to illustrate.

il·lus·tri·ous *adj.* Greatly celebrated; renowned. **illustriousness** *n.*

ill will *n.* Unfriendly or hostile feelings; malice.

I'm *contr.* I am.

im·age *n.* A representation of the form and features of someone or something; an optically formed representation of an object made by a mirror or lens; a mental picture of something imaginary. *v.* To make a likeness of; to reflect; to depict vividly.

im·age·ry *n.*, *pl.* **-ies** Mental pictures; existing only in the imagination.

im·ag·in·a·ble *adj.* Capable of being imagined. **imaginably** *adv.*

im·ag·i·nar·y *adj.* Existing only in the imagination.

im·ag·i·na·tion *n.* The power of forming mental images of unreal or absent objects; such power used creatively; resourcefulness.
imaginative *adj.*, **imaginatively** *adv.*

im·ag·ine *v.* To form a mental picture or idea of; to suppose; to guess.

i·ma·go *n.*, *pl.* **-goes** *or* **-gines** An insect in its sexually mature adult stage.

i·mam *n.* A prayer leader of Islam; rulers that claim descent from Muhammad.

im·bal·ance *n.* A lack of functional balance; defective coordination.

im·be·cile *n.* A mentally deficient person. **imbecilic** *adj.*, **imbecility** *n.*

im·bibe *v.* To drink; to take in. **-er** *n.*

im·bri·cate *adj.* With edges over-lapping in a regular arrangement, as roof tiles or fish scales.

im·bro·glio *n.*, *pl.* **-glios** A complicated situation or disagreement; a confused heap; a tangle.

im·bue *v.* To saturate, as with a stain or dye.

im·i·ta·ble *adj.* Capable or worthy of imitation.

im·i·tate *v.* To copy the actions or appearance of another; to adopt the style of; to duplicate; to appear like. **imitator** *n.*

im·i·ta·tion *n.* An act of imitating; something copied from an original.

im·mac·u·late *adj.* Free from sin, stain, or fault; impeccably clean. **immaculately** *adv.*

im·ma·nent *adj.* Existing within; restricted to the mind; subjective. **immanence, immanency** *n.*, **-ly** *adv.*

im·ma·te·ri·al *adj.* Lacking material body or form; of no importance or relevance. **-ly** *adv.*, **immaterialness** *n.*

im·ma·ture *adj.* Not fully grown; undeveloped; suggesting a lack of maturity. **-ly** *adv.*, **immaturity** *n.*

im·meas·ur·a·ble *adj.* Not capable of being measured. **immeasurably** *adv.*

im·me·di·a·cy *n.*, *pl.* **-ies** The quality of being immediate; directness; something of urgent importance.

im·me·di·ate *adj.* Acting or happening without an intervening object, agent, or cause; directly perceived; occurring at once; close in time, location, or relation. **immediately** *adv.*

im·me·mo·ri·al *adj.* Beyond the limits of memory, tradition, or records.

im·mense *adj.* Exceptionally large. **immensely** *adv.*, **immensity** *n.*

im·merse *v.* To put into a liquid; to baptize by submerging in water; to engross; to absorb. **-ible** *adj.*, **-ion** *n.*

im·mi·grant *n.* One who leaves his country to settle in another.

im·mi·grate *v.* To leave one country and settle in another. **immigration** *n.*

im·mi·nent *adj.* About to happen. **imminence** *n.*

im·mo·bile *adj.* Not moving or incapable of motion **immobility** *n.*

im·mo·bi·lize *v.* To render motionless. **immobilization** *n.*

im·mod·er·ate *adj.* Exceeding normal bounds. **immoderately** *adv.*

im·mod·est *adj.* Lacking modesty; indecent; boastful. **-ly** *adv.*, **- y** *n.*

im·mo·late *v.* To kill, as a sacrifice; to destroy completely. **immolator** *n.*

im·mor·al *adj.* Not moral. **-ly** *adv.*

im·mo·ral·i·ty *n.*, *pl.* **-ies** Lack of morality; an immoral act or practice.

im·mor·tal *adj.* Exempt from death; lasting forever, as in fame. *n.* A person of lasting fame. **immortality** *n.*, **immortally** *adv.*

im·mov·a·ble *adj.* Not capable of moving or being moved. **-ly** *adv.*

im·mune *adj.* Not affected or responsive; resistant, as to a disease. **immunity** *n.*

im·mu·nize *v.* To make immune. **immunization** *n.*

im·mu·nol·o·gy *n.* The study of immunity to diseases. **-ic, -ical** *adj.*, **-ly** *adv.*

im·mu·no·sup·pres·sive *adj.* Acting to

suppress a natural immune response to an antigen.

im-mure v. To confine by or as if by walls; to build into a wall.

im-mu-ta-ble adj. Unchanging or unchangeable. **immutability** n., **-y** adv.

imp n. A mischievous child.

im-pact n. A collision; the impetus or force produced by a collision; an initial, usually strong effect. v. To pack firmly together; to strike or affect forcefully.

im-pac-ted adj. Wedged together at the broken ends, as an impacted bone; wedged inside the gum in such a way that normal eruption is prevented, as an impacted tooth.

im-pac-tion n. Something wedged in a part of the body.

im-pair v. To diminish in strength, value, quantity, or quality. **impairment** n.

im-pa-la n. A large African antelope, the male of which has slender curved horns.

im-pale v. To pierce with a sharp stake or point; to kill by piercing in this fashion. **impalement** n.

im-pal-pa-ble adj. Not perceptible to touch; not easily distinguished. **impalpability** n., **impalpably** adv.

im-part v. To grant; to bestow; to make known; to communicate.

im-par-tial adj. Not partial; unbiased. **impartiality** n., **impartially** adv.

im-pass-a-ble adj. Impossible to travel over or across.

im-passe n. A road or passage having no exit; a difficult situation with no apparent way out; a deadlock.

im-pas-sioned adj. Filled with passion.

im-pas-sive adj. Unemotional; showing no emotion; expressionless. **impassively** adv.

im-pa-tient adj. Unwilling to wait or tolerate delay; expressing or caused by irritation at having to wait; restlessly eager; intolerant. **impatiently** adv.

im-peach v. To charge with misconduct in public office before a proper court of justice; to make an accusation against. **-able** adj., **impeachment** n.

im-pec-ca-ble adj. Having no flaws; perfect; not capable of sin. **-ly** adv.

im-pe-cu-ni-ous adj. Having no money. **impecuniousness** n.

im-ped-ance n. A measure of the total opposition to the flow of an electric current, especially in an alternating current circuit.

im-pede v. To obstruct or slow down the progress of.

im-ped-i-ment n. One that stands in the way; something that impedes, especially an organic speech defect.

im-ped-i-men-ta pl., n. Things that impede or encumber, such as baggage.

im-pel v. To spur to action; to provoke; to drive forward; to propel. **impeller** n.

im-pend v. To hover threateningly; to be about to happen.

im-pen-e-tra-ble adj. Not capable of being penetrated; not capable of being seen through or understood; unfathomable. **-ility** n., **-ly** adv.

im-pen-i-tent adj. Not sorry; unrepentant. **impenitence** n.

im-per-a-tive adj. Expressing a command or request; empowered to command or control; compulsory. **imperative** n., **imperatively** adv.

im-per-cep-ti-ble adj. Not perceptible by the mind or senses; extremely small or slight. **imperceptibly** adv.

im-per-fect adj. Not perfect; of or being a verb tense which shows an uncompleted or continuous action or condition. n. The imperfect tense. **imperfectly** adv.

im-per-fec-tion n. The quality or condition of being imperfect; a defect.

im-pe-ri-al adj. Of or relating to an empire or emperor; designating a nation or government having dependent colonies; majestic; regal. n. A pointed beard on the lower lip or chin. **imperially** adv.

im-pe-ri-al-ism n. The national policy or practice of acquiring foreign territories or establishing dominance over other nations. **imperialist** n., **imperialistic** adj.

imperial moth n. A large New World moth with yellow wings and brownish or purplish markings.

im-per-il v. To put in peril; endanger.

im-pe-ri-ous adj. Commanding; domineering; urgent. **imperiousness** n., **imperiously** adv.

im-per-ish-a-ble adj. Not perishable. **imperishably** adv.

im-per-ma-nent adj. Not permanent; temporary. **impermanence** n., **impermanently** adv.

im-per-me-a-ble adj. Not permeable. **impermeability** n., **impermeably** adv.

im-per-mis-si-ble adj. Not permissible; not allowed.

im-per-son-al adj. Having no personal reference or connection; showing no emotion or personality. **-ly** adv.

im-per-son-ate v. To assume the character or manner of. **-ation**, **-tor** n.

im-per-ti-nent adj. Overly bold or disrespectful; not pertinent; irrelevant. **impertinence** n., **impertinently** adv.

im-per-turb-a-ble adj. Unshakably calm. **imperturbability** n., **imperturbably** adv.

im-per-vi-ous adj. Incapable of being penetrated or affected. **imperviously** adv., **imperviousness** n.

im-pe-ti-go n. A contagious skin disease marked by pustules.

im-pet-u-ous adj. Marked by sudden action or emotion; impulsive. **impetuosity** n., **impetuously** adv.

im-pe-tus n. A driving force; an incitement; a stimulus; momentum.

im-pi-e-ty n., pl. **-ies** The quality of being impious; irreverence.

im-pinge v. To strike or collide; to impact; to encroach. **impingement** n.

im-pi-ous adj. Not pious; irreverent; disrespectful. **impiously** adv.

imp-ish adj. Mischievous. **impishly** adv.,

impishness *n.*

im-pla-ca-ble *adj.* Not capable of being placated or appeased.
implacability *n.,* **implacably** *adv.*

im-plant *v.* To set in firmly; to fix in the mind; to insert surgically. **-ation** *n.*

im-plau-si-ble *adj.* Difficult to believe; unlikely. **implausibility** *n.,* **-ly** *adv.*

im-ple-ment *n.* A utensil or tool. *v.* To put into effect; to carry out; to furnish with implements. **implementation** *n.*

im-pli-cate *v.* To involve, especially in illegal activity; to imply.

im-pli-ca-tion *n.* The act of implicating or state of being implicated; the act of implying; an indirect expression; something implied.

im-plic-it *adj.* Contained in the nature of someone or something but not readily apparent; understood but not directly expressed; complete; absolute.

im-plode *v.* To collapse or burst violently inward. **implosion** *n.*

im-plore *v.* To appeal urgently to. **implorer** *n.,* **imploringly** *adv.*

im-ply *v.* To involve by logical necessity; to express indirectly; to suggest.

im-po-lite *adj.* Rude.

im-pon-der-a-ble *adj.* Incapable of being weighed or evaluated precisely. **imponderable** *n.*

im-port *v.* To bring in goods from a foreign country for trade or sale; to mean; to signify; to be significant. *n.* Something imported; meaning; significance; importance. **importer** *n.*

im-por-tance *n.* The quality of being important; significance.

im-por-tant *adj.* Likely to determine or influence events; significant; having fame or authority. **importantly** *adv.*

im-por-ta-tion *n.* The act or business of importing goods; something imported.

im-por-tu-nate *adj.* Persistent in pressing demands or requests. **-ly** *adv.*

im-por-tune *v.* To press with repeated requests. **importunity,** **importuner** *n.*

im-pose *v.* To enact or apply as compulsory; to obtrude or force oneself or a burden on another; to take unfair advantage; to palm off. **imposition** *n.*

im-pos-ing *adj.* Awesome; impressive. **imposingly** *adv.*

im-pos-si-ble *adj.* Not capable of existing or happening; unlikely to take place or be done; unacceptable; difficult to tolerate or deal with.
impossibility *n.,* **impossibly** *adv.*

im-post *n.* A tax or duty.

im-pos-tor *or* **im-pos-ter** *n.* One who assumes a false identity or title for the purpose of deception.

im-pos-ture *n.* Deception by the assumption of a false identity.

im-po-tent *adj.* Without strength or vigor; having no power; ineffectual; incapable of sexual intercourse. **impotence, impotency** *n.,* **-ly** *adv.*

im-pound *v.* To confine in or as if in a pound; to seize and keep in legal custody; to hold water, as in a reservoir. **impoundment** *n.*

im-pov-er-ish *v.* To make poor; to deprive or be deprived of natural richness or fertility. **impoverishment** *n.*

im-prac-ti-ca-ble *adj.* Incapable of being done or put into practice. **-ness, impracticability** *n.,* **impracticably** *adv.*

im-prac-ti-cal *adj.* Unwise to put into effect; unable to deal with practical or financial matters efficiently. **impracticality** *n.*

im-pre-cise *adj.* Not precise.

im-preg-nate *v.* To make pregnant; to fertilize, as an ovum; to fill throughout; to saturate. **-ion, -or** *n.*

im-pre-sa-ri-o *n., pl.* **-os** A theatrical manager or producer, especially the director of an opera company.

im-press *v.* To apply or produce with pressure; to stamp or mark with or as if with pressure; to fix firmly in the mind; to affect strongly and usually favorably. *n.* The act of impressing; a mark made by impressing; a stamp or seal for impressing. **impressible** *adj.,* **impresser** *n.*

im-pres-sion *n.* A mark or design made on a surface by pressure; an effect or feeling retained in the mind as a result of experience; an indistinct notion or recollection; a satiric or humorous imitation; the copies of a publication printed at one time.

im-pres-sion-a-ble *adj.* Easily influenced.

im-pres-sion-ism *n.* A style of late nineteenth century painting in which the immediate appearance of scenes is depicted with unmixed primary colors applied in small strokes to simulate reflected light.
impressionist *n.,* **impressionistic** *adj.*

im-pres-sive *adj.* Making a strong impression; striking. **impressively** *adv.,* **impressiveness** *n.*

im-pri-ma-tur *n.* Official permission to print or publish; authorization.

im-print *v.* To make or impress a mark or design on a surface; to make or stamp a mark on; to fix firmly in the mind. *n.* A mark or design made by imprinting; a lasting influence or effect; a publisher's name, often with the date and place of publication, printed at the bottom of a title page.

im-pris-on *v.* To put in prison. **imprisonment** *n.*

im-prob-a-ble *adj.* Not likely to occur or be true. **improbability** *n.,* **improbably** *adv.*

im-promp-tu *adj.* Devised or performed without prior planning or preparation. **impromptu** *adv.*

im-prop-er *adj.* Unsuitable; indecorous; incorrect. **improperly** *adv.*

improper fraction *n.* A fraction having a numerator larger than or the same as the denominator.

im-pro-pri-e-ty *n., pl.* **-ies** The quality or state of being improper; an improper act or remark.

im-prove *v.* To make or become better; to increase something's productivity or value. **improvable** *adj.*

im-prove-ment *n.* The act or process of improving or the condition of being improved; a change that improves.

im-prov-i-dent *adj.* Not providing for the future. **-ence** *n.*, **improv.dently** *adv.*

im-pro-vise *v.* To make up, compose, or perform without preparation; to make from available materials. **-ation, -er, -or** *n.*, **-ory, -orial** *adj.*, **-ally** *adv.*

im-pru-dent *adj.* Not prudent; unwise. **imprudence** *n.*, **imprudently** *adv.*

im-pu-dent *adj.* Marked by rude boldness or disrespect. **-ence** *n.*, **-ly** *adv.*

im-pugn *v.* To attack as false; to cast doubt on.

im-pulse *n.* A driving force or the motion produced by it; a sudden spontaneous urge; a motivating force; a general tendency. *Physiol.* A transfer of energy from one neuron to another.

im-pul-sive *adj.* Acting on impulse rather than thought; resulting from impulse; uncalculated. **impulsively** *adv.*, **impulsiveness** *n.*

im-pu-ni-ty *n.* Exemption from punishment.

im-pure *adj.* Not pure; unclean; unchaste or obscene; mixed with another substance; adulterated; deriving from more than one source or style. **impurely** *adv.*, **impurity** *n.*

im-pute *v.* To attribute something as a mistake, to another; to charge. **imputation** *n.*

in ab-sen-tia *adv.* In the absence of.

in-ac-ces-si-ble *adj.* Not accessible. **inaccessibility** *n.*, **inaccessibly** *adv.*

in-ac-tive *adj.* Not active or inclined to be active; out of current use or service. **inactively** *adv.*, **inactivity, -ness** *n.*

in-ad-e-quate *adj.* Not adequate. **inadequacy** *n.*, **inadequately** *adv.*

in-ad-ver-tent *adj.* Unintentional; accidental; inattentive. **-ly** *adv.*

in-al-ien-a-ble *adj.* Not capable of being given up or transferred. **inalienably** *adv.*, **inalienability** *n.*

in-ane *adj.* Without sense or substance. **inanely** *adv.*, **inanity** *n.*

in-an-i-mate *adj.* Not having the qualities of life; not animated. **inanimately** *adv.*, **inanimateness** *n.*

in-a-ni-tion *n.* Exhaustion, especially from malnourishment.

in-ap-pre-cia-ble *adj.* Too slight to be significant. **inappreciably** *adv.*

in-ar-tic-u-late *adj.* Not uttering or forming intelligible words or syllables; unable to speak; speechless; unable to speak clearly or effectively; unexpressed. **-ly** *adv.*, **inarticulateness** *n.*

in-as-much *as conj.* Because of the fact that; since.

in-au-gu-rate *v.* To put into office with a formal ceremony; to begin officially. **inauguration, inaugurator** *n.*

in--be-tween *adj.* Intermediate. *n.* An intermediate or intermediary.

in between *adv. & prep.* Between.

in-bound *adj.* Incoming.

in-cal-cu-la-ble *adj.* Not calculable; indeterminate; unpredictable; very large. **incalculably** *adv.*

in-can-des-cent *adj.* Giving off visible light when heated; shining brightly; ardently emotional or intense. **incandescence** *n.*

incandescent lamp *n.*

A lamp in which a filament is heated to incandescence by an electric current.

in-can-ta-tion *n.* A recitation of magic charms or spells; a magic formula for chanting or reciting.

in-ca-pac-i-tate *v.* To render incapable; to disable; in law, to disqualify. **incapacitation** *n.*

in-ca-pac-i-ty *n., pl.* **-ies** Inadequate ability or strength; a defect; in law, a disqualification.

in-car-cer-ate *v.* To place in jail. **incarceration** *n.*

in-car-na-tion *n.* The act of incarnating or state of being incarnated; the embodiment of God in the human form of Jesus; one regarded as personifying a given abstract quality or idea.

in-cen-di-ar-y *adj.* Causing or capable of causing fires; of or relating to arson; tending to inflame; inflammatory. **incendiary** *n.*

in-cense *v.* To make angry. *n.* A substance, as a gum or wood, burned to produce a pleasant smell; the smoke or odor produced.

in-cen-tive *n.* Something inciting one to action or effort; a stimulus.

in-cep-tion *n.* A beginning; an origin. **inceptive** *adj.*

in-cer-ti-tude *n.* Uncertainty; lack of confidence; instability.

in-ces-sant *adj.* Occurring without interruption; continuous. **incessantly** *adv.*

in-cest *n.* Sexual intercourse between persons so closely related that they are forbidden by law to marry. **incestuous** *adj.*, **incestuously** *adv.*

inch *n.* A unit of measurement equal to 1/12th of a foot. *v.* To move slowly.

in-cho-ate *adj.* In an early stage; incipient. **-ly** *adv.*, **inchoateness** *n.*

in-ci-dence *n.* The extent or rate of occurrence.

in-ci-dent *n.* An event; an event that disrupts normal procedure or causes a crisis.

in-ci-den-tal *adj.* Occurring or likely to occur at the same time or as a result; minor; subordinate. *n.* A minor attendant occurrence or condition. **incidentally** *adv.*

in-cin-er-ate *v.* To burn up. **-ation** *n.*

in-cin-er-a-tor *n.* One that incinerates; a furnace for burning waste.

in-cip-i-ent *adj.* Just beginning to appear or occur. **incipience** *n.*, **-ly** *adv.*

in-cise *v.* To make or cut into with a sharp tool; to carve into a surface; to engrave.

in-ci-sion *n.* The act of incising; a cut or notch, especially a surgical cut.

in-ci-sive *adj.* Having or suggesting sharp intellect; penetrating; cogent and effective; telling. **-ly** *adv.*, **-ness** *n.*

in-ci-sor *n.*

A cutting tooth at the front of the mouth.

in-cite *v.* To provoke to action. **incitement, inciter** *n.*

in-clem-ent *adj.* Stormy or rainy; unmerciful. **inclemency** *n.*

in-cli-na-tion *n.* An attitude; a disposition; a tendency to act or think in a certain way; a preference; a bow or tilt; a slope.

in-cline *v.* To deviate or cause to deviate from the horizontal or vertical; to slant; to dispose or be disposed; to bow or nod. *n.* An inclined surface.

in-clude *v.* To have as a part or member; to contain; to put into a group or total. **inclusion** *n.*, **inclusive** *adj.*, **-ly** *adv.*

in-cog-ni-to *adv.* & *adj.* With one's identity hidden.

in-co-her-ent *adj.* Lacking order, connection, or harmony; unable to think or speak clearly or consecutively. **incoherence** *n.*, **incoherently** *adv.*

in-com-bus-ti-ble *adj.* Incapable of burning. **incombustible** *n.*

in-come *n.* Money or its equivalent received in return for work or as profit from investments.

income tax *n.* A tax on income earned by an individual or business.

in-com-ing *adj.* Coming in or soon to come in.

in-com-men-su-rate *adj.* Not commensurate; disproportionate. **-ly** *adv.*

in-com-mode *v.* To inconvenience; to disturb.

in-com-mu-ni-ca-do *adv.* & *adj.* Without being able to communicate with others.

in-com-pa-ra-ble *adj.* Incapable of being compared; without rival. **incomparably** *adv.*

in-com-pat-i-ble *adj.* Not suited for combination or association; inconsistent. **incompatibility** *n.*, **incompatibly** *adv.*

in-com-pe-tent *adj.* Not competent. **incompetence, incompetency,** **in-com-plete** *adj.* Not complete. **incompletely** *adv.*, **incompleteness** *n.*

in-con-gru-ous *adj.* Not corresponding; disagreeing; made up of diverse or discordant elements; unsuited to the surrounding or setting. **-ity** *n.*, **-ly** *adv.*

in-con-se-quen-tial *adj.* Without importance; petty. **inconsequentially** *adv.*

in-con-sid-er-a-ble *adj.* Unimportant; trivial. **inconsiderably** *adv.*

in-con-sid-er-ate *adj.* Not considerate; thoughtless. **-ly** *adv.*, **-ness** *n.*

in-con-sol-a-ble *adj.* Not capable of being consoled. **inconsolably** *adv.*

in-con-spic-u-ous *adj.* Not readily seen or noticed. **-ly** *adv.*, **-ness** *n.*

in-con-stant *adj.* Likely to change; unpredictable; faithless; fickle. **inconstancy** *n.*, **inconstantly** *adv.*

in-con-ti-nent *adj.* Not restrained; uncontrolled; unable to contain or restrain something specified; incapable of controlling the excretory functions. **-ence** *n.*, **incontinently** *adv.*

in-con-tro-vert-i-ble *adj.* Unquestionable; indisputable. **-ly** *adv.*

in-con-ven-ience *n.* The quality or state of being inconvenient; something inconvenient. *v.* To cause inconvenience to; to bother.

in-con-ven-ient *adj.* Not convenient. **inconveniently** *adv.*

in-cor-po-rate *v.* To combine into a unified whole; to unite; to form or cause to form a legal corporation; to give a physical form to; to embody. **incorporation, incorporator** *n.*

in-cor-po-re-al *adj.* Without material form or substance. **incorporeally** *adv.*

in-cor-ri-gi-ble *adj.* Incapable of being reformed or corrected. **incorrigibility,** **incorrigible** *n.*, **incorrigibly** *adv.*

in-cor-rupt-i-ble *adj.* Not capable of being corrupted morally; not subject to decay. **-ifity** *n.*, **incorruptibly** *adv.*

in-crease *v.* To make or become greater or larger; to have offspring; to reproduce. *n.* The act of increasing; the amount or rate of increasing. **increasingly** *adv.*

in-cred-i-ble *adj.* Too unlikely to be believed; unbelievable; extraordinary; astonishing. **-ility** *n.*, **incredibly** *adv.*

in-cred-u-lous *adj.* Skeptical; disbelieving; expressive of disbelief. **incredulity** *n.*, **incredulously** *adv.*

in-cre-ment *n.* An increase; something gained or added, especially one of a series of regular additions. **-al** *adj.*

in-crim-i-nate *v.* To involve in or charge with a wrongful act, as a crime. **incrimination** *n.*, **incriminatory** *adj.*

in-cu-bus *n.*, *pl.* **-buses** or **-bi** An evil spirit believed to seize or harm sleeping persons; a nightmare; a nightmarish burden.

in-cul-cate *v.* To impress on the mind by frequent repetition or instruction. **inculcation, inculcator** *n.*

in-cul-pate *v.* To incriminate.

in-cum-bent *adj.* Lying or resting on something else; imposed as an obligation; obligatory; currently in office. *n.* A person who is currently in office. **incumbency** *n.*, **incumbently** *adv.*

in-cu-nab-u-lum *n.*, *pl.* **-la** A book printed before 1501.

in-cur *v.* To become liable or subject to, especially because of one's own actions. **incurrence** *n.*

in-cu-ri-ous *adj.* Lacking interest; detached.

in-cur-sion *n.* A sudden hostile intrusion into another's territory.

in-cus *n.*, *pl.* **incudes** An anvil-shaped bone in the middle ear of mammals.

in-debt-ed *adj.* Obligated to another, as for money or a favor; beholden.

indebtedness n.

in-de-cent adj. Morally offensive or contrary to good taste. **-cy** n., **-ly** adv.

in-de-ci-pher-a-ble adj. Not capable of being deciphered or interpreted.

in-de-ci-sion n. Inability to make up one's mind; irresolution.

in-de-ci-sive adj. Without a clear-cut result; marked by indecision.
indecisively adv., **indecisiveness** n.

in-dec-o-rous adj. Lacking good taste or propriety. **-ly** adv., **indecorousness** n.

in-deed adv. Most certainly; without doubt; in reality; in fact. interj. Used to express surprise, irony, or disbelief.

in-de-fat-i-ga-ble adj. Tireless.
indefatigably adv.

in-de-fin-a-ble adj. Not capable of being defined. **-ness** n., **indefinably** adv.

in-def-i-nite adj. Not decided or specified; vague; unclear; lacking fixed limits. **-ly** adv., **indefiniteness** n.

in-del-i-ble adj. Not able to be erased or washed away; permanent. **-ly** adv.

in-del-i-cate adj. Lacking sensitivity; tactless. **indelicacy** n., **indelicately** adv.

in-dem-ni-fy v. To secure against hurt, loss, or damage; to make compensation for hurt, loss, or damage.
indemnification, **indemnifier** n.

in-dem-ni-ty n., pl. **-ties** Security against hurt, loss, or damage; a legal exemption from liability for damages; compensation for hurt, loss, or damage.

in-dent v. To set in from the margin, as the first line of a paragraph; to notch the edge of; to serrate; to make a dent or depression in; to impress; to stamp. n. An indentation.

in-den-ta-tion n. The act of indenting or the state of being indented; an angular cut in an edge; a recess in a surface.

in-den-ture n. A legal deed or contract; a contract obligating one party to work for another for a specified period of time. v. To bind into the service of another.

in-de-pend-ence n. The quality or state of being independent.

in-de-pend-ent adj. Politically self-governing; free from the control of others; not committed to a political party or faction; not relying on others, especially for financial support; providing or having enough income to enable one to live without working. n. One who is independent, especially a candidate or voter not committed to a political party. **independently** adv.

in--depth adj. Thorough; detailed.

in-de-scrib-a-ble adj. Surpassing description; incapable of being described.
indescribably adv.

in-de-ter-mi-nate adj. Not determined; not able to be determined; unclear or vague.
indeterminacy n., **indeterminately** adv.

in-dex n., pl. **-dexes** or **-dices** A list for aiding reference, especially an alphabetized listing in a printed work which gives the pages on which various names, places, and subjects are mentioned; something serving to guide or point out, especially a printed character calling attention to a paragraph or section; something that measures or indicates; a pointer, as in an instrument; in mathematics, a small number just above and to the left of a radical sign indicating what root is to be extracted; any number or symbol indicating an operation to be performed on a expression; a number or scale indicating change in magnitude, as of prices, relative to the magnitude at some specified point usually taken as one hundred (100). v. To provide with or enter in an index; to indicate; to adjust through.

in-dex-a-tion n. The linkage of economic factors, as wages or prices, to a cost-of-living index so they rise and fall within the rate of inflation.

in-dex fin-ger n.

The finger next to the thumb.

in-dex of re-frac-tion n. The quotient of the speed of light in a vacuum divided by the speed of light in a medium under consideration.

in-di-cate v. To point out; to show; to serve as a sign or symptom; to signify; to suggest the advisability of; to call for. **indication**, **indicator** n.

in-dic-a-tive adj. Serving to indicate; of or being a verb mood used to express actions and conditions that are objective facts. n. The indicative mood; a verb in the indicative mood.

in-dict v. To accuse of an offense; to charge; to make a formal accusation against by the findings of a grand jury.
indictable adj., **indicter**, **indictor**, **indictment** n.

in-dif-fer-ent adj. Having no marked feeling or preference; impartial; neither good nor bad.
indifference n., **indifferently** adv.

in-dig-e-nous adj. Living or occurring naturally in an area; native.

in-di-gent adj. Impoverished; needy.
indigence n.

in-di-ges-tion n. Difficulty or discomfort in digesting food.

in-dig-nant adj. Marked by or filled with indignation. **indignantly** adv.

in-dig-na-tion n. Anger aroused by injustice, unworthiness, or unfairness.

in-dig-ni-ty n., pl. **-ies** Humiliating treatment; something that offends one's pride.

in-di-go n., pl. **-gos** or **-goes** A blue dye obtained from a plant or produced synthetically; a dark blue.

in-di-go bunt-ing n. A small North American bird, the male of which has deep-blue plumage.

in-di-go snake n. A non-venomous bluish-black snake found in the southern United States and northern Mexico.

in-di-rect *adj.* Not taking a direct course; not straight to the point. **indirection** *n.,* **indirectly** *adv.*

in-dis-creet *adj.* Lacking discretion. **indiscreetly** *adv.,* **indiscretion** *n.*

in-dis-pen-sa-ble *adj.* Necessary; essential. **indispensability, indispensable** *n.*

in-dis-posed *adj.* Mildly ill. **indisposition** *n.*

in-dite *v.* To write; to compose; to put down in writing. **inditer** *n.*

in-di-um *n.* A soft, silver-white, metallic element used for mirrors and transistor compounds, symbolized by In.

in-di-vid-u-al *adj.* Of, for, or relating to a single human being. **individually** *adv.*

in-di-vis-i-ble *adj.* Not able to be divided.

in-doc-tri-nate *v.* To instruct in a doctrine or belief; to train to accept a system of thought uncritically. **indoctrination** *n.*

in-do-lent *adj.* Disinclined to exert oneself; lazy. **indolence** *n.*

in-dom-i-ta-ble *adj.* Incapable of being subdued or defeated. **indomitably** *adv.*

In-do-ne-sia *n.* A country of southeastern Asia. **Indonesian** *adj. & n.*

in-du-bi-ta-ble *adj.* Too evident to be doubted. **indubitably** *adv.*

in-duce *v.* To move by persuasion or influence; to cause to occur; to infer by inductive reasoning. **inducer** *n.*

in-duce-ment *n.* The act of inducing; something that induces.

in-duct *v.* To place formally in office; to admit as a new member; to summon into military service. **inductee** *n.*

in-duc-tance *n.* A circuit element, usually a conducting coil, in which electromagnetic induction generates electromotive force.

in-duc-tion *n.* The act of inducting or of being inducted; reasoning in which conclusions are drawn from particular instances or facts; the generation of electromotive force in a closed circuit by a magnetic field that changes with time; the production of an electric charge in an uncharged body by bringing a charged body close to it.

in-dulge *v.* To give in to the desires of, especially to excess; to yield to; to allow oneself a special pleasure. **indulger** *n.*

in-dus-tri-al *adj.* Of, relating to, or used in industry. **industrially** *adv.*

in-dus-tri-ous *adj.* Working steadily and hard; diligent. **-ly** *adv.,* **-ness** *n.*

in-dus-try *n., pl.* **-tries** The commercial production and sale of goods and services; a branch of manufacture and trade; industrial management as distinguished from labor; diligence.

in-e-bri-ate *v.* To make drunk; to intoxicate. **-ed, -iant** *adj.,* **inebriation** *n.*

in-ef-fa-ble *adj.* Beyond expression; indescribable. **ineffably** *adv.*

in-ef-fi-cient *adj.* Wasteful of time, energy, or materials. **inefficiency** *n.,*

inefficiently *adv.*

in-e-luc-ta-ble *adj.* Not capable of being avoided or overcome. **ineluctably** *adv.*

in-ept *adj.* Awkward or incompetent; not suitable. **ineptitude, ineptness** *n.,* **ineptly** *adv.*

in-e-qual-i-ty *n., pl.* **-ies** The condition or an instance of being unequal; social or economic disparity; lack of regularity.

in-eq-ui-ty *n., pl.* **-ies** Injustice; unfairness.

in-ert *adj.* Not able to move or act; slow to move or act; sluggish; displaying no chemical activity. **-ly** *adv.,* **-ness** *n.*

in-er-tia *n.* The tendency of a body to remain at rest or to stay in motion unless acted upon by an external force; resistance to motion or change. **inertial** *adj.,* **inertially** *adv.*

in-ev-i-ta-ble *adj.* Not able to be avoided or prevented. **inevitably** *adv.*

in-ex-o-ra-ble *adj.* Not capable of being moved by entreaty; unyielding. **inexorably** *adv.*

in-ex-pe-ri-ence *n.* Lack of experience.

in-ex-pli-ca-ble *adj.* Not capable of being explained. **inexplicably** *adv.*

in ex-tre-mis *adj.* At the point of death.

in-ex-tri-ca-ble *adj.* Not capable of being untied or untangled; too complex to resolve. **inextricably** *adv.*

in-fal-li-ble *adj.* Not capable of making mistakes; not capable of failing; never wrong. **infallibility** *n.,* **infallibly** *adv.*

in-fa-mous *adj.* Having a very bad reputation; shocking or disgraceful.

in-fa-my *n., pl.* **-ies** Evil notoriety or reputation; the state of being infamous; a disgraceful, publicly known act.

in-fan-cy *n., pl.* **-ies** The condition or time of being an infant; an early stage of existence; in law, minority.

in-fant *n.* A child in the first period of life; a very young child; in law, a minor.

in-fan-ti-cide *n.* The killing of an infant.

in-fan-tile *adj.* Of or relating to infants or infancy; immature; childish.

in-fan-tile pa-ra-ly-sis *n.* Poliomyelitis.

in-farct *n.* An area of dead tissue caused by an insufficient supply of blood. **infarcted** *adj.,* **infarction** *n.*

in-fat-u-ate *v.* To arouse an extravagant or foolish love in. **infatuated** *adj.,* **infatuation** *n.*

in-fect *v.* To contaminate with disease-causing microorganisms; to transmit a disease to; to affect as if by contagion.

in-fec-tion *n.* Invasion of a bodily part by disease-causing microorganisms; the condition resulting from such an invasion; an infectious disease.

in-fe-lic-i-tous *adj.* Not happy; unfortunate; not apt, as in expression. **infelicity** *n.,* **infelicitously** *adv.*

in-fer *v.* To conclude by reasoning; to deduce; to have as a logical consequence; to lead to as a result or conclusion. **inferable** *adj.*

in-fer-ence *n.* A conclusion based on

facts and premises.

in-fe-ri-or *adj.* Located under or below; low or lower in order, rank, or quality. **inferior, inferiority** *n.*

in-fer-nal *adj.* Of, like, or relating to hell; damnable; abominable. **infernally** *adv.*

in-fer-no *n.* A place or condition suggestive of hell.

in-fest *v.* To spread in or over so as to be harmful or offensive. **infestation** *n.*

in-fi-del *n.* One who has no religion; an unbeliever in a religion, especially Christianity.

in-fil-trate *v.* To pass or cause to pass into something through pores or small openings; to pass through or enter gradually or stealthily. **infiltration** *n.*

in-fi-nite *adj.* Without boundaries; limitless; immeasurably great or large; in mathematics, greater in value than any specified number, however large; having measure that is infinite. **infinite** *n.*, **infinitely** *adv.*

in-fin-i-tes-i-mal *adj.* Immeasurably small. **infinitesimally** *adv.*

in-fin-i-ty *n.*, *pl.* **-ies** The quality or state of being infinite; unbounded space, time, or amount; an indefinitely large number.

in-firm *adj.* Physically weak, especially from age; feeble; not sound or valid.

in-fir-ma-ry *n.*, *pl.* **-ries** An institution for the care of the sick or disabled.

in-flame *v.* To set on fire; to arouse to strong or excessive feeling; to intensify; to produce, affect or be affected by inflammation.

in-flam-ma-ble *adj.* Tending to catch fire easily; easily excited.

in-flam-ma-tion *n.* Localized redness, swelling, heat, and pain in response to an injury or infection.

in-flate *v.* To fill and expand with a gas; to increase unsoundly; to puff up; to raise prices abnormally. **inflatable** *adj.*

in-fla-tion *n.* The act or process of inflating; a period during which there is an increase in the monetary supply, causing a continuous rise in the price of goods.

in-flect *v.* To turn; to veer; to vary the tone or pitch of the voice, especially in speaking; to change the form of a word to indicate number, tense, or person. **inflective** *adj.*, **inflection** *n.*

in-flex-i-ble *adj.* Not flexible; rigid; not subject to change; unalterable. **inflexibility** *n.*, **inflexibly** *adv.*

in-flict *v.* To cause to be suffered; to impose. **inflicter, inflictor, infliction** *n.*

in-flo-res-cence *n.*

A characteristic arrangement of flowers on a stalk. **inflorescent** *adj.*

in-flu-ence *n.* The power to produce effects, especially indirectly or through an intermediary; the condition of being affected; one exercising indirect power to sway or affect. *v.* To exert influence over; to modify. **influential** *adj.*

in-flu-en-za *n.* An acute, infectious viral disease marked by respiratory inflammation, fever, muscular pain, and often intestinal discomfort; the flu.

in-flux *n.* A stream of people or things coming in.

in-form-ant *n.* One who discloses or furnishes information which should remain secret.

in-for-ma-tive *adj.* Providing information; instructive.

in-frac-tion *n.* A violation of a rule.

in-fra-red *adj.* Of, being, or using electromagnetic radiation with wave lengths longer than those of visible light and shorter than those of microwaves.

in-fra-son-ic *adj.* Producing or using waves or vibrations with frequencies below that of audible sound.

in-fra-struc-ture *n.* An underlying base or foundation; the basic facilities needed for the functioning of a system.

in-fringe *v.* To break a law; to violate; to encroach; to trespass. **infringement** *n.*

in-fu-ri-ate *v.* To make very angry or furious; to enrage. **-ly** *adv.*, **-ation** *n.*

in-fuse *v.* To introduce, instill or inculcate, as principles; to obtain a liquid extract by soaking a substance in water. **infusion** *n.*

-ing *suff.* Used in forming the present participle of verbs and adjectives resembling participles; activity or action; the result or a product of an action.

in-gen-ious *adj.* Showing great ingenuity; to have inventive ability; clever. **ingeniously** *adv.*, **ingeniousness** *n.*

in-ge-nu-i-ty *n.*, *pl.* **-ies** Cleverness; inventive skill.

in-gen-u-ous *adj.* Frank and straightforward; lacking sophistication.

in-gest *v.* To take or put food into the body by swallowing. **-ion** *n.*, **-ive** *adj.*

in-gle-nook *n.* A recessed area or corner near or beside a fireplace.

in-glo-ri-ous *adj.* Not showing courage or honor; dishonorable. **-ly** *adv.*

in-got *n.* A mass of cast metal shaped in a bar or block.

in-grate *n.* A person who is ungrateful.

in-gra-ti-ate *v.* To gain favor or confidence of others by deliberate effort or manipulation. **ingratiating** *adv.*, **ingratiation** *n.*, **ingratiatory** *adj.*

in-grat-i-tude *n.* Lack of gratitude.

in-gre-di-ent *n.* An element that enters into the composition of a mixture; a part of anything.

in-gress *n.* A going in or entering of a building. **ingression** *n.*, **ingressive** *adj.*

in-grown *adj.* Growing into the flesh; growing abnormally within or into.

in-gui-nal *adj.*, *Anat.* Of, pertaining to, or located in the groin.

in-hab-it *v.* To reside in; to occupy as a home. **inhabitability, inhabiter, inhabitation** *n.*, **inhabitable** *adj.*

in-hab-i-tant *n.* A person who resides permanently, as distinguished from a visitor.

in-ha-la-tion *n.* The act of inhaling.

in-here *v.* To be an essential or permanent feature; to belong.

in-her-ent *adj.* Forming an essential element or quality of something.

in-hib-it *v.* To restrain or hold back; to prevent full expression. **inhibitable** *adj.*, **inhibitor, inhibiter** *n.*, **inhibitive, inhibitory** *adj.*

in-hi-bi-tion *n.* The act of restraining, especially a self-imposed restriction on one's behavior; a mental or psychological restraint.

in-hu-man *adj.* Lacking pity, emotional warmth, or kindness; monstrous; not being of the ordinary human type.

in-hu-mane *adj.* Lacking compassion or pity; cruel. **inhumanely** *adv.*

in-hu-man-i-ty *n.*, *pl.* **-ties** The lack of compassion or pity; an inhumane or cruel act.

in-im-i-cal *adj.* Harmful opposition; hostile; malign. **inimically** *adv.*

in-im-i-ta-ble *adj.* Incapable of being matched; unique. **inimitably** *adv.*

in-iq-ui-ty *n.*, *pl.* **-ies** The grievous violation of justice; wickedness; sinfulness.

in-i-tial *adj.* Of or pertaining to the beginning. *n.* The first letter of a name or word. *v.* To mark or sign with initials. **initially** *adv.*

in-i-ti-ate *v.* To begin or start.

in-i-ti-a-tive *n.* The ability to originate or follow through with a plan of action.

in-ject *v.* To force a drug or fluid into the body through a blood vessel or the skin with a hypodermic syringe; to throw in or introduce a comment abruptly. **injection** *n.*

in-jure *v.* To cause physical harm, damage, or pain.

in-ju-ri-ous *adj.* Causing injury, damage or hurt; slanderous; abusive. **injuriously** *adv.*, **injuriousness** *n.*

in-ju-ry *n.*, *pl.* **-ies** Damage or harm inflicted or suffered.

in-jus-tice *n.* The violation of another person's rights; an unjust act; a wrong.

ink *n.* Any of variously colored liquids or paste, used for writing, drawing, and printing. **inker** *n.*

in-laid *adj.* Ornamented with wood, ivory, or other materials embedded flush with the surface.

in-law *n.* A relative by marriage.

in-lay *v.* To set or embed something, as gold or ivory, into the surface of a decorative design.

in-let *n.* A bay or stream that leads into land; a passage between nearby islands.

in-mate *n.* A person who dwells in a building with another; one confined in a prison, asylum, or hospital.

in-nards *pl. n.*, *Slang* The internal organs or parts of the body; the inner parts of a machine.

in-nate *adj.* Inborn and not acquired; having as an essential part; inherent.

in-ner *adj.* Situated or occurring farther inside; relating to or of the mind or spirit.

in-ner-most *adj.* Most intimate.

in-no-cent *adj.* Free from sin, evil, or moral wrong; pure; legally free from blame or guilt; not maliciously intended; lacking in experience or knowledge; naive. **innocence, innocent** *n.*, **innocently** *adv.*

in-noc-u-ous *adj.* Having no harmful qualities or ill effect; harmless.

in-nom-i-nate bone *n.*, *Anat.* One of the two large, irregular bones which form the sides of the pelvis.

in-no-vate *v.* To introduce or begin something new. **innovative** *adj.*, **innovator** *n.*

in-nu-en-do *n.*, *pl.* **-dos** or **-does** An indirect or oblique comment, suggestion or hint.

in-nu-mer-a-ble *adj.* Too numerous or too much to be counted; countless.

in-oc-u-late *v.* To introduce a mild form of a disease or virus to a person or animal in order to produce immunity.

in-op-er-a-ble *adj.* Unworkable; incapable of being treated or improved by surgery.

in-op-er-a-tive *adj.* Not working; not functioning.

in-op-por-tune *adj.* Inappropriate; untimely; unsuitable. **-ly** *adv.*,

in-or-di-nate *adj.* Exceeding proper or normal limits; not regulated; unrestrained. **inordinately** *adv.*

in-or-gan-ic *adj.* Not having or involving living organisms, their remains, or products.

in-pa-tient *n.* A patient admitted to a hospital for medical treatment.

in-put *n.* The amount of energy delivered to a machine; in computer science, information that is put into a data processing system. *Elect.* The voltage, current, or power that is delivered to a circuit.

in-quest *n.* A legal investigation into the cause of death.

in-quire *v.* To ask a question; to make an investigation. **inquirer** *n.*, **inquiringly** *adv.*

in-quir-y *n.*, *pl.* **-ies** The act of seeking or inquiring; a request or question for information; a very close examination; an investigation or examination of facts or evidence.

in-quis-i-tive *adj.* Curious; probing; questioning. **inquisitively** *adv.*,

in-sane *adj.* Afflicted with a serious mental disorder impairing a person's ability to function; the characteristic of a person who is not sane. **insanely** *adv.*, **insanity** *n.*

in-san-i-tar-y *adj.* Not sanitary; not hygienic and dangerous to one's health.

in-scribe *v.* To write, mark, or engrave on a surface.

in-scru-ta-ble *adj.* Difficult to interpret or understand; incomprehensible.
inscrutability, -ness *n.*, -ly *adv.*

in-sec-tiv-o-rous *adj.* Feeding on insects.

in-se-cure *adj.* Troubled by anxiety and apprehension; threatened; not securely guarded; unsafe; liable to break, fail, or collapse.
insecurely *adv.*, insecurity *n.*

in-sem-i-nate *v.* To introduce semen into the uterus of; to make pregnant; to sow seed. -ion, inseminator *n.*

in-sen-sate *adj.* Showing a lack of humane feeling; unconscious.

in-sen-si-ble *adj.* Deprived of consciousness; unconscious; incapable of perceiving or feeling; unmindful; unaware. insensibility *n.*,
insensibly *adv.*

in-sen-ti-ent *adj.* Without sensation or consciousness. insentience *n.*

in-sep-a-ra-ble *adj.* Incapable of being separated or parted. inseparability *n.*,
inseparably *adv.*

in-sert *v.* To put in place; to set. *n.* In printing, something inserted or to be inserted. insertion *n.*

in-set *v.* To set in; to implant; to insert.

in-shore *adj.* Near or moving toward the shore. inshore *adv.*

in-side *n.* The part, surface, or space that lies within. insides *n.* The internal parts or organs. inside *adj.*

in-sid-er *n.* One having special knowledge or access to confidential information.

in-sid-i-ous *adj.* Cunning or deceitful; treacherous; seductive; attractive but harmful. -ly *adv.*, insidiousness *n.*

in-sight *n.* Perception into the true or hidden nature of things.
insightful *adj.*, insightfully *adv.*

in-sig-ni-a *n.*, *pl.* -nia *or* -nias A badge or emblem used to mark membership, honor, or office.

in-sin-cere *adj.* Not sincere; hypocritical.
insincerely *adv.*, insincerity *n.*

in-sin-u-ate *v.* To suggest something by giving a hint; to introduce by using ingenious and sly means.
insinuating *adv.*, insinuation *n.*

in-sip-id *adj.* Lacking of flavor; tasteless; flat; dull; lacking interest.
insipidly *adv.*, insipidness *n.*

in-sist *v.* To demand or assert in a firm way; to dwell on something repeatedly, as to emphasize.
insistence *n.*, insistent *adj.*, -ly *adv.*

in-so-far *adv.* To such an extent.

in-sole *n.* The fixed inside sole of a shoe or boot; a removable strip of material put inside a shoe for protection or comfort.

in-sol-u-ble *adj.* Incapable of being dissolved; not soluble; not capable of being solved. insolubility,
insolubleness *n.*, insolubly *adv.*

in-sol-vent *adj.* In law, unable to meet debts; bankrupt.

in-som-ni-a *n.* The chronic inability to sleep. insomniac *n.*

in-sou-ci-ant *adj.* Lighthearted and cheerful; unconcerned; not bothered.
insouciance *n.*

in-spect *v.* To examine or look at very carefully for flaws; to examine or review officially.
inspection, inspector *n.*

in-spi-ra-tion *n.* The stimulation within the mind of some idea, feeling, or impulse which leads to creative action; a divine or holy presence which inspires; the act of inhaling air.
inspirational *adj.*, inspirationally *adv.*

in-spire *v.* To exert or guide by a divine influence; to arouse and create high emotion; to exalt; to inhale; breathe in. inspirer *n.*, inspiringly *adv.*

in-sta-bil-i-ty *n.*, *pl.* -ties Lacking stability.

in-stall *or* in-stal *v.* To put in position for service; to place into an office or position; to settle. Installation,
installer *n.*

in-stall-ment *or* in-stal-ment *n.* One of several payments due in specified amounts at specified intervals.

in-stance *n.* An illustrative case or example; a step in proceedings. *v.* To illustrate.

in-stant *n.* A very short time; a moment; a certain or specific point in time. *adj.* Instantaneously; immediate; urgent.

in-stan-ta-ne-ous *adj.* Happening with no delay; instantly; completed in a moment. instantaneously *adv.*

in-stant-ly *adv.* Immediately; at once.

in-stead *adv.* In lieu of that just mentioned.

in-step *n.*, *Anat.*

The arched upper part of the human foot.

in-sti-gate *v.* To urge forward; to stir up; to foment; to provoke.
instigation, instigator *n.*

in-still *or* in-stil *v.* To introduce by gradual instruction or effort; to pour in slowly by drops.
instillation, instiller *n.*

in-stinct *n.* The complex and normal tendency or response of a given species to act in ways essential to its existence, development, and survival.
instinctive, instinctual *adj.*, -ly *adv.*

in-sti-tute *v.* To establish or set up; to find; to initiate; to set in operation; to start. *n.* An organization set up to promote or further a cause; an institution for educating.

in-sti-tu-tion *n.* The principle custom that forms part of a society or civilization; an organization which performs a particular job or function, such as research, charity, or education; a place of confinement such as a prison or mental hospital. -ize *v.*,
institutional *adj.*, institutionally *adv.*

in-struct *v.* To impart skill or knowledge; to teach; to give orders or direction.
instructive *adj.*

in-struc-tion *n.* The act of teaching or instructing; important knowledge; a lesson; an order or direction.

in-struc-tor *n.* One who instructs; a teacher; a low-rank college teacher, not having tenure.
instructorship, instructress *n.*

in-stru-ment *n.* A mechanical tool or implement; a device used to produce music; a person who is controlled by another; a dupe; in law, a formal legal document, deed, or contract.

in-stru-men-tal *adj.* Acting or serving as a means; pertaining to, composed for, or performed on a musical instrument. **instrumentally** *adv.*

in-stru-men-tal-ist *n.* A person who plays or performs with a musical instrument.

in-stru-men-tal-i-ty *n., pl.* **-ies** Anything that serves to accomplish a purpose; means or agency.

in-stru-men-ta-tion *n.* The use of instruments or work performed with instruments. *Mus.* The arrangement of music for instruments.

in-sub-or-di-nate *adj.* Not obedient; not obeying orders. **insubordinately** *adv.,* **insubordination** *n.*

in-sub-stan-tial *adj.* Unreal; imaginary; not solid or firm; flimsy.
insubstantiality *n.*

in-suf-fi-cient *adj.* Inadequate; not enough. **-ly** *adv.,* **insufficiency** *n.*

in-su-lar *adj.* Of or related to an island; typical or suggestive of life on an island; narrow-minded; limited in customs, opinions, and ideas. **insularity** *n.*

in-su-late *v.* To isolate; to wrap or surround with nonconducting material in order to prevent the passage of heat, electricity, or sound into or out of; to protect with wrapping or insulation. **insulation, insulator** *n.*

in-su-lin *n., Biochem.* The hormone released by the pancreas, essential in regulating the metabolism of sugar; a preparation of this hormone removed from the pancreas of a pig or an ox, used in the treatment of diabetes.

in-sult *v.* To speak or to treat with insolence or contempt; to abuse verbally. *n.* An act or remark that offends someone. **insulter** *n.,* **insulting** *adj.,* **insultingly** *adv.*

in-su-per-a-ble *adj.* Insurmountable; not able to be overcome. **insuperability** *n.,* **insuperably** *adv.*

in-sur-ance *n.* Protection against risk, loss, or ruin; the coverage an insurer guarantees to pay in the event of death, loss, or medical bills; a contract guaranteeing such protection on future specified losses in return for annual payments; any safeguard against risk or harm. **insurability** *n.,* **insurable** *adj.*

in-sure *v.* To guarantee against loss of life, property, or other types of losses; to make certain; to ensure; to buy or issue insurance.
insurability *n.,* **insurable** *adj.*

in-sured *n.* A person protected by an insurance policy.

in-sur-er *n.* The person or company which insures someone against loss or damage.

in-sur-mount-a-ble *adj.* Incapable of being overcome. **insurmountably** *adv.*

in-sur-rec-tion *n.* An open revolt against an established government. **-al** *adj.,* **insurrectionary** *adj.,* **insurrectionist** *n.*

in-sus-cep-ti-ble *adj.* Immune; incapable of being infected. **insusceptibility** *n.*

in-tact *adj.* Remaining whole and not damaged in any way. **intactness** *n.*

in-take *n.* The act of taking in or absorbing; the amount or quantity taken in or absorbed.

in-tan-gi-ble *adj.* Incapable of being touched; vague or indefinite to the mind. **-ility, -ness** *n.,* **intangibly** *adv.*

in-te-ger *n.* Any of the numbers 1, 2, 3, etc., including all the positive whole numbers and all the negative numbers and zero; a whole entity.

in-te-gral *adj.* Being an essential and indispensable part of a whole; made up, from, or formed of parts that constitute a unity.

in-te-grate *v.* To make into a whole by joining parts together; to unify; to be open to people of all races or ethnic groups. **-ion** *n.,* **integrative** *adj.*

in-teg-ri-ty *n.* Uprightness of character; honesty; the condition, quality, or state of being complete or undivided.

in-tel-lect *n.* The power of the mind to understand and to accept knowledge; the state of having a strong or brilliant mind; a person of notable intellect.

in-tel-lec-tu-al *adj.* Pertaining to, possessing, or showing intellect; inclined to rational or creative thought. *n.* A person who pursues and enjoys matters of the intellect and of refined taste. **-ity** *n.,* **intellectually** *adv.*

in-tel-lec-tu-al-ize *v.* To examine objectively so as not to become emotionally involved. **-ation, intellectualizer** *n.*

in-tel-li-gence *n.* The capacity to perceive and comprehend meaning; information; news; the gathering of secret information, as by military or police authorities; information so collected.

in-tel-li-gent *adj.* Having or showing intelligence. **intelligently** *adv.*

in-tel-li-gi-ble *adj.* Having the capabilities of being understood; understanding.

in-tend *v.* To have a plan or purpose in mind; to design for a particular use. **intended** *adj.*

in-tense *adj.* Extreme in strength, effect, or degree; expressing strong emotion, concentration, or strain; profound. **intensely** *adv.,* **intenseness** *n.*

in-ten-si-fy *v.* To become or make more intense or acute. **intensification** *n.*

in-ten-si-ty *n., pl.* **-ies** The quality of being intense or acute; a great effect, concentration, or force.

in-ten-sive *adj.* Forceful and concentrated; marked by a full and complete application of all resources.

intensively adv.

intensive care n. The hospital care provided for a gravely ill patient in specially designed rooms with monitoring devices and life-support systems.

in-tent n. A purpose, goal, aim, or design. intently adv., intentness n.

in-ten-tion n. A plan of action; purpose, either immediate or ultimate.

in-ten-tion-al adj. Deliberately intended or done. -ity n., intentionally adv.

in-ter v. To place in a grave; bury.

inter- pref. Mutually; with each other; together; among or between.

in-ter-act v. To act on each other or with each other. -ion n., interactive adj.

in-ter-breed v. To crossbreed; to breed together two different species.

in-ter-cede v. To argue or plead on another's behalf. interceder n.

in-ter-cept v. To interrupt the path or course of; to seize or stop. intercept, interception n.

in-ter-cep-tor or in-ter-cept-er n. One who or that which intercepts; a fighter plane designed for the pursuit and interception of enemy aircraft.

in-ter-ces-sion n. An entreaty or prayer on behalf of others. intercessor n., intercessional, intercessory adj.

in-ter-change v. To put each in the place of another; to give and receive in return. n. The intersection of a highway which allows traffic to enter or turn off without obstructing other traffic. -able adj., -ably adv., -er n.

in-ter-col-le-gi-ate adj. Involving or pertaining to two or more colleges.

in-ter-com n., Informal A two-way communication system, as used in different areas of a home or business.

in-ter-com-mu-ni-cate v. To communicate with each other. -tion n., intercommunicative adj.

in-ter-con-ti-nen-tal adj. Pertaining to or involving two or more continents.

in-ter-course n. Mutual exchange between persons or groups; communication; sexual intercourse.

in-ter-dict v. To forbid or prohibit by official decree. -tion, -or n., -ory adj.

in-ter-est n. Curiosity or concern about something; that which is to one's benefit; legal or financial right, claim, or share, as in a business; a charge for a loan of money, usually a percent of the amount borrowed.

in-ter-est-ed adj. Having or displaying curiosity; having a right to share in something. interestedly adv.

in-ter-est-ing adj. Stimulating interest, attention, or curiosity. interesting adv., interestingness n.

in-ter-face n. A surface forming a common boundary between adjacent areas; in computer science, the software or hardware connecting one device or system to another. interface v., interfacial adj.

in-ter-fere v. To come between; to get in the way; to be an obstacle or obstruc-

tion. interference n.

in-ter-ga-lac-tic adj. Between galaxies.

in-ter-im n. A time between events or periods. adj. Temporary.

in-te-ri-or adj. Of, or contained in the inside; inner; away from the coast or border; inland; private; not exposed to view.

in-ter-ject v. To go between other parts or elements; to add something between other things. interjector n., interjectory adj.

in-ter-jec-tion n. A word used as an exclamation to express emotion, as Oh! Heavens! Super! interjectional adj.

in-ter-lace v. To join by weaving together; to intertwine; to blend.

in-ter-lin-e-ar adj. Situated or inserted between lines of a text.

in-ter-lock v. To join closely.

in-ter-loc-u-tor n. One who takes part in a conversation.

in-ter-loc-u-to-ry adj. Having the nature of a dialogue; in law, pronounced while a suit is pending and temporarily in effect.

in-ter-lope v. To intrude or interfere in the rights of others.

in-ter-lude n. A period of time that occurs in and divides some longer process; light entertainment between the acts of a show, play, or other more serious entertainment.

in-ter-mar-ry v. To marry someone who is not a member of one's own religion, class, race, or ethnic group. intermarriage n.

in-ter-me-di-ar-y n., pl. -ies A mediator. adj. Coming between; intermediate.

in-ter-me-di-ate adj. Situated or occurring in the middle or between. intermediately adv. intermediateness n.

in-ter-min-gle v. To blend or become mixed together.

in-ter-mis-sion n. A temporary interval of time between events or activities; the pause in the middle of a performance.

in-ter-mit-tent adj. Ceasing from time to time; coming at intervals.

in-tern or in-ferne n. A medical school graduate undergoing supervised practical training in a hospital. v. To confine, as in wartime. internship n.

in-ter-nal adj. Of or pertaining to the inside; pertaining to the domestic affairs of a country; intended to be consumed by the body from the inside.

in-ter-nal—com-bus-tion en-gine n. An engine in which fuel is burned inside the engine.

in-ter-nal med-i-cine n. The branch of medicine that studies and treats the nonsurgical diseases.

in-ter-na-tion-al adj. Pertaining to or involving two or more nations. -ly adv.

in-ter-na-tion-al-ism n. The policy of cooperation among nations where politics and economics are concerned. internationalist n.

in-ter-nec-ine adj. Mutually destructive to both sides; involving struggle within a group.

in-tern-ee *n.* A person who is confined or interned.

in-ter-nist *n.* A physician who is a specialist in internal medicine.

in-ter-play *n.* Action, movement, or influence between or among people.

in-ter-po-late *v.* To insert between other things or elements; to change something by introducing additions or insertions. interpolation, interpolator *n.*

in-ter-pose *v.* To put between parts; to put in or inject a comment into a conversation or speech; to intervene. interposer, interposition *n.*

in-ter-pret *v.* To convey the meaning of something by explaining or restating; to present the meaning of something, as in a picture; to take words spoken or written in one language and put them into another language. -able *adj.*, interpretation, interpreter *n.*

in-ter-pre-ta-tive *or* **in-ter-pre-tive** *adj.* Of or based on interpreting; to provide an interpretation. -ly *adv.*

in-ter-ra-cial *adj.* Between, among, or affecting different races.

in-ter-reg-num *n., pl.* **-nums** *or* **-na** An interval between two successive reigns; a break in continuity.

in-ter-re-late *v.* To have or to put into a mutual reltionship. -ationship *n.*

in-ter-ro-gate *v.* To question formally. interrogation, interrogator *n.*

in-ter-rog-a-tive *adj.* Asking or having the nature of a question. *n.* A word used to ask a question. -ly *adv.*

in-ter-rupt *v.* To break the continuity of something; to intervene abruptly while someone else is speaking or performing. -er, -ion *n.*, interruptive *adj.*

in-ter-scho-las-tic *adj.* Conducted between or among schools.

in-ter-sect *v.* To divide by cutting through or across; to form an intersection; to cross.

in-ter-sperse *v.* To scatter among other things. interspersion *n.*

in-ter-state *adj.* Between, involving, or among two or more states.

in-ter-stel-lar *adj.* Among or between the stars.

in-ter-stice *n.* The small space between things. interstitial *adj.*

in-ter-twine *v.* To unite by twisting together. intertwinement *n.*

in-ter-ur-ban *adj.* Between or among connecting urban areas.

in-ter-val *n.* The time coming between two points or objects; a period of time between events or moments. *Mus.* The difference in pitch between two tones.

in-ter-vene *v.* To interfere or take a decisive role so as to modify or settle something; to interfere with force in a conflict. intervention *n.*

in-ter-view *n.* A conversation conducted by a reporter to elicit information from someone; a conversation led by an employer who is trying to decide whether to hire someone. interview *v.*, interviewer *n.*

in-ter-weave *v.* To weave together; to intertwine.

in-tes-tate *adj.* Having made no valid will; not disposed of by a will. intestacy *n.*

in-tes-tine *or* **in-tes-tines** *n. Anat.*
The section of the alimentary canal from the stomach to the anus. intestinal *adj.*, intestinally *adv.*

in-ti-mate *adj.* Characterized by close friendship or association. -ly *adv.*, intimacy, intimateness *n.*

in-tim-i-date *v.* To make timid or fearful; to frighten; to discourage or suppress by threats or by violence. infimidation, intimidator *n.*

in-to *prep.* To the inside of; to a form or condition of; to a time in the midst of.

in-tol-er-a-ble *adj.* Not tolerable; unbearable. -ility, -ness *n.*, -ly *adv.*

in-tol-er-ant *adj.* Not able to endure; not tolerant of the rights or beliefs of others. intolerance *n.*, -ly *adv.*

in-to-na-tion *n.* The manner of speaking, especially the meaning and melody given to speech by changing levels of pitch.

in-tone *v.* To utter or recite in a monotone; to chant. intoner *n.*

in-tox-i-cate *v.* To make drunk; to elate or excite. intoxicant, intoxication *n.*

intra- *prefix* Within.

in-tra-cel-lu-lar *adj.* Within a cell or cells.

in-tra-cra-ni-al *adj.* Within the skull.

in-tra-ta-ble *adj.* Hard to manage; difficult to cure or treat.

in-tra-dos *n., pl.* **-dos** *or* **-doses** The interior curve of an arch or vault.

in-tra-mu-ral *adj.* Taking place within a school, college, or institution; competition limited to a school community.

in-tra-mus-cu-lar *adj.* Within a muscle.

in-tran-si-gent *adj.* Refusing to moderate a position; uncompromising. intransigence, intransigency, *n.*

in-tra-oc-u-lar *adj.* Within the eyeball.

in-tra-state *adj.* Within a state.

in-tra-u-ter-ine *adj.* Within the uterus.

in-tra-u-ter-ine de-vice *n.* A metal or plastic loop, ring, or spiral inserted into the uterus as a means of contraception.

in-tra-ve-nous *adj.* Within a vein. intravenously *adv.*

in-trep-id *adj.* Courageous; unshaken by fear; bold. -y *adv.*, intrepidness *n.*

in-tri-cate *adj.* Having many perplexingly entangled parts or elements; complex; difficult to solve or understand. intricacy *n.*, intricately *adv.*

in-trigue *v.* To arouse the curiosity or interest; to fascinate; to plot; to conspire; to engage in intrigues. *n.* A secret or illicit love affair; a secret plot or plan. **intriguer** *n.*

in-trin-sic *adj.* Belonging to the true or fundamental nature of a thing; inherent. **intrinsically** *adv.*

in-tro-duce *v.* To present a person face to face to another; to make acquainted; to bring into use or practice for the first time; to bring to the attention of. **-er, -tion** *n.*, **-tory** *adj.*

in-tro-it *or* **In-tro-it** *n.* A hymn or psalm sung at the beginning of a Roman Catholic Mass.

in-tro-vert *n.*, *Psychol.* A person who directs his interest to himself and not to friends or social activities. **introversion** *n.*, **introversive, -ed** *adj.*

in-trude *v.* To thrust or push oneself in; to come in without being asked or wanted.

in-tu-it *v.* To understand through intuition.

in-tu-i-tion *n.* The direct knowledge or awareness of something without conscious attention or reasoning; knowledge that is acquired in this way. **intuitive** *adj.*, **intuitively** *adv.*

in-un-date *v.* To overwhelm with abundance or excess, as with work. **inundation** *n.*

in-ure *v.* To become used to accepting something which is undesirable. **inurement** *n.*

in-vade *v.* To enter by force with the intent to conquer or pillage; to penetrate and overrun harmfully; to violate; to encroach upon. **invader** *n.*

in-va-lid *n.* A chronically sick, bedridden, or disabled person. **invalid** *adj.* & *v.*

in-val-id *adj.* Disabled by injury or disease; not valid; unsound. **invalidity** *n.*, **invalidly** *adv.*

in-val-i-date *v.* To nullify; to make invalid. **invalidation, invalidator** *n.*

in-val-u-able *adj.* Priceless; of great value; to be of great help or use. **invaluably** *adv.*, **invaluableness** *n.*

in-var-i-a-ble *adj.* Constant and not changing. **invariably** *adv.*

in-va-sion *n.* The act of invading; an entrance made with the intent of overrunning or occupying. **invasive** *adj.*

in-veigh *v.* To angrily protest. **inveigher** *n.*

in-vei-gle *v.* To win over by flattery. **inveiglement, inveigler** *n.*

in-vent *v.* To devise or create by original effort or design. **inventor** *n.*

in-ven-tion *n.* The act or process of inventing; a new process, method, or device conceived from study and testing.

in-ven-tive *adj.* Skillful at invention or contrivance; ingenious.

in-ven-to-ry *n.*, *pl.* **-ies** A list of items with descriptions and quantities of each; the process of making such a list. **inventory** *v.*

in-verse *adj.* Reversed in order or sequence; inverted. *n.* Something opposite. **inversely** *adv.*

in-ver-sion *n.* The act of inverting or the state of being inverted; that which is inverted.

in-vert *v.* To turn upside down; to reverse the position, condition, or order of something. **-er** *n.*, **-ible** *adj.*

in-ver-te-brate *adj.* Lacking a backbone or spinal column. **invertebrate** *n.*

in-vest *v.* To use money for the purchase of stocks or property in order to obtain profit or interest; to place in office formally; to install; to make an investment. **investor** *n.*

in-ves-ti-gate *v.* To search or inquire into; to examine carefully. **investigative** *adj.*, **-tion, investigator** *n.*

in-ves-ti-ture *n.* The ceremony or act of investing or installing someone in a high office.

in-vest-ment *n.* The act of investing money or capital to gain interest or income; property acquired and kept for future benefit.

in-vig-o-rate *v.* To give strength or vitality to. **-ingly** *adv.*, **invigoration** *n.*

in-vin-ci-ble *adj.* Incapable of being defeated. **-ility** *n.*, **invincibly** *adv.*

in-vi-o-la-ble *adj.* Secure from profanation; safe from assault. **inviolability** *n.*

in-vi-o-late *adj.* Not violated. **inviolately** *adv.*, **inviolateness** *n.*

in-vis-i-ble *adj.* Not capable of being seen; not visible; not open to view; hidden. **invisibility** *n.*, **invisibly** *adv.*

in-vi-ta-tion *n.* The act of inviting; the means or words that request someone's presence or participation.

in-vite *v.* To request the presence or participation of; to make a formal or polite request for; to provoke; to entice; to issue an invitation.

in-vit-ing *adj.* Tempting; attractive. **invitingly** *adv.*

in-vo-ca-tion *n.* An appeal to a deity or other agent for inspiration, witness, or help; a prayer used at the opening of a ceremony or service.

in-voice *n.* An itemized list of merchandise shipped or services rendered, including prices, shipping instructions, and other costs; a bill. **invoice** *v.*

in-voke *v.* To call upon for aid, support, or inspiration; to conjure. **invoker** *n.*

in-vol-un-tar-y *adj.* Not done by choice or willingly. *n.* *Physiol.* Muscles which function without an individual's control. **involuntariness** *n.*

in-volve *v.* To include as a part; to make

in-vul-ner-a-ble *adj.* To be immune to attack; impregnable; not able to be physically injured or wounded. **invulnerability** *n.*, **invulnerably** *adv.*

in-ward *adj.* Situated toward the inside, center, or interior; of or existing in the mind or thoughts. **-ness** *n.*, **-ly** *adv.*

i-o-dine *n.* A grayish-black, corrosive, poisonous element, symbolized by I; a solution made up of iodine, alcohol, and sodium iodide or potassium iodide which is used as an antiseptic.

i-on *n.*, *Physics.* An atom or group of atoms which carries a positive or negative electric charge as a result of having lost or gained one or more electrons.

i-on-ize *v.* To convert completely or partially into ions. **ionization** *n.*

ip-so fac-to *adv., L.* By that very fact or act.

i-ras-ci-ble *adj.* Easily provoked to anger; quick-tempered. **irascibly** *adv.*

i-rate *adj.* Raging; angry. **irately** *adv.*

ir-i-des-cent *adj.* Displaying the colors of the rainbow in shifting hues and patterns. **iridescence** *n.*

i-ris *n., pl.* **Irises** *or* **irides**

The pigmented part of the eye which regulates the size of the pupil by contracting and expanding around it. *Bot.* A plant with narrow sword-shaped leaves and large, handsome flowers, as the gladiolus and crocus.

irk *v.* To annoy or to weary.

i-ron-bound *adj.* Bound with iron; unyielding.

i-ron-clad *adj.* Covered with protective iron plates; strict; unbreakable.

iron curtain *n.* An impenetrable political and ideological barrier between the Soviet bloc and the rest of the world.

i-ron-ic *adj.* Marked by or characterized by irony. **ironical** *adj.,* **ironically** *adv.*

iron lung *n.* A tank which encloses the entire body with the exception of the head and regulates the respiration of a patient by alternately increasing and decreasing air pressure.

i-ron-stone *n.* A heavy, white, glazed pottery.

i-ro-ny *n., pl.* **-ies** A literary device for conveying meaning by saying the direct opposite of what is really meant.

ir-ra-di-ate *v.* To subject to ultraviolet light, radiation, or similar rays.

ir-ra-tion-al *adj.* Unable to reason; contrary to reason; absurd; in mathematics, a number which is not expressible as an integer or a quotient of integers. **-ity** *n.,* **irrationally** *adv.*

ir-rec-on-cil-a-ble *adj.* Not able or willing to be reconciled.

ir-re-deem-a-ble *adj.* Not capable of being recovered, bought back, or paid off; not convertible into coin.

ir-re-duc-i-ble *adj.* Not having the capabilities of reduction, as to a smaller amount. **-ility** *n.,* **-ly** *adv.*

ir-ref-ra-ga-ble *adj.* Cannot be refuted or disproved. **irrefragably** *adv.*

ir-re-fut-able *adj.* Cannot be disproved

ir-reg-u-lar *adj.* Not according to the general rule or practice; not straight, uniform, or orderly; uneven. *n.* One who is irregular. **-ity** *n.,* **-ly** *adv.*

ir-rel-e-vant *adj.* Not pertinent or related to the subject matter. **-ly** *adv.,* **irrelevance, irrelevancy** *n.*

ir-re-lig-ious *adj.* Lacking in religion; opposed to religion. **irreligiously** *adv.*

ir-re-mis-si-ble *adj.* Unpardonable, as for sin. **irremissibility** *n.*

ir-re-mov-a-ble *adj.* Not removable.

ir-rep-a-ra-ble *adj.* Unable to be set right or repaired. **-ility** *n.,* **-ly** *adv.*

ir-re-place-a-ble *adj.* Unable to be replaced.

ir-re-press-i-ble *adj.* Impossible to hold back or restrain. **-ility** *n.,* **-ly** *adv.*

ir-re-proach-a-ble *adj.* Blameless; not meriting reproach. **-ness** *n.,* **-ly** *adv.*

ir-re-sist-i-ble *adj.* Completely fascinating; impossible to resist. **-bility** *n.*

ir-res-o-lute *adj.* Lacking resolution; indecisive; lacking firmness of purpose.

ir-re-spec-tive *adj.* Regardless of.

ir-re-spon-si-ble *adj.* Lacking in responsibility; not accountable.

ir-re-triev-a-ble *adj.* Unable to be retrieved or recovered.

ir-rev-er-ence *n.* A lack of reverence; a disrespectful action. **irreverent** *adj.*

ir-re-vers-i-ble *adj.* Impossible to reverse. **-ility** *n.,* **irreversibly** *adv.*

ir-rev-o-ca-ble *adj.* Unable or incapable of being turned in the other direction; incapable of being repealed, annulled or undone. **-ility** *n.,* **irrevocably** *adv.*

ir-ri-gate *v.* To water the land or crops artificially, as by means of ditches or sprinklers; to refresh with water. *Med.* To wash out with a medicated fluid or water. **-ation, -or** *n.,* **irrigational** *adj.*

ir-ri-ta-ble *adj.* Easily annoyed; ill-tempered. *Pathol.* To respond abnormally to stimuli.

ir-ri-tate *v.* To annoy or bother; to provoke; to be sore, chafed, or inflamed. **-ation** *n., -ant* *adj.,* **-ingly** *adv.*

ir-rupt *v.* To burst or rush in; to invade. **-ion** *n.,* **irruptive** *adj.,* **irruptively** *adv.*

is *v.* Third person, singular, present tense of the verb to be.

-ish *suffix* Of or belonging to a nationality or ethnic group; characteristic of; the approximate age of; the approximate time of; somewhat.

is-land *n.* A piece of land smaller than a continent, completely surrounded by water. **islander** *n.*

isle *n.* A small island.

-ism *suffix* Practice; process; a manner of behavior characteristic of person or thing; a system of principles.

is-n't *contr.* Is not.

i-so-late *v.* To set apart from the others; to put by itself; to place or be placed in quarantine. **isolation, isolator** *n.*

i-so-la-tion-ism *n.* A national policy of avoiding political or economic alliances or relations with other countries. **isolationist** *n.*

i-so-mer *n.* A compound having the same kinds and numbers of atoms as another compound but differing in chemical or physical properties due to the linkage or arrangement of the atoms. **isomeric** *adj.*

i-son-o-my *n.* equal rights and privileges under law

i-sos-ce-les tri-an-gle *n.*

A triangle which has two equal sides.

i-so-therm *n.* A line on a map linking points that have the same temperature. **isothermal** *adj.*

i-so-tope *n.* Any of two or more species of atoms of a chemical element which contain in their nuclei the same number of protons but different numbers of neutrons. **-ic** *adj.*, **-ically** *adv.*

i-so-trop-ic *adj.* Having the same value in all directions. **isotropy** *n.*

is-sue *n.* The act of giving out; something that is given out or published; a matter of importance to solve. *Med.* A discharge as of pus or blood. *v.* To come forth; to flow out; to emerge; to distribute or give out, as supplies.

isth-mus *n.* A narrow strip of land which connects two larger pieces of land.

it *pron.* Used as a substitute for a specific noun or name when referring to places, things, or animals of unspecified sex; used to refer to the general state of something.

i-tal-ic *adj.* A style of printing type in which the letters slant to the right. **Italics** *pl.* Italic typeface.

i-tal-i-cize *v.* To print in italics.

itch *n.* A skin irritation which causes a desire to scratch; a contagious skin disease accompanied by a desire to scratch; a restless desire or craving.

-ite *suffix* A native or inhabitant of; an adherent of; a sympathizer or follower; a descendant of; a rock or mineral.

i-tem *n.* A separately-noted unit or article included in a category or series; a short article, as in a magazine or newspaper.

i-tem-ize *v.* To specify by item; to list. **itemizer, itemization** *n.*

it-er-ate *v.* To state or do again; to repeat. **iteration** *n.*

i-tin-er-ant *adj.* Traveling from place to place; wandering. **itinerant** *n.*

i-tin-er-ar-y *n.*, *pl.* **-ies** A scheduled route of a trip.

it'll *contr.* It will; it shall.

its *adj.* The possessive case of the pronoun it.

I've *contr.* I have.

i-vo-ry *n.*, *pl.* **-ies** A hard, smooth, yellowish-white material which forms the tusks of elephants, walruses, and other animals; any substance similar to ivory. **ivories** The teeth; the keys on a piano. **ivory** *adj.*

i-vo-ry–billed wood-peck-er *n.* A type of large and almost extinct woodpecker living in the southeastern U.S.

i-vo-ry black *n.* A type of black pigment which can be made by calcining ivory.

i-vo-ry tow-er *n.* A condition or attitude of withdrawal from the world and reality.

i-vo-ry tow-ered *adj.* To be divorced from practical matters.

i-vy *n.*, *pl.* **-ies** A climbing plant having glossy evergreen leaves.

iz-zard *n.* The letter Z.

J, j *n.* The tenth letter of the English alphabet.

jab *v.* To poke or thrust sharply with short blows; a rapid punch.

jab-ber *v.* To speak quickly or without making sense.

jab-ot *n.* A ruffle or decoration on the front of a blouse, dress, or shirt.

ja-cal *n.* A small hut found in the southwestern United States and Mexico, with wall made of rows and rows of thin vertical poles filled in with mud.

jac-a-mar *n.* A tropical, brilliantly colored, insectivorous bird.

jack *n.* The playing card that ranks just below a queen and bears a representation of a knave; any of various tools or devices used for raising heavy objects; the male of certain animals; a man or boy; fellow; a small flag on a ship that indicates nationality. *Electr* A socket into which a plug is inserted to make an electric circuit.

jacks *n.* A game played with a set of six-pronged metal pieces and a small ball.

jack-al *n.* An African or Asian dog-like, carnivorous mammal.

jack-ass *n.*

A male donkey or ass; a stupid person or one who acts in a stupid fashion.

jack-et *n.* A short coat worn by men and women; an outer protective cover for a book; the skin of a cooked potato.

jack-hammer *n.* A tool operated by air pressure, used to break pavement and to drill rock.

jack–in–the–box *n.* A toy consisting of a small box from which a puppet springs up when the lid is unfastened.

jack–in–the–pul-pit *n.* A common herb which grows from a turnip-shaped bulb.

jack-knife *n.* A large pocketknife; a dive executed by doubling the body forward with the knees unbent and the hands touching the ankles and then straightening before entering the water. *v.* To bend in the manner of a jackknife.

jack-leg *adj.* Deficient in skill or training; having questionable practices; below professional quality or standards.

jack-light *n.* A light used for hunting or fishing at night. *v.* To fish or hunt with a light. **jacklighter** *n.*

jack–of–all–trades *n.* A person who is able to do many types of work.

jack–o–lan-tern *n.* A lantern made from a hollowed out pumpkin which has been carved to resemble a face.

jack-pot *n.* Any post, prize, or pool in which the amount won is cumulative.

jack rabbit *n.* A large American hare with long back legs and long ears.

jade *n.* A hard, translucent, green

gemstone; an old, worn-out unmanageable horse; a mean old woman; hussy. *adj.* Worn-out; exhausted. **jade** *v.*

jag *n.* A very sharp projection or point. *Slang* A binge or spree.

jag-ged *adj.* Having jags or sharp notches; serrated. **jaggedness** *n.*

jag-uar *n.* A large, spotted, feline mammal of tropical America with a tawny coat and black spots.

jai alai *n.* A game similar to handball in which players catch and throw a ball with long, curved, wicker baskets strapped to their arms.

jail *n.* A place of confinement for incarceration

jail-bird *n.*, *Slang* A prisoner or ex-prisoner.

jail-er *n.* The officer in charge of a jail and its prisoners.

ja-lop-y *n.*, *pl.* **-ies** *Slang* An old, rundown automobile.

ja-lou-sie *n.* A window, blind, or door having adjustable horizontal slats.

jam *v.* To force or wedge into a tight position; to apply the brakes of a car suddenly; to be locked in a position; to block; to crush. *Mus.* To be a participant in a jazz session. *Slang* To be in a difficult situation or to be crowded together, as of people, cars; a difficult situation. **jam** *v.*

jam *n.* A preserve of whole fruit boiled with sugar.

jamb *n.* The vertical sidepiece of a door.

jam-bo-ree *n.* A large, festive gathering.

jam session *n.* An informal gathering of a group of jazz musicians.

jan-gle *v.* To make a harsh unmusical sound. *n.* A discordant sound. **-er** *n.*

jan-i-tor *n.* A person who cleans and cares for a building. **janitorial** *adj.*

ja-pan *n.* A black varnish used for coating objects.

jape *v.* To joke; to make fun of or mock by words or actions. **jape, -er, -ery** *n.*

jar *n.* A deep, cylindrical vessel with a wide mouth; a harsh sound. *v.* To strike against or bump into; to affect one's feelings unpleasantly.

jar-di-niere *n.* A decorative pot or stand for flowers or plants.

jar-gon *n.* The technical or specialized vocabulary used among members of a particular profession. **jargonistic** *adj.*

jas-mine *or* **jes-sa-mine** *n.* A shrub with fragrant yellow or white flowers.

jas-per *n.* An opaque red, brown, or yellow variety of quartz, having a high polish.

ja-to *n.* A takeoff of an airplane which is assisted by an auxiliary rocket engine.

jaun-dice *n.*, *Pathol.* A diseased condition of the liver due to the presence of bile pigments in the blood and characterized by yellowish staining of the eyes, skin, and body fluids.

jaun-diced *adj.* To be affected with jaundice.

jaunt *n.* A short journey for pleasure.

jaun-ty *adj.* Having a buoyantly carefree

and self-confident air or matter about oneself. **jauntily** *adv.*, **jauntiness** *n.*

jave-lin *n.* A light spear thrown as a weapon; a long spear with a wooden shaft, used in competitions of distance throwing.

jaw *n.*, *Anat.* Either of the two bony structures forming the framework of the mouth and holding the teeth.

jaw-bone *n.* One of the bones of the jaw, especially the lower jaw.

jay *n.* Any of various corvine birds of brilliant coloring, as the blue jay.

jay-walk *v.*, *Slang* To cross a street carelessly, violating traffic regulations and or signals. **jaywalker** *n.*

jazz *n.* A kind of music which has a strong rhythmic structure with frequent syncopation and often involving ensemble and solo improvisation. *Slang* Lying and exaggerated talk; idle and foolish talk; liveliness. *Jazz up* To make more interesting; to enliven.

jeal-ous *adj.* Suspicious or fearful of being replaced by a rival; resentful or bitter in rivalry; demanding exclusive love. **-ly** *adv.*, **jealousness, jealousy** *n.*

jean *n.* A strong, twilled cotton cloth. **jeans** Pants made of denim.

jeer *v.* To speak or shout derisively.

Je-ho-vah *n.* God, in the Christian translations of the Old Testament.

je-june *adj.* Lacking in substance or nourishment; immature.

je-ju-num *n.*, *pl.* **-na** *Anat.* The part of the small intestine which extends from the duodenum to the ileum.

jel-ly *n.* *pl.* **-ies** Any food preparation made with pectin or gelatin and having a somewhat elastic consistency; a food made of boiled and sweetened fruit juice and used as a filler or spread. *v.* To make into jelly; to become or take the form of jelly; to become gelatinous; to assume or cause to assume definite form.

jel-lybean *n.* A small candy having a hard, colored coating over a gelatinous center.

jel-ly-fish *n.*, *pl.* **fishes** Any of a number of freeswimming marine animals of jellylike substance, often having bell or umbrella-shaped bodies with trailing tentacles. *Slang* A person lacking determination; a spineless weakling.

jeop-ard-ize *v.* To put in jeopardy; to expose to loss or danger.

jeop-ard-y *n.* Exposure to loss or danger.

jer-bo-a *n.*

Any of a type of small, nocturnal rodent of Asia and Africa with long hind legs.

jer-e-mi-ad *n.* A lament or prolonged complaint.

jerk *v.* To give a sharp twist or pull to. *n.*

A sudden movement, as a tug or twist. *Physiol.* An involuntary contraction of a muscle resulting from a reflex action. Slang An annoying or foolish person. **jerky,** -lly *adv.,* **jerkiness** *n.*

jer-kin *n.* A close-fitting jacket, usually sleeveless.

jerk-wa-ter *adj.* Of little importance.

jer-ry--build *v.* To build flimsily and cheaply. **jerry--builder** *n.*

jer-sey *n., pl.* -seys A soft ribbed fabric of wool, cotton, or other material; a knitted sweater, jacket, or shirt; fawn-colored, small dairy cattle which yield milk rich in butter fat.

jest *n.* An action or remark intended to provoke laughter; a joke; a playful mood. **jester** *n.*

Je-sus *n.* The founder of Christianity, son of Mary and regarded in the Christian faith as Christ the son of God, the Messiah; also referred to as Jesus Christ or Jesus of Nazareth.

jet *n.*

A sudden spurt or gush of liquid or gas emitted through a narrow opening; a jet airplane; a hard, black mineral which takes a high polish and is used in jewelry; a deep glossy black.

jet lag *n.* Mental and physical fatigue resulting from rapid travel through several time zones.

jet stream *n.* A high-velocity wind near the troposphere, generally moving from west to east often at speeds exceeding 250 mph.; a high-speed stream of gas or other fluid expelled from a jet engine or rocket.

jet-ti-son *v.* To throw cargo overboard; to discard a useless or hampering item.

jet-ty *n., pl.* -ies A wall made of piling rocks, or other material which extends into a body of water to protect a harbor or influence the current; a pier.

jew-el *n.* A precious stone used for personal adornment; a person or thing of very rare excellence or value. *v.* To furnish with jewels. **jewelry** *n.*

jew-eler *or* **jew-el-ler** *n.* A person who makes or deals in jewelry.

jib *n., Naut.* A triangular sail set on a stay extending from the head of the foremast to the bowsprit. *v.* To swing or shift from one side of a vessel to the other.

jif-fy *or* **jiff** *n., pl.* -ies, **jiffs** A very short time.

jig *n.* Any of a variety of fast, lively dances; the music for such a dance. *Mech.* A device used to hold and guide a tool. **jig** *v.*

jig-ger *n.* A small measure holding 1 1/2 oz. used for measuring liquor. *Naut.* A small sail in the stern of a sailing craft. *Slang* Any small item which does not have a particular name.

jig-gle *v.* To move or jerk lightly up and down. *n.* A jerky, unsteady movement.

jig-saw *n.* A saw having a slim blade set vertically, used for cutting curved or irregular lines.

jig-saw puz-zle *n.* A puzzle consisting of many irregularly shaped pieces which fit together and form a picture.

jilt *v.* To discard a lover. *n.* A woman or girl who discards a lover.

jim-my *n., pl.* -ies A short crowbar, often used by a burglar. *v.* To force open or break into with a jimmy.

jim-son-weed *n.* A tall, coarse, foul-smelling, poisonous annual weed with large, trumpet-shaped purplish or white flowers.

jin-gle *v.* To make a light clinking or ringing sound. *n.* A short, catchy song or poem, as one used for advertising.

jin-go-ism *n.* Extreme nationalism which is marked by a belligerent foreign policy. **jingoist** *n.,* **jingoistic** *adj.*

jinn *n., pl.* **jin-ni** In the Moslem legend, a spirit with supernatural powers.

jinx *n., Slang* A person or thing thought to bring bad luck; a period of bad luck.

jit-ney *n.* A vehicle carrying passengers for a small fee.

jit-ter *v., Slang* To be intensely nervous.

jit-ter-bug *n., Slang* A lively dance or one who performs this dance.

jit-ters *n.* Nervousness.

jive *n., Slang* Jazz or swing music and musicians.

job *n.* Anything that is done; work that is done for a set fee; the project worked on; a position of employment.

job-ber *n.* One who buys goods in bulk from the manufacturer and sells them to retailers; a person who works by the job; a pieceworker.

job-name *n.* Computer Science. A code that is assigned to a specific job instruction in a computer program, for the operator's use.

jock *n., Slang* A male athlete in college; a person who participates in athletics.

jock-ey *n.* A person who rides a horse as a professional in a race; one who works with a specific object or device.

joc-u-lar *adj.* Marked by joking; playful.

joc-und *adj.* Cheerful; merry; suggestive of high spirits and lively mirthfulness.

jog *n.* A slight movement or a slight shake; the slow steady trot of a horse, especially when exercising or participating in a sport; a projecting or retreating part in a surface or line. *v.* To shift direction abruptly; to exercise by running at a slow but steady pace.

jog-gle *v.* To move or shake slightly.

john *n., Slang* Toilet; a prostitute's client.

john-ny-cake *n.* A thin bread made with cornmeal.

john-ny--come--late-ly *n., pl.* -ies Slang A late or recent arrival.

join *v.* To bring or put together so as to form a unit; to become a member of an organization; to participate.

join-er *n.* A person whose occupation is to build articles by joining pieces of wood; a cabinetmaker; a carpenter.

joint *n.*

The place where two or more things or parts are joined; a point where bones are connected. *Slang* A disreputable or shabby place of entertainment. *adj.* Marked by cooperation, as a joint effort.

join-ture *n.*, *Law* A settlement of property arranged by a husband which is to be used for the support of his wife after his death.

joist *n.* Any of a number of small parallel beams set from wall to wall to support a floor.

joke *n.* Something said or done to cause laughter, such as a brief story with a punch line; something not taken seriously. *v.* To tell or play jokes.

jok-er *n.* A person who jokes; a playing card, used in certain card games as a wild card; an unsuspected or unapparent fact which nullifies a seeming advantage.

jol-li-fi-ca-tion *n.* Merrymaking; festivity.

jol-ly *adj.* Full of good humor; merry.

jolt *v.* To knock or shake about. *n.* A sudden bump or jar, as from a blow.

jon-quil *n.* A widely grown species of narcissus related to the daffodil, having fragrant white or yellow flowers and long narrow leaves.

josh *v.*, *Slang* To make good-humored fun of someone; to tease; to joke.

joss *n.* A Chinese idol or image.

joss stick *n.* A stick of incense burnt by the Chinese.

jos-tle *v.* To make one's way through a crowd by pushing, elbowing, or shoving. **jostler** *n.*

jot *v.* To make a brief note of something. *n.* A tiny bit.

jounce *v.* To bounce; to bump; to shake. **jounce** *n.*, **jouncy** *adj.*

jour *abbr.* Journal; journalist.

jour-nal *n.* A diary or personal daily record of observations and experiences; in bookkeeping, a book in which daily financial transactions are recorded. *Mech.* The part of an axle which rotates in or against a bearing.

jour-nal-ese *n.* The vocabulary and style of writing supposedly characteristic of most newspapers.

jour-nal-ism *n.* The occupation, collection, writing, editing, and publishing of newspapers and other periodicals. **journalist** *n.*, **journalistic** *adj.*, **journalistically** *adv.*

jour-ney *n.* A trip from one place to another over a long distance; the distance that is traveled. *v.* to make a trip; to travel a long distance.

jour-ney-man *n.*, *pl.* **-men** A worker who has served an apprenticeship in a skilled trade.

joust *n.* A formal combat between two knights on horseback as a part of a medieval tournament.

jo-vi-al *adj.* Good-natured; good-humored; jolly. **joviality** *n.*

jowl *n.* The fleshy part of the lower jaw; the cheek. **jowly** *adj.*

joy *n.* A strong feeling of great happiness; delight; a state or source of contentment or satisfaction; anything which makes one delighted or happy. **joyfully** *adv.*, **joyfulness** *n.*, **joyless** *adj.*, **joylessly** *adv.*, **joylessness** *n.*

joy-ous *adj.* Joyful; causing or feeling joy. **joyously** *adv.*, **joyousness** *n.*

joy ride *Slang* A ride taken for pleasure only.

joy stick *Slang* The control stick of an airplane or video game.

ju-bi-lant *adj.* Exultantly joyful or triumphant; expressing joy. **jubilance** *n.*, **jubilantly** *adv.*

ju-bi-la-tion *n.* Rejoicing; exultation.

ju-bi-lee *n.* A special anniversary of an event; any time of rejoicing.

judge *v.*, *Law* A public officer who passes judgment in a court. *v.* To decide authoritatively after deliberation.

judg-ment or judge-ment *n.* The ability to make a wise decision or to form an opinion; the act of judging. *Law* The sentence or determination of a court. **judgmental** *adj.*

ju-di-ca-ture *n.* The function or action of administration of justice; law, courts, or judges as a whole.

ju-di-cial *adj.* Pertaining to the administering of justice, to courts of law, or to judges; enforced or decreed by a court of law. **judicially** *adv.*

ju-di-ci-ar-y *adj.* Of or pertaining to judges, courts, or judgments. *n.* The department of the government which administers the law; a system of courts of law.

ju-di-cious *adj.* Having, showing, or exercising good sound judgment. **judiciously** *adv.*, **judiciousness** *n.*

ju-do *n.* A system or form of self-defense, developed from jujitsu in Japan in 1882, which emphasizes principles of balance and leverage.

jug *n.* A small pitcher or similar vessel for holding liquids. *Slang* A jail.

jug-gle *v.* To keep several objects continuously moving from the hand into the air; to practice fraud or deception. **juggler** *n.*

jug-u-lar *adj.*, *Anat.* Of or pertaining to the region of the throat or the jugular vein.

jug-u-lar vein *n.*, *Anat.* One of the large veins on either side of the neck.

juice *n.* The liquid part of a vegetable, fruit, or animal. *Slang* Electric current.

juic-er *n.* A device for extracting juice from fruit.

juic-y *adj.* Full of; abounding with juice; full of interest; richly rewarding, especially financially. **juiciness** *n.*

juke box *n.* A large, automatic, coin-operated record player equipped with push buttons for the selection of records.

jum-ble *v.* To mix in a confused mass; to throw together without order; to confuse or mix something up in the mind.

jump *v.* To spring from the ground, floor, or other surface into the air by using a muscular effort of the legs and feet; to move in astonishment; to leap over; to increase greatly, as prices. *Informal* To attack by surprise. *Computer Science* To move from one set of instructions in a program to another set further behind or ahead.

jump-er *n.* One who or that which jumps; a sleeveless dress, usually worn over a blouse. *Electr.* A short wire used to bypass or join parts of a circuit.

junc-tion *n.* The place where lines or routes meet, as roads or railways; the process of joining or the act of joining.

jun-gle *n.* A densely covered land with tropical vegetation, usually inhabited by wild animals. **jungle** *adj.*

jun-ior *adj.* Younger in years or rank, used to distinguish the son from the father of the same first name; the younger of two. *n.* The third year of high school or college.

junk *n.* Discarded material, as glass, scrap iron, paper, or rags; a flat-bottomed Chinese ship with battened sails; rubbish; worthless matter. *Slang* Heroin, narcotics or dope.

junk-ie *or* **junk-y** *n. Slang* A drug addict that uses heroin.

jun-ta *n.* A body of men or persons, as military officers, in power following a coup d'etat.

ju-rid-i-cal *or* **ju-rid-ic** *adj.* Of or pertaining to the law and to the administration of justice.

ju-ris-dic-tion *n.* The lawful right or power to interpret and apply the law; the territory within which power is exercised. **jurisdictional** *adj.*

ju-ror *n.* A person who serves on a jury.

ju-ry *n., pl.* **-ies** A group of legally qualified persons summoned to serve on a judicial tribunal to give a verdict according to evidence presented.

just *adj.* Fair and impartial in acting or judging; morally right; merited; deserved; based on sound reason. *adv.* To the exact point; precisely; exactly right. **justly** *adv.,* **justness** *n.*

jus-tice *n.* The principle of moral or ideal rightness; conformity to the law; the abstract principle by which right and wrong are defined; a judge.

jus-ti-fy *v.* To be just, right, or valid; to declare guiltless; to adjust or space lines to the proper length. **-iable** *adj.*

jut *v.* To extend beyond the main portion; to project.

ju-ve-nile *adj.* Young; youthful; not yet an adult. *n.* A young person; an actor who plays youthful roles; a child's book.

K, k The eleventh letter of the English alphabet. In Computer science, a unit of storage capacity equal to 1024 bytes.

Kaá-ba *n.* Building in the Great Mosque at Mecca.

ka-bob *n.* Cubed meat and vegetables placed on a skewer.

ka-bu-ki *n.* A traditional Japanese drama in which dances and songs are performed in a stylized fashion.

kaf-fee klatsch *n.* An informal get-together to drink coffee and talk.

kai-nite *n.* A mineral that is used as a fertilizer and a source of magnesium and potassium.

kai-ser *n.* An Austrian ruler from 1804-1918; an emperor.

ka-ka-po *n.* A large parrot.

ka-lie-do-scope *n.* A tubular instrument rotated to make successive symmetrical designs by using mirrors reflecting the changing patterns made by pieces of loose colored glass at the end of a tube. **-ic, -ical** *adj.,* **-ally** *adv.*

kame *n.* A short ridge of gravel and sand that remains after glacial ice melts.

kam-ik *n.* Boot made of sealskin, knee-high in length.

ka-mi-ka-ze *n.* A Japanese pilot in World War II trained to make a suicidal crash; an aircraft loaded with explosives used in a suicide attack.

kan-ga-roo *n., pl.* **-roo, roos**

Any of various herbivorous marsupials, of Australia, with short forelegs, large hind limbs, capable of jumping, and a large tail.

ka-o-lin *or* **ka-o-line** *n.* A fine clay used in ceramics.

ka-pok *n.* A silky fiber manufactured from the fruit of the silk-cotton tree and used for stuffing cushions and life preservers.

ka-put *adj., Slang* Destroyed or out of order.

kar-a-kul *n.* Any of a breed of fat-tailed sheep of central Asia having a narrow body and coarse wiry, brown fur.

kar-at *n.* A unit of measure for the fineness of gold; a measure of weight for precious gems.

ka-ra-te *n.* A Japanese art of self-defense.

kar-ma *n.* The over-all effect of one's behavior, held in Hinduism and Buddhism to determine one's destiny in a future existence. **karmic** *adj.*

ka-ross *n.* Animal skins sewn together worn by natives.

ka-ty-did *n.* Any of various green insects related to grasshoppers and crickets, having specialized organs on the wings of the male that make a shrill sound when rubbed together.

katz-en-jam-mer *n.* A feeling of uneasiness, worry, or nervousness.

kay-ak n. A watertight Eskimo boat with a light frame and covered with sealskin.

kay-o n. To knock our an opponent, in boxing.

ka-zoo n. A toy musical instrument with a paper membrane which vibrates when a player hums into the tube.

ke-a n. A New Zealand parrot.

kedge n. A small anchor. v. Pull a ship by the rope of an anchor.

keel n. The central main stem on a ship or aircraft which runs lengthwise along the center line from bow to stern, to which a frame is built upwards. v. To capsize. **keel over**. To fall over suddenly; turn upside down.

keen adj. Having a sharp edge or point; acutely painful or harsh; intellectually acute; strong; intense. Slang Great. **-ly** adv., **keenness** n., **keener** n.

keep v. To have and hold; to not let go; to maintain, as business records; to know a secret and not divulge it; to protect and defend. **-er** n., **-ing** n.

keep back v. To withhold things; to prevent one from coming forward.

keep-er n. One who keeps, guards, or maintains something; a person who respects or observes a requirement; a device for holding something in place, as a latch, or clasp.

keep-ing n. Charge or possession; conformity or harmony; maintenance or support; be consistent with.

keep off v. To fend or avert off. v. To stay back or remain at a distance.

keep-sake n. A memento or souvenir; a token or remembrance of friendship.

kef n. A tranquil and dreamy state; a narcotic.

keg n. A small barrel usually having the capacity of five to ten gallons; the unit of measure for nails which equals 100 pounds.

Keller, Helen n. 1880-1968 American author and lecturer who was deaf, mute, and blind.

kelp n. Any of a large brown seaweeds.

kel-pie n. A sheep dog originally bred in Australia.

Kel-vin adj. Designating or relating to the temperature scale having a zero point of approximately -273. 15 degree C.

kemp n. A course hairlike fiber used in the making of carpet.

ken-nel n. A shelter for or a place where dogs or cats are bred, boarded, or trained. **kenneled, kenneling.** v.

Ken-ny meth-od n., Med. A treatment for poliomyelitis that involves both exercise and hot applications.

ke-no n. A game of chance resembling bingo; a lottery game.

kep-i n. A French military cap having a flat, round top and a visor.

ker-a-tin n. A fibrous protein which forms the basic substance of nails, hair, horns, and hoofs. **keratinous** adj.

ker-chief n. A piece of cloth usually

worn around the neck or on the head; scarf. **kerchiefed, kerchiefs** adj.

ker-mis n. An annual fair of the Netherlands.

ker-nel n. A grain or seed, as of corn, enclosed in a hard husk; the inner substance of a nut; the central, most important part. **kernelly** adj.

ker-o-sene or **ker-o-sine** n. An oil distilled from petroleum or coal and used for illumination.

kes-trel n. A small falcon, with gray and brown plumage.

ketch n. A small sailing vessel with two masts.

ketch-up n. A thick, smooth sauce made form tomatoes.

ke-tene n. A gas which is colorless and poisonous.

ke-to adj. Having a ketone.

ke-tol n. Organic compound having a ketone and alcohol group.

ke-tone n. An organic compound; used as a solvent; acetone. **-ic** adj., **-sis** n.

ket-tle n. A pot, usually made of metal, used for stewing or boiling.

ket-tle-drum n. A musical instrument with a parchment head which can be tuned by adjusting the tension.

ket-tle of fisk n. A mess; an awkward situation; matter of consideration.

key n. An object used to open a lock; button or level pushed on a keyboard of a typewriter, piano, etc.; the crucial or main element. **keyed** adj.

Key, Francis Scott n. 1779-1843. American poet and lawyer.

key-board n. A bank of keys, as on a piano, typewriter, or computer terminal. v. To set by means of a keyed typesetting machine; to generate letters by means of a word processor.

key club n. A private club that offers entertainment and serves liquor.

key-hole n. Lock; area that a key is inserted into.

key-note n., Mus. The first and harmonically fundamental tone of a scale; main principle or theme.

key-note ad-dress n. An opening speech that outlines issues for discussion.

key-punch n. A machine operated from a keyboard that uses punched holes in tapes or cards for data processing systems. **keypunch** n., **keypuncher** v.

key-stone n. The wedge-shaped stone at the center of an arch that locks its parts together; an essential part.

key-stroke n. A stroke of a key, as of a typewriter.

kg abbr. Kilogram.

khad-dar n. Cloth made from cotton.

khak-i n. A yellowish brown or olive-drab color; a sturdy cloth being khaki in color. **khakis** A uniform of khaki cloth. **khaki** adj.

khan n. An Asiatic title of respect; a medieval Turkish, Mongolian or Tartar ruler. **khanate** n.

khe-dive n. A ruler of Egypt from 1867 to 1914 governing as a viceroy of the sultan of Turkey.

kib-itz *v. Slang* To look on and offer meddlesome advice to others. **kibitzer** *n.*

kick *v.* To strike something with a force by the foot. **kick in** To put in money. **kick out** To expel with force. **kicker** *n.*

kick-back *n.* A secret payment to a person who can influence a source of income; repercussion; a strong reaction.

kick-off *n.* The play that begins a game of soccer or football.

kick-stand *n.* The swiveling bar for holding a two-wheeled vehicle upright.

kid *n.* A young goat; leather made from the skin of a young goat. *Slang* A child; youngster *v.* To mock or tease playfully to deceive for fun; to fool. **kiddish** *adj.*, **kiddishness**, **kidder** *n.*

kid-nap *v.* To seize and hold a person; unlawfully, often for ransom. **kidnapper** *n.*, **kidnaping**, **kidnapping** *v.*

kid-ney *n.*, *pl.* -neys

Either of two organs situated in the abdominal cavity of vertebrates whose function is to keep proper water balance in the body and to excrete wastes in the form of urine.

kidney bean *n.* A bean grown for its edible seeds.

kidvid *n.*, *Slang* Television programming for kids.

kiel-ba-sa *n.* A smoked Polish sausage.

kill *n.* To put to death; nullify; cancel; to slaughter for food; to deprive of life; to neutralize or destroy the active qualities. **killer** *n.*

kill-deer *n.*, *pl.* -deer, -deers A bird characterized by a plaintive, penetrating cry.

kill-er whale *n.* A black and white carnivorous whale, found in the colder waters of the seas.

kil-lick *n.* An anchor for a boat sometimes consisting of a stone secured by wood.

kil-li-fish *n.* A fish found in North America belonging to the family Cyprinodontidea.

kill-ing *n.* The act of a person who kills; a slaying. **killingly** *adv.*

kill-joy *n.* One who spoils the enjoyment of others.

kiln *n.* An oven or furnace for hardening or drying a substance, especially one for firing ceramics, pottery, etc.

ki-lo *n.* A kilogram.

kil-o-bit *n.* In computer science, one thousand binary digits.

kil-o-cal-o-rie *n.* One thousand gram calories.

ki-lo-cy-cle *n.* A unit equal to one thousand cycles, one thousand cycles per second.

kil-o-gram *n.* A measurement of weight in the meteoric system equal to slightly more than one third of a pound.

kil-o-li-ter *n.* Metric measurement equal to one thousand liters.

kil-o-me-ter *n.* Metric measurement equal to one thousand meters.

kil-o-ton *n.* One thousand tons; an explosive power equal to that of one thousand tons of TNT.

kil-o-volt *n.* One thousand volts.

kil-o-watt *n.* A unit of power equal to one thousand watts.

kil-o-watt-hour *n.* A unit of electric power consumption of one thousand watts throughout one hour.

kilt *n.* A knee-length wool skirt with deep pleats, usually of tartan, worn especially by men in the Scottish Highlands.

kil-ter *n.* Good condition; proper or working order.

ki-mo-no *n.* A loose, Japanese robe with a wide sash; a loose robe worn chiefly by women.

kin *n.* One's relatives by blood; relatives collectively.

kind *n.* A characteristic; a variety.

kind *adj.* Of a friendly, or good-natured disposition; coming from a good-natured readiness to please others. **kindness** *n.*

kin-der-gar-ten *n.* A school or class for young children from the ages of four to six to further their social, mental and physical development.

kin-der-gart-ner *n.* A child who attends kindergarten.

kind-heart-ed *adj.* Having much generosity and kindness.

kin-dle *v.* To ignite; to catch fire; to stir up; to arouse; to excite, as the feelings.

kind-less *adj.* Mean, cruel, unkind, unfriendly. **kindlessly** *adv.*

kin-dling *n.* Easily ignited material such as, sticks, wood chips, etc. used to start a fire.

kind-ly *adv.* A kind nature, disposition, or character; benevolent. **kindliness** *n.*

kind-ness *n.* An act of good will; state or quality of being kind.

kin-dred *n.* A person's relatives by blood. *adj.* Having a like nature; similar. **kindredness** *n.*

kin-e-mat-ics *n.* The branch of dynamics that deals with motion considered apart from force and mass. **kinematic, kinematical** *adj.*, **kinematically** *adv.*

kin-e-scope *n.* A cathode-ray tube in a television set which translates received electrical into a visible picture on a screen; a film of a television on broadcast.

ki-ne-sics *n.* To study the relationship between communication and body language. **kinesic** *adj.*, **-ally** *adv.*

ki-ne-si-ol-o-gy *n.* Science that investigates organic and anatomy process in reference to human motion.

kin-es-the-sia *n.* The sense of muscular movement or effort. **-is**, **-tic** *adj.*

ki-net-ic *adj.* Of, or pertaining to, or produced by motion.

ki-net-ic art *n.* The type of modern abstract art that attempts to present or indicate a sense of motion.

ki-ne-to-scope *n.* The early form of the motion picture, where a series of pictures pass beneath a small opening for viewing, at a high rate of speed.

king *n.* One who rules over a country; a male ruler; a playing card with a picture of a king; the main piece in the game of chess; a crowned checker in the game of checkers. **kingship** *n.*

king-bird *n.* A North American bird belonging to the genus Tyrannus.

king-bolt *n.* A vertical central vehicle to the front axle.

king crab *n.* A large crab-like crustacean common in the coastal waters of Japan, Alaska, and Siberia.

king-craft *n.* The art of ruling as a king; the profession and techniques used by a king.

king-dom *n.* The area or the country which is ruled by a king or queen. **kingdomless** *adj.*

king-fish *n.* A large fish used for food.

king-fish-er *n.* A bright colored bird having a long stout bill and short tails and feeds on fish and insects.

King James Bible *n.* An English translation of the Bible from Hebrew and Greek published in 1611 authorized by King James I of England.

king-let *n.* A very small bird; a king of little importance.

king-ly *adj.* Pertaining to or belonging to a king or kings; monarchical; splendid; befitting a king.

king-pin *n.* The foremost pin of a set arranged in order for playing bowling or tenpins; the most important or essential person.

king post *n.* A post located between the tie beam and the apex of a roof truss.

king-ship *n.* A monarchy; the state, or dignity of a king.

king--size *adj.* Very large; larger than the standard size.

king snake *n.* Large snake found in the southern United States which is non-poisonous.

king-wood *n.* Wood of Brazil with violet-colored stripes.

kink *n.* A tight twist or knot-like curl; a sharp painful muscle cramp; a mental quirk. *v.* To form or cause to form a kink.

kink-y *adj.* Tightly curled; sexually uninhibited. **kinkily** *adv.*, **kinkiness** *n.*

kin-ka-jou *n.* A tropical American mammal having large eyes, brown fur and a long prehensile tail.

ki-osk *n.* A small building used as a refreshment booth or newsstand.

kip *n.* The untanned skin of a calf, a lamb and or an adult of any small breed; a bundle of such hides.

kip-per *n.* A salted and smoked herring or salmon. *v.* To cure by salting, smoking, or drying.

kirk *n.* The Presbyterian Church of Scotland as opposed to the Episcopal Church of Scotland.

Kir-man *n.* An elaborate Persian rug having elaborate floral designs and soft colors.

kir-tle *n.* A woman's long skirt or petticoat; a man's tunic or coat.

kis-met *n.* Fate; appointed lot.

kiss *v.* To touch two lips together in greeting, between two people. **kissable** *adj.*

kit *n.* A collection of tools, supplies, or items for a special purpose.

kitch-en *n.* A room in a house or building used to prepare and cook food.

kitch-en-ette *n.* A small area that functions ar a kitchen.

kitch-en-ware *n.* Dishes, pots, pans, and other utensils that are used in a kitchen.

kite *n.* A light-weight framework of wood and paper designed to fly in a steady breeze at the end of a string; any of various predatory birds of the hawk family having a long, usually forked tail.

kith *or* **kin** *n.* Acquaintances or family.

kitsch *n.* Anything that is pretentious and in poor taste.

kit-ten *n.*

A young cat. **-ish** *adj.*

kit-ty *n.* A small collection or accumulation of objects or money; a young cat or kitten.

kit-ty-cor-nered *adj.* Diagonally; catty-cornered.

ki-va *n.* A Pueblo Indian chamber, used in ceremonies, often underground.

Ki-wa-ni-an *n.* A member of a major national and international service club organized to promote higher business standards and provides service to the community.

ki-wi *n.* A flightless bird, of New Zealand having vestigial wings and a long, slender bill; a vine, native to Asia, which yields a fuzzy-skinned, edible fruit; the fruit of this vine; a student who has not piloted a plane solo.

kl *abbr.* Kiloliter.

klatch, klatsch *n.* A social gathering devoted primarily to small talk and gossip.

klep-to-ma-ni-a *n.* Obsessive desire to steal or impulse to steal, especially without economic motive. **-iac** *n.*

kloof *n.* A ravine; gorge; deep mountain cleft.

klutz *n., Slang* A stupid or clumsy person. **klutziness** *n.*, **klutzy** *adj.*

km *abbr.* Kilometer.

knack *n.* A natural talent; aptitude.

knack-wurst *or* **knock-wurst** *n.* A thick or short, heavily seasoned sausage.

knap-sack *n.* A supply or equipment bag, as of canvas or nylon, worn strapped across the shoulders.

knave *n.* Tricky; or dishonest person; a rascal. **-ish** *adj.*, **-ly** *adv.*, **-ry** *n.*

knead *v.* To work dough into a uniform mass; to shape by or as if by kneading.

knee *n.* The joint in the human body

which connects the calf with the thigh.

knee-cap *n.* Patella; bone covering the joint of the knee.

knee-deep *adj.* So deep that it reaches ones knees.

kneel *v.* To go down upon one's knees. **kneeler** *n.*

knell *v.* To sound a bell, especially when rung for a funeral; to toll. *n.* An act or instance of knelling; a signal of disaster.

knick-ers *pl. n.* Short loose-fitting pants gathered at the knee.

knick-knack *n.* A trinket; trifling article.

knife *n.* An instrument used to cut an item. **knifed, knifing** *v.*

knife edge *n.* A very sharp edge; the edge of a knife.

knife switch *n.* A switch used to close a circuit.

knight *n.* A medieval soldier serving a monarch; a chess piece bearing the shape of a horse's head.

knight-hood *n.* The character of a knight.

knight-ly *adj.* Dealing with a knight.

knish *n.* Baked or fried dough stuffed with meat, cheese, or potatoes.

knit *v.*

To form by intertwining thread or yarn, by interlocking loops of a single yarn by means of needles; to fasten securely; to draw together.

knitting needle *n.* A long, slender, pointed rod for knitting.

knob *n.* A rounded protuberance; a lump; a rounded mountain; a rounded handle. **knobbed** *adj.*, **knobby** *adj.*

knock *v.* To hit or strike with a hard blow; to criticize; to collide; to make a noise, as that of a defective engine.

knock-down *adj.* Designed to be easily assembled for storage or shipment. **knockdown** *n.*

knock down *v.* To strike to the ground with or as with a sharp blow.

knock down drag out *adj.* Extremely violent or bitter.

knock-er *n.* One who or that which knocks; as a metal ring for knocking on a door.

knock-knee *n.* A condition in which one or both knees turn inward and knock or rub together while walking.

knoll *n.* A small round hill; a mound.

knot *n.* A interwinding as of string or rope; a fastening made by tying together lengths of material, as string; a unifying bond, especially of marriage; a hard node on a tree from which a branch grows. *Naut.* A unit of speed, also called a nautical mile which equals approximately 1.15 statute miles per hour. **-ted, -ting** *v.*

knot-hole *n.* A hole in lumber left by the falling out of a knot.

knout *n.* A whip or scourge for flogging criminals. **knout** *v.*

know *v.* To perceive directly as fact or truth; to believe to be true; to be certain of; to be familiar with or have experience of. **-able** *adj.*, **-ledge, -er** *n.*

know-how *n.* Knowing how to do something.

know-ing *adj.* To be astute; to know secret knowledge. **knowingly** *adv.*

knowl-edge *n.* Having ability to know facts, information.

knowl-edge-a-ble *adj.* The state of being intelligent.

know--noth-ing *n.* An extremely stupid person.

knuck-le *n.* On the finger; the joint of the finger. **knuckly** *adj.*

knuck-le ball *n.* A pitch used in baseball that is a slow pitch.

knuck-le-bone *n.* The bone of the finger which forms the knuckle.

knuck-le-head *n.* A person who is not very smart; dumb.

knur *n.* A lump or knot of a tree.

knurl *n.* A ridge. **knurled, knurly** *adj.*

ko-a-la *n.*

An Australian marsupial which has large hairy ears, gray fur, and feeds on eucalyptus leaves.

Ko-di-ak bear *n.* A type of large bear that is found in Alaska.

kohl *n.* Dark powder used as cosmetics to darken under the eyes.

kohl-ra-bi *n., pl.* **-ies** A variety of cabbage having a thick stem and eaten as a vegetable.

ko-la *n.* The tree which produces the kola nut.

ko-la nut *n.* The brownish nut used as a tonic and stimulant.

ko-lin-sky *n.* A mink found in Asia.

kook *n., Slang* A crazy or eccentric person. **kookiness** *n.*, **kooky** *adj.*

Ko-ran *n.* The sacred book of Islam, accepted as containing the revelations made to Mohammed by Allah through the angel Gabriel.

ko-sher *adj.* Conformant to eat according to Jewish dietary laws. *Slang* Appropriate; proper.

kow-tow *v.* To show servile deference.

kph *abbr.* Kilometers per hour.

kraal *n.* A village of southern African natives; and enclosure for animals in southern Africa.

kryp-ton *n.* A white, inert gaseous chemical used mainly in fluorescent lamps; symbolized by Kr.

kum-quat *n.* A small, round orange fruit having a sour pulp and edible rind.

kung fu *n.* A Japanese art of self-defense similar to karate.

ku-miss *n.* The fermented camel's milk drank by Asiatic nomads.

ky-pho-sis *n.* Abnormal curving of the spine.

L, l *n.* The twelfth letter of the English alphabet; the Roman numeral for fifty.

la-bel *n.* Something that identifies or describes. **label** *v.* To attach a label to.

la-bi-al *adj.* Pertaining to or of the labia or lips.

la-bi-um *n., pl.* **labia** Any of the four folds of the vulva.

la-bor *n.* Physical or manual work done for hire. *Med.* The physical pain and efforts involved in childbirth. *v.* To work; to progress with great effort.

lab-o-ra-to-ry *n., pl.* **-ies** A place equipped for conducting scientific experiments, research, or testing; a place where drugs and chemicals are produced.

lab-y-rinth *n.*

A system of winding, intricate passages; a maze. **-ine** *adj.*

lac *n.* The resinous secretion left on certain trees by the lac insect and used in making paints and varnishes.

lace *n.* A delicate open-work fabric of silk, cotton, or linen made by hand or on a machine.

lac-er-ate *v.* To open with a jagged tear; to wound the flesh by tearing. **-tion** *n.*

lach-ry-mal or **lac-ri-mal** *adj.* Relating to or producing tears; relating to the glands that produce tears.

lack *n.* The deficiency or complete absence of something. *v.* To have little of something or to be completely without.

lack-ey *n.* A male servant of very low status.

lack-lus-ter *adj.* Lacking sheen; dull.

lac-quer *n.* A transparent varnish which is dis-solved in a volatile solution and dries to give surfaces a glossy finish.

lac-tate *v.* To secrete or to milk. **-tion** *n.*

lac-te-al *adj.* Of, resembling, or like milk. *n., Anat.* Any of the lymphatic vessels carrying chyle from the small intestine to the blood.

lac-tic acid *n.* A limpid, syrupy acid that is present in sour milk, molasses, some fruits, and wines.

lac-tose *n., Biochem.* A white, odorless crystal-line sugar that is found in milk.

la-cu-na *n., pl.* **-nas, -nae** A space from which something is missing; a gap.

lad-der *n.* An implement used for climbing up or down in order to reach another place or area.

lad-en *adj.* Heavily burdened; oppressed; weighed down; loaded. **laden** *v.*

lad-ing *n.* Cargo; freight.

la-dle *n.*

A cup-shaped vessel with a deep bowl and a long handle, used for dipping or conveying liquids. **ladle** *v.*

la-dy *n., pl.* **ladies** A woman showing refinement, cultivation, and often high social position; the woman at the head of a household; an address or term of reference for any woman.

lag *v.* To stray or fall behind; to move slowly; to weaken gradually. *n.* The process or act of retardation or falling behind; the amount or period of lagging.

la-gniappe *n.* A small gift which is given to a purchaser by a storekeeper. *Informal* Anything given as an extra bonus.

la-goon *n.* A body of shallow water separated from the ocean by a coral reef or sandbars. **lagoonal** *adj.*

laid Past tense of lay.

lain *v.* Past tense of lie.

lais-sez--faire *n.* A policy stating that a government should exercise very little control in trade and industrial affairs; noninterference.

la-i-ty *n.* Laymen, as distinguished from clergy.

lake *n.* A large inland body of either salt or fresh water.

La-maze meth-od *n.* A method of childbirth in which the mother is prepared psychologically and physically to give birth without the use of drugs.

lamb *n.* A young sheep; the meat of a lamb used as food; a gentle person.

lam-baste or **lambast** *v., Slang* To thrash or beat.

lam-bent *adj.* Lightly and playfully brilliant; flickering gently; softly radiant. **lambency** *n.,* **lambently** *adv.*

lame *adj.* Disabled or crippled, especially in the legs or feet so as to impair free movement; weak; ineffective; unsatisfactory. **-ly** *adv.,* **lameness** *n.*

la-me *n.* A brocaded fabric woven with gold or silver thread, sometimes mixed with other fiber.

la-ment *v.* To express sorrow; to mourn. *n.* An expression of regret or sorrow. **lamentable** *adj.,* **-ably** *adv.,* **-ation** *n.*

lam-i-na *n., pl.* **-nae, -nas** A thin scale or layer. *Bot.* The blade or flat part of a leaf.

lam-i-nate *v.* To form or press into thin sheets; to form layers by the action of pressure and heat. **lamination** *n.,* **laminated** *adj.,* **laminator** *n.*

lamp *n.* A device for generating heat or light.

lam-poon *n.* A satirical, but often humorous, attack in verse or prose, especially one that ridicules a group, person, or institution. **lampoonery** *n.*

lam-prey *n.*, *pl.* **preys** An eel-like fish having a circular, suctorial mouth with rasping teeth and no jaw.

lance *n.* A spear-like implement used as a weapon by mounted knights or soldiers. *lance* *v.*

land *n.* The solid, exposed surface of the earth as distinguished from the waters. *v.* To arrive at a destination; to catch a fish; to receive a new job. **landless** *adj.*

lan-dau *n.* A four-wheeled vehicle with a closed carriage and a back seat with a collapsible top.

land-er n. A space vehicle for landing on a celestial body.

land-ing n. The act of coming, going, or placing ashore from any kind of vessel or craft; the act of descending and settling on the ground in an airplane.

land-locked adj. Almost or completely surrounded by land.

land-mark n. A fixed object that serves as a boundary marker.

land-scape n. A view or vista of natural scenery as seen from a single point. v. To change or improve the features of a section of ground by contouring the land and planting shrubs, trees, or flowers.

lane n. A small or narrow path between walls, fences, or hedges.

lan-guage n. The words, sounds, pronunciation and method of combining words used and understood by people.

lan-guid adj. Lacking in energy; drooping; weak. **-ly** adv., **languidness** n.

lan-guish v. To become weak; to be or live in a state of depression. **languisher** n., **languishment** n.

lank adj. Slender; lean. **-y** adv., **-ness** n.

lan-o-lin n. Wool grease obtained from sheep's wool and refined for use in ointments and cosmetics.

lan-tern n. A portable light having transparent or translucent sides.

lan-yard n. A piece of rope or line used to secure objects on ships.

la-pel n.

The front part of a garment, especially that of a coat, that is turned back, usually a continuation of the collar.

lap-in n. Rabbit fur that is sheared and dyed.

lap-is laz-u-li n. A semi-precious stone that is azure blue in color.

lap-pet n. A flap or fold on a headdress or on a garment.

lapse n. A temporary deviation or fall to a less desirable state. **lapse** v.

lar-ce-ny n., pl. **-ies** The unlawful taking of another person's property. **-ous** adj.

lard n. The soft, white, solid or semi-solid fat obtained after rendering the fatty tissue of the hog.

lar-der n. A place, such as a pantry or room, where food is stored.

large adj. Greater than usual or average in amount or size. **at large** To be free and not confined.

large in-tes-tine n. The portion of the intestine that extends from the end of the small intestine to the anus.

large--scale adj. Larger than others of the same kind; extensive; of or relating to a scale drawing to show detail.

lar-gess or **lar-gesse** n. Liberal or excessive giving to an inferior; generosity.

lar-go adv., Mus. In a very slow, broad, and solemn manner. **largo** adj. & n.

lar-i-at n. A long, light rope with a running noose at one end to catch livestock.

lark n. A bird having a melodious ability to sing; a merry or carefree adventure.

lar-va n., pl. **larvae** The immature, wingless, often worm-like form of a newly hatched insect; the early form of an animal that differs greatly from the adult, such as the tadpole. **larval** adj.

lar-yn-gi-tis n. Inflammation of the larynx.

lar-ynx n., pl. **larynges** or **larynxes** The upper portion of the trachea which contains the vocal cords. **-al** adj.

la-sa-gna or **la-sa-gne** n. Traditional Italian dish of wide flat noodles baked with a sauce of tomatoes, meat, and cheese.

la-ser n. A device which utilizes the natural oscillations of molecules or atoms between energy levels for generating coherent electromagnetic radiation in the visible, ultraviolet, or infrared parts of the spectrum.

lash v. To strike or move violently or suddenly; to attack verbally; to whip. n. Eyelash. **lasher** n.

lass n. A young girl or woman.

las-si-tude n. A condition of weariness; fatigue.

las-so n., pl. **-sos**, **-soes** A long rope or long leather thong with a running noose used to catch horses and cattle. **lasso** v.

last adj. Following all the rest; of or relating to the final stages, as of life; worst; lowest in rank. adv. After all others in sequence or chronology. v. To continue. n. A form in the shape of a foot used to hold a shoe while it is repaired or to shape a shoe as it is being made.

latch n. A device used to secure a gate or door, consisting of a bar that usually fits into a notch. **latch onto** To grab onto.

latch-et n. A narrow leather strap or thong used to fasten a shoe or sandal.

latch-key n. A key for opening an outside door.

latch-key child n. A child whose parent or parents work during the day and who carries a key to the front door because he or she returns home from school to an empty house.

late adj. Coming, staying, happening after the proper or usual time; having recently died. **lateness** n., **lately** adv.

lat-er-al adj. Relating to or of the side. n. In football, an underhand pass thrown sideways or away from the line of scrimmage. **laterally** adv.

la-tex n. The milky, white fluid that is produced by certain plants, such as the rubber tree; a water emulsion of synthetic rubber or plastic globules used in paints and adhesives.

lath n. A thin, narrow strip of wood nailed to joists, rafters, or studding and used as a supporting structure for plaster.

lathe n. A machine for holding material while it is spun and shaped by a tool.

lath-er *n.* A foam formed by detergent or soap and water. **-er** *n.*, **lathery** *adj.*

lat-i-tude *n.* The angular distance of the earth's surface north or south of the equator, measured in degrees along a meridian; freedom to act or to choose.

la-trine *n.* A public toilet, as in a camp or in a barracks.

lat-ter *adj.* Being the second of two persons or two things.

lat-tice *n.* A structure made of strips of wood, metal, or other materials, interlaced or crossed, framing regularly spaced openings. **lattice** *v.*

laud *v.* To praise; to extol. **laudable** *adj.*

laugh *v.* To express amusement, satisfaction, or pleasure with a smile and inarticulate sounds. **laughable** *adj.*

laugh-ter *n.* The expression, sound, or act produced by laughing.

launch *v.* To push or move a vessel into the water for the first time; to set a rocket or missile into flight. **-er** *n.*

launch *n.* A large boat carried by a ship.

laun-der *v.* To wash clothes or other materials in soap and water. **launderer, laundress** *n.*

laun-dro-mat *n.* A place to wash and dry clothes in coin operated automatic machines.

laun-dry *n., pl.* **-ies** An establishment where laundering is done professionally; clothes or other articles to be or that have been laundered.

lau-re-ate A person honored for his accomplishment. **laureate** *v.*

la-va *n.* Molten rock which erupts or flows from an active volcano; the rock formed after lava has cooled and hardened.

lav-a-to-ry *n., pl.* **-ies** A room with permanently installed washing and toilet facilities.

lav-en-der *n.* An aromatic plant having spikes of pale violet flowers; light purple in color. **lavender** *adj.*

lav-ish *adj.* Generous and extravagant in giving or spending. **lavisher** *n.*, **lavishly** *adv.*, **lavishness** *n.*

law *n.* A rule of conduct or action, recognized by custom or decreed by formal enactment, considered binding on the members of a nation, community, or group; a system or body of such rules.

law--a-bid-ing *adj.* Abiding by the laws.

lawn *n.* A stretch of ground covered with grass that is mowed regularly near a house, park, or building.

law-ren-ci-um *n.* A short-lived radioactive element, symbolized by LR.

law-suit *n.* A case or proceeding brought before a court of law for settlement.

law-yer *n.* A person trained in the legal profession who acts for and advises clients or pleads in court.

lax *adj.* Lacking disciplinary control; lacking rigidity or firmness. **laxity**, **laxness** *n.*, **laxly** *adv.*

lax-a-tive *n.* A medicine taken to stimulate evacuation of the bowels.

laxative *adj.*

lay *v.* To cause to lie; to place on a surface; past tense of lie.

lay-er *n.* A single thickness, coating, or covering that lies over or under another. **layered** *adj.*, **layer** *v.*

lay-ette *n.* The clothing, bedding, and equipment for a newborn child.

lay-man *n.* A person not belonging to a particular profession or specialty; one who is not a member of the clergy.

lay-off *n.* A temporary dismissal of employees.

lay-out *n.* A planned arrangement of something, such as a street, room, park, or building.

la-zy *adj.* Unwilling to work; moving slowly; sluggish. **lazily** *adv.*, **laziness** *n.*

la-zy-bones *n. Slang* A lazy person.

lea *n., Poetic.* A grassy field or meadow.

leach *v.* To cause a liquid to pass through a filter; to remove or wash out by filtering. **leachable** *adj.*

lead *v.* To go ahead so as to show the way; to control the affairs or action of. *n.* A soft, malleable, heavy, dull gray metallic element symbolized by Pb, used in solder, paints, and bullets; a graphite stick used as the writing material in pencils; in printing, the thin strip of type metal used to provide space between printed lines. **leadenness** *n.*, **leading**, **leaden** *adj.*

lead poisoning *n.* Poisoning of a person's system by the absorption of lead or any of its salts.

leaf *n., pl.* **leaves**

A flat outgrowth from a plant structure or tree, usually green in color and functioning as the principal area of photosynthesis; a single page in a book. *v.* To turn the pages of a book. **leafless**, **leafy** *adj.*

leaf-let *n.* A part or a segment of a compound leaf; a small printed handbill or circular, often folded.

league *n.* An association of persons, organizations, or states for common action or interest; an association of athletic competition; an underwater measurement of distance that equals 3 miles or approximately 4.8 km.

leak *n.* An opening, as a flaw or small crack, permitting an escape or entrance of light or fluid. **leakage** *n.*, **leakiness** *n.*, **leaky** *adj.*

lean *v.* To rest or incline the weight of the body for support; to rest or incline anything against a large object or wall; to rely or depend on; to have a tendency or preference for; to tend towards a suggestion or action. *adj.* having little or no fat; thin. **leanly** *adv.*, **leanness** *n.*

lean-ing *n.* An inclination; a predispositon.

lean--to *n.* A structure of branches, sloping to the ground from a raised support, usually an outside wall.

leap *v.* To rise or project oneself by a sudden thrust from the ground with a spring of the legs; to spring, to jump. **leap, leaper** *n.*

leap-frog *n.* A game in which two players leap over each other by placing one's hands on the back of another who is bending over and leaping over him in a straddling position.

leap year *n.* A year containing 366 days, occurring every 4th year, with the extra day added to make 29 days in February.

learn *n.* The process of acquiring knowledge, understanding, or mastery of a study or experience. **learner** *n.*, **learnable** *adj.*, **learn** *v.*

lease *n.* A contract for the temporary use or occupation of property or premises in exchange for payment of rent.

leash *n.* A strong cord or rope for restraining a dog or other animal.

least-wise *adv., Slang* At least; at any rate.

leath-er *n.* An animal skin or hide with the hair removed, prepared for use by tanning.

leath-er-neck *n., Slang* A United States Marine.

leave *v.* To go or depart from; to permit to remain behind or in a specified place or condition; to forsake; to abandon; to bequeath, as in a will. *n.* Official permission for absence from duty.

leav-en *n.* An agent of fermentation, as yeast, used to cause batters and doughs to rise; any pervasive influence that produces a significant change.

lech-er-y *n.* Unrestrained indulgence in sexual activity. **lecher** *n.*, **lecherous** *adj.*, **lecherously** *adv.*

lec-i-thin *n.* Any of a group of phosphorus containing compounds found in plant and animal tissues, commercially derived from egg yolks, corn, and soybeans, and used in the production of foods, cosmetics, pharmaceuticals, and plastics.

lec-tern *n.* A stand or tall desk, usually with a slanted top, on which a speaker or instructor may place books or papers.

lec-ture *n.* A speech on a specific subject, delivered to an audience for information or instruction. *v.* To give a speech or lecture; to criticize or reprimand.

led *v., p.t. & p.p.* Past tense of lead.

ledge *n.* A narrow, shelf-like projection forming a shelf, as on a wall or the side of a rocky formation.

ledg-er *n.* A book in which sums of money received and paid out are recorded.

lee *n.* The side of a ship sheltered from the wind.

leech *n.* Any of various carnivorous or bloodsucking worms; a person who clings or preys on others.

leek *n.* A culinary herb of the lily family,

related to the onion, with a slender, edible bulb.

leer *n.* A sly look or sideways glance expressing desire or malicious intent.

lee-way *n., Naut.* The lateral drift of a plane or ship away from the correct course.

left *adj.* Pertaining to or being on the side of the body that faces north when the subject is facing east.

leg *n.* A limb or appendage serving as a means of support and movement in animals and man; a part or division of a journey or trip. **leg** *v.*

leg-a-cy *n., pl.* **-ies** Personal property, money, and other valuables that are bequeathed by will; anything that is handed down from an ancestor, predecessor, or earlier era.

le-gal *adj.* Of, pertaining to, or concerned with the law or lawyers; something based on or authorized by law. **-ity, -ization** *n.*, **-ize** *v.*, **-ly** *adv.*

le-gal-ism *n.* A strict conformity to the law, especially when stressing the letter and forms of the law rather than the spirit of justice. **-ist** *n.*, **-istic** *adj.*

le-ga-tion *n.* The official diplomatic mission in a foreign country, headed by a minister; the official residence or business premises of a diplomatic minister of lower rank than an ambassador.

le-ga-to *adv., Music* Smooth and flowing with successive notes connected.

leg-end *n.* An unverifiable story handed down from the past; a body of such stories, as those connected with a culture or people.

leg-en-dar-y *adj.* Presented as, based on, or of the nature of a legend.

leg-horn *n.* A hat made from finely plaited wheat straw.

leg-i-ble *adj.* Capable of being read or deciphered. **legibility** *n.*, **legibly** *adv.*

leg-is-late *v.* To pass or make laws.

leg-is-la-tion *n.* The act or procedures of passing laws; lawmaking; an officially enacted law.

leg-is-la-tive *adj.* Of or pertaining to legislation or a legislature; having the power to legislate.

leg-is-la-ture *n.* A body of persons officially constituted and empowered to make and change laws.

leg-ume *n.* A plant of the pea or bean family, that bears pods which split when mature; the seeds or pod of a legume used as food. **leguminous** *adj.*

leg-work *n., Slang* A chore, task, or gathering of information accomplished by going about on foot.

lei *n., pl.* **leis**

A wreath of flowers worn around the neck; the customary greeting of welcome in the state of Hawaii.

lei-sure *n.* The time of freedom from work or duty. **leisured** *adj.*

lem-on *n.* An oval citrus fruit grown on a tree, having juicy, acid pulp and a yellow rind that yields an essential oil used as a flavoring and as a perfuming agent. *Slang* Something, as an automobile, that proves to be defective or unsatisfactory.

lem-on-ade *n.* A drink made from water, lemon juice, and sugar.

lend *v.* To allow the temporary use or possession of something with the understanding that it is to be returned; to offer oneself as to a specific purpose.

length *n.* The linear extent of something from end to end, usually the longest dimension of a thing as distinguished from its thickness and width; the measurement of something to estimate distance. **lengthy** *adj.*

length-en *v.* To make or become longer.

length-wise *adv. & adj.* Of or in the direction or dimension of length; longitudinally.

le-ni-ent *adj.* Gentle, forgiving, and mild; merciful; undemanding; tolerant. **leniency, lenience** *n.*

len-i-tive *adj.* Having the ability to ease pain or discomfort. **lenitive** *n.*

lens *n.*

In optics, the curved piece of glass or other transparent substance that is used to refract light rays so that they converge or diverge to form an image; the transparent structure in the eye, situated behind the iris, which serves to focus an image on the retina.

lent *v.* Past tense of lend.

len-til *n.* A leguminous plant, having broad pods and containing edible seeds.

leop-ard *n.*

A large member of the cat family of Africa and Asia, having a tawny coat with dark brown or black spots grouped in rounded clusters, also called a panther. **leopardess** *n.*

le-o-tard *n.* A close-fitting garment worn by dancers and acrobats.

lep-er *n.* One who suffers from leprosy.

lep-re-chaun *n.* A mischief-making elf of Irish folklore, supposed to own hidden treasure.

lep-ro-sy *n.*, *Pathol.* A chronic communicable disease characterized by nodular skin lesions and the progressive destruction of tissue. **-otic** *adj.*

les-bi-an *n.* A homosexual woman.

lese maj-es-ty *or n.* An offense against a ruler or supreme power of state.

le-sion *n.*, *Pathol.* An injury; a wound; any well-defined bodily area where the tissue has changed in a way that is characteristic of a disease.

less *adj.* Smaller; of smaller or lower importance or degree. *prep.* With the subtraction of; minus.

-less *suffix.* Without; lacking.

les-see *n.* One who leases a property.

les-son *n.* An instance from which something is to be or has been learned; an assignment to be learned or studied as by a student.

les-sor *n.* One who grants a lease to another.

let *v.* To give permission; to allow. *n.* An invalid stroke in a game such as tennis, that must be repeated because of some interruption or hindrance of playing conditions.

let-down *n.* A decrease or slackening, as in energy or effort. *Slang* A disappointment.

le-thal *adj.* Pertaining to or being able to cause death. **lethally** *adv.*

leth-ar-gy *n.*, *Pathol.* A state of excessive drowsiness or abnormally deep sleep; laziness. **-ic** *adj.*, **-ically** *adv.*

let's *contr.* Let us.

let-ter *n.* A standard character or sign used in writing or printing to represent an alphabetical unit or speech sound; a written or printed means of communication sent to another person.

let-ter-head *n.* Stationery printed with a name and address, usually of a company or business establishment.

let-ter--perfect *adj.* Absolutely correct; perfect.

let-tuce *n.* A plant having crisp, edible leaves that are used especially in salads.

leu-ke-mi-a *n.*, *Pathol.* A generally fatal disease of the blood in which white blood cells multiply in uncontrolled numbers. **leukemic** *adj.*

le-vee *n.* An embankment along the shore of a body of water, especially a river, built to prevent over-flowing.

lev-el *n.* A relative position, rank, or height on a scale; a standard position from which other heights and depths are measured. *adj.* Balanced in height; even. *v.* To make or become flat or level. **-er, levelness** *n.*, **levelly** *adv.*

lev-el--head-ed *adj.* Showing good judgment and common sense. **-ness** *n.*

lever *n.* A handle that projects and is used to operate or adjust a mechanism.

lever-age *n.* The use of a lever; the mechanical advantage gained by using a lever; power to act effectively.

lev-i-tate *v.* To rise and float in the air in apparent defiance of gravity. **-ion** *n.*

lev-i-ty *n.*, *pl.* **-ies** Lack of seriousness; frivolity; lightness.

lev-y *v.* To impose and collect by authority or force, as a fine or tax; to draft for military service; to prepare for, begin, or wage war. **levy** *n.*

lewd *adj.* Preoccupied with sex; lustful. **lewdly** *adv.*, **lewdness** *n.*

lex-i-cog-ra-phy *n.* The practice or profession of compiling dictionaries. **lexicographer** *n.*, **lexicographical** *adj.*

lex-i-con *n.* A dictionary; a vocabulary or

list of words that relate to a certain subject, occupation, or activity. lexical adj.

li-a-bil-i-ty n., pl. -ies The condition or state of being liable; that which is owed to another.

li-a-ble adj. Legally or rightly responsible.

li-ai-son n. A communication, as between different parts of an armed force or departments of a government; a close connection or relationship; an illicit love affair.

li-ar n. A person who tells falsehoods.

lib n., Slang Liberation.

li-bel n., Law A written statement in published form that damages a person's character or reputation. libel v., libelous adj.

lib-er-al adj. Characterized by generosity or lavishness in giving; abundant; ample; inclining toward opinions or policies that favor progress or reform, such as religion or politics. liberalism, liberality n., -ize v., liberally adv.

liberal arts pl. n. Academic courses that include literature, philosophy, history, languages, etc., which provide general cultural information.

lib-er-ate v. To set free, as from bondage, oppression, or foreign control. liberation n.

lib-er-ty n., pl. -ies The state of being free from oppression, tyranny, confinement, or slavery; freedom; in Navy terms, the permission to be absent from one's ship or duty for less that 48 hours.

li-bi-do n. One's sexual desire or impulse; the psychic energy drive that is behind all human activities. -inous adj.

li-brar-i-an n. A person in charge of a library; one who specializes in library work.

li-brar-y n., pl. -ies A collection of books, pamphlets, magazines, and reference books kept for reading, reference, or borrowing; a commercial establishment, usually in connection with a city or school, which rents books.

lice n. Plural of louse.

li-cense n. An official document that gives permission to engage in a specified activity or to perform a specified act. license v., licenser n.

li-cen-ti-ate n. A person licensed to practice a specified profession.

li-cen-tious adj. Lacking in moral restraint; immoral. licentiously adv., licentiousness n.

li-chen n. Any of various flowerless plants consisting of fungi, commonly growing in flat patches on trees and rocks. lichened, lichenous adj.

lic-it adj. Lawful. -ly adv., licitness n.

lick v. To pass the tongue over or along the surface of. Slang To beat; to thrash.

lick-e-ty-split adv. Full speed; rapidly.

lic-o-rice n. A perennial herb of Europe, the dried root of which is used to flavor medicines and candy.

lid n. A hinged or removable cover for a container; an eyelid. lidded, lidless adj.

lie v. To be in or take a horizontal recumbent position; to recline. n. A false or untrue statement.

liege n. A feudal lord or sovereign. adj. Loyal; faithful.

lien n. The legal right to claim, hold, or sell the property of another to satisfy a debt or obligation.

lieu n. Place; stead. in lieu of In place of.

lieu-ten-ant n. A commissioned officer in the U.S. Army, Air Force, or Marine Corps who ranks below a captain.

life n., pl. lives The form of existence that distinguishes living organisms from dead organisms or inanimate matter in the ability to carry on metabolism, respond to stimuli, reproduce, and grow.

life-guard n. An expert swimmer employed to protect people in and around water.

lifer n. Slang A person sentenced to life in prison.

life-sup-port sy-stem n. A system giving a person all or some of the items, such as oxygen, water, food, and control of temperature, necessary for a person's life and health while in a spacecraft or while exploring the surface of the moon; a system used to sustain life in a critical health situation.

life-time n. The period between one's birth and death.

life-work n. The main work of a person's lifetime.

life zone n. A biogeographic zone.

lift v. To raise from a lower to a higher position; to elevate; to take from; to steal. n. The act or process of lifting; force or power available for lifting; an elevation of spirits; a device or machine designed to pick up, raise, or carry something; an elevator. lifter n.

lift-off n. The vertical takeoff or the instant of takeoff of an aircraft or spacecraft.

lig-a-ment n. A tough band of tissue joining bones or holding a body organ in place. ligamentous adj.

li-gate v. To tie with a ligature.

lig-a-ture n.

Something, as a cord, that is used to bind; a thread used in surgery; something that unites or connects; a printing character that combines two or more letters.

light n. Electromagnetic radiation that can be seen by the naked eye; brightness; a source of light; spiritual illumination; enlightenment; a source of fire, such as a match. adj. Having light; bright; of less force, quantity, intensity, weight, than normal; having less calories or alcoholic content; dizzy; giddy. light v., lightness n.

light-er n. A device used to light a pipe,

cigar or cigarette; a barge used to load and unload a cargo ship.

light-ning *n.* The flash of light produced by a high-tension natural electric discharge into the atmosphere. *adj.* Moving with or as if with the suddenness of lightning.

light-ning bug *n.* A firefly.

light-ning rod *n.* A grounded metal rod positioned high on a building to protect it from lightning.

light op-er-a *n.* An operetta.

lights *pl. n.* The lungs, especially of a slaughtered animal.

light-ship *n.* A ship, having a powerful light or horn, that is anchored in dangerous waters to warn other vessels.

light show *n.* A display of colored lights in kaleidoscopic patterns, often accompanied by film, slides, or music.

light-weight *n.* A person who weighs very little; a boxer or wrestler weighting between 127 and 135 pounds.

light--year *or* **light year** *n.* A measure equal to the distance light travels in one year, approximately 5.878 trillion miles.

lig-ne-ous *adj.* Of or resembling wood; woody.

lig-ni-fy *v.* To make or become woody or wood-like.

lig-nite *n.* A brownish-black soft coal, especially one in which the texture of the original wood is distinct.

lig-ro-in *n.* A volatile, flammable fraction of petroleum used as a solvent.

lik-en *v.* To describe as being like; to compare.

like-ness *n.* Resemblance; a copy.

like-wise *adv.* In a similar way.

li-lac *n.* A shrub widely grown for its large, fragrant purplish or white flower cluster; a pale purple. **lilac** *adj.*

Lil-li-pu-tian *n.* A very small person. *adj.* Tiny.

lilt *n.* A light song; a rhythmical way of speaking.

lil-y *n., pl.* **-ies**

Any of various plants bearing trumpet-shaped flowers; a plant similar or related to the lily, as the water lily.

lil-y--liv-ered *adj.* Timid; cowardly.

lily of the valley *n., pl.* **lilies** A widely cultivated plant which bears fragrant, bell-shaped white flowers on a short stem.

Li-ma *n.* The capital of Peru.

li-ma bean *n.* Any of several varieties of tropical American plants having flat pods with light green edible seeds.

limb *n.* A large bough of a tree; an animal's appendage used for movement or grasping; an arm or leg.

lim-ber *adj.* Bending easily; pliable; moving easily; agile. *v.* To make or become limber. **-ly** *adv.*, **limberness** *n.*

lim-bo *or* **Lim-bo** *n.* The abode of souls kept from entering Heaven; a place or condition of oblivion or neglect.

lime *n.* A tropical citrus tree with evergreen leaves, fragrant white flowers, and edible green fruit; calcium oxide. **limy** *adj.*

lime-light *n.* A focus of public attention; the center of attention.

lim-er-ick *n.* A humorous verse of five lines.

lime-stone *n.* A form of sedimentary rock composed mainly of calcium carbonate which is used in building and in making lime and cement.

lim-it *n.* A boundary; a maximum or a minimum number or amount; a restriction on frequency or amount. *v.* To restrict; to establish bounds or boundaries. **limitation** *n.*

li-mo-nite *n.* A natural iron oxide used as an ore of iron.

lim-ou-sine *n.* A luxurious large vehicle; a small bus used to carry passengers to airports and hotels.

limp *v.* To walk lamely. *adj.* Lacking or having lost rigidity; not firm or strong. **limply** *adv.*, **limpness** *n.*

lim-pet *n.* Any of numerous marine gastropod mollusks having a conical shell and adhering to tidal rocks.

lim-pid *adj.* Transparently clear. **limpidity** *n.*, **limpidly** *adv.*

linch-pin *n.* A locking pin inserted through a shaft to keep a wheel from slipping off.

lin-den *n.* Any of various shade trees having heart-shaped leaves.

lin-e-age *n.* A direct line of descent from an ancestor.

lin-e-a-ment *n.* A contour, shape, or feature of the body and especially of the the face.

lin-e-ar *adj.* Of, pertaining to, or resembling a line; long and narrow.

lin-e-ar per-spec-tive *n.* A technique in painting and drawing in which parallel lines converge to give the illusion of distance and depth.

line-back-er *n.* In football, one of the defensive players positioned directly behind the line of scrimmage.

line drive *n.* In baseball, a ball hit with force whose path approximates a straight line parallel or nearly parallel to the ground.

line-man *n.* A person who works on telephone or electric power lines; a player on the forward line of a team, especially football.

lin-en *n.* Thread, yarn, or fabric made of flax; household articles, such as sheets and pillow cases, made of linen or a similar fabric. **linen** *adj.*

line of scrim-mage *n.* In football, an imaginary line that extends across the field from the position of the football on any given play.

lin-er *n.* A ship belonging to a ship line or an aircraft belonging to an airline; one that lines or serves as a lining.

line score *n.* In baseball, a statistical record of each inning of a game.

lines-man *n.* An official in a court game,

as tennis or volleyball, who calls shots which fall out-of-bounds; an official in football who marks the downs.

line-up n. A line of persons formed for the purpose of inspection or identification; the members of a team who take part in a game; a group of television programs that are aired sequentially.

ling n. Any of various marine food fishes related to the cod.

lin-ger v. To be slow in parting or reluctant to leave; to be slow in acting; to procrastinate. **-er** n., **lingeringly** adv.

lin-ge-rie n. Women's undergarments.

lingo n., pl. **goes** Language that is unfamiliar; a specialized vocabulary.

lin-guist n. One who is fluent in more than one language; A person specializing in linguistics.

lin-i-ment n. A liquid or semi-liquid medicine applied to the skin.

lin-ing n. A material which is used to cover an inside surface.

link n. One of the rings forming a chain; something in the form of a link; a tie or bond; a cuff link. v. To connect or or as if by a link or links.

link-age n. The act or process of linking; a system of connecting structures.

links pl., n. A golf course.

li-no-le-um n. A floor covering consisting of a surface of hardened linseed oil and a filler, as wood or powdered cork, on a canvas or burlap backing.

lin-seed n. The seed of flax, used in paints and varnishes.

lin-sey-wool-sey n. A coarse, sturdy fabric of wool and linen or cotton.

lin-tel n. A horizontal beam across the top of a door which supports the weight of the structure above it.

li-on n.

A large carnivorous mammal of the cat family, found in Africa and India, having a short, tawny coat and a long, heavy mane in the male; a person of great importance or prestige. **lioness** n.

li-on-heart-ed adj. Very courageous.

li-on-ize v. To treat someone as a celebrity.

lip service n. An expression of acquiescence that is not acted upon.

liq-ue-fy or **liq-ui-fy** v. To make liquid. **liquefaction**, **liquefier** n.

li-queur n. A sweet alcoholic beverage; a cordial.

liq-ui-date v. To settle a debt by payment or other settlement; to close a business by settling accounts and dividing up assets; to get rid of, especially to kill. **-ion**, **liquidator** n.

liq-uor n. A distilled alcoholic beverage; a liquid substance, as a watery solution of a drug.

lisle n. A fine, tightly twisted cotton thread.

lisp n. A speech defect or mannerism marked by lisping. v. To mispronounce the s and z sounds, usually as th. **lisper** n.

lis-some adj. Nimble. **lissomely** adv., **lissomeness** n.

list n. A series of numbers or words; a tilt to one side. **list** v.

list-less adj. Lacking energy or enthusiasm. **-ly** adv., **listlessness** n.

lit abbr. Literary; literature.

lit-a-ny n., pl. **-ies** A prayer in which phrases recited by a leader are alternated with answers from a congregation.

li-tchi or **li-chee** n. A Chinese tree, bearing edible fruit; the fruit of the tree.

lit-er-al adj. Conforming to the exact meaning of a word; concerned primarily with facts; without embellishment or exaggeration.

literally adv., literalistic adj.

lit-er-al-ism n. Adherence to the explicit sense of a given test; literal portrayal; realism. **-ist** n., literalistic adj.

lit-er-ar-y adj. Pertaining to literature; appropriate to or used in literature; of or relating to the knowledge of literature. literarily adv.

lit-er-ate adj. Having the ability to read and write; showing skill in using words. **literacy**, **literate** n.

lit-er-a-ti pl., n. The educated class.

lit-er-a-ture n. Printed material, as leaflets for a political campaign; written words of lasting excellence.

lithe adj. Bending easily; supple.

lithely adv., litheness n.

lith-i-um n. A silver-white, soft metallic element symbolized by Li.

li-thog-ra-phy n. A printing process in which a flat surface is treated so that the ink adheres only to the portions that are to be printed.

lithograph n. & v., lithographer n., lithographic, lithographical adj.

li-thol-o-gy n. The microscopic study and classification of rocks. **lithologist** n.

lit-i-gate v. To conduct a legal contest by judicial process. **-ant**, **-ion**, **-or** n.

lit-mus n. A blue powder obtained from lichens which turns red in acid solutions and blue in alkaline solutions, used as an acid-base indicator.

lit-mus pa-per n. Unsized paper that is treated with litmus and used as an indicator.

lit-ter n. A covered and curtained couch, mounted on shafts and used to carry a single passenger; a stretcher used to carry a sick or injured person; material used as bedding for animals; the offspring at one birth of a multiparous animal; an accumulation of waste material. **litter** v., **litterer** n.

lit-ter-bug n. One who litters a public area.

Little Dipper n. Ursa Minor.

lit-to-ral adj. Relating to or existing on a shore. n. A shore.

lit-ur-gy n., pl. **-ies** A prescribed rite or

body of rites for public worship.
litur-gical adj., **liturgically** adv.
live-li-hood n. A means of support or subsistence.
live-ly adj. Vigorous. **liveliness** n.
liv-er n. The large, very vascular, glandular organ of vertebrates which secretes bile.
liv-er-wurst n. A kind of sausage made primarily of liver.
liv-er-y n., pl. -ies A uniform worn by servants; the care and boarding of horses for pay; a concern offering horses and vehicles for rent. -**ied** adj.
liv-er-y-man n. A keeper or employee of a livery stable.
live-stock n. Farm animals raised for human use.
live wire n., Slang An energetic person.
liv-id adj. Discolored from a bruise; very angry.

liz-ard n.

One of various reptiles, usually with an elongated scaly body, four legs, and a tapering tail.
liz-ard fish n. A bottom-dwelling fish, having a lizard-like head and dwelling in warm waters of the seas.
lla-ma n. A South American ruminant, related to the camel family and raised for its soft wool.
load n. A mass or weight that is lifted or supported; anything, as cargo, put in a ship, aircraft, or vehicle for conveyance; something that is a heavy responsibility; a burden.
loader, loading n. **load** v.
load-ed adj. Intended to trick or trap. Slang Drunk; rich.
loaf n., pl. **loaves** A food, especially bread, that is shaped into a mass. v. To spend time in idleness. **loafer** n.
loam n. Soil that consists chiefly of sand, clay, and decayed plant matter. -**y** adj.
loan n. Money lent with interest to be repaid; something borrowed for temporary use. v. To lend.
loan shark n. One who lends money to individuals at exorbitant rates of interest. **loan sharking** n.
loath adj. Averse.
loathe v. To dislike intensely.
loath-ing n. Intense dislike; abhorrence.
loath-some adj. Arousing disgust. **loathsomely** adv., **loathsomeness** n.
lob v. To hit or throw in a high arc.
lob-by n., pl. -ies A foyer, as in a hotel or theatre; a group of private persons trying to influence legislators.
lobbyist n. **lobby** v.
lobe n. A curved or rounded projection or division, as the fleshy lower part of the ear. **lobar, lobed** adj.
lob-lol-ly n., pl. -ies A mudhole; mire.
lo-bo n. The gray wolf, as referred to by those who reside in the western United States.
lo-bot-o-my n., pl. -mies Surgical

severance of nerve fibers by incision into the brain.

lob-ster n.

Any of several large, edible marine crustaceans with five pairs of legs, the first pair being large and claw-like.
lob-ule n. A small lobe; a subdivision of a lobe. **lobular** adj.
lo-cal adj. Pertaining to, being in, or serving a particular area or place. **locally** adv.
lo-cale n. A locality where a particular event takes place; the setting or scene, as of a novel.
lo-cal-i-ty n., pl. -ties A specific neighborhood, place, or district.
lo-cate v. To determine the place, position, or boundaries of; to look for and find; to establish or become established; to settle. **locator** n.
loch n., Scot. A lake.
lock-et n. A small, ornamental case for a keepsake, often a picture, worn as a pendant on a necklace.
lock-jaw n. Tetanus; a form of tetanus in which a spasm of the jaw muscles locks the jaws closed.
lock-smith n. A person who makes or repairs locks.
lo-co adj., Slang Insane.
lo-co-mo-tion n. The act of moving; the power to move from place to place.
lo-co-mo-tive n. A self-propelled vehicle that is generally electric or diesel-powered and is used for moving railroad cars.
lode-star n. A star; the North Star, used as a reference point.
lodge n. A house, such as a cabin, used as a temporary or seasonal dwelling or shelter; an inn; the den of an animal, such as a beaver; a local chapter of a fraternal organization; the meeting hall of such a chapter.
lodg-er n. One who rents a room in another's house.
lodg-ment or **lodge-ment** n. An act of lodging; a place for lodging; an accumulation or deposit.
log-gi-a n. A roofed but open arcade along the front of a building; an open balcony in a theatre.
log-ic n. The science dealing with the principles of reasoning, especially of the method and validity of deductive reasoning; something that forces a decision apart from or in opposition to reason. **logician** n.
lo-go-type n. Identifying symbol for a company or publication.
lo-gy adj. Something marked by sluggishness. **loginess** n.
loin n. The area of the body located between the ribs and pelvis; a cut of meat from an animal.
loi-ter v. To stay for no apparent reason; to dawdle or delay. **loiterer** n.

loll v. To move or act in a lax, lazy or in-dolent manner; to hang loosely or laxly. **loller** n.

lol-li-pop or **lol-ly-pop** n. A piece of flavored hard candy on a stick.

lol-ly-gag v., Slang To fool around.

lone adj. Single; isolated; sole; unfrequented.

lone-ly adj. Being without companions; dejected from being alone. **-iness** n.

lon-er n. A person who avoids the company of others.

lone-some adj. Dejected because of the lack of companionship. **-ness** n.

long-bow n. A wooden bow that is approximately five to six feet in length.

lon-gev-i-ty n. Long life; long duration; seniority.

long-hand n. Cursive handwriting.

lon-gi-tude n. The angular distance that is east and west of the prime meridian at Greenwich, England.

lon-gi-tu-di-nal adj. Of or relating to the length; relating to longitude. **-ly** adv.

loose adj. Not tightly fastened; not confined or fitting; free.

loot n. Goods, usually of significant value, taken in time of war; goods that have been stolen. v. To plunder; to steal. **looter** n.

lop v. To remove branches from; to trim.

lope v. To run with a steady gait. **lope, lopper** n.

lop-sid-ed adj. Larger or heavier on one side than on the other; tilting to one side. **lopsidedly** adv., **lopsidedness** n.

lo-qua-cious adj. Overly talkative. **loquaciously** adv., **loquacity** n.

Lord n. God. A man having dominion and power over other people; the owner of a feudal estate.

lore n. Traditional fact; knowledge that has been gained through education or experience.

lor-gnette n. A pair of opera glasses with a handle.

lose v. To mislay; to fail to keep. **loser** n.

loss n. The suffering or damage used by losing; someone or something that is lost. **losses** pl. n. Killed, wounded, or captured soldiers; casualties.

lost adj. Unable to find one's way.

lot n. Fate; fortune; a parcel of land having boundaries; a plot.

lo-tion n. A liquid medicine for external use on the hands and body.

lot-ter-y n., pl. **-ies** A contest in which winners are selected by a random drawing.

lo-tus n. An aquatic plant having fragrant pinkish flowers and large leaves; any of several plants similar or related to the lotus.

lo-tus-eater n. One of a people represented in the Odyssey of Homer as eating the lotus fruit and living in the dreamy indolence it produced.

loud adj. Marked by intense sound and high volume. **loudly** adv., **loudness** n.

lounge v. To move or act in a lazy, relaxed manner. n. A room, as in a hotel or theatre, where people may wait; a couch. **lounger** n.

louse n., pl. **lice**

A small, wingless biting or sucking insect which lives as a parasites on various animals and also on human beings. Slang A mean, contemptible person.

lous-y adj. Lice-infested. Slang Mean; poor; inferior; abundantly supplied. **lousily** adv.

lout n. An awkward, stupid person. **loutish** adj.

lou-ver or **lou-vre** n. An opening in a wall fitted with movable, slanted slats which let air in, but keep precipitation out; one of the slats used in a louver. **louvered** adj.

love n. Intense affection for another arising out of kinship or personal ties; a strong feeling of attraction resulting from sexual desire; enthusiasm or fondness; a score of zero in tennis. **love** v., **lovable, loving** adj.

love-bird n. Any of various Old World parrots which show great affection for their mates.

love-ly adj. Beautiful. **loveliness, lovely** n.

lov-er n. A person who loves another; a sexual partner.

love seat n. A small couch which seats two.

love-sick adj. Languishing with love; expressing a lover's yearning. **-ness** n.

loving cup n. A large, ornamental cup with two or more handles, often given as an award or trophy.

low adj. Not high; being below or under normal height, rank, or level; depressed. v. To moo, as a cow.

low-brow n. An uncultured person.

low-down n. The whole truth; all the facts adj. Despicable; mean; depressed.

low-er-case adj. Having as its typical form a, b, c, or u, v, w rather than A, B, C, or U, V, W.

low-er class n. The group in society that ranks below the middle class in social and economic status.

low-est com-mon de-nom-i-na-tor n. The least common multiple of the denominators of a set of fractions.

low-est com-mon mul-ti-ple n. Least common multiple.

low fre-quen-cy n. A radio-wave frequency between 30 and 300 kilohertz.

low-land n. Land that is low and level in relation to the surrounding countryside.

low-ly adj. Low in position or rank.

low-rise adj. Having one or two stories and no elevator.

low-ten-sion adj. Having a low voltage; built to be used at low voltage.

lox n. Smoked salmon; liquid oxygen.

loy-al adj. Faithful in allegiance to one's country and government; faithful to a person, cause, ideal, or custom.

loy-al-ist *n.* One who is or remains loyal to political cause, party, government, or sovereign.

loz-enge *n.* Small medicated candy, normally having the shape of a lozenge.

lu-au *n.* A traditional Hawaiian feast.

lub-ber *n.* An awkward, clumsy or stupid person; an inexperienced sailor.

lu-bri-cant *n.* A material, as grease or oil, applied to moving parts to reduce friction.

lu-bri-cious *or* **lu-bri-cous** *adj.* Smooth, unstable; shifty. **lubricity** *n.*

lu-cid *adj.* Easily understood; mentally clear; rational; shining. **lucidity, lucidness** *n.*, **lucidly** *adv.*

luck *n.* Good fortune; the force or power which controls odds and which brings good fortune or bad fortune. **lucky** *adj.*, **luckily** *adv.*, **luckiness** *n.*

lu-cra-tive *adj.* Producing profits or great wealth. **lucratively** *adv.*

lu-cre *n.* Money; profit.

lu-cu-brate *v.* To study or work laboriously.

lu-di-crous *adj.* Amusing or laughable through obvious absurdity; ridiculous. **ludicrously** *adv.*, **ludicrousness** *n.*

luff *v.* To turn a sailing vessel toward the wind.

lug *n.* An ear-like handle or projection used as a hold; a tab. *v.* To carry with difficulty.

luge *n.* A small sled similar to a toboggan which is ridden in a supine position and used especially in competition.

lu-gu-bri-ous *adj.* Mournful; dejected; especially exaggeratedly or affectedly so. **-ly** *adv.*, **lugubriousness** *n.*

luke-warm *adj.* Mildly warm; tepid; unenthusiastic; soothing. **-ly** *adv.*

lull *v.* To cause to rest or sleep; to cause to have a false sense of security. *n.* A temporary period of quiet or rest.

lul-la-by *n.*, *pl.* **-bies** A song to lull a child to sleep.

lum-ba-go *n.* Painful rheumatic pain of the muscles and tendons of the lumbar region.

lum-bar *adj.* Part of the back and sides between the lowest ribs and the pelvis.

lu-mi-nar-y *n.*, *pl.* **-ies** A celestial body, as the sun; a notable person.

lu-mi-nes-cence *n.* An emission of light without heat, as in fluorescence.

lu-mi-nous *adj.* Emitting or reflecting light; bathed in steady light; illuminated; easily understood; clear.

lum-mox *n.* A clumsy oaf.

lump *n.* A projection; a protuberance; a swelling, as from a bruise or infection. *v.* To group things together. **-y** *adj.*

lu-na-cy *n.*, *pl.* **-ies** Insanity.

lu-nar *adj.* Of, relating to, caused by the moon.

lu-nar e-clipse *n.* An eclipse where the moon passes partially or wholly through the umbra of the earth's shadow.

lu-na-tic *n.* A crazy person.

lunch-eon *n.* A lunch.

lunch-eon-ette *n.* A modest restaurant at which light meals are served.

lung *n.*

One of the two spongy organs that constitute the basic respiratory organ of air-breathing vertebrates.

lunge *n.* A sudden forward movement.

lu-pus *n.* A bacterial disease of the skin.

lure *n.* A decoy; something appealing; an artificial bait to catch fish. *v.* To attract or entice with the prospect of reward or pleasure.

lurk *v.* To lie in concealment, as in an ambush.

lus-cious *adj.* Very pleasant to smell or taste; appealing to the senses. **lusciously** *adv.*, **lusciousness** *n.*

lush *adj.* Producing luxuriant growth or vegetation. *Slang* An alcoholic. **lushly** *adv.*, **lushness** *n.*

lust *n.* Intense sexual desire; an intense longing; a craving. **-ful** *adj.*

lust-y *adj.* Vigorous; healthy; robust; lively. **lustily** *adv.*, **lustiness** *n.*

lute *n.* A medieval musical stringed instrument with a fretted finger board, a pear-shaped body, and usually a bent neck.

lu-te-ti-um *or* **lu-te-ci-um** *n.* A silvery rare-earth metallic element symbolized by Lu.

lux-u-ri-ant *adj.* Growing or producing abundantly; lush; plentiful.

lux-u-ri-ate *v.* To enjoy luxury or abundance; to grow abundantly.

ly-ce-um *n.* A hall where public programs are presented; an organization which sponsors such programs as lectures and concerts.

lye *n.* A powerful caustic solution yielded by leaching wood ashes; potassium hydroxide; sodium hydroxide.

ly-ing-in *n.* Confinement in childbirth.

lymph node *n.* A roundish body of lymphoid tissue; lymph gland.

lynch *v.* To execute without authority or the due process of law.

lynx *n.*

A wildcat. *adj.* Having acute eyesight.

lyre *n.* An ancient Greek stringed instrument related to the harp.

lyr-ic *adj.* Concerned with thoughts and feelings; romantic; appropriate for singing. *n.* A lyric poem. **lyrics** The words of a song. **-al** *adj.*, **-ally** *adv.*

ly-ser-gic acid di-eth-yl-am-ide *n.* An organic compound which induces psychotic symptoms similar to those of schizophrenia; LSD.

M, m The thirteenth letter of the English alphabet; the Roman numeral for 1,000.

ma'am n. Madam.

mac n. An address for a man whose name is unknown.

ma-ca-bre adj. Suggesting death and decay.

mac-ad-am n. Pavement for roads consisting of layers of compacted, broken stone, usually cemented with asphalt and tar. **macadamize** v.

mac-a-ro-ni n. Dried pasta made into short tubes and prepared as food.

mac-a-roon n. A small cookie made of sugar, egg whites, coconut, and ground almonds.

ma-caw n. Any of various tropical American parrots with long tails, brilliant plumage, and harsh voices.

mace n. An aromatic spice made by grinding the cover of the nutmeg.

mac-er-ate v. To make a solid substance soft by soaking in liquid; to cause to grow thin. **maceration** n.

ma-chet-e n. A large, heavy knife with a broad blade, used as a weapon.

mach-i-nate v. To plot. **machination, machinator** n.

ma-chine n. A device or system built to use energy to do work; a political organization. v. To produce precision tools.

ma-chine lan-guage n., In Computer Science, the system of numbers or instructions for coding input data.

ma-chin-er-y n., pl. **-ies** A collection of machines as a whole; the mechanism or operating parts of a machine.

ma-chin-ist n. One skilled in the operation or repair of machines.

ma-chis-mo n. An exaggerated sense of masculinity.

ma-cho adj., Slang Exhibiting machismo.

mack-er-el n. A fish with dark, wavy bars on the back and a silvery belly, found in the Atlantic Ocean.

mac-ra-me n. The craft or hobby of tying knots into a pattern.

mac-ro-bi-ot-ic adj. Relating to or being an extremely restricted diet to promote longevity, consisting mainly of whole grain, vegetables and fish.

ma-cron n. A mark (-) placed over a vowel to indicate a long sound.

mac-ro-scop-ic or **ma-cro-scop-i-cal** adj. Large enough to be seen by the naked eye.

mad adj. Angry; afflicted with a mental disorder; insane.

mad-am n., pl. **mes-dames** A title used to address a married woman; used without a name as a courtesy title when addressing a woman.

mad-cap adj. Impulsive, rash or reckless.

mad-den v. To craze; to enrage; to make mad. v. To become mad.

mad-ding adj. Behaving senselessly; acting mad.

made v. Past tense of make.

mad-e-moi-selle n., pl. **mademoiselles** or **mesdemoiselles** An unmarried French girl or woman.

made--up adj. Fabricated; invented; having only makeup on.

mad-house n., Slang A place of confusion and disorder.

mad-ri-gal n., Music An unaccompanied song, usually for four to six voices, developed during the early Renaissance.

mael-strom n. Any irresistible or dangerous force.

maes-tro n., pl. **-tros** or **-tri** A person mastering any art, but especially a famous conductor of music.

mag-a-zine n. A publication with a paper cover containing articles, stories, illustrations and advertising; the part of a gun which holds ammunition ready for feeding into the chamber.

ma-gen-ta n. A purplish red color.

mag-got n. The legless larva of any of various insects, as the housefly, often found in decaying matter.

mag-ic n. The art which seemingly controls foresight of natural events and forces by means of supernatural agencies. **-al** adj., **-ly** adv., **-ian** n.

mag-is-trate n. A civil officer with the power to enforce the law.

mag-nan-i-mous adj. Generous in forgiving insults or injuries. **magnanimity, magnanimousness** n., **-ly** adv.

mag-nate n. A person notable or powerful, especially in business.

mag-ne-sia n., Chem. A light, white powder used in medicine as an antacid and laxative.

mag-ne-si-um n. A light, silvery metallic element which burns with a very hot, bright flame and is used in lightweight alloys, symbolized by Mg.

mag-net n.

A body having the property of attracting iron and other magnetic material.

magnetism n.

mag-net-ic adj. Pertaining to magnetism or a magnet; capable of being attracted by a magnet; having the power or ability to attract. **magnetically** adv.

magnetic field n. The area in the neighborhood of a magnet or of an electric current, marked by the existence of a detectable magnetic force in every part of the region.

mag-net-ite n. A black iron oxide in mineral form, which is an important iron ore.

mag-net-ize v. To have magnetic properties; to attract by personal charm or influence. **magnetizable** adj., **magnetization, magnetizer** n.

mag-ne-to n. A small alternator which works by means of magnets that are permanently attached, inducing an electric current for the spark in some engines.

mag-ne-tom-e-ter n. An instrument used for measuring the direction and intensity of magnetic forces.

mag-ne-to-sphere n., Physics A region of the upper atmosphere extending from about 500 to several thousand km above the surface, forming a band of ionized particles trapped by the earth's magnetic field.

mag-nif-i-cent adj. Having an extraordinarily imposing appearance; beautiful; outstanding; exceptionally pleasing.

mag-ni-fy v. To increase in size; to cause to seem more important or greater; to glorify or praise someone or something. magnification, magnifier n.

mag-nil-o-quent adj. Speaking or spoken in a lofty and extravagant manner. magniloquence n., magniloquently adv.

mag-ni-tude n. Greatness or importance in size or extent. Astron. The relative brightness of a star expressed on a numerical scale, ranging from one for the brightest to six for those just visible.

mag-no-lia n. An ornamental flowering tree or shrub with large, fragrant flowers of white, pink, purple, or yellow.

mag-num n. A wine bottle holding about two quarts or approximately 2/5 gallon.

mag-num o-pus n. A great work of art; literary or artistic masterpiece; the greatest single work of an artist, writer, or other creative person.

mag-pie n. Any of a variety of large, noisy bird found the world over having long tapering tails and black and white plumage.

ma-ha-ra-ja or **ma-ha-ra-jah** n. A king or prince who rules an Indian state.

ma-ha-ra-ni or **ma-ha-ra-nee** n. The wife of a maharajah.

ma-hat-ma n. In some Asian religions, a person venerated for great knowledge; a title of respect.

ma-hog-a-ny n., pl. -ies Any of various tropical trees having hard, reddish-brown wood, much used for cabinet work and furniture.

maid n. A young unmarried woman or girl; a female servant. maiden n.

maid-en-hair n. A delicate fern with dark stems and light-green, feathery fronds.

maid-en name n. A woman's family name before marriage.

maid of hon-or n. An unmarried woman who is the main attendant of a bride at a wedding.

mail n. Letter, printed matter, or parcel handled by the postal system. -er n.

mail or-der n. Goods which are ordered and sent by mail.

maim v. To disable or to deprive of the use of a bodily part; to impair.

main adj. Being the most important part of something. n. A large pipe used to carry water, oil, or gas. mainly adv.

Maine n. A state located in the northeastern corner of the United States.

main-land n. The land part of a country as distinguished from an island.

main-line v., Slang To inject a drug directly into a vein.

main-stream n. A main direction or line of thought. mainstream adj. & v.

main-tain v. To carry on or to keep in existence; to preserve in a desirable condition. -able adj., maintenance n.

maize n. Corn.

maj-es-ty n., pl. -ies Stateliness; exalted dignity. majestic adj., -ically adv.

ma-jor adj. Greater in importance, quantity, number, or rank; serious. n. An officer in the U.S. Army, Air Force or Marines who ranks above a captain and below a lieutenant colonel; a subject or field of academic study. Music A major musical scale, interval, key, or mode.

ma-jor-ette n. A young woman or girl who marches and twirls a baton with a band.

ma-jor-i-ty n., pl. -ies The greater number of something; more than half; the age at which a person is considered to be an adult, usually 21 years old.

make v. To cause something to happen; to create; to provide, as time; to manufacture a line of goods. n. A brand name, as a make of a car. make a-way with To carry off. make hay To take advantage of a given opportunity in the early stages. make no bones To perform unhesitating.

make--be-lieve n. A pretending to believe. v. To pretend.

make up n. The manner in which something is formed together or assembled; con-structions; the qualities of physical or mental constitution; cosmetics. v. To invent a story.

mal-a-chite n. A green basic copper carbonate, used as a common ore of copper and for decorating stoneware.

mal-a-droit adj. Lacking skill; awkward; clumsy. -ly adv., maladroitness n.

mal-a-dy n., pl. -ies A chronic disease or sickness.

mal-aise n. The vague discomfort sometimes indicating the beginning of an illness.

mal-ap-prop-ism n. A foolish misuse of a word.

mal-ap-ro-pos adj. Not appropriate.

ma-lar-i-a n., Pathol. The infectious disease introduced into the blood by the bite of the infected female anopheles mosquito and characterized by cycles of fever, chills, and profuse sweating. malarial adj.

ma-lar-key n., Slang Foolish or insincere talk; nonsense.

mal-con-tent adj. Unhappy with existing conditions or affairs. malcontent n.

mal de mer n. Seasickness.

male adj. Of or belonging to the sex that has organs to produce spermatozoa. Bot. A plant with stamens but no pistil. n. A male person or animal.

mal-e-dic-tion n. A curse; execration. maledictory adj.

mal-e-fac-tor n. A person who commits a crime or an unlawful act; a criminal.

malefaction n.

ma-lev-o-lent adj. Full of spite or ill will for another; malicious.
malevolently adv., **malevolence** n.

mal-func-tion n. Failure to function correctly. **malfunction** v.

mal-ice n. The direct intention or desire to harm others. Law The willfully formed design to injure another without just reason or cause.

ma-lign v. To speak slander or evil of. **maligner** n.

ma-lig-nant adj., Pathol. Of or relating to tumors and abnormal or rapid growth, and tending to metastasize; opposed to benign; causing death or great harm. **malignancy**, **malignity** n., **malignantly** adv.

mall n. A walk or other shaded public promenade; a street with shops, restaurants, and businesses which is closed to vehicles.

mal-lard n., pl. mallard or -ards. A wild duck having brownish plumage, the male of which has a green head and neck.

mal-le-a-ble adj. Able to be bent, shaped, or hammered without breaking; capable of being molded, altered, or influenced. **malleability**, **malleableness** n., **malleably** adv.

mal-let n. A hammer with a head made of wood or rubber and a short handle; a tool for striking an object without marring it.

mal-le-us n., pl. -lei Anat. The club-shaped bone of the middle ear or the largest of three small bones; also called the hammer.

mal-nour-ished adj. Undernourished.

mal-nu-tri-tion n. Insufficient nutrition.

mal-oc-clu-sion n. Improper alignment of the teeth.

mal-o-dor-ous adj. Having a disagreeable or foul odor. **-ly** adv., **-ness** n.

mal-prac-tice n. Improper treatment of a patient by his doctor during surgery or treatment which results in damage or injury; failure to perform a professional duty in a proper, careful, or correct fashion, resulting in injury, loss, or other problems.

malt n. Grain, usually barley, used chiefly in brewing and distilling; an alcoholic beverage.

mal-tose n. A white, crystalline sugar found in malt.

mal-treat v. To treat badly, unkindly, or roughly. **maltreatment** n.

ma-ma n. Mother.

mam-ba n. A venomous snake found in the tropics and in southern Africa.

mam-bo n. A dance resembling the rumba of Latin America.

mam-mal n. Any member of a class whose females secrete milk for nourishing their young, including man. **mammalian** adj. & n.

mam-ma-ry gland n. The milk-producing organ of the female mammal, consisting of small cavity clusters with ducts ending in a nipple.

mam-mog-ra-phy n. An x-ray examination of the breast for early detection of cancer.

mam-moth n. An extinct, early form of elephant whose tusks curved upwards and whose body was covered with long hair; anything of great or huge size.

man n., pl. **men** An adult or fully-grown male; the human race; any human being, regardless of sex. Slang Husband; an expression of pleasure or surprise.

man-a-cle n. A device for restraining the hands; handcuffs. **manacle** v.

man-age v. To direct or control the affairs or use of; to organize. **manageability** n., **-able** adj., **-ably** adv.

man-ag-er n. One in charge of managing an enterprise or business. **managerial** adj., **managership** n.

man-a-tee n. An aquatic mammal of the coastal waters of Florida, West Indies, and the Gulf of Mexico.

man-date n. An authoritative order or command. Law A judicial order issued by a higher court to a lower one. **mandate** v.

man-da-to-ry adj. Required by, having the nature of, or relating to a mandate; obligatory.

man-di-ble n. The lower jaw bone. Biol. Either part of the beak of a bird. **mandibular** adj.

man-do-lin n. A musical instrument having a pear-shaped body and a fretted neck.

man-drake n. A plant having purplish flowers and a branched root sometimes resembling the human form.

man-drel or **man-dril** n. A spindle or shaft on which material is held for working on a lathe.

man-drill n. A large, fierce West African baboon.

mane n.

The long hair growing on the neck of some animals, as the lion, and horse.

man-eat-er n. An animal which feeds on human flesh, such as a shark or a tiger.

ma-nege n. The art of training and riding horses; the performance of a horse so trained.

ma-neu-ver n., Milit. A planned strategic movement or shift, as of warships, or troops; any planned, skillful, or calculated move. **maneuver** v., **maneuverability** n., **maneuverable** adj.

man Fri-day n. A person devoted to another as a servant, aide, or employee.

man-ful adj. Having a manly spirit. **manfully** adv., **manfulness** n.

man-ga-nese n. A hard, brittle, gray-white metallic element which forms an important component of steel alloys, symbolized by Mn.

mange *n.* A contagious skin disease of dogs and other domestic animals caused by parasitic mites and marked by itching and hair loss. **mangy** *adj.*

man-ger *n.* A trough or box which holds livestock feed.

man-gle *v.* To disfigure or mutilate by bruising, battering, or crushing; to spoil. **mangler** *n.*

man-go *n., pl.* **-goes** *or* **-gos** A tropical evergreen tree that produces a fruit having a slightly acid taste.

man-grove *n.* A tropical evergreen tree or shrub having aerial roots which form dense thickets along tidal shores.

man-han-dle *v.* To handle very roughly.

man-hole *n.* A circular covered, opening usually in a street, through which one may enter a sewer, drain, or conduit.

man-hood *n.* The state of being an adult male.

man--hour *n.* The amount of work that one person can complete in one hour.

ma-ni-a *n.* An extraordinary enthusiasm or craving for something; intense excitement and physical overactivity, often a symptom of manic-depressive psychosis.

-mania *suffix.* Unreasonable or intense desire or infatuation with.

ma-ni-ac *n.* A violently insane person. **maniac, maniacal** *adj.*

man-ic--de-pres-sive *adj.* Of a mental disorder characterized by alternating periods of manic excitation and depression. **manic-depressive** *n.*

man-i-cot-ti *n.* Pasta shaped like a tube, filled with meat or ricotta cheese and served with hot tomato sauce.

man-i-cure *n.* The cosmetic care of the hands and fingernails. **manicurist** *n.*

man-i-fest *adj.* Clearly apparent; obvious. *v.* To display, reveal or show. *n.* A list of cargo or passengers. **manifestly** *adv.*

man-i-fes-ta-tion *n.* The act or state of being manifest.

man-i-fes-to *n., pl.* **-toes** *or* **-tos** A public or formal explanation of principles or intentions, usually of a political nature.

man-i-fold *adj.* Having many and varied parts, forms, or types; having an assortment of features. *Mech.* A pipe with several or many openings, as for the escaping of exhaust gas. **manifoldly** *adv.*, **manifoldness** *n.*

man-i-kin *or* **man-ni-kin** *n.* A little man; a dwarf; a mannequin.

ma-nip-u-late *v.* To handle or manage shrewdly and deviously for one's own profit. **manipulation, manipulator** *n.*, **manipulative** *adj.*

man-kind *n.* The human race; men collectively, as opposed to women.

man-ly *adj.* Pertaining to or having qualities which are traditionally attributed to a man. **manliness** *n.*

man--made *adj.* Made by human beings and not developed by nature.

man-na *n.* The food which was miraculously given to the Israelites in the wilderness on their flight from Egypt; anything of value that one receives unexpectedly.

manned *adj.* Operated by a human being.

man-ne-quin *n.* A life-sized model of a human figure, used to fit or display clothes; a woman who models clothes.

man-ner *n.* The way in which something happens or is done; an action or style of speech; one's social conduct and etiquette. **mannered** *adj.*

man-ner-ism *n.* A person's distinctive behavioral trait or traits. **mannerist** *n.* **manneristic, manneristical** *adj.*

man-ner-ly *adj.* Well-behaved; polite. **mannerliness** *n.*

man-nish *adj.* Resembling a man; masculine. **-ly** *adv.*, **mannishness** *n.*

man--of--war *n., pl.* **men--of--war** A warship.

ma-nom-e-ter *n.* An instrument used to measure pressure, as of gases or liquids. **manometric** *adj.*

man-or *n.* A landed estate; the house or hall of an estate. **manorial** *adj.*

man pow-er *n.* The force of human physical power; the number of men whose strength and skill are readily available to a nation, army, project, or other venture.

man-que *adj.* Lacking fulfillment; frustrated.

man-sard *n., Archit.* A curved roof with the lower slope almost vertical and the upper almost horizontal.

manse *n.* The house of a clergyman.

man-sion *n.* A very large, impressive house.

man--size *or* **man--sized** *adj., Slang* Quite large.

man-slaugh-ter *n., Law* The unlawful killing without malice of a person by another.

man-ta *n.* A rough-textured cotton fabric; any of several very large fishes having large, very flat bodies with winglike fins.

man-teau *n., pl.* **-teaus** *or* **-teaux** A robe or cloak.

man-tel *also* **man-tle** *n.* A shelf over a fireplace; the ornamental brick or stone around a fireplace.

man-til-la *n.* A light scarf worn over the head and shoulders by women in Latin America and Spain.

man-tis *n., pl.* **mantises** *or* **mantes** A tropical insect with a long body, large eyes, and swiveling head, which stands with its forelegs folded as if in prayer.

man-tle *n.* A loose-fitting coat which is usually sleeveless; something that covers or conceals; a device consisting of a sheath of threads, used in gas lamps to give off brilliant illumination when heated by a flame. **mantle** *v.*

man-u-al *adj.* Used or operated by the hands. *n.* A small reference book which gives instructions on how to operate or work something. **-ly** *adv.*

man-u-fac-ture *v.* To make a product; to invent or produce something. **-er** *n.*

ma-nure *n.* The fertilizer used to fertilize land, obtained from animal dung.

man-u-script *n.* A typed or written material copy of an article, book, or document, which is being prepared for publication.

man-y *adj.* Amounting to a large or indefinite number or amount.

map *n.* A plane surface representation of a region. *v.* To plan anything in detail. mapmaker, mapper *n.*

ma-ple *n.* A tall tree having lobed leaves and a fruit of two joined samaras; the wood of this tree, amber-yellow in color when finished and used for furniture and flooring.

ma-ple su-gar *n.* Sugar made from the sap of the maple tree.

ma-ple sy-rup *n.* The refined sap of the sugar maple.

mar *v.* To scratch or deface; to blemish; to ruin; to spoil.

mar-a-bou *n.* A stork of Africa, whose soft down is used for trimming women's garments.

ma-ra-ca *n.*

A percussion instrument made from gourds containing dried beans or pebbles.

mar-a-schi-no *n.* A cherry preserved in a cordial distilled from the fermented juice of the small wild cherry and flavored with cracked cherry pits.

mar-a-thon *n.* A foot race of 26 miles, usually run on the streets of a city; any contest of endurance.

mar-ble *n.* A limestone which is partly crystallized and irregular in color. *v.* To contain sections of fat, as in meat. marbles A game played with balls of glass. *Slang* A person's common sense or sanity marble *v.*, marbly *adj.*

march *v.* To walk with measured, regular steps in a solemn or dignified manner. *Mus.* A musical composition.

mare *n.* The female of the horse and other equine animals.

ma-re *n., pl. Astron.* Any of the dark areas on the surface of the moon.

mar-ga-rine *n.* A butter substitute made from vegetable oils and milk.

mar-gin *n.* The edge or border around the body of written or printed text; the difference between the selling price and cost of an item.

mar-gi-na-li-a *pl., n.* The notes in the margin of a book.

ma-ri-a-chi *n.* A Mexican band; the music performed by a musician playing in a mariachi.

mar-i-gold *n.* Any of a variety of plants having golden-yellow flowers.

mar-i-jua-na *or* **marihuana** *n.* Hemp; the dried flower tops and leaves of this plant, capable of producing disorienting or hallucinogenic effects when smoked in cigarettes or ingested.

ma-ri-na *n.* A docking area for boats, furnishing moorings and supplies for small boats.

mar-i-nade *n.* A brine made from vinegar or wine and oil with various herbs and spices for soaking meat, fowl, or fish before cooking.

mar-i-nate *v.* To soak meat in a marinade.

ma-rine *adj.* Of, pertaining to, existing in, or formed by the sea. *n.* A soldier trained for service on land and at sea. **Marine** *n.* A member of the Marine Corps.

mar-i-tal *adj.* Pertaining to marriage. maritally *adv.*

mar-i-time *adj.* Located or situated on or near the sea; pertaining to the sea and its navigation and commerce.

mark *n.* A visible impression, trace, dent, or stain; an identifying seal, inscription, or label.

mar-ket *n.* The trade and commerce in a certain service or commodity; a public place for purchasing and selling merchandise; the possible consumers of a particular product. *v.* To sell. marketability *n.*, marketable *adj.*

mar-ket-place *n.* A place, such as a public square, where ideas, opinions, and works are traded and tested.

marks-man *n.* A person skilled in firing a gun and hitting the mark. -woman *n.*

mark-up *n.* The amount of increase in price from the cost to the selling price. *v.* To raise the price.

mar-lin *n.* A large marine game fish of the Atlantic; the striped marlin found in the Pacific.

mar-line-spike *n., Naut.* A pointed tool used in splicing ropes.

mar-ma-lade *n.* A preserve made from the pulp and rind of fruits.

ma-roon *v.* To put ashore and abandon on a desolate shore. *n.* A dull purplish red.

mar-que-try *n.* Inlaid work of wood or ivory used for decorating furniture.

mar-quis *n.* The title of a nobleman ranking below a duke.

mar-qui-sette *n.* A fabric of cotton, silk, nylon, or a combination of these, used in curtains, clothing, and mosquito nets.

mar-riage *n.* The state of being married; wedlock; the act of marrying or the ceremony entered into by a man and woman so as to live together as husband and wife. -ability *n.*, -able *adj.*

mar-row *n.* The soft, vascular tissue which fills bone cavities; the main part or essence of anything.

mar-ry *v.* To take or join as husband or wife; to unite closely.

marsh *n.* An area of low, wet land; a swamp. marshy *adj.*

mar-shal *n.* A military officer of high rank in foreign countries; the person in the U.S. in charge of a police or fire department. *v.* To bring troops together to prepare for a battle.

marsh-mal-low *n.* A soft, white confection made of sugar, corn syrup, starch, and gelatin and coated with powdered sugar.

mar-su-pi-al *n.* An animal, such as a kangaroo, koala, or opossum, which has no placenta, but which in the female has an abdominal pouch with teats to feed and carry the offspring.

mart *n.* A trading market; a center.

mar-ten *n.*

A weasel-like mammal of eastern North America with arboreal habits; the valuable brown fur of the marten.

mar-tial *adj.* Of, pertaining to, or concerned with war or the military life.

mar-tial arts *pl., n.* Oriental arts of self-defense, such as karate or judo, which are practiced as sports.

mar-tial law *n.* Temporary rule by military forces over the citizens in an area where civil law and order no longer exist.

mar-tin *n.* A bird of the swallow family with a tail that is less forked than that of the common swallow.

mar-ti-ni *n., pl.* -nis A cocktail of gin and dry vermouth, served with an olive or lemon peel.

mar-tyr *n.* A person who would rather die than renounce his religious principles; one making great sacrifices to advance a cause, belief, or principle. **martyr** *v.,* **martyrdom** *n.*

mar-vel *n.* Anything causing surprise, wonder, or astonishment. **marvel** *v.*

mar-vel-ous *or* **marvellous** *adj.* Causing astonishment and wonder; wondrous. *Informal* Excellent; very good, admirable. -ly *adv.,* **marvelousness** *n.*

mar-zi-pan *n.* A confection of grated almonds, sugar, and egg whites.

mas-car-a *n.* A cosmetic preparation used for coloring or darkening the eyelashes.

mas-cot *n.* A person, animal, or object thought to bring good luck.

mas-cu-line *adj.* Of or pertaining to the male sex; male; the masculine gender. **masculinity** *n.*

ma-ser *n., Physics* One of several devices which are similar to the laser but which operate with microwaves rather than light.

mash *n.* A soft, pulpy mass or mixture used to distill alcohol or spirits. *v.* To crush into a soft, pulpy mass. -er *n.*

mask *n.* A covering used to conceal the face in order to disguise or protect. *v.* To hide or conceal.

mas-o-chism *n.* A condition in which sexual gratification is marked by pleasure in being subjected to physical pain or abuse. -ist *n.,* -istic *adj.*

ma-son *n.* A person working with brick or stone.

ma-son-ic *adj.* Pertaining to or like freemasonry or Freemasons.

masque *n.* An elaborately staged dramatic performance, popular during the 16th and 17th centuries in England; a masquerade.

mas-quer-ade *n.* A costume party in which the guests are masked and dressed in fancy costumes. *v.* To disguise oneself. **masquerader** *n.*

mass *n.* A body of matter that does not have definite shape but is relatively large in size; physical volume; the measure of a body's resistance to acceleration.

mas-sa-cre *n.* The indiscriminate and savage killing of human beings in large numbers. **massacre** *v.*

mas-sage *n.* The manual or mechanical manipulation of the skin to improve circulation and to relax muscles.

mas-seur *n.* A man who gives massages.

mas-seuse *n.* A woman who gives massages.

mas-sive *adj.* Of great intensity, degree, and size. -ly *adv.,* **massiveness** *n.*

mast *n.* The upright pole or spar which supports the sails and running rigging of a sail boat.

mas-tec-to-my *n., pl.* -ies The surgical removal of breast.

mas-ter *n.* A person with control or authority over others; one who is exceptionally gifted or skilled in an art, science, or craft; the title given for respect or in address. *v.* To learn a skill, craft, or job; to overcome defeat. **mastership** *n.*

mas-ter key *n.* A key which will open many different locks whose keys are not the same.

mas-ter-ly *adj.* Characteristic of a master. **masterliness** *n.*

mas-ter-mind *n.* A person who plans and directs at the highest levels of policy and strategy. *v.* To plan or direct an undertaking.

mas-ter of cer-e-mo-nies *n.* A person who hosts a formal event or program.

mas-ter-piece *n.* Something having notable excellence; an unusually brilliant achievement which is considered the greatest achievement of its creator.

mas-ter plan *n.* A plan providing complete instructions.

mast-head *n.* The top of a mast; the listing in a periodical giving the names of the editors, staff, and owners.

mas-ti-cate *v.* To chew. **mastication** *n.*

mas-to-don *n.* A large, extinct mammal which resembles an elephant.

mas-toid *n., Anat.* The nipple shaped portion at the rear of the temporal bone behind the ear.

mas-tur-ba-tion *n.* The act of stimulating the sexual organs by hand or other means without sexual intercourse. **masturbate** *v.,* **masturbator** *n.*

mat *n.* A flat piece of material made of fiber, rubber, rushes, or other material and used to cover floors; the border around a picture, which serves as a contrast between the picture and the frame.

mat-a-dor *n.* A bullfighter who kills the bull after completing various maneuvers with a cape.

match *n.* Anything that is similar or identical to another; a short, thin piece of wood or cardboard with a specially treated tip which ignites as a result of friction. *v.* To equal; to oppose successfully. **-able** *adj.*, **-er** *n.*

match-maker *n.* A person who arranges a marriage.

mate *n.* A spouse; something matched, joined, or paired with another; in chess, a move which puts the opponent's king in jeopardy. *Naval* A petty officer. **mate** *v.*

ma-te-ri-al *n.* The substance from which anything is or may be composed or constructed of; anything that is used in creating, working up, or developing something.

ma-te-ri-al-ism *n.* The doctrine that physical matter is the only reality and that everything, including thought, feeling, will, and mind, is explainable in terms of matter; a preference for material objects as opposed to spiritual or intellectual pursuits. **materialist** *n.*, **materialistic** *adj.*, **materialistically** *adv.*

ma-te-ri-al-ize *v.* To give material or actual form to something; to assume material or visible appearance; to take form or shape. **-ation**, **materializer** *n.*

ma-te-ri-el *n.* The equipment and supplies of a military force, including guns and ammunition.

ma-ter-nal *adj.* Relating to a mother or motherhood; inherited from one's mother.

ma-ter-ni-ty *n.* The state of being a mother; the qualities of a mother; the department in a hospital for the prenatal and postnatal care of babies and their mothers.

math *n.* Mathematics.

math-e-mat-ics *n.* The study of form, arrangement, quantity, and magnitude of numbers and operational symbols. **-al** *adj.*, **-ally** *adv.*, **mathematician** *n.*

mat-i-nee *n.* An afternoon performance of a play, concert, movie, etc.

ma-tri-arch *n.* A woman ruler of a family, tribe, or clan. **-al** *adj.*, **-y** *n.*

mat-ri-cide *n.* The killing of one's own mother; one who kills his mother. **matricidal** *adj.*

ma-tric-u-late *v.* To enroll, or to be admitted into a college or university. **matriculation** *n.*

mat-ri-mo-ny *n.* The condition of being married; the act, sacrament, or ceremony of marriage. **matrimonial** *adj.*, **matrimonially** *adv.*

ma-trix *n.*, *pl.* **-rixes** *or* **-rices.** Something within which something else develops, originates, or takes shape; a mold or die.

ma-tron *n.* A married woman or widow of dignity and social position; the woman supervisor in a prison.

matronliness *n.*, **matronly** *adj. & adv.*

mat-ter *n.* Something that makes up the substance of anything; that which is material and physical, occupies space, and is perceived by the senses; something that is sent by mail; something that is written or printed.

mat-tock *n.* A tool having a blade on one side and a pick on the other or one with a blade on each side.

mat-tress *n.* A large cloth case filled with soft material and used on or as a bed.

mat-u-rate *v.* To ripen or mature.

ma-ture *adj.* Completely developed; at full growth; something, as a bond at a bank, that is due and payable. **mature** *v.*, **maturely** *adv.*, **maturity** *n.*

mat-zo *n.*, *pl.* **-zos** *or* **-zot.** A large, flat piece of unleavened bread eaten during Passover.

maud-lin *adj.* Overly sentimental; tearfully and overwhelmingly emotional.

maul *n.* A heavy hammer or mallet used to drive wedges, piles, and other materials. *v.* To handle roughly; to abuse.

maun-der *v.* To wander or talk in an incoherent manner.

mau-so-le-um *n.*, *pl.* **-leums** *or* **-lea.** A large and stately tomb.

mauve *n.* A purplish rose shade; a moderately reddish to gray purple.

mav-er-ick *n.* An unbranded or orphaned calf or colt. *Slang* A person who is unorthodox in his ideas or attitudes.

maw *n.* The jaws, mouth, or gullet of a hungry or ferocious animal; the stomach.

mawk-ish *adj.* Disgustingly sentimental; sickening or insipid. **mawkishly** *adv.* **mawkishness** *n.*

max *abbr.* Maximum.

max-i *n.* A floor-length garment, such as a skirt or coat.

max-il-la *n.*, *pl.* **-lae** *or* **-las.** The upper jaw or jawbone. **maxillary** *adj.*

max-im *n.* A brief statement of truth, general principle, or rule of conduct.

max-i-mize *v.* To increase as greatly as possible; to intensify to the maximum.

max-i-mum *n.*, *pl.* **-mums** *or* **-ma.** The greatest possible number, measure, degree, or quantity. **maximum** *adj.*

may *v.* To be permitted or allowed; used to express a wish, purpose, desire, contingency, or result.

may-be *adv.* Perhaps; possibly.

may-flow-er *n.* A wide variety of plants which blossom in May.

may-hem *n.*, *Law* The offense of injuring a person's body; any situation brought on by violence, confusion, noise, or disorder.

may-o *n.*, *Slang* Mayonnaise.

may-on-naise *n.* A dressing for salads, made by beating raw egg yolk, oil, lemon juice, or vinegar and seasonings.

may-or *n.* The chief magistrate of a town, borough, municipality, or city. **mayoral** *adj.*, **mayoralty**, **mayorship** *n.*

may-pole *n.* A decorated pole hung with streamers around which May Day dancing takes place.

maze *n.* A complicated, intricate network of passages or pathways; a labyrinth; a state of uncertainty, bewilderment, or perplexity. **maze** *v.*

me *pron.* The objective case of the pronoun I.

mead *n.* An alcoholic beverage made from fermented honey and water with yeast and spices added.

mead-ow *n.* A tract of grassland used for grazing or growing hay.

mead-ow-lark *n.* A songbird of North America.

mea-ger *or* **mea-gre** *adj.* Thin; lean; deficient in quantity, richness, vigor, or fertility. **-ly** *adv.*, **meagerness** *n.*

meal *n.* The edible seeds of coarsely ground grain; any powdery material; the food served or eaten at one sitting at certain times during the day; the time or occasion of taking such food.

meal-tick-et *n.*, *Slang* One who is a source of financial support for another; a ticket or card bought for a specified price and redeemable at a restaurant for food.

meal-y--mouthed *adj.* Unable to speak plainly and frankly; evasive.

mean *v.* To have in mind as a purpose or intent; to be of a specified importance or significance. *adj.* Poor or inferior in appearance or quality. *n.* The medium point. **means** The method or instrument by which some end is or may be accomplished; the available resources.

me-an-der *v.* To wander about without a certain course or a fixed direction.

mean-ing *n.* That which is meant or intended; the aim, end, or purpose; the significance; an interpretation. **meaningful, meaningfulness** *adj.*

mean-time *n.* The time or period between or during the intervening time.

mean-while *adv.* At the same time.

mea-sles *n.* A contagious viral disease usually occurring in children, characterized by the eruption of red spots.

mea-sly *adj.*, *Slang* Very small; meager.

meas-ure *n.* The range, dimension, extent, or capacity of anything. *Mus.* The group of beats marked off by regularly recurring primary accents; the notes and rests between two successive bars on a musical staff. *v.* To determine the range, dimension, extent, volume, or capacity of anything. **measurable** *adj.*, **measurably** *adv.*, **measurer** *n.*

meas-ure-ment *n.* The process or act of measuring.

meat *n.* The flesh of an animal which is used as food; the core or essential part of something. **-iness** *n.*, **meaty** *adj.*

mech *abbr.* Mechanical; mechanics.

me-chan-ic *n.* A person skilled in the making, operation, or repair of machines or tools.

me-chan-i-cal *adj.* Involving or having to do with the construction, operation, or

design of tools or machines; produced or operated by a machine. **-ly** *adv.*

me-chan-i-cal draw-ing *n.* A drawing done with the aid of squares, compasses, or other instruments.

me-chan-ics *pl.*, *n.* The scientific study and analysis of the action of forces and motion on material bodies.

mech-a-nism *n.* The arrangement or parts of a machine; the technique or process by which something works.

mech-a-nize *v.* To make mechanical; to equip with tanks, trucks, mechanical and other equipment, as in the military. **mechanization** *n.*

med *abbr.* Medical.

med-al *n.*

A small piece of metal with a commemorative image or inscription which is presented as an award.

med-al-ist *n.* A person who designs, collects, or makes medals; one who has been awarded or received a medal.

me-dal-lion *n.* A large circular or oval medal which is used as a decorative element.

med-dle *v.* To interfere or participate in another person's business or affairs. **meddler** *n.*, **meddlesome** *adj.*

med-i-a *pl.*, *n.* The instruments of news communication, as radio, television, and newspapers.

me-di-al *adj.* Pertaining to or situated in the middle; ordinary.

me-di-ate *v.* To help settle or reconcile opposing sides in a dispute. **mediation, mediator** *n.*

med-i-cal *adj.* Relating to the study or practice of medicine. **medically** *adv.*

med-i-cate *v.* To treat an injury or illness with medicine. **medication** *n.*

med-i-cine *n.* Any agent or substance used in the treatment of disease or in the relief of pain; the science of diagnosing and treating disease; the profession of medicine.

med-i-cine ball *n.* A large, heavy ball used for physical exercise.

me-di-e-val *or* **mediaeval** *adj.* Like or characteristic of the Middle Ages. **-ism, medievalist** *n.*, **medievally** *adv.*

me-di-o-cre *adj.* Common; fair; undistinguished.

med-i-tate *v.* To be in continuous, contemplative thought; to think about doing something. **-tive** *adj.*, **-tion** *n.*

me-dul-la *n.*, *pl.* **-las** *or* **-lae** *Anat.* The center of certain vertebrate structures, such as bone marrow.

me-dul-la ob-lon-ga-ta The mass of nerve tissue found at the base of the brain, controlling bodily functions such as breathing and circulation.

meek *adj.* Showing patience and a gentle disposition; lacking spirit or backbone; submissive. **-ly** *adv.*, **-ness** *n.*

meet *v.* To come upon; to encounter.

meg-a-bucks *n.*, *Slang* One million dollars; a lot of money.

meg·a·hertz *n., pl.* **-hertz** *Physics.* One million cycles per second, used as a radio-frequency unit.

meg·a·lo·ma·ni·a *n., Psychiatry* A mental disorder marked by fantasies of power, wealth, or omnipotence. **megalomaniac** *n.,* **megalomaniacal** *adj.*

meg·a·lop·o·lis *n.* A very large urban complex.

meg·a·ton *n.* One million tons; the unit equal to the explosive power of one million tons of TNT.

meg·a·watt *n.* A unit of electrical power equal to one million watts.

mei·o·sis *n., pl.* **-ses** *Biol.* The process by which undeveloped sex cells, sperm and ovum, mature by reduction division so that they contain only half of the full number of chromosomes.

mel·an·cho·li·a *n., Psychiatry* A mental disorder of great depression of spirits and excessive brooding without apparent cause. **melancholiac** *adj. & n.*

mel·an·chol·ic *adj.* Depressed; sad.

mel·an·chol·y *adj.* Excessively gloomy or sad.

me·lange *n., French* A medley or mixture.

mel·a·nin *n., Biochem.* The brownish-black pigment which is contained in animal tissues, as the hair and skin.

mel·a·nism *n.* An abnormally dark pigmentation of the skin.

mel·a·no·ma *n., pl.* **-mas** *or* **-mata** A dark-colored tumor or malignant mole.

mel·io·rate *v.* To cause to improve or to improve. **melioration** *n.,* **-ive** *adj.*

mel·lif·er·ous *adj.* Producing or bearing honey.

mel·lo *adj.* Sweet and soft; rich and full-flavored; rich and soft in quality, as in sounds or colors.

mel·lo·di·ous *adj.* Characterized by a melody; tuneful; pleasant to hear.

mel·o·dy *n., pl.* **-ies** An agreeable succession of pleasing sounds. **melodic** *adj.,* **melodically** *adv.*

mel·on *n.* The large fruit of any of various plants of the gourd family, as the watermelon.

melt *v.* To change from a solid to a liquid as a result of pressure or heat.

melt-down *n.* The melting of a nuclear-reactor core.

mem·brane *n.* A thin, pliable, sheet-like layer of tissue which covers body surfaces and separates or connects body parts. **membranous** *adj.*

me·men·to *n., pl.* **-tos** *or* **-toes** A keepsake.

mem·o *n.* A memorandum.

mem·oir *n.* Personal records or reminiscences; an autobiography.

mem·o·ra·ble *adj.* Worth remembering or noting. **memorably** *adv.*

mem·o·ran·dum *n., pl.* **-dums** *or* **-da** A brief, informal note written as a reminder.

me·mo·ri·al *n.* Something that serves to keep in remembrance, as a person or event. *adj.* Perpetuating remembrance.

mem·o·rize *v.* To commit something to memory. **memorization, memorizer** *n.*

mem·o·ry *n., pl.* **-ries** The mental function or capacity of recalling or recognizing something that has been previously learned or experienced.

men *pl. n.* The plural of man.

men·ace *n.* Something or someone who threatens; an annoying person. **menace** *v.,* **menacingly** *adv.*

me·nar·che *n.* The beginning or the first occurrence of menstruation.

mend *v.* To fix; to repair; to correct.

men·da·cious *adj.* Prone to lying; deceitful; untrue; false. **-ly** *adv.,* **-ity** *n.*

men·de·le·vi·um *n.* A short-lived radioactive element of the actinide series, symbolized by Md.

me·ni·al *adj.* Relating to a household servant or household chores requiring little responsibility or skill.

men·in·gi·tis *n., Pathol.* An inflammation of the membranes which enclose the brain and spinal cord.

me·ninx *n., pl.* **meninges** The membrane which encloses the spinal cord and brain. **meningeal** *adj.*

men·ses *pl., n.* The blood and dead cell debris which are discharged from the uterus through the vagina by women who are not pregnant; menstruation, occurring at monthly intervals between puberty and menopause.

men·stru·a·tion *n., Physiol.* The process, act, or periodical flow of bloody fluid from the uterus, also called period.

-ment *suffix* The result or product of achievement; action; process.

men·tal *adj.* Relating to or of the mind.

men·tal de·fi·cien·cy *n.* Subnormal intellectual development, marked by deficiencies ranging from impaired learning ability to social incompetence.

men·tal·i·ty *n., pl.* **-ies** Mental faculties or powers; mental activity; habit of mind.

men·tal re·tar·da·tion *n.* A mental deficiency.

men·thol *n., Chem.* The white, waxy crystalline alcohol which is obtained from and has the odor of peppermint oil. **mentholated** *adj.*

men·tion *v.* To refer to incidentally, in passing, or briefly. **-able** *adj.,* **-er** *n.*

men·tor *n.* A wise and trusted person.

me·ow *n.* The cry of a cat. **meow** *v.*

me·phi·tis *n.* A sickening or foul smell; a stench emitted from the earth.

mer·can·tile *adj.* Of or relating to merchants, trading, or commerce.

mer·cer·ize *v.* To treat cotton yarn or thread with sodium hydroxide so as to give strength and receptiveness to dyes.

mer·chan·dise *n.* Commodities or goods that are bought and sold. *v.* To buy and sell.

mer·chant *n.* A person who operates a retail business for profit.

mer·chant·man *n.* A ship used for commercial shipments.

mer-cu-ry *n.* A silvery, metallic, liquid element used in thermometers and barometers, symbolized by Hg.

mer-cy *n., pl.* **-ies** Compassionate and kind treatment. **merciful,** **merciless** *adj.,* **-ifully, mercilessly** *adv.*

mere *adj.* Absolute; no more than what is stated. **merest** *adj.,* **merely** *adv.*

merge *v.* To unite or bring together as one; in Computer Science, to combine two or more files into one, retaining the internal order of both.

me-ri-no *n., pl.* **-nos** A Spanish breed of hardy, white, fine-wooled sheep; a soft, lightweight fabric originally made of merino wool. **merino** *adj.*

mer-it *n.* A characteristic act or trait which is worthy of praise. *v.* To earn; to be worthy of.

mer-i-toc-ra-cy *n., pl.* **-ies** A system which bases advancement on ability or achievement.

mer-i-to-ri-ous *adj.* Deserving honor, praise or reward. **meritoriously** *adv.*

mer-maid *n.* An imaginary sea creature having the upper body of a woman and the tail of a fish. **merman** *n.*

me-sa *n.* A flat-topped hill or small plateau with steep sides.

mes-mer-ize *v.* To hypnotize or put into a trance.

mes-sen-ger *n.* A person who carries a message or does an errand for another person or company.

mess-y *adj.* Untidy; upset; dirty; lacking neatness. **messily** *adv.,* **messiness** *n.*

met *v., p.t. & p.p.* Past tense of meet.

me-tab-o-lism *n.* The chemical and physical changes in living cells which involve the maintenance of life.

metabolic *adj.,* **metabolize** *v.*

meta-car-pus *n.* The part of the forefoot or hand which connects the bones of the toes or fingers to the ankle or wrist.

met-a-gal-ax-y *n.* The universe; the entire system of galaxies.

metal *n.* One of a category of opaque, fusible, ductile, and typically lustrous elements. **-lic** *adj.,* **metallically** *adv.*

met-al-lur-gy *n.* The technology and science which studies methods of extracting metals from their ores and of preparing them for use.

metallurgical *adj.,* **metallurgist** *n.*

met-a-mor-pho-sis *n.* The transformation and change in the structure and habits of an animal during normal growth, as the metamorphosis of a tadpole into a frog. **-ism** *n.,* **metamorphose** *v.*

met-a-phor *n.* A figure of speech in which the context demands that a word or phrase not be taken literally, as the sun is smiling; a comparison which doesn't use like or as.

me-tas-ta-sis *n.* A spread of cancer cells from the original tumor to one or more additional sites within the body.

metastasize *v.,* **-static** *adj.*

met-a-tar-sus *n., pl.* **-si** The part of the human foot which forms the instep and contains five bones between the ankle and the toes; the hind foot of four-legged animals. **metatarsal** *adj.*

me-te-or *n.* A moving particle in the solar system which appears as a trail or streak in the sky as it comes into contact with the atmosphere of the earth.

me-te-or-ic *adj.* Of or relating to a meteor or meteors; resembling a meteor in speed, brilliance, or brevity.

me-te-or-ite *n.* A stony or metallic mass of a meteor which reaches the earth after partially burning in the atmosphere.

me-te-or-ol-o-gy *n.* The science concerned with the study of weather, weather conditions and weather forecasting. **-ical, meteorologic** *adj.,* **meteorologically** *adv.,* **meteorologist** *n.*

me-ter *n.* The arrangement of words, syllables, or stanzas in verse or poetry; a measure equaling 39.37 inches.

meth-a-done *n.* A man-made narcotic used in the treatment of heroin addiction.

meth-ane *n.* A colorless, odorless flammable gas used as a fuel; a product of the decomposition of organic matter.

meth-a-nol *n.* A colorless, odorless flammable alcohol that is used as an antifreeze, as a fuel, and as a raw material in chemical synthesis.

me-thinks *v.* It seems to me.

meth-od *n.* A manner, a process, or the regular way of doing something; the orderly arrangement, development, or classification.

meth-yl *n.* An alkyl radical derived from methane which occurs in several organic compounds.

me-tic-u-lous *adj.* Very precise; careful; concerned with small details.

meticulously *adv.,* **meticulousness** *n.*

me-tis *n.* A person of mixed blood, usually of French and Indian ancestry.

met-ric *adj.* Of or relating to the metric system. **metrical** *adj.,* **metrication** *n.*

met-ric sys-tem *n.* A decimal system of weights and measures based on the meter as a unit of length and the kilogram as a unit of mass, originated in France around 1790.

met-ri-fy *v.* To adopt or convert to the metric system. **metrification** *n.*

met-ro *n.* A subway system for transportation.

met-ro-nome *n.* An instrument designed to mark time by means of a series of clicks at exact intervals. **-ic** *adj.*

me-trop-o-lis *n.* A large or capital city of a state, region, or country.

metropolitan *adj.*

mew *n.* A hideaway; a secret place.

mez-za-nine *n.* A low story between two main stories of a building; the lowest balcony in a theatre.

mice *pl. n.* The plural of mouse.

mi-crobe *n.* A germ, plant, or animal so small that is can be seen only with the aid of a microscope.

mi-cro-bi-ol-o-gy *n.* The scientific study

of microorganisms.
microbiological *adj.*, **microbiologist** *n.*

mi-cro-ceph-a-ly *n.* A condition of abnormal smallness of the head, usually associated with mental defects.

mi-cro-cir-cuit *n.* An electronic circuit composed of very small components.

mi-cro-com-put-er *n.* A computer which uses a microprocessor.

mi-cro-film *n.* A film used to photograph printed matter at a greatly reduced size.

micro-or-gan-ism *n.* An organism too small to see without the aid of a microscope.

mi-cro-phone *n.*

An instrument which converts acoustical waves into electrical signals and feeds them into a recorder, amplifier or broadcasting transmitter. **-ic** *adj.*

mi-cro-proc-es-sor *n.* In Computer Science, a semiconductor processing unit which is contained on an integrated circuit chip.

mi-cro-scope *n.*

An optical instrument consisting of a lens or combination of lenses, used to produce magnified images of very small objects.

mi-cro-scop-ic *adj.* Too small to be seen by the eye alone. **microscopical** *adv.*

mi-cro-sur-ger-y *n.* Surgery performed by means of a microscope and laser beam. **microsurgical** *adj.*

mi-cro-wave *n.* A very short electromagnetic wave.

mid *adj.* In the middle or center; central.

mid-air *n.* A point in the air just above the ground surface.

mid-day *n.* Noon; the middle of the day.

mid-den *n.* A refuse heap or dunghill.

mid-dle *adj.* Being equally distant from extremes or limits; the central. *n.* Anything which occupies a middle position; the waist.

mid-dle age *n.* A period of life from about 40 to 60 years.

mid-dle class *n.* The social class of people between a high income and low income status.

mid-dle ear *n.* A small membrane-lined cavity between the tympanic membrane and the inner ear through which sound waves are carried.

mid-dle-man *n.* A person who serves as an agent between the producer and the consumer.

midg-et *n.* A very small person.

mid-i *n.* *Slang* A dress, skirt, or coat which extends to the calf.

mid-night *n.* 12 o'clock p.m.; the middle of the night.

mid-point *n.* A point at or near the middle.

mid-riff *n.* The midsection of the human torso; the diaphragm.

midst *n.* The central or middle part or position; a person positioned among others in a group.

mid-sum-mer *n.* The middle of summer.

mid-term *n.* The middle of an academic term.

mid-way *n.* The section of a carnival or fair where shows and rides are located.

mid-wife *n.* A woman who gives assistance in the birth of a baby.

mid-year *n.* The middle of a calendar year; academic examinations which are given in the middle of the academic year.

miff *n.* Ill humor; displeasure. **miff** *v.*

might *n.* Force, power, or physical strength. *v.* To indicate a present condition contrary to fact; to ask permission politely.

might-y *adj.* Showing or having great power.

mi-graine *n.* A condition of severe, recurring headaches often accompanied by nausea.

mi-grant *n.* A person who moves from one place to another to find work in the fields.

mi-grate *v.* To move from one place to another or from one climate to another. **-ion** *n.*, **-ional**, **-ory** *adj.*

mike *n.*, *Slang* Microphone.

mil *n.* A unit of measure equal to 1/1000 of an inch, used in measuring wire.

milch *adj.* Giving milk.

mild *adj.* Gentle in manner, behavior, or disposition; not severe or extreme. **mildly** *adv.*, **mildness** *n.*

mil-dew *n.* A fungal growth which is usually white in color. **mildew** *v.*, **mildewy** *adj.*

mile *n.* A unit of measurement equaling 5,280 feet.

mile-age *n.* The distance traveled or measured in miles; an allowance given for traveling expenses at a set rate per mile; the average distance of miles a vehicle will travel on a gallon of gas.

mil-i-tant *adj.* Engaged in warfare or combat; aggressive. **militancy,**

mil-i-ta-rize *v.* To train or equip for war.

mil-i-tar-y *adj.* Of or related to arms, war, or soldiers. *n.* A nation's armed forces. **militarily** *adv.*

mi-li-tia *n.* A military service or armed forces called upon in case of an emergency.

milk *n.* A whitish fluid produced by the mammary glands of all mature female mammals as a source of food for their young. *v.* To draw milk from the breast or udder. *Slang* To take advantage of every possibility in a given situation. **milkiness** *n.*, **milky** *adj.*

milk-sop *n.* A man who lacks manly qualities.

milk-weed *n.* Any of various plants which secrete latex and have pointed pods that open to release seeds and downy flowers.

mill *n.* A building housing machinery for grinding grain into meal or flour; any of various machines which grind, crush, or press; a unit of money which equals 1/1000 of a U.S. dollar. *v.* To grind.

mill-er *n.* A person who operates, works, or owns a grain mill; a moth whose wings are covered with a powdery substance.

mil-li-ner *n.* Someone who designs, sells, or makes women's hats.

mil-lion *n.* A very large number equal to 1,000 x 1,000. **million** *adj.*, **millionth** *n.*, *adj.*

mime *v.* To act a part or performance without using words. *n.* An actor who portrays a part, emotion, or situation using only gestures and body language. **mimer** *n.*

mim-e-o-graph *n.* A duplicating machine that makes duplicates of typed or drawn information from a stencil through which ink is pressed.

mim-ic *v.* To imitate another person's behavior or speech.

mince *v.* To cut or chop something into small pieces.

mind *n.* The element of a human being which controls perception, thought, feeling, memory, and imagination. *v.* To obey; to take care of; to bring; to remember; to object to.

mine *n.* A pit or underground excavation from which metals or coal can be uncovered and removed. **miner** *n.*

mine *pron.* The one that belongs to me.

min-er-al *n.* A solid inorganic substance, such as silver, diamond, or quartz, which is taken from the earth. **mineral** *adj.*, **mineralize** *v.*

min-e-stro-ne *n.* A very thick vegetable soup that may contain pasta and beans.

min-gle *v.* To mix or come together.-er *n.*

min-i-a-ture *n.* A copy or model of something that has been greatly reduced in size.

min-i-com-put-er *n.* In Computer Science, a computer designed on a very small scale.

mini-disk *n.* *Computer Science* The 5 1/4 inch floppy disk which is used for storing information.

min-i-mum *n.*, *pl.* -ums *or* -uma The least, smallest, or lowest amount, degree, number, or position.

min-is-ter *n.* The pastor of a Protestant church; a high officer of state who is in charge of a governmental division.

mink *n.*, *pl.* **mink** *or* **minks**

A semiaquatic animal of the weasel family whose thick, lustrous fur is used for making fur coats.

min-now *n.* A small, fresh-water fish used as bait.

mi-nor *adj.* Not of legal age; lesser in degree, size or importance.

mi-nor-i-ty *n.*, *pl.* -ies The smaller in number of two groups constituting a whole; a part of the population that differs, as in race, sex, or religion.

min-ster *n.* A large cathedral or church.

min-strel *n.* A medieval traveling musician or poet.

mint *n.* A place where coins are made by a government; any of a variety of aromatic plants used for flavoring; candy flavored by such a plant. -y *adj.*

min-u-end *n.* A number of quantity from which another is to be subtracted.

min-u-et *n.* A slow, stately dance.

mi-nus *prep.*, *Math.* Reduced by subtraction. *n.* The minus sign (-); a negative number.

min-ute *n.* The unit of time which equals 60 seconds.

mi-nute *adj.* Extremely small in size.

mir-a-cle *n.* A supernatural event or happening regarded as an act of God.

mi-rage *n.* An optical illusion in which nonexistent bodies of water with reflections of objects are seen.

mire *n.* Soil or heavy mud.

mir-ror *n.* A surface of glass which reflects light, forming the image of an object.

mirth *n.* Merriment or joyousness expressed by laughter.

mis- *prefix* Wrong, bad, or ill.

mis-ad-ven-ture *n.* An unlucky mishap; a misfortune.

mis-an-thrope *n.* Someone who hates mankind.

mis-ap-pre-hend *v.* To understand something incorrectly; to misunderstand. **misapprehension** *n.*

mis-ap-pro-pri-ate *v.* To embezzle money; to use wrongly for one's own benefit. **misappropriation** *n.*

misc *abbr.* Miscellaneous.

mis-car-riage *n.* The premature birth of a fetus from the uterus.

mis-ce-ge-na-tion *n.* The marriage between two people of different races.

mis-cel-la-ne-ous *adj.* Consisting of a mixed variety of parts, elements, or characteristics.

mis-chance *n.* Bad luck or mishap.

mis-chief *n.* Behavior which causes harm, damage, or annoyance.

mis-chie-vous *adj.* Tending to behave in a playfully annoying way. -ly *adv.*

mis-ci-ble *adj.*, *Chem.* Capable of being mixed. **miscibility** *n.*

mis-con-ceive *v.* To misunderstand the meaning. **misconceiver**, -eption *n.*

mis-con-duct *n.* Improper conduct or behavior; bad management.

mis-count *v.* To count incorrectly; to miscalculate.

mis-cre-ant *n.* A person who is involved in criminal or evil acts; a heretic. **miscreant** *adj.*

mis-cue *n.* An error; a mistake.

mis-deed *n.* A wrong or improper act; an

evil deed.

mis-de-mean-or *n.*, *Law* A crime less serious than a felony.

mis-er *n.* A person who hoards money; a person who lives a meager life in order to hoard his money.

mis-er-a-ble *adj.* Very uncomfortable or unhappy; causing misery. **miserableness** *n.*, **miserably** *adv.*

mis-er-y *n.* A state of great unhappiness, distress, or pain.

mis-feed *n.* In computer science, the failure of paper or other media to pass through a printer or other device properly.

mis-fire *v.* To fail to explode, ignite, or fire. **misfire** *n.*

mis-fit *n.* A person who is not adjusted to his environment; anything which does not fit correctly.

mis-for-tune *n.* Bad luck or fortune.

mis-giv-ing *n.* A feeling of doubt.

mis-guide *v.* To guide incorrectly; to misdirect. **-ance** *n.*, **misguidedly** *adv.*

mis-han-dle *v.* To handle clumsily; to manage inefficiently.

mis-hap *n.* An unfortunate accident; bad luck.

mish-mash *n.* A jumble or hodgepodge.

mis-in-ter-pret *v.* To understand or explain incorrectly. **misinterpretation** *n.*

mis-judge *v.* To make a mistake in judgment. **misjudgment** *n.*

mis-lay *v.* To lose; to put something in a place and not remember where.

mis-lead *v.* To lead in a wrong direction; to deliberately deceive. **misleader** *n.*, **misleading** *adj.*

mis-no-mer *n.* A wrong or inappropriate name.

mis-pro-nounce *v.* To pronounce a word incorrectly.

mi-sog-a-my *n.* Hatred of marriage.

mi-sog-y-ny *n.* Hatred of women.

mis-place *v.* To mislay; to put in a wrong place.

mis-read *v.* To read or interpret incorrectly.

mis-rep-re-sent *v.* To represent wrongly, misleadingly, or falsely. **-ation** *n.*

mis-rule *n.* Misruling; the condition of being misruled; disorder.

mis-sal *n.* A book containing prayers and services, used in the Roman Catholic Church throughout the year.

mis-shape *v.* To deform; to shape badly; to distort. **misshapen** *adj.*

mis-sile *n.* An object that is thrown or shot at a target. **missilery** *n.*

mis-sion *n.* An instance or the act of sending; an assignment or task to be carried out.

mis-sion-ar-y *n.*, *pl.* **-ies** A person sent to do religious or charitable work, usually in a foreign country.

mis-spell *v.* To spell a word incorrectly. **misspelling** *n.*

mis-take *n.* A wrong statement, action, or decision. **mistaken**, **mistakable** *adj.*, **-ably** *adv.*, **mistake** *v.*

mis-tle-toe *n.* A parasitic plant with thick leaves, small yellowish flowers and white berries.

mis-treat *v.* To treat badly or wrongly. **mistreatment** *n.*

mis-tress *n.* A woman having authority, ownership, or a position of control; a woman having a sexual relationship with a man who is not her husband.

mis-tri-al *n.* A trial that is invalid because of an error during the procedure.

mis-trust *v.* To have doubt; to lack trust in something or someone. **mistrust** *n.* **mistrustful** *adj.*, **mistrustfully** *adv.*

mis-un-der-stand *v.* To interpret incorrectly; to fail to understand.

mite *n.* A very small insect; a small amount of money.

mi-ter *n.*

A joint made by cutting two pieces at an angle and then fitting them together.

mit-i-gate *v.* To make or become less severe or painful.

mi-to-sis *n.*, *pl.* **mitoses** A process of cell division in which chromatin divides into chromo-somes.

mitt *n.* A women's glove that covers only the wrist and hand, leaving the fingers exposed; in baseball, a glove for a catcher or first baseman made in the style of a mitten.

mix *v.* To blend or combine into one; to come or bring together. **mixable** *adj.*

mixed num-ber *n.* A number representing the sum of an integer and a fraction, such as 5 1/2.

mix-ture *n.* The state of being mixed; the process or act of mixing; a combination of two or two substances.

mix-up *n.* An instance or state of confusion.

moan *n.* A very low, dull sound indicative of pain or grief.

moat *n.* A deep and wide trench surrounding a castle, usually filled with water.

mob *n.* A large, unruly crowd. *v.* To overcrowd.

mo-bi-lize *v.* To put into motion; to make ready. **mobilization** *n.*

moc-ca-sin *n.* A shoe or slipper made of a soft leather.

mo-cha *n.* An Arabian coffee of superior quality; a flavoring with coffee, often used with chocolate.

mock *v.* To treat with contempt or scorn; to imitate a mannerism or sound closely; to mimic. *adv.* In an insincere manner. *n.* An imitation; a copy. **mockingly** *adv.*

mock-er-y *n.*, *pl.* **-ies** Insulting or contemptuous action or speech; a subject of laughter or sport; a false appearance.

mock--he-ro-ic *n.* A satirical imitation of the heroic manner or style.

mock-ing-bird *n.* A common bird that is remarkable for its exact imitations of the notes of other birds.

mock orange *n.* Any of several deciduous

shrubs.

mock-up or **mock--up** *n.* A model of a structure used for study, testing, or demonstration.

mod *n.* A modern and unusual style of dress. *adj.* Modern.

mode *n.* A way or method of doing something; a particular manner or form; the value or score that occurs most frequently in a set of data; the current fashion or style, as in dress.

mod-el *n.* A small representation of an object; a pattern that something will be based on; a design or type; one serving as an example; one who poses for an artist or photographer. **model** *v.*, **modeler** *n.*

mod-er-ate *adj.* Not excessive; tending toward the mean or average extent or quality; opposed to extreme political views. **moderate** *v.*, **moderation** *n.*

mod-er-a-tor *n.* A person who moderates; a person who presides over a discussion or meeting but takes no sides.

mod-ern *adj.* Typical of the recent past or the present; advanced or up-to-date. **modernity** *n.*, **modernly** *adv.*

mod-ern-ism *n.* A thought, action, or belief characteristic of modern times. **modernistic** *adj.*

mod-ern-ize *v.* To make or become modern. **modernization** *n.*

mod-est *adj.* Placing a moderate estimate on one's abilities or worth; retiring or reserved; limited in size or amount. **modesty** *n.*

mod-i-cum *n.* A small amount.

mod-i-fy *v.* To alter; to make different in character or form; to change to less extreme; to moderate. **modified**, **modifiable** *adj.*, **-ication**, **modifier** *n.*

mod-ish *adj.* Fashionable. **modishly** *adv.*, **modishness** *n.*

mo-diste *n.* A person dealing in fashionable clothing for women.

mod-u-late *v.* To soften; to temper; to vary the intensity of. *Music* To change from one key to another; to vary the tone or intensity of. **-ation**, **-or** *n.*, **modulative**, **modulatory** *adj.*

mod-ule *n.* One of a series of standardized components which work together in a system. *Electr.* A self-contained subassembly of electronic components, as a computer stage; the self-contained area of a spacecraft for performing a particular task. **-ar** *adj.*

mod-us op-er-an-di *n.* A method of operating or proceeding.

mod-us vi-ven-di *n.* A compromise which avoids difficulties.

mo-gul *n.* A very great or important person; a small hill or bump of ice and snow on a ski slope.

mo-hair *n.* The fabric or yarn made from the silky hair of the Angora goat.

moi-e-ty *n.*, *pl.* **-ies** A half; any portion; part or share.

moil *v.* To work hard; to drudge. **moil** *n.*

moi-re *n.* Fabric, especially silk or rayon having a wavy pattern.

moist *adj.* Slightly wet; damp; saturated with moisture or liquid. **moistly** *adv.*, **moistness** *n.*

mois-ten *v.* To make or become moist or slightly wet. **moistener** *n.*

mois-ture *n.* Liquid diffused or condensed in a relatively small quantity; dampness. **-ize** *v.*, **moisturizer** *n.*

mo-lar *n.* A grinding tooth which has a broad surface for grinding food, located in the back of the mouth.

mo-las-ses *n.* A thick, dark syrup produced when sugar is refined.

mold *n.* A superficial, often woolly growth produced on damp or decaying organic matter or on living organisms; a fungus that produces such a growth; crumbling, soft, friable earth suited to plant growth; distinctive nature or character; the frame on or around which an object is constructed; a cavity in which an object is shaped; general shape; form. **moldable** *adj.*

mold-board *n.* The curved blade of a plow.

mold-er *v.* To crumble or decay gradually and turn to dust.

mole *n.* A pigmented spot or mark on the human skin; a small, insectivorous mammal that lives mostly underground and has a narrow snout, small eyes, and silky fur; a large wall of stone or masonry used as a breakwater or pier.

mo-lec-u-lar *adj.* Of, relating to, or caused by molecules.

mo-lec-u-lar bi-ol-o-gy *n.* The branch of biology dealing with the structure and development of biological systems which are studied in terms of their molecular constituents.

mol-e-cule *n.* The simplest structural unit into which a substance can be divided and still retain its identity.

mo-lest *v.* To bother, annoy, or persecute; to accost sexually. **molestation**, **molester** *n.*

mol-li-fy *v.* To make less angry; to soften; to make less intense or severe. **mollification** *n.*

mol-lusk or **mol-lusc** *n.* Any of various largely marine invertebrates, including the edible shellfish.

mol-ly-cod-dle *v.* To spoil by pampering; to coddle.

molt *v.* To cast off or shed an external covering, as horns, feathers, or skin, which is periodically replaced by new growth. **molt** *n.*

mol-ten *adj.* Transformed to liquid form by heat.

mo-lyb-de-num *n.* A hard, gray metallic element used to harden steel alloys, symbolized by Mo.

mo-men-tar-i-ly *adv.* For just a moment; soon; from moment to moment.

mo-men-tar-y *adj.* Lasting just a moment; occurring presently or at every moment.

mo-men-tous *adj.* Of great importance or consequence; significant. **momentously** *adv.*, **momentousness** *n.*

mo-men-tum *n.*, *pl.* **-ta** *or* **-tums** A property of a moving body which determines the length of time required to bring it to rest when under the action of a constant force.

mon-arch *n.* A person who reigns over a kingdom or empire; a large orange and black butterfly.
monarchic, monarchical *adj.*

mon-ar-chism *n.* The principles or system of a monarchic government.
monarchist *n.*, **monarchistic** *adj.*

mon-ar-chy *n.*, *pl.* **-chies** Government by a monarch; sovereign control; a government or nation ruled by a monarch.

mon-as-ter-y *n.*, *pl.* **-ies** A house for persons under religious vows. **-ial** *adj.*

mo-nas-tic *adj.* Of, relating to, or typical of monasteries, monks, or life in monasteries.

mo-nas-ti-cism *n.* The monastic lifestyle or system.

mon-au-ral *adj.* Of or relating to a system of transmitting or recording sound by techniques in which one or more sources are channeled into one carrier.

mon-e-tar-y *adj.* Of or relating to money or how it is circulated. **-ily** *adv.*

mon-ey *n.* Anything which has or is assigned value and is used as a medium of exchange.

mon-ey-lend-er *n.* Someone whose business is lending money to others with interest.

mon-ger *n.* One who attempts to stir up or spread something that is undesirable; one who deals.

mon-goose *n.*, *pl.* **-ses** A chiefly African or Asian mammal which has the ability to kill venomous snakes.

mon-grel *n.* An animal or plant, especially a dog, produced by interbreeding.

mo-ni-tion *n.* A caution or warning, as for an impending danger.

mon-i-tor *n.* A student assigned to assist a teacher; a receiver used to view the picture being picked up by a television camera; the image being generated by a computer. **monitorial** *adj.*

mon-i-to-ry *adj.* Giving a caution or conveying a warning.

monk *n.* A man who is a member of a religious order and lives in a monastery. **monkish** *adj.*,
monkishly *adv.*, **monkishness** *n.*

mon-key *n.*, *pl.* **-keys**

A member of the older primates, excluding man, having a long-tail; a smaller species as distinguished from the larger apes. *v.* To play or fool around; to tamper with.

monk's cloth *n.* A sturdy cotton cloth having a coarse basket weave.

monks-hood *n.* A normally poisonous plant of the genus Aconitum, having variously colored hooded flowers.

mon-o *n.* Mononucleosis.

mon-o-chro-mat-ic *adj.* Of, consisting of, or having one color. **-ally** *adv.*

mon-o-cle *n.* An eyeglass for one eye.

mon-o-cot-y-le-don *n.* Any of various plants having a single embryonic seed leaf appearing at germination.
monocotyledonous *adj.*

mo-noc-u-lar *adj.* Of, relating to, or having one eye.

mo-nog-a-my *n.* Marriage or sexual relationship with only one person at a time. **monogamist** *n.*, **-ous** *adj.*

mon-o-gram *n.* A design consisting of one or more initials. **monogram** *v.*

mon-o-graph *n.* A scholarly pamphlet or book on a particular and usually limited subject. **monographic** *adj.*

mon-o-lin-gual *adj.* Knowing only one language.

mon-o-lith *n.* A single block of stone, as one used in architecture or sculpture.
monolithic *adj.*

mon-o-logue *or* **mon-o-log** *n.* A speech by one person which precludes conversation; a series of jokes and stories delivered by a comedian. **-ist** *n.*

mon-o-ma-ni-a *n.* A pathological obsession or mental disorder in which a person is totally obsessed with a single idea. **-c** *n.*, **monomaniacal** *adj.*

mo-no-mi-al *n.* An algebraic expression consisting of only one term.

mon-o-nu-cle-ar *adj.* Having only one nucleus.

mon-o-nu-cle-o-sis *n.* An infectious disease marked by an abnormal increase of too many cells having one nucleus.

mon-o-nu-cle-o-tide *n.* A nucleotide containing one molecule each of a phosphoric acid, a pentose, and either a purine or pyrimidine base.

mon-o-phon-ic *adj.* Having only one part; a solo voice with accompaniment, as a piano.

mon-o-plane *n.* An aircraft with one wing or one set of wings.

mo-nop-o-ly *n.*, *pl.* **-ies** Exclusive ownership or control, as of a service or commodity, by a single group, person, or company; a group, person, or company having a monopoly; exclusive possession; a service or commodity controlled by a single group. **-ist**, **-ization** *n.*, **-istic** *adj.*, **monopolize** *v.*

mon-o-rail *n.* A single rail serving as a track on which a wheeled vehicle can travel; a vehicle that travels on such a rail.

mon-o-so-di-um glu-ta-mate *n.* Sodium glutamate used as a seasoning, abbreviated as MSG.

mon-o-syl-la-ble *n.* A word of one syllable. **-ic** *adj.*, **monosyllabically** *adv.*

mon-o-the-ism *n.* The belief that there is just one God. **monotheist** *n.*, **monotheistic** *adj.*

mon-o-tone *n.* The utterance of sounds, syllables, or words in a single unvarying tone.

mo-not-o-nous *adj.* Spoken in a monotone; lacking in variety. **monotonously** *adv.*, **monotony** *n.*

mon-ox-ide *n.* An oxide that contains one oxygen atom per molecule.

mon-soon *n.* A periodic wind, especially in the Indian Ocean and southern Asia; the season of the monsoon in India and parts of Asia.

mon-ster *n.* An animal or plant having an abnormal form or structure; an animal, plant, or object having a frightening or deformed shape; one unusually large for its kind. **-ity, -ousness** *n.*, **-ous** *adj.*, **-ously** *adv.*

mon-tage *n.* A composite picture made by combining several separate pictures or parts of several pictures; a rapid succession of images in a motion picture, designed to illustrate an association of ideas.

month *n.* One of the twelve divisions of a calendar year.

month-ly *adj.* Occurring, done, or payable each month. *n.* A publication issued once a month. **monthly** *adv.*

mon-u-ment *n.* An object, such as a statue, built as a memorial to a person or an event; a burial vault; an area set aside for public use by a government because of its aesthetic, historical, or ecological significance.

mon-u-men-tal *adj.* Serving as or similar to a monument; massive; extremely important. **monumentally** *adv.*

mooch *v. Slang* To acquire by begging; to steal. **moocher** *n.*

mood *n.* A conscious yet temporary state of mind or emotion; the prevailing spirit; a verb form or set of verb forms inflected to show the understanding of the person speaking regarding the condition expressed.

mood-y *adj.* Subject to moods, especially depression; gloomy **-ily** *adv.*, **-iness** *n.*

moon *n.* The earth's only natural satellite; a natural satellite which revolves around a planet. *v.* To dream.

moon-beam *n.* A ray of moonlight.

moon-light *n.* The light of the moon. *v.* To hold a second job in addition to a regular one. **moonlighter** *n.*

moon-lit *adj.* Lit by the moon.

moon-rise *n.* The rising of the moon above the horizon; the time of the moon's rising.

moon-scape *n.* The surface of the moon as seen or as depicted.

moon-set *n.* The descent of the moon below the horizon; the time of the moon's setting.

moon-shine *n.* Moonlight; empty talk; nonsense; intoxicating liquor, especially illegally distilled corn whiskey.

moon shot *n.* The launching of a spacecraft to the moon or its vicinity.

moon-stone *n.* A transparent or translucent feldspar of pearly or opaline luster used as a gem.

moor *v.* To make fast with cables, lines, or anchors. *n.* An expanse of open, rolling, infertile land. **moorage** *n.*

moor-ing *n.* A place where a ship or aircraft can be secured; a stabilizing device.

moose *n., pl.* **moose**

A very large North American deer having a large broad muzzle.

moot *v.* To bring up as for debate or discussion; to argue. *adj.* Open to debate; having no legal significance.

mope *v.* To be uncaring or dejected; to move in a leisurely manner. **moper** *n.*

mop-pet *n.* A child; a darling baby.

mop--up *n.* The process of completing a task.

mo-raine *n.* An accumulation of earth and stones carried and finally deposited by a glacier.

mor-al *adj.* Of or pertaining to conduct or character from the point of right and wrong; teaching a conception of right behavior. *n.* The lesson to be learned from a story, event, or teaching. **morals** Standards of right and wrong. **morally** *adv.*

mo-rale *n.* An individual's state of mind with respect to the tasks he or she is expected to perform; esprit de corps.

mor-al-ist *n.* Someone concerned with moral principles and questions; someone who practices morality. **moralism** *n.*, **-ic** *adj.*, **-ally** *adv.*

mo-ral-i-ty *n., pl.* **-ies** The quality of being morally right; moral behavior.

mor-al-ize *v.* To think, discuss, or judge in a moral sense. **moralization, moralizer** *n.*

mo-rass *n.* A marsh or bog; low-lying wet, soft ground; something which hinders or overwhelms.

mor-a-to-ri-um *n., pl.* **-iums** or **-ia** A temporary pause in activity; an authorization given legally to a debtor to suspend payments for a period of time.

mo-ray *n.* Any of various marine eels found usually in tropical waters.

mor-bid *adj.* Of, pertaining to, or affected by disease; suggesting an unhealthy mental state of being; gruesome. **-ity, -ness** *n.*, **-ly** *adv.*

mor-da-cious *adj.* Violent in action; prone to biting. **mordacity** *n.*

mor-dant *adj.* Biting and caustic in thought, manner, or style. **mordancy** *n.*, **mordantly** *adv.*

mo-rel *n.* An edible mushroom having a sponge-like cap or hood.

more-o-ver *adv.* Furthermore; besides.

mo-res *n., pl.* The moral customs and traditional customs of a social group.

morgue *n.* A place in which dead bodies are kept until claimed or identified; the reference file at a newspaper or magazine office.

mor-i-bund *adj.* Approaching extinction; at the point of death. **moribundity** *n.*

morn *n.* Morning.

morn-ing *n.* The early part of the day; the time from midnight to noon.

mo-roc-co *n.* A soft, textured leather made of goatskin.

mo-rose *adj.* Having a sullen disposition; marked by gloom. **morosely** *adv.*, **moroseness** *n.*

mor-pheme *n.* A meaningful unit which cannot be divided into smaller meaningful parts. **morphemic** *adj.*, **morphemically** *adv.*

mor-phi-a *n.* Morphine.

mor-phine *n.* A highly addictive narcotic derived from opium which can be used as either a sedative or to dull pain.

mor-phol-o-gy *n.* The study of the form and structure of living organisms, considered separate from function; the study and description of word formation in a language. **morphological, morphologically** *adj.*, **morphologist** *n.*

mor-ris *n.* An old English folk dance.

mor-row *n.* The next day.

mor-tal-i-ty *n.*, *pl.* **-ies** The state or condition of being mortal; the death rate; deaths.

mor-tar *n.* A strong vessel in which materials can be crushed or ground with a pestle; a muzzle-loading cannon for firing shells at short ranges and at high angles; a mixed building material, as cement with sand and water, which hardens and is used in masonry or plaster.

mor-tar-board *n.*

A square board with a handle, for holding mortar; an academic cap topped by a stiff, flat square.

mort-gage *n.* A temporary conveyance of property to a creditor as security for the repayment of a debt; a contract or deed defining the terms of a mortgage. *v.* To pledge or transfer by means of a mortgage. **mortgagee, mortgagor** *n.*

mor-ti-cian *n.* An undertaker.

mor-ti-fy *v.* To destroy the strength or functioning of; to subdue or deaden through pain or self-denial; to subject to severe humiliation; to become gangrenous. **-ication** *n.*, **-ingly** *adv.*

mor-tise *n.* A usually hollowed out rectangular hole in a piece of wood which receives a tenon of another piece to form a joint.

mor-tu-ar-y *n.*, *pl.* **-ies** A place in which dead bodies are temporarily held until burial or cremation.

mo-sa-ic *n.* A decorative inlaid design of small pieces, as of colored glass or tile, in cement. **mosaic** *adj.*

mo-sey *v.* *Slang* To move slowly; to shuffle along.

mosque *n.* A Moslem house of worship.

mos-qui-to *n.*, *pl.* **-toes** or **-tos** Any of various winged insects of which the females suck the blood of animals or humans.

mos-qui-to net *n.* A fine net or screen to keep out mosquitoes.

moss *n.* Delicate, small green plants which often form a dense, mat-like growth. **mossiness** *n.*, **mossy** *adj.*

moss-back *n.* An old-fashioned person.

most *adj.* The majority of. *n.* The greatest amount. *pron.* The largest part or number. *adv.* In or to the highest degree.

most-ly *adv.* For the most part; principally.

mot *n.* A short, witty saying.

mote *n.* A particle, as of dust; a speck of dust.

mo-tet *n.* A polyphonic vocal composition, based on a religious text and usually sung without accompaniment.

moth-er *n.* A female parent; one who holds a maternal relationship toward another; an old or elderly woman; a woman in a position of authority. *adj.* Of, relating to, or being a mother. *v.* To give birth to; to care for or protect like a mother. **motherhood, motherliness** *n.*, **mothery** *adj.*

moth-er-in-law *n.* The mother of one's spouse.

moth-er-land *n.* The country or land of one's birth.

moth-er-of-pearl *n.* The pearly iridescent internal layer of a mollusk shell.

mo-tif *n.* An underlying main element or theme that recurs in a musical, artistic, or literary work.

mo-tile *adj.* Exhibiting or capable of movement.

mo-tion *n.* The act or process of changing position; a purposeful movement of the body or a bodily part; a formal proposal or suggestion that action be taken. **motion** *v.*, **motionless** *adj.*

mo-ti-vate *v.* Causing to act.

mo-tive *n.* Something, as a need or desire, which causes a person to act; a musical motif. *adj.* Causing or having the power to cause motion.

mot-ley *adj.* Composed of a variety of components.

mo-tor *n.* Any of various devices which develop energy or impart motion.

mo-tor-bike *n.* A small motorcycle.

mo-tor-car *n.* An automobile.

mo-tor-cy-cle *n.* A two-wheeled automotive vehicle. **motorcycle** *v.*,

mo-tor-ize *v.* To equip with a motor; to supply with motor-propelled vehicles.

mo-tor-man *n.* An operator of a locomotive engine, streetcar, or subway train.

mo-tor scoo-ter *n.* A small two-wheeled vehicle similar to a scooter but having a low-powered gasoline engine.

mo-tor ve-hi-cle *n.* A motor-powered vehicle which travels freely without the need for rails.

mot-tle *v.* To mark or be marked with spots or streaks of different colors or shades; to blotch. *n.* A blotch.

mot-to *n.*, *pl.* **-toes** or **-tos** A sentence, phrase, or word expressing purpose, character, or conduct; an appropriate phrase inscribed on something.

moue *n.* A grimace, as of disapproval or

disdain.

mound *n.* A small hill of earth, sand, gravel or debris.

mount *n.* To rise or ascend; to get up on; climb upon; to increase in amount or extent; to organize and equip; to launch and carry out. *n.* A horse or other animal used for riding; a support to which something is fixed.

moun-tain *n.* A land mass that rises above its surroundings and is higher than a hill.

moun-tain-eer *n.* An inhabitant of a mountainous region; one who climbs mountains for sport. **mountaineer** *v.*

moun-tain goat *n.* A long-haired Rocky Mountain goat.

moun-tain laurel *n.* A low-growing evergreen shrub with poisonous leaves and clusters of pink or white flowers.

moun-tain lion *n.* A large wildcat; puma.

moun-tain-ous *adj.* Of or relating to a region with many mountains.

moun-tain-side *n.* The side of a mountain.

moun-tain-top *n.* The top of a mountain.

moun-te-bank *n.* A quack doctor; a false and boastful pretender; a charlatan.

mount-ing *n.* A supporting frame or structure of an article.

mourn *v.* To express grief; to feel grief or sorrow; to follow the religious customs and rituals surrounding the death of a loved one.

mouse *n.,* *pl.* **mice**

A small rodent that frequents human habitations; a timid person.

mousse *n.* A light frozen dessert.

mouth *n.,* *pl.* **mouths** The bodily opening through which food is taken in.

mouth-off *v.* To speak disrespectfully.

mouth--to--mouth *adj.* Pertaining to a method of artificial resuscitation.

mov-ie *n.* A motion picture; motion picture industry.

mow *v.* To cut down, as with a machine. *n.* The part of the barn where hay or grain is stored. **mower** *n.*

moz-za-rel-la *n.* A soft white cheese with a mild flavor.

much *adj.* In great amount, quantity, degree, or extent. *adv.* To a great extent. *n.* Something impressive.

mu-ci-lage *n.* A sticky substance that is similar to plant gums.

muck *n.* Moist farmyard manure; moist, sticky soil or filth. *v.* To dirty with or as with muck. **mucky** *adj.*

muck-rake *v.* To search out and publicly expose real or apparent misconduct on the part of well-known persons.

mu-co-sa *n.* A mucous membrane.

mu-cous *adj.* Of, pertaining to, or secreting mucus.

mu-cous mem-brane *n.* A membrane secreting mucus which lines bodily channels that come into contact with air.

mu-cus *n.* The viscous liquid secreted by glands by the mucous membrane.

mu-lat-to *n.,* *pl.* **-tos** *or* **-toes** A person with one white parent and one black parent; a person of mixed black and white ancestry.

mulct *n.* A financial penalty or fine. *v.* To punish by fining; to obtain by fraud or theft.

mull *v.* To mix or grind thoroughly; to ponder; to think about.

mul-lah *n.* A Muslim leader and clergyman.

mul-lein *n.* A plant having yellow flowers and downy leaves.

mul-let *n.* An edible marine and freshwater fish.

mul-li-gan stew *n.* A stew made of various vegetables and meats.

multi- *prefix* Much, many, multiple; more than two.

mul-ti-dis-ci-plin-ary *adj.* Using or related to a combination of several disciplines for a common cause.

mul-ti-far-i-ous *adj.* Having much diversity. **multifariously** *adv.*

mul-ti-form *adj.* Having many appearances or forms. **multiformity** *n.*

mul-ti-lane *adj.* Having several lanes.

mul-ti-lat-er-al *adj.* Having many sides; involving or participated in by more than two parties or nations. **-ly** *adv.*

mul-ti-lin-gual *adj.* Expressed in several languages. **multilingualism** *n.*

mul-ti-mil-lion-aire *n.* A person whose fortune is worth many millions of dollars.

mul-ti-na-tion-al *adj.* Involving or relating to several countries.

mul-tip-a-rous *adj.* Producing more than one at a birth.

mul-ti-ple *adj.* Relating to or consisting of more than one individual, part, or element. *Math.* A number into which another number can be divided with no remainders.

mul-ti-ple scle-ro-sis *n.* A degenerative condition marked by patches of hardened tissue in the spinal cord or the brain.

mul-ti-pli-ca-tion *n.* The mathematical operation by which a number indicates how many times another number is to be added to itself.

mul-ti-plic-i-ty *n.,* *pl.* **-ies** A large number or variety.

mul-ti-pli-er *n.* A number that is or is to be multiplied by another number.

mul-ti-ply *v.* To increase in amount or number; to combine by multiplication.

mul-ti-sense *adj.* Having several meanings.

mul-ti-stage *adj.* Consisting of propulsion units which operate in turn.

mul-ti-tude *n.* A very large amount or number. **multitudinous** *adj.*

mul-ti-vi-ta-min *n.* A pill containing several vitamins that are essential to health.

mum-mer *n.* A performer who acts in a pantomime.

mum-mery *n.*, *pl.* **-ies** A hypocritical or ridiculous ceremony.

mum-mi-fy *v.* To dry and embalm as a mummy; to cause to shrivel and dry up. **mummification** *n.*

munch *v.* To chew noisily. **muncher** *v.*

mun-dane *adj.* Pertaining to or relating to the world; characterized by the ordinary and practical. **mundanely** *adv.*

mu-nic-i-pal *adj.* Relating to or typical of a municipality; having self-government in local affairs. **municipally** *adv.*, **municipality** *n.*

mu-nif-i-cent *adj.* Very liberal in giving; lavish. **-ence** *n.*, **munificently** *adv.*

mu-ni-tions *pl. n.* Guns and ammunition.

mu-ral *n.* A painting created on a wall.

murk *n.* Darkness; gloom. **murkily** *adv.*,

mur-rain *n.* A plague affecting plants or domestic animals.

mus-cae vo-li-tan-tes *n.* A condition of spots before the eyes due to cells and cell fragments in the vitreous humor and lens.

mus-cle *n.* Bodily tissue which consists of long cells that contract when stimulated. **muscle** *v.*

mus-cu-lar *adj.* Relating to or consisting of muscle; brawny; having well-developed muscles. **muscularity** *n.*

mus-cu-lar dys-tro-phy *n.* A noncontagious hereditary disease characterized by gradual but irreversible muscular deterioration.

mus-cu-la-ture *n.* The muscles of an animal's body.

muse *n.* A state of deep thought.

mu-sette *n* A small bagpipe having a soft, sweet tone or sound; a small bag with a shoulder strap.

mu-sic *n.* Organized tones in sequences and combinations which make up a continuous composition. **musical** *adj.*

mu-si-cian *n.* A composer or performer of music. **-ly** *adj.*, **musicianship** *n.*

mu-si-col-o-gy *n.* The scientific and historical study of music. **musicological** *adj.*, **musicologist** *n.*

mus-ket *n.* A heavy, large-caliber shoulder gun with a long barrel.

musk-mel-on *n.* A sweet melon having a rough rind and juicy, edible flesh.

musk-rat *n.*

A rodent of North America with brown fur.

muss *v.* To make messy or untidy. *Slang* A confused conflict. **mussily** *adv.*, **mussiness** *n.*, **mussy** *adj.*

mus-sel *n.* A freshwater bivalve mollusk.

must *v.* To be forced to; to have to.

mus-tang *n.* A wild horse of the western plains.

mus-ter *v.* To come or bring together; to convene; to bring or call forth.

mustn't *contr.* Must not.

mus-ty *adj.* Moldy or stale in odor or taste. **mustily** *adv.*, **mustiness** *n.*

mu-ta-ble *adj.* Prone to or capable of change. **mutability**, **mutableness** *n.*

mu-tant *n.* An individual or organism which differs from the parental strain as a result of mutation. **mutant** *adj.*

mu-tate *v.* To undergo or cause to undergo mutation. **mutative** *adj.*

mu-ta-tion *n.* A change in form. *Biol.* A sudden change in the hereditary makeup of an organism in which there is a physical or chemical change in the genes.

mute *adj.* Unable to speak. *n.* A person who cannot speak. **-ly** *adv.*, **-ness** *n.*

mu-ti-late *v.* To deprive of an essential part, as a limb of the body; to maim or cripple; to make imperfect. **mutilation**, **mutilator** *n.*

mu-ti-ny *n.*, *pl.* **-ies** Open revolt against lawful authority. **mutineer** *n.*,

mut-ter *v.* To speak or utter in a low voice; to grumble; to complain.

mut-ton *n.* The flesh of a fully grown sheep, used for food. **muttony** *adj.*

mu-tu-al *adj.* Having the same relationship; received and directed in equal amounts. **mutuality** *n.*

my *adj.* Relating to or of myself or one. *interj.* Used to express surprise, dismay, or pleasure.

my-ce-li-um *n.*, *pl.* **-lia** A mass of interwoven filaments which form the main growing structure of a fungus. **-ial** *adj.*

my-col-o-gy *n.* A branch of botany; the scientific study of fungi. **mycological** *adj.*, **mycologist** *n.*

my-e-li-tis *n.* An inflammation of the spinal cord or bone marrow.

my-elo-ma *n.* A tumor of the bone marrow.

my-na *or* **my-nah** *n.* A dark brown, slightly crested bird of south-eastern Asia.

myo-car-dio-graph *n.* A recording tool which traces the action of the heart muscles.

myo-car-di-um *n.* The muscular layer of the heart, located in the middle of the heart wall.

myr-i-a-pod *n.* An arthropod, having a segmented body and many legs.

myr-mi-don *n.* A loyal follower.

my-self *pron.* The one identical with me; used reflexively; my normal, healthy state or condition.

mys-ter-y *n.*, *pl.* **-ies** Something not understood; a problem or puzzle; an enigma; a Christian sacrament.

mys-ti-cism *n.* The spiritual discipline of communion with God.

mys-ti-fy *v.* To perplex, to bewilder. **mystification** *n.*, **mystifyingly** *adv.*

mys-tique *n.* A body of beliefs connected with a group, person, idea, or thing.

my-thol-o-gy *n.*, *pl.* **-ies** A body of myths dealing with gods and heroes. **mythological** *adj.*, **mythologist** *n.*

myx-e-de-ma *n.* A disease caused by decreased activity of the thyroid gland and marked by loss of mental and physical vigor.

N, n The fourteenth letter of the English alphabet.

nab *v.*, *Slang* To seize; to arrest.

na-cho *n.* A tortilla, often small and triangular in shape, topped with cheese or chili sauce and baked.

nag *v.* To bother by scolding or constant complaining. *n.* A worthless horse. **nagger** *n.*, **nagging** *adj.*, **naggingly** *adv.*

nai-ad *n.*, Gr. Mythol. A nymph presiding over and living in springs, brooks, and fountains.

nail *n.* A thin pointed piece of metal for hammering into wood and other materials to hold pieces together.

nail-brush *n.* A small brush with frim bristles used to clean the hands and nails.

nail file *n.* A small instrument with a rough surface, used to shape the fingernails.

na-ive *adj.* Simple and trusting; not sophisticated. **-ly** *adv.*, **naiveness** *n.*

na-ked *adj.* Without clothes on the body; nude. **nakedly** *adv.*, **nakedness** *n.*

nam-by--pam-by *adj.* Weak; indecisive.

name *n.* A title or word by which something or someone is known. *v.* To give a name. **namable**, **namable** *adj.*

name--call-ing *n.* The use of offending names to induce condemnation or rejection.

name-less *adj.* Having no name; anonymous. **namelessly** *adv.*, **-ness** *n.*

nan-ny *n.* A child's nurse; one who cares for small children.

nan-ny goat *n.* A female domestic goat.

nap *n.* A short rest or sleep, often during the day. *v.* The surface of a piece of leather or fabric. **napless**, **napped** *adj.*

na-palm *n.* A mixture of aluminum soaps used in jelling gasoline for use in bombs or by flame throwers.

nape *n.* The back of the neck.

nar-cis-sus *n.* A widely grown type of bulbous plant which includes the jonquil, narcissus, and daffodil.

nar-co-sis *n.* A deep drug induced state of stupor or unconsciousness.

nar-cot-ic *n.* A drug which dulls the senses, relieves pain, and induces a deep sleep; if abused, it can become habit-forming and cause convulsions or comas. **narcotically** *adv.*

nar-rate *v.* To tell a story or give a description in detail. **narration** *n.*, **narrator** *v.*

nar-row *adj.* Slender or small in width; of less than standard width. **narrowly** *adj.*, **narrowness** *n.*

nar-whal *n.*

An aquatic mammal of the Arctic regions, closely related to the white whale, having a long, twisted, protruding tusk in the male.

na-sal *adj.* Of or pertaining to the nose.

na-stur-tium *n.* A five-petaled garden plant usually having red, yellow, or orange flowers.

nas-ty *adj.* Dirty, filthy, or indecent; unpleasant. **nastily** *adv.*, **nastiness** *n.*

na-tal *adj.* Pertaining to or associated with birth.

na-tion *n.* A group of people made up of one or more nationalities under one government. **-al** *adj.*, **-ally** *adv.*

na-tion-al-ism *n.* Devotion to or concern for one's nation.

na-tion-al-i-ty *n.* The fact or condition of belonging to a nation.

na-tion-al-ize *v.* To place a nation's resources and industries under the control of the state.

na-tive *n.* A person born in a country or place.

na-tiv-i-ty *n.* Birth, circumstances, or conditions.

nat-ty *adj.* Tidy and trimly neat. **nattily** *adv.*, **nattiness** *n.*

nat-u-ral *adj.* Produced or existing by nature. *Mus.* A note that is not sharp or flat. **naturalness** *n.*, **naturally** *adv.*

nat-u-ral child-birth *n.* Childbirth with little stress or pain, requiring training for the mother and father and medical supervision, but without the use of drugs, anesthesia, or surgery.

nat-u-ral-ize *v.* To confer the privileges and rights of full citizenship. **naturalization** *n.*

na-ture *n.* The universe and its phenomena; one's own character or temperament. **natured** *adj.*

naught *n.* Nothing; the number 0; zero.

naugh-ty *adj.* Unruly; not proper; ill-behaved. **naughtily** *adv.*, **-iness** *n.*

nau-se-a *n.* An upset stomach with a feeling that one needs to vomit. **-ous** *adj.*, **nauseate** *v.*, **-tingly** *adv.*

nau-ti-cal *adj.* Pertaining to ships or seamanship. **nautically** *adv.*

na-val *adj.* Of or relating to ships; maritime.

na-vel *n.* A small mark or scar on the abdomen where the umbilical cord was attached.

nav-i-ga-ble *adj.* Sufficiently deep and wide enough to allow ships to pass. **navigableness** *n.*, **navigably** *adv.*

nav-i-gate *v.* To plan the course of a ship or aircraft; to steer a course. **-tion**, **navigator** *n.*, **navigational** *adj.*

na-vy *n.* One of a nation's organizations for defense; a nation's fleet of ships; a very dark blue.

neap tide *n.* A tide in the minimum range which occurs during the first and third quarter of the moon.

near *adv.* At, to, or within a short time or distance. **nearness** *n.*

near-by *adj. & adv.* Close by; near at hand; adjacent.

near-sight-ed *adj.* Able to see clearly at short distances only. **-ly** *adv.*, **nearsightedness** *n.*

neat *adj.* Tidy and clean; free from disorder and dirt. **neatly** *adv.*, **neatness** *n.*

neat-en *v.* To make neat; to set in order.

neb-u-lous *adj.* Confused or vague;

hazy. **-ly** *adv.*, **nebulousness** *n.*

nec·es·sar·y *adj.* Unavoidable; required; essential; needed. **necessarily** *adv.*

ne·ces·si·tate *v.* To make necessary; to oblige.

ne·ces·si·ty *n.*, *pl.* **-ies** The condition of being necessary; the condition making a particular course of action necessary.

neck *n.* The part of the body which connects the head and trunk; a narrow part or projection, as of land, a stringed instrument, or bottle. *v.* To caress and kiss.

neck·tie *n.* A narrow strip of material worn around the neck and tied.

nec·tar *n.* A sweet fluid in various flowers, gathered by bees to help make honey. **nectarous** *adj.*

nee *n.* The surname a woman was born with.

need *n.* The lack of something desirable, useful, or necessary.

need·ful *adj.* Necessary. *n.* Something needed. **needfully** *adv.*, **needfulness** *n.*

nee·dle *n.* A slender, pointed steel implement which contains an eye through which thread is passed. *v.* To tease. **needlelike** *adj.*

needle·point *n.* Decorative stitching done on canvas in even stitches across counted threads. **needlepoint** *adj.*

need·less *adj.* Unnecessary; not needed. **needlessly** *adv.*, **needlessness** *n.*

need·n't *contr.* Need not.

ne·far·i·ous *adj.* Extremely wicked; despicable. **-le** *adv.*, **-ness** *n.*

neg *abbr.* Negative.

ne·gate *v.* To nullify; to deny. **-tor** *n.*

ne·ga·tion *n.* A judgement; a negative statement, or doctrine.

neg·a·tive *adj.* Expressing denial or disapproval; not positive. In photography, a negative photo. **negatively** *adj.*, **negativeness** *n.*

neg·lect *v.* To ignore; to pay no attention to; to fail to perform. **neglectful** *adj.*

neg·li·gee *n.* A woman's loose-fitting dressing gown.

neg·li·gent *adj.* To neglect what needs to be done.

ne·go·ti·ate *v.* To confer with another person to reach an agreement. **negotiation**, **negotiator** *n.*

ne·groid *adj.* Of or relating to the Black race.

neigh·bor *n.* One who lives near another. **neighboring** *adj.* **neighbor** *v.*

neigh·bor·hood *n.* A section or small region that possesses a specific quality.

neigh·bor·ly *adj.* Characteristic of congenial neighbors; friendly. **neighborliness** *n.*

nei·ther *adj.* Not one or the other. *pron.* Not the one or the other.

nel·son *n.* A wrestling hold using the application of leverage against an opponent's arm, head, and neck.

neo *prefix* Recent; new.

neo·dym·i·um *n.* A metallic element of the rare-earth group, symbolized by Nd.

ne·on *n.* An inert gaseous element used in lighting fixtures, symbolized by Ne. **neon**, **neoned** *adj.*

ne·o·nate *n.* A newborn child less than a month old.

ne·o·na·tol·o·gy *n.* The medical study of the first 60 days of a baby's life.

neo·phyte *n.* A novice; a beginner.

ne·o·plasm *n.* A tumor tissue serving no physiologic function. **neoplastic** *adj.*

neph·ew *n.* The son of one's sister, brother, sister-in-law, or brother-in-law.

ne·phrit·ic *adj.* Relating to the kidneys; afflicted with an inflammation of the kidneys.

nep·o·tism *n.* The act of showing favoritism to relatives or friends in the work force. **nepotist** *n.*

nep·tu·ni·um *n.* A radioactive metallic element.

nerve *n.* The bundles of fibers which convey sensation and originate motion through the body. *Slang* Impudent.

nerve·less *adj.* Lacking courage or strength. **-ly** *adv.*, **nervelessness** *n.*

nerv·ous *adj.* Affecting the nerves or the nervous system; agitated; worried. **nervously** *adv.*, **nervousness** *n.*

nervous system *n.*, *Physiol.* The body system that coordinates, regulates, and controls the various internal functions and responses to stimuli.

nest *n.* A place, shelter, or home built by a bird to hold its eggs and young.

nest egg *n.* A supply of money accumulated or saved for future use.

nes·tle *v.* To lie close to. **nestler** *n.*

net *n.* A meshed fabric made of cords, ropes, threads, or other material knotted or woven together; the profit, weight, or price which remains after all additions, subtractions, or adjustments have been made. **net** *v.*

neth·er *adj.* Situated below or beneath.

neth·er·most *adj.* Lowest; farthest down.

net·tle *n.* A plant having toothed leaves covered with stinging hairs.

net·work *n.* A system of interlacing tracks, channels, or lines; an interconnected system.

neu·ral *adj.* Relating to a nerve or the nervous system. **neurally** *adv.*

neu·ral·gia *n.* Pain that occurs along the course of a nerve.

neu·ri·tis *n.* An inflammation of a nerve which causes pain, the loss of reflexes, and muscular decline. **neurotic** *adj.*

neu·rol·o·gy *n.* The medical and scientific study of the nervous system and disorders. **neurological** *adj.*, **neurologist** *n.*

neu·ron *or* **neu·rone** *n.*, *Anat.* A granular cell nerve which is the main functional unit of the nervous system.

neu·ro·sis *n.* Any one of various functional disorders of the mind or emotions having no physical cause. **neurotic** *adj.* *n.*, **neurotically** *adv.*

neu-ro-sur-geon n. A surgeon that specializes in neurosurgery.

neu-ro-surgery n. Surgery of the brain.

neu-ter adj. Neither feminine nor masculine. n. A castrated animal. **neuter** v.

neu-tral adj. Not supporting either side of a debate, quarrel, or party; a color which does not contain a decided hue. Chem. Neither alkaline nor acid. **neutrality** n., **neutrally** adv.

neu-tral-ize v. To make or declare neutral.

neu-tron n. An uncharged particle in the nucleus of an atom present in all atomic nuclei except the hydrogen nucleus.

nev-er adv. Not ever; absolutely not.

nev-er-the-less adv. Nonetheless; however.

new adj. Not used before; unaccustomed; unfamiliar. **newness** n.

news n., pl. Current information and happenings.

news-cast n. A television or radio news broad-cast.

news-pa-per n. A weekly or daily publication which contains recent news and information.

news-print n. An inexpensive machine-finished paper made from wood pulp and used chiefly for newspapers and some paperback books.

New Test-a-ment n. The second part of the Christian Bible containing the Gospels, Acts, Epistles, and the Book of Revelation.

next adj. Immediately following or proceeding; nearest in space or position.

nib-ble v. To bite a little at a time; to take small bites. **nibble**, **nibbler** n.

nice adj. Pleasing; enjoyable; polite and courteous; refined. **-ly** adv.

niche n. A recess or alcove in a wall.

nick n. A small chip or cut on a surface; the final critical moment.

nick-el n. A hard, silver, metallic element used in alloys and symbolized by Ni; a United States coin worth five cents.

nic-o-tine or **nicotin** n. A poisonous alkaloid found in tobacco and used in insecticides and medicine.

niece n. A daughter of one's sister or brother or one's sister-in-law or brother-in-law.

nigh adv. Near in relationship, time, or space.

night n. The time between dusk and dawn and the hours of darkness.

night-cap n. An alcoholic drink usually taken before retiring for the night.

night-in-gale n.

A songbird with brownish plumage, noted for the sweet, nocturnal song of the male.

night-mare n. A frightening and horrible dream.

nim-ble adj. Marked by a quick, light movement; quick-witted. **nimbleness** n., **nimbly** adv.

nin-com-poop n. A silly or stupid person.

nine n. The cardinal number that is equal to $8 + 1$. **nine** adj., pron.

ni-o-bi-um n. A gray, metallic element used in alloys, symbolized by Nb.

nip v. To pinch, bite, or grab something. n. A pinch, bite, or grab; a sharp, stinging feeling caused by cold temperatures. **nipper** n.

ni-tro-gen n. A nonmetallic gaseous element which is essential to life.

ni-tro-glyc-er-in n. A highly flammable, explosive liquid, used to make dynamite and, in medicine, to dilate blood vessels.

no adv. Used to express rejection, disagreement, or denial; not so; not at all.

no-bel-i-um n. A radioactive element.

no-bil-i-ty n., pl. ies The state or quality of being noble.

no-ble adj. Morally good; superior in character or nature. n. A person of rank or noble birth. **nobleman**, **nobleness** n., **nobly** adv.

no-bod-y pron. Not anybody; no person.

noc-tur-nal adj. Pertaining to or occurring during the night. **nocturnally** adv.

node n. A swollen or thickened enlargement.

noise n. A sound which is disagreeable or loud; in computer science, unwanted data in an electronic signal. **noisy** adj., **noisily** adv.

no-mad n. A member of a group of people who wander from place to place. **nomadic** adj., **nomadism** n.

no-men-cla-ture n. The set of names used to describe the elements of art, science, and other fields.

nom-i-nal adj. Of or relating to something that is in name or form only. **nominally** adv.

nom-i-nate v. To select a candidate for an elective office. **-tion**, **-tor** n.

nom-i-nee n. A person nominated for a position or office.

non- prefix Not.

non-a-ge-nar-i-an adj. A person between the ages of 90 and 100 years.

non-cha-lant adj. Giving an effect of casual unconcern. **nonchalance** n., **nonchalantly** adv.

non com-pos men-tis adj. Mentally unbalanced.

non-con-form-ist n. A person who does not feel compelled to follow or accept his community's traditions. **-ity** n.

none pron. Not any; not one.

non-sec-tar-i-an adj. Not associated with or restricted to one religion, faction, or sect.

non-sense n. Something that seems senseless or foolish. **nonsensical** adj.

non seq-ui-tur n. An inference that does not follow as the logical result of what has preceded it.

non-sex-ist adj. Not discriminating on the basis of gender.

noo-dle *n.* A flat strip of dried dough made with eggs and flour.

noon *n.* The middle of the day; 12:00 o'clock.

nor *conj.* Not either; or not.

norm *n.* A rule, model, or pattern typical for a particular group.

nor-mal *adj.* Ordinary, average, usual; having average intelligence. **normalcy, normality** *n.*, **normally** *adv.*

north *n.* The direction to a person's left while facing east.

nose *n.* The facial feature containing the nostrils; the sense of smell.

nose-dive *n.* A sudden plunge as made by an aircraft.

nos-tal-gia *n.* A yearning to return to the past. **nostalgic** *adj.*

nos-tril *n.* The external openings of the nose.

nos-y *or* **nos-ey** *adj.* Snoopy; inquisitive; prying.

not *adv.* In no manner; used to express refusal or denial.

no-ta-ble *adj.* Remarkable, distinguished. **notably** *adv.*

no-ta-rize *v.* To acknowledge and certify as a notary public.

notary public *n.* A person who is legally authorized as a public officer to witness and certify documents.

no-ta-tion *n.* A process or system of figures or symbols used in specialized fields to represent quantities, numbers, or values. **notational** *adj.*

notch *n.* A v-shaped indentation or cut.

note *n.*
A record or message in short form. *Mus.* A tone or written character. **note** *v.*

not-ed *adj.* Famous; well-known.

noth-ing *n.* Not any thing; no part or portion.

no-tice *n.* An announcement; a notification. **noticeable** *adj.*, **noticeably** *adv.*

no-ti-fy *v.* To give notice of; to announce. **notifier, notification** *n.*

no-tion *n.* An opinion; a general concept; an idea.

notions *pl.*, *n.* Small useful articles, as thread or buttons.

no-to-ri-ous *adj.* Having a widely known and usually bad reputation.

not-with-stand-ing *prep.* In spite of. *adv.* Nevertheless; anyway. *conj.* Although.

noun *n.* A word which names a person, place, or thing.

nour-ish *v.* To furnish with the nutriment and other substances needed for growth and life; to support. **nourishing** *adj.*, **nourishment** *n.*

nou-veau riche *n.* A person who has recently become rich.

no-va *n.*, *pl.* **-vae** *or* **-vas** A star which flares up and fades away after a few years or months.

nov-el *n.* An inventive narrative dealing with human experiences; a book. **-ist** *n.*

nov-el-ty *n.*, *pl.* **-ies** Something unusual or new.

nov-ice *n.* A person who is new and unfamiliar with an activity or business.

now *adv.* At the present time; immediately.

no-where *adv.* Not in or at any place.

nox-ious *adj.* Harmful; obnoxious; corrupt.

nu-ance *n.* A slight variation.

nub *n.* A knob; a small piece or lump.

nu-bile *adj.* Suitable or ready for marriage.

nu-cle-ar *adj.* Pertaining to and resembling a nucleus; relating to atomic energy.

nu-cle-us *n.*, *pl.* **-clei** *or* **-cleuses** A central element around which other elements are grouped.

nude *adj.* Unclothed; naked. **-ity, -ist** *n.*

nudge *v.* To poke or push gently.

nug-get *n.* A lump, as of precious metal.

nui-sance *n.* A source of annoyance.

null *adj.* Invalid; having no value or consequence. **nullification** *n.*

nul-li-fy *v.* To counteract.

nu-meral *n.* A symbol, figure, letter, word, or a group of these which represents a number.

nu-mer-a-tor *n.* The term in mathematics indicating how many parts are to be taken; the number in a fraction which appears above the line.

nu-mer-ous *adj.* Consisting or made up of many units.

nup-tial *adj.* Of or pertaining to a wedding.

nuptials *pl.*, *n.* A wedding.

nurse *n.* A person who is specially trained to care for disabled or sick persons. *v.* To feed a baby from a mother's breast.

nurs-er-y *n.*, *pl.* **-ies** A room reserved for the special use of infants or small children; a business or place where trees, shrubs, and flowers are raised.

nur-ture *n.* The upbringing, care, or training of a child. **nurture** *v.*, **nurturer** *n.*

nut *n.* A hard-shelled fruit or seed which contains an inner, often edible kernal.

nut-crack-er *n.* A hinged tool for cracking nuts.

nut-let *n.* A type of small fruit that is similar to a nut.

nu-tri-ent *n.* A substance which nourishes. **nutrient** *adj.*

nu-tri-tion *n.* The process by which a living being takes in food and uses it to live and grow. **-tive, -tional** *adj.*, **nutritionally** *adv.*, **nutritionist** *n.*

nuts *adj.*, *Slang* Foolish, crazy.

nuz-zle *v.* To gently rub against something with the nose; to cuddle.

ny-lon *n.* A strong, elastic material; yarn or fabric made from nylon. **nylons** Stockings made of nylon.

nymph *n.*, *Gr. & Rom. Mythol.* Nature goddesses who lived in woods, rivers, and trees; various immature insects, especially the larva which undergoes incomplete metamorphosis. **-al** *adj.*

O, o The 15th letter of the English alphabet.

O *n.* A word used before a name when talking to that person; an interjection.

oaf *n.* A stupid or clumsy person. **oafish** *adj.*, **oafishly** *adv.*

oak *n.* A large tree of durable wood bearing acorns. **oaken** *adj.*

oak apple *n.* The round gall which is made on oak leaves by the gall wasp.

oak-moss *n.* A type of lichens that will grow on oak trees.

oak wilt *n.* A type of disease of the oak tree that will cause wilting and defoliation and is caused by a fungus.

oar *n.* A long pole, flat at one end, used in rowing a boat.

oars-man *n.* A person who rows in a racing crew. **oarsmanship** *n.*

oa-sis *n., pl.* **oases** A fertile section in the desert which contains water.

oat *n.* A cultivated cereal grass whose grain or seed is used as food.

oat-en *adj.* To be pertaining to oats.

oath *n.* A solemn promise in the name of God or on a Bible that a person will speak only the truth.

oat-meal *n.* A cooked cereal food made from rolled oats.

ob-du-rate *adj.* Stubborn; hard-hearted; not giving in. **obduracy** *n.*

o-be-di-ent *adj.* Obeying or willing to do what one is told. **obedience** *n.*

o-be-lisk *n.* A tall, four-sided stone pillar which slopes from a pointed top.

o-bese *adj.* Very fat. **obesity** *n.*

o-bey *v.* To carry out instructions; to be guided or controlled; to follow directions. **obeyer** *n.*

o-bit *n.* *Slang* An obituary.

o-bit-u-ar-y *n., pl.* **-ies** A published announcement that a person has died, often containing a short biography of the person's life. **obituary** *adj.*

ob-ject *v.* To voice disapproval; to protest. *n.* Something that is visible or can be touched. *Grammar* A word in a sentence which explains who or what is acted upon. **objectless** *adj.*

ob-jec-tion *n.* A feeling of opposition or disagreement, etc.; the reason for a disagreement. **objective** *adj.*

ob-la-tion *n.* A religious offering or the act of sacrifice; that which is offered.

ob-li-ga-tion *n.* A promise or feeling of duty; something one must do because one's conscience or the law demands it; a debt which must be repaid.

o-blige *v.* To constrain; to put in one's debt by a service or favor; to do a favor. **obliger** *n.*, **obligingly** *adv.*

ob-li-gee *n.* The person to whom another is obligated.

o-blique *adj.*

Inclined; not level or straight up and down; slanting; indirect. **-ness, obliquity** *n.*

o-blit-er-ate *v.* To blot out or eliminate completely; to wipe out. **obliteration, obliterator** *n.*, **obliterative** *adj.*

o-bliv-i-on *n.* The condition of being utterly forgotten; the act of forgetting.

ob-liv-i-ous *adj.* Not aware or conscious of what is happening; unmindful. **obliviously** *adv.*, **obliviousness** *n.*

ob-long *adj.* Rectangular; longer in one direction than the other; normally, the horizontal dimension; the greater in length. **oblong** *n.*

ob-lo-quy *n.* Abusive language; a stonly condemnatory utterance.

ob-nox-ious *adj.* Very unpleasant; repugnant. **obnoxiousness** *n.*

o-boe *n.* A double-reed, tube-shaped woodwind instrument. **oboist** *n.*

ob-scene *adj.* Indecent; disgusting. **obscenity** *n.*

ob-scure *adj.* Remote; not clear; faint. *v.* To make dim; to conceal by covering. **-ly** *adv.*, **obscurity, obscureness** *n.*

ob-serve *v.* To pay attention; to watch. **observable, observant** *adj.*, **observably** *adv.*, **observer** *n.*

ob-ser-vant *adj.* Paying strict attention to someting. **observantly** *adv.*

ob-ser-va-tion *n.* The act of observing some-thing; that which is observed; a judgment or opinion. **observational** *adj.*, **-ly** *adv.*

ob-ser-va-to-ry *n., pl.* **-ies** A building or station furnished with instruments for studying the natural phenomenon; a high tower affording a panoramic view.

ob-sess *v.* To preoccupy the mind with an idea or emotion; to be abnormally preoccupied. **obsession** *n.*

ob-so-lete *adj.* No longer in use; out-of-date. **obsolescence** *n.*, **obsolescent** *adj.*

ob-sta-cle *n.* An obstruction; anything which opposes or stands in the way of.

ob-ste-tri-cian *n.* A physician who specializes in the care of a woman during pregnancy and childbirth.

ob-stet-rics *pl.*, *n.* The branch of medicine which deals with pregnancy and childbirth.

ob-sti-nate *adj.* Stubbornly set to an opinion or course of action; difficult to control or manage; hardheaded. **obstinacy** *n.*, **obstinately** *adv.*

ob-strep-er-ous *adj.* Noisy, unruly, or boisterous in resistance to advice or control. **obstreperousness** *n.*

ob-struct *v.* To block, hinder or impede. **obstructor, obstruction** *n.*, **-ive** *adj.*

ob-struc-tion-ism *n.* The deliberate interference the progress or business. **obstructionist** *n.*, **obstructionistic** *adj.*

ob-tain *v.* To acquire or gain possession of. **obtainable** *adj.*, **obtainer** *n.*

ob-trude *v.* To thrust forward without request or warrant; to call attention to oneself. **obtruder, obtrusion** *n.*

ob-tuse *adj.* Lacking acuteness of feeling; insensitive; not distinct or clear to the senses, as pain or sound. *Bot.* Rounded or blunt at the end, as a petal or leaf. **-ly** *adv.*, **obtuseness** *n.*

ob-vert *v.* To turn in order to present a different view or surface.

ob-vi-ate *v.* To counter or prevent by effective measures; to provide for.

ob-vi-ous *adj.* Easily seen, discovered, or understood. **obviously** *adv.*, **-ness** *n.*

oc-ca-sion *n.* The time an event occurs; the event itself; a celebration. *v.* To bring about; to cause.

oc-ca-sion-al *adj.* Appearing or occurring irregularly or now and then; intended, made, or suitable for a certain occasion; incidental.

oc-ci-den-tal *adj.* Western. **-ly** *adv.*

oc-cip-i-tal bone *n. Anat.* The bone which forms the back of the skull.

oc-cult *adj.* Concealed. *n.* The action or influence of supernatural agencies or secret knowledge of them. **occultist** *n.*

oc-cult-ism *n.* Study or belief in the influence or action of supernatural powers.

oc-cu-pan-cy *n.* The state or act of being occupied; the act of holding in possession; the time or term during which something is occupied.

oc-cu-pant *n.* A person who acquires title by occupancy.

oc-cu-pa-tion *n.* A job, profession, or vocation; a foreign military force which controls an area.

oc-cu-pa-tion-al ther-a-py *n. Med.* The treatment of mental, nervous, or physical disabilities by means of work designed to promote recovery or re-adjustment. **occupational therapist** *n.*

oc-cu-py *v.* To take and retain possession of; to live in. **occupier** *n.*

oc-cur *v.* To suggest; to have something come to mind; to happen. **occurrence** *n.*, **occurrent** *adj.*

o-cean *n.* An immense body of salt water which covers 3/4 of the earth's surface; one of the oceans. **oceanic** *adj.*

ocean-ar-i-um *n.* A large contained marine aquarium.

o-ce-an-og-ra-phy *n.* The science of oceanic phenomena dealing with underwater research. **oceanographer** *n.*, **oceanographic** *adj.*

o'clock *adv.* Of, or according to the clock.

oc-ta-gon *n.* A polygon with eight angles and eight sides. **octagonal** *adj.*, **octagonally** *adv.*

oc-tane *n.* Any of several hydrocarbon compounds which occur in petroleum.

oc-tave *n.*, *Music* A tone on the eighth degree above or below another tone.

oc-to-ge-nar-i-an *n.* A person between the ages of 80 and 90.

oc-to-pus *n.*, *pl.* **-es** *or* **-pi**

A cephalopod with a sac-like body and eight tentacles containing double rows of suckers.

oc-u-lar *adj.* Of or relating to the eye; perceived or done by the eye.

odd *adj.* Unusual; strange; singular; left over; not even. **oddly** *adv.*, **oddness** *n.*

odd-ball *n.* One who displays an eccentric behavior.

odds *pl, n.* An equalizing advantage given to a weaker opponent; a ratio between the probability against and the probability for something happening or being true.

odds and ends *n.* Miscellaneous things; remnants; scraps.

ode *n.* A lyric poem usually honoring a person or event.

o-dom-e-ter *n.* A device in a vehicle used to measure distance traveled. **odometry** *n.*

o-dor *n.* A smell; a sensation which occurs when the sense of smell is stimulated.

od-ys-sey *n.* A long voyage marked by many changes of fortune; a spiritual quest.

of *prep.* Proceeding; composed of; relating to.

off *adv.* From a position or place; no longer connected or on. *adj.* Canceled. *prep.* Away from. *interj.* Go away.

of-fend *v.* To make angry; to arouse resentment; to break a law. **offender** *n.*

of-fense *n.* A violation of a duty, rule, or a propriety; the act of causing displeasure; the act of assaulting or attacking; in football and other sports, the team having possession of the ball.

of-fen-sive *adj.* Disagreeable or unpleasant; causing resentment; insulting.

of-fer *v.* To present for acceptance or rejection; to present as an act of worship; to make available; to present in order to satisfy a requirement.

of-fer-ing *n.* The act of one who offers; a contribution, as money, given to the support of a church.

off-hand *adv. or adj.* Without preparation or premeditation.

of-fice *n.* A place where business or professional duties are conducted; an important job, duty, or position.

of-fi-cer *n.* A person who holds a title, position of authority, or office; a policeman.

of-fi-cial *adj.* Something derived from proper authority. *n.* One who holds a position or office; a person who referees a game such as football, basketball, or soccer. **officialism** *n.*, **officially** *adv.*

of-fi-ci-ate *v.* To carry out the duties and functions of a position or office.

of-fi-cious *adj.* Offering one's services or advice in an unduly forward manner. **officiously** *adv.*, **officiousness** *n.*

off-spring *n.*, *pl.* **-springs** The descendants of a person, plant, or animal.

of-ten *adv.* Frequently; many times.

oh *interj.* Used to express surprise, fear, or pain.

ohm *n.* A unit of electrical resistance equal to the resistance of a conductor in which one volt produces a current of one ampere.

oil *n.* Any of various substances, usually

thick, which can be burned or easily melted; a lubricant. **v.** To lubricate.

oil-cloth *n.* A cloth treated with oil which therefore becomes waterproof.

oil field *n.* An area rich in petroleum; an area which has been made ready for oil production.

oil slick *n.* A layer of oil floating on water.

oint-ment *n.* An oily substance used on the skin as an aid to healing or to soften the skin.

o-kra *n.* A tall tropical and semitropical plant with green pods that can be either fried or cooked in soups.

old *adj.* Having lived or existed for a long time; of a certain age. *n.* Former times.

old-en *adj.* Of or relating to times long past; ancient.

old--fash-ioned *adj.* Pertaining to or characteristic of former times or old customs; not modern or up-to-date.

Old Tes-ta-ment *n.* The first of two parts of the Christian Bible, containing the history of the Hebrews, the laws of Moses, the writings of the prophets, the Holy Scriptures of Judaism, and other material.

ol-fac-tory *adj.* Pertaining to the sense of smell.

oli-gar-chy *pl., n.* -ies A government controlled by a small group for corrupt and selfish purposes; the group exercising such control.

ol-ive *n.*

A small oval fruit from an evergreen tree with leathery leaves and yellow flowers, valuable as a source of oil.

om-buds-man *pl. n.* -men A government official appointed to report and receive grievances against the government.

om-e-let *or* **om-e-lette** *n.* A dish made from eggs and other items, such as bacon, cheese, and ham, and cooked until set.

o-men *n.* A phenomenon which is thought of as a sign of something to come, whether good or bad.

om-i-nous *adj.* Foreshadowed by an omen or by a presentiment of evil; threatening.

o-mis-sion *n.* The state or act of being omitted; anything neglected or left out.

o-mit *v.* To neglect; to leave out; to overlook.

om-ni-bus *n.* A public vehicle designed to carry a large number of people; a bus. *adj.* Covering a complete collection of objects or cases.

om-nip-o-tent *adj.* Having unlimited or infinite power or authority.

om-nis-cient *adj.* Knowing all things; having universal or complete knowledge.

om-niv-or-ous *adj.* Feeding on both

vegetable and animal substances; absorbing everything. **omnivorously** *adv.*

on *prep.* Positioned upon; indicating proximity; indicating direction toward; with respect to. *adv.* In a position of covering; forward.

once *adv.* A single time; at any one time. *conj.* As soon as.

once-over *n., Slang* A swift but comprehensive glance.

on-col-o-gy *n.* The study of tumors. **oncological, oncologic** *adj., -ist n*

one *adj.* Single; undivided. *n.* A single person; a unit; the first cardinal number (1).

one-self *pron.* One's own self.

one--sid-ed *adj.* Partial to one side; unjust. **one-sidedness** *n.*

on-ion *n.* An edible bulb plant having a pungent taste and odor.

on--line *adj. Computer Science* Controlled directly by a computer.

on-ly *adj.* Sole; for one purpose alone. *adv.* Without anyone or anything else. *conj.* Except; but.

on-o-mat-o-poe-ia *n.* The use of a word, as buzz or hiss, which vocally imitates the sound it denotes. **onomatopoeic, onomatopoetic** *adj.*

on-shore *adj.* Moving or coming near or onto the shore. **onshore** *adv.*

on-slaught *n.* A fierce attack.

on-to *prep.* To a position or place; aware of.

o-nus *n.* A burden; a responsibility or duty which is difficult or unpleasant; the blame.

on-ward *adv.* Moving forward in time or space. **onwards** *adj.*

on-yx *n.* A gemstone; a chalcedony in layers of different colors.

oo-dles *pl., n., Slang* A great or large quantity.

ooze *n.* A soft deposit of slimy mud on the bottom of a body of water; muddy or marshy ground; a bog. *v.* To flow or leak slowly; to disappear little by little.

o-pal *n.* A translucent mineral composed of silicon, often marked with an iridescent play of colors. **opaline** *adj.*

o-paque *adj.* Not transparent; dull; obscure. **opacity, opaqueness** *n.*

o-pen *adj.* Having no barrier; not covered, sealed, locked, or fastened. *n.* A contest for both amateurs and professionals. *v.* To begin or start. **openness** *n.,* **openly** *adv.*

open--and--shut *adj.* Easily settled; simple to decide.

op-era *n.* A drama having music as a dominant factor, an orchestral accompaniment, acting, and scenery.

op-er-ate *v.* To function, act, or work effectively; to perform an operation, as surgery. **operative** *adj.*

op-er-a-tion *n.* The process of operating; the system or method of operating; a series of acts to effect a certain purpose; a process; a procedure performed on the human body with surgical instruments to restore health; various mathematical or logical processes.

op·er·a·tor n. A person who operates a machine; the owner or person in charge of a business. *Slang* A shrewd person.

oph·thal·mol·o·gy n. A branch of medical science dealing with diseases of the eye, its structure, and functions.

o·pin·ion n. A judgment held with confidence; a conclusion held without positive knowledge.

o·pi·um n. A bitter, highly addictive drug; a narcotic.

o·pos·sum n., pl. -sum or -sums

A nocturnal animal which hangs by its tail and carries its young in a pouch.

op·po·nent n. An adversary; one who opposes another.

op·por·tune adj. Occurring at the right or appropriate time. **opportunist** n., **opportunely** adv.

op·por·tu·ni·ty n., pl. -ies A favorable position; a chance for advancement.

op·pose v. To be in direct contention with; to resist; to be against. **opposable** adj., **opposition** n.

op·po·site adj. Situated or placed on opposing sides. **oppositeness** n.

op·press v. To worry or trouble the mind; to weigh down; to burden as if to enslave. **oppression, oppressor** n.

op·pres·sive adj. Unreasonably severe or burdensome.

op·tic adj. Pertaining or referring to sight or the eye.

op·ti·cal adj. Pertaining to sight; constructed or designed to assist vision. **optically** adv.

op·ti·cian n. A person who makes eyeglasses and other optical articles.

op·ti·mism n. A doctrine which emphasizes that everything is for the best.

op·ti·mum n., pl. -ma The degree or condition producing the most favorable result. adj. Conducive to the best result.

op·tion n. The act of choosing or the power of choice; a choice. **optionally** adv.

op·tion·al adj. Left to one's decision; elective; not required.

op·tom·e·try n. The occupation or profession of examining the eyes and prescribing corrective lenses.

op·u·lence n. Wealth in abundance; affluence.

or conj. A word used to connect the second of two choices or possibilities, indicating uncertainty. *suffix* Indicating a person or thing which does something.

or·a·cle n. A seat of worship where ancient Romans and Greeks consulted the gods for answers; a person of unquestioned wisdom. **oracular** adj.

o·ral adj. Spoken or uttered through the mouth; taken or administered through the mouth. **orally** adv.

o·ral con·tra·cep·tive n. A pill containing hormones, taken monthly to prevent pregnancy.

or·ange n. A citrus fruit which is round and orange in color. adj. Yellowish red.

o·rang·u·tan n., pl. -tans A large, anthropoid ape, having brownish-red hair and very long arms.

o·rate v. To speak in an elevated manner.

orb n. A globe or sphere.

or·bit n. The path of a celestial body or a manmade object. v. To revolve or move in an orbit; to circle. **orbital** adj.

or·chard n. Land that is devoted to the growing of fruit trees.

or·ches·tra n. A group of musicians performing together on various instruments. **orchestral** adj.

or·ches·tra pit n. In theatres, the space reserved for musicians.

or·chid n. A plant found the world over having three petals in various colors.

or·dain v. To appoint as a minister, priest, or rabbi by a special ceremony; to decree.

or·deal n. A painful or severe test of character or endurance.

or·der n. A condition where there is a logical arrangement or disposition of things; sequence or succession; method; an instruction for a person to follow; a request for certain objects. v. To command; to demand.

or·der·ly adj. Neat, tidy.

or·di·nance n. A command, rule, or order; a law issued by a municipal body.

or·di·nar·y adj. Normal; having no exceptional quality; common; average; plain.

ore n. A natural underground substance, as a mineral or rock, from which valuable matter is extracted.

o·reg·a·no n. A bushy perennial herb of the mint family, used as a seasoning for food.

or·gan·dy or **or·gan·die** n., pl. -ies A translucent, stiff fabric of cotton or silk.

or·gan·i·za·tion n. The state of being organized or the act of organizing; a group of people united for a particular purpose. **organizational** adj.

or·gan·ize v. To assemble or arrange with an orderly manner; to arrange by planning. **organization** n.

o·ri·ent v. To determine the bearings or right direction with respect to another source.

or·i·fice n. An opening through which something may pass; a mouth.

or·i·gin n. The cause or beginning of something; the source; a beginning place.

o·rig·i·nal adj. Belonging to the first or beginning. n. A new idea produced by one's own imagination; the first of a kind. **originality** n., **originally** adv.

or-i-ole n. A songbird having brightly colored yellow and black plumage in the males.

or-na-ment n. A decoration. v. To adorn or beautify. **ornamental** adj., **ornamentally** adv., **ornamentation** n.

or-nate adj. Excessively ornamental; elaborate; showy, as a style of writing.

or-phan n. A child whose parents are deceased. **orphan** v., **orphanage** n.

or-ris n. Any of several species having a fragrant root and used in medicine, perfumes, and cosmetics.

or-tho-don-tics n. The branch of dentistry dealing with the correction and prevention of irregularities of the teeth.

or-tho-dox adj. Following established traditions and beliefs, especially in religion.

or-tho-pe-dics or **or-tho-pae-dics** n. The branch of surgery or manipulative treatment concerned with the disorders of the bones, joints, and muscles.

os-cil-late v. To swing back and forth with regular motion, as a pendulum. **oscillation, -tor** n., **oscillatory** adj.

os-mi-um n. A hard, but brittle metallic element symbolized as OS.

os-mo-sis n. The tendency of fluids separated by a semipermeable membrane to pass through it and become mixed and equal in strength. **osmotic** adj.

os-ten-ta-tion n. The act of displaying pretentiously in order to excite.

os-teo n. comb. form Bone; pertaining to the bones.

os-teo-po-ro-sis n. A disorder causing gradual deterioration of bone tissue, usually occurring in older women.

os-tra-cize v. To exile or exclude from a group; to shut out.

oth-er adj. Additional; alternate; different from what is implied or specified. pron. A different person or thing.

oth-er-wise adv. Under different conditions of circumstances.

ot-ter n., pl. **-ter** or **-ters** web-footed aquatic mammals, related to the weasel.

ouch n. interj. An exclamation to express sudden pain.

ought v. Used to show or express a moral duty or obligation; to be advisable or correct.

ounce n. A unit of weight which equals 1/16 of a pound.

our adj. Of or relating to us ourselves. pron. The possessive case of the pronoun we. **ourselves** Our own selves.

oust v. To eject; to remove with force.

out adv. Away from the center or inside. adj. Away. n. A means of escape. prep. Through; forward from.

out-age n. A loss of electricity.

out-break n. A sudden outburst; an occurrence.

out-cast n. A person who is excluded; a homeless person.

out-come n. A consequence or result.

out-dated adj. Old-fashioned and obsolete.

out-do v. To excel in achievement.

out-fit n. The equipment or tools required for a specialized purpose; the clothes a person is dressed in. v. To supply.

out-land-ish adj. Extremely ridiculous, unusual, or strange.

out-let n. An exit.

out-line n. A rough draft showing the main features of something. **outline** v.

out-look n. A person's point of view; an area offering a view of something.

out-num-ber v. To go over or exceed in number.

out-pa-tient n. A patient who visits a clinic or hospital for treatment but does not spend the night.

out-put n. Production or yield during a given time.

out-rage n. An extremely violent act of violence or cruelty; the violent emotion such an act engenders. **outrageous** adj., **outrage** v.

out-right adj. Free from reservations or complications; complete; entire.

out-side n. The area beyond the boundary lines or surface; extreme. adv. Outdoors.

out-spo-ken adj. Spoken without reserve; candid. **outspokenly** adv.

out-stand-ing adj. Excellent; prominent; unsettled, as a bill owed; projecting.

out-ward adj. Pertaining to the outside or exterior; superficial. **outwards** adv.

out-wit v. To trick, baffle, or outsmart with ingenuity.

o-val adj. Having the shape of an egg; an ellipse.

o-va-ry n., pl. **-ies** One of the pair of female reproductive glands.

o-va-tion n. An enthusiastic display of approval for a person or a performance; applause.

ov-en n. An enclosed chamber used for baking, drying, or heating.

o-ver prep. Above; across; upon. adv. Covering completely; thoroughly; again; repetition. adj. Higher; upper. prefix Excessive, as **overstuffed** or **overcrowded**.

o-ver-act v. To act in an exaggerated way.

o-ver-arm adj. Thrown or executed with the arms raised above the shoulders.

o-ver-bear v. To crush or bear down by superior force or weight.

o-ver-board adv. Over the side of a boat or ship into the water.

o-ver-cast adj. Gloomy; obscured. Meteor. Clouds covering more than 9/10 of the sky.

o-ver-coat n. A coat worn over a suit for extra warmth.

o-ver-come v. To prevail; to conquer or defeat. **overcomer** n.

o-ver-con-fi-dence n. Extreme or excessive confidence.

o-ver-do v. To do anything excessively; to

overcook.

o-ver-dose *n.* To take an excessive dose of medication, especially narcotics.

o-ver-draw *v.* To withdraw money over the limits of one's credit.

o-ver-due *adj.* Past the time of return or payment.

o-ver-flow *v.* To flow beyond the limits of capacity; to overfill.

o-ver-hand *v.* To execute something with the hand above the level of the elbow or shoulder. **over-handed** *adv.*

o-ver-haul *v.* To make all needed repairs.

o-ver-head *n.* The operating expenses of a company, including utilities, rent, and up-keep. *adj.* Situated above the level of one's head.

o-ver-look *v.* To disregard or fail to notice something purposely; to ignore.

o-ver-night *adj.* Lasting the whole night; from dusk to dawn. **overnight** *adv.*

o-ver-rule *v.* To put aside by virtue of higher authority.

o-ver-run *v.* To spread out; to extend or run beyond.

o-ver-see *v.* To supervise workers; to direct. **overseer** *n.*

o-ver-shoe *n.* A cover worn over a shoe for protection from snow or water.

o-ver-sight *n.* A mistake made inadvertently.

o-ver-size or **o-ver-sized** *adj.* Larger than the average size of something.

o-ver-step *v.* To go beyond a limit or restriction.

o-vert *adj.* Open to view.

o-ver-whelm *v.* To overcome completely; to make helpless.

o-void *adj.* Having the shape of an egg.

ovu-late *n.* To discharge or produce eggs from an ovary.

o-vum *n.*, *pl.* **ova** The female reproductive cell.

owe *v.* To be in debt for a certain amount; to have a moral obligation.

owl *n.*

A predatory nocturnal bird, having large eyes, a short hooked bill, and long powerful claws. **owlish** *adj.*

own *adj.* Belonging to oneself. *v.* To possess; to confess; to admit. **owner** *n.*

ox *n.*, *pl.* **oxen** A bovine animal used domestically in much the same way as a horse; an adult castrated bull.

ox-ide *n.* A compound of oxygen and another element.

ox-y-gen *n.* A colorless, odorless, tasteless gaseous element essential to life, symbolized by O.

ox-y-gen mask *n.* A device worn over the mouth and nose through which a person can receive oxygen as an aid to breathing.

oys-ter *n.* An edible marine mollusk.

o-zone *n.* A pale-blue gas formed of oxygen with an odor like chlorine, formed by an electrical discharge in the air. *Slang* Fresh air.

P, p The 16th letter of the English alphabet.

pace *n.* A person's step in walking or the length of a person's step; stride; the gait of a horse in which the legs on the same side are moved at the same time. **pace** *v.*, **pacer** *n.*

pace-mak-er *n.* The person who sets the pace for another in a race; a surgically implanted electronic instrument used to stabilize or stimulate the heartbeat.

pac-er *n.* One that sets a particular speed or pace.

pac-i-fy *v.* To quiet or soothe anger or distress; to calm. **pacification** *n.*

pack *n.* A bundle; a group or number of things tied or wrapped up; a full set of associated or like things, such as a pack of cards; a group of wolves or wild dogs that hunt together. *v.* To put things together in a trunk, box, or suitcase; to put away for storage. **to send packing** To force to leave with haste and without ceremony. **packability** *n.*, **packable** *adj.*

pack-age *n.* Something tied up, wrapped or bound together.

pack-age store *n.* A retail establishment that sells alcoholic beverages only in sealed containers.

pack animal *n.* An animal used to carry heavy packs.

pack-board *n.* A metal frame that is usually covered with canvas, used to carry goods and equipment over ones shoulder.

pact *n.* An agreement between nations, groups, or people.

pad *n.* Anything stuffed with soft material and used to protect against blows; a cushion; a drawing or writing tablet of paper gummed together at one edge; the cushion-like part of the foot on some animals, as the dog. *Slang* A person's home. *v.* To stuff, line, or protect with soft material; to extend or lengthen something by inserting unnecessary matter; to travel by foot in a soft and nearly inaudible way.

pad-dle *n.* A broad-bladed implement usually made from wood, used to steer and propel a small boat; a tool used for mixing, turning, or stirring; a small wooden, rounded racket used in table tennis. **paddle** *v.*, **paddler** *n.*

paddle-wheel *n.* A wheel with boards for propelling vessels.

pad-dy wag-on *n.*, *Slang* A police vehicle for transporting suspects.

pad-lock *n.* A detachable lock, having a pivoted u-shaped hasp which can be inserted through a ring and then locked. **padlock** *v.*

pa-dre *n.* A title used in Spain and Italy for a priest.

pa-gan *n.* A person who does not acknowledge God in any religion; a heathen. **pagan** *adj.*, **paganism** *n.*

page *n.* A person hired to deliver messages or run errands; one side of the leaf of a book or letter. *v.* To call or summon a person.

pag-eant n. An elaborate exhibition or spectacular parade for public celebration. **pageantry** n.

pa-go-da n. A sacred Buddhist tower built as a memorial or shrine.

paid v. Past tense of pay.

pail n. A cylindrical container usually having a handle; a bucket.

pain n. The unpleasant feeling resulting from injury or disease; any distress or suffering of the mind; sorrow. v. To cause or experience pain. **painful, painless** adj.

pain-kell-er n. Medication that relieves pain. **painkilling** adj.

paint n. A mixture of colors or pigments which are spread on a surface as protection or as a decorative coating; makeup for the face, as rouge. v. To apply paint to a surface; the practice of using paint to express oneself on canvas. **painter, painting** n.

pair n., pl. **pairs** or **pair** Two things which are similar and used together; something made of two parts which are used together; two persons or animals which live or work together.

pa-ja-mas pl. n. A loose fitting garment for sleeping, consisting of a jacket and pants.

pal-ace n. The royal residence of a sovereign, as of a king; a mansion. **palatial** adj.

pal-at-a-ble adj. Pleasant to the taste; agreeable to one's feelings or mind.

pale n. The pointed stake of a fence; a picket; an area that is enclosed within bounds. adj. Having a whitish or lighter than normal complexion; pallid; weak. **palely, adv.**

pal-ette n. A thin oval board with a hole for the thumb, on which an artist lays and mixes colors.

pal-in-drome n. A word, number, or sentence which reads the same backward or forward, such as toot or 1991.

pal-i-sade n. A fence made of stakes for protection. **palisade** v.

pall n. A heavy cloth used to cover a bier or coffin; a very gloomy atmosphere.

pal-la-di-um n. A silvery-white metallic element symbolized by Pd.

pall-bear-er n. A person who assists in carrying a coffin at a funeral.

pal-let n. A wooden platform on which material for freight shipments can be moved or stored.

pal-lid adj. Deficient in color; lacking sparkle. **pallidly** adv., **pallidness** n.

pal-lor n. Lacking color; paleness.

palm n. The inner area of the hand between the fingers and the wrist; any of a large group of tropical evergreen trees, having an unbranched trunk with a top or crown of fan-like leaves. v. To hide something small in or about the hand.

pal-sy n., pl. **-ies** Paralysis; the loss of ability to control one's movements.

pam-per v. To treat with extreme care.

pam-phlet n. A brief publication which is not permanently bound.

pan-a-ce-a n. A remedy for all diseases, difficulties, or ills; a cure-all.

pan-cake n. A thin, flat cake made from batter and fried on a griddle, served with butter, powdered sugar, syrup, and other toppings.

pan-cre-as n., Anat. A large, irregularly shaped gland situated behind the stomach which releases digestive enzymes and produces insulin. **-ic** adj.

pan-cre-atec-to-my n. The surgical removal of any part or all of the pancreas.

pan-da n.

A large bear-like animal of China and Tibet with black and white fur and rings around the eyes; a racoon-like animal of the south-eastern Himalayas with a ringed tail and reddish fur.

pan-de-mo-ni-um n. A place marked with disorder and wild confusion; disorder; confusion.

pan-der or **panderer** n. A go-between in sexual affairs; a pimp; one who profits from the base desires or passions of others. v. To act as a panderer for someone.

pan-el n. A flat, rectangular piece of material, often wood, which forms a part of a surface; a group of people selected to participate in a discussion group or to serve on a jury. **panelist** n., **panel** n.

pan-ic n. A sudden unreasonable fear which overpowers. v. To cause or to experience panic. **panicky** adj.

pan-nier n. One of a pair of large baskets which are carried on either side of an animal or over a person's back.

pan-ni-kin n. A small cup or pan.

pan-o-ply n., pl. **-lies** The complete equipment of a warrior, including his armor and weapons.

pan-o-ram-a n. An unlimited or complete view in all directions of what is visible.

pan-sy n., pl. **-ies** A garden plant with flowers bearing blossoms in a variety of colors.

pant v. To breathe in rapid or short gasps; to yearn. n. A short breath.

pan-the-ism n. The belief that the laws and forces of nature are all manifestations of God. **pantheist** n., **pantheistic** adj.

pan-ther n. A black leopard in its unspotted form. **pantheress** n.

pan-to-mime n. Communication done solely by means of facial and body gestures. v. To express or act in pantomime.

pan-try n., pl. **-ies** A closet or room for the storage of food, dishes, and other kitchen items.

pants pl. n. Trousers; underpants.

pap n. A soft food for invalids or babies.

pa·pa·cy *n.*, *pl.* **-ies** The dignity or jurisdiction of a pope; a pope's term in office.

pa·per *n.* A substance made of pulp from wood and rags, formed into sheets for printing, wrapping and writing.

pa·pier—ma·che *n.* A material consisting of wastepaper mixed with glue or paste which can be molded when wet and becomes hard when dry.

pa·poose *n.* A North American Indian child or baby.

pa·pri·ka *n.* A dark red seasoning powder made by grinding red peppers.

Pap test *n.* A test in which a smear of bodily secretion from the uterus is examined for the early detection of cancer.

par·a·ble *n.* A short, fictitious story which illustrates a moral lesson.

par·a·chute *n.*

A folding umbrella shaped apparatus of light fabric used to make a safe landing after a free fall from an airplane. **parachute** *v.*, **parachutist** *n.*

pa·rade *n.* An organized public procession; a march. **parader** *n.*

par·a·dise *n.* A state or place of beauty, bliss or delight; heaven. **paradisiac**, **paradisiacal** *adj.*

par·a·dox *n.* A statement which seems opposed to common sense or contradicts itself, but is perhaps true. **paradoxical** *adj.*, **paradoxically** *adv.*

par·af·fin *n.* A white, waxy substance derived from petroleum and used to make lubricants, candles, and sealing materials. **paraffin** *v.*

par·a·gon *n.* A pattern or model of excellence or perfection.

par·a·graph *n.* A section of a composition dealing with a single idea, containing one or more sentences with the first line usually indented.

par·a·keet *n.*

A small parrot with a long, wedge-shaped tail.

par·al·lel *adj.* Moving in the same direction but separated by a distance, as railroad tracks. *n.* A parallel curve, line, or surface; a comparison; one of the imaginary lines which circle the earth paralleling the equator and mark the latitude. **parallel** *v.*, **parallelism** *n.*

par·al·lel·o·gram *n.* A four-sided figure having parallel opposite sides which are equal.

pa·ral·y·sis *n.*, *pl.* **-ses** Complete or partial loss of the ability to feel any sensation or to move. **paralytic** *adj. & n.*

par·a·lyze *v.* To cause to be inoperative or powerless.

par·a·med·ic *n.* A person trained to give emergency medical treatment until a doctor is available.

par·a·mount *adj.* Superior to all others in rank, importance, and power.

par·a·noi·a *n.* Mental insanity marked by systematic delusions of persecution or grandeur.

par·a·pher·na·lia *n.* Personal effects or belongings; the apparatus or articles used in some activities; equipment.

par·a·phrase *v.* To put something written or spoken into different words while retaining the same meaning.

par·a·site *n.*, *Biol.* An organism which lives, grows, feeds, and takes shelter in or on another organism; a person depending entirely on another without providing something in return.

par·a·sol *n.* A small umbrella used as protection from the sun.

par·a·troops *pl.*, *n.* Troops which are equipped and trained to parachute behind enemy lines.

par·boil *v.* To precook something in boiling water.

par·cel *n.* A wrapped package; a bundle; a portion or plat of land. **parcel** *v.*

parch *v.* To become very dry from intense heat; to become dry from thirst or the lack of water.

parch·ment *n.* Goatskin or sheepskin prepared with a pumice stone and used as a material for writing or drawing.

par·don *v.* To forgive someone for an offense. In law, to allow a convicted person freedom from the penalties of an office or crime. **pardonable** *adj.*, **pardoning** *adv.*, **pardon** *n.*

pare *v.* To cut away or remove the outer surface gradually. **parer** *n.*

par·e·go·ric *n.* A medication used to relieve stomach pains.

par·ent *n.* A mother or father; a forefather; an ancestor; a source; a cause. **parentage**, **parenthood** *n.*, **parental** *adj.*

pa·ren·the·sis *n.*, *pl.* **-ses** One of a pair of curved lines () used to enclose a qualifying or explanatory remark.

par·ish *n.* In association with the Roman Catholic Church, the district under the charge of a priest; the members of a parish.

park *n.* A tract of land used for recreation. *v.* To leave something temporarily in a parking garage or lot, as a car. **parker** *n.*

par·ka *n.* A cloth jacket with an attached hood.

par·lia·ment *n.* The assembly which constitutes the lawmaking body of various countries, as the United Kingdom.

par·lor *n.* A room for entertaining visitors or guests; a business offering a personal service, as beauty parlor, ice cream parlor, or funeral parlor.

pa·ro·chi·al *adj.* Belonging to a local parish; having to do with a parish.

par·o·dy *n.*, *pl.* **-ies** A composition, song, or poem which mimics another in a ridiculous way.

pa-role *n.* The conditional release of a prisoner before his sentence expires.
parole *v. & adj.*

par-ox-ysm *n.* A violent attack or outburst; a spasm.

par-ri-cide *n.* A person who murders his mother or father; the crime of murdering one's parents. **-al** *adj.*

par-rot *n.*

A brightly colored, semitropical bird with a strong, hooked bill. *v.* To imitate or repeat.

par-ry *v.* To avoid something; to turnaside. **parry** *n.*

parse *v.* To identify the parts of speech in a sentence and to indicate their relationship to each other.

par-si-mo-ny *n.* Extreme reluctance to use one's resources or to spend money. **parsimonious** *adj.*, **-ly** *adv.*

pars-ley *n.* An herb with curly leaves which is used for seasoning and garnishing.

pars-nip *n.* A plant from the carrot family cultivated for its long, edible root.

par-son *n.* A pastor or clergyman.

par-son-age *n.* The home provided by a church for its parson.

part *n.* A segment, portion, or division of a whole; a component for a machine; the role of a character, as in a play; the line which forms where the hair is parted by combing or brushing. *v.* To leave or go away from; to be separated into pieces; to give up control or possession.

par-take *v.* To have a share or part; to take; to take a part in something.

par-tial *adj.* Incomplete; inclined to favor one side more than the other. **partiality** *n.*, **partially** *adv.*

par-tic-i-pate *v.* To join in or share; to take part. **participant, participation, participator** *n.*, **participatory** *adj.*

par-ti-cle *n.* A very small piece of solid matter. *Gram.* A group of words, such as articles, prepositions, and conjunctions which convey very little meaning but help to connect, specify, or limit the meanings of other words.

par-tic-u-lar *adj.* Having to do with a specific person, group, thing, or category; noteworthy; precise. **particularly** *adv.*

part-ing *n.* A division; a separation; the place where a division or separation occurs. *adj.* Done, given, or said on departing.

par-ti-tion *n.* A separation or division. *v.* To divide.

part-ner *n.* One who shares something with another.

part-ner-ship *n.* Two or more persons who run a business together and share in the profits and losses.

par-tridge *n.*, *pl.* **partridges** A plump or stout-bodied game bird.

par-ty *n.*, *pl.* **-ies** A group of persons who gather for pleasure or entertainment; a group of persons associated together for a common purpose; a group which unites to promote or maintain a policy, a cause, or other purposes, as a political group. In law, a person or group of people involved in a legal proceeding.

pass *v.* To proceed; to move; to transfer; to go away or come to an end; to get through a course, trial or test; to approve; to vote for; to give as an opinion or judgment; to hit or throw a ball to another player. *n.* A ticket or note that allows a person to come and go freely. **come to pass** To happen. **pass away** To die or cease to live. **pass over** To leave out, to ignore.

pas-sage *n.* The act of going, proceeding, or passing; the enactment by a legislature of a bill into law; a small portion or part of a whole book or speech; something, as a path or channel, through, over or along which something else may pass.

pas-sen-ger *n.* One who travels in a vehicle, car, plane, boat, or other conveyance.

pas-sion *n.* A powerful feeling; lust; sexual desire; an outburst of strong feeling; violence or anger. **Passion** The suffering of Christ which followed the Last Supper to the time of his death. **passionless, passionate** *adj.*

pas-sive *adj.* Not working, acting, or operating; inactive; acted upon, influenced, or affected by something external. *Gram.* Designating the form of a verb which indicates the subject is receiving the action. **passively** *adv.*, **passivity, passiveness** *n.*

pass-port *n.* An official permission issued to a person allowing him to travel out of this country and to return; a document of identification.

past *adj.* Having to do with or existing at a former time. *n.* Before the present time; a person's history or background. *adv.* To go by. *prep.* After; beyond in time; beyond the power, reach, or influence.

paste *n.* A mixture usually made from water and flour, used to stick things together; dough used in making pastry; a brilliant glass used in imitating precious stones. **paste** *v.*

pas-tel *n.* A crayon made of ground pigments; a drawing made with crayons of this kind. *adj.* Pale and light in color or shade.

pas-teur-i-za-tion *n.* The process of killing disease-producing microorganisms by heating the liquid to a high temperature for a period of time.

pas-time *n.* Spending spare time in a pleasant way; a diversion.

pas-tor *n.* A Christian clergyman in charge of a church or congregation.

pas-tor-al *adj.* Referring to the duties of a pastor; pertaining to life in the country; rural or rustic. *n.* A poem dealing with country life.

past par-ti-ci-ple *n.* A participle used with reference to actions and conditions in the past.

pas-try *n.* Food made with dough or having a crust made of dough, as pies, tarts, or other desserts.

pas-ture *n.* An area for grazing of domestic animals. pastured, pasturing *v.*, pasturage, pasturer *n.*

pat *v.* To tap lightly with something flat. *n.* A soft, caressing stroke.

patch *n.* A piece of fabric used to repair a weakened or torn area in a garment; a piece of cloth with an insignia which represents an accomplishment. *v.* to repair or put together hastily. patchy, patchable *adj.*, patcher *n.*

pat-ent *n.* A governmental protection assuring an inventor the exclusive right of manufacturing, using, exploiting, and selling an invention. *adj.* Evident; obvious. patentee, patency *n.* patently *adv.*

pa-ter-nal *adj.* Relating to or characteristic of a father; inherited from a father. -ly *adv.*, -ism *n.*

pa-thet-ic *adj.* Arousing pity, tenderness, or sympathy. pathetically *adv.*

pa-thol-o-gy *n.* The science that deals with facts about diseases, their nature and causes. pathologic, pathological *adj.*, pathologist *n.*

pa-thos *n.* A quality in a person that evokes sadness or pity.

pa-tience *n.* The quality, state, or fact of being patient; the ability to be patient.

pa-tient *adj.* Demonstrating uncomplaining endurance under distress. *n.* A person under medical care. -ly *adv.*

pa-tri-arch *n.* The leader of a tribe or family who rules by paternal right; a very old and revered man. patriarchal *adj.*, patriarchy *n.*

pa-tri-ot *n.* A person who loves and defends his country. patriotic *adj.*, patriotically *adv.*, patriotism *n.*

pa-trol *n.* Walking around an area for the purpose of maintaining or observing security; a person or group carrying out this action. patrol *v.*

pa-tron *n.* A person who fosters, protects, or supports some person, enterprise, or thing; a regular customer.

pat-sy *n., pl.* -ies *Slang* A person who is taken advantage of.

pat-tern *n.* Anything designed or shaped to serve as a guide in making something else; a sample. *v.* To make according to a pattern.

pat-ty *n., pl.* -ies A small, flat piece of chopped meat.

pau-per *n.* A very poor person who depends on charity. pauperism *n.*, pauperize *v.*

pause *v.* To linger, hesitate, or stop for a time. pause *n.*

pave *v.* To surface with gravel, concrete, asphalt, or other material.

pave-ment *n.* A surface that has been paved.

pa-vil-ion *n.* A large, roofed structure used for shelter.

paw *n.* The foot of an animal. *v.* To handle clumsily or rudely.

pawn *n.* Something given as security for a loan; a hostage; a chessman of little value. pawn *v.*

pay *v.* To give a person what is due for a debt, purchase, or work completed; to compensate; to suffer the consequences.

pay-ment *n.* The act of paying.

pea *n.* A round edible seed contained in a pod and grown on a vine.

peace *n.* A state of physical or mental tranquillity; calm; serenity; the absence of war; the state of harmony between people. peaceable, -ful *adj.*, peaceably, peacefully *adv.*

peach *n.* A round, sweet, juicy fruit having a thin, downy skin, a pulpy yellow flesh, and a hard, rough single seed.

pea-cock *n.*

A male bird with brilliant blue or green plumage and a long iridescent tail that fans out to approximately six feet.

peak *n.* A projecting edge or point; the summit of a mountain; the top. *v.* To bring to the maximum.

peal *n.* The ring of bells; the long, loud sound of thunder or laughter. *v.* To ring.

pea-nut *n.* A nut-like seed which ripens underground; the plant bearing this nut.

pear *n.* A juicy, edible fruit which grows on a tree.

pearl *n.* A smooth, rounded deposit formed around a grain of sand in the shell of various mollusks, especially the oyster; anything which is precious, rare, or fine. pearly *adj.*

peas-ant *n.* A farmhand or rustic workman; an uneducated person of the lowest class. *Slang* Uneducated or uncouth.

peat *n.* The black substance formed when plants begin to decay in wet ground, as bogs. peaty *adj.*

peat moss *n.* A moss which grows in very wet areas, used as plant food and mulch.

peb-ble *n.* A small, smooth stone. *v.* To treat, as to give a rough texture.

pe-can *n.* A large tree of the central and southern United States with an edible oval, thin-shelled nut.

peck *v.* To strike with the beak; to eat without an appetite, taking only small bites. *n.* A measure which equals 1/4 of a bushel.

pec-tin *n.* A complex carbohydrate found in ripe fruits and used in making jelly. pectic *adj.*

pe-cu-liar *adj.* Odd; strange. peculiarity *n.*, peculiarly *adv.*

ped-al *n.* A lever usually operated by the

foot. **pedal** v.

ped-dle v. To travel around in an attempt to sell merchandise.

ped-es-tal n. A support or base for a statue. to put on a pedestal To hold something in high respect.

pe-des-tri-an n. A person traveling by foot.

pe-di-at-rics n. The branch of medicine dealing with the care of children and infants. **pediatric** adj., **pediatrician** n.

ped-i-cure n. The cosmetic care of the toenails and feet. **pedicurist** n.

ped-i-gree n. A line of ancestors, especially of an animal of pure breed.

ped-i-ment n. A broad, triangular architectural or decorative part above a door.

pe-dom-e-ter n. An instrument which indicates the number of miles one has walked.

pe-dun-cle n., *Biol.* A stalk-like support in some plants and animals.

peek v. To look shyly or quickly from a place of hiding; to glance. **peek** n.

peel n. The natural rind or skin of a fruit. v. To pull or strip the skin or bark off; to remove in thin layers. *Slang* To undress. **peeler** n.

peen n. The ball-shaped end of a hammer opposite the flat, striking surface.

peep v. To utter a very small and weak sound, as of a young bird.

peer v. To look searchingly; to come partially into one's view. n. An equal; a member of the British nobility, as a duke or earl.

pee-vish adj. Irritable in mood; cross. **peevishly** adv., **peevishness** n.

peg n. A small pin, usually of wood or metal; a projecting pin on which something may be hung. *Slang* An artificial leg, often made of wood. **peg** v.

pei-gnoir n. A woman's loose fitting dressing gown.

pe-koe n. A superior black tea made from young or small leaves.

pel-i-can n. A large, web-footed bird with a large pouch under the lower bill for the temporary storage of fish.

pel-let n. A small round ball made from paper or wax; a small bullet or shot.

pelt n. The skin of an animal with the fur.

pel-vis n., pl. **-vises** or **-ves** The structure of the vertebrate skeleton which rests on the lower limbs, supporting the spinal column.

pen n. An instrument used for writing.

pe-nal adj. Of or pertaining to punishment or penalties.

pen-al-ty n., pl. **-ties**. The legal punishment for an offense or crime; something which is forfeited when a person fails to meet a commitment; in sports, a punishment or handicap imposed for breaking a rule.

pen-ance n. A voluntary act to show sorrow or repentance for sin.

pen-dant or **pen-dent** n. An ornament which hangs from a necklace.

pend-ing adj. Not yet decided; imminent.

prep. During; until.

pen-du-lous adj. Hanging downward so as to swing; wavering.

pen-du-lum n. A suspended object free to swing back and forth.

pen-e-trate v. To force a way through or into; to pierce; to enter; to pass through something. **penetrable** n, **penetrating** adj., **penetration** n.

pen-guin n. A web-footed, flightless, marine bird of the southern hemisphere.

pen-i-cil-lin n. A powerful antibiotic derived from mold and used to treat certain types of bacterial infections.

pen-in-su-la n. A piece of land projecting into water from a larger land mass. **peninsular** adj.

pe-nis n., pl. **-nises** or **-nes** The male sex organ; the male organ through which urine leaves the body.

pen-i-tent adj. Having a feeling of guilt or remorse for one's sins or misdeeds; sorry. **penitence** n., **penitential** adj.

pen-ny n., pl. **-ies** A United States coin worth one cent ($.01).

pen-sion n. The amount of money a person receives regularly after retirement. **pensioner** n.

pen-sive adj. Involved in serious, quiet reflection; causing melancholy thought. **pensively** adv., **pensiveness** n.

pen-ta-gon n.

Any object or building having five sides and five interior angles. **Pentagon** The five-sided office building in Arlington, Va. which houses the Defense Department.

pent-house n. An apartment built on the roof of a building.

pe-o-ny n., pl. **-nies** A plant with a large, fragrant red, white, or pink flower.

peo-ple n., pl. **people** Human beings; a body of persons living in the same country, under the same government, and speaking the same language; one's relatives or family. **people** v.

pep-per n. A strong, aromatic condiment. v. To pelt or sprinkle.

pep-tic adj. Pertaining to or aiding digestion.

per an-num adv. For, by, or in each year; annually.

per-cale n. A closely woven cotton fabric.

per--cap-i-ta adj. & adv., *Latin* Of each individual.

per-ceive v. To become aware of by the senses; to understand; to feel or observe. **-able** adj., **perceivably** adv.

per-cent-age n. The rate per hundred; a part or proportion in relation to a whole. *Slang* Profit; advantage.

per-cept n. A mental impression of something perceived; the immediate knowledge obtained from perceiving.

perch n. A place on which birds rest or alight; any place for standing or sitting; a small, edible freshwater fish having tender white meat.

per-cip-i-ent *adj.* Having the power of perception. **percipience, percipiency** *n.*

per-co-late *v.* To pass or cause to pass through a porous substance; to filter. **percolation, percolator** *n.*

per-cus-sion *n.* The sharp striking together of one body against another; the striking of a cap in a firearm. *Music.* An instrument which makes music when it is struck, as a drum or cymbal.

per-en-ni-al *adj.* Lasting from year to year; perpetual. *n.* A plant which lives through the winter and blooms again in the spring. **perennially** *adv.*

per-fect *adj.* Having no defect or fault; flawless; accurate; absolute. *v.* To make perfect. **-ly** *adv.*, **perfectness** *n.*

per-form *v.* To execute or carry out an action; to act or function in a certain way; to act; to give a performance or exhibition. **performable** *adj.*, **performer, performance** *n.*

per-fume *n.* A fragrant substance which emits a pleasant scent; one distilled from flowers. **perfume** *v.*

per-haps *adv.* Possibly; maybe; not sure.

per-i-gee *n.* The point of an orbit when a satellite of the earth is closest to the earth; the lowest part of an orbit.

per-il *n.* A source of danger; exposure to the chance of injury; danger. **perilous** *adj.*, **perilously** *adv.*

pe-ri-od *n.* An interval of time marked by certain conditions; an interval of time that is regarded as a phase in development; menstruation; the punctuation mark (.) which indicates the end of a sentence or an abbreviation.

pe-riph-er-y *n., pl.* **-ies** The outer part, boundary, or surface. **peripheral** *adj.*

per-ish *v.* To ruin or spoil; to suffer an untimely or violent death.

per-i-win-kle *n.* Any of several edible marine snails; a trailing evergreen plant with blue and sometimes white flowers.

per-jure *v.* To give false testimony while under oath. **perjury** *n.*

per-ma-nent *adj.* Continuing in the same state; lasting indefinitely; enduring. *n.* A hair wave which gives long lasting curls or body to the hair. **permanence, permanency** *n.*, **permanently** *adv.*

per-me-ate *v.* To spread through; to pervade; to pass through the pores. **permeation** *n.* **permeable** *adj.*

per-mis-sion *n.* The act of permitting something; consent.

per-mit *v.* To consent to; to allow. *n.* An official document giving permission for a specific activity.

per-ni-cious *adj.* Very harmful; malicious. **-ly** *adv.*, **perniciousness** *n.*

per-ox-ide *n., Chem.* Oxide containing the highest proportion of oxygen for a given series; a chemical used with other ingredients to bleach the hair.

per-pen-dic-u-lar *adj.* Being at right angles to the plane of the horizon.

Math. Meeting a plane or given line at right angles. **perpendicular, perpendicularity** *n.*, **-ly** *adv.*

per-pe-trate *v.* To perform; to commit; to be guilty of. **petration, perpetrator** *n.*

per-pet-u-al *adj.* Lasting or continuing forever or an unlimited time. **perpetually** *adv.*

per-plex *v.* To confuse or be confused; to make complicated. **perplexing** *adj.*, **-ly, perplexedly** *adv.*, **perplexity** *n.*

per-se-cute *v.* To harass or annoy persistently; to oppress because of one's religion, beliefs, or race. **persecution, persecutor** *n.*, **persecutive** *adj.*

per-se-vere *v.* To persist in any purpose or idea; to strive in spite of difficulties or obstacles. **perseverance** *n.*, **perseveringly** *adv.*

per-sim-mon *n.* A tree having reddish orange, edible fruit.

per-sist *v.* To continue firmly despite obstacles; to endure. **persistence, persistency** *n.*, **persistent** *adj.*, **persistently** *adv.*

per-son *n.* A human being; an individual; the personality of a human being. *Law* Any human being, corporation, or other entity having legal rights and duties.

per-son-al *adj.* Belonging to a person or persons; of the body or person; relating to oneself; done by oneself.

per-son-i-fy *v.* To think of or represent as having human qualities or life; to be a symbol of. **personifier, -fication** *n.*

per-son-nel *n.* The body of people working for a business or service.

per-spec-tive *n.*

A painting or drawing technique in which objects seem to have depth and distance.

per-spi-ra-tion *n.* The salty fluid excreted from the body by the sweat glands.

per-spire *v.* To give off perspiration.

per-suade *v.* To cause to convince or believe by means of reasoning or argument. **persuader, persuasiveness** *n.*, **persuasive** *adj.*

per-tain *v.* To relate to; to refer to; to belong as a function, adjunct or quality; to be appropriate or fitting.

per-ti-na-cious *adj.* Adhering firmly to an opinion, belief, or purpose; stubbornly persistent. **pertinaciously** *adv.*, **pertinacity** *n.*

per-ti-nent *adj.* Relating to the matter being discussed.

per-turb *v.* To disturb, make anxious, or make uneasy; to cause confusion. **perturbation** *n.*

per-vade *v.* To spread through every part of something; to permeate. **pervasive** *adj.*

per-ver-sion *n.* The act of being led away from the accepted course; a deviant form of sexual behavior.

per-vert *v.* To lead away from the proper cause; to use in an improper way. *n.* A person practicing or characterized by sexual perversion. **perverted**, **pervertible** *adj.*

pes-si-mism *n.* The tendency to take a gloomy view of affairs or situations and to anticipate the worst. **-ist** *n.*, **pessimistic** *adj.*, **pessimistically** *adv.*

pest *n.* A person or thing which is a nuisance; an annoying person or thing; a destructive insect, plant, or animal.

pes-ter *v.* To harass with persistent annoyance; to bother.

pes-ti-cide *n.* A chemical substance used to destroy rodents, insects, and pests. **pesticidal** *adj.*

pes-ti-lence *n.* A widespread and often fatal infectious disease, as bubonic plague or cholera.

pet *n.* An animal, bird, or fish one keeps for companionship; any favorite or treasured thing. *adj.* Treated or tamed as a pet. *v.* To stroke or caress gently. *Slang* To make love by fondling and caressing.

pet-al *n.*, *Bot.* One of the leaf-like parts of a flower.

pe-tite *adj.* Small in size; little. **petiteness** *n.*

pet-it four *n.*, *pl.* **petits fours** *or* **petit fours** A small decorated cake.

pe-ti-tion *n.* A solemn request or prayer; a formal written request addressed to a group or person in authority. **petitioner** *n.*

pet-ri-fy *v.* To convert into a stony mass; to make fixed or immobilize, as in the face of danger or surprise. **petrification** *n.* **petrifactive** *adj.*

pe-tro-le-um *n.* An oily, thick liquid which develops naturally below the ground surface, used in products such as gasoline, fuel oil, and kerosene.

pet-ti-coat *n.* A woman's skirt-like garment worn as an underskirt.

pet-ty *adj.* To have little importance or value; insignificant; trivial; having a low position or rank; minor; small-minded. **pettiness** *n.*

pet-ty cash *n.* Cash held on hand for minor bills or expenditures.

pe-tu-nia *n.* A widely grown tropical plant having a funnel-shaped flower in various colors.

pew *n.* A row of bench-like seats for seating people in church.

pew-ter *n.* An alloy of tin with copper, silver-gray in color and used for tableware and kitchen utensils.

pfen-nig *n.*, *pl.* **-nigs** *or* **-nige** A small coin of Germany, equal to one hundredth of a Deutschemark.

phal-lus *n.*, *pl.* **-li** *or* **-luses** A representation of the penis, often as a symbol of generative power. **phallic** *adj.*

phan-tasm *n.* The creation of an imaginary image; a fantasy; a phantom. **phantasmal**, **phantasmic** *adj.*

phan-tom *n.* Something which exists but has no physical reality; a ghost. **phantom** *adj.*

phar-ma-ceu-ti-cal *adj.* Pertaining or relating to a pharmacy or pharmacists.

phar-ma-cy *n.*, *pl.* **-cies** A place of business which specializes in preparing, identifying, and disbursing drugs; a drugstore.

phar-ynx *n.*, *pl.* **-ynges** *or* **-ynxes**. The part of the throat located between the palate and the esophagus, serving as a passage for air and food. **pharyngeal** *adj.*

phase *n.* Any decisive stage in development or growth. *Astron.* One of the forms or appearances of a planet.

pheas-ant *n.* A long-tailed game bird noted for the beautiful plumage of the male.

phe-nom-e-non *n.*, *pl.* **-na** *or* **-nons.** Something that can be observed or perceived; a rare occurrence. *Slang* An outstanding person with remarkable power, ability, or talent.

phi-lan-der *v.* To make love without feeling or serious intentions. **-er** *n.*

phi-lat-e-ly *n.* The collection and study of postage stamps and postmarked material. **philatelic** *adj.*, **philatelist** *n.*

phil-har-mon-ic *adj.* Pertaining to a symphony orchestra. **philharmonic** *n.*

phi-los-o-phy *n.*, *pl.* **-ies** The logical study of the nature and source of human knowledge or human values; the set of values, opinions, and ideas of a group or individual.

pho-bi-a *n.* A compulsive fear of a specified situation or object.

phone *n.*, *Slang* A telephone. *v.* To call or communicate by telephone.

phon-ic *adj.* Pertaining to sounds in speech; using the same symbol for each sound. **-ally** *adv.*, **phonetics** *n.*

pho-no-graph *n.* A machine which uses a needle to reproduce sound from a grooved disc or record.

pho-ny *adj.* *Informal* Counterfeit; fraudulent; not real or genuine.

phos-phate *n.*, *Chem.* A salt or phosphoric acid which contains mostly phosphorus and oxygen.

phos-pho-rus *n.* A highly flammable, poisonous, nonmetallic element used in safety matches, symbolized by P.

pho-to *n.* *Slang* A photograph.

pho-to-cop-y *v.* To reproduce printed material using a photographic process. **photocopier**, **photocopy** *n.*

pho-to-graph *n.* A picture or image recorded by a camera and then reproduced on a photosensitive surface. **photography** *n.*

pho-to-stat *n.* A trademark for a camera designed to reproduce documents and graphic material.

pho-to-syn-the-sis *n.*, *Biochem.* The chemical process by which plants use light to change carbon dioxide and water into carbohydrates, releasing oxygen as a by-product. **photosynthesize** *v.*, **photosynthetic** *adj.*

phrase *n.*, *Gram.* A brief or concise expression which does not contain a predicate.

phre-nol-o-gy *n.* The study of or the theory that the conformation of the human skull indicates the degree of intelligence and character.

phys-i-cal *adj.* Relating to the human body apart from the mind or emotions; pertaining to material rather than imaginary subjects. *n.* A medical exam to determine a person's physical condition. physically *adv.*

phy-si-cian *n.* A person licensed to practice medicine.

phys-ics *n.* The scientific study which deals with energy, matter, motion, and related areas of science.

phys-i-ol-o-gy *n., pl.* -ies The scientific study of living animals, plants, and their activities and functions; the vital functions and processes of an organism. physiological, physiologic *adj.,* physiologist *n.*

phys-i-o-ther-a-py *n.* The treatment of disease or physical defects by the use of heat and massage.

pi-an-o *n.* A musical instrument with a manual keyboard and felt-covered hammers which produce musical tones when struck upon steel wires.

pi-az-za *n.* A public square or an open area in an Italian town or city.

pi-ca *n.* A printer's type size of 12 points, equal to about 1/6 inch; a typewriter type size with 10 characters to an inch.

pic-co-lo *n.* A small flute with a brilliant sound pitched an octave above the flute.

pick *v.* To select or choose from a number or group; to remove the outer area of something with the fingers or a pointed instrument; to remove by tearing away little by little; to open a lock without using a key; to harass or tease someone or something; to pluck a musical instrument. *n.* A pointed metal tool sharpened at both ends, used to break up hard surfaces. *Music* A small flat piece of plastic or of bone, used to pluck or strum the strings of an instrument, as a guitar or banjo.

pick-et *n.* A pointed stake driven into the ground as support for a fence; a person positioned outside of a place of employment during a strike. *Mil.* A soldier posted to guard a camp.

pick-le *n.* A cucumber preserved in a solution of brine or vinegar. *Slang* A troublesome situation.

pick-pock-et *n.* A person who steals from another's purse or pocket.

pic-nic *n.* An outdoor social gathering where food is provided usually by the people attending. picnicker *n.*

pic-ture *n.* A visual representation on a surface, which is printed, drawn or photographed; the mental image or impression of an event or situation.

piece *n.* An element, unit, or part of a whole; a musical or literary work. *Slang* A firearm.

piecemeal *adv.* Gradually, bit by bit.

pier *n.* A structure extending into the water, used to secure, protect, and provide access to vessels.

pierce *v.* To penetrate or make a hole in something; to force into or through. piercing *adj.*

pi-e-ty *n., pl.* -ties. Devoutness toward God.

pig *n.*

A cloven-hoofed mammal with short legs, bristly hair, and a snout for rooting; the edible meat of a pig; pork. *Slang* A greedy or gross person.

pi-geon *n.* A bird with short legs, a sturdy body, and a small head.

pig-gy-back *adv.* Carried on the back and shoulders. piggyback *adj.*

pig-head-ed *adj.* Stubborn. -ly *adv.*

pig-ment *n.* A material used as coloring matter, suitable for making paint. *Biol.* Any substance such as melanin and chlorophyll which imparts color to vegetable tissue or animals.

pig-skin *n.* Something made from the skin of a pig. *Slang* A football.

pike *n.* A long pole with a sharp, pointed steel head; a large edible fresh-water fish with a long snout and a slender body. *Slang* A turnpike or a major highway.

pile *n.* A quantity of anything thrown in a heap; a massive or very large building or a group of buildings.

pil-fer *v.* To steal in little quantities; to steal items of little value. pilferage *n.*

pil-grim *n.* A person who travels to a sacred place; a wanderer. Pilgrims The English Puritans who founded the Plymouth colony in New England in the year 1620.

pill *n.* A small tablet containing medicine which is taken by mouth; someone or something which is disagreeable but must be dealt with. the pill *Slang* An oral contraceptive drug taken by women.

pil-lar *n.* A freestanding column which serves as a support.

pi-men-to *n.* A sweet pepper used as a stuffing for olives or as a relish.

pim-ple *n.* A small eruption of the skin, having an inflamed base. pimpled, pimply *adj.*

pine *n., Bot.* Any of various cone-bearing evergreen trees; the wood of such a tree.

pink *n.* Any of various plants related to the carnation, having fragrant flowers; a light or pale hue of crimson; the highest or best possible degree.

pink-eye *n., Pathol.* An acute, contagious conjunctivitis of the eye.

pin-na-cle *n.* The highest peak; a sharp point; a pointed summit.

pi-noch-le *or* pi-noc-le *n.* A card game for two, three, or four people, played with a double deck of 48 cards.

pint *n.* A liquid or dry measurement equal to half of a quart or two cups.

pin-to *n.*, *pl.* **-tos** *or* **-toes** A horse with spots; a spotted bean of the southwestern United States.

pi-o-neer *n.* One of the first settlers of a new region or country; the first developer or investigator in a new field of enterprise, research, or other endeavor.

pi-ous *adj.* Reverently religious; devout. **piously** *adv.*, **piousness** *n.*

pipe *n.* A hollow cylinder for conveying fluids; a small bowl with a hollow stem for smoking tobacco. *Music* A tubular flute.

pique *n.* A feeling of resentment or irritation.

pi-rate *n.* A robber of the high seas. *Slang* Someone who uses or reproduces someone else's work without authorization. **piracy** *n.*, **pirate** *v.*, **piratical** *adj.*

pis-ta-chi-o *n.* A small tree of western Asia; the edible fruit from this tree.

pis-til *n.* The seed-producing female reproductive organ of a flower.

pis-tol *n.* A small hand-held firearm.

pis-ton *n.*, *Mech.* A solid cylinder fitted into a larger cylinder, moving back and forth under liquid pressure.

pitch-fork *n.* A large fork with a wide prong span, used as a garden or farm tool.

pith *n.*, *Bot.* The sponge-like soft tissue at the center of the branch or stem of many plants.

pit-i-ful *adj.* Evoking or meriting pity. **pitifully** *adv.*

pit-y *n.*, *pl.* **-ies.** A feeling of compassion or sorrow for another's misfortune.

piv-ot *n.* A thing or person upon which development, direction, or effect depends. *v.* To turn.

pla-cen-ta *n.*, *pl.* **-tas** *or* **-tae** *Anat.* The vascular, membranous structure which supplies a fetus with nourishment before its birth.

plague *n.* Anything that is troublesome. *Pathol.* A highly contagious and often fatal epidemic disease, as the bubonic plague.

plain *adj.* Level; flat; clear; open, as in view; not rich or luxurious; not highly gifted or cultivated.

plainly *adv.*, **plainness** *n.*

plain-tiff *n.* A person who brings suit.

plan *n.* A scheme or method for achieving something; a drawing to show proportion and relationship to parts. *v.* To have in mind as an intention or purpose.

plane *n.* A tool for smoothing or leveling a wood surface. *Geom.* A surface as a straight line that joins any two points on it. *Slang* Airplane. **plane** *v.*

plan-et *n.*, *Astron.* A celestial body which is illuminated by light from the star around which it revolves. **-tary** *adj.*

plan-e-tar-i-um *n.*, *pl.* **-iums** *or* **-ia** A device for exhibiting celestial bodies as they exist at any time and for any place on earth.

plank *n.* A broad piece of wood; one of

the issues or principles of a political platform.

plant *n.* A living organism belonging to the vegetable kingdom, having cellulose cell walls. *v.* To place a living organism in the ground for growing; to place so as to deceive or to spy.

plaque *n.* A flat piece, made from metal, porcelain, ivory, or other materials, engraved for mounting; the bacteria deposit which builds up on the teeth.

plas-ma *n.* The clear fluid part of blood, used for transfusions.

plas-ter-board *n.* A building material of layered gypsum bonded to outer layers of paper.

plas-tic *adj.* Pliable; capable of being molded. *n.* A synthetically made material which is molded and then hardened into objects.

plasticity *n.* **plasticize** *v.*

plastic surgery *n.* Surgery dealing with the restoration or repair of deformed or destroyed parts of the body or skin.

plate *n.* A flat flexible, thin piece of material, as metal; a shallow, flat vessel made from glass, crockery, plastic, or other material from which food is served or eaten; a piece of plastic, metal, or vulcanite fitted to the mouth to hold one or more artificial teeth. *Baseball* The place or object marking home base. *v.* To cover something, as jewelry, with a thin layer of gold, silver, or other metal.

pla-teau *n.* An extensive level expanse of elevated land; a period or stage of stability.

plat-form *n.* Any elevated or raised surface used by speakers, or by other performers or for display purposes; a formal declaration of principles or policy of a political party.

plat-i-num *n.* A silver-white, metallic element which is corrosive-resistant, used in jewelry; symbolized by Pt.

pla-toon *n.* A military unit subdivision commanded by a lieutenant.

plat-ter *n.* A large, oblong, shallow dish for serving food.

plau-si-ble *adj.* Seeming to be probable; appearing to be trustworthy or believable.

play *v.* To amuse or entertain oneself, as in recreation; to take part in a game; to perform in a dramatic role; to perform with a musical instrument; in fishing, to allow a hooked fish to tire itself out; to pretend to do something. *n.* A dramatic presentaton.

play-ful *adj.* Lightly humorous; full of high spirits.

play-ground *n.* The area set aside for children's recreation.

play-off *n.* A sports contest to break a tie; a series of games to decide the winner or championship.

pla-za *n.* An open-air marketplace or square; a shopping mall.

plea *n.* An urgent request. In law, an allegation made by either party in a law suit.

plead *v.* To argue for or against something in court; to ask earnestly.

pleas-ant *adj.* Giving or promoting the feeling of pleasure; very agreeable. **pleasantly** *adv.* **pleasantness** *n.*

please *v.* To make happy; to give pleasure; to be the will or wish of; to prefer.

pleas-ur-a-ble *adj.* Pleasant; gratifying.

pleas-ure *n.* A feeling of satisfaction or enjoyment; one's preference or wish.

pleat *n.* A fold in a cloth made by doubling the cloth back and fastening it down.

plebe *n.* A freshman or first year student at the United States Naval Academy.

pledge *n.* A solemn promise; a deposit of something as security for a loan; a promise to join a fraternity; a person who is pledged to join a fraternity. *v.* To promise or vow.

plen-ti-ful *adj.* Having great abundance. **plentifully** *adv.* **plentifulness** *n.*

plen-ty *n.* An ample amount; prosperity or abundance.

pleu-ra *n., pl.* **pleurae** *Anat.* The membranous sac which envelops the lungs and provides a lining for the thoracic cavity.

pli-a-ble *adj.* Flexible; easily controlled or persuaded. **pliability,** **pliableness** *n.* **pliably** *adv.*

pli-ers *pl. n.* A pincers-like implement used for holding, bending, or cutting.

plight *n.* A distressing circumstance, situation, or condition.

plod *n.* To walk in a heavy, slow way.

plot *n.* A small piece of ground usually used for a special purpose; the main story line in a piece of fiction; a plan; an intrigue; a conspiracy. *v.* To represent something by using a map or chart; to scheme secretly. **plotter** *n.*

plow *n.* An implement for breaking up or turning over the soil. *v.* To dig out. *Slang* To hit with force.

pluck *v.* To remove by pulling out or off; to pull and release the strings on a musical instrument. *Slang* To swindle.

plug *n.* Anything used to stop or close a hole or drain. *Electr.* A two-pronged device attached to a cord and used in a jack or socket to make an electrical connection. *Slang* To advertise favorably; to give a recommendation or a piece of publicity for someone.

plum *n.* A small tree bearing an edible fruit with a smooth skin and a single hard seed; the fruit from such a tree.

plum-age *n.* The feathers of a bird.

plumb *n.* A lead weight tied to the end of a string, used to test the exact perpendicular line of something.

plumb-er *n.* A person who repairs or installs plumbing in a home or business.

plume *n.* A feather used as an ornament.

plun-der *v.* To deprive of goods or property in a violent way. **plunderer** *n.*

plunge *v.* To thrust or cast something, as into water; to submerge; to descend sharply or steeply.

plunk *v.* To put down or place suddenly; to pluck or strum a banjo.

plunk, plunker *n.*

plu-ral *adj.* Consisting of or containing more than one. **plural** *n.*

plus *prep.* Add the symbol (+) which indicates addition; increase; extra quantity.

plu-to-ni-um *n.* A radioactive metallic element symbolized by Pu.

ply *v.* To mold, bend, or shape. *n.* A layer of thickness; the twisted strands of thread, yarn,, or rope.

ply-wood *n.* A structural material consisting of thin layers of wood which have been glued and pressed together.

pneu-mo-nia- *n.* An inflammation caused by bacteria, virus of the lungs, or irritation.

poach *v.* To cook in a liquid just at the boiling point; to trespass on another's property with the intent of taking fish or wild game. **poacher** *n.*

pock-et *n.* A small pouch within a garment, having an open top and used for carrying items. *v.* To put in or deposit in a pocket.

pod *n., Bot.*

A seed vessel, as of a bean or pea. *Aeron* A separate and detachable compartment in a spacecraft.

po-di-a-try *n.* Professional care and treatment of the feet.

po-di-um *n.,pl.* **-ia** *or* **-iums** A small raised platform for an orchestra conductor or a speaker.

po-em *n.* A composition in verse with language selected for its beauty and sound.

po-et *n.* A person who writes poetry.

po-et-ry *n.* The art of writing stories, poems, and thoughts into verse.

point *n.* The sharp or tapered end of something; a mark of punctuation, as a period (.); a geometric object which does not have property or dimensions other than locaton; a degree, condition, or stage; a particular or definite spot in time. *v.* To aim; to indicate direction by using the finger.

poin-set-ti-a *n.* A tropical plant having large scarlet leaves, used in Christmas decorations.

poise *v.* To bring into or hold one's balance. *n.* Equilibrium; self-confidence; the ability to stay calm in all social situations.

poi-son *n.* A substance which kills, injures, or destroys. **poisoner** *n.,* **poisonous** *adj.*

poke *v.* To push or prod at something with a finger or other implement.

po-lar *adj.* Having to do with the poles of a magnet or sphere; relating to the geographical poles of the earth.

po-lar-ize *v.* To cause something to vibrate in an exact pattern; to break up into opposite groups. **-ation** *n.*

pole *n.* Either of the two ends of the axis of a sphere, as the earth; the two points called the North and South Poles, where the axis of the earth's rotation meets the surface; a long, slender rod.

pol-i-o-my-e-li-tis *n.* Inflammation of the spinal cord causing paralysis; also *polio.*

po-lice *n.* A division or department organized to maintain order; the members of such a department. *v.* To patrol; to enforce the law and maintain order. **policewoman** *n.*

po-liceman *n.* A member of the police force. **policewoman** *n.*

pol-i-cy *n., pl.* -ies Any plan or principle which guides decision making.

pol-ish *v.*

To make lustrous and smooth by rubbing; to become refined or elegant.

po-lite *adj.* Refined, mannerly, and courteous.

po-lit-i-cal *adj.* Concerned with or pertaining to government; involved in politics.

pol-i-ti-cian *n.* A person active in governmental affairs or politics.

pol-i-tics *n.* The activities and methods of a political party.

poll *n.* The recording of votes in an election; a public survey taken on a given topic. **poll** *v.*

pol-len *n.* The yellow dust-like powder which contains the male reproductive cells of a flowering plant.

pol-lute *v.* To contaminate; to make unclear or impure; to dirty. **pollution** *n.*

po-lo-ni-um *n.* A radioactive metallic element symbolized by PO.

pol-ter-geist *n.* A mischievous ghost or spirit which makes much noise.

pol-y-es-ter *n.* A strong lightweight synthetic resin used in fibers.

pol-y-graph *n.* A machine designed to record different signals given off by the body, as respiration, blood pressure, or heartbeats; may be used to detect a person who may be lying.

pol-y-he-dron *n., pl.* -dra *or* -drons *Geom.* A solid bounded by polygons.

pom-pa-dour *n.* A hairstyle which is pulled over the forehead.

pomp-ous *adj.* A showing or appearance of dignity or importance.

pond *n.* A body of still water, smaller in size than a lake.

pon-der *v.* To weigh or think about very carefully; to meditate.

pon-der-ous *adj.* Massive; having great weight.

pon-tiff *n.* A pope.

po-ny *n., pl.* -ies A small horse.

poor *adj.* Lacking possessions and money; not satisfactory; broke; needy; destitute.

pop *v.* To cause something to burst; to make a sharp, explosive sound. *Slang* Soda. **popper** *n.*

pope *n.* The head of the Roman Catholic Church.

pop-lar *n.* A rapid growing tree having a light, soft wood.

pop-u-lar *adj.* Approved of; widely liked; suited to the means of the people.

pop-u-la-tion *n.* The total number of people in a given area, country, or city.

por-ce-lain *n.* A hard, translucent ceramic which has been fired and glazed.

porch *n.* A covered structure forming the entrance to a house.

por-cu-pine *n.*

A clumsy rodent covered with long sharp quills.

pore *v.* To ponder or meditate on something. *n.* A minute opening, as in the skin.

pork *n.* The edible flesh of swine. *Informal* Favors given by a government for political reasons and not public necessity.

por-nog-ra-phy *n.* Pictures, films, or writing which deliberately arouse sexual excitement.

por-poise *n.*

An aquatic mammal with a blunt, rounded snout.

port *n.* A city or town with a harbor for loading and unloading cargo from ships; the left side of a ship; a dark-red, sweet, fortified wine.

port-a-ble *adj.* Capable of being moved easily.

por-ter *n.* A person hired to carry baggage.

port-fo-li-o *n.* A carrying case for holding papers, drawings, and other flat items.

port-hole *n.* A small opening in the side of a ship providing light and ventilation.

por-tion *n.* A section or part of a whole; a share. *v.* To allot; to assign.

por-tray *v.* To represent by drawing, writing, or acting.

pose *v.* To place or assume a position, as for a picture.

po-si-tion *n.* The manner in which something is placed; an attitude; a viewpoint; a job; employment. *v.* To place in proper order.

pos-i-tive *adj.* Containing, expressing, or characterized by affirmation; very confident; absolutely certain; not negative. **positively** *adv.,* **positiveness** *n.*

pos-se *n.* A deputized group or squad.

pos-ses-sion *n.* The fact or act of possessing property; the state of being possessed, as by an evil spirit.

pos-ses-sive *adj.* Having a strong desire to possess; not wanting to share. *n.* The noun or pronoun case which indicates ownership.

pos-si-ble *adj.* Capable of being true,

happening, or being accomplished. possibility n., possibly adv.

post-age n. The charge or fee for mailing something.

pos-te-ri-or adj. Located in the back. n. The buttocks.

post-mor-tem adj. The examination of a body after death; an autopsy.

post-op-er-a-tive adj. Following surgery.

post-pone v. To put off; to defer to a later time. postponable adj., postponement, postponer n.

post-script n. A short message added at the end of a letter.

pos-ture n. The carriage or position of the body.

po-tas-si-um n. A silvery-white, highly reactive metallic element symbolized by K.

po-ta-to n., pl. -toes A thick, edible, underground tuber plant native to America.

po-tent adj. Having great strength or physical powers; having a great influence on the mind or morals; sexually competent.

po-ten-tial adj. Possible, but not yet actual; having the capacity to be developed. Electr. The potential energy of an electric charge that depends on its position in an electric field. potentiality n., potentially adv.

pot-pour-ri n. A mixture of sweet-smelling dried flower petals and spices, kept in an airtight jar.

pot-ter-y n., pl. -ies Objects molded from clay and fired by intense heat.

poul-try n. Domestic fowl as ducks and hens, which are raised for eggs or meat.

pov-er-ty n. The condition or state of being poor and needing money.

pow-er-ful adj. Possessing energy or great force; having authority.

power of attorney n. A legal document in which one person gives another the authority to act for him.

prac-ti-cal adj. Serving an actual use or purpose; inclined to act instead of thinking or talking about something; useful.

pract-ice n. A custom or habit of doing something. v. To work at a profession; to apply; to put into effect; to exercise or rehearse.

prai-rie n. A wide area of level or rolling land with grass and weeds but no trees.

praise v. To express approval; to glorify.

prank n. A mischievous, playful action or trick. prankster n.

pra-seo-dym-i-um n. A metallic element of the rare-earth group, symbolized by Pr.

prawn n. An edible shrimp-like crustacean found in both salt and fresh water.

pray v. To address prayers to God; to ask or request.

prayer n. A devout request; the act of praying; a formal or set group of words used in praying.

praying mantis n. An insect which holds its front legs folded as, in prayer.

pre- pref Earlier or prior to something; in front.

preach v. To advocate; to proclaim; to deliver a sermon. preacher, preachment n., preachy adj.

pre-cau-tion n. A measure of caution or care taken in advance to guard against harm.

pre-cede v. To be or go before in time, position, or rank. precedence n.

prec-e-dent n. An instance which may serve as a rule or example in the future.

pre-cept n. A rule, order, or commandment meant to guide one's conduct.

pre-cinct n. An electoral district of a county, township, city, or town; an enclosure with definite boundaries.

pre-cious adj. Having great worth or value; beloved; cherished.

pre-cip-i-ta-tion n. Condensed water vapor which falls as snow, rain, sleet or hail. Chem. The act of causing crystals to separate and fall to the bottom of a liquid.

pre-cip-i-tous adj. Very steep; marked with very steep cliffs.

pre-cise adj. Exact; definite; strictly following rules; very strict.

pre-ci-sion n. Exactness; the quality of being precise; accuracy.

pre-clude v. To shut out; to make impossible; to prevent.

pre-co-cious adj. Showing and developing skills and abilities very early in life.

pre-con-ceive v. To form a notion or conception before knowing all the facts. preconception n.

pre-da-cious adj. Living by preying on other animals.

pre-des-ti-na-tion n. Destiny; fate; the act by which God has predestined all events.

pred-i-ca-ble adj. Capable of being predicated; to foretell.

pred-i-cate n. Gram. The word or words which say something about the subject of a clause or sentence; the part of a sentence which contains the verb. v. To establish.

pre-dict v. To tell beforehand; to foretell; to forcast. predictability n., -able adj., -ably adv., prediction n.

pre-dom-i-nant adj. Superior in strength, authority, number, or other qualities.

pree-mie n. Slang A baby born before the expected due date.

pre-empt v. To take or get hold of before someone else; to take the place of; to do something before someone else has a chance to do it. -ion n., -ive adj.

pre-fab-ri-cate v. To construct in sections beforehand. prefabrication n.

pref-ace n. The introduction at the beginning of a book or speech.

pre-fect n. A high administrative official.

pre-fer v. To select as being the favorite; to promote; to present.

pref-er-ence n. A choice; a special liking for anything over another.

pre-fix v. To put at the beginning; to put before.

preg-nant adj. Carrying an unborn fetus; significant. **pregnancy** n.

pre-his-tor-i-cal adj. Of or related to the period before recorded history.

pre-judge v. To judge before one knows all the facts. **prejudgment** n.

prej-u-dice n. A biased opinion based on emotion rather than reason; bias against a group, race, or creed.

pre-lim-i-nar-y adj. Leading up to the main action. **preliminaries** n.

prel-ude n. An introductory action. *Music* The movement at the beginning of a piece of music.

pre-med-i-tate v. To plan in advance or beforehand.

pre-mi-er adj. First in rank or importance. n. The chief executive of a government. **premiership** n.

pre-na-tal adj. Existing prior to birth.

pre-oc-cu-py v. To engage the mind or attention completely.

prep *Slang* Preparatory school; preparation.

prep-a-ra-tion n. The process of preparing for something.

pre-par-a-to-ry adj. Serving as preparation.

pre-pare v To make ready or qualified; to equip. **preparedly** adv.

pre-pay v. To pay for in advance.

pre-pon-der-ate v. To have superior importance, weight, force, influence, or other qualities. **preponderance, preponderancy** n., **preponderantly** adv.

prep-o-si-tion n., *Gram.* A word placed in front of a noun or pronoun to show a connection with or to something or someone.

pre-pos-ter-ous adj. Absurd; ridiculous; beyond all reason.

prep-pie n. *Slang* A student attending a prep school; a young adult who behaves and dresses very traditionally.

pre-rog-a-tive n. The unquestionable right belonging to a person.

pres-age n. An omen or indication of something to come; a premonition.

pre-scribe v. To impose as a guide; to recommend.

pre-scrip-tion n., *Med.* A physician's written order for medicine.

pres-ence n. The state of being present; the immediate area surrounding a person or thing; poise.

pres-en-ta-tion n. A formal introduction of one person to another; to present something as an exhibition, show, or product.

pre-serv-a-tive adj. Keeping something from decay or injury. **preservation** n., **preservable** adj.

pre-serve v. To keep or save from destruction or injury; to prepare fruits or vegetables to prevent spoilage or decay. **preserves** Fruit which has been preserved with sugar.

pres-i-dent n. The chief executive officer of a government, corporation, or association. **presidency** n., **-ial** adj.

pres-sure n. The act of or the state of being pressed; a constraining moral force; any burden, force, painful feeling, or influence; the depressing effect of something hard to bear.

pres-tige n. Importance based on past reputation and achievements.

pres-to adv., *Music* Very fast and quick; at once.

pre-sume v. To take for granted; to take upon oneself without permission; to proceed overconfidently. **-able** adj., **presumably** adv., **presumer** n.

pre-sump-tion n. Arrogant conductor speech; something that can be logically assumed true until disproved.

pre-tend v. To make believe; to act in a false way. **pretender** n.

pre-tense n. A deceptive and false action or appearance; a false purpose.

pre-ten-tions n. Having or making claims to worth, excellence, etc.; showy.

pre-text n. A motive assumed in order to conceal the true purpose.

pret-ty adj. Pleasant; attractive; characterized by gracefulness; pleasing to look at. **sitting pretty** In a favorable position; good circumstances. **prettier, prettiest** adj.

pre-vail v. To succeed; to win control over something; to predominate. **prevailer** n., **prevailingly** adv.

pre-vent v. To keep something from happening; to keep from doing something.

pre-ven-tive or **preventative** adj. Protecting or serving to ward off harm, disease, or other problems. **preventive** n.

pre-view or **prevue** n. An advance showing or viewing to invited guests.

pre-vi-ous adj. Existing or occurring earlier. **previously** adv.

price n. The set amount of money expected or given for the sale of something.

pride n. A sense of personal dignity; a feeling of pleasure because of something achieved, done, or owned.

priest n. A clergyman in the Catholic church who serves as mediator between God and His worshipers.

pri-ma-ry adj. First in origin, time, series, or sequence; basic; fundamental.

prim-i-tive adj. Of or pertaining to the beginning or earliest time; resembling the style or manners of an earlier time.

primp v. To dress or arrange with superfluous attention to detail.

prince n. The son of a king; a king.

prin-cess n. The daughter of a king.

prin-ci-pal adj. Chief; most important. n. The head-master or chief official of a school; a sum of money invested or owed which is separate from the interest.

prin-ci-ple n. The fundamental law or truth upon which others are based; a moral standard.

print n. An impression or mark made with ink; the design or picture which is transferred from an engraved plate or other impression. v. To stamp designs; to publish something in print, as a book or magazine.

print-er n. A person whose occupation is printing.

print-out n. Computer Science The output of a computer, printed on paper.

pri-or adj. Previous in order or time.

pri-or-i-ty n. Something which takes precedence; something which must be done or taken care of first.

prism n.

A solid figure with triangular ends and rectangular sides, used to disperse light into a spectrum.

pris-on n. A place of confinement where people are kept while waiting for a trial or while serving time for breaking the law; jail. **prisoner** n.

pri-vate adj. Secluded or removed from the public view; secret; intimate.

priv-i-lege n. A special right or benefit granted to a person. **privileged** adj.

prize n. An award or something given to the winner of a contest; something exceptional or outstanding.

pro n. An argument in favor of or supporting something. Slang A professional or an expert in a given field.

prob-a-bil-i-ty n., pl. -ies The state or quality of being probable; a mathematical statement or prediction of the odds of something happening or not happening.

prob-a-ble adj. Likely to become a reality, but not certain or proved.

pro-bate n. The act of legally proving that a will is genuine.

probe n. An instrument used for investigating an unknown environment; a careful investigation or examination.

prob-lem n. A perplexing situation or question; a question presented for consideration, solution, or discussion. **problem, problematic** adj.

pro-ce-dure n. A certain pattern or way of doing something; the normal methods or forms to be followed.

pro-ceed v. To carry on or continue an action or process. Law To begin or institute legal action.

pro-ceeds pl., n. The profits received from a fund-raising venture.

proc-ess n. The course, steps, or methods toward a desired result. Law Any judicial request or order. Computer Science The sequence of operations which gives a desired result. v. To compile, compute, or assemble; data.

pro-ces-sion n. A group which moves along in a formal manner; a parade.

pro-ces-sor n. Computer Science The central unit of a computer which processes data.

pro-claim v. To announce publicly.

proc-la-ma-tion n. An official public declaration or announcement.

pro-cras-ti-nate v. To put off, defer, or postpone to a later time. **procrastination, procrastinator** n.

proc-tor n. A person in a university or college whose job it is to see that order is maintained during exams.

pro-cure v. To acquire; to accomplish.

prod v. To arouse mentally; to poke with a pointed instrument. n. A pointed implement used to prod or poke.

prod-i-gal adj. Wasteful expenditure of money, strength, or time; extravagance. n. One who is a spendthrift or is wasteful.

pro-duc-tion n. The process or act of producing; something produced, as a play.

pro-fane adj. Manifesting disrespect toward sacred things; vulgar.

pro-fess v. To admit or declare openly; to make an open vow.

pro-fes-sor n. A faculty member of the highest rank in a college or university; a highly skilled teacher.

pro-fi-cient adj. Highly skilled in a field of knowledge. **proficiency** n.,

prof-it n. The financial return after all expenses have been accounted for. v. To gain an advantage or a financial reward. **profitable** adj.

pro-found adj. Deeply held or felt; intellectually penetrating.

pro-fuse adj. Extravagant; giving forth lavishly; overflowing. **profusely** adv., **profuseness** n.

prog-e-ny n., pl. -ies One's offspring, children, or descendants.

prog-no-sis n., pl. -noses A prediction of the outcome and course a disease may take.

pro-gram n. Any prearranged plan or course; a show or performance, as one given at a scheduled time. Computer Science A sequence of commands which tell a computer how to perform a task or sequence of tasks. **program** v.

prog-ress n. Forward motion or advancement to a higher goal; an advance; steady improvement.

pro-hib-it v. To forbid legally; to prevent.

pro-ject n. A plan or course of action; a proposal; a large job. v. To give an estimation on something.

pro-jec-tile n. Anything hurled forward through the air.

pro-jec-tion n. The act or state of being projected; the state or part that sticks out.

pro-lif-er-ate v. To grow or produce with great speed, as cells in tissue formation.

prom-i-nent adj. Jutting out; widely known; held in high esteem.

pro-mis-cu-ous adj. Lacking selectivity or discrimination, especially in sexual relationships.

prom-ise n. An assurance given that one will or will not do something; a pledge. **promise** v.

prompt adj. Arriving on time; punctual; immediate. v. To suggest or inspire.

pro-noun n., Gram. A word which can be used in the place of a noun or noun phrase.

pro-nounce v. To deliver officially; to articulate the sounds.

prop-a-gate v. To reproduce or multiply by natural causes; to pass on qualifies or traits. propagation n.

prop-er-ty n., pl. -ies Any object of value owned or lawfully acquired, as real estate; a piece of land.

proph-e-cy n., pl. -ies A prediction made under divine influence.

proph-et n. One who delivers divine messages; one who foretells the future.

pro-pi-ti-ate v. To win the goodwill of; to stop from being angry. propitiation n.

pro-po-nent n. One who supports or advocates a cause.

pro-por-tion n. The relation of one thing to another in size, degree, or amount. v. To adjust or arrange with balance and harmony. proportional, -ate adj., proportionally adv.

prop-o-si-tion n. A scheme or plan offered for consideration; a subject or idea to be proved or discussed. v. To make a sexual suggestion.

pro-pri-e-ty n., pl. -ies The quality or state of being proper in accordance with recognized principles or usage.

pro-pul-sion n. The act or process of propelling. propulsive adj.

pro-rate v. To distribute or divide proportionately. proration n.

pro-scribe v. To banish; to outlaw; to prohibit.

prose n. Ordinary language, speech, or writing which is not poetry.

pros-e-cute v. To carry on. Law To bring suit against a person; to seek enforcement for legal process. prosecution n.

pros-pect n. Something that has the possibility of future success; a possible customer. v. To explore. prospective adj., prospectively adv.

pros-tate n. A small gland at the base of the male bladder.

pros-ti-tute n. One who sells the body for the purpose of sexual intercourse.

pros-trate adj. Lying with the face down to the ground. v. To overcome; to adopt a submissive posture. prostrative adj., prostration n.

pro-tect v. To guard or shield from attack or injury; to shield. protective adj., protectively adv.

pro-test v. To make a strong formal objection; to object to. n. The act of protesting. protester n.

pro-to-col n. The code and rules of diplomatic and state etiquette.

pro-ton n., Physics A unit of positive charge equal in magnitude to an electron.

pro-tract v. To extend in space; to protrude.

pro-trude v. To project; to thrust outward. protrusion n.

prove v. To show with valid evidence that something is true. provable adj., provably adv.

pro-vide v. To supply or furnish with what is needed.

pro-vi-sion n. A supply of food or needed equipment.

pro-voke v. To cause to be angry; to annoy. provocation n.

prox-i-mate adj. Immediate; direct; close.

prox-y n., pl. -ies The authority, usually written, to act for another.

prude n. A person who is very modest, especially in matters related to sex. prudery, prudishness n., prudish adj.

pru-dent adj. Cautious; discreet; managing very carefully.

psalm n. A sacred hymn, taken from the Book of Psalms in the Old Testament.

pso-ri-a-sis n., Pathol. A non-contagious, chronic, inflammatory skin disease characterized by reddish patches and white scales.

psych v., Slang To prepare oneself emotionally or mentally; to outwit or outguess.

psy-chi-a-try n. The branch of medicine which deals with the diagnosis and treatment of mental disorders.

psy-chol-o-gy n., pl. -ies The science of emotions, behavior, and the mind. psychological adj., psychologist n.

psy-cho-path n. A person suffering from a mental disorder characterized by aggressive antisocial behavior. -ic adj.

pu-ber-ty n. The stage of development in which sexual reproduction can first occur; the process of the body which culminates in sexual maturity.

pub-lic adj. Pertaining to or affecting the people or community; for everyone's use; widely or well known.

pub-lish v. To print and distribute a book, magazine, or any printed matter to the public. -able adj., -er n.

pud-dle n. A small pool of water.

puff n. A brief discharge of air or smoke. v. To breathe in short heavy breaths.

pulp n. The soft juicy part of a fruit; a soft moist mass; inexpensive paper.

pul-sate v. To beat rhythmically. pulsation, pulsator n.

pulse n., Physiol. The rhythmical beating of the arteries caused by the action of the heart. pulse v.

pul-ver-ize v. To be reduced to dust or powder by crushing.

punc-tu-al adj. Prompt; arriving on time.

pun-ish v. To subject a person to confinement or impose a penalty for a crime.

punishment n. A penalty which is imposed for breaking the law or a rule.

punt n. A narrow, long, flat-bottomed boat; in football, a kick of a football dropped from the hands. v. To kick a football.

pup n.

A puppy, young dog, or the young of other animals.

pupil n. A person who attends school and receives instruction by a teacher.

pup-pet *n.* A small figure of an animal or person which is manipulated by hand or by strings. **puppeteer, puppetry** *n.*

pur-chase *v.* To receive by paying money as an exchange. **purchaser** *n.*

pure *adj.* Free from anything that damages, weakens, or contaminates; innocent; clean.

purge *v.* To make clean; to free from guilt or sin; to rid of anything undesirable, as unwanted persons. *Med.* To cause or induce emptying of the bowels. **purge** *n.*

pu-ri-fy *v.* To make clean or pure. **purification, purifier** *n.*

pu-ri-ty *n.* The quality of being pure; freedom from guilt or sin.

pur-ple *n.* A color between red and violet. **purplish** *adj.*

pur-port *v.* To give the appearance of intending; to imply, usually with the intent to deceive.

pur-pose *n.* A desired goal; an intention. **-ful, purposeless** *adj.*, **purposely** *adv.*

purr *n.* The low, murmuring sound characteristic of a cat. **purr** *v.*

pur-sue *v.* To seek to achieve; to follow in an attempt to capture. **pursuer** *n.*

pur-suit *n.* The act of pursuing an occupation.

pur-vey *v.* To supply provisions as a service. **purveyance, purveyor** *n.*

pus *n.* A yellowish secretion formed in infected tissue which contains bacteria.

put *v.* To cause to be in a location; to bring into a specific relation or state; to bring forward for debate or consideration, as to put up for. **put down** To humiliate.

pu-ta-tive *adj.* Commonly supposed.

pu-tre-fy *v.* To cause to decay; to decay. **putrefaction** *n.*, **putrefactive** *adj.*

putt *n.* In golf, a light stroke made on a putting green to get the ball into the hole.

pyg-my *n., pl.* **-ies** A very small person or animal; a dwarf.

py-lon *n.* A tower serving as a support for electrical power lines.

py-or-rhe-a *n., Pathol.* Inflammation of the gums and sockets of the teeth.

pyr-a-mid *n.*

A solid structure with a square base and triangular sides which meet at a point.

pyre *n.* A pile of combustible material for burning a dead body.

py-ro-ma-ni-a *n.* A compulsion to set fires.

pyr-rhic *n.* A type of ancient Greecian dance of war that simulated the movements of battle.

py-u-ri-a *n. Pathol.* The condition where there is pus in the urine.

pyx-ie *n.* A type of evergreen plant that is located in the eastern U.S.

pyx-is *n.* A small box, used by the Romans to hold jewelry.

Q, q The seventeenth letter of the English alphabet.

qua *adv.* The character or capacity of.

quack *n.* To make crying sounds as of a duck; someone who pretends or makes believe he knows how to perform something.

qat *n.* A small plant found in Africa, the fresh leaf is chewed for a stimulating effect.

qi-vi-ut *n.* Yarn spun from the fine, soft hair of the musk ox.

quack *n.* The harsh, croaking cry of a duck; someone who pretends to be a doctor. **quack** *v.*, **quackery** *n.*

quack grass *n.* A quickly growing weed.

quack-sal-ver *n.* A doctor who is quacked.

quad-ran-gle *n., Math* A plane figure with four sides and four angles.

quad-rant *n.*

A quarter section of a circle, subtending or enclosing a central angle of 90 degrees.

quad-rate *adj.* Being square.

quad-ri-ceps *n.* The great muscle of the front of the thigh.

quad-rille *n.* A square dance consisting of four couples.

quad-ril-lion *n.* A thousand trillions; one followed by fifteen zeros.

quad-ru-ple *adj.* Consisting of four parts; multiplied by four.

quaff *v.* To drink with abundance.

quag-mire *n.* An area of soft muddy land that gives away underfoot; a marsh.

quail *n., pl.* A small game bird.

quaint *adj.* Pleasing in an old-fashioned, unusual way.

quake *v.* To shake or tremble violently.

quak-er *n.* The religious sect called the Society of Friends.

qual-i-fi-ca-tion *n.* An act of qualifying; the ability, skill, or quality which makes something suitable for a given position.

qual-i-fy *v.* To prove something able.

qual-i-ty *n., pl.*, **ties** A distinguishing character which makes something such as it is; a high degree of excellence.

qualm *n.* A sudden feeling of sickness; sensation of uneasiness or doubt.

quan-da-ry *n.* A state of perplexity.

quan-ti-ty *n.* Number; amount; bulk; weight; a portion; as a large amount.

quar-an-tine *n.* A period of enforced isolation for a specified period of time used to prevent the spread of a contagious disease. **quarantine** *v.*

quar-rel *n.* An unfriendly, angry disagreement.

quar-ry *n., pl.* **quar-ries** An animal hunted for food; an open pit or excavation from which limestone or other material is being extracted.

quart *n.* A unit of measurement equaling four cups.

quar-ter *n.* One of four equal parts into

which anything may be divided; a place of lodging, as a barracks; a U.S. coin equal to 1/4 of a dollar.

quar-ter-back n. Football The offensive player who directs the plays for his team.

quar-ter-mas-ter n. The officer in charge of supplies for army troops; a navy Od officer who steers a ship and handles signaling equipment.

quar-tet n. A musical composition for four voices or instruments; any group or set of four.

quartz n. A hard, transparent crystallized mineral.

qua-sar n. One of the most distant and brightest bodies in the universe; a quasar producing intense visible radiation but not emitting radio signals.

quea-sy adj. Nauseated; sick. **-iness** n.

queen n. The wife of a king; a woman sovereign or monarch; in chess, the most powerful piece on the board, which can move any number of squares in any direction; the fertile female in a colony of social insects.

queer adj. Strange; unusual; different from the normal. Slang Homosexual.

quell v. To put down with force; to quiet; to pacify.

quench v. To extinguish or put out; to cool metal by thrusting into water; to drink to satisfy a thirst.

quer-u-lous adj. Complaining or fretting; expressing complaints.

que-ry n. An injury; a question. v. To question.

quest n. A search; pursuit; an expedition to find something.

ques-tion n. An expression of inquiry which requires an answer; a problem; an unresolved matter; the act of inquiring or asking.

ques-tion mark n. A mark of punctuation, (?), used in writing to indicate a question.

ques-tion-naire n. A written series of questions to gather statistical information often used for a survey.

queue n. Computer Science A sequence of stored programs or data on hold for processing.

quib-ble v. To raise trivial objection. **quibble, quibbler** n.

quiche n. Unsweetened custard baked in a pastry shell, usually with vegetables or seafood.

quick adj. Moving swiftly; occurring in a short time; responding, thinking, or understanding something rapidly and easily. **quickly** adv., **quickness** n.

quick-sand n. A bog of very fine, wet sand of considerable depth, that engulfs and sucks down objects, people, or animals.

quid n. A small portion of tobacco; a cow's cud.

qui-es-cent adj. Being in a state of quiet repose.

qui-et adj. Silent; making very little sound; still; tranquil; calm. v. To become or make quiet. n. The state of being quiet.

quill n.

A strong bird feather; a spine from a porcupine; a writing instrument made from a long stiff feather.

quilt n. A bed coverlet made of two layers of cloth with a soft substance between and held in place by lines of stitching.

qui-nine n., Chem. A very bitter, colorless, crystalline powder used in the treatment of malaria.

quin-sy n., Pathol. A severe inflammation of the tonsils, which is accompanied by fever.

quin-tes-sence n. The most essential and purest form of anything.

quin-tet n. A musical composition written for five people; any group of five.

quin-til-lion n. A thousand quadrillions, one followed by eighteen zeros.

quin-tu-ple adj. Increased five times; multiplied by five; consisting of five parts.

quip n. A sarcastic remark. **quipster** n.

quirk n. A sudden, sharp bend or twist; a personal mannerism.

quis-ling n. A person who is a traitor, working against his own country from within.

quit v. To cease; to give up; to depart; to abandon; to resign or leave a job or position.

quite adv. To the fullest degree; really; actually; to a great extent.

quiv-er v. To shake with a trembling motion. n. The arrows used in archery; the case in which arrows are kept.

quix-ot-ic adj. Extravagantly romantic; impractical.

quiz v. To question, as with an informal oral or written examination. **quiz, quizzer** n.

quiz-zi-cal adj. Being odd; teasing; questioning.

quod n. Slang For a jail.

quoit n. A game in which a metal ring connected to a rope is thrown in an attempt to encircle a stake.

quon-dam adj. Former.

quo-rum n. The number of members needed in order to validate a meeting.

quot-a-ble adj. To be suitable for being quoted.

quo-ta-tion n. The exact quoting of words as a passage; the stated current price.

quo-ta-tion mark n. The marks of punctuation (" ") showing a direct quote.

quote v. To repeat exactly what someone else has previously stated.

quo-tid-i-an adj. Occurring or recurring daily.

quo-tient n., Math The amount or number which results when one number is divided by another.

R, r The eighteenth letter of the English alphabet.

rab-bet *n.* A recess or groove along the edge of a piece of wood cut to fit another piece to form a joint. **-ed** *v.*

rab-bi *n.* An ordained leader of Jews; the leader and teacher of a Jewish congregation. **rabbinic** *adj.*

rab-bin-i-cal *adj.* To be referring or pertaining to the rabbis. **rabbinically** *adv.*

rab-bit *n.*

A burrowing mammal related to but smaller than the hare.

rab-ble *n.* A disorderly crowd. **-ing, -ed** *v.*

rab-id *adj.* Affected with rabies; mad; furious. **rabidly** *adv.* **rabidness** *n.*

ra-bies *n.* An acute, infectious viral disease of the central nervous system, often fatal, which is transmitted by the bite of an infected animal.

rac-coon *n., pl.* **-coons, -coon**

A nocturnal mammal with a black, mask-like face and a black-and-white ringed, bushy tail.

race *n.* The zoological division of the human population having common origin and other physical traits, such as hair form and pigmentation; a group of people having such common characteristics or appearances; people united by a common nationality.

race *n.* A contest which is judged by speed; any contest, such as a race for an elective office. **raced, racer** *n.*

ra-ceme *n.* A type of plant bearing flowers along its stalk.

ra-chis *n.* A type of axial structure.

ra-cial *adj.* A characteristic of a race of people.

rac-ism *n.* A thought or belief that one race is better than another race. **-ist** *n.*

rack *n.* An open framework or stand for displaying or holding something; an instrument of torture used to stretch the body; a triangular frame used to arrange the balls on a pool table. *Mech.* A metal bar with teeth designed to move a cogged gear and produce a rotary or linear motion. *v.* to strain, as with great effort in thinking.

rack-et or **racquet** *n.* A light-weight bat-like object with netting stretched over an oval frame, used in striking a tennis ball or a shuttlecock.

rack-et-eer *n.* A person who engages in acts which are illegal.

rac-on-teur *n.* One who is skilled in the act of telling stories.

rac-y *adj.* Having a spirited or strongly marked quality; slightly improper or immodest. **racily** *adv.,* **raciness** *n.*

ra-dar *n.* A system which uses radio signals to detect the presence of an object or the speed the object is traveling.

ra-dar as-tron-o-my *n.* Astronomy that deals with investigations of the celestial bodies of the solar system by comparing characteristics of reflected radar wave with characteristics of ones transmitted from earth.

ra-dar-scope *n.* A screen or oscilloscope that serves as a visual indicator in a radar receiver.

rad-dled *adj.* To be in a state of confusion; broken down; worn; lacking composure.

ra-di-al *adj.* Pertaining to or resembling a ray or radius; developing from a center axis.

ra-di-ance *n.* The quality of being shiny; the state of being radiant; relating or emitting to radiant heat.

ra-di-ant *adj.* Emitting rays of heat or light; beaming with kindness or love; projecting a strong quality. **-ly** *adv.*

ra-di-ant heat *n.* Heat that is transmitted by radiation.

ra-di-ate *v.* To move out in rays, such as heat moving through the air. **-ly** *adv.*

ra-di-a-tion *n.* An act of radiating; the process or action of radiating; the process of emitting radiant energy in the form of particles or waves. **radiationless** *adj.,* **radiative** *adj.*

ra-di-a-tor *n.* Something which radiates.

rad-i-cal *adj.* Proceeding from a foundation or root; drastic; making extreme changes in views, conditions, or habits; carrying convictions or theories to their fullest application. **radically** *adv.,* **radicalness** *n.*

ra-di-o *n.* The technique of communicating by radio waves; the business of broadcasting programmed material to the public via radio waves. **radioing, radioed** *v.*

ra-dio-ac-tive *adj.* Exhibiting radioactivity. **radioactively** *adv.*

ra-di-o-ac-tiv-i-ty *n., Physics* A spontaneous emission of electromagnetic radiation, as from a nuclear reaction.

ra-di-o-fre-quen-cy *n.* A frequency which is above 15,000 cycles per second that is used in radio transmission.

ra-di-o-gram *n.* A type of radiograph.

ra-di-ol-o-gy *n.* A science which deals with rays for a radioactive substance and use for medical diagnosis. **-ist** *n.*

ra-di-um *n.* A radioactive metallic element symbolized by Ra.

ra-di-us *n., pl.* **-dii** or **-uses**

A line from the center of a circle to its surface or circumference.

ra-don *n.* A heavy, colorless, radioactive gaseous element symbolized by Rn.

raf-fi-a *n.* A fiber from an African palm tree used for making baskets, hats, and other woven articles.

raff-ish *adj.* Something that is marked by crudeness or flashy vulgarity. **raffishly** *adv.,* **raffishness** *n.*

raf-fle *n.* A game of chance; a lottery in

which one buys chances to win something.

raft *n.* A floating structure made from logs or planks and used for water transportation.

raft-er *n.* A timber of a roof which slopes.

rag *n.* A cloth which is useless and sometimes used for cleaning purposes.

rag-a-muf-fin *n.* A child who is unkempt.

rag-bag *n.* A miscellaneous grouping or collection; a bag for holding scrap pieces of material.

rag doll *n.* A child's doll that is usually made from scrap material and has a hand painted face.

rage *n.* Violent anger. -ing *adj.*, -ly *adv.*

rag-ged *adj.* To be torn or ripped. raggedness *n.*, raggedly *adv.*

rag-weed *n.* A type of plant whose pollen can cause hay fever.

raid *n.* A sudden invasion or seizure.

rail *n.* A horizontal bar of metal, wood, or other strong material supported at both ends or at intervals; the steel bars used to support a track on a railroad.

rail-ing *n.* A barrier of wood.

rain *n.* The condensed water from atmospheric vapor, which falls to earth in the form of drops.

rain-bow *n.* An arc that contains bands of colors of the spectrum and is formed opposite the sun and reflects the sun's rays, usually visible after a light rain shower.

rain check *n.* A coupon or stub for merchandise which is out of stock; the assurance of entrance or availability at a later date.

rain-coat *n.* A water-resistant or waterproof coat.

rain-fall *n.* The amount of measurable precipitation.

rain gauge *n.* An instrument used to measure rain fall.

rain-making *n.* The act or process of producing or attempting to produce rain by the use of artificial means.

raise *v.* To cause to move upward; to build; to make greater in size, price, or amount; to increase the status; to grow; as plants; to rear as children; to stir ones emotions; to obtain or collect as funds or money.

rai-sin *n.* A grape dried for eating.

rake *n.* A tool with a long handle at the end and a set of teeth at the other end used to gather leaves and other matter; a slope or incline, as the rake of an auditorium. rake *v.*

ral-ly *v.* To call together for a purpose. *n.* A rapid recovery, as from depression, exhaustion, or any setback; in a meeting whose purpose is to rouse or create support.

ram *n.* A male sheep; an implement used to drive or crush by impact; to cram or force into place.

RAM *abbr.* Random access memory.

ram-ble *v.* To stroll or walk without a special destination in mind; to talk without sequence of ideas.

ramble *n.*, **ramblingly** *adv.*

ram-bunc-tious *adj.* Rough or boisterous. rambunctiousness *n.*

ramp *n.* An incline which connects two different levels; movable staircase allows passengers to enter or leave an aircraft.

ram-page *n.* A course of destruction or violent behavior. *v.* To storm about in a rampage. rampageous *adj.*, rampageously *adv.*, rampageousness *n.*

ram-pan-cy *n.* The state or quality of being rampant.

ram-pant *adj.* Exceeding or growing without control; wild in actions; standing on the hind legs and elevating both forelegs. rampantly *adv.*

ram-rod *n.* A metal rod used to drive or plunge the charge into a muzzle-loading gun or pistol; the rod used for cleaning the barrels of a rifle or other firearm.

ram-shack-le *adj.* Likely to fall apart from poor construction or maintenance.

ranch *n.* A large establishment for raising cattle, sheep, or other livestock; a large farm that specializes in a certain crop or animals. rancher *n.*

ran-cid *adj.* Having a rank taste or smell. rancidness *n.*

ran-dom *adj.* Done or made in a way that has no specific pattern or purpose; to select from a group whose members all had an even chance of being chosen.

rang *v.* Past tense of ring.

range *n.* An area over which anything moves; an area of activity; a tract of land over which animals such as cattle and horses graze; an extended line or row especially of mountains; an open area for shooting at a target; large cooking stove with burners and oven. *v.* to arrange in a certain order; to extend or proceed in a particular direction.

range finder *n.* Instrument that is used in gunnery to determine the distance of a target.

rank *n.* A degree of official position or status. *v.* To place in order, class, or rank. *adj.* A strong and disagreeable odor, smell, or taste.

ran-sack *v.* To search or plunder through every part of something.

ran-som *n.* The price demanded or paid for the release of a kidnaped person; the payment for the release of a person or property detained. ransom *v.*

rant *v.* To talk in a wild, loud way.

ra-pa-cious *adj.* Living on prey seized alive; taking by force; plundering. rapaciously *adv.*, -ness, rapacity *n.*

rape *n.* The crime of forcible sexual intercourse; abusive treatment.

rap-id *adj.* Having great speed; completed quickly or in a short time. rapidity, rapidness *n.*

ra-pi-er *n.* A long, slender, straight sword with two edges.

rap-ine *n.* The forcible taking of another's property.

rap-port *n.* A harmonious relationship.

rapt *adj.* Deeply absorbed or carried away with something and not to noticing anything else; engrossed.
raptness *n.*, **raptly** *adv.*

rare *adj.* Scarce; infrequent; often held in high esteem or admiration because of infrequency. **rareness** *n.*

ras-cal *n.* A person full of mischief; a person who is not honest. **rascally** *adj.*

rash *adj.* Acting without consideration or caution. *n.* A skin irritation or eruption caused by an allergic reaction.

rasp *n.*

A file with course raised and pointed projections. *v.* To scrape or rub with a course file; to utter something in a rough, grating voice.
rasper *n.*, **raspy** *adj.*

rasp-berry *n.* A small edible fruit, red or black in color and having many small seeds. *Slang* Contemptuous sound made by expelling air with the tongue between the lips in order to make a vibration.

raspy *adj.* Grating; irritable.

rat *n.*

A rodent similar to the mouse, but having a longer tail.
Slang A despicable person who betrays his friends or associates.

rat-a-tat *n.* A sharp tapping, or repeated knocking.

ratch-et *n.* A mechanism consisting of a pawl that allows a wheel or bar to move in one direction only.

ratch-et wheel *n.* A wheel with teeth that is held place with a engaging handle.

rate *n.* The measure of something to a fixed unit; the degree of price or value; a fixed ratio or amount. *v.* To appraise.

rath-er *adv.* Preferably; with more reason or justice; more accurate or precise.

rat-i-fy *v.* To approve something in an official way. **ratification** *n.*

rat-ing *n.* A relative evaluation or estimate of something.

ra-tio *n.*, *pl.* **-tios** The relationship between two things in amount, size, degree, expressed as a proportion.

ra-tion *n.* A fixed portion or share. *v.* To provide or allot in rations. **rationing** *n.*

ra-tio-nal *adj.* Having the faculty of reasoning; being of sound mind.
-ity *n.*, **rationally** *adv.*, **rationalness** *n.*

rat-tan *n.* An Asian palm whose strong stems are used to make wickerworks.

rat-tle *v.* To make a series of rapid, sharp noises in quick succession; to talk rapidly; chatter. *n.* A baby's toy made to rattle when shaken.

rat-tler *n.*, *Slang* A venomous snake

which has a series of horny, modified joints which make a rattling sound when moved; a rattlesnake; one that rattle.

rat-tle-trap *n.* Something that is rickety or ratly.

rau-cous *adj.* Loud and rowdy; having a rough hoarse sound; disorderly.
raucously *adv.*, **raucousness** *n.*

rav-age *v.* To bring on heavy destruction; devastate.

rave *v.* To speak incoherently; to speak with enthusiasm. *n.* The act of raving.

rav-el *v.* To separate fibers or threads; to unravel. **ravelment** *n.*

ra-ven *n.* A large bird, with shiny black feathers. *adj.* Of or relating to the glossy sheen or color of the raven.

ra-vine *n.* A deep gorge with steep sides in the earth's surface, usually created by flowing water.

rav-ish *v.* To seize and carry off; to rape.
ravishment *n.*, **ravisher** *n.*

raw *adj.* Uncooked; in natural condition; not processed. inexperienced; damp, sharp, or chilly. **rawly** *adv.*, **rawness** *n.*

ray *n.* A thin line of radiation or light; a small trace or amount; one of several lines coming from a point.

ray-on *n.* A synthetic cellulose yarn; any fabric made from such yarn.

ra-zor *n.* A sharp cutting instrument used especially for shaving.

ra-zor-back *n.* A wild hog of the southeastern United States; the mascot of the University of Arkansas.

razz *v.*, *Slang* To heckle; to tease.

raz-zle--daz-zel *n.* A state of complete confusion.

re- *prefix* Again, anew or reverse action.

reach *v.* To stretch out; to be able to grasp. *n.* The act of stretching out.

re-act *v.* To act in response to. *Chem.* To undergo a chemical change; to experience a chemical reaction.

re-ac-tor *n.* A person, object, device, or substance which reacts to something.

read *v.* To visually go over something, as a book, and to understand its meaning; to learn or be informed; to perceive something in a meaning which may or may not actually be there.

read-y *adj.* Prepared for use or action; quick or prompt; willing.

re-a-gent *n* Any substance which causes a chemical reaction.

re-al *adj.* Something which is existing, genuine, true, or authentic. *Law* Property which is regarded as permanent or immovable.

reel-to-reel *adj.* Pertaining to magnetic tape which is threaded to a take-up reel, which moves from one reel to another.

real estate *n.* Land and whatever is attached such as natural resources or buildings.

re-al-ism *n.* Concern or interest with actual facts and things as they really are.
realist *n.*, **-tic** *adj.*, **realistically** *adv.*

re-al-i-ty *n.*, *pl.* The fact or state of being real or genuine; an actual situation or event.

re-al-ize v. To understand correctly; to make real. **realizable** adj., **realization** n., **realizer** n.

re-al-ly adv. Actually; truly; indeed.

realm n. A scope or field of any power or influence.

ream n. A quantity of paper containing 500 sheets.

reap v. To harvest a crop with a sickle or other implement.

rear n. The back. adj. Of or at the rear. v. To raise up on the hind legs; to raise as an animal or child.

rea-son n. A statement given to confirm or justify a belief, promise, or excuse; the ability to decide things, to obtain ideas, to think clearly, and to make logical and rational choices and decisions. v. To discuss something logically. **reasoning** n.

rea-son-a-ble adj. Moderate; rational. **reasonableness** n., **reasonably** adv.

re-a-sur-ance n. The act of reassuring; reinsurance.

re-bate n. A deduction allowed on items sold; a discount; money which is returned to the purchaser from the original payment. v. To return part of the payment. **rebater** n.

re-bel v. To refuse allegiance; to resist any authority; to react with violence.

re-bel-lion n. An organized uprising to change or overthrow an existing authority.

re-bel-lious adj. Engaged in rebellion; relating to a rebel or rebellion. **rebelliously** adv., **rebelliousness** n.

re-birth n. A revival or renaissance; reincarnation.

re-bound v. To spring back; to recover from a setback or frustration. n. Recoil.

re-broad-cast v. To repeat or broadcast again. **rebroadcast** n.

re-buff v. To refuse abruptly; to snub.

re-build v. To make extensive repairs to something; to reconstruct; remodel.

re-buke v. To criticize something sharply; to turn back. **rebuker** n.

re-but v. To try and prove someone wrong by argument or evidence. **rebuttal** n., **rebutable** adj.

re-call v. To order or summon to return to ask for something to be returned; so that defects can be fixed or repaired; to remember; to recollect.

re-cant v. To formally admit that a previously held belief was wrong by making public confession.

re-cap v. To restore an old tire; to review or summarize something.

re-cede v. To move back; as floodwater; to withdraw from an agreement.

re-ceipt n. The written acknowledgment of something received. pl., **receipts** The amount of money received.

re-ceive v. To take or get something; to greet customers or guests; to accept as true or correct. **receiver** n.

re-cent adj. Happening at a time just before the present. **recently** adv.

re-cep-ta-cle n. Anything which holds something; an electrical outlet designed to receive a plug.

re-cep-tion n. The act or manner of receiving something; a formal entertainment of guests, as a wedding reception.

re-cep-tion-ist n. An employee who greets callers and answers the telephone for a business.

re-cep-tive adj. Able to receive. **-ly** adv., **receptiveness, receptivity** n.

re-cess n. A break in the normal routine of something; a depression or niche in a smooth surface.

re-ces-sion n. The act of receding; withdrawal; a period or time of reduced economic activity. **-ary** adj.

rec-i-pe n. The directions and a list of ingredients for preparing food.

re-cip-ro-cate v. To give and return mutually, one gift or favor for another.

re-cite v. To repeat something from memory; give an account of something in detail.

reck-less adj. State of being careless and rash when doing something. **-ness** n.

reck-on v. To calculate; to compute; to estimate; to consider; to assume.

reck-on-ing n. The act of calculation or counting.

re-claim v. To redeem; to reform; to recall; to change to a more desirable condition or state.

rec-la-ma-tion n. The state of being reclaimed.

re-cline v. To assume a prone position. **recliner** n.

re-cluse n. A person who chooses to live in seclusion.

rec-og-ni-tion n. An acknowledgment which is formal.

re-cog-ni-zance n. An amount of money which will be forfeited for a nonperformance of an obligation.

rec-og-nize v. To experience or identify something or someone as having been known previously; to appreciative. **recognizable** adj., **recognizably** adv.

re-coil v. To fall back or to rebound. **recoilless** adj.

rec-ol-lect v. To remember or recall to the mind. **recollection** n.

rec-om-mend v. To suggest to another as desirable; advise. **recommendation** n., **recommedable** adj.

rec-om-pense v. To reward with something for a service.

rec-on-cile v. To restore a friendship after an estrangement. **-ably** adv.

rec-on-dite adj. Being obscure.

re-con-di-tion v. To return to a good condition.

re-con-firm v. Confirm something again.

re-con-nais-sance n. An observation of territory such as that of the enemy.

re-con-noi-ter v. To survey a region.

re-con-sid-er v. To think about again with a view to changing a previous action or decision. **reconsideration** n.

re-con-struct v. To build something again.

re-con-struc-tion *n.* Something which has been reconstructed or rebuilt.

re-cord *v.* To write down for future use or permanent reference; to preserve sound on a tape or disk for replay; a phonograph record. *n.* Information which is recorded and kept permanently.

re-cord-er *n.* A person who records things such as official transactions.

re-cord-ing *n.* The act of making a transcription of sounds.

rec-ord play-er *n.* The machine which is used to play recordings.

re-count *v.* To tell the facts; narrate or describe in detail; to count again. *n.* A second count to check the results of the first count.

re-coup *v.* To be reimbursed; to recover.

re-course *n.* A turning to or an appeal for help.

re-cov-er *v.* To regain something which was lost; to be restored to good health. *Law* To obtain a judgment for damages.

re-cov-er-y *n.* The power to regain something.

rec-re-ant *adj.* Cowardly; unfaithful. recreant *n.*

re-cre-ate *v.* To create again.

rec-re-a-tion *n.* Refreshment of body and mind; a pleasurable occupation or exercise. recreational *adj.*

re-crim-i-nate *v.* The charging of another of the same account. -tory, recriminative *adj.*, recrimination *n.*

re-cruit *v.* To enlist someone for military or naval purposes; to look for someone as for a service or employment. *n.* A newly enlisted person.

rec-tal *adj.* Referring to the rectum of the body.

rec-tan-gle *n.*

A parallelogram with all right angles. rectangular *adj.*, rectangularity *n.*

rec-ti-fi-er *n.* That which rectifies something.

rec-ti-fy *v.* To make correct. *Chem.* To purify by repeated distillations. *Electr.* To make an alternating current a direct current.

rec-ti-lin-e-ar *adj.* Made up of or indicated by straight lines; bounded by straight lines.

rec-ti-tude *n.* Rightness in principles and conduct; correctness.

rec-to *n.* The right-hand page of a book.

rec-tor *n.* A member of the clergy in charge of a parish; a priest in charge of a congregation, church, or parish; the principal or head of a school or of a college.

rec-tum *n.*, *pl.* -tums, -ta *Anat.* The lower terminal portion of the large intestine connecting the colon and anus.

re-cum-bent *adj.* Lying down or reclining.

re-cu-per-ate *v.* To regain strength or to regain one's health; to recover from a financial loss. recuperation *n.*, recuperative *adj.*

re-cur *v.* To happen, to return, or to appear again. recurrence, recurrent *adj.*

re-deem *v.* To buy back; to pay off; to turn something in, as coupons or rain checks and receive something in exchange.

re-doubt *n.* A small enclosed fortification.

re-doubt-a-ble *adj.* To be dreaded.

re-dound *v.* To have an effect on something.

re-dress *v.* To put something right.

red-start *n.* An American warbler which is brightly colored.

re-duce *v.* To decrease; lessen in number, degree, or amount.

re-duc-tion *n.* The state of being reduced.

re-dun-dant *adj.* Exceeding what is necessary; repetitive.

re-du-pli-cate *v.* To repeat something.

re-ech-o *v.* To reverberate again.

reef *n.* A chain of rocks, coral, or sand at or near the surface of the water.

reef-er *n.* A jacket which is close-fitting.

reek *v.* To emit vapor or smoke; to give off a strong offensive odor.

re-e-lect *v.* The act of electing someone again for an office.

re-em-pha-size *v.* To stress something or an idea again.

re-en-list *v.* To enlist or join a group or an armed force again. reenlistment *n.*

re-enter *v.* To enter a room or area again.

re-ex-am-ine *v.* Examine something or someone another time or again.

re-fec-to-ry *n.* The place in colleges where the students dine.

re-fer *v.* To direct for treatment, information, or help.

ref-e-ree *n.* A person who supervises a game, making sure all the rules are followed.

ref-er-ence *n.* The act of referring someone to someplace or to something.

ref-er-en-dum *n.* A public vote on an item for final approval or for rejection.

ref-er-ent *n.* What is referred to such as a person.

re-fill *v.* To fill something with an item again.

re-fine *v.* To purify by removing unwanted substances or material; to improve. refined *adj.*, refinement *n.*

re-fin-ish *v.* The act of putting a new surface onto something, such as wood.

re-fit *v.* To repair something.

re-flect *v.* To throw back rays of light from a surface; to give an image, as from a mirror; to ponder or think carefully about something. reflection *n.* reflective *adj.*

re-flec-tor *n.* Something which is able to reflect things, such as light.

re-flex *adj.* Turning, casting, or bending backward. *n.* An involuntary reaction of the nervous system to a stimulus.

re-for-est *v.* The act of replanting a forest or wooded area with trees.

re-form *v.* To reconstruct, make over, or change something for the better; improve; to abandon or give up evil ways. reformer *n.*, reformed *adj.*

re-for-ma-to-ry *n.* A jail-like institution for young criminals.

re-fract *v.* The deflecting something, such as a ray of light. refractive *adj.*

re-frac-tion *n.* The state of being refracted or deflected.

re-frac-to-ry *adj.* Unmanageable; obstinate; difficult to melt; resistant to heat. *n.* Something which does not change significantly when exposed to high temperatures.

re-frain *v.* To hold back.

re-fresh *v.* To freshen something again.

re-frig-er-ant *n.* An agent which cools something.

re-fu-el *v.* To put fuel into something again.

ref-uge *n.* Shelter or protection from harm; any place one may turn for relief or help.

ref-u-gee *n.* A person who flees to find safety.

re-ful-gent *adj.* State of being radiant or putting off a bright light.

re-fund *v.* To return or pay back; to reimburse. refundable *adj.* refund *n.*

re-fur-bish *v.* To make clean; to renovate.

re-fus-al *n.* The denial of something which is demanded.

re-fuse *v.* To decline; to reject; to deny.

ref-use *n.* Rubbish; trash.

re-fute *v.* To overthrow or to disprove with the use of evidence.

re-gain *v.* To recover; to reach again.

re-gal *adj.* Of or appropriate for royalty. regally *adv.*

re-gale *v.* To entertain or delight; to give pleasure.

re-ga-li-a *n.* Something which represents royalty such as a septer.

re-gard-less *adj.* State of being careless or showing no regard towards something or someone.

re-gat-ta *n.* A boat race.

re-gen-cy *n., pl.* **-ies** The jurisdiction or office of a regent.

re-gen-er-ate *v.* To reform spiritually or morally; to make or create anew; to refresh or restore.

re-gime *n.* An administration.

reg-i-men *n.* Government control; therapy.

reg-i-ment *n.* A military unit of ground troops which is composed of several battalions. -al *adj.*, regimentation *n.*

re-gion *n.* An administrative, political, social, or geographical area.

re-gion-al *adj.* Typical or pertaining to a geographic region; limited to a particular region.

reg-is-ter *n.* Something which contains names or occurrences.

reg-is-trar *n.* The person who keeps a register.

reg-is-tra-tion *n.* An act of recording things or names.

re-gress *v.* To return to a previous state or condition. regress, regression *n.*

re-gret *v.* To feel disappointed or distressed about. *n.* A sense of loss or expression of grief; a feeling of sorrow. regretfully, regretably *adv.*, regretful, regretable *adj.*

reg-u-lar *adj.* Usual; normal; customary; conforming to set principles, procedures, or discipline; well-ordered; not varying. regularity *n.*, regularly *adv.*

reg-u-late *v.* To adjust to a specification or requirement. regulative, regulatory *adj.*, regulator *n.*

reg-u-la-tion *n.* A rule that is set down in order to govern an area or people.

re-gur-gi-tate *v.* To pour something forth.

re-ha-bil-i-tate *v.* To restore; to a former state, by education and therapy. rehabilitation *n.*, rehabilitative *adj.*

re-hash *v.* To rework or go over old material.

re-hears-al *n.* The act of practicing for a performance. rehearse *v.*

reign *n.* The period in time when the monarch rules over an area.

re-im-burse *v.* To repay. -ment *n.*

re-in-state *v.* To restore something to its former position or condition. -ment *n.*

re-it-er-ate *v.* To say or do something over and over again.

re-ject *v.* To refuse; to discard as useless. reject, rejection *n.*

re-joice *v.* To fill with joy; to be filled with joy.

re-join *v.* To respond or to answer someone.

re-join-der *n.* The answer to a reply made by someone to another.

re-ju-ve-nate *v.* To restore to youthful appearance or vigor. rejuvenation *n.*

re-kin-dle *v.* To inflame something again.

re-lapse *v.* To fall back or revert to an earlier condition. relapse *n.*

re-late *v.* To tell the events of; to narrate; to bring into natural association.

re-lat-ed *adj.* To be in the same family; connected to each other by blood or by marriage.

re-la-tion *n.* The relationship between people by marriage or blood lines.

re-la-tion-ship *n.* A connection by blood or family; kinship; friendship; a natural association.

rel-a-tive *adj.* Relevant; connected; considered in comparison or relationship to other. *n.* A member of one's family.

rel-a-tiv-i-ty *n.* A condition or state of being relative.

re-lay *n.* A race in which a fresh team replaces another. *v.* To pass from one group to another.

re-lease *v.* To set free from confinement; to unfasten; to free; to relinquish a claim on something. releaser *n.*

rel-e-gate *v.* To banish someone or something.

re-lent *v.* To soften in temper, attitude, or determination; to slacken.

relentless adj.

rel-e-vant adj. Related to matters at hand.

re-li-a-ble adj. Dependable; capable of being relied upon.

re-li-ance n. Confidence and trust; something which is relied upon.

re-li-ant adj. State of being confident or having reliance.

re-lic n. Something which is very old.

re-lieve v. To lessen or ease pain, anxiety, embarrassment, or other problems; to release or free from a duty by providing a replacement. reliever n., relievable adj.

re-lig-ion n. An organized system of beliefs, rites, and celebrations centered on a supernatural being power; belief pursued with devotion -ious adj.

re-lin-quish v. To release something or someone.

re-lish n. Pleasure; a spicy condiment taken with food to lend it flavor.

re-live v. To experience something again.

re-lo-cate v. To move to another area.

re-luc-tance n. An unwillingness.

re-luc-tant adj. Unwilling; not yielding.

re-ly v. To trust or depend.

re-main v. To continue without change; to stay after the departure of others.

re-mains pl., n. What is left after all other parts have been taken away; corpse.

re-mand n. State of being remanded.

re-mark n. A brief expression or comment; to take notice; to observe; to comment.

re-mark-a-ble adj. Extraordinary. remarkably adv.

re-me-di-a-ble adj. Being able to be remedied.

rem-e-dy n., pl. -ies A therapy or medicine which relieves pain; something which corrects an error or fault. v. To cure or relieve. To rectify.

re-mem-ber v. To bring back or recall to the mind; to retain in the mind carefully.

re-mem-brance n. Something which is remembered by someone.

re-mind v. To cause or help to remember.

rem-i-nisce v. To recall the past things which have happened.

rem-i-nis-cence n. The practice or process of recalling the past. reminiscent adj.

re-miss adj. Lax in performing one's duties; negligent. remissness n.

re-mis-sion n. A forgiveness; act of remitting.

rem-nant n. A small piece or a scrap or something.

re-mod-el v. To reconstruct something making it like new.

re-mon-strance n. Statement of reasons against an idea or something.

re-mon-strate v. Giving strong reasons against an act or an idea.

re-morse n. Deep moral regret for past misdeeds. remorseful adj.

re-mote adj. Distant in time; space or relation. remotely adv., remoteness n.

re-mount v. To mount something again.

re-mov-a-ble adj. Being able to be removed.

re-mov-al n. The change of a site or place.

re-move v. To get rid of; to extract; to dismiss from office; to change one's business or residence. n. An act of moving. removable adj., removal n.

re-moved adj. State of being separate from others.

re-mu-ner-ate v. Pay an equivalent for a service.

re-nal adj. Of or relating to the kidneys.

re-nas-cence n. A revival or a rebirth.

rend v. To remove from with violence; to split.

ren-dez-vous n. A meeting place that has been prearranged. v. To meet at a particular time and place.

ren-di-tion n. An interpretation or a translation.

ren-e-gade n. A person who rejects one allegiance for another; an outlaw; a traitor. renegade adj.

re-nege v. To fail to keep one's word.

re-new v. To make new or nearly new by restoring; to resume. renewable adj.

re-nounce v. To reject something or someone.

ren-o-vate v. To return or to restore to a good condition.

re-nown n. The quality of being widely honored. renowned adj.

rent n. The payment made for the use of another's property. v. To obtain occupancy in exchange for payment. rental n.

re-nun-ci-a-tion n. Renouncing.

re-or-gan-i-za-tion n. The process of reorganizing something.

rep. n., Slang Representative. v. Represent.

re-pair v. To restore to good or usable condition; to renew; refresh. repairable adj.

re-pair-man n. The person who makes repairs of things that are broken.

rep-a-ra-ble adj. Being able to be corrected.

rep-a-ra-tion n. The act of repairing something.

rep-ar-tee n. A quick, witty response or reply.

re-pa-tri-ate v. To go back to one's own country.

re-pay v. To pay back money; to do something in return.

re-peal v. To withdraw officially. repeal n., repealer n.

re-peat v. To utter something again; to do an action again.

re-pel v. To discourage; to force away; to create aversion.

re-pel-lent adj. Able to repel.

re-pent v. To feel regret for something which has occurred; to change one's sinful way. -ance n., repentant adj.

re-per-cus-sion n. An unforeseen effect produced by an action. -ive adj.

rep-er-toire n. The accomplishments or skills of a person.

rep-er-to-ry n. A collection of things.

rep-e-ti-tion n. The act of doing something over and over again; the act of repeating.

re-place v. To return something to its previous place. **replaceable** adj., **replacement** n., **replacer** n.

re-plen-ish v. To add to something to replace what has gone or been used.

re-plete adj. Having plenty; abounding; full.

rep-li-ca n. A reproduction or copy of something. **replicate** v.

re-ply v. To give an answer to either verbally or in writing. **reply** n.

re-port n. A detailed account; usually in a formal way. v. To tell about; to make oneself available; to give details of. **reportable** adj., **reporter** n.

re-port-ed-ly adv. To be according to a report.

re-pose n. The act of being at rest. v. To lie at rest. **reposeful** adj.

re-pos-i-tor-y n. The location where things may be placed for preservation.

re-pos-sess v. To restore ownership of something.

rep-re-hend v. To show or express disapproval of. **reprehension** n., **-sible** adj.

rep-re-sent v. To stand for something; to serve as the official representative for.

rep-re-sen-ta-tion n. The act of representing.

rep-re-sent-a-tive n. A person or thing serving as an example or type. adj. Of or relating to government by representation; typical.

re-press v. To restrain; hold back; to remove from the conscious mind. **repression** n., **repressive** adj.

re-prieve v. To postpone punishment; to provide temporary relief. **-able** adj., **reprieve** n., **reprieve**, **reprieving** v.

rep-ri-mand v. To censure severely; rebuke. **reprimand** n.

re-print n. An additional printing of a book exactly as the previous one. **reprint** v., **reprinter** n.

re-pri-sal n. Retaliation with intent to inflict injury in return for injury received.

re-proach v. To blame; to rebuke. **reproachful** adj.

rep-ro-bate adj. The state of being morally depraved.

re-pro-duce v. To produce an image or copy. Biol. To produce an offspring; to recreate or produce again. **-er** n., **reproducible** adj., **reproduction** n.

re-proof n. A censure.

re-prove v. To tell or express a disapproval of something.

rep-tile n.
A cold-blooded, egg-laying vertebrate, as a snake, lizard, or turtle. **reptilian** n., adj.

re-pub-lic n. A political unit or state where representatives are elected to exercise the power.

re-pub-li-can adj. Having the character of a republic.

re-pub-li-can-ism n. The Republican principles.

re-pu-di-ate v. To cast away; to refuse to pay something.

re-pug-nance n. The state or condition of being opposed.

re-pug-nant adj. Distasteful; repulsive; offensive.

re-pulse v. To repel or drive back; to repel or reject rudely; to disgust or be disgusted. **repulsion** n.

re-pul-sive adj. State of causing aversion.

rep-u-ta-ble adj. To be honorable. **reputability** n.

re-put-a-tion n. The commonly held evaluation of a person's character.

re-pute v. To account or to consider something.

re-quest v. To ask for something.

re-qui-em n. The Roman Catholic mass for a deceased person.

re-quire v. To demand or insist upon. **requirement** n.

req-ui-site adj. Absolutely needed; necessary.

req-ui-si-tion n. A demand or a request.

re-quit-al n. The act of requiting something.

re-quite v. To reward; to repay someone.

re-run n. A television show which is shown again.

re-sale n. The act of selling something again.

re-scind v. To repeal; to void. **rescindable** adj., **rescission** n.

res-cue v. To free from danger. n. An act of deliverance. **rescuer** n.

re-search n. A scientific or scholarly investigation; to carefully seek out. **researcher** n.

re-sem-ble v. To have similarity to something. **resemblance** n.

re-sent v. To feel angry about. **-ful** adj., **resentfully** adv., **resentment** n.

res-er-va-tion n. The act of keeping something back.

re-serve v. To save for a special reason; to set apart; to retain; to put off. n. Something that is saved for a future point in time; the portion of a country's fighting force kept inactive until called upon.

res-er-voir n. A body of water stored for the future; large reserve; a supply.

re-side v. To dwell permanently; to exist as a quality or attribute. **residence** n.

res-i-due n. Matter remaining after treatment or removal of a part; something which remains.

re-sign v. To give up; to submit to something as being unavoidable; to quit. **resignation** n.

res-in n. A plant substance from certain plants and trees used in varnishes and lacquers. **resinous** adj.

re-sist v. To work against or actively oppose; to withstand. **resistible** adj.

res-o-lute *adj.* Coming from or characterized by determination.
resolutely *adv.*, resolution *n.*

re-solve *v.* To make a firm decision on something; to find a solution.
resolvable *adj.*, resolver *n.*, -tion *n.*

re-sort *v.* To go frequently or customarily. *n.* A place, or recreation, for rest, and for a vacation.

re-sound *v.* To be filled with echoing sounds; to reverberate; to ring or sound loudly. resounding *adj.*, resoundingly *adv.*

re-source *n.* A source of aid or support which can be drawn upon if needed. resources One's available capital or assets. resourceful *adj.*

re-spect *v.* To show consideration or esteem for; to relate to. *n.* Courtesy or considerate treatment.
respectfully *adv.* respectful *adj.*

res-pi-ra-tion *n.* The process or act of inhaling and exhaling; the act of breathing; the process in which an animal or person takes in oxygen from the air and releases carbon dioxide.
respirator *n.*

res-pite *n.* A temporary postponement.

re-spond *v.* To answer or reply; to act when promted by something or someone.

re-sponse *n.* A reply; the act of replying.
responsive *adj.*

re-spon-si-ble *adj.* Trustworthy; in charge; having authority; being answerable for one's actions or the actions of others. responsibility *n.*

rest *n.* A cessation of all work, activity, or motion. *Mus.* An interval of silence equal in time to a note of same value. *v.* To stop work; to place or lay.
restful *adj.*, restfully *adv.*

res-tau-rant *n.* A place which serves meals to the public.

res-ti-tu-tion *n.* The act of restoring something to its rightful owner; compensation for injury, loss, or damage.

res-tive *adj.* Nervous or impatient because of a delay. restively *adv.*, restiveness *n.*

re-store *v.* To bring back to a former condition; to make restitution of. restoration *n.*

re-strain *v.* To hold back or be held back; to control, limit, or restrict.
restraint *n.*

re-strict *v.* To confine within limits.
restriction *n.*, restrictive *adj.*, restrictively *adv.*

re-sult *v.* To happen or exist in a particular way. *n.* The consequence of an action, course, or operation.

re-sume *v.* To start again after an interruption. resumption *n.*

res-u-me *n.* A summary of one's personal history, background, work, and education.

re-sus-ci-ate *v.* To return to life; to revive. resuscitation *n.*, resuscitator *n.*

re-tail *v.* The sale of goods or commodities to the public. *v.* To sell to the consumer. retail *adj.*, retailer *n.*

re-tain *v.* To hold in one's possession; to remember; to employ someone, as for his services.

re-tain-er *n.* A person or thing that retains; a fee paid for one's services.

re-tard *v.* To delay or slow the progress of. retardant *n.* & *adj.*

re-tar-da-tion *n.* A condition in which mental development is slow or delayed; a condition of mental slowness.

re-ten-tion *n.* The act or condition of being retained.

ret-i-na *n.*, *pl.* -nas,- nae The light sensitive membrane lining the inner eyeball connected by the optic nerve to the brain. retinal *adj.*

re-tire *v.* To depart for rest; to remove oneself from the daily routine of working. *Baseball* To put a batter out. retirement *n.*, retired *adj.*, retiree *n.*

re-trace *v.* To go back over.

re-tract *v.* To draw back or to take back something that has been said.
retractable *adj.*, retraction *n.*

re-tread *v.* To replace the tread of a worn tire. retread *n.*

re-treat *n.* The act of withdrawing from danger; a time of study; prayer; and meditation in a quiet; isolated location.

re-trieve *v.* To regain; to find something and carry it back. retrievable *adj.*, retrieval *n.*

ret-ro-ac-tive *adj.* Taking effect on a date prior to enactment.

ret-ro-spect *n.* A review of things in the past. -ively *adv.*, retrospective *adj.*

re-turn *v.* To come back to an earlier condition; to reciprocate. *n.* The act of sending, bringing, or coming back. returns *n.* A yield or profit from investments; a report on the results of an election. returnable *adj.*, returnee *n.*, returner *n.*

re-un-ion *n.* A reuniting; the coming together of a group which has been separated for a period of time.

re-veal *v.* To disclose or make known; to expose or bring into view.

rev-eil-le *n.* The sounding of a bugle used to awaken soldiers in the morning.

rev-el *v.* To take great delight in. -er *n.*

rev-e-la-tion *n.* An act of or something revealed; a manifestation of divine truth. **Revelation** The last book in the New Testament.

re-venge *v.* To impose injury in return for injury received. revengeful *adj.*, revenger *n.*

re-verse *adj.* Turned backward in position. *n.* The opposite of something; a change in fortune usually from better to worse; change or turn to the opposite direction; to transpose or exchange the positions of. *Law* To revoke a decision. reverser *n.*

re-vert *v.* To return to a former practice or belief. reversion *n.*

re-view *v.* To study or look over something again; to give a report on. *n.* A reexamination; a study which gives a critical estimate of something.

reviewer n.

re-vise v. To look over something again with the intention of improving or correcting it. **reviser** n., **revision** n.

re-viv-al n. The act or condition or reviving; the return of a film or play which was formerly presented; a meeting whose purpose is religious reawakening.

re-vive v. To restore, refresh, or recall; to return to consciousness or life.

re-voke v. To nullify or make void by recalling. **revocation** n.

re-volt n. To try to overthrow authority; to fill with disgust.

rev-o-lu-tion n. The act or state of orbital motion around a point; the abrupt overthrow of a government; a sudden change in a system.

re-volve v. To move around a central point; to spin; to rotate. **-able** adj.

re-vue n. A musical show consisting of songs, dances, skits, and other similar entertainment.

re-ward n. Something given for a special service. v. To give a reward.

R.F.D. abbr. Rural free delivery.

rhap-so-dy n., pl. **-ies** An excessive display of enthusiasm.

rhe-ni-um n. A metallic element symbolized by Re.

rhet-o-ric n. Effective expression in writing or speech; language which is not sincere.

Rh fac-tor n. A substance found in the red blood cells of 85% of all humans; the presence of this factor is referred to as PH positive; the absence as PH negative.

rhi-noc-er-os n.

A very large mammal with one or two upright horns on the snout.

rho-di-um n. A metallic element symbolized by Rh.

rhu-barb n. A garden plant with large leaves and edible stalks used for pies.

rhyme or **rime** n. A word or verse whose terminal sound corresponds with another. **rhyme** v., **rhymer** n.

rhy-thm n. Music, speech, or movements which are characterized by equal or regularly alternating beats.

rhythmical, rhythmic adj. **-ly** adv.

rib n. One of a series of curved bones enclosed in the chest of man and animals. Slang To tease.

rib-bon n. A narrow band or strip of fabric, such as satin, used for trimming.

rice n. A cereal grass grown extensively in warm climates.

rich adj. Having great wealth; of great value; satisfying and pleasing in voice, color, tone, or other qualities; extremely productive; as soil or land.

rick-ets n., Pathol. A disease occurring in early childhood resulting from a lack

of vitamin D and insufficient sunlight, characterized by defective bone growth and deformity.

rid v. To make free from anything objectionable.

rid-dle v. To perforate with numerous holes. n. A puzzling problem or question which requires a clever solution.

ride v. To travel in a vehicle or on an animal; to sit on and drive, as a motorcycle.

rid-er n. One who rides as a passenger; a clause, usually having little relevance, which is added to a document.

ridge n. A long, narrow crest; a horizontal line formed where two sloping surfaces meet. **ridge** v.

rid-i-cule n. Actions or words intended to make a person or thing the object of mockery.

ri-dic-u-lous adj. To be causing derision or ridicule.

rife adj. State of being abundant or abounding.

rif-fle n. Ripply water which is caused by a ridge.

riff-raff n. The rabble; low persons in society.

ri-fle n. A firearm having a grooved bore designed to be fired from the shoulder.

ri-fling n. The act of putting or cutting spiral grooves in the barrel of a gun.

rift n. A fault; disagreement; a lack of harmony.

rig v. To outfit with necessary equipment. n. The arrangement of sails, masts, and other equipment on a ship; the apparatus used for drilling water or oil wells.

right adj. In accordance with or conformable to law, justice, or morality; proper and fitting; properly adjusted, disposed, or placed; orderly; sound in body or mind. n. The right side, hand, or direction; the direction opposite left. adv. Immediately; completely; according to justice, morality, or law.

rightness n.

right an-gle n., Geom.

An angle of 90 degrees; an angle with two sides perpendicular to each other.

rig-id adj. Not bending; inflexible; severe; stern. rigidity, rigidness n.

rig-or n. The condition of being rigid or stiff; stiffness of temper; harshness. rigorous adj., rigorously adv.

rind n. A tough outer layer which may be taken off or pealed off.

ring n. A circular mark, line, or object; a small circular band worn on a finger; a group of persons acting together; especially in an illegal way. v. To make a clear resonant sound, as a bell when struck. n. The sound made by a bell.

ring-worm n., Pathol. A contagious skin disease caused by fungi and marked by discolored, ring-shaped, scaly patches on the skin.

ri-ot *n.* A wild and turbulent public disturbance. *Slang* An irresistibly amusing person. **riotous** *adj.*

rip *v.* To tear apart violently; to move violently or quickly. *n.* A torn place. **rip-off** *Slang* To steal.

rip-cord *n.* A cord which, when pulled, releases a parachute from its pack.

ripe *adj.* Fully developed or aged; mature. **ripeness** *n.*

rip-ple *v.* To cause to form small waves on the surface of water; to waver gently.

ris-i-ble *adj.* Being inclined to or causing laughter.

risk *n.* A chance of suffering or encountering harm or loss; danger. **risky** *adj.*

rite *n.* A formal religious ceremony; any formal custom or practice.

rit-u-al *n.* A prescribed method for performing a religious ceremony. *adj.* Pertaining to or practiced as a rite. **ritual** *adj.*, **ritualism** *n.*

ri-val *n.* One who strives to compete with another; one who equals or almost equals another.

riv-er *n.* A relatively large natural stream of water, usually fed by another body of water.

riv-et *n.* A metal bolt used to secure two or more objects.

roach *n.* A European freshwater fish; cockroach. *Slang* The butt of a marijuana cigarette.

roam *v.* To travel aimlessly or without a purpose. **roamer** *n.*

roar *v.* To utter a deep prolonged sound of excitement; to laugh loudly. **roar, roarer** *n.*

roast *v.* To cook meat by using dry heat in an oven. *n.* A cut of meat.

rob *v.* To take property unlawfully from another person. **robber** *n.*, **robbery** *n.*

robe *n.* A long loose garment usually worn over night clothes; a long flowing garment worn on ceremonial occasions.

rob-in *n.* A large North American bird with a black head and reddish breast.

ro-bot *n.* A machine capable of performing human duties.

ro-bust *adj.* Full of strength and health; rich; vigorous. **robustly** *adv.*, **-ness** *n.*

rock *n.* A hard naturally formed material. *Slang* One who is dependable.

rock-et *n.*

A device propelled with the thrust from a gaseous combustion. *v.* To move rapidly.

rode *v.* Past tense of ride.

ro-dent *n.* A mammal, such as a rat, mouse, or beaver having large incisors used for gnawing.

ro-de-o *n.* A public show, contest, or demonstration of ranching skills, as riding and roping.

roe *n.* The eggs of a female fish.

rogue *n.* A scoundrel or dishonest person; an innocently or playful person.

roll *v.* To move in any direction by turning over and over; to sway or rock from side to side, as a ship; to make a deep prolonged sound as thunder. *n.* A list of names. *Slang* A large amount of money.

roll-er *n.* A cylinder for crushing, smoothing or rolling something; any of a number of various cylindrical devices.

ro-mance *n.* A love affair, usually of the young, characterized by ideals of devotion and purity; a fictitious story filled with extravagant adventures. **romance** *v.*, **romancer** *n.*

Ro-man nu-mer-al *n.* The letter or letters of the Roman system of numbering still used in formal contexts, as: V=5, X=10, L=50, C=100, D=500, M=1000.

romp *v.* To run, play, or frolic in a carefree way.

rood *n.* A measurement of land which equals 1/4 acre.

rook-ie *n.* An untrained person; a novice or inexperienced person.

room *n.* A section or area of a building set off by partitions or walls. *v.* To occupy or live in a room.

roost *n.* A place or perch on which birds sleep or rest; a piece of meat which has been or is to be roasted.

root *n.*

The part of a plant which grows in the ground. *Math* A number which, when multiplied by itself, will produce a given quantity. *v.* To search or rummage for something; to turn up the earth with the snout, as a hog. **rootless** *adj.*, **rootless** *adj.*

rope *n.* A heavy cord of twisted fiber. know the ropes. To be familiar with all of the conditions at hand.

ro-sa-ry *n.*, *pl.* **-ies** A string of beads for counting prayers; a series of prayers.

rose *n.* A shrub or climbing vine having sharp prickly stems and variously colored fragrant flowers.

ro-sette *n.* An ornament gathered to resemble a rose and made of silk or ribbon.

Rosh Ha-sha-nah *n.* The Jewish New Year.

ros-ter *n.* A list of names.

ro-ta-ry *adj.* Turning or designed to turn; of or relating to axial rotation.

ro-tate *v.* To turn on an axis; to alternate something in sequence. **rotatable** *adj.*, **rotation, rotator** *n.*, **rotatory** *adj.*

ro-tis-ser-ie *n.* A rotation device with spits for roasting food.

ro-tor *n.* A rotating part of a mechanical device.

rot-ten *adj.* Decomposed; morally corrupt; very bad.

ro-tund *adj.* Plump; rounded.

rouge *n.* A cosmetic coloring for the cheeks.

rough *adj.* Having an uneven surface; violent or harsh. The part of a golf course with tall grass. *v.* To treat roughly. *adv.* In a very rude manner. **roughly** *adv.*, **roughness** *n.*

round *adj.* Curved; circular; spherical. *v.* To become round; to surround. *adv.* Throughout; prescribed duties, places, or actions. **roundness** *n.*

rouse *v.* To awaken or stir up.

route *n.* A course of travel. *v.* To send in a certain direction.

rou-tine *n.* Activities done regularly. *adj.* Ordinary.

rove *v.* To wander over a wide area. **rover** *n.*, **roving** *adj.*

row *n.* A number of things positioned next to each other; a continuous line. *v.* To propel a boat with oars.

roy-al *adj.* Relating to a king or queen.

roy-al-ty *n.*, *pl.* **-ies** Monarchs and or their families; a payment to someone for the use of his invention, copyright, or services.

rub *v.* To move over a surface with friction and pressure; to cause to become worn or frayed.

rub-ber *n.* A resinous elastic material obtained from the coagulated and processed sap of tropical plants or produced synthetically. **rubbery** *adj.*

rub-ber ce-ment *n.* A type of adhesive that is liquid and made of rubber.

rub-ber-ize *v.* Coat or cover something with rubber.

rub-ber plant *n.* Type of plant that is found in East India and yields rubber.

rub-bish *n.* Worthless trash; nonsense. **rubbishy** *adj.*

rub-ble *n.* The pieces of broken material or stones.

ru-bel-la *n.* The German measles.

ru-bi-cund *adj.* State of being of a red color or hue.

ru-bid-i-um *n.*, *Symbol* A silvery, highly reactive element symbolized by Rb.

ru-bric *n.* A heading, title, or initial letter of a manuscript which appears in red.

ru-by *n.*, *pl.* **-ies** A deep-red precious stone.

ruck-us *n.*, *Slang* A noisy uproar, or commotion.

rud-der *n.*, *Naut.* A broad, flat, hinged device attached to the stern of a boat used for steering.

rud-dy *adj.* Being red in color or hue. **ruddiness** *n.*

rude *adj.* Discourteous; offensively blunt. **rudeness** *n.*

ru-di-ment *n.* A first step, element, skill, or principle. *Biol.* An undeveloped organ.

rue *v.* To repent.

rue-ful *adj.* To be causing sorrow or remorse.

ruff *n.* A stiff collar which has pleats in it.

ruf-fi-an *n.* A lawless, rowdy person.

ruf-fle *n.* A pleated strip or frill; a decorative band. *v.* To disturb or destroy the smoothness.

rug *n.* A heavy textile fabric used to cover a floor.

rug-ged *adj.* Strong; rough; having an uneven or rough surface. **ruggedness** *n.*, **ruggedly** *adv.*

ru-in *n.* Total destruction. *v.* To destroy. **ruination** *n.*, **ruinous** *adj.*

rule *n.* Controlling power; an authoritative direction or statement which regulates the method of doing something; a standard procedure. *v.* To have control over; to make a straight line using a ruler; to be in command.

rum *n.* A type of liquor made from molasses and is distilled.

rum-ba *n.* A type of dance which has a complex rhythm.

rum-ble *v.* To make a heavy, continuous sound. *n.* A long deep rolling sound.

ru-mi-nate *v.* To chew a cud; to ponder at length. **rumination** *n.*, **ruminative** *adj.*, **ruminator** *n.*

rum-mage *v.* To look or search thoroughly by digging or turning things over; to ransack.

rum-mage sale *n.* A sale of second-hand objects, conducted to make money.

ru-mor *n.* An uncertain truth which is circulated from one person to another; gossip. *v.* To speed by rumor.

ru-mor-mon-ger *n.* One who aids in the spreading of rumors.

rump *n.* The fleshy hind quarter of an animal; the human buttocks.

rum-ple *v.* To form into creases or folds; to wrinkle.

rum-pus room *n.* A type of room which is used for parties.

rund-let *n.* A type of barrel which is small in size.

rung *n.* A bar or board which forms a step of a ladder.

runt *n.* The smallest animal in a litter.

run-through *n.* The rehearsal of a play.

rup-ture *n.* A state of being broken; the act of bursting.

ru-ral *adj.* Pertaining to the country or country life.

ruse *n.* A type of trick.

rush *v.* To move quickly; to hurry; to be in a hurry.

rus-tic *adj.* Characteristic of country life. *n.* A simple person. **rustically** *adv.*

rus-ti-cate *v.* Living and staying in the country or rural area. **rusticator**, **rusticity** *n.*

rus-tle *v.* To move making soft sounds, such as those made by leaves of a tree.

rus-tler *n.* A person who steals cattle.

rust-proof *adj.* Being unable to rust.

rust-y *adj.* To be covered by rust. **rustiness** *n.*, **rustily** *adv.*

rut *n.* An indented track made by the wheels of vehicles.

ru-the-ni-um *n.* A metallic element symbolized by Ru.

ruth-less *adj.* Merciless. **ruthlessly** *adv.*

rye *n.* A cultivated cereal grass whose seeds are used to make flour and whiskey.

S, s The nineteenth letter of the English alphabet.

sa-ber *n.* A lightweight sword.

sa-ber rat-tling *n.* An aggressive show of military force or power.

sa-ber--toothed ti-ger *n.* A cat like animal with excessively long upper canine teeth, having a saberlike look or appearance.

sa-ble *n.* A carnivorous mammal having soft, black or dark fur.

sab-o-tage *n.* An act of malicious destruction, intended to obstruct production of war material by the opposing side.

sab-o-teur *n.* A person who practices or commits sabotage.

sac *n., Biol.* A membranous pouch in an animal or plant, containing a liquid.

sac-cha-rin *n.* A white, crystalline powder used as a noncaloric sugar substitute.

sa-chet *n.* A small bag of a sweet-smelling powder used to scent clothes.

sack *n.* A strong bag for holding articles. *Slang* Dismissal from a position or job; sleeping bag or bed.

sac-ra-ment *n., Eccl.* A formal Christian rite performed in a church, as a baptism. **Sacrament** The consecrated bread and wine of the Eucharist; the Lord's Supper.

sa-cred *adj.* Dedicated to worship; holy. **sacredly** *adv.,* **sacredness** *n.*

sac-ri-fice *n.* The practice of offering something, as an animal's life, to a deity. *v.* To give up something of value for something else. **sacrificial** *adj.*

sad *adj.* Marked by sorrow; unhappy; causing sorrow; deplorable. **sadly** *adv.,* **sadness** *n.*

sad-dle *n.*

A seat for a rider, as on the back of a horse or bicycle; a cut of meat which includes the backbone. *v.* To put a saddle on; to load down; to burden.

sa-dism *n., Psychol.* A condition in which sexual gratification comes from inflicting pain on others; cruelty. **sadist** *n.,* **sadistic** *adj.,* **-ly** *adv.*

sa-fa-ri *n., pl.* **-ris.** A trip or journey; a hunting expedition in Africa.

safe *adj.* Secure from danger, harm, or evil. *n.* A strong metal container used to protect and store important documents or money. **safely** *adv.,* **safeness** *n.*

sag *v.* To droop; to sink from pressure or weight; to lose strength. **sag** *n.*

sa-ga *n.* A long heroic story.

sage *n.* A person recognized for judgment and wisdom. **sage** *adj.*

said *v.* Past tense of say.

sail *n.* A strong fabric used to catch the wind and cause a ship to move; a trip on a sailing vessel or boat. *v.* To travel on a sailing vessel.

saint *n.* A person of great purity who has been officially recognized as such by the Roman Catholic Church; a person who has died and is in heaven. **sainted** *adj.* **sainthood** *n.*

sake *n.* Motive or reason for doing something.

sal-ad *n.* A dish usually made of green vegetables, fruit, or meat tossed with dressing.

sal-a-man-der *n.* A lizard-like amphibian with porous, scaleless skin.

sa-la-mi *n.* A spiced sausage made of beef and pork.

sal-a-ry *n., pl.* **-ies** A set compensation paid on a regular basis for services rendered. **salaried** *adj.*

sale *n.* An exchange of goods for a price; disposal of items at reduced prices. **salable** *adj.*

sa-li-ent *adj.* Projecting beyond a line; conspicuous.

sa-li-va *n.* Tasteless fluid secreted in the mouth which aids in digestion.

Salk vac-cine *n.* A vaccine used to immunize against polio.

salm-on *n., pl.* **-on** *or* **-ons** A large game fish with pinkish flesh.

sa-lon *n.* A large drawing room; a business establishment pertaining to fashion.

sa-loon *n.* A place where alcoholic drinks are sold; a barroom.

salt *n.* A white crystalline solid, mainly sodium chloride, found in the earth and sea water, used as a preservative and a seasoning. *adj.* Containing salt.

salt-pe-ter *n.* Potassium nitrate.

sal-u-tar-y *adj.* Wholesome; healthful.

sal-u-ta-tion *n.* An expression; a greeting of good will, as used to open a letter.

sa-lute *v.* To show honor to a superior officer by raising the right hand to the forehead. *n.* An act of respect or greeting by saluting.

sal-vage *v.* The act of rescuing a ship, its cargo, or its crew; property which has been saved. *v.* To save from destruction; to rescue.

salve *n.* A medicated ointment used to soothe the pain of a burn or wound.

sal-vo *n., pl.* **-vos** *or* **-voes** The discharge of a number of guns at the same time.

same *adj.* Identical; exactly alike; similar; not changing. *pron.* The very same one or thing. **sameness** *n.*

sam-ple *n.* A portion which represents the whole. *v.* To try a little.

san-a-to-ri-um *n., pl.* **-ums** *or* **-ria** An institution for treating chronic diseases.

sanc-ti-fy *v.* To make holy. **-fication** *n.*

sanc-tion *n.* Permission from a person of authority; a penalty to ensure compliance. *v.* To officially approve an action.

sanc-tu-ar-y *n., pl.* **-ies.** A sacred, holy place, as the part of a church, where services are held; a safe place; a refuge.

sand *n.* Fine grains of disintegrated rock found in deserts and on beaches. *v.* To smooth or polish with sandpaper.

sandy *adj.*

san-dal *n.*
A shoe which is fastened to the foot by straps attached to the sole; a low shoe or slipper with an ankle strap.

san-dal-wood *n.* A fragrant Asian tree used in wood carving and cabinet making.

sand-bag *n.* A sand-filled bag, used to hold back water.

sand-wich *n.* Two or more slices of bread between which a filling, such as cheese or meat, is placed.

sane *adj.* Having a healthy, sound mind; showing good judgment. **sanely** *adv.,* **sanity** *n.*

san-i-tar-y *adj.* Free from bacteria or filth which endanger health.

san-i-tize *v.* To make sanitary; to make clean or free of germs.

sap *n.* The liquid which flows or circulates through plants and trees. *v.* To weaken or wear away gradually. *Slang* A gullible person; fool.

sa-pi-ent *adj.* Wise.

sap-phire *n.* A clear, deep-blue gem, used in jewelry.

sar-casm *n.* An insulting or mocking statement or remark. **sarcastic** *adj.,* **sarcastically** *adj.*

sar-dine *n.* A small edible fish of the herring family, often canned in oil.

sar-don-ic *adj.* Scornful; mockingly cynical.

sa-ri *n.* A garment consisting of a long piece of lightweight material wrapped around the body and over the shoulder of Hindu women.

sar-sa-pa-ril-la *n.* The dried root of a tropical American plant, which is used as flavoring.

sash *n.* A band worn over the shoulder or around the waist.

sass *n., Slang* Rudeness; a disrespectful manner of speech. *v.* To talk with disrespect.

sas-sa-fras *n.* The dried root of a North American tree, used as flavoring.

Sa-tan *n.* The devil.

sat-el-lite *n.* A natural or man-made object which orbits a celestial body.

sat-in *n.* A smooth, shiny fabric made of silk, nylon, or rayon, having a glossy face and dull back.

sat-ire *n.* The use of mockery, sarcasm, or humor in a literary work to ridicule or attack human vice.

sat-is-fac-tion *n.* Anything which brings about a happy feeling; the fulfillment of a need, appetite, or desire; a source of gratification.

sat-is-fy *v.* To fulfill; to give assurance to.

sat-u-rate *v.* To make completely wet; to soak or load to capacity. **saturable** *adj.,* **saturation** *n.*

sat-yr *n., Gr. Myth.* A Greek woodland god having a human body and the legs, horns, and ears of a goat.

sauce *n.* A liquid or dressing served as an accompaniment to food. **saucing** *v.*

sau-cer *n.* A small shallow dish for holding a cup.

sau-er-kraut *n.* Shredded and salted cabbage cooked in its own juices until tender and sour.

sau-na *n.* A steam bath in which one is subjected to heat produced by water poured over heated rocks.

sau-sage *n.* Chopped meat, usually pork, which is highly seasoned, stuffed into a casing and cooked.

sav-age *adj.* Wild; not domesticated; uncivilized; brutal. **savagely** *adv.,* **savagery** *n.*

save *v.* To rescue from danger, loss, or harm; to prevent loss or waste; to keep for another time in the future; to be delivered from sin. **saver** *n.*

sav-ior *n.* One who saves. Christ Savior.

sa-voir--faire *n.* Social skill; the ability to say and do the right thing.

sa-vor *n.* The taste or smell of something. *v.* To have a particular smell; to truly enjoy. **savory** *adj.*

saw *n.* A tool with a sharp metal blade edged with teeth-like points for cutting. *v.* Past tense of see; to cut with a saw.

sax-o-phone *n.* A brass wind instrument having finger keys and a reed mouthpiece. **saxophonist** *n.*

say *v.* To speak aloud; to express oneself in words; to indicate; to show. *n.* The chance to speak; the right to make a decision.

scab *n.* The stiff, crusty covering which forms over a healing wound. *Slang* A person who continues to work while others are on strike.

sca-bies *n.* A contagious skin disease characterized by severe itching, caused by a mite under the skin.

scaf-fold *n.* A temporary support of metal or wood erected for workers who are building or working on a large structure.

scal-a-wag *n., Slang* A rascal.

scald *v.* To burn with steam or a hot liquid; to heat a liquid to a temperature just under boiling.

scale *n.* A flat plate which covers certain animals, especially fish and reptiles; a device for weighing; a series of marks indicating the relationship between a map or model and the actual dimensions. *Music* A sequence of eight musical notes in accordance with a specified scheme of intervals. **-ly** *adj.*

scal-lop *n.* A marine shellfish with a fan-shaped, fluted bivalve shell; the fleshy edible muscle of the scallop.

scalp *n.* The skin which covers the top of the human head where hair normally grows. *v.* To tear or remove the scalp from. *Slang* To buy or sell something at a greatly inflated price. **scalper** *n.*

scal-pel *n.* A small,straight knife with a narrow,pointed blade, used in surgery.

scamp *n.* A scheming or tricky person.

scan v. To examine all parts closely; to look at quickly; to analyze the rhythm of a poem. *Electron.* To move a beam of radar in search of a target.
scan, scanner n.

scan-dal n. Something which brings disgrace when exposed to the public; gossip.

scan-di-um n. A metallic element symbolized by Sc.

scant adj. Not plentiful or abundant; inadequate. **scantly** adv., **scantness** n.

scant-ling n. The dimensions of material used in building, as wood and brick.

scap-u-la n., pl. **-lae** One pair of large, flat, triangular bones which form the back of the shoulder. **scapular** adj.

scar n. A permanent mark which remains on the skin after a sore or injury has healed. **scar** v.

scarce adj. Not common or plentiful; rare. **scarceness** n.

scarf n. A wide piece of cloth worn around the head, neck, and shoulders for warmth.

scar-la-ti-na n. A mild form of scarlet fever.

scar-let n. A bright or vivid red.

scarlet fever n. A communicable disease caused by streptococcus and characterized by a sore throat, vomiting, high fever, and a rash.

scat-ter v. To spread around; to distribute in different directions.

scav-en-ger n. An animal, as a vulture, which feeds on decaying or dead animals or plant matter.

sce-nar-i-o n. A synopsis of a dramatic plot.

scene n. A view; the time and place where an event occurs; a public display of temper; a part of a play.

scent n. A smell; an odor. v. To smell; to give something a scent.

scep-ter n. A rod or staff carried by a king as a sign of authority.

sched-ule n. A list or written chart which shows the times at which events will happen, including a plan given for work and specified deadlines.

scheme n. A plan of action; an orderly combination of related parts; a secret plot.

schol-ar n. A student with a strong interest in learning. **scholarly** adj.

school n. A place for teaching and learning; a group of persons devoted to similar principles.

schoon-er n. A sailing vessel with two or more masts.

sci-ence n. The study and theoretical explanation of natural phenomena in an orderly way; knowledge acquired through experience. **scientific** adj., **scientifically** adv., **scientist** n.

scis-sors pl., n. A cutting tool consisting of two blades joined and pivoted so that the edges are close to each other.

scle-ro-sis n., pl. **-ses** A hardening of a part of the body, as an artery.

scold v. To accuse or reprimand harshly.

sconce n. A wall bracket for holding candles.

scoop n. A small, shovel-like tool. v. To lift up or out. *Slang* An exclusive news report.

scoot v. To go suddenly and quickly.

scope n. The range or extent of one's actions; the space to function or operate in.

-scope suff. A device for seeing or discovering.

scorch v. To burn slightly, changing the color and taste of something; to parch with heat.

scorcher n., *Slang* A very hot day.

scorn n. Contempt; disdain. v. To treat with scorn. **scornful** adj.

scor-pi-on n.

An arachnid having an upright tail tipped with a poisonous sting.

scour v. To clean by rubbing with an abrasive agent; to clean thoroughly.

scout v. To observe activities in order to obtain information. n. A person whose job is to obtain information; a member of the Boy Scouts or Girl Scouts.

scow n. A large barge with a flat bottom and square ends, used to transport freight, gravel, or other cargo.

scowl v. To make an angry look; to frown. **scowl** n.

scrab-ble v. To scratch about frantically, as if searching for something. **scrabble, scrabbler** n.

scrag-gly adj. Messy; irregular.

scrap n. A small section or piece. v. To throw away waste.

scrape v. To rub a surface with a sharp object in order to clean. *Slang* An embarrassing situation.

scratch v. To mark or make a slight cut on; to mark with the fingernails. n. The mark made by scratching; a harsh, unpleasant sound.

scrawl v. To write or draw quickly and often illegibly. **scrawl** n.

scraw-ny adj. Very thin; skinny.

scream v. To utter a long, sharp cry, as of fear or pain. n. A long piercing cry. *Slang* A very funny person.

screech v. To make a shrill, harsh noise. **screech** n.

screen n. A movable object used to keep something from view, to divide, or to decorate; a flat reflecting surface on which a picture is projected. v. To keep from view.

screw n.

A metal piece that resembles a nail, having a spiral thread which is used for fastening things together; a propeller on a ship. v. To join by twisting. **screw up** To make a mess of.

scribe n. A person whose profession is to

copy documents and manuscripts.

scrim-mage *n.* In football, a practice game. **scrimmage** *v.*

scrim-shaw *n.* The art of carving designs on whale ivory or whalebone.

scrip-ture *n.* A sacred writing. Scriptures The Bible.

scroll *n.* A roll of parchment or similar material used in place of paper.

scro-tum *n.*, *pl.* -ta The external sac of skin which encloses the testes. -al *adj.*

scrub *v.* To clean something by rubbing. *Slang* To cancel.

scrump-tious *adj.*, *Slang* Delightful.

scru-ple *n.* A principle which governs one's actions. **scrupulous** *adj.*

scu-ba *n.* An apparatus used by divers for underwater breathing; from the initials for self-contained underwater breathing apparatus.

scuff *v.* To drag or scrape the feet while walking. *n.* A rough spot.

scuf-fle *v.* To struggle in a confused manner. **scuffle** *n.*

scull *n.* An oar mounted at the stern of a boat, which is moved back and forth to produce forward motion.

sculp-tor *n.* A person who creates statues from clay, marble, or other material.

scum *n.* A thin layer of waste matter floating on top of a liquid.

scurf *n.* Flaky dry skin; dandruff.

scur-ry *v.* To move quickly; to scamper.

scythe *n.* A tool with a long handle and curved, single-edged blade, used for cutting hay, grain and grass.

seal *n.*

A device having a raised emblem, displaying word or symbol, used to certify a signature or the authenticity of a document; a tight closure which secures; a large aquatic mammal with a sleek body and large flippers; the fur or pelt of a seal. *v.* To hunt seals. **sealer, sealant** *n.*

sea level *n.* The level of the sea's surface, used as a standard reference point in measuring the height of land or the depth of the sea.

seam *n.* The line formed at the joint of two pieces of material.

sear *v.* To wither or dry up; to shrivel; to burn or scorch.

search *v.* To look over carefully; to find something; to probe. **searcher** *n.*

sea-son *n.* One of the four parts of the year; spring, summer, fall or autumn and winter; a time marked by particular activities or cele-brations. *v.* To add flavorings or spices; to add interest or enjoyment. **seasonal** *adj.*, **seasonally** *adj.*

seat *n.* A place or spot, as a chair, stool, or bench, on which to sit; the part of the body used for sitting; the buttocks.

se-cede *v.* To withdraw from an organization or group. **secession, secessionist** *n.*

se-clude *v.* To isolate; to keep apart.

sec-ond *n.* A unit of time equal to 1/60 of a minute; a very short period of time; an object which does not meet first class standards. *Math* A unit of measure equal to 1/60 of a minute of angular measurement.

sec-on-dar-y *adj.* Not being first in importance; inferior; pertaining to a secondary school; high school.

se-cret *n.* Knowledge kept from others; a mystery. **secretly** *adv.* **secret, secrecy** *n.*

sec-re-tar-y *n.*, *pl.* -ies A person hired to write and keep records for an executive or an organization; the head of a government department. **secretarial** *adj.*

se-crete *v.* To produce and give off; to release or discharge.

sec-tion *n.* A part or division of something; a separate part. *v.* To divide or separate into sections.

sec-tor *n.* An area or zone in which a military unit operates; the part of a circle bounded by two radii and the arc they cut. *Math v.* To divide.

sec-u-lar *adj.* Relating to something worldly; not sacred or religious.

se-cure *adj.* Safe and free from doubt or fear; sturdy or strong; not likely to fail. *v.* To tie down, fasten, lock, or otherwise protect from risk or harm; to ensure. **securely** *adv.*

se-cu-ri-ty *n.*, *pl.* -ies The state of being safe and free from danger or risk; protection; an object given to assure the fulfillment of an obligation; in computer science, the prevention of unauthorized use of a device or program.

se-dan *n.* A closed, hardtop automobile with a front and back seat.

se-date *adj.* Serene and composed. *v.* To keep or be kept calm through the use of drugs. **sedative** *n.*

sed-i-ment *n.* Material which floats in or settles to the bottom of a liquid. **sedimentary** *adj.*, **sedimentation** *n.*

se-duce *v.* To tempt and draw away from proper conduct; to entice someone to have sexual intercourse. **seducer, seduction** *n.*, **seductive** *adj.*

see *v.* To have the power of sight; to understand; to experience; to imagine; to predict. **see red** To be extremely angry.

seed *n.* A fertilized plant ovule with an embryo, capable of producing an offspring. *v.* To plant seeds; to remove the seeds from.

seek *v.* To search for; to try to reach; to attempt. **seeker** *n.*

seem *v.* To appear to be; to have the look of. **seeming** *adj.*, **seemingly** *adv.*

seep *v.* To leak or pass through slowly. **seepage** *n.*

seer *n.* A person who predicts the future.

see-saw *n.* A board supported in the center which allows children to alternate being up and down.

seg-ment *n.* Any of the parts into which a thing is divided. *v.* To divide.

segmental *adj.*, **segmentation** *n.*

seg-re-gate *v.* To separate or isolate from others.

seg-re-ga-tion *n.* The act of separating people based on the color of their skin.

seine *n.* A fishing net with weights on one edge and floats on the other.

seize *v.* To grasp or take possession forcibly.

sel-dom *adv.* Not often.

se-lect *v.* To choose from a large group; to make a choice. **select**, **selection** *adj.*, **selector**, **selectness** *n.*

se-le-ni-um *n.* An element symbolized by Se.

self *n.*, *pl.* **-selves**. The complete and essential being of a person; personal interest, advantage or welfare.

self-de-fense *n.* To act of defending oneself or one's belongings.

sell *v.* To exchange a product or service for money; to offer for sale. **seller** *n.*

se-man-tics *n.* The study of word meanings and the relationships between symbols and signs.

sem-a-phore *n.* A system for signaling by using flags, lights or arms in various positions. **semaphore** *v.*

se-men *n.* The secretion of the male reproductive system, thick and whitish in color and containing sperm.

se-mes-ter *n.* One of two periods of time in which a school year is divided.

sem-i-an-nu-al *adj.* Occurring twice a year.

sem-i-co-lon *n.* A punctuation mark (;) having a degree of separation stronger than a comma but less than a period.

sem-i-nar *n.* A course of study for students engaged in advanced study of a particular subject.

sem-i-nar-y *n.*, *pl.* **-ies** A school that prepares ministers, rabbis, or priests for their religious careers. **seminarian** *n.*

sen-ate *n.* The upper house of a legislature, as the United States Senate.

send *v.* To cause something to be conveyed from one place to another; to dispatch.

se-nile *adj.* Having a mental deterioration often associated with old age. **senility** *n.*

sen-ior *adj.* Being the older of two; of higher office or rank; referring to the last year of high school or college. *n.* One who is older or of higher rank.

sen-ior-i-ty *n.* Priority over others based on the length of time of service.

sen-sa-tion *n.* An awareness associated with a mental or bodily feeling; something that causes a condition of strong interest.

sense *n.* Sensation; feeling; the physical ability which allows a person to be aware of things around him; the five senses: taste, smell, touch, sight, and hearing; an ethical or moral attitude; the meaning of a word; *v.* To feel through the senses; to have a feeling about.

sen-si-bil-i-ty *n.*, *pl.* **-ies** The ability to receive sensations.

sen-si-ble *adj.* Capable of being perceived through the senses; sensitive; having good judgment. **sensibly** *adv.*

sen-si-tive *adj.* Capable of intense feelings; affected by the emotions or circumstances of others; tender-hearted; of or relating to secret affairs of state. **sensitively** *adv.*, **sensitivity**, **sensitiveness** *n.*

sen-sor *n.* A device which responds to a signal.

sen-su-al *adj.* Preoccupied with the gratification of the senses. **sensualist**, **sensuality** *n.*, **sensuous** *adj.*

sent *v.* Past tense of send.

sen-tence *n.* A series of words arranged to express a single complete thought; a prison term for a convicted person, determined by a judge or jury. *v.* To impose or set the terms of punishment.

sen-ti-ment *n.* Feelings of affection; an idea, opinion, thought, or attitude based on emotion rather than reason.

sen-ti-men-tal *adj.* Emotional; affected by sentiment.

sen-ti-nel *n.* One who guards.

se-pal *n.* One of the leaves which forms a calyx in a flower.

sep-a-rate *v.* To divide or keep apart by placing a barrier between; to go in different directions; to set apart from others. *adj.* Single; individual.

sep-a-ra-tion *n.* The process of separating or being separated; an interval which separates.

se-quel *n.* A new story which follows or comes after an earlier one and which uses the same characters.

se-quence *n.* A set arrangement; a number of connected events; the regular order; the order in which something is done. **sequential** *adj.*, **sequentially** *adv.*

ser-e-nade *n.* Music performed as a romantic expression of love.

se-rene *adj.* Calm; peaceful. **serenity** *n.*

serf *n.* A slave owned by a lord during the Middle Ages.

serge *n.* A twilled, durable woolen cloth.

ser-geant *n.* A noncommissioned officer who ranks above a corporal but below a lieutenant.

se-ri-al *adj.* Arranged in a series with one part presented at a time.

se-ries *pl. n.* A number of related items which follow one another.

se-ri-ous *adj.* Sober; grave; not trivial; important. **seriously** *adv.*, **-ness** *n.*

ser-mon *n.* A message or speech delivered by a clergyman during a religious service.

ser-pent *n.* A snake.

ser-rate *adj.* Having sharp teeth; having a notched edge. **serrate** *v.*, **serration** *n.*

se-rum *n.*, *pl.* **-rums** *or* **-ra** The yellowish fluid part of the blood which remains after clotting; the fluid extracted from immunized animals and used for the prevention of disease.

ser·vant n. One employed to care for someone or his property.

serve v. To take care of; to wait on; to prepare and supply; to complete a term of duty; to act in a certain capacity; to start the play in some sports. n. The manner of serving or delivering a ball.

serv·ice n. Help given to others; a religious gathering; the military; a set of dishes or utensils. v. To repair; to furnish a service to something or someone.

ses·a·me n. A tropical plant and its edible seeds.

ses·sion n. A meeting or series of meetings; a meeting set for a specific purpose; the period during the day or year during which a meeting takes place.

set v. To put or place; to cause to do; to regulate; to adjust; to arrange; to place in a frame or mounting; to go below the horizon; to establish or fix. n. A group of things which belong together; a piece of equipment made up of many pieces; a young plant. adj. Established; ready.

set·tee n. A small couch or bench with arms and a back.

set·ting n. The act of placing or putting something somewhere; the scenery for a show or other production; the place where a novel, play, or other fictional work takes place; a jewelry mounting.

set·tle v. To arrange or put in order; to restore calm or tranquility to; to come to an agreement on something; to resolve a problem or argument; to establish in a new home or business.

sev·en n. The cardinal number 7, after 6 and before 8. **seven** adj. & pron., **seventh** adj., adv. & n.

sev·en·teen n. The cardinal number 17, after 16 and before 18. **seventeen** adj., **seventeenth** adj., adv. & n.

sev·en·ty n., pl. -ies The cardinal number 70, after 69 and before 71. **seventy** adj. **seventieth** adj., adv. & n.

sev·er v. To cut off or separate. **severance** n.

sev·er·al adj. Being more than one or two, but not many; separate. -ly adv.

se·vere adj. Strict; stern; hard; not fancy; extremely painful; intense. **severely** adv., **severity** n.

sew v. To fasten or fix; to make stitches with thread and needle.

sew·age n. The solid waste material carried away by a sewer.

sew·er n. A conduit or drain pipe used to carry away waste.

sex n. One of two divisions, male and female, into which most living things are grouped; sexual intercourse.

sex·tet n. A group of six people or things; music written for six performers.

shab·by adj. Worn-out; ragged. **shabbily** adv., **shabbiness** n.

shack n. A small, poorly built building.

shack·le n. A metal band locked around the ankle or wrist of a prisoner; anything that restrains or holds. v. To restrain with shackles.

shad·ow n. An area from which light is blocked; a shaded area. v. To cast or throw a shadow on. **shadowy** adj.

shake v. To move or to cause a back-and-forth or up and down motion; to tremble; to clasp hands with another, as to welcome or say farewell; to upset or disturb. **shake** n., **shaky** adj.

shall v., p.t. Past tense of should; used with the pronouns I or we to express future tense; with other nouns or pronouns to indicate promise, determination or a command.

shal·low adj. Not deep; lacking intellectual depth.

sham n. A person who is not genuine but pretends to be; a cover for pillows. v. To pretend to have or feel something.

sham·ble v. To walk while dragging one's feet.

shambles A scene or state of complete destruction.

shame n. A painful feeling of embarrassment or disgrace brought on by doing something wrong; dishonor; disgrace; a disappointment.

sham·poo n. A soap used to cleanse the hair and scalp; a liquid preparation used to clean upholstery and rugs.

sham·rock n. A form of clover with three leaflets on a single stem; regarded as the national flower and emblem of Ireland.

shank n. The portion of the leg between the ankle and the knee; a cut of meat from the leg of an animal, such as a lamb.

shape n. The outline or configuration of something; the form of a human body; the condition of something; the finished form in which something may appear. v. To cause to take a particular form.

share n. A part or portion given to or by one person; one of equal parts, as the capital stock in a corporation **sharer** n.

shark n.

A large marine fish which eats other fish and is dangerous to man; a greedy, crafty, person.

sharp adj. Having a thin edge or a fine point; capable of piercing or cutting; clever; quick-witted; intense; painful. Slang Nice looking. n. Music A note raised half a tone above a given tone. **sharpness** n., **sharply** adv.

shat·ter v. To burst suddenly into pieces.

shave v. To remove a thin layer; to cut body hair, as the beard, by using a razor; to come close to.

shawl n. An oblong or square piece of fabric worn over the head or shoulders.

she *pron.* A female previously indicated by name.

shear *v.* To trim, cut, or remove the fleece or hair with a sharp instrument; to clip. **shearer** *n.*

sheath *n.* A cover or case for a blade, as a sword.

shed *v.* To pour out or cause to pour; to throw off without penetrating; to cast off or leave behind, especially by a natural process. *n.* A small building for shelter or storage.

sheen *n.* Luster.

sheep *n., pl.* **sheep**

A cud-chewing thick-fleeced mammal, widely domesticated for meat and wool; a meek or timid person.

sheer *adj.* Very thin; almost transparent; complete; absolute; very steep, almost perpendicular.

sheet *n.* A large piece of cloth for covering a bed; a single piece of paper; a continuous, thin piece of anything.

shelf *n., pl.* **shelves** A flat piece of wood, metal, plastic, or other rigid material attached to a wall or within another structure, used to hold or store things; something which resembles a shelf, as a ledge of rocks.

shell *n.* The hard outer covering of certain organisms; something light and hollow which resembles a shell; the framework of a building under construction; a case containing explosives which are fired from a gun. **sheller** *n.*

shel-lac *n.* A clear varnish used to give a smooth, shiny finish to furniture and floors. *Slang* To defeat. **shellac** *v.*

shel-ter *n.* Something which gives protection or cover. *v.* To give protection.

shelve *v.* To put aside; to place on a shelf.

shep-herd *n.* A person who takes care of a flock of sheep; a person who takes care of others.

sher-bet *n.* A sweet frozen dessert made with fruit juices, milk or water, egg white, and gelatin.

sher-iff *n.* A high ranking law-enforcement officer.

shield *n.* A piece of protective metal or wood held in front of the body; anything which serves to conceal or protect; a badge or emblem. **shield** *v.*, **shielder** *n.*

shift *n.* A group of people who work together; a woman's loose-fitting dress. *v.* To change direction or place; to change or move the gears in an automobile.

shim-mer *v.* To shine with a faint sparkle. **shimmer** *n.*, **shimmery** *adj.*

shin *n.* The front part of the leg from the knee to the ankle. *v.* To climb a rope or pole by gripping and pulling with the hands and legs.

shine *v.* To give off light; to direct light; to make bright or glossy; to polish shoes. *n.* Brightness.

shiner *n.* A black eye.

shin-gle *n.* A thin piece of material, as asbestos, used to cover a roof or side of a house. *v.* To apply shingles to. **shingler** *n.*

shin-gles *pl., n., Pathol.* An acute, inflammatory viral infection, characterized by skin eruptions along a nerve path.

ship *n.* A large vessel for deep-water travel or transport. *v.* To send or transport.

ship-wreck *n.* The loss of a ship; destruction; ruin. *v.* To wreck.

ship-yard *n.* A place where ships are built or repaired.

shirt *n.* A garment worn on the upper part of the body.

shiv-er *v.* To tremble or shake with excitement or chill **shiver** *n.*, **-ery** *adj.*

shock *n.* A sudden blow or violent impact; an unexpected, sudden upset of mental or emotional balance; a serious weakening of the body caused by the loss of blood pressure or sudden injury. *v.* To strike with great surprise, disgust, or outrage; to give an electric shock.

shoe *n.* An outer cover for a foot; the part of a brake which presses against the drum or wheel to slow or stop the motion. *v.* To put on shoes.

shone *v.* Past tense of shine.

shoot *v.* To kill or wound with a missile, as a bullet, fired from a weapon; to discharge or throw rapidly; to push forward or begin to grow by germinating. *Slang* To inject drugs directly into the veins. **shooter** *n.*

shop *n.* A small business or small retail store; a place where certain goods are produced. *v.* To visit a store in order to examine or buy things. **shopper** *n.*

shore *n.* The land bordering a body of water.

short *adj.* Having little height or length; less than normal in distance, time, or other qualities; less than the needed amount. **shorts** Underpants or outerpants which end at the knee or above. **shortage** A lack in the amount needed. **short-change** To give less than the correct amount, as change for money. **short circuit** An electrical malfunction.

short-en-ing *n* A fat, such as butter, used to make pastry rich and light.

short order *n.* An order, usually for food, which can be quickly prepared and served.

shot *n.* The discharging of a gun, rocket, or other device; an attempt; a try; an injection; a photograph. *Slang* Useless; ruined.

should *v.* Past tense of shall, used to express obligation, duty, or expectation.

shoul-der *n.* The part of the body located between the neck and upper arm; the side of the road. *v.* To use the shoulder to push or carry something; to take upon oneself.

should-n't *contr.* Should not.

shout *v.* To yell. *n.* A loud cry.

shov-el *n.* A tool with a long handle and a scoop, used for picking up material or for digging. *v.* To move, dig, or scoop up with a shovel; to push or move large amounts rapidly.

show *v.* To put within sight; to point out; to explain; to put on display. *n.* A display; a movie, play or similar entertainment.

show-er *n.* A short period of rain; a party with gifts given in honor of someone; a bath with water spraying down on the bather. *v.* To take a shower; to be extremely generous. **showery** *adj.*

shrank *v.* Past tense of shrink.

shrap-nel *n., pl.* **shrapnel** A large shell containing metal fragments; fragments of metal that are exploded with great force.

shrew *n.* A small mouse-like mammal, having a narrow, pointed snout.

shriek *n.* A loud, sharp scream or noise.

shrill *adj.* A high-pitched, sharp sound.

shrimp *n., pl.* **shrimp** *or* **shrimps** A small, edible shellfish. *Slang* A small person.

shrine *n.* A place for sacred relics; a place considered sacred because of an event or person associated with it.

shrink *v.* To make or become less or smaller; to pull back from; to flinch. *Slang* A psychiatrist.

shroud *n.* A cloth in which a body is wrapped for burial. *v.* To cover.

shrug *v.* To raise the shoulders briefly to indicate doubt or indifference **shrug** *n.*

shrunk *v.* Past tense of shrink.

shuck *n.* The outer husk that covers an ear of corn. *v.* To remove.

shud-der *v.* To tremble uncontrollably, as from fear. **shudder** *n.*

shuf-fle *v.* To drag or slide the feet; to mix together in a haphazard fashion; to rearrange or change the order of cards. **shuffle** *n.*

shun *v.* To avoid deliberately.

shut-tle *n.* A device used to move thread in weaving; a vehicle, as a train or plane, which travels back and forth from one location to another.

shy *adj.* Bashful; timid; easily frightened. *v.* To move suddenly from fear. **shyly** *adv.,* **shyness** *n.*

sib-ling *n.* One of two or more children from the same parents.

sick *adj.* In poor health; ill; nauseated; morbid. **sickness** *n.*

sick-le *n.*

A tool with a curved blade attached to a handle, used for cutting grass or grain.

side *n.* A surface between the front and back or top and bottom of an object; either surface of a flat object; the part to the left or right of a vertical axis; the right or left portion of the human body; the space beside someone or something; an opinion or point of view which is the opposite of another. *v.* To take a stand and support the opinion of a particular side. *adj.* Supplementary; peripheral.

siege *n.* The action of surrounding a town or port in order to capture it; a prolonged sickness.

si-er-ra *n.* A rugged chain of mountains or hills.

si-es-ta *n.* A rest or short nap.

sieve *n.* A meshed or perforated device which allows small particles to pass through but which holds back larger particles; a device for separating liquids from solids. **sieve** *v.*

sift *v.* To separate coarse particles from small or fine ones by passing through a sieve. **sift through** To carefully examine. **sifter** *n.*

sigh *v.* To exhale a long, deep breath, usually when tired, sad, or relieved.

sight *n.* The ability to see with the eyes; the range or distance one can see; a view; a device mounted on a firearm used to guide the eye or aim.

sign *n.* A piece of paper, wood, metal, etc., with information written on it; a gesture that tells or means something. *v.* To write one's name on.

sig-nal *n.* A sign which gives a warning; the image or sound sent by television or radio.

sig-na-ture *n.* The name of a person, written by that person; a distinctive mark which indicates identity. *Music* A symbol indicating the time and key.

sig-nif-i-cance *n.* The quality of being important; the meaning of something which is considered important.

sig-ni-fy *v.* To express or make known by a sign; to indicate. **signification** *n.,* **significant** *adj.*

sign language *n.* A means of communicating by using hand gestures; the language of deaf people.

si-lence *n.* The state or quality of being silent; quiet. *v.* To make quiet. **silencer** *n.*

silent *adj.* Making no sound; not speaking; mute; unable to speak; an unpronounced letter, as the "g" in gnat. **silently** *adv.*

sil-hou-ette *n.*

The outline of something, as a human profile, filled in with a solid color, as black; the outline of an object.

sil-i-con *n.* The second most common chemical element, found only in combination with another substance, symbolized as Si.

silk *n.* A soft, thread-like fiber spun by silkworms; thread or fabric made from silk. silken, silky adj.

sill n. The horizontal support that forms the bottom part of the frame of a window or door.

sil-ly adj. Foolish; lacking good sense, seriousness, or substance. silliness n.

si-lo n. A tall, cylindrical structure for storing food for farm animals; an underground shelter or storage for guided missiles.

sil-ver n. A soft, white metallic element used in tableware, jewelry, and coins, symbolized by Ag. v. To coat with silver. adj. Of the color silver.

sim-i-lar adj. Almost the same, but not identical.

sim-mer v. To cook just below boiling; to be near the point of breaking, as with emotion.

sim-ple adj. Easy to do or understand; not complicated; ordinary; not showy; lacking intelligence or education. simpleness n., simply adv.

sim-plic-i-ty n. The state of being easy to understand; naturalness; sincerity.

sim-pli-fy v. To make easy or simple. simplification n.

sim-u-late v. To have the appearance, effect, or form of. -tion, simulator n.

si-mul-ta-ne-ous adj. Occurring at exactly the same time. -ly adj.

sin n. The breaking of a religious law or a law of God. v. To do something which is morally wrong. sinless adj., sinner n.

since adv. At a time before the present. prep. During the time later than; continuously from the time when something occurs.

sin-cere adj. Honest; not deceitful; genuine; true. sincerely adv., sincerity n.

sing v. To use the voice to make musical tones; to make a humming or whistling sound. singer n.

singe v. To slightly burn the surface of something; to remove feathers.

sin-gle adj. Of or referring to only one, separate; individual; unmarried. n. A separate, individual person or item; a dollar bill; in baseball, a hit that allows the batter to progress to first base. singly adv.

sin-gu-lar adj. Separate; one; extraordinary; denoting a single unit, thing or person.

sink v. To submerge beneath a surface; to go down slowly; to become less forceful or weaker. n. A basin for holding water, attached to a wall and connected to a drain. sinkable adj.

si-nus n., pl. sinuses Anat. A body cavity; one of eight air spaces in the bones of the face which drain into the nasal cavity.

sip v. To drink in small amounts. sip n.

si-phon also syphon n. A tube through which liquid from one container can be drawn into another by forced air pressure. siphon v.

sir n. A respectful term used when addressing a man.

si-ren n. A whistle which makes a loud wailing noise, as a warning or signal; a seductive woman.

sis-ter n. A female having the same parents as another; a woman in membership with others, as in a church group or sorority. sisterly adj., sisterhood n.

sit v. To rest the body with the weight on the buttocks; to cover eggs for hatching; to pose for a portrait.

six n. The cardinal number 6, after five and before seven.

six-teen n. The cardinal number 16, after fifteen and before seventeen.

six-ty n. The cardinal number 60, after fifty nine and before sixty one.

siz-a-ble adj. Large in size or dimensions.

size n. The measurement or dimensions of something; a sticky substance used to glaze walls, before applying wall paper.

siz-zle v. To make a hissing sound, as of fat frying. sizzle n.

skel-e-ton n. The framework of bones that protects and supports the soft tissues and organs.

skep-tic n. A person who doubts or questions. skepticism n., skeptical adj., skeptically adv.

sketch n. A rough drawing or outline; a brief literary composition. sketchy adj.

skew v. To turn or slant. n. A slant.

ski n., pl. skis One of a pair of long, narrow pieces of wood worn on the feet for gliding over snow or water. v. To travel on skis. skier n.

skid v. To slide to the side of the road; to slide along without rotating. skid n.

skill n. Ability gained through practice; expertise. skilled adj.

skim v. To remove the top layer; to remove floating matter; to read over material quickly; to travel over lightly and quickly. skimmer n.

skimp v. To economize; to hold back. skimpy adj.

skin n. The tough, outside covering of man and some animals; the outside layer of a vegetable or fruit; the fur or pelt of an animal. skin v., skinless adj.

skip v. To move in light jumps or leaps; to go from one place to another, missing what is between. skip n.

skirt n. A piece of clothing that extends down from the waist. v. To extend along the boundary; to avoid the issue.

skull n. The bony part of the skeleton which protects the brain.

skunk n.

A black mammal with white streaks down its back, which sprays an unpleasant smelling liquid when annoyed or frightened.

sky n., pl. skies The upper atmosphere above the earth; the celestial regions.

slab n. A thick piece or slice.

slack *adj.* Not taut or tense; sluggish; lacking in strength. *v.* To make slack. *n.* A part of something which hangs loose. **slacks** Long pants or trousers.

slain *v.* Past tense of slay.

slam *v.* To shut with force; to strike with a loud impact. *n.* A loud noise produced by an impact.

slam-mer *n.*, *Slang* Jail or prison.

slan-der *n.* A false statement that deliberately does harm to another's reputation. **slanderous** *adj.*

slang *n.* Informal language that contains made-up words or common words used in a different or uncommon way.

slant *v.* To lie in an oblique position; to slope; to report on something giving only one side or viewpoint. *n.* An incline or slope.

slap *n.* A sharp blow with an open hand.

slash *v.* To cut with a fast sweeping stroke; to reduce or limit greatly. *n.* A long cut.

slate *n.* A fine grained rock that splits into thin layers, often used as a writing surface or roofing material. **slate** *v.*

slaugh-ter *v.* To kill livestock for food; to kill in great numbers. *Slang* To soundly defeat. **slaughterer** *n.*

slave *n.* A person held against his will and made to work for another.

sled *n.* A vehicle with runners, used to travel on snow or ice.

sleek *adj.* Smooth and shiny; neat and trim. **sleekly** *adv.*, **sleekness** *n.*

sleep *n.* A natural state of rest for the mind and body. *v.* To rest in sleep.

sleet *n.* Rain that is partially frozen; a combination of snow and rain. **sleet** *v.*, **sleety** *adj.*

sleeve *n.* The part of a garment which covers the arm; a case for something.

sleigh *n.* A vehicle mounted on runners, usually pulled over ice and snow by horses.

slen-der *adj.* Slim; inadequate in amount. **slenderly** *adv.*, **slenderness** *n.*

slept *v.* Past tense of sleep.

slice *n.* A thin cut; a portion or share; in sports, a ball in flight that curves off to the right of its target. *v.* To cut into slices. **slicer** *n.*

slick *adj.* Smooth and slippery; quick; smart; clever; attractive for the present time but without quality or depth. *n.* Water with a thin layer of oil floating on top.

slick-er *n.* A raincoat made of yellow oilcloth.

slide *v.* To move smoothly across a surface without losing contact. *n.* The act of sliding; a slanted smooth surface usually found on playgrounds; a transparent picture which can be projected on a screen; a small glass plate for examining specimens under a microscope.

slight *adj.* Minor in degree; unimportant. *v.* To ignore. **-ly** *adv.*

slim *adj.* Slender; meager; not much. **slimness** *n.*

slime *n.* A wet, slippery substance.

slimy *adj.*

sling *n.* A piece of material, as leather, or a strap which secures something; a piece of fabric worn around the neck used to support an injured hand or arm; a weapon made of a strap, used to throw a stone.

slip *v.* To move in a smooth, quiet way; to fall or lose one's balance. *Slang* To become less active, alert, or strong. *n.* The action of slipping; the place between two piers used for docking a boat; a woman's undergarment; a small piece of paper; a portion of a plant used for grafting.

slith-er *v.* To slide or slip in an indirect manner; to move like a snake. **slithery** *adj.*

sliv-er *n.* A thin, narrow piece of something that has been broken off.

slob-ber *v.* To dribble from the mouth. **slobber** *n.*

slo-gan *n.* A phrase used to express the aims of a cause.

slope *v.* To slant upward or downward. *n.* An upward or downward incline, as a ski slope.

slosh *v.* To splash in a liquid, as water. **sloshy** *adj.*

slot *n.* A narrow, thin groove or opening. *Slang* A place or scheduled time for an event.

sloth *n.* Laziness; a slow mammal found in South America.

slouch *n.* A drooping or sagging posture; a lazy person. *v.* To sit or walk with poor posture.

slow *adj.* Moving at a low rate of speed; requiring more time than usual; not lively; sluggish; not interesting. *adv.* At less speed; in a slow manner. **slowly** *adv.*, **slowness** *n.*

slug *n.* A slow animal related to the snail; a bullet or a lump of metal. *v.* To strike forcefully with the fist or a heavy object.

sluice *n.* A man-made ditch used to move water; a sloping trough used for floating logs. *v.* To wash with flowing water.

slum *n.* A crowded urban neighborhood marked by poverty. **slum** *v.*

slum-ber *v.* To sleep; to doze. **-er** *n.*

slump *v.* To fall or sink suddenly.

slung *v.* Past tense of sling.

slur *v.* To slide over without careful consideration; to pronounce unclearly. *n.* An insult. *Music* Two or more notes connected with a curved line to indicate they are to be slurred.

slush *n.* Melting snow; snow which is partially melted. **slushy** *adj.*

slut *n.* A woman of bad character; a prostitute. **sluttish** *adj.*

sly *adj.* Cunning; clever; sneaky; underhanded. **slyly** *adv.*, **slyness** *n.*

smack *v.* To slap; to press and open the lips with a sharp noise. *n.* The act or noise of slapping something. *adv.* Directly.

small *adj.* Little in size, quantity, or extent; unimportant. *n.* The part that is less than the other. **smallness** *n.*

small-pox *n.* An acute, contagious disease marked by high fever and sores on the skin.

smart *adj.* Intelligent; clever.

smash *v.* To break into small pieces; to move forward violently, as to shatter; to ruin. *n.* The act or sound of crashing. *adj.* Outstanding. **smasher** *n.*

smear *v.* To spread or cover with a sticky, oily, or moist substance. *Slang* To discredit one's reputation. **smear** *n.*

smell *v.* To notice an odor by means of the olfactory sense organs. *n.* An odor; the ability to perceive an odor; the scent of something.

smelt *v.* To heat metals or their ores to a high temperature in order to obtain pure metallic constituents.

smile *n.* A grin; a facial expression in which the corners of the mouth turn upward, indicating pleasure. **smile** *v.*

smirk *v.* To smile in a conceited way. **smirk, smirker** *n.*

smite *v.* To hit with great force using the hand.

smith *n.* One who repairs or shapes metal.

smock *n.* A loose-fitting garment worn as a protection for one's clothes while working. *v.* To gather fabric into very small pleats or gathers.

smog *n.* A mixture of smoke and fog. **smoggy** *adj.*

smoke *n.* A cloud of vapor released into the air when something is burning. *v.* To preserve or flavor meat by exposing it to smoke. **smokeless, smoky** *adj.*, **smoker** *n.*

smolder *v.* To burn slowly without a flame and with little smoke.

smooth *adj.* Not irregular; flat; without lumps, as in gravy; without obstructions or impediments. *adv.* Evenly. *v.* To make less difficult; to remove obstructions.

smor-gas-bord *n.* A buffet meal with a variety of foods to choose from.

smother *n.* Failure to receive enough oxygen to survive. *v.* To conceal; to be overly protective. **smothery** *adj.*

smudge *v.* To soil by smearing with dirt. *n.* A dirty mark or smear.

smug *adj.* Complacent with oneself; self-satisfied. **smugly** *adv.*, **smugness** *n.*

smug-gle *v.* To import or export goods illegally without paying duty fees. **smuggler** *n.*

snack *n.* A small amount of food taken between meals. **snack** *v.*

snag *n.* A stump or part of a tree that is partly hidden under the surface of water; a pull in a piece of fabric. *v.* To tear on a rough place. *Slang* To catch unexpectedly; to snatch.

snake *n.* Any of a large variety of scaly reptiles, having a long tapering body. *Slang* An untrustworthy person.

snap *v.* To break suddenly with a sharp, quick sound; to fly off under tension; to snatch something suddenly.

snare *n.* Anything that entangles or entraps; a trap with a noose, used to catch small animals.

snarl *v.* To speak in an angry way; to cause confusion; to tangle or be tangled. *n.* A growl.

snatch *v.* To seize or grasp something suddenly. *n.* The act of taking something; a brief or small part.

sneak *v.* To act or move in a quiet, sly way. *n.* A person who acts in a secret, underhanded way.

sneer *v.* To express scorn by the look on one's face.

sneeze *v.* To expel air from the nose suddenly and without control.

sniff *v.* To inhale through the nose in short breaths with a noise; to show scorn. **sniff** *n.*

snip *v.* To cut off in small pieces and with quick strokes. *n.* A small piece.

snipe *n., pl.* snipe *or* snipes A bird with a long bill which lives in marshy places. *v.* To shoot at people from a hidden position. **sniper** *n.*

snob *n.* A person who considers himself better than anyone else and who looks down on those he considers to be his inferiors.

snoop *v., Slang* To prowl or spy. *n.* One who snoops.

snore *v.* To breath with a harsh noise while sleeping. **snore, snorer** *n.*

snor-kel *n.* A tube that extends above the water, used for breathing while swimming face down.

snort *v.* To force air through the nostrils with a loud, harsh noise. *Slang* To inhale a narcotic through the nose.

snow *n.* Vapor that forms crystals in cold air and falls to the ground in white flakes. *Slang* To charm or overwhelm.

snub *v.* To treat with contempt or in an unfriendly way. **snub** *n.*

snuff *v.* To draw air in through the nostrils. **snuff** *n.*

snug *adj.* Warm, pleasant, comfortable and safe.

so *adv.* To a degree or extent as a result; likewise; also; indeed. *conj.* In order that; therefore.

soap *n.* A cleansing agent made of an alkali and a fat, and used for washing. *v.* To rub with soap.

soar *v.* To glide or fly high without any noticeable movement; to rise higher than usual.

sob *v.* To weep with short, quick gasps.

so-ber *adj.* Not drunk or intoxicated; serious; solemn; quiet. **soberly** *adv.*, **soberness** *n.*

soc-cer *n.* A game in which two teams of eleven men each try to kick a ball into the opposing team's goal.

so-cia-ble *adj.* Capable of friendly social relations; enjoying the company of others. **sociableness** *n.*, **sociably** *adv.*

so-cial *adj.* Having to do with people living in groups; enjoying friendly companionship with others. *n.* An informal party or gathering.

so-cial-ism *n.* A system in which people as a whole, and not individuals, control and own all property.

so-ci-e-ty n., pl. **-ies** People working together for a common purpose; companionship.

so-ci-ol-o-gy n. The study of society and the development of human society. **sociologic, sociological** adj.

sock n. A short covering for the foot, ankle, and lower part of the leg; a hard blow. Slang To hit with force.

sock-et n. A hollow opening into which something is fitted.

Soc-ra-tes n. Greek philosopher.

so-da n. Sodium carbonate; a flavored, carbonated drink.

sod-den adj. Completely saturated; very wet; lacking in expression.

so-di-um n. A metallic element symbolized by Na.

sod-om-y n. Anal sexual intercourse.

so-fa n. An upholstered couch with arms and a back.

soft adj. Not stiff or hard; not glaring or harsh; mild or pleasant; gentle in sound.

soft-ball n. A game played on a smaller diamond than baseball, with a larger, softer ball.

soft-ware n. In computer science, data, as routines, programs and languages, which is essential to the operation of computers.

sog-gy adj. Saturated with a liquid or moisture.

sol-ace n. Comfort in a time of trouble, grief, or misfortune. **solacer** n.

so-lar adj. Relating to or connected with the sun; utilizing the sun for power or light; measured by the earth's movement around the sun.

so-lar-i-um n., pl. **-ia** or **-ums** A glassed-in room exposed to the sun's rays.

solar system n. The sun and the planets, asteroids, and comets that orbit it.

sol-der n. Any alloy, as lead or tin, which is melted and used to mend or join other pieces of metal. **soldered** adj.

soldier n. An enlisted person who serves in the military.

sole n. The bottom of a foot or shoe; single, the only one; a flat fish very popular as seafood.

sol-emn adj. Very serious; characterized by dignity; sacred. **solemnity, solemnness** n.

so-lic-it v. To try to obtain; to ask earnestly; to beg or entice a person persistently. **solicitation** n.

sol-id adj. Having a definite firm shape and volume; having no crevices; not hollow; having height, weight and length; without interruption; reliable, sound and upstanding. n. A solid substance. **solidification, solidness** n., **solidify** v.

sol-i-taire n. A single gemstone set by itself; a card game played by one person.

sol-i-tude n. The act of being alone or secluded; isolation.

so-lo n. A musical composition written for and performed by one single person or played by one instrument.

sol-stice n. Either of the two times in a twelve month period at which the sun reaches an extreme north or south position.

sol-u-ble adj. Capable of being dissolved; able to be solved or explained. **solubility** n., **solubly** adv.

solve v. To find the answer to. **solvable** adj.

som-ber adj. Dark; gloomy; melancholy.

some adj. Being an indefinite number or quantity; unspecified. pron. An undetermined or indefinite quantity. adv. An approximate degree. **somebody** n. A person unknown. **someday** adv. At an unspecified future time. **somehow** adv. In a way.

som-er-sault n. The act or acrobatic stunt in which one rolls the body in a complete circle, with heels over head.

som-nam-bu-lism n. The act of walking during sleep. **somnambulant** adj.

son n. A male offspring.

so-na-ta n. An instrumental composition with movements contrasting in tempo and mood but related in key.

song n. A piece of poetry put to music; the act or sound of singing.

son-ic adj. Pertaining to sound or the speed of sound.

son-net n. A poem made up of fourteen lines.

soon adv. In a short time; in the near future; quickly.

soot n. The black powder generated by incomplete combustion of a fuel, such as coal or wood.

soothe v. To make comfortable; to calm.

sop v. To soak up a liquid; to absorb. n. Anything softened by a liquid; something given as a conciliatory offering.

soph-o-more n. A second year college or high school student.

so-pran-o n., pl. **-nos** or **-ni** The highest female singing voice.

sor-cery n. The use of supernatural powers.

sor-did adj. Filthy, very dirty; morally corrupt.

sore adj. Tender or painful to the touch, as an injured part of the body; severe or extreme. n. A place on the body which has been bruised, inflamed, or injured in some way. **sorely** adv.

sor-ghum n. A cane-like grass grown for its sweet juices and used as fodder for animals; the syrup prepared from the sweet juices.

so-ror-i-ty n., pl. **-ies** A social organization for women.

sor-rel n. Any of several herbs with sour-tasting leaves, used in salads.

sor-row n. Anguish; mental suffering; an expression of grief. **sorrowful** adj., **sorrowfully** adv.

sor-ry adj. Feeling or showing sympathy or regret; worthless.

sort n. A collection of things having common attributes or similar qualities. v. to arrange according to class, kind, or size.

sor-tie *n.*, *Mil.* An attack on enemy forces; a combat mission flown by an aircraft.

souf-fle *n.* A fluffy dish made of egg yolks, whipped egg whites, and other ingredients, served as a main dish or sweetened as a dessert.

sought *v.* Past tense of seek.

soul *n.* The spirit in man that is believed to be separate from the body and is the source of a person's emotional, spiritual, and moral nature. *Slang* A spirit or attitude derived from Blacks and their culture.

sound *n.* A sensation received by the ears from air, water, noise, and other sources. *v.* To make a sound; to make noise. *adj.* Free from flaw, injury, disease, or damage. **-less** *adj.*, **-ly** *adv.*

soup *n.* A liquid food made by boiling meat and/or vegetables, in water.

sour *adj.* Sharp to the taste; acid; unpleasant; disagreeable. *v.* To become sour or spoiled. **sourly** *adv.*

source *n.* Any point of origin or beginning; the beginning or place of origin of a stream or river.

south *n.* The direction opposite of north. *adv.* To or towards the south. *adj.* From the south **southerly** *adj.* & *adv.*, **southern, southward** *adj.*, **-er** *n.*

south-paw *n.* A left-handed person.

south-west *n.* The direction between south and west. **southwestern** *adj.*

sou-ve-nir *n.* An item kept as a remembrance of something or someplace.

sov-er-eign *n.* A ruler with supreme power; a monarch. *adj.* Possessing supreme jurisdiction or authority.

sow *v.* To scatter or throw seeds on the ground for growth. *n.* A female pig.

space *n.* The unlimited area in all directions in which events occur and have relative direction; an interval of time; the area beyond the earth's atmosphere. **space** *v.*

spade *n.* A tool with a flat blade used for digging, heavier than a shovel **spade** *v.*

spa-ghet-ti *n.* Pasta made in long, thin pieces.

span *n.* The extent of space from the end of the thumb to the end of the little finger of a spread hand; the section between two limits or supports. *v.* To extend across.

span-iel *n.* A dog with large drooping ears and short legs.

spank *v.* To strike or slap the buttocks with an open hand as a means of punishment.

spare *v.* To refrain from injuring, harming or destroying; to refrain from using; to do without. *n.* An extra, as a spare tire.

spar-kle *v.* To emit or reflect light.

spar-row *n.* A small bird with grayish or brown plumage.

sparse *adj.* Scant; thinly distributed. **sparsely** *adv.*, **sparsity** *n.*

spasm *n.* An involuntary muscle contraction.

spat-ter *v.* To scatter or splash a liquid.

spat-u-la *n.* A kitchen utensil with a flexible blade for mixing soft substances.

spawn *n.* The eggs of fish or other water animals, as oysters or frogs. *v.* To lay eggs.

speak *v.* To utter words; to express a thought in words. **speaker** *n.*

spear *n.* A weapon with a long shaft and a sharply pointed head. *v.* To strike, pierce, or stab with a spear.

spear-mint *n.* A mint plant yielding an aromatic oil used as a flavoring.

spe-cial-ist *n.* A person, such as a doctor, who devotes his practice to one particular field. **spe-cial-ize** *v.*

spec-i-men *n.* A sample; a representative of a particular thing.

speck *n.* A small particle, mark, or spot. *v.* To cover or dot with specks.

spec-ta-cle *n.* A public display of something unusual. *pl.* Eyeglasses. **spectacled** *adj.*

spec-trum *n.*, *Physics* The band of colors produced when light is passed through a prism or other means, separating the light into different wave lengths.

spec-u-late *v.* To reflect and think deeply; to take a chance on a business venture in hopes of making a large profit. **speculation** *n.*

speech *n.* The ability, manner, or act of speaking; a talk before the public. **speechless** *adj.*

speed *n.* Rate of action or movement; quickness; rapid motion. *Slang* A drug used strictly as a stimulant.

spell *v.* To say out loud or write in proper order the letters which make up a word; to relieve. *n.* The state of being controlled by magic; a short period of time; a time or period of illness; an attack.

spend *v.* To give out; to use up; to pay; to exhaust.

sperm *n.* The male cell of reproduction; semen. **spermatic** *adj.*

sphere *n.*, *Math* A round object with all points the same distance from a given point; globe, ball, or other rounded object. **spherical** *adj.*, **spherically** *adv.*

sphinx *n.*, *pl.* **sphinxes** *or* **sphinges** An ancient Egyptian figure having the head of a man, male sheep, or hawk and the body of a lion; a very mysterious person.

spice *n.* A pungently aromatic plant used as flavoring in food, as nutmeg, cinnamon, pepper, or curry. **spicy** *adj.*

spi-der *n.*

An eight-legged insect with a body divided into two parts spinning webs as a means of capturing and holding its prey.

spike *n.* A large, thick nail; a pointed metal piece on the sole of a shoe to prevent slipping, as on a sports shoe.

spill *v.* To allow or cause something to

flow or run out of something. *Slang n.* A fall from a horse; to make known.

spin *v.* To draw out fibers and twist into thread; to run something around and around; to resolve. *Slang* A short drive or ride in an auto. **spinner** *n.*

spin-ach *n.* A widely cultivated plant with dark green leaves which are used in salads.

spin-dle *n.* A rod with a slit in the top and a piece of wood at the other end, used to hold yarn or thread; a needle-like rod mounted on a base, used to hold papers.

spine *n.* The spinal column; the back-bone; the back of a bound book, in-scribed with the title.

spin-ster *n.* An unmarried woman; an old maid.

spir-it *n.* The vital essence of man, con-sidered divine in origin; the part of a human being characterized by per-sonality and self-consciousness; the mind; the Holy Ghost; the creative power of God; a supernatural being, as a ghost or angel.

spir-i-tual *adj.* Of, like, or pertaining to the nature of spirit; relating to religion; sacred. *n.* A religious song originating among the Negroes of the southern United States. **spirituality** *n.*, **spiritualize** *v.*

spite *n.* Hatred or malicious bitterness; a grudge. **spite** *v.*, **spiteful** *adj.*, **spitefully** *adv.*

spit-toon *n.* A cuspidor or receptacle for spit.

spitz *n.* A small dog with a tail which curls over its back.

splash *v.* To spatter a liquid; to wet or soil with liquid; to make a splash. **splash** *n.*, **splashy** *adj.*

splash-down *n.* The landing of a missile or spacecraft in the ocean.

spleen *n.*, *Anat.* A highly vascular, flat-tened organ which filters and stores blood, located below the diaphragm.

splen-did *adj.* Illustrious; magnificent.

splice *v.* To join together by wearing, overlapping, and binding the ends. **splice** *n.*

splint *n.* A device used to hold a frac-tured or injured limb in the proper position for healing. **splint** *v.*

splut-ter *v.* To make a slight, short spit-ting sound. **splutter** *n.*

spoil *v.* To destroy the value, quality, or usefulness; to overindulge as to harm the character. **spoils**, **spoilage**, **-er** *n.*

spoke *n.* One of the rods that serve to connect and support the rim of a wheel.

spokes-man *n.* One who speaks on be-half of another.

sponge *n.* Any of a number of marine creatures with a soft, porous skeleton which soaks up liquid. *v.* To clean with a sponge. **sponger** *n.*, **spongy** *adj.*

spon-sor *n.* A person who is responsible for a debt or duty of another; a busi-ness that finances a television or radio program that in turn advertises its product. **sponsor** *v.*, **sponsorship** *n.*

spon-ta-ne-ous *adj.* Done from one's own impulse without apparent exter-nal cause. **spontaneity** *n.*, **spontaneously** *adv.*

spook *n.*, *Slang* A ghost. *v.* To scare or frighten. **spooky** *adj.*

spool *n.* A small cylinder for holding thread, tape or wire.

spoon *n.* An eating or cooking utensil; a shiny metallic fishing lure. *Slang* To make love, as by kissing or caressing. **spoonful** *n.*

spo-rad-ic *adj.* Occurring occasionally or at irregular intervals. **sporadically** *adv.*

spore *n.*, *Bot.* The reproductive singlecelled structure produced by nonflowering plants; any cell capable of developing into a new organism, seed, or germ.

sport *n.* An interesting diversion; a par-ticular game or physical activity with set rules; a person who leads a fast life. *Slang* To amuse and have a good time. **sporting** *adj.*

sport-ing *adj.* Of or relating to risk taking or gambling; displaying sportsmanship.

sports-man-ship *n.* Fair play; the ability to win or lose graciously.

spot *n.* A small area that differs in size, portion, or color. *adj.* Delivered or made immediately. *Slang* A dangerous or difficult situation. **spot** *v.*, **spotless** *adj.*, **spotlessly** *adv.*

spot-light *n.* A powerful light thrown directly at one area.

spouse *n.* One's husband or wife; a mar-riage partner.

spout *v.* To pour out forcibly, as under pressure; to cause to shoot forth. *Slang* To orate pompously; to declaim. **spouter** *n.*

sprain *n.* A wrenching or twisting of a muscle or joint.

sprawl *v.* To sit or lie in an ungraceful manner; to develop haphazardly. **sprawl**, **sprawler** *n.*

spray *n.* A liquid dispersed in a fine mist or droplets. **sprayer** *n.*

spread *v.* To unfold or open fully; to apply or distribute over an area; to force apart; to extend or expand.

spree *n.* An excessive indulgence in an activity; a binge.

sprin-kle *v.* To scatter in small particles or drops; to rain in small drops.

sprint *n.* A short, fast race. **sprinter** *n.*

sprock-et *n.*, *Mech.* A tooth-like projec-tion from the rim of a wheel.

spruce *n.* An evergreen tree with needle-like foliage, cones, and soft wood.

spry *adj.* Quick; brisk; energetic.

spud *n.*, *Slang* A potato.

spur *n.* A sharp, projecting device worn on a rider's boot, used to nudge a horse.

sput-nik *n.* An unmanned Soviet earth satellite.

sput-ter *v.* To throw off small particles in short bursts; to speak in a confused or agitated manner.

spy *n., pl.* **spies** A secret agent who obtains information; one who watches other people secretly.

squab-ble *v.* To engage in a petty argument. **squabble** *n.*

squad *n.* A small group organized to perform a specific job.

squan-der *v.* To spend extravagantly or wastefully.

square *n.* A parallelogram with four equal sides; an implement having a T or L shape used to measure right angles. *Math.* To multiply a number by itself. *Slang* An unsophisticated person; a person who is not aware of the latest fads or trends.

square root *n.* A number which when multiplied by itself gives the given number.

squash *n.*

An edible fruit of the gourd family; a sport played in a walled court with a hard rubber ball and racket. *v.* To press or squeeze into a soft pulp.

squat *v.* To sit on the heels; to crouch; to settle on a piece of land in order to obtain legal title squatter, squatness *n.*

squaw *n.* An American Indian woman.

squeak *v.* To utter a sharp, penetrating sound. **squeak** *n.,* **squeaky** *adj.*

squea-mish *adj.* Easily shocked or nauseated. **-ly** *adv.,* **squeamishness** *n.*

squee-gee *n.* A tool having a stout rubber blade across a wooden handle, used to wash windows. **squeegee** *v.*

squeeze *v.* To press together; to extract by using pressure. *n.* An instance of squeezing for pleasure; a hug.

squib *n.* A firecracker that does not explode.

squint *v.* To view through partly closed eyes; to close the eyes in this manner.

squire *n.* An old-fashioned title for a rural justice of the peace, lawyer, or judge; a man who escorts a woman; a young man who ranks just below a knight. **squire** *v.*

squirm *v.* To twist the body in a wiggling motion. **squirm** *v.*

squir-rel *n.*

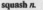

A rodent with gray or brown fur, having a long bushy tail and dark eyes. **squirrel** *v.*

squirt *v.* To eject in a thin stream or jet; to wet with a squirt. *n.* The act of squirting.

sta-bi-lize *v.* To make firm; to keep from changing. **stabilization, stabilizer** *n.*

sta-ble *n.* A building for lodging and feeding horses or other farm animals. *adj.* Standing firm and resisting change. **stable** *v.*

stac-ca-to *adj., Music* Marked by sharp emphasis. **staccato** *n. & adv.*

stack *n.* A large pile of straw or hay; any systematic heap or pile; a chimney. *v.* To fix cards so as to cheat.

sta-di-um *n., pl.* **-dia** A large structure for holding athletic events or other large gatherings.

staff *n., pl.* **staffs** *or* **staves** A pole or rod used for a specific purpose; the people employed to assist in the day-to-day affairs of running a business, organization, or government. *Mil.* A group of people on an executive or advisory board. *Music* The horizontal lines on which notes are written.

stag *n.* The adult male of various animals; a man who attends a social gathering without a woman companion; a social event for men only. *adj.* For men only.

stag-ger *v.* To walk unsteadily; to totter. *adj.* Strongly affected by defeat, misfortune, or loss of strength.

stag-nant *adj.* Not flowing; standing still; foul from not moving; inactive. **stagnate** *v.*

stair *n.* A step or a series of steps.

stair-case *n.* A series or a flight of steps that connect one level to another.

stake *n.* A bet placed on a game of chance; a sharpened piece of wood for driving into the ground. **stake** *v.*

stale *adj.* Having lost freshness; deteriorated; lacking in interest; dull; inactive.

stale-mate *n.* A position in chess when a player cannot move without placing his king in check.

stalk *n.* The main axis of a plant. *v.* To approach in a stealthy manner.

stall *n.* An enclosure in a barn, used as a place to feed and confine animals; a sudden loss of power in an engine; a booth used to display and sell. *v.* To try to put off doing something; to delay.

stal-lion *n.* An uncastrated, fully grown male horse.

sta-men *n., pl.* **stamens** *Bot.* The pollen-producing organs of a flower.

stam-i-na *n.* Physical or moral endurance.

stam-mer *v.* To make involuntary halts or repetitions of a sound or syllable while speaking **stammerer** *n.*

stamp *v.* To put the foot down with force; to imprint or impress with a die, mark, or design. *n.* The act of stamping; the impression or pattern made by a stamp; a postage stamp.

stam-pede *n.* A sudden rush of panic, as of a herd of horses or cattle. *v.* To cause a stampede.

stance *n.* The posture or position of a standing person or animal.

stand *v.* To be placed in or maintain an erect or upright position; to take an upright position; to remain unchanged; to maintain a conviction; to resist. *n.* The act of standing; a device on which something rests; a small booth for selling or displaying items.

stand-ard *n.* A model which stands for

or is accepted as a basis for comparison. **standard** *adj.*

stand-ing *n.* A status, reputation, or achievement; a measure of esteem. *adj.* Unchanging; stationary; not moving.

sta-ple *n.* A principle commodity grown in an area; a major element; a metal fastener designed to hold materials such as cloth or paper. **staple** *v.*, **stapler** *n.*

star *n.*, *Astron.* A self-luminous body that is a source of light; any of the celestial bodies that can be seen in the night sky; a symbol having five or six points and resembling a star.

star-board *n.* The right side of a ship or boat. **starboard** *adj.* & *adv.*

starch *n.* Nutrient carbohydrates that are found in foods such as rice and potatoes. *v.* To stiffen clothing by using starch. **-iness** *n.*, **starchy** *adj.*

stare *v.* To look with an intent, direct gaze. **stare, starer** *n.*

stark *adj.* Bare; total; complete; forbidding in appearance. **starkness** *n.*, **starkly** *adv.*

star-ling *n.* A common black or brown bird.

star-tle *v.* To cause a sudden surprise; to shock. **startle** *n.*

starve *v.* To suffer or die from not having food or love. **starvation** *n.*

state *n.* A situation, mode, or condition of something; a nation; the governing power or authority of; one of the subdivisions or areas of a federal government, as the United States. *v.* To make known verbally.

stat-ic *adj.* Not moving. *n.* A random noise heard on a radio. **statically** *adv.*

sta-tion-ar-y *adj.* Not movable; unchanging.

sta-tion-er-y *n.* Writing paper and envelopes.

sta-tis-tic *n.* An estimate using an average or mean on the basis of a sample taken; numerical data.

stat-ue *n.* A form sculpted from wood, clay, metal, or stone.

stave *n.* A narrow piece of wood used in forming part of a container, as a barrel. **stave** *v.*

stay *v.* To remain; to pause; to maintain a position; to halt or stop; to postpone or delay an execution. *n.* A short visit.

stead-fast *adj.* Not changing or moving; firm in purpose; true. **steadfastly** *adv.*, **steadfastness** *n.*

stead-y *adj.* Firmly placed, fixed or set; not changing; constant; uninterrupted.

steal *v.* To take another person's property; to move in a sly way; to move secretly. *Baseball* To take a base without the ball being hit. *Slang* A real bargain.

steam *n.* Water in the form of vapor; the visible mist into which vapor is condensed by cooling. **steamy** *adj.*

steel *n.* A various mixture of iron, carbon, and other elements; a strong material that can be shaped when heated. **steely** *adj.*

stem *n.* The main stalk of a plant; the main part of a word to which prefixes and suffixes may be added. *v.* To stop or retard the progress or flow of something.

sten-cil *n.* A form cut into a sheet of material, as cardboard or plastic, so that when ink or paint is applied, the pattern will reproduce on paper or another material.

ste-nog-ra-phy *n.* The skill of writing in shorthand. **stenographer** *n.*

ste-re-o *n.* A record player with stereophonic sound. **stereo** *adj.*

ste-reo-phon-ic *adj.* Relating to or giving a three-dimensional effect of auditory perspective.

ster-e-o-type *n.* A conventional opinion or belief; a metal printing plate.

ster-ile *adj.* Free from microorganisms; sanitary; unable to reproduce.

ster-ling *n.* An alloy of 92.5% silver and another metal, as copper.

stern *adj.* Inflexible; harsh. *n.* The rear of a boat or ship. **sternly** *adv.*, **sternness** *n.*

ster-num *n.*, *pl.* **-nums** *or* **-na** A long, flat bone located in the chest wall, connecting the collarbones and the cartilage of the first seven pairs of ribs. **sternal** *adj.*

steth-o-scope *n.*

An instrument used to listen to the internal sounds of the body.

stew *v.* To cook slowly; to simmer; to boil. *n.* A dish of stewed meat and potatoes. *Slang* To worry.

stew-ard *n.* A manager of another's financial affairs; a person responsible for maintaining household affairs; a male attendant on an airplane or ship. **stewardess, stewardship** *n.*

stick *n.* A slender piece of wood; a club, rod, or walking stick. *v.* To put a hole in something; to pierce; to cling; to become jammed.

stiff *adj.* Not flexible; not easily bent; awkward. *n.*, *Slang* A dead body. **stiffness** *n.*

sti-fle *v.* To suffocate; to cut off; to suppress; to keep back.

stig-ma *n.*, *pl.* **-mata** *or* **-mas** A mark of disgrace. **stigmata** The part of a flower where pollen is deposited at pollination; wounds resembling the crucifixion scars of Jesus Christ. **stigmatic** *adj.*

still *adj.* Silent; calm; peaceful; until now or another time. **still** *v.*, **stillness** *n.*

still-birth *n.* The birth of a dead fetus.

stilt *n.* One of a pair of long poles with foot supports, used for walking.

stim-u-lant *n.* An agent which arouses or accelerates physiological activity.

stim-u-late *v.* To excite to a heightened activity; to quicken. **stimulation** *n.*

stim-u-lus *n.*, *pl.* **-li** Something that excites to action.

sting *v.* To prick with something sharp; to feel or cause to feel a smarting pain; to cause or feel sharp pain, either physical or mental. *n.* The act of stinging; the injury or pain caused by the stinger of a bee or wasp. **stinger** *n.*

stin-gy *adj.* Not giving freely; cheap.

stink *v.* To give off a foul odor that is highly offensive.

stip-u-late *v.* To settle something by agreement; to establish conditions of agreement. **stipulation** *n.*

stir *v.* To mix a substance by moving round and round; to agitate or provoke. **stirrer** *n.*

stir-rup *n.* A loop extending from a horse's saddle, used to support the rider's foot.

stitch *n.* In sewing, a single loop formed by a needle and thread; the section of loop of thread, as in sewing. *v.* To join with a stitch.

stock *n.* A supply of goods kept on hand; animals living on a farm; a share in ownership, as in a company or corporation; the raw material or the base used to make something. *v.* To provide with stock. *adj.* Regular, common, or typical.

stock-ade *n.* A barrier placed around a fort for protection.

stock-ing *n.* A knitted covering for the foot.

stock-y *adj.* Short and plump; built sturdily.

stole *n.* A long, narrow scarf that is usually worn around a woman's shoulders, as a mink stole. *v.* Past tense of steal.

stom-ach *n., Anat.* The organ into which food passes from the esophagus; one of the primary organs of digestion. *v.* To tolerate or stand; to put up with.

stone *n.* Rock; compacted earth or mineral matter; a gem or jewel; the seed or pit of certain fruits. *Med.* A hard rock that forms inside a body organ, as the kidney. **stoned** To be overcome by an excessive amount of alcohol or drugs.

stool *n.* A seat without a backrest and arms; a small version of this on which to rest the feet; a bowel movement.

stoop *v.* To bend the body forward and downward from the waist. *n.* A porch attached to a house.

stop *v.* To cease; to halt; to refrain from moving, operating, or acting; to block or obstruct; to visit for a short time. *v.* A location where a bus, train, or other means of mass transportation may pick up or drop off passengers. **stoppage** *n.*

stor-age *n.* The act of storing or keeping; in Computer Science, the part of a computer in which all information is held; the memory.

store *n.* A business offering merchandise for sale; a supply to be used in the future. *v.* To supply; to accumulate.

stork *n.* A large, wading bird.

storm *n.* An atmospheric condition marked by strong winds with rain, sleet, hail, or snow. *v.* To attack with a powerful force. **stormy** *adj.*

sto-ry *n., pl.* **-ies.** A narration of a fictional tale or account; a lie; a level in a building.

stout *adj.* Strong; sturdy; substantial; courageous. **stoutly** *adv.*

stove *n.* An apparatus in which oil, electricity, gas, or other fuels are consumed to provide the heat for cooking.

stow *v.* To pack or put away.

strad-dle *v.* To sit or stand with the legs on either side of something; to favor both sides of an issue. **straddler** *n.*

straight *adj.* Being without bends, angles, or curves; upright; erect; honest; undiluted; unmodified; heterosexual. *n.* In poker, a numerical sequence of five cards not of the same suit. **straightly** *adv.*, **straightness** *n.*

strain *v.* To stretch beyond a proper limit; to injure by putting forth too much effort; to pass through a sieve to separate small particles from larger ones.

strait *n.* A narrow passageway which connects two bodies of water.

strand *n.* Land that borders a body of water; one of the threads that are twisted together to form a rope. *v.* To leave in a difficult situation.

strange *adj.* Not previously known or experienced; odd; peculiar; inexperienced; alien. **strangely** *adv.*, **strangeness** *n.*

stran-ger *n.* A person unknown; a newcomer.

stran-gle *v.* To kill by choking. **-er** *n.*

strap *n.* A long, narrow strip of leather or other material used to secure objects. **strap** *v.*

strat-e-gy *n., pl.* **-ies** The skillful planning and managing of an activity. **strategic** *adj.*, **strategist** *n.*

stra-tum *n., pl.* **-ta** *or* **-tums** A horizontal layer, as of the earth's crust.

straw *n.* A stalk of dried, threshed grain; a slender, plastic or paper straw used to suck up a liquid. *adj.* Yellowish brown.

straw-ber-ry *n.*

A low plant with white flowers and red fruit; the fruit of this plant.

stray *v.* To roam or wander. *n.* A lost or wandering animal or person. **strayer** *n.*

streak *n.* A narrow line or stripe that is different from the surrounding area; a run of good or bad luck. *v.* To rush or move rapidly; to make a streak. **streaky** *adj.*

stream *n.* A small body of flowing water; a steady or continuous succession or procession. *v.* To flow in or like a stream.

stren-u-ous *adj.* Necessitating or characterized by vigorous effort or exertion.

stretch v. To extend fully; to extend forcibly beyond proper limits; to prolong. n. The state or act of stretching. **stretchable, stretchy** adj.

strick-en adj. Suffering, as from an emotion, illness, or trouble.

strict adj. Holding to or observing rules exactly; imposing absolute standards. **strictly** adv. **strictness** n.

stride v. To walk with a long, sweeping step.

strin-gent adj. Of or relating to strict requirements; marked by obstructions or scarcity. **stringency** n., **-ly** adv.

stroll v. To walk in a slow, leisurely way.

strong adj. Exerting or possessing physical power; durable; difficult to break. **strongly** adv.

stron-ti-um n. A metallic element symbolized by Sr.

struc-ture n. A construction made up of a combination of related parts. **structure** v., **structural** adj.

strug-gle v. To put forth effort against opposition. **struggle, struggler** n., **strugglingly** adv.

stub n. A short, projecting part; the short end of something after the main part has been removed or used. **stub** v.

stub-born adj. Inflexible; difficult to control, handle, or manage.

stu-dent n. A person who studies at a school or college.

stu-di-o n. The place of work for an artist, photographer, or other creative person; a place for filming movies.

stud-y n., pl. **-ies** The process of applying the mind to acquire knowledge.

stum-ble v. To trip and nearly fall over something; to come upon unexpectedly. **stumble** v.

stun v. To render senseless by or as if by a blow.

stu-pen-dous adj. Astonishing or impressive. **-ness** n., **-ly** adv.

stu-pid adj. Slow in apprehension or understanding. **stupidity** n.

stur-dy adj. Possessing robust strength and health. **sturdily** adv., **sturdiness** n.

stur-geon n. A large freshwater fish highly valued as a source of caviar.

stut-ter v. To speak with involuntary repetitions of sound. **stutter** n.

sty n., pl. **sties** An inflammation of the edge of an eyelid.

suave adj. Ingratiating; smoothly pleasant in manner.

sub-con-scious adj. Below the level of consciousness. **subconscious** n.

sub-due v. To bring under control by influence, training, persuasion or force.

sub-jec-tive adj. Taking place within; relating to or preceding from an individual's emotions or mind. **subjectively** adv., **subjectivity** n.

sub-merge v. To plunge under the surface of the water. **submergible** adj., **submergence** n.

sub-mit v. To give into or surrender to another's authority. **submission, submittal** n.

sub-or-di-nate adj. Being of lower class or rank; minor; inferior. **subordination** n., **subordinative** adj.

sub-poe-na n. A legal document requiring a person to appear in court for testimony.

sub-se-quent adj. Following in time, place, or order. **subsequently** adv., **subsequentness** n.

sub-side v. To move to a lower level or sink; to become less intense.

sub-sid-i-ar-y adj., pl., n. **-ies**. Providing assistance in a lesser capacity. **subsidiaries** pl., n.

sub-si-dy n., pl. **-dies**. Financial aid granted directly to a private commercial enterprise from the gov-ernment.

sub-sist v. To have continued existence.

sub-soil n. The layer of earth that comes after the surface soil. **subsoiler** n.

sub-stance n. Matter or material of which anything consists.

sub-sti-tute n. Something or someone that takes the place of another.

sub-ten-ant n. A person who rents property from a tenant.

sub-ter-rä-ne-an adj. Located, situated, or operating underground.

sub-tract v. To deduct or take away from.

sub-trop-i-cal adj. Pertaining to regions adjacent to the tropics.

sub-urb n. A residential community near a large city. **suburban** adj.

suc-ceed v. To accomplish what is attempted; to come next or to follow.

suc-cess n. Achievement of something intended or desired; attaining wealth, or fame.

suc-ces-sive adj. Following in order or sequence. **-ly** adv., **successiveness** n.

suc-cu-lent adj. Juicy; full of juice or sap. **succulence** n., **succulently** adv.

such adj. Of this or that kind or thing; a great degree or extent in quality.

su-crose n. Sugar obtained from the sugar beet or sugar cane.

suc-tion n. The process or act of sucking.

sud-den adj. Happening very quickly without warning or notice; sharp; abrupt; marked by haste. **suddenly** adv., **suddenness** n.

suede n. Leather with a soft, napped finish.

su-et n. The hard fat around the kidney and loins of sheep.

suf-fer v. To feel pain or distress; to sustain injury, loss, or damage. **sufferer** n.

suf-fi-cient adj. As much that is needed or desired. **sufficiency** n., **-ly** adv.

suf-fix n. A form affixed to the end of a word.

suf-fo-cate v. To kill by depriving something or someone of oxygen. **-tion** n.

sugar n. A sweet, watersoluble, crystalline carbohydrate. Slang A nickname for someone.

sug-gest v. To give an idea for action or consideration; to imply; hint or intimate.

sug-ges-tion n. The act of suggesting; a slight insinuation; hint.

su-i-cide *n.* The act of taking one's own life. **suicidal** *adj.*

sulk *v.* To be sullenly silent.

sul-len *adj.* Ill-humored, melancholy; gloomy; depressing.

sul-try *adj.* Hot and humid; muggy.

sum *n.* The result obtained by adding; the whole amount, quantity, or number; summary.

sum-ma-ry *n., pl.* **-ries.** Giving the sum or substance. *adj.* A statement covering the main points. **summarily** *adv.*

sum-mer *n.* The warmest of the four seasons, following spring and coming before autumn. **summery** *adj.*

sum-mit *n.* The top and highest point, or degree.

sum-mons *n., pl.* **-monses.** An order or command to perform a duty; a notice to appear at a certain place.

sunk-en *adj.* Submerged or deeply depressed in.

su-per-fi-cial *adj.* Pertaining to a surface; concerned only with what is not necessarily real.

su-pe-ri-or *adj.* Of higher rank, grade, or dignity. *n.* A person who surpasses another in rank or excellence. **superiority** *n.*, **superiorly** *adv.*

su-per-la-tive *adj.* Of the highest degree of excellence; pertaining to the degree of comparison of an adverb or adjective that shows extreme extent or level.

su-per-sede *v.* To take the place of; to set aside.

su-per-son-ic *adj.*, *Aero.* Characterized by a speed greater than that of sound.

su-per-sti-tion *n.* A belief founded, despite evidence that it is irrational; a belief, resulting from faith in magic or chance. **-tious** *adj.*, **-ly** *adv.*

su-per-vise *v.* To have charge in directing the work of other people. **supervision,** **supervisor** *n.*, **supervisory** *adj.*

sup-per *n.* The last or evening meal of the day.

sup-ple-ment *n.* A part that compensates for what is lacking. **supplementary,** **supplemental** *adj.*

sup-ply *v., pl., n.* **-plies.** To provide with what is needed; to make available.

sup-port *v.* To bear or hold the weight of; to tolerate; to give assistance or approval. **supportable,** **supportive** *adj.*, **supporter** *n.*

sup-pose *v.* To think or assume as true; to consider probable. **supposed** *adj.*, **supposedly** *adv.*

sup-pos-i-to-ry *n., pl.* **-ries.** A medication, in solid form, that melts when inserted into the body cavity, as the rectum.

sup-press *v.* To put an end to something by force.

su-preme *adj.* Of the highest authority, rank, or power.

sur-charge *n.* An extra fee added to the cost of something; to overcharge.

sure *adj.* Firm and sturdy; being impossible to doubt; inevitable; not liable to fail. **surer, surest** *adj.*, **surely** *adv.*

sur-face *n.* The exterior or outside boundary of something; outward appearance. **surface** *v.*

surge *v.* To increase suddenly. *n.* A large swell of water.

sur-geon *n.* A physician who practices surgery.

sur-ger-y *n., pl.* **-ies.** The branch of medicine in which physical deformity or disease is treated by an operative procedure.

sur-mise *v.* To guess; to conjecture.

sur-mount *v.* To overcome; to be at the top.

sur-name *n.* A person's family's last name.

sur-pass *v.* To go beyond the limits of; to be greater than. **surpassingly** *adv.*

sur-plus *n.* An amount beyond what is needed.

sur-prise *v.* To come upon unexpectedly or suddenly. **-er** *n.*, **surprisingly** *adv.*

sur-ren-der *v.* To give up or yield possession or power. *n.* The act of surrendering.

sur-rey *n., pl.* **-reys.** A four-wheeled, horse-driven carriage.

sur-ro-gate *n.* A person who puts himself in the place of another. **surrogate** *v.*

sur-round *v.* To extend around all edges of something; to enclose or shut in.

sur-veil-lance *n.* Close observation kept over one, especially as a suspect.

sur-vey *v., pl., n.* **-veys.** To examine in detail; to determine area, boundaries.

sur-vive *v.* To continue to exist; to outlast; to outlive. **surviving** *adj.*, **survival, survivor** *n.*

su-shi *n.* A Japanese dish of thin slices of fresh, raw fish.

sus-pect *v.* To have doubt or distrust.

sus-pense *n.* The feeling of being insecure or undecided, resulting from uncertainty.

sus-pi-cion *n.* The instance of suspecting something wrong without proof. **suspicious** *adj.*, **suspiciously** *adv.*

sus-tain *v.* To hold up and keep from falling; to suffer or undergo an injury.

su-ture *n.* The stitching together or joining the edges of an incision or cut.

swad-dle *v.* To wrap closely, using a long strip of flannel or linen.

swag-ger *v.* To walk with a proud or conceited air.

swal-low *v.* To cause food to pass from the mouth to the stomach; to retract or take back, as words spoken. *n.* The act of swallowing.

swan *n.*

A mostly pure white bird having a long neck and heavy body, related to geese.

swap *v.* To trade something for something in return. **swap** *n.*

swarm *n.* A large number of insects, as bees; a large group of persons or things. **swarm** *v.*, **swarmer** *n.*

swat *v.* To hit something with a sharp blow.

swath *n.* The area or width of grass cut by a machine. **swathe** *v.*

sway *v.* To move or swing from right to left or side by side; to exert influence or control.

swear *v.* To make an affirmation under oath. **swearer** *n.*

sweat gland *n., Anat.* One of the tubular glands that secrete sweat externally through pores.

swift *adj.* Moving with great speed; accomplished or occurring quickly. **swiftly** *adv.,* **swiftness** *n.*

swirl *v.* To move with a whirling, rotating motion. **swirl** *n.,* **swirly** *adj.*

swiv-el *n.* A coupling device, ring, or pivot that allows attached parts to rotate or move freely. **swivel** *v.*

syl-la-ble *n., Phonet.* A word or part of one that consists of a single vocal impulse, usually consisting of one or more vowels or consonants.

syl-lo-gism *n.* An argument with a major premise, a minor premise and a conclusion that is logically drawn from the premises.

sym-bol *n.* Something that stands for or represents something else. **symbolic, symbolical** *adj.,* **symbolically** *adv.*

sym-me-try *n., pl.* **-tries.** Balance in form, size, and position of parts that are on two sides of an axis.

sym-pa-thet-ic *adj.* Having or showing kindness or sympathy for others. **sympathetically** *adv.,* **sympathize** *v.*

sym-pa-thy *n., pl.* **-thies.** Mutual understanding or affection during a time of sadness or loss.

sym-pho-ny *n., pl.* **-nies.** A large orchestra with wind, percussion and string sections. **symphonic** *adj.*

symp-tom *n.* A sign of change in a body's functions or appearance. **-tic** *adj.*

syn-a-gogue *n.* A place for Jewish worship and prayer.

syn-chro-nize *v.* To operate or take place at the same time.

syn-drome *n.* A set of concurrent symptoms that indicate or characterize a disorder or disease.

syn-o-nym *n.* A word that means the same or nearly the same as another. **synonymous** *adj.,* **synonymy** *n.*

syn-op-sis *n., pl.* **-ses.** A shortened statement or narrative.

syn-tax *n.* The way in which words are put together or arranged to form sentences and phrases.

syph-i-lis *n.* An infectious venereal disease transmissible by direct contact and usually progressing in severity.

sy-ringe *n.* A medical instrument used to inject or draw fluids from the body.

syr-up *n.* A sticky, thick, sweet liquid, used as a topping for food.

sys-tem *n.* A method or way of doing something; the human body or related parts of the body that perform vital functions; an orderly arrangement. **systematic** *adj.,* **systematically** *adv.*

sys-to-le *n., Physiol.* The regular rhythmic contraction of the heart that pumps blood through the aorta and pulmonary artery. **systolic** *adj.*

T, t The twentieth letter of the English alphabet.

tab *n.* A strip, flap, or small loop that projects from something. *Slang* A bill or total.

tab-er-na-cle *n.* A portable shelter or structure used by the Jews during their journey out of Egypt; a place of worship.

ta-ble *n.* An article of furniture having a flat top, supported by legs; a collection of related signs, values, or items. *v.* To put off or postpone.

ta-ble-spoon *n.* A unit of measure; a large spoon for serving food. **tablespoonful** *n., pl.,* **tablespoonsful**

tab-leau *n., pl.* **-leaux** *or* **-leaus** A vivid representation; a stage scene represented by motionless and silent people who stand in an appropriate arrangement.

tab-let *n.* A pad used for writing; a thin, flat piece of stone or wood which is fit for or has an inscription.

tab-loid *n.* A small newspaper.

ta-boo *n.* A custom or rule against doing, using, or mentioning something. *adj.* Forbidden by social authority, convention, or custom.

tab-u-lar *adj.* Pertaining to or arranged in a table or list. **tabularly** *adv.*

ta-chom-e-ter *n.* An instrument for measuring velocity and speed.

tac-it *adj.* Understood; expressed or implied nonverbally; implicit. **tacitly** *adv.,* **taciitness** *n.*

tack *n.* A small, short nail with a flat head; a sewing stitch used to hold something temporarily; the changing of a sailboat from one direction to another. *v.* to change the direction in which a sailboat is going. **tacker** *n.*

tack claw *n.* A small tool used to remove tacks.

tacki-ness *n.* The state of being tacky.

tack-le *n.* Equipment used for fishing or other sports or occupations; an apparatus of ropes and pulley blocks for pulling and hoisting heavy loads. In football, a position on a football team; the lineman between the guard and end. **tackled** *v.,* **tackler** *n.*

tack-y *adj.* Slightly sticky; shabby; lacking style or good taste; flashy.

tact *n.* Having the ability to avoid what would disturb someone. **tactful, tactless** *adj.,* **tactfully, tactlessly** *adv.,* **tactfulness, -nessness** *n.*

tac-tic *n.* A way or method of working toward a goal; the art of using strategy to gain military objectives or other goals. **tactical** *adj.,* **tactician** *n.*

tad *n.* A small boy; an insignificant degree or amount.

tad-pole *n.*

The early stage in the growth of a frog or toad during which it breathes by external gills, has a long tail, and lives in the water; a polliwog.

taf-fe-ta *n.* A stiff, smooth fabric of rayon, nylon, or silk. **taffetized** *adj.*

taff-rail *n.* The rail around the stern of a boat or ship.

tag *n.* A piece of plastic, metal, paper, or other material that is attached to something in order to identify it; a children's game in which one child is "it" and tries to catch another child, who then becomes "it." **tag** *v.*, **-ger** *n.*

tail *n.* The posterior extremity, extending from the end or back of an animal. **Tails** The opposite side of a coin from heads; formal evening dress for men. *v.* To follow or keep close watch on someone.

tail-gate *n.* The hinged gate at the back of a truck or automobile for loading and unloading. *v.* To follow very closely in a car.

tai-lor *n.* One whose profession is making, mending, and altering clothing. *v.* To adapt for a specific purpose.

taint *v.* To spoil, contaminate, or pollute. *n.* A blemish or stain.

take *v.* To seize or capture; to get possession of; to receive, swallow, absorb, or accept willingly; to attack and surmount; to move, convey, or conduct to a different place; to require; to choose or pick. *n.* The process of acquiring; the total receipts for admission at an event. *Slang* To cheat; to subtract.

talc *n.* A soft, fine-grained, smooth mineral used in making talcum powder.

tal-ent *n.* The aptitude, disposition, or characteristic ability of a person. **talented, talentless** *adj.*

tal-ent scout *n.* A person who discovers and recruits people with talent for a specialized activity or field.

talk *v.* To communicate by words or speech; to engage in chatter or gossip. *n.* A speech or lecture, usually given to a group of people. *Slang* To boast; to brag. **talker, talkativeness** *n.*, **talkative** *adj.*, **talkatively** *adv.*

tall *adj.* Of greater than average height; of a designated or specified height; imaginary, as a tall tale. **tallness** *n.*, **tallish** *adj.*

tal-low *n.* Hard fat rendered from sheep or cattle, used to make candles, lubricants, and soap. **tallow** *adj.*

tal-ly *n., pl.* **-ies** A record or counting of money, amounts, or scores. *v.* To agree with; to reckon or figure a score; to count.

tal-on *n.* A long, curved claw found on birds or animals. **taloned** *adj.*

tam-bou-rine *n.*

A percussion instrument made of a small drum with jingling metal disks around the rim.

tame *adj.* Not wild or ferocious; domesticated or manageable. *v.* To make docile or calm. **tamely** *adv.*, **tamer, tameness** *n.*

tam-per *v.* To change, meddle, or alter something; to use corrupt measures to scheme. **tamperproof** *adj.*, **tamperer** *n.*

tan *v.* To cure a hide into leather by using chemicals. *n.* A brownish skin tone caused by exposure to the sun.

tan-dem *n.* Any arrangement that involves two or more things, animals or persons arranged one behind the other.

tang *n.* A sharp, distinct taste, smell, or quality; a slender shank that projects from a tool and connects to a handle. **tangy** *adv.*

tan-gent *n.* A line that touches a curved line but does not intersect or cross it; a sudden change from one course to another. **tangency** *n.*, **tangential** *adj.*

tan-ger-ine *n.* A small citrus fruit with an easily peeled orange skin, resembling an orange.

tan-gi-ble *adj.* Capable of being appreciated or felt by the sense of touch; capable of being realized. **tangibility, tangibleness** *n.*, **tangibly** *adv.*

tan-gle *v.* To mix, twist, or unite in a confused manner making separation difficult. **tangle, tanglement** *n.*

tan-go *n.* A ballroom dance with long, gliding steps. **tango** *v.*

tank *n.* A large container for holding or storing a gas or liquid. **tankful** *n.*

tank-ard *n.* A large drinking mug, usually with a hinged top.

tan-ta-lize *v.* To tease or tempt by holding or keeping something just out of one's reach. **tantalizer** *n.*, **-ingly** *adv.*

tan-ta-lum *n.* A metallic element symbolized by Ta.

tan-trum *n.* A fit; an outburst or a rage of bad temper.

tap *v.* To strike repeatedly, usually while making a small noise; to strike or touch gently; to make secret contact with something. In medicine, to remove liquid from the body. **tapper** *n.*

tape *n.* A narrow strip of woven fabric; a string or ribbon stretched across the finish line of a race. **tape** *v.*

ta-per *n.*

A very slender candle. *v.* To become gradually smaller or thinner at one end.

tap-es-try *n., pl.* **-ies** A thick fabric woven with designs and figures.

tap-i-o-ca *n.* A bead-like substance used for thickening and for puddings.

taps *n. pl. Mil.* A bugle call that signals lights out, also sounded at memorial and funeral services.

tar-dy *adj.* Late; not on time. **tardily** *adv.*, **tardiness** *n.*

tar-get *n.* An object marked to shoot at; an aim or goal.

tar-iff *n.* Duty or tax on merchandise coming into or going out of a country.

tar-nish *v.* To become discolored or dull; to lose luster; to spoil.

tarnish n., tarnishable adj.

tar-ot n. A set of 22 cards used for fortune-telling, each card showing a virtue, an elemental force, or a vice.

tar-pau-lin n. A sheet of waterproof canvas used as a protective covering.

tar-ry v. To linger, delay, or hesitate.

tart adj. Sharp; sour; cutting, biting in tone or meaning. tartly adv., -ness n.

tar-tan n. A plaid fabric pattern of Scottish origin. tartan adj.

tar-tar n. The reddish, acidic, crust-like deposit which forms as grape juice turns to wine; a hard deposit which forms on the teeth, composed of secretions, food, and calcium salts. tartaric adj.

task n. A bit of work, usually assigned by another; a job.

tas-sel n.

An ornamental decoration made from a bunch of string or thread.

taste n. The ability to sense or determine flavor in the mouth; a personal liking or disliking. v. To test or sense flavors in the mouth. tasteful, tasteless adj., taster n.

tat-ter n. A torn scrap of cloth. v. To become or make ragged.

tat-tle v. To reveal the secrets of another by gossiping. tattler n.

tat-tle-tale n. One who betrays secrets concerning others; a person, usually a child, who informs on others.

tat-too n. A permanent design or mark made on the skin by pricking and inserting an indelible dye. tattoo v., tattooer n.

taught v. Past tense of teach.

taut adj. Tight; emotionally strained. tautly adv., tautness n.

tau-tol-o-gy n., pl. -ies Redundancy; a statement which is an unnecessary repetition of the same idea.

tav-ern n. An inn; an establishment or business licensed to sell alcoholic drinks. taverner n.

tax n. A payment imposed and collected from individuals or businesses by the government. v. To strain. taxable adj., taxation, taxer, taxpayer n.

tax-ex-empt adj. Exempted from tax; bearing tax-free interest on federal or state income.

tax shel-ter n. A credit or allowance that reduces taxes on current earnings for an individual investor or corporation.

tax-i v. To move along the ground or water surface on its own power before taking off.

taxi-cab n. A vehicle for carrying passengers for money.

tax-i-der-my n. The art or profession of preparing, stuffing, and mounting animal skins. taxidermist n.

tea n. A small tree or bush which grows where the climate is very hot and damp; a drink made by steeping the dried leaves of this shrub in boiling water.

teach v. To communicate skill or knowledge; to give instruction or insight. teachability, teachableness, teaching n., teachable adj.

teach-er n. A person who teaches; one who instructs.

team n. Two or more players on one side in a game; a group of people trained or organized to work together; two or more animals harnessed to the same implement. v. To join or work together.

team-ster n. A person who drives a team of animals or a vehicle as an occupation.

tear v. To become divided into pieces; to separate; to rip into parts or pieces; to move fast; to rush. n. A rip or torn place.

tear n. A fluid secreted by the eye to moisten and cleanse. v. To cry. teary adj.

tease v. To make fun of; to bother; to annoy; to tantalize. n. A person who teases. teaser n., teasingly adv.

tech abbr. Technical; technician.

tech-ne-tium n. A metallic element symbolized by Tc.

tech-ni-cal adj. Expert; derived or relating to technique; relating to industry or mechanics. technically adv.

tech-nique n. A technical procedure or method of doing something.

tech-nol-o-gy n., pl. -ies The application of scientific knowledge to serve man in industry, commerce, medicine and other fields.

te-di-ous adj. Boring; taking a long time. tediously adv.

tee n.

A peg used to hold a golf ball on the first stroke toward a hole or goal post; a peg used to support a football during a field goal attempt. tee v.

teem v. To abound; to be full of; to swarm or crowd.

teens pl., n. The ages between 13 and 19; the years of one's life between 13 and 19.

teeth pl., n. The plural of tooth.

tel-e-cast n. A television broadcast.

tel-e-gram n. A message sent or received by telegraph. telegram v.

tel-e-graph n. A system for communicating; a transmission sent by wire or radio. v. To send messages by electricity over wire. telegrapher, telegraphist n., telegraphic adj.

te-lep-a-thy n. Communication by means of mental processes rather than ordinary means. telepathic adj., -ist n.

tel-e-phone n. A system or device for transmitting conversations by wire. telephone v., telephoner n.

tel-e-pho-to adj. Relating to a camera lens which produces a large image of a distant object. telephotograph n.

tel-e-scope n. An instrument which con-

tains a lens system which makes distant objects appear larger and nearer.
telescopic *adj.*

tel-e-thon *n.* A long telecast used to raise money for a worthy cause.

tel-e-vi-sion *n.* Reception and transmission of images on a screen with sound; the device that reproduces television sounds and images.

tel-ex *n.* Teletype communications by means of automatic exchanges.

tell *v.* To relate or describe; to command or order. **tellable, telling** *adj.*, **teller** *n.*

tel-lu-ri-um *n.* An element symbolized by Te.

temp *abbr.* Temperature.

tem-per *n.* The state of one's feelings. *v.* To modify something, making it flexible or hard. **temperable** *adj.*

tem-per-a-ment *n.* Personality; a characteristic way of thinking, reacting, or behaving. **temperamental** *adj.*

tem-per-ance *n.* Moderation; restraint; moderation or abstinence from drinking alcoholic beverages.

tem-per-ate *adj.* Avoiding extremes; moderate. **-ly** *adv.*, **temperateness** *n.*

tem-per-a-ture *n.* A measure of heat or cold in relation to the body or environment; an elevation in body temperature above the normal 98.6 degrees Fahrenheit.

tem-pest *n.* A severe storm, usually with snow, hail, rain, or sleet.

tem-ple *n.* A place of worship; the flat area on either side of the forehead.

tem-po *n., pl.* **-pos** *or* **-pi** *Mus.* The rate of speed at which a musical composition is to be played.

tem-po-rar-y *adj.* Lasting for a limited amount of time; not permanent.

tempt *n.* To encourage or draw into a foolish or wrong course of action; to lure. **temptation, tempter** *n.*

ten *n.* The cardinal number equal to 9 + 1; the number before eleven.

te-na-cious *adj.* Persistent; stubborn. **tenaciously** *adv.*, **tenaciousness** *n.*

ten-ant *n.* A person who pays rent to occupy another's property. **tenantless, tenantable** *adj.*

Ten Commandments *n.* The ten rules of moral behavior which were given to Moses by God.

tend *v.* To be inclined or disposed; to be directed; to look after.

ten-den-cy *n., pl.* **-ies** A disposition to act or behave in a particular way; a particular dir-ection, mode, outcome, or direction.

ten-der *adj.* Fragile; soft; not hard or tough; painful or sore when touched. *n.* Something offered as a formal bid or offer; compassionate; a supply ship. *v.* To make an offer to buy or purchase; to present, as a resignation. **-hearted, tenderly** *adv.*, **tenderness** *n.*

ten-der-loin *n.* A cut of tender pork or beef.

ten-don *n.* A band of tough, fibrous tissues that connect, a muscle and bone.

ten-dril *n.*

A thread-like part of a climbing plant which attaches itself to a support. **-led** *or* **tendrilled** *adj.*

ten-nis *n.* A sport played with a ball and racket by 2 or 4 people on a rectangular court.

ten-or *n.* An adult male singing voice, above a baritone.

tense *adj.* Taut or stretched tightly; nervous; under strain. **tense** *v.*

ten-sion *n.* The condition of stretching or the state of being stretched. **tensional, tensionless** *adj.*

tent *n.* A portable shelter made by stretching material over a supporting framework.

ten-ta-cle *n.* A long, unjointed, flexible body part that projects from certain invertebrates, as the octopus. **tentacular, tentacled** *adj.*

ten-ta-tive *adj.* Experimental; subject to change; not definite. **tentatively** *adv.*

ten-ure *n.* The right, state, or period of holding something, as an office or property. **-ed, -ial** *adj.*, **tenurially** *adv.*

te-pee *n.* A tent made of hides or bark used by the Indians of North America.

tep-id *adj.* Lukewarm. **-ly** *adv.*, **-ness** *n.*

ter-bi-um *n.* A metallic element of the rare-earth group symbolized by Tb.

ter-cen-ten-a-ry *n., pl.* **-ries.** The time span of 300 years; a 300th anniversary. **tercentenary** *adj.*

term *n.* A phrase or word; a limited time or duration; a phrase having a precise meaning. *Math* The quantity of two numbers either added together or subtracted.

ter-mi-nal *adj.* Of, forming, or located at the end; final. *n.* A station at the end of a bus line, railway, or airline; In Computer Science, the instrument through which data enters or leaves a computer.

ter-mi-nate *v.* To bring to a conclusion or end; to finish. **termination** *n.*

ter-mite *n.* The winged or wingless insect which lives in large colonies feeding on wood.

ter-race *n.* An open balcony or porch; a level piece of land that is higher than the surrounding area; a row of houses built on a sloping or raised site.

ter-ra cot-ta *n.* A hard, baked clay used in ceramic pottery.

ter-rain *n.* The surface of an area, as land.

ter-ra-pin *n.* An edible turtle of North America, living in both fresh and salt water.

ter-res-tri-al *adj.* Something earthly; not heavenly; growing or living on land.

ter-ri-ble *adj.* Causing fear or terror; intense; extreme; horrid; difficult. **terribly** *adv.*, **terribleness** *n.*

ter-ri-er *n.* A very active small dog, originally bred by hunters to dig for burrowing game, now kept as a family pet.

ter-rif-ic *adj.* Terrifying. *Informal* Excellent; causing amazement. -ally *adv.*

ter-ri-fy *v.* To fill with fear or terror; to frighten; to menace. terrified, terrifying *adj.*

ter-ri-to-ry *n., pl.* -ies An area, usually of great size, which is controlled by a particular government; a district or area assigned to one person or group. territorial *adj.*, territorially *adv.*

ter-ror *n.* Extreme fear; one who causes terror.

ter-ror-ism *n.* The state of being terrorized or the act of terrorizing; the use of intimidation to attain one's goals or to advance one's cause.

terse *adj.* Brief; using as few words as possible without loss of force or clearness. tersely *adj.*, terseness *n.*

test *n.* An examination or evaluation of something or someone; an examination to determine one's knowledge, skill, intelligence or other qualities. test *v.*, tester *n.*

tes-ta-ment *n.* A legal document which states how one's personal property is to be distributed upon his death.

Testament *n.* One of the two sections of the Bible: the Old Testament and the New Testament.

tes-tate *adj.* Having left a valid will.

tes-ti-fy *v.* To give evidence while under oath; to serve as proof. testifier *n.*

tes-ti-mo-ni-al *n.* A formal statement; a gift, dinner, reception, or other sign of appreciation given to a person as a token of esteem. testimonial *adj.*

tes-ti-mo-ny *n., pl.* -ies A solemn affirmation made under oath; an outward expression of a religious experience.

tes-tis *n., pl.* testes The sperm producing gland of the male.

test tube *n.*

A thin glass tube closed at one end, used in biology and chemistry.

test--tube ba-by *n.* A baby conceived outside of a mother's womb by fertilizing an egg removed from the mother and then returning the fertilized egg to the mother's womb.

tet-a-nus *n., Pathol* An often fatal disease marked by muscular spasms, commonly known as lockjaw.

teth-er *n.* A rope or chain which fastens an animal to something but allows limited freedom to wander within its range.

text *n.* The actual wording of an author's work distinguished his from notes; the main part or body of a book. textual *adj.*, textually *adv.*

text-book *n.* A book used by students to prepare their lessons.

tex-tile *n.* A cloth made by weaving; yarn or fiber for making cloth. textile *adj.*

tex-ture *n.* The look, surface, or feel of something; the basic makeup.

textural *adj.*, texturally *adv.*

thal-li-um *n.* A metallic element resembling lead, symbolized by Tl.

than *conj.* In comparison with or to something.

thank *v.* To express one's gratitude; to credit.

thank-ful *adj.* Feeling or showing gratitude; grateful. thankfully *adv.*, thankfulness *n.*, thankless *adj.*

thanks *pl., n.* An expression of one's gratitude.

that *adj., pl.* those The person or thing present or being mentioned. *conj.* Used to introduce a clause stating what is said.

thatch *n.* Grass, straw, or similar material used to make a roof. *v.* To overlay or cover with or as if with thatch.

thaw *v.* To change from a frozen state to a liquid or soft state; to grow warmer; to melt. thaw *n.*

the *definite adj.* or *article* Used before nouns and noun phrases as a determiner, designating particular persons or things. *adv.* Used to modify words in the comparative degree; by so much; by that much.

the-a-tre *n.* A building adapted to present dramas, motion pictures, plays, or other performances; a performance.

the-at-ri-cal *adj.* Extravagant; designed for show, display, or effect.

theft *n.* The act or crime of stealing; larceny.

their *adj. & pron.* The possessive case of they; belonging to two or more things or beings previously named.

the-ism *n.* The belief in the existence of God. theist *n.*, theistic *adj.*

them *pron.* The objective case of they.

theme *n.* The topic or subject of something. *Mus.* A short melody of a musical composition. thematic *adj.*

them-selves *pron.* Them or they; a form of the third person plural pronoun.

then *adv.* At that time; soon or immediately. *adj.* Being or acting in or belonging to or at that time.

thence *adv.* From that place, event, fact, or origin.

thence-forth, thence-for-ward *adv.* From that time on.

the-oc-ra-cy *n., pl.* -ies Government by God or by clergymen who think of themselves as representatives of God. theocrat *n.*, theocratic *adj.*, -ically *adv.*

the-ol-o-gy *n., pl.* -ies The religious study of the nature of God, beliefs, practices, and ideas. theologian *n.*

the-o-rize *v.* To analyze theories. theoretician, -ation, -er, theorist *n.*

the-o-ry *n., pl.* -ies A general principle or explanation which covers the known facts; an offered opinion which may possibly, but not positively, be true.

ther-a-peu-tics *n.* The medical treatment of disease. therapeutist *n.*

ther-a-py *n., pl.* -ies The treatment of certain diseases; treatment intended to

remedy an undesirable condition.
therapist n.

there adv. In, at, or about that place; toward, into, or to.
thereabouts, thereafter, thereby, therefore, therefrom, therein adv.

ther-mal adj. Having to do with or producing heat.

ther-mom-e-ter n. A glass tube containing mercury which rises and falls with temperature changes. -metric adj.

ther-mo-plas-tic adj. Pliable and soft when heated or warm but hard when cooled. **thermoplastic** n.

ther-mo-stat n.

A device that automatically responds to temperature changes and activates equipment such as air conditioners and furnaces to adjust the temperature to correspond with the setting on the device.

the-sau-rus n., pl. -ruses or -ri A book which contains synonyms.

these pron. The plural of this.

the-sis n., pl. -ses A formal argument or idea; a paper written by a student that develops an idea or point of view.

they pron. The two or more beings just mentioned.

they'd contr. They had.

they'll contr. They will.

they're contr. They are.

they've contr. They have.

thick adj. Having a heavy or dense consistency; having a considerable extent or depth from one surface to its opposite. Slang Excessive.
thickly adv., **thickness, thicken** n.

thief n., pl. **thieves** A person who steals.

thieve v. To take by theft. **thievery** n.

thigh n. The part of the leg between the hip and the knee of man.

thim-ble n.

A small cap-like protection for the finger, worn while sewing.
thimbleful n.

thin adj. Having very little depth or extent from one side or surface to the other; not fat; slender.
thinly adv., **thinness** n.

thing n. Something not recognized or named; an idea, conception, or utterance; a material or real object.

things One's belongings.

think v. To exercise thought; to use the mind; to reason and work out in the mind; to visualize.
thinkable adj., **thinker** n.

third n. Next to the second in time or place; the last in a series of three.

thirst n. An uncomfortably dry feeling in the throat and mouth accompanied by an urgent desire for liquids. -y adj.

thir-teen n. The cardinal number equal to 12 + 1.

this pron., pl. **these** The person or thing

that is near, present, or just mentioned; the one under discussion.

this-tle n. A prickly plant usually producing a purplish or yellowish flower.

thith-er adv. To that place; there; on the farthest side.

thong n. A narrow strip of leather used for binding.

tho-rax n., pl. -raxes or -races The section or part of the human body between the neck and abdomen, supported by the ribs and breastbone.
thoracic adj.

tho-ri-um n. A radioactive metallic element symbolized by Th.

thorn n. A sharp, pointed, woody projection on a plant stem.
thorniness n., **thorny** adj.

thor-ough adj. Complete; intensive; accurate; very careful; absolute.
thoroughness n., **thoroughly** adv.

thor-ough-bred adj. Being of a pure breed of stock.

thor-ough-fare n. A public highway, road or street.

those adj. & pron. The plural of that.

though adv. Nevertheless; in spite of.

thought n. The process, act, or power of thinking; a possibility; an idea.
thoughtful, thoughtless adj.

thou-sand n. The cardinal number equal to 10 X 100. **thousand** adj. & pron.

thrash v. To beat or strike with a whip; to move violently about; to defeat.

thread n. A thin cord of cotton or other fiber; the ridge going around a bolt, nut or screw. v. To pass a thread through, as to thread a needle.

thread-bare adj. Shabby.

threads pl., n. Slang Clothes.

threat n. An expression or warning of intent to do harm; anything holding a possible source of danger. **threaten** v., **threatener** n., **threateningly** adv.

three n. The cardinal number equal to 2 + 1.

three-D or **3-D** n. A three-dimensional form.

thresh v. To separate seed from a harvested plant mechanically; to strike severely.

thresh-old n. A horizontal piece of wood or other material which forms a doorsill; a beginning point.

threw v. Past tense of throw.

thrice adv. Three times.

thrift n. The careful use of money and other resources. **thriftily** adv., **thriftiness** n., **thrifty** adj.

thrill n. A feeling of sudden intense excitement, fear, or joy.
thrilling adj., **thrillingly** adv.

thrive v. To prosper; to be healthy; to do well in a position.

throat n. The front section or part of the neck containing passages for food and air.

throb v. To beat, move, or vibrate in a pulsating way; to pulsate. **throb** n.

throm-bo-sis n., pl. -ses The development of a blood clot in a blood vessel or in the heart cavity.

throng *n.* A large group or crowd. *v.* To crowd around or into.

throt-tle *n.* The valve which controls the flow of fuel to an engine. *v.* To control the speed or fuel with a throttle.

through *prep.* From the beginning to the end; in one side and out the opposite side. *Slang* Completed; finished.

through-out *prep., adv.* In every place; everywhere; at all times.

throw *v.* To toss or fling through the air with a motion of the arm; to hurl with force. *Slang* To entertain, as to throw a party. **throw up** To vomit. **throw out** To discard something.

thru *prep., adv., & adj.* Through.

thrush *n.* A small songbird having a brownish upper body and spotted breast.

thrust *v.* To push; to shove with sudden or vigorous force. *n.* A sudden stab or push.

thru-way *or* **through-way** *n.* A major highway; an expressway.

thud *n.* A heavy, dull thumping sound.

thug *n.* A tough or violent gangster. **thuggish** *adj.*

thumb *n.* The short first digit of the hand; the part of the glove that fits over the thumb. *v.* To browse through something quickly.

thump *n.* A blow with something blunt or heavy. **thump** *v.*

thun-der *n.* The loud explosive sound made as air is suddenly expanded by heat and then quickly contracted again.

thun-der-bolt *n.* A flash of lightning immediately followed by thunder.

thun-der-cloud *n.* A dark cloud carrying an electric charge and producing lightning and thunder.

thun-der-show-er *n.* A brief rainstorm with thunder and lightning.

thus *adv.* In this or that way; therefore.

thwack *v.* To strike hard, using something flat.

thwart *v.* To prevent from happening; to prevent from doing something. *n.* A seat positioned crosswise in a boat.

thy *adj.* Pertaining to oneself; your.

thyme *n.* An aromatic mint herb whose leaves are used in cooking.

thy-roid *adj. Anat.* Pertaining to the thyroid gland. *n.* The gland in the neck of man that produces hormones which regulate food use and body growth.

thy-rox-ine *n.* A hormone secreted by the thyroid gland.

ti-ar-a *n.* A bejeweled crown in the form of a half circle and worn by women at formal occasions.

tick *n.* One of a series of rhythmical tapping sounds made by a clock; a small bloodsucking parasite, many of which are carriers of disease.

tick-et *n.* A printed slip of paper or cardboard allowing its holder to enter a specified event or to enjoy a privilege; a list of candidates who represent a political party.

tick-le *v.* To stroke lightly so as to cause laughter; to amuse or delight. **tickle, tickler** *n.*

tidal wave *n.* An enormous rise of destructive ocean water caused by a storm or earthquake.

tid-bit *n.* A choice bit of food, news, or gossip.

tide *n.* The rise and fall of the surface level of the ocean which occurs twice a day due to the gravitational pull of the sun and moon on the earth.

tid-ings *pl., n.* News; information about events.

ti-dy *adj.* Well arranged; neat; orderly. *v.* To make orderly and neat. **tidily** *adv.,* **tidiness** *n.*

tie *v.* To secure or bind with a rope, line, cord or other similar material; to make secure or fasten with a rope; to make a bow or knot in; to match an opponent's score. *n.* A string, rope, cord or other material used to join parts or hold something in place. A necktie; a beam that gives structural support. **railroad tie** A device, as timber, laid crosswise to support train tracks.

tier *n.* A layer or row placed one above the other. **tiered** *adj.*

ti-ger *n.*

A large carnivorous cat having tawny fur with black stripes.

tiger-eye *n.* A yellow-brown gemstone.

tight *adj.* Set closely together; bound or securely firm; not loose; taut; difficult. *adv.* Firmly. *Slang* Intoxicated.

tight-en *v.* To become or make tighter. **tightener** *n.*

tight-rope *n.* A tightly stretched horizontal rope high above the ground for the use of acrobats.

till *prep. & conj.* Until; unless or before. *v.* To cultivate; to plow. *n.* A small cash register or drawer for holding money.

tilt *v.* To tip, as by raising one end. *n.* The state of tilting or being tilted.

tim-ber *n.* Wood prepared for building; a finished piece of wood or plank.

time *n.* A continuous period measured by clocks, watches, and calendars; the period or moment in which something happens or takes place.

tim-id *adj.* Lacking self-confidence; shy.

tinc-ture *n.* A tinge of color; an alcohol solution of some medicinal substance. *v.* To tint.

tin-der *n.* A readily combustible substance or material used for kindling.

tine *n.* A narrow pointed spike or prong, as of a fork or antler.

tinge *v.* To impart a faint trace of color; to tint. *n.* A slight trace of added color.

tin-gle *v.* To feel a stinging or prickling sensation. **tingle** *n.,* **tingly** *adj.*

tin-kle *v.* To produce a slight, sharp

series of metallic ringing sounds.

tin-ny *adj.* Pertaining to or composed of tin.

tin-sel *n.* Thin strips of glittering material used for decorations.

tint *n.* A slight amount or trace of color. *v.* To color.

ti-ny *adj.* Minute; very small.

tip *v.* To slant from the horizontal or vertical. *n.* Extra money given as an acknowledgment of a service; a gratuity; a helpful hint.

tip-ple *v.* To drink an alcoholic beverage to excess.

tip-sy *adj.* Partially intoxicated -iness *n.*

ti-rade *n.* A long, violent speech or outpouring, as of censure.

tire-less *adj.* Untiring. tirelessly *adv.*

tis-sue *n., Biol.* Similar cells and their products developed by plants and animals; a soft, absorbent piece of paper, consisting of two layers.

ti-ta-ni-um *n.* A metallic element symbolized by Ti.

tithe *n.* A tenth of one's income given voluntarily for the support of a church. **tithe** *v.*, **tither** *n.*

tit-il-late *v.* To excite or stimulate in a pleasurable way.
titillating, **titillative** *adj.*,
titillatingly *adv.*, **titillation** *n.*

to *prep.* Toward, opposite or near; in contact with; as far as; used as a function word indicating an action, movement, or condition suggestive of movement; indicating correspondence, dissimilarity, similarity, or proportion; indicating the one for which something is done or exists. *adv.* In the state, direction, or condition.

to-bac-co *n.* A tropical American plant widely cultivated for its leaves, which are prepared in various ways, as for chewing or smoking.

to-bog-gan *n.* A long sled-like vehicle without runners, having long thin boards curved upwards at the forward end. **tobogganist** *n.*, **toboggan** *v.*

to-day *adv.* On or during the present day. *n.* The present time, period, or day.

tod-dle *v.* To walk unsteadily with short steps.

tod-dler *n.* A small child learning to walk.

tod-dy *n., pl.* -ies A drink made with hot water, sugar, spices, and liquor.

tof-fee *n.* A chewy candy made of butter and brown sugar.

to-geth-er *adv.* In or into one group, mass, or body; regarded jointly; in time with what is happening or going on. **togetherness** *n.*

toil *v.* To labor very hard and continuously. *n.* A difficult task -some *adj.*

to-ken *n.* A keepsake; a symbol of authority or identity; a piece of imprinted metal used in place of money. *adj.* Done as a pledge or indication.

tol-er-ate *v.* To put up with; to recognize and respect the opinions and rights of others; to endure; to suffer.

toleration *n.*, **tolerance**, **tolerant** *adj.*

toll *n.* A fixed charge for travel across a bridge or along a road. *v.* To sound a bell in repeated single, slow tones.

tom *n.* A male turkey or cat.

tom-a-hawk *n.* An ax used as a weapon or tool by North American Indians.

to-ma-to *n., pl.* -toes A garden plant cultivated for its edible fruit; the fruit of such a plant.

tomb *n.* A vault for burying the dead; a grave.

tom-boy *n.* A girl whose behavior is characteristic of a boy. **tomboyish** *adj.*

tomb-stone *n.* A stone used to mark a grave.

tom-cat *n.* A male cat.

to-mor-row *n.* The day after the present day. *adv.* On the day following today.

ton *n.* A measurement of weight equal to 2,000 pounds. *Slang* A large amount.

tongs *pl., n.* An implement with two long arms joined at one end, used for picking up or lifting.

tongue *n.* The muscular organ attached to the floor of the mouth, used in tasting, chewing, and speaking; anything shaped like a tongue, as the material under the laces or buckles of a shoe.

to-night *n.* This night; the night of this day; the night that is coming. *adv.* On or during the present or coming night.

ton-sil *n.* One of a pair of tissue similar to lymph nodes, found on either side of the throat.

ton-sil-lec-to-my *n.* The surgical removal of tonsils.

too *adv.* Also; as well; more than is needed.

tool *n.* An implement used to perform a task; anything needed to do one's work. *v.* To make or shape with a tool.

tooth *n., pl.* teeth One of the hard, white structures rooted in the jaw and used for chewing and biting; the small, notched, projecting part of any object, such as a gear, comb or saw.
toothed, **toothless** *adj.*

top *n.* The highest part or surface of anything; a covering or lid; the aboveground part of a rooted plant; the highest degree; a toy having a symmetric body with a tapered end upon which it spins. **top** *v.*

to-paz *n.* A gemstone, usually yellow in color.

top-coat *n.* An outer coat.

top-ic *n.* The subject discussed in an essay, thesis, speech or other discourse; the theme.

top-most *adj.* Uppermost.

to-pog-ra-phy *n., pl.* -ies A detailed description of a region or place; a physical outline showing the features of a region or place.

top-ple *v.* To fall; to overturn.

top-sy--tur-vy *adv.* With the top side down; upside down. *adj.* In a confused state. *n.* Confusion.

To-rah *n.* The body of law and wisdom contained in Jewish Scripture and oral tradition; a parchment scroll that contains the first five books of the Old Testament.

torch *n.* A stick of resinous wood which is burned to give light; any portable device which produces hot flame. *Slang* To set fire to.

tor-ment *n.* Extreme mental anguish or physical pain; a source of trouble or pain. *v.* To cause terrible pain; to pester, harass, or annoy. tormentingly *adv.*, tormentor *n.*

tor-na-do *n., pl.* -does *or* -dos A whirling, violent windstorm accompanied by a funnel-shaped cloud that travels a narrow path over land; a whirlwind.

tor-pe-do *n., pl.* -oes A large, self-propelled, underwater missile launched from a ship, containing an explosive charge.

tor-pid *adj.* Having lost the power of motion or feeling; dormant. torpidity *n.*, torpidly *adv.*

tor-rent *n.* A swift, violent stream; a raging flood. torrential *adj.*

tor-rid *adj.* Parched and dried by the heat. torridly *adv.*

tor-sion *n.* The act or result of twisting; the stress produced when one end is held fast and the other turned.

tor-so *n., pl.* -sos *or* -si The trunk of the human body.

tort *n., Law* A wrongful act requiring compensation for damages.

tor-toise *n.* A turtle that lives on the land; a person or thing regarded as slow.

tor-tu-ous *adj.* Marked by repeated bends, turns, or twists; devious.

tor-ture *n.* The infliction of intense pain as punishment; something causing anguish or pain. *v.* To subject or cause intense suffering; to wrench or twist out of shape. -er *n.*, torturously *adv.*

toss *v.* To fling or throw about continuously; to throw up in the air. *n.* A throw.

tot *n.* A young child; a toddler.

to-tal *n.* The whole amount or sum; the entire quantity. *adj.* Absolute; complete. total *v.*, totally *adv.*

to-tal-i-tar-i-an *adj.* Characteristic of a government controlled completely by one party; exercising complete political control. totalitarian *n.*

tote *v.* To carry something on one's arm or back.

to-tem *n.* An animal or plant regarded as having a close relationship to some family clan or group; a representation or symbol.

tot-ter *v.* To walk unsteadily; to shake or sway as if about to fall.

tou-can *n.*

A brightly colored tropical bird having a very large thin bill.

touch *v.* To allow a part of the body, as the hands, to feel or come into contact with; to hit or tap

lightly; to join; to come next to; to have an effect on.

tough *adj.* Resilient and strong enough to withstand great strain without breaking or tearing; strong; hardy.

tour-ni-quet *n.* A device used to temporarily stop the flow of blood through an artery.

tou-sle *v.* To mess up; to disarrange.

to-ward *or* **to-wards** *prep.* In the direction of; just before; somewhat before; regarding; with respect to.

tow-el *n.* An absorbent piece of cloth used for drying or wiping. towel *v.*

tox-e-mi-a *n., Pathol.* Blood poisoning; a condition in which the blood contains toxins.

tox-ic *adj.* Relating to a toxin; destructive, deadly, or harmful.

tox-in *n.* A poisonous substance produced by chemical changes in plant and animal tissue.

tra-di-tion *n.* The doctrines, knowledge, practices, and customs passed down from one generation to another. traditional *adj.*, traditionally *adv.*

tra-duce *v.* To betray. traducement *n.*, traducer *n.*

trait *n.* A quality or distinguishing feature, such as one's character.

tra-jec-to-ry *n., pl.* -ies The curved line or path of a moving object.

tram-mel *n.* A long, large net used to catch birds or fish; something that impedes movement. trammeler *n.*

tram-ple *v.* To tread heavily; to stomp.

trance *n.* A stupor, daze, mental state, or condition, such as produced by drugs or hypnosis.

tran-quil *adj.* Very calm, quiet, and free from disturbance. tranquillity *n.*, tranquilly *adv.*, tranquilize *v.*

trans-act *v.* To perform, carry out, conduct, or manage business in some way. transaction, transactor *n.*

tran-scend *v.* To pass beyond; to exceed; to surpass. transcendent *adj.*, transcendence *n.*

tran-scribe *v.* To make copies of something; to adopt or arrange.

tran-script *n.* A written copy.

trans-crip-tion *n.* The process or act of transcribing.

trans-fer *v.* To remove, shift, or carry from one position to another. transferable *adj.*, -ence, transferer *n.*

trans-fig-ure *v.* To change the outward appearance or form; to exalt; to glorify. transfiguration *n.*

trans-fix *v.* To pierce; to hold motionless, as with terror, awe or amazement.

trans-form *v.* To change or alter completely in nature, form or function. -able *adj.*, -ation, transformer *n.*

tran-sient *adj.* Not staying or lasting very long; moving from one location to another. transient *n.*, transiently *adv.*

trans-lu-cent *adj.* Diffusing and admitting light but not allowing a clear view of the object.

trans-mit *v.* To dispatch or convey from one thing, person, or place to another.

transmissible, -table *adj.*, -ter *n.*

trans-mute *v.* To change in nature, kind, or substance. transmutation *n.*

trans-par-ent *adj.* Admitting light so that images and objects can be clearly viewed; easy to understand; obvious. transparency *n.*, transparently *adv.*

tran-spire *v.* To give off waste products through plant or animal pores in the form of vapor; to happen; to take place. transpiration *n.*

trans-sex-u-al *n.* A person whose sex has been changed surgically.

tra-peze *n.* A short horizontal bar suspended by two ropes, used for acrobatic exercise or stunts.

trau-ma *n.*, *pl.* -mas *or* -mata A severe wound caused by a sudden physical injury; an emotional shock causing lasting and substantial damage to a person's psychological development.

tra-vail *n.* Strenuous mental or physical exertion; labor in childbirth. *v.* To undergo the sudden sharp pain of childbirth.

trav-el *v.* To journey or move from one place to another. *n.* The process or act of traveling. traveler *n.*

trawl *n.* A strong fishing net which is dragged through water.

tray *n.* A flat container having a low rim, used for carrying, holding, or displaying something.

treach-er-ous *adj.* Diskoyal; deceptive; unreliable. -ly *adv.*, treachery *n.*

treas-ure *n.* Hidden riches; something regarded as valuable. *v.* To save and accumulate for future use; to value.

treasurer *n.* A person having charge and responsibilities for funds.

treas-ur-y *n.*, *pl.* -ies A place where public or private funds are kept.

treat-ment *n.* The manner or act of treating; medical care.

tre-foil *n.* Any of various plants having three leaflets with red, purple, yellow, or pink flowers.

trek *v.* To make a slow and arduous journey. trek, trekker *n.*

trel-lis *n.* A latticework frame used for supporting vines and other climbing plants.

trem-ble *v.* To shake involuntarily, as with fear or from cold; to express or feel anxiety.

tremble, trembler *n.*, trembly *adj.*

tre-men-dous *adj.* Extremely huge, large, or vast. *Slang* Wonderful.

trem-or *n.* A quick, shaking movement; any continued and involuntary trembling or quavering of the body.

trench *n.* A ditch; a long, narrow excavation in the ground. *v.* To cut deep furrows for protection. trencher *n.*

trend *n.* A general inclination, direction, or course; a fad. *v.* To have or take a specified direction. trendsetter *n.*

tres-pass *v.* To infringe upon another's property. In law, to invade the rights, property, or privacy of another without consent or knowledge.

tres-tle *n.* A bar or beam supported by four legs, used as a support, as for a table.

tri-al *n.* In law, the examination and hearing of a case before a court of law in order to determine the case; an attempt or effort.

tri-an-gle *n.*, *Geom.*

A plane figure bounded by three sides and having three angles. triangular *adj.*, triangularity *n.*

tribe *n.* A group of people composed of several villages, districts, or other groups which share a common language, culture, and name.

trib-u-la-tion *n.* Great distress or suffering caused by oppression.

trib-un-al *n.* A decision-making body.

trib-ute *n.* An action of respect or gratitude to someone; money or other goods given by one country to another showing obedience and insuring against invasion.

tri-ceps *n.*, *Anat.* The large muscle at the back of the upper arm.

trick *n.* An action meant to fool, as a scheme; a prank; a feat of magic. *v.* To deceive or cheat. tricky *adj.*

trick-er-y *n.* Deception.

trick-le *v.* To flow in droplets or a small stream. trickle *n.*

tri-col-or *n.* The French color in the flag. tricolored *adj.*

tri-cy-cle *n.* A small vehicle having three wheels, propelled by pedals.

tri-dent *n.* A long spear with three prongs, used as a weapon.

tried *adj.* Tested and proven reliable or useful.

tri-en-ni-al *adj.* Happening every third year; lasting for a time period of three years. triennial *n.*, triennially *adv.*

tri-fle *n.* Something of little value or importance; a dessert made with cake, jelly, wine, and custard. *v.* To use or treat without proper concern.

trig-ger *n.* A lever pulled to fire a gun; a device used to release or start an action. *v.* To start.

trill *n.* A tremulous utterance of successive tones. *v.* To utter with a fluttering sound.

tril-lion *n.* The cardinal number equal to one thousand billion.

trim *v.* To clip or cut off small amounts in order to make neater; to decorate. *adj.* Neat. trim *n.*

tri-ni-tro-tol-u-ene *n.* A very powerful explosive, abbreviated as TNT.

trin-ket *n.* A small piece of jewelry.

tri-o *n.* A set or group of three.

trip *n.* Travel from one place to another; a journey; a loss of balance. *v.* To stumble. *Slang* A hallucinatory effect induced by drugs.

tripe *n.* The stomach lining of oxen or similar animals, used as food. *Slang* Nonsense.

trip-le *adj.* Having three parts. *v.* To

multiply by three; in baseball, a three-base hit.

trip-let *n.* One of three born at the same time.

trip-li-cate *adj.* A group of three identical things. **triplicate** *v.*

tri-pod *n.* A three-legged stand or frame.

trite *adj.* Used too often; common.

tri-umph *v.* To be victorious. *n.* A victory. **triumphant** *adj.*, **-ly** *adv.*

triv-i-al *adj.* Insignificant; of little value or importance; ordinary.

troll *v.* To fish by pulling a baited line slowly behind a boat; to sing with a loud, full voice. *n.* The act of trolling for fish; dwarf or elf.

trol-ley *n.* A streetcar powered by electricity from overhead lines; a small container or basket used to convey material, as in an underground tunnel or mine.

trom-bone *n.* A brass musical instrument, larger and lower in pitch than a trumpet.

troop *n.* A group or assembly of people or animals; a group of Boy Scouts or Girl Scouts having an adult leader; a military unit. **trooper** *n.*

tro-phy *n.*, *pl.* **-ies** A prize or object, such as a plaque, awarded to someone for his success, victory, or achievement.

trop-ic *n.* Either of two imaginary parallel lines which constitute the Torrid Zone. **Tropics** The very warm region of the earth's surface between the Tropic of Cancer and the Tropic of Capricorn. **tropical** *adj.*

tro-po-sphere *n.* The lowest atmosphere between the earth's surface and the stratosphere.

trot *n.* The gait of a horse or other four-footed animal, between a walk and a run, in which the hind leg and opposite front leg move at about the same time. **trot** *v.*

trou-ble *n.* Danger; affliction; need; distress; an effort; physical pain, disease or malfunction. *v.* To bother; to worry; to be bothered; to be worried. **troubler** *n.*, **troublingly** *adv.*

trough *n.* A long, narrow, shallow container, especially one that holds food or water for animals.

trounce *v.* To whip or beat; to defeat decisively.

troupe *n.* A group, especially of the performing arts. **troupe** *v.*

trou-sers *pl.*, *n.* An outer garment that covers the body from the waist down.

trous-seau *n.*, *pl.* **-seaux** or **-seaus** The wardrobe, linens, and other similar articles of a bride.

trout *n.* A freshwater game or food fish.

trowel *n.* A flat-bladed garden tool with a pointed blade, used for digging.

tru-ant *n.* A person who is absent from school without permission. **truancy** *n.*, **truant** *adj.*

truce *n.* An agreement to stop fighting; a cease fire.

trudge *v.* To walk heavily; to plod.

true *adj.* In accordance with reality or fact; not false; real; loyal; faithful. *adv.* Truthfully. **truly** *adv.*

trump *n.* In cards, a suit of any cards which outrank all other cards for a selected period of time.

trum-pet *n.*, *Mus.* A brass instrument having a flared bell, valves, and a mouthpiece. *v.* To proclaim something loudly.

trunk *n.*

The main part of a tree; the human body, excluding the head, arms and legs; a sturdy box for packing clothing, as for travel or storage; the long snout of an elephant. **trunks** Men's clothing worn for swimming or athletics.

truss *v.* To fasten or tie securely. *Med.* A support or device worn to keep a hernia in place.

trust *n.* Confidence or faith in a person or thing; care or charge. *Law* The confidence or arrangement by which property is managed and held for the good or benefit of another person. *v.* To have confidence or faith in; to believe; to expect; to entrust; to depend on.

truth *n.*, *pl.* **truths** The facts corresponding with actual events or happenings; sincerity or honesty. **truthful** *adj.*, **truthfully** *adv.*, **truthfulness** *n.*

try *v.* To make an attempt; to make an effort; to strain; to hear or conduct a trial; to place on trial. **trying** *adj.*, **tryout** *n.*

tsu-na-mi *n.* An extensive and destructive ocean wave caused by an underwater earthquake.

tub *n.* A round, low, flat-bottomed, vessel with handles on the side, as one used for washing.

tu-ba *n.* A large, brass wind instrument having a low range.

tube *n.* A hollow cylinder, made of metal, rubber, glass or other material, used to pass or convey something through. **tube**, **tubal** *adj.*

tu-ber *n.*

The underground stem of certain plants, as the potato, with buds from which new plants arise.

tu-ber-cu-lo-sis *n.* A contagious lung disease of humans and animals caused by microorganisms; abbreviated as TB.

tug *v.* To strain and pull vigorously. *n.* A hard pull; a strong force.

tu-i-tion *n.* Payment for instruction, as at a private school or college.

tum-brel *n.* A cart which can discharge its load by tilting.

tu-mor *n.*, *Pathol.* A swelling on or in

any part of the body; an abnormal growth which may be malignant or benign.

tu-mult *n.* The confusion and noise of a crowd; a riot; any violent commotion.

tu-na *n., pl.* -na *or* -nas Any of several large marine food fish.

tun-nel *n.* An underground or underwater passageway. **tunnel** *v.*

tur-bu-lent *adj.* Marked by a violent disturbance.

tur-moil *n.* A state of confusion or commotion.

tur-quoise *n.* A blue-green gemstone; a light bluish-green color. **turquoise** *adj.*

tusk *n.* A long, curved tooth, as of an elephant or walrus.

tus-sle *n.* A hard fight or struggle with a problem or person. **tussle** *v.*

tu-tu *n.* A very short ballet skirt.

tux-e-do *n.* A semiformal dress suit worn by men.

tweak *v.* To pinch and twist sharply.

twelve *n.* The cardinal number equal to 11 + 1. **twelve** *adj. & pron.*

twen-ty *n.* The cardinal number equal to 19 + 1 or 2 X 10. **twenty** *adj. & pron.*

twice *adv.* Double; two times.

twid-dle *v.* To turn or twirl in an aimless way.

twig *n.* A small branch which grows from a larger branch on a tree.

twill *n.* A weave that produces the parallel rib on the surface of a fabric.

twinge *n.* A sudden, sharp pain; a brief emotional or mental pang. **twinged** *v.*

twin-kle *v.* To gleam or shine with quick flashes; to sparkle. **twinkle** *n.*

twirl *v.* To rotate or cause to turn around and around. **twirl** *n.*

twit *v.* To tease about a mistake. *n.* A taunting reproach.

twitch *v.* To move or cause to move with a jerky movement. *n.* A sudden tug.

tyke *n.* A small child.

ty-phoid *n., Path.* An acute, infectious disease caused by germs in drink or food. **typhoid** *adj.*

typ-i-cal *adj.* Exhibiting the characteristics of a certain class or group.

typ-i-fy *v.* To be characteristic or typical of; to show all the traits or qualities of. **typified, typifying** *adj.*

typ-ist *n.* The operator of a typewriter.

ty-po *n., Slang* An error in typewriting or in setting type; any printed error which was not the fault of the author.

ty-ran-no-sau-rus *n.*

A large, flesh-eating dinosaur which walked on its hind legs.

tyr-an-ny *n.* Harsh, absolute, and unfair rule by a king or other ruler; complete control.

tyr-an-nize *v.* To rule or control completely.

ty-ro *also* **ti-ro** *n.* A novice or a beginner.

U, u The twenty-first letter of the English alphabet.

ud-der *n.* The milk-producing organ pouch of some female animals, having two or more teats.

ugh *interj.* Used to express disgust or horror.

ug-ly *adj.* Offensive; unpleasant to look at -lily *adv.* -liest, -lier *adj.*, -liness *n.*

uh *interj.* To express hesitation.

u-ku-le-le *n.* A small, four-stringed musical instrument, orginally from Hawaii.

ul-cer *n.* A festering, inflamed sore on a mucous membrane or on the skin that results in the destruction of the tissue. **ulcerous** *adj.* **ulceration** *n.*, **ulcerate** *v.*

ul-na *n., Anat.* One of the two bones of the forearm.

ul-ti-mate *adj.* Final; ending; most extreme. **ultimately** *adv.*, **ultimateness** *n.*, **ultimacy** *n.*

ul-ti-ma-tum *n., pl* -tums, -ta A final demand, proposal, or choice, as in negotiating.

ultra- *prefix.* Beyond the scope, range, or limit of something.

ul-tra-mod-ern *adj.* Extremely advanced or modern in style or ideas.

ul-tra-son-ic *adj.* Relating to sound frequencies inaudible to humans.

ul-tra-vi-o-let *adj.* Producing radiation having wave-lengths just shorter than those of visible light and longer than those of X rays. **ultraviolet** *n.*

um-bil-i-cal cord *n.*

The structure by which a fetus is attached to its mother, serving to supply food and dispose of waste.

um-brel-la *n.* A collapsible frame covered with plastic or cloth, held above the head as protection from sun or rain.

um-pire *n.* In sports, the person who rules on plays in a game. *v.* To act as an umpire.

ump-teen *adj., Slang* An indefinitely large number. **umpteenth** *adj.*

un- *prefix* The reverse or opposite of an act; removal or release from.

un-a-ble *adj.* Not having the mental capabilities.

un-ac-com-pa-nied *adj.* Alone; without a companion. *Mus.* Solo.

un-ac-count-a-ble *adj.* Without an explanation; mysterious; not responsible. **unaccountably** *adv.*, -bility *n.*

un-ac-cus-tomed *adj.* Not used to or in the habit of; not ordinary.

u-nan-i-mous *adj.* Agreed to completely; based on the agreement of all. **unanimously** *adv.*

un-armed *adj.* Lacking means for protection.

un-as-sum-ing *adj.* Modest and not showy. **unassumingness** *n.*

un-at-tach-ed *adj.* Not engaged, going steady, or married.

un-a-void-able adj. Inevitable; unstoppable. unavoidably adv.

un-a-ware adj. Not realizing. -ness n.

un-bear-a-ble adj. Not possible to endure; intolerable. unbearably adv.

un-be-com-ing adj. Unattractive; not pleasing; notproper. -ness n.

un-be-known or unbeknownst adj. Not known; without one's knowledge.

un-be-liev-able adj. Incredible; hard to accept; not to be believed. -ly adv.

un-called for adj. Not necessary or needed; not requested.

un-can-ny adj. Strange, odd, or mysterious; exceptional. uncannily adv., uncanniness n.

un-cer-tain adj. Doubtful; not sure; not known; hard to predict. uncertainly adv., uncertainness n.

un-changed adj. Having nothing new or different.

un-civ-il-ized adj. Without culture or refinement; without an established cultural and social way of living.

un-cle n. The brother of one's mother or father; the husband of an aunt.

un-clean adj. Immoral; dirty; not decent. uncleanness n., uncleanly adv.

un-clothe v. To uncover or undress. unclothed adj.

un-com-fort-a-ble adj. Disturbed; not at ease physically or mentally; causing discomfort. uncomfortably adv.

un-com-mon adj. Rare; odd; unusual. uncommonly adv., uncommonness n.

un-com-pro-mis-ing adj. Firm; unwilling to give in or to compromise. uncompromisingly adv.

un-con-cern n. Lack of interest; disinterest; indifference.

un-con-cerned adj. the state of not having any interest in something or someone. -ness n., -ly adv.

un-con-di-tion-al adj. Without conditions or limits. unconditionally adv.

un-con-scious adj. Not mentally aware; done without thought; not on purpose. unconsciously adv. unconsciousness n.

un-con-sti-tu-tion-al adj. Contrary to the constitution or the basic laws of a state or country.

un-couth adj. Acting or speaking crudely, unrefined; clumsy or awkward. uncouthness n., -ly adv.

un-cov-er v. To remove the cover from something; to disclose. uncovered adj.

un-de-cid-ed adj. Unsettled; having made no firm decision; open to change. undecidedly adv.

un-de-ni-able adj. Not open to doubt or denial; not possible to contradict. undeniably adv.

un-der prep. Below, in place or position; in a place lower than another; less in degree, number, or other quality; inferior in rank, quality, or character; during the reign or period; in accordance with. less than the required amount; insufficient.

un-der prefix. Location beneath or below; lower in importance or rank, degree or amount.

un-der-brush n. Small bushes, vines, and plants that grow under tall trees.

un-der-clothes pl., n. Clothes worn next to the skin; underwear.

un-der-de-vel-oped adj. Not fully mature or grown; lacking modern communications and industry.

un-der-foot adj. Underneath or below the feet; being so close to one's feet as to be in the way.

un-der-go v. To have the experience of; to be subjected to.

un-der-grad-u-ate n. A college or university student studying for a bachelor's degree.

un-der-hand adj. Done deceitfully and secretly; sneaky. -ed adj. -edly adv.

un-der-line v. To draw a line directly under something. underline n.

un-der-mine v. To weaken; to make less strong.

un-der-neath adv. Beneath or below; on the under side; lower. prep. Under; below.

un-der-priv-i-leged adj. Deprived of economic and social advantages.

un-der-rate v. To rate or value below the true worth.

un-der-score v. To emphasize.

un-der-sell v. To sell for less than a competitor.

un-der-side n. The side or part on the bottom.

un-der-stand v. To comprehend; to realize; to know the feelings and thoughts of. understanding v.

un-der-stand-a-ble adj. Able to sympathize or comprehend. -ably adv.

un-der-state v. To make too little of the actual situation. understatement n.

un-der-stood adj. Agreed upon by all.

un-der-stud-y v. To learn another person's part or role in order to be able to replace him if necessary.

un-der-take v. To set about to do a task; to pledge oneself to a certain job; to attempt. undertaking n.

un-der-tak-er n. A person who prepares the dead for burial.

un-der-tone n. A low, quiet voice; a pale or subdued color visible through other colors.

un-der-tow n. The underwater current which runs in the opposite direction of the surface current.

un-der-wa-ter adj. Occurring, happening or used beneath the surface of the water. underwater adv.

un-de-sir-a-ble adj. Offensive; not wanted. undesirably adv.

un-do v. To cancel; to reverse; to loosen or unfasten; to open a package.

un-done adj. Not finished; unfastened; ruined.

un-du-late v. To move from side to side with a flowing motion; to have a wavy shape. undulation n.

un-dy-ing adj. Without end.

un-earth v. To dig up from the earth; to find or discover.

un-earth-ly adj. Strange; not from this world.

un-eas-y *adj.* Feeling or causing distress or discomfort; embarrassed; awkward; uncertain. **uneasily** *adv.*, **uneasiness** *n.*

un-em-ployed *adj.* Without a job; without work. **unemployment** *n.*

un-e-qual *adj.* Not even; not fair; not of the same size or time; lacking sufficient ability. **unequaled** *adj.*

un-e-ven *adj.* Not equal; varying in consistency or form; not balanced. **-ly** *adv.*

un-e-vent-ful *adj.* Lacking in significance; calm. **uneventfully** *adv.*

un-expect-ed *adj.* Surprising; happening without warning. **unexpectedly** *adv.*

un-fail-ing *adj.* Constant, unchanging.

un-fair *adj.* Not honest; marked by a lack of justice. **-ly** *adv.*, **unfairness** *n.*

un-faith-ful *adj.* Breaking a promise or agreement; without loyalty; guilty of adultery. **-ness** *n.*, **unfaithfully** *adv.*

un-fa-mil-iar *adj.* Not knowing; strange; foreign. **unfamiliarity** *n.*

un-fa-vor-able *adj.*, Not desired; harmful; unpleasant.

un-feel-ing *adj.* Without sympathy; hardhearted; without sensation. **unfeelingly** *adv.*

un-fit *adj.* Not suitable; not qualified; in poor body or mental health. **unfitly** *adv.*, **unfitness** *n.*

un-fold *v.* To open up the folds of and lay flat; to reveal gradually. **-ment** *n.*

un-fore-seen *adj.* Not anticipated or expected.

un-for-get-ta-ble *adj.* Impossible or hard to forget; memorable. **-ably** *adv.*

un-for-tu-nate *adj.* Causing or having bad luck, damage, or harm. *n.* A person who has no luck. **-ly** *adv.*

un-found-ed *adj.* Not founded or based on fact; groundless; lacking a factual basis.

un-friend-ly *adj.* Showing a lack of kindness; not friendly; not favorable. **unfriendliness** *n.*

un-furl *v.* To unroll or unfold; to open up or out.

un-fur-nished *adj.* Without furniture.

un-god-ly *adj.* Wicked; evil; lacking reverence for God. **ungodliness** *n.*

un-grate-ful *adj.* Not thankful; showing no appreciation. **ungratefully** *adv.*

un-guent *n.* A healing or soothing salve; ointment.

un-heard *adj.* Not heard; not listened to.

un-heard--of *adj.* Not known or done before; without precedent.

un-hook *v.* To release or undo from a hook.

u-ni-corn *n.*

A mythical animal resembling a horse, with a horn in the center of its forehead.

u-ni-cy-cle *n.* A one wheeled vehicle with pedals.

un-i-den-ti-fied fly-ing ob-ject *n.* A flying object that cannot be explained or identified, abbreviated as UFO.

u-ni-form *n.* Identical clothing worn by the members of a group to distinguish them from the general population. **uniformly** *adv.*

u-ni-fy *v.* To come together as one; to unite. **unifier** *n.*

un-in-hab-it-ed *adj.* Not lived in; empty.

un-in-ter-est-ed *adj.* Having no interest or concern in; not interested.

un-ion *n.* The act of joining together of two or more groups or things.

u-nique *adj.* Unlike any other; sole. **uniqueness** *n.*, **uniquely** *adv.*

u-ni-sex *adj.* Adaptable and appropriate for both sexes.

u-ni-son *n.* In music, the exact sameness of pitch, as of a tone; harmonious agreement.

u-nite *v.* To join or come together for a common purpose.

u-ni-ty *n.*, *pl.* **-ies** The fact or state of being one; accord; agreement; harmony.

u-ni-valve *n.* A mollusk having a one-piece shell, such as a snail.

u-ni-ver-sal *adj.* Having to do with the world or the universe in its entirety. **universally** *adv.*, **universalness** *n.*

u-ni-verse *n.* The world, stars, planets, space, and all that is contained.

u-ni-ver-si-ty *n.*, *pl.* **-ies** An educational institution offering undergraduate and graduate degrees in a variety of academic areas.

un-just *adj.* Not fair; lacking justice or fairness. **unjustly** *adv.*

un-kempt *adj.* Poorly groomed; messy; untidy.

un-kind *adj.* Harsh; lacking in sympathy, concern, or understanding. **unkindly** *adj.* **unkindness** *n.*

un-known *adj.* Strange; unidentified; not known; not familiar or famous.

un-lead-ed *adj.* Containing no lead.

un-like *prep.* Dissimilar; not alike; not equal in strength or quantity; not usual for.

un-lim-it-ed *adj.* Having no boundaries or limitations.

un-load *v.* To take or remove the load; to unburden; to dispose or get rid of by selling in volume.

un-lock *v.* To open, release, or unfasten a lock; open with a key.

un-loose *v.* To loosen or undo; to release.

un-luck-y *adj.* Unfortunate; having bad luck; disappointing or unsuitable.

un-manned *adj.* Designed to operate or be operated without a crew of people.

un-men-tion-a-ble *adj.* Improper or unsuitable.

un-mis-tak-a-ble *adj.* Very clear and evident; understood; obvious.

un-mor-al *adj.* Having no moral knowledge.

un-nat-u-ral *adj.* Abnormal or unusual; strange; artificial. **unnaturally** *adv.*

un-nec-es-sar-y *adj.* Not needed; not appropriate. **unnecessarily** *adv.*

un-nerve *v.* To frighten; to upset. **unnervingly** *adv.*

un-num-bered *adj.* Countless; not identified by number.

un-oc-cu-pied *adj.* Empty; not occupied.

un-pack *v.* To remove articles out of trunks, suitcases, boxes, or other storage places.

un-pleas-ant *adj.* Not agreeable; not pleasant. **-tly** *adv.*, **unpleasantness** *n.*

un-pop-u-lar *adj.* Not approved or liked. **unpopularity** *n.*

un-pre-dict-a-ble *adj.* Not capable of being foretold; not reliable. **unpredictably** *adj.*

un-pre-pared *adj.* Not equipped or ready.

un-pro-fes-sion-al *adj.* Contrary to the standards of a profession; having no professional status.

un-prof-it-a-ble *adj.* Showing or giving no profit; serving no purpose.

un-qual-i-fied *adj.* Lacking the proper qualifications; unreserved.

un-rav-el *v.* To separate threads; to solve; to clarify; to come apart.

un-re-al *adj.* Having no substance or reality.

un-rea-son-a-ble *adj.* Not according to reason; exceeding all reasonable limits.

un-re-li-a-ble *adj.* Unable to be trusted; not dependable.

un-re-served *adj.* Done or given without reserve; unlimited.

un-re-strained *adj.* Not held back, forced, or affected.

un-ru-ly *adj.* Disorderly; difficult to subdue or control.

un-sat-is-fac-to-ry *adj.* Unacceptable; not pleasing.

un-screw *v.* To loosen or unfasten by removing screws from.

un-scru-pu-lous *adj.* Without morals, guiding principles, or rules. **unscrupulously** *adv.*, **-ness** *n.*

un-seat *v.* To cause to lose one's seat; to force out of office.

un-sel-fish *adj.* Willing to share; thinking of another's well-being before one's own. **unselfishly** *adv.*, **unselfishness** *n.*

un-set-tle *v.* To cause to be upset or excited; to disturb. **unsettled** *adj.*

un-sheathe *v.* To draw a sword from a sheath or other case.

un-sight-ly *adj.* Not pleasant to look at; ugly.

un-skilled *adj.* Having no skills or training in a given kind of work.

un-skill-ful *adj.* Lacking in proficiency. **unskillfully** *adv.*, **unskillfulness** *n.*

un-sound *adj.* Having defects; not solidly made; unhealthy in body or mind. **unsoundly** *adv.*, **unsoundness** *n.*

un-speak-a-ble *adj.* Of or relating to something which cannot be expressed or described. **unspeakably** *adv.*

un-sta-ble *adj.* Not steady or firmly fixed; having the tendency to fluctuate or change.

un-stead-y *adj.* Not secure; unstable;

variable. **unsteadily** *adv.*, **-diness** *n.*

un-sub-stan-tial *adj.* Lacking strength, weight, or solidity; unreal.

un-suit-a-ble *adj.* Unfitting; not suitable; not appropriate for a specific circumstance. **-bly** *adv.*, **-ness** *n.*

un-tan-gle *v.* To free from snarls or entanglements.

un-thank-ful *adj.* Ungrateful.

un-think-a-ble *adj.* Unimaginable.

un-ti-dy *adj.* Messy; showing a lack of tidiness. **untidily** *adv.*, **untidiness** *n.*

un-tie *v.* To unfasten or loosen; to free from a restraint or bond.

un-til *prep.* Up to the time of. *conj.* To the time when; to the degree or place.

un-time-ly *adj.* Premature; before the expected time.

un-told *adj.* Not revealed; not told; inexpressible; cannot be described or revealed.

un-touch-a-ble *adj.* Cannot be touched; incapable of being obtained or reached.

un-true *adj.* Not true; contrary to the truth; not faithful; disloyal.

un-truth *n.* Something which is not true; the state of being false. **untruthful** *adj.*, **-fully** *adv.*, **-ness** *n.*

un-used *adj.* Not put to use; never having been used.

un-u-su-al *adj.* Not usual; uncommon. **unusually** *adv.*, **unusualness** *n.*

un-ut-ter-a-ble *adj.* Incapable of being described or expressed; unpronounceable. **unutterably** *adv.*

un-veil *v.* To remove a veil from; to uncover; to reveal.

un-war-y *adj.* Not cautious or careful; careless.

un-whole-some *adj.* Unhealthy; morally corrupt or harmful.

un-will-ing *adj.* Reluctant; not willing. **unwillingly** *adv.*, **unwillingness** *n.*

un-wind *v.* To undo or reverse the winding of; to untangle.

un-wise *adj.* Lacking good judgment or common sense. **unwisely** *adv.*

un-wor-thy *adj.* Not deserving; not becoming or befitting; lacking merit or worth; shameful. **unworthiness** *n.*

up *adv.* From a lower position to a higher one; on, in, or to a higher level, position, or place.

up-beat *n.*, *Mus.* The relatively unaccented beat preceding the down beat. *adj.* Optimistic; happy.

up-bring-ing *n.* The process of teaching and rearing a child.

up-com-ing *adj.* About to take place or appear.

up-date *v.* To revise or bring up-to-date; to modernize. **update** *n.*

up-draft *n.* An upward current of air.

up-grade *v.* To increase the grade, rank, or standard of. *n.* An upward slope.

up-hill *adv.* Up an incline. *adj.* Hard to accomplish; going up a hill or incline.

up-keep *n.* The cost and work needed to keep something in good condition.

up-lift *v.* To raise or lift up; to improve the social, economic, and moral level of a group or of a society.

up-on *prep.* On.

up-per *adj.* Higher in status, position or location.

up-right *adj.* Having a vertical direction or position; honest. *n.* Something standing vertically, such as a beam in a building.

up-ris-ing *n.* A revolt; a rebellion; an insurrection.

up-roar *n.* A confused, loud noise; a commotion.

up-root *v.* To detach completely by pulling up the roots. **uprooter** *n.*

up-stairs *adv.* Up one or more flights of stairs. *adj.* Situated on the upper floor.

up-stand-ing *adj.* Straightforward; honest; upright.

up-tight *adv.* Nervous, tense, or anxious.

up--to--date *adj.* Most current or recent; appropriate to the present time.

up-town *adv.* Toward or in the upper part of town. **uptown** *adv.*

up-ward *or* **up-wards** *adv.* From a lower position to or toward a higher one. *adj.* Directed toward a higher positon.

u-ra-ni-um *n.* A hard, heavy, shiny metallic element that is radioactive, used especially in research and in nuclear weapons and fuels, symbolized by U.

ur-ban *adj.* Pertaining to a city or having characteristics of a city; living or being in a city. **urbanite** *n.*, **urbanize** *v.*

urge *v.* To encourage, push, or drive; to recommend persistently and strongly. *n.* An influence, impulse, or force.

ur-gent *adj.* Requiring immediate attention. **urgency** *n.*, **urgently** *adv.*

urine *n.* In man and other mammals, the yellowish fluid waste produced by the kidneys.

Us *pl., pron.* The objective case of we; used as an indirect object, direct object, or object of a preposition.

us-a-ble *or* **use-a-ble** *adj.* Fit or capable of being used. **usability** *n.*, **usably** *adv.*

us-age *n.* The way or act of using something; the way words are used.

use *v.* To put into action; to emply for a special purpose; to employ on a regular basis; to exploit for one's own advantage. **used** *adj.*, **useful** *adj.*

u-su-al *adj.* Ordinary or common; regular; customary. **usually** *adv.*, **usualness** *n.*

u-surp *v.* To take over by force without authority. **usurpation, usurper** *n.*

u-ten-sil *n.* A tool, implement, or container, especially one for the kitchen.

u-ter-us *n.* An organ of female mammals within which young develop and grow before birth. **uterine** *adj.*

u-til-ize *v.* To make or put to use.

ut-most *adj.* Of the greatest amount or degree; most distant. **utmost** *n.*

ut-ter *v.* To say or express verbally; to speak. *adv.* Absolute; complete. **utterly** *adv.*, **utterance** *n.*

u-vu-la *n.* The fleshy projection which hangs above the back of the tongue. **uvular** *adj.*

V, v The twenty-second letter of the English alphabet; the Roman numeral for 5.

va-cant *adj.* Empty; not occupied; without expression or thought.

va-cate *v.* To leave; to cease to occupy.

va-ca-tion *n.* A period of time away from work for pleasure, relaxation, or rest.

vac-ci-nate *v.* To inject with a vaccine so as to produce immunity to an infectious disease, as measles or smallpox.

vac-ci-na-tion *n.* The inoculation with a vaccine.

vac-cine *n.* A solution of weakened or killed microorganisms, as bacteria or viruses, injected into the body to produce immunity to a disease.

vac-u-um *n., pl.* **-ums, -ua** A space which is absolutely empty; a void; a vacuum cleaner.

vag-a-bond *n.* A homeless person who wanders from place to place; a tramp.

va-gar-y *n., pl.* **-ies** An eccentric or capricious action or idea. **vagarious** *adj.*

va-gi-na *n., pl.* **-nas, -nae** *Anat.* The canal or passage extending from the uterus to the external opening of the female reproductive system.

vag-i-ni-tis *n.* An inflammation of the vagina.

va-grant *n.* A person who wanders from place to place. *adj.* Roaming from one area to another without a job.

vague *adj.* Not clearly expressed; not sharp or definite. **vaguely** *adv.*

vain *adj.* Conceited; lacking worth or substance; having too much pride in oneself. **in vain** Irreverently. **-ly** *adv.*

val-ance *n.* A decorative drapery across the top of a window.

vale *n.* A valley.

val-e-dic-to-ri-an *n.* The student ranking highest in a graduating class, who delivers a speech at the commencement.

val-et *n.* A man who takes care of another man's clothes and other personal needs; a hotel employee who attends to personal services for guests.

val-iant *adj.* Brave; exhibiting valor. **valiance, valor** *n.*

val-id *adj.* Founded on facts or truth. *Law* Binding; having legal force. **validity, validate** *n.*

val-ley *n., pl.* **-leys** Low land between ranges of hills or mountains.

val-or *n.* Bravery. **-ous** *adj.*, **-ously** *adv.*

val-u-a-ble *adj.* Of great value or importance; having a high monetary value.

val-ue *n.* The quality or worth of something that makes it valuable; material worth; a principle regarded as worthwhile or desirable. *Math* A calculated numerical quantity. *v.* To estimate the value or worth of; to regard very highly; to rate according to importance, worth, or usefulness. **valueless** *adj.*

valve *n.* The movable mechanism which opens and closes to control the flow of a substance through a pipe or other passageway. *Anat.* A membranous

structure in a vein or artery that prevents or slows the backward movement of fluid.

va-moose v. *Slang* To leave in a hurry.

vam-pire n. In folklore, a dead person believed to rise from the grave at night to suck the blood of sleeping persons; a person who preys on others.

vam-pire bat n.

A tropical bat that feeds on the blood of living mammals.

van n. A large closed wagon or truck.

va-na-di-um n. A metallic element symbolized by V.

van-dal-ism n. The malicious defacement or destruction of private or public property.

vane n. A metal device that turns in the direction the wind is blowing; a thin rigid blade of an electric fan, propeller, or windmill.

va-nil-la n. A flavoring extract used in cooking and baking; prepared from the vanilla bean.

van-ish v. To disappear suddenly; to drop out of sight; to go out of existence.

van-i-ty n., pl., -ies Conceit; extreme pride in one's ability, possessions, or appearance.

van-tage n. A superior position; an advantage.

va-por n. Moisture or smoke suspended in air, as mist or fog. **vaporish, vaporous** adj., **vaporize** v.

var-i-able adj. Changeable; tending to vary; inconstant. n. A quantity or thing which can vary. **-ness** n., **-ly** adv.

var-i-ance n. The state or act of varying; difference; conflict.

var-i-a-tion n. The result or process of varying; the degree or extent of varying. *Mus.* A different form or version of a given theme, with modifications in rhythm, key, or melody.

var-i-e-gat-ed adj. Having marks of different colors. **variegate** v.

va-ri-e-ty n., pl., -ies The state or character of being varied or various; a number of different kinds; an assortment.

var-i-ous adj. Of different kinds.

var-mint n., *Slang* A troublesome animal; an obnoxious person.

var-nish n. A solution paint used to coat or cover a surface with a hard, transparent, shiny film. v. To put varnish on.

var-si-ty n., pl., -ies The best team representing a college, university, or school.

var-y v. To change; to make or become different; to be different; to make of different kinds.

vas-cu-lar adj., *Biol.* Having to do with vessels circulating fluids, as blood.

va-sec-to-my n., pl. -ies Method of male sterilization involving the surgical excision of a part of the tube which conveys semen.

vast adj. Very large or great in size. **vastly** adv., **vastness** n.

vault n. An arched structure that forms a ceiling or roof; a room for storage and safekeeping, as in a bank, usually made of steel; a burial chamber. v. To supply or construct with a vault; to jump or leap with the aid of a pole.

veg-e-ta-ble n. A plant, as the tomato, green beans, lettuce, raised for the edible part. adj. Resembling a vegetable in activity; passive; dull.

veg-e-tar-i-an n. A person whose diet is limited to vegetables. adj. Consuming only plant products. **vegetarianism** n.

veg-e-ta-tion n. Plants or plant life which grow from the soil.

ve-hi-cle n. A motorized device for transporting goods, equipment, or passengers; any means by which something is transferred, expressed, or applied.

veil n. A piece of transparent cloth worn on the head or face for concealment or protection; anything that conceals from view. v. To cover or conceal, as with a veil.

vein n., *Anat.*

A vessel which transports blood back to the heart after passing through the body; one of the branching support tubes of an insect's wing; a long wavy, ir regularly colored streak, as in marble, or wood. **vein** v.

ve-lour n. A soft velvet-like woven cloth having a short, thick nap.

vel-vet n. A fabric made of rayon, cotton, or silk, having a smooth, dense pile.

vend-er or **vend-or** n. A person who sells, as a peddler.

ven-det-ta n. A fight or feud between blood-related persons, involving revenge killings.

ven-er-a-ble adj. Meriting or worthy of respect by reason of dignity, position, or age.

ve-ne-re-al dis-ease n. A contagious disease, as syphilis, or gonorrhea, which is typically acquired through sexual intercourse.

ve-ne-tian blind n. A window blind having thin, horizontal slats which can be adjusted to desired angles so as to vary the amount of light admitted.

ven-i-son n. The edible flesh of a deer.

ven-om n. A poisonous substance secreted by some animals, as scorpions or snakes, usually transmitted to their prey or an enemy through a bite or sting. **venomous** adj.

ve-nous adj. Of or relating to veins. *Physiol.* Returning blood to the heart after passing through the capillaries, supplying oxygen for the tissues, and becoming charged with carbon dioxide. **venously** adv.

vent *n.* A means of escape or passage from a restricted area; an opening which allows the escape of vapor, heat, gas, or liquid.

ven-ti-late *v.* To expose to a flow of fresh air for refreshing, curing, or purifying purposes; to cause fresh air to circulate through an area; to expose to public discussion or examination. **ventilation, ventilator** *n.*

ven-ture *n.* A course of action involving risk, chance, or danger, especially a business investment. *v.* To take a risk.

ven-ue *n.* The place where a crime or other cause of legal action occurs; the locale of a gathering or public event.

verb *n.* The part of speech which expresses action, existence, or occurrence.

ver-bal *adj.* Expressed in speech; expressed orally; not written; relating to or derived from a verb. *n.* An adjective, noun, or other word which is based on a verb and retains some characteristics of a verb. **verbally** *adv.*, **verbalize** *v.*

ver-ba-tim *adv.* Word for word.

ver-be-na *n.* An American garden plant having variously colored flower clusters.

verge *n.* The extreme edge or rim; margin; the point beyond which something begins. *v.* To border on.

ver-min *n., pl.* **vermins** A destructive, annoying animal which is harmful to one's health.

ver-sa-tile *adj.* Having the capabilities of doing many different things; having many functions or uses. **versatility** *n.*

verse *n.* Writing that has a rhyme; poetry; a subdivision of a chapter of the Bible. *v.* To make verse; to tell or celebrate in verse; to familiarize by close association or study.

ver-so *n., pl.* **-sos** The left-hand page.

ver-sus *prep.* Against; in contrast to; as an alternative of.

ver-te-bra *n., pl.* **-brae, -bras** One of the bony or cartilaginous segments making up the spinal column. **-al** *adj.*

ver-tex *n., pl.* **-es, -tices** The highest or topmost point; the pointed top of a triangle, opposite the base; the point at which two lines meet to form an angle.

ver-ti-cal *adj.* In a straight up-and-down direction; being perpendicular to the plane of the horizon or to a primary axis; upright. **vertically** *adv.*

ver-y *adv.* To a high or great degree; truly; absolutely; exactly; actually; in actual fact.

ves-per *n.* An evening prayer service; a bell to call people to such a service.

vest *n.* A sleeveless garment open or fastening in front, worn over a shirt.

ves-tige *n.* A trace or visible sign of something that no longer exists. **vestigial** *adj.*, **vestigially** *adj.*

ves-try *n., pl.* **vestries** A room in a church used for meetings and classes.

vet *n., Slang* A veterinarian; a veteran.

vet-er-an *n.* A person with a long record or experience in a certain field; one who has served in the military.

vet-er-i-nar-i-an *n.* One who is trained and authorized to give medical treatment to animals.

vet-er-i-nar-y *adj.* Pertaining to or being the science and art of prevention and treatment of animals.

ve-to- *n., pl.* **vetoes** The power of a government executive, as the President or a governor, to reject a bill passed by the legislature. *v.* To reject a bill passed by the legislature.

vex *v.* To bother; or annoy. **vexation** *n.*

vi-a *prep.* By way of; by means of.

vi-a-duct *n.* A bridge, resting on a series of arches, carrying a road or railroad.

vi-al *n.* A small, closed container used especially for liquids.

vi-brate *v.* To move or make move back and forth or up and down. **vibration** *n.*

vi-car-i-ous *adj.* Undergoing or serving in the place of someone or something else; experienced through sympathetic or imaginative participation in the experience of another.

vice *n.* An immoral habit or practice; evil conduct. *prefix* One who takes the place of another.

vi-ce ver-sa *adv.* With the order or meaning of something reversed.

vi-chy-ssoise *n.* A soup made from potatoes, chicken stock, and cream, flavored with leeks or onions and usually served cold.

vi-cin-i-ty *n., pl.* **-ies** The surrounding area or district; the state of being near in relationship or space.

vi-cious *adj.* Dangerously aggressive; having the quality of immorality. **viciously** *adv.*, **viciousness** *n.*

vic-tim *n.* A person who is harmed or killed by another; a living creature which is slain and offered as sacrifice; one harmed by circumstance or condition. **victimize** *v.*

vic-tor *n.* A person who conquers; the winner.

vic-to-ri-ous *adj.* Being the winner in a contest. **victoriously** *adv.*

vic-to-ry *n., pl.* **-ies** A defeat of those on the opposite side.

vid-e-o *adj.* Being, related to, or used in the reception or transmission of television.

vid-e-o disc *n.* A disc containing recorded images and sounds which may be played on a television set.

vid-e-o game *n.* A computerized game displaying on a display screen, controlled by a player or players.

vid-e-o ter-mi-nal *n. Computer Science* A computer device having a cathoderay tube for displaying data on a screen.

vie *v.* To strive for superiority.

vig-or *n.* Energy or physical strength; intensity of effect or action. **-ous** *adj.*

vile *adj.* Morally disgusting, miserable, and unpleasant. **vilely** *adv.*, **vileness** *n.*

vil-la *n.* A luxurious home in the country; a country estate.

vil-lage *n.* An incorporated settlement, usually smaller than a town. **villager** *n.*

vil-lain *n.* An evil or wicked person; a criminal; an uncouth person. **villainous** *adj.*, **villainy** *n.*

vin-ai-grette *n.* A small ornamental bottle with a perforated top, used for holding an aromatic preparation such as smelling salts.

vin-di-cate *v.* To clear of suspicion; to set free; to provide a defense or justification for. **vindication** *n.*

vin-dic-tive *adj.* Showing or possessing a desire for revenge; spiteful.

vine *n.* A plant whose stem needs support as it climbs or clings to a surface.

vin-tage *n.* The grapes or wine produced from a particular district in one season.

vi-nyl *n.* A variety of shiny plastics, similar to leather, often used for clothing and for covering furniture.

vi-o-la *n.* A stringed instrument, slightly larger and deeper in tone than a violin.

vi-o-late *v.* To break the law or a rule; to disrupt or disturb a person's privacy.

vi-o-lence *n.* Physical force or activity used to cause harm, damage, or abuse.

vi-o-let *n.* A small, low-growing plant with blue, purple, or white flowers; a purplish-blue color.

vi-o-lin *n.* A small stringed instrument, played with a bow.

vi-per *n.* A poisonous snake; an evil or treacherous person.

vir-gin *n.* A person who has never had sexual intercourse. *adj.* In an unchanged or natural state.

vir-ile *adj.* Having the qualities and nature of a man; capable of sexual performance in the male. **virility** *n.*

vir-tu *n.* The love or knowledge of fine objects of art.

vir-tue *n.* Morality, goodness or uprightness; a special type of goodness. **virtuous** *adj.*, **virtuously** *adv.*

vi-rus *n.* Any of a variety of microscopic organisms which cause diseases.

vi-sa *n.* An official authorization giving permission on a passport to enter a specific country.

vis-cid *adj.* Sticky; having an adhesive quality.

vise *or* **vice** *n.* A tool in carpentry and metalwork having two jaws to hold things in position.

vis-i-bil-i-ty *n.*, *pl.* -ies The degree or state of being visible; the distance that one is able to see clearly.

vis-i-ble *adj.* Apparent; exposed to view.

vi-sion *n.* The power of sight; the ability to see; an image created in the imagination.

vis-it *v.* To journey to or come to see a person or place.

vi-su-al *adj.* Visible; relating to seeing or sight.

vi-tal *adj.* Essential to life; very important. **vitally** *adv.*

vi-tal signs *pl.*, *n.*, *Med.* The pulse rate, body temperature, blood pressure, and respiratory rate of a person.

vi-ta-min *n.* Any of various substances which are found in foods and are essential to good health.

vit-re-ous *adj.* Related to or similar to glass.

vit-ri-fy *v.* To convert into glass or a substance similar to glass, by heat and fusion.

vi-va-cious *adj.* Filled with vitality or animation; lively. **vivaciously** *adv.*

viv-id *adj.* Bright; brilliant; intense; having clear, lively, bright colors.

viv-i-fy *v.* To give life to. **vivification** *n.*

vo-cab-u-lar-y *n.*, *pl.* -ies A list or group of words and phrases, usually in alphabetical order; all the words that a person uses or understands.

vo-cal *adj.* Of or related to the voice; uttered by the voice; to speak freely and loudly. *n.* A vocal sound. **-ly** *adv.*

vo-ca-tion *n.* A career, occupation, or profession.

vo-cif-er-ate *v.* To utter or cry out loudly; to shout. **vociferation** *n.*, **vociferous** *adj.*, **vociferously** *adv.*

vogue *n.* The leading style or fashion; popularity. **vogue** *adj.*

voice *n.* The sounds produced by speaking; the ability or power to produce musical tones. *v.* To express; to utter; to give voice.

void *adj.* Containing nothing; empty; not inhabited; useless; vain; without legal force or effect; null.

voile *n.* A fine, soft, sheer fabric used for making light clothing and curtains.

volt-age *n.* The amount of electrical power, given in terms of the number of volts.

vol-ume *n.* The capacity or amount of space or room; a book; a quantity; the loudness of a sound.

vol-un-tar-y *adj.* Done cooperatively or willingly; from one's own choice.

vo-lup-tu-ous *adj.* Full of pleasure; delighting the senses; sensuous; luxury. **voluptuousness** *n.*

vo-ra-cious *adj.* Having a large appetite; insatiable. **voraciously** *adv.*

vote *n.* The expression of one's choice by voice, by raising one's hand, or by secret ballot. *v.* To express one's views. **voteless** *adj.*, **voter** *n.*

vo-tive *adj.* Performed in fulfillment of a vow or in devotion.

vouch *v.* To verify or support as true; to guarantee. **voucher** *n.*

vow-el *n.* A sound of speech made by voicing the flow of breath within the mouth; a letter representing a vowel, as a, e, i, o, u, and sometimes y.

voy-age *n.* A long trip or journey.

vul-gar *adj.* Showing poor manners; crude; improper; immoral or indecent.

vul-ner-a-ble *adj.* Open to physical injury or attack. **vulnerability** *n.*, **-ably** *adv.*

vul-ture *n.* A large bird of the hawk family, living on dead animals; a greedy person; one who feeds on the mistakes or bad luck of others.

W, w The twenty-third letter of the English alphabet.

wacky *adj.* Amusingly or absurdly irrational. **wackily** *adj.*, **wackiness** *n.*

wad *n.* A small crumpled mass or bundle; a soft plug used to hold shot or gunpowder charge in place. *Slang* A large roll of money. **wad** *v.*

wad-dle *v.* To walk with short steps and swing from side to side. **waddle, waddler** *n.*

wade *v.* To walk through a substance as mud or water which hampers one's steps.

wa-fer *n.* A small, thin, crisp cracker, cookie, or candy.

waf-fle *n.* Pancake batter cooked in a waffle iron.

waft-age *n.* The state or act of being wafted.

wag *v.* To move quickly from side to side or up and down. *n.* A playful, witty person. **waggish** *adj.*, **wagger** *n.*

wage *n.* A payment of money for labor or services. *v.* To conduct. **-less** *adj.*

wa-ger *v.* To make a bet. **wager** *n.*

wag-on *n.* A four-wheeled vehicle used to transport goods; a station wagon; a child's four-wheeled cart with a long handle.

wail *n.* A loud, mournful cry or weep. *n.* To make such a sound.

waist *n.* The narrow part of the body between the thorax and hips; the middle part or section of something which is narrower than the rest. **waisted** *adj.*

wait-er *n.* A man who serves food at a restaurant.

wait-ress *n.* A woman who serves food at a restaurant.

wake *v.* To come to consciousness, as from sleep. *n.* A vigil for a dead body; the surface turbulence caused by a vessel moving through water.

walk *v.* To move on foot over a surface; to pass over, go on, or go through by walking; in baseball, to advance to first base after four balls have been pitched. **walker** *n.*

walk-out *n.* A labor strike against a company.

wall *n.* A vertical structure to separate or enclose an area. *v.* To provide or close up, as with a wall.

wal-la-by *n.* A small or medium-sized kangaroo.

wal-let *n.* A flat folding case for carrying paper money.

wal-lop *n.* A powerful blow; an impact. *v.* To move with disorganized haste. **walloper** *n.*

wal-nut *n.* An edible nut with a hard, light-brown shell; the tree on which this nut grows.

wal-rus *n.*

A large marine mammal of the seal family, having flippers, tusks, and a tough hide.

waltz *n.* A ballroom dance in 3/4 time;

music for a waltz. *v.* To dance a waltz; to advance successfully and easily.

wam-pum *n.* Polished shells, once used as currency by North American Indians. *Slang* Money.

wand *n.* A slender rod used by a magician.

wan-der *v.* To travel about aimlessly; to roam; to stray. **wanderer** *n.*

wane *v.* To decrease in size or extent; to decrease gradually. *n.* A gradual deterioration.

wan-gle *v.* To resort to devious methods in order to obtain something wanted. **wangler** *n.*

want *v.* To wish for or desire; to need; to lack; to fail to possess a required amount; to hunt in order to apprehend. *n.* The state of lacking a required or usual amount. **wanting** *adj.*

war *n.* An armed conflict among states or nations; a state of discord; the science of military techniques or procedures.

ward *n.* A section in a hospital for certain patients requiring similar treatment; a person under protection or surveillance. *v.* To keep watch over someone or something.

ware *n.* Manufactured items of the same general kind; items or goods for sale.

ware-house *n.* A large building used to store merchandise. **warehouse** *v.*

warm *adj.* Moderate heat; neither hot or cold; comfortably established; marked by a strong feeling; having pleasant feelings.

warn *v.* To give notice or inform beforehand; to call to one's attention; to alert.

warp *v.* To become bent out of shape; to deviate from a proper course. *n.* The condition of being twisted or bent; threads running down the length of a fabric.

war-rant *n.* A written authorization giving the holder legal power to search, seize, or arrest. *v.* To provide a reason; to give proof. **warrantable** *adj.*, **warrantor** *n.*

war-ri-or *n.* One who fights in a war or battle.

war-y *adj.* Marked by caution.

wash *v.* To cleanse by the use of water; to remove dirt; to move or deposit as if by the force of water. *n.* A process or instance of washing; a group of soiled clothes or linens.

wash-and-wear *adj.* Requiring little or no ironing after washing.

wash-board *n.* A corrugated board on which clothes are rubbed in the process of washing; an uneven surface as a washboard.

washed-out *adj.*, *Slang* Tired.

wash-er *n.* A small disk usually made of rubber or metal having a hole in the center, used with nuts and bolts; a washing machine.

wash-ing *n.* Clothes and other articles that are washed or to be washed; cleaning.

was-n't *contr.* Was not.

wasp *n.* Any of various insects, having a slim body with a constricted abdomen, the female capable of inflicting a painful sting.

waste *v.* To be thrown away; to be available but not used completely. *n.* A barren region; the instance of wasting; useless material produced as a byproduct. *Slang* To destroy or murder. **wasteful** *adj.*, **waster** *n.*

watch *v.* To view carefully; to guard; to keep informed. *n.* The act of staying awake to guard or protect; a small timepiece worn on the wrist, designed to keep the correct time of day.

watch-dog *n.* A dog trained to guard someone or his property.

watch-ful *adj.* Carefully observant or attentive. **watchfully** *adv.*

watch-man *n.* A person hired to keep watch; a guard.

wa-ter *n.* The clear liquid making up oceans, lakes, and streams; the body fluids as tears or urine. *v.* To pour or spray on water on something or someone; to give water to drink; to weaken or dilute with water.

wa-ter moc-ca-sin *n.* A venomous snake from the lowlands and swampy areas of the southern United States.

wa-ter po-lo *n.* A water game between two teams, the object of which is to get a ball into the opponent's goal.

wa-ter pow-er *n.* The power or energy produced by swift-moving water.

wa-ter-proof *adj.* Capable of preventing water from penetrating. *v.* To make or treat in order to make waterproof. *n.* A material or fabric which is waterproof.

wa-ter--re-pel-lant *adj.* A material or product treated to resist water, but not completely waterproof.

wa-ter-shed *n.* The raised area between two regions that divides two sections drained by different river sources.

wa-ter--ski *v.* To travel over water on a pair of short, broad skis while being pulled by a motorboat.

wa-ter-spout *n.* A tube or pipe through which water is discharged; a funnel-shaped column of spray and mist whirling over an ocean or lake.

wa-ter ta-ble *n.* The upper limit of the portion of the ground completely saturated with water.

wa-ter-tight *adj.* Closed or sealed so tightly that no water can enter, leaving no chance for evasion.

wa-ter-way *n.* A navigable body of water; a channel for water.

wa-ter-y *adj.* Containing water; diluted; lacking effectiveness. **wateriness** *n.*

watt *n.* A unit of electrical power represented by current of one ampere, produced by the electromotive force of one volt.

wave *v.* To move back and forth or up and down; to motion with the hand. *n.* A swell or moving ridge of water; a curve or curl, as in the hair.

wa-ver *v.* To sway unsteadily; to move back and forth; to weaken in force. **waver** *n.*, **waveringly** *adv.*

wax *n.* A natural yellowish substance made by bees, solid when cold and easily melted or softened when heated. **waxy** *adj.*

way *n.* A manner of doing something; a tendency or characteristic; a habit or customary manner of acting or living; a direction; freedom to do as one chooses.

way-lay *v.* To attack by ambush.

way-ward *adj.* Unruly; unpredictable.

we *pl., pron.* Used to refer to the person speaking and one or more other people.

weak *adj.* Having little energy or strength; easily broken; having inadequate skills; not reasonable or convincing. **weakness** *n.*, **weakly** *adv.*

wealth *n.* An abundance of valuable possessions or property; all goods and resources having monetary value.

wealth-y *adj.* Having much wealth or money; abundant; rich.

wean *v.* To accustom an infant or small child to food other than a mother's milk or bottle.

weap-on *n.* A device used in fighting a war; a device which can be used to harm another person.

wear *v.* To have on or put something on the body; to display. *n.* The act of wearing out or using up; the act of wearing, as clothing. **wearable** *adj.*

wea-ri-some *adj.* Tedious, boring or tiresome.

wea-ry *adj.* Exhausted; tired; feeling fatigued. *v.* To make or become tired; to become fatigued. **-ily** *adv.*, **-iness** *n.*

wea-sel *n.* A mammal with a long tail and short legs; a sly, sneaky person.

weath-er *n.* The condition of the air or atmosphere in terms of humidity, temperature, and similar features. *v.* To become worn by the actions of weather; to survive.

weather vane *n.*

A device that turns, indicating the direction of the wind.

weave *v.* To make a basket, cloth, or 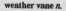 other item by interlacing threads or other strands of material. **weaver** *n.*

web *n.*

A cobweb; a piece of interlacing material which forms a woven structure; something constructed as an entanglement; a thin membrane that joins the toes of certain water birds.

wed *v.* To take as a spouse; to marry.

we'd *contr.* We had; we should.

wed-ding *n.* A marriage ceremony; an act

of joining together in close association.

wedge n. A tapered, triangular piece of wood or metal used to split logs, to add leverage, and to hold something open or ajar. v. To force or make something fit tightly.

wed-lock n. Marriage; the state of being married.

weed n. An unwanted plant which interferes with the growth of grass, vegetables, or flowers.

week n. A period of seven days, beginning with Sunday and ending with Saturday; the time or days normally spent at school or work.

week-day n. Any day of the week except Saturday or Sunday.

week-end n. The end of the week from the period of Friday evening through Sunday evening.

week-ly adv. Every week; once a week. adj. Taking place or done every week of or relating to a week.

weep v. To shed tears; to express sorrow, joy, or emotion; by shedding tears; to cry. **weeper** n.

wee-vil n. A small beetle having a downwardcurving snout, which damages plants.

weigh v. To determine the heaviness of an object by using a scale; to consider carefully in one's mind; to be of a particular weight; to oppress or burden.

weight n. The amount that something weighs; heaviness; a heavy object used to hold or pull something down; an overpowering force; the quality of a garment for a particular season. v. To make heavy.

weight-less adj. Lacking the pull of gravity; having little weight.

weight-y adj. Burdensome; important.

weird adj. Having an extraordinary or strange character. **weirdly** adv.

weird-o n., Slang A person who is very strange.

wel-come v. To extend warm hospitality; to accept gladly. adj. Received warmly. n. A greeting upon one's arrival.

weld v. To unite metallic parts by applying heat and sometimes pressure, allowing the metals to bond together. n. A joint formed by welding.

wel-fare n. The state of doing well; governmental aid to help the disabled or disadvantaged.

well n. A hole in the ground which contains a supply of water; a shaft in the ground through which gas and oil are obtained. adj. Being in good health; in an agreeable state.

we'll contr. We will; we shall.

well--be-ing n. The state of being healthy, happy, or prosperous.

well--done adj. Completely cooked; done properly.

well--groomed adj. Clean, neat, and properly cared for.

well--known adj. Widely known.

well--man-nered adj. Polite; having good manners.

well--mean-ing adj. Having good intentions.

well--to--do adj. Having more than enough wealth.

welsh v., Slang To cheat by avoiding a payment to someone; to neglect an obligation. **welsher** n.

welt n. A strip between the sole and upper part of a shoe; a slight swelling on the body, usually caused by a blow to the area. v. To hit severly.

wel-ter-weight n. A boxer weighing between 136 and 147 pounds.

went v. Past tense of go.

wept v. Past tense of weep.

were v. Second person singular past plural of be.

we're contr. We are.

were-n't contr. Were not.

west n. The direction of the setting sun; the direction to the left of a person standing north. adj. At, of, or from the west. adv. To or toward the west.

western adj.

whack v. To strike with a hard blow, to slap. n. An attempt.

whale n.

A very large mammal resembling a fish which lives in salt water. Slang An outstanding or impressive example.

wharf n. A pier or platform built at the edge of water so that ships can load and unload.

what pron. Which one; which things; which type or kind. adv. In which way. adj. Which particular one.

what-ev-er pron. Everything or anything. adj. No matter what. Slang Which thing or things.

what's contr. What is.

wheat n. A grain ground into flour, used to make breads and similar foods.

wheel n. A circular disk which turns on an axle; an apparatus having the same principles of a wheel; something which resembles the motion or shape of a wheel. v. To move on or as if by wheels; to turn around a central axis; to rotate, pivot, or turn around.

wheel-bar-row n. A vehicle having one wheel, used to transport small loads.

wheel-chair n. A mobile chair for disabled persons.

wheel-er n. Anything that has wheels.

wheeze v. To breathe with a hoarse whistling sound. n. A high whistling sound.

whelk v. Any of various large water snails, sometimes edible.

when adv. At what time; at which time. pron. What or which time. conj. While; at the time that; although.

whence adv. From what source or place; from which.

when-ev-er adv. At any time; when. conj. At whatever time.

where adv. At or in what direction or place; in what direction or place.

where-a-bouts *adv.* Near, at, or in a particular location. *n.* The approximate location.

where-as *conj.* It being true or the fact; on the confrary.

where-by *conj.* Through or by which.

wher-ev-er *adv.* In any situation or place.

whet *v.* To make sharp; to stimulate.

weth-er *conj.* Indicating a choice; alternative possibilities; either.

whet-stone *n.* A stone used to sharpen scissors, knives, and other implements.

whew *n., interj.* Used to express relief; or tiredness.

whey *n.* The clear, water-like part of milk that separates from the curd.

which *pron.* What one or ones; the one previously; whatever one or ones; whichever. *adj.* What one; any one of.

which-ev-er *pron.* Any; no matter which or what.

whiff *n.* A slight puff; a light current of air; a slight breath or odor.

while *n.* A length or period of time.
conj. During the time that; even though; at the same time; although.

whim *n.* A sudden desire or impulse.

whim-per *v.* To make a weak, soft crying sound. **whimper** *n.*

whim-si-cal *adj.* Impulsive; erratic; light and spontaneous. **whimsically** *adv.*

whine *v.* To make a squealing, plaintive sound; to complain in an irritating, childish fashion.

whin-ny *v.* To neigh in a soft gentle way.

whip *v.* To spank repeatedly with a rod or stick; to punish by whipping; to move in a motion similar to whipping or beating. *n.* A flexible stick or rod used to herd or beat animals; a dessert made by whipping ingredients; the utensil used to do so. *Slang* To overcome. **whipper** *n.*

whip-lash *n.* An injury to the spine or neck caused by a sudden jerking motion of the head.

whip-poor-will *n.* A brownish nocturnal bird of North America.

whir *v.* To move with a low purring sound.

whirl *v.* To rotate or move in circles; to twirl; to move, drive, or go very fast. *n.* A rapid whirling motion. **whirler** *n.*

whirl-pool *n.* A circular current of water.

whirl-wind *n.* A violently whirling mass of air; a tornado.

whirl-y-bird *n., Slang* A helicopter.

whisk *v.* To move with a sweeping motion; to move quickly or lightly. *n.* A sweeping movement; a utensil used in cooking; to stir.

whisk-er *n.*

The hair that grows on a man's face; the long hair near the mouth of dogs, cats, and other animals. **whiskers** A man's beard.

whis-key *n.* An alcoholic beverage distilled from rye, barley, or corn.

whis-per *v.* To speak in a very low tone;

to tell in secret. *n.* A low rustling sound; the act of whispering.

whis-tle *v.* To make a clear shrill sound by blowing air through the teeth, through puckered lips, or through a special instrument. *n.* A device used to make a whistling sound. **whistler** *n.*

white-cap *n.* A wave having a top of white foam.

with-er *adv.* To what state, place, or circumstance; wherever.

whit-tle *v.* To cut or carve off small shavings from wood with a knife; to remove or reduce gradually. -**ler** *n.*

who *pron.* Which or what certain individual, person, or group; referring to a person previously mentioned.

who'd *contr.* Who would; who had.

who-ev-er *pron.* Whatever person; all or any persons.

whole *adj.* Complete; having nothing missing; not divided or in pieces; a complete system or unity; everything considered. *Math* Not a fraction.
wholeness *n.*

whole-heart-ed *adj.* Sincere; totally committed; holding nothing back.

whole-sale *n.* The sale of goods in large amounts to a retailer. *adj.* Relating to or having to do with such a sale. *v.* To sell wholesale. **wholesaler** *n.*

whole-some *adj.* Contributing to good mental or physical health.
wholesomely *adv.*, **wholesomeness** *n.*

whole wheat *adj.* Made from the wheat kernel with nothing removed.

who'll *contr.* Who shall; who will.

whol-ly *adv.* Totally; exclusively.

whom *pron.* The form of who used as the direct object of a verb or the object of the preposition.

whom-ev-er *pron.* The form of whoever used as the object of a preposition or the direct object of a verb.

whoop-ing cough *n.* An infectious disease of the throat and breathing passages in which the patient has spasms of coughing often followed by gasps for breath.

whoop-ing crane *n.* A large bird of North America, nearly extinct, having long legs and a high, shrill cry.

whoosh *v.* To make a rushing or gushing sound, as a rush of air.

whop-per *n.* Something of extraordinary size. *Slang* A lie.

whore *n.* A prostitute.

who's *contr.* Who is; who has.

whose *pron.* Belonging to or having to do with one's belongings. *adj.* Relating to *which* or *whom.*

why *adj.* For what reason or purpose. *conj.* The cause, purpose, or reason for which. *interj.* Expressing surprise or disagreement.

wick *n.* The soft strand of fibers which extends from a candle or lamp and draws up the fuel for burning.

wick-er *n.* A thin, pliable twig used to make furniture and baskets.

wick-et *n.* A wire hoop in the game of croquet; a small door, window, or opening used as a box office.

wide *adj.* Broad; covering a large area; completely extended or open. *adv.* Over a large area; full extent.

wide-spread *adj.* Fully spread out; over a broad area.

wid-ow *n.* A woman whose husband is no longer living.

wid-ow-er *n.* A man whose wife is no longer living.

width *n.* The distance or extent of something from side to side.

wield *v.* To use or handle something skillfully; to employ power effectively.

wie-ner *n.* A frankfurter; a hot dog.

wife *n.* A married female.

wig *n.* Artificial or human hair woven together to cover baldness or a bald spot on the head.

wig-gle *v.* To squirm; to move with rapid side-to-side motions. **wiggler** *n.*

wig-wam *n.* An Indian dwelling place.

wild *adj.* Living in a natural, untamed state; not occupied by man; not civilized; strange and unusual.

wil-der-ness *n.* An unsettled area; a region left in its uncultivated or natural state.

wild-life *n.* Animals and plants living in their natural environments.

wil-low *n.* A large tree, usually having narrow leaves and slender flexible twigs.

wilt *v.* To cause or to become limp; to lose force; to deprive of courage or energy.

win *v.* To defeat others; to gain victory in a contest; to receive. *n.* Victory; the act of winning. **winner** *n.*

winch *n.* An apparatus with one or more drums on which a cable or rope is wound, used to lift heavy loads.

wind *n.* A natural movement of air. *v.* To become short of breath. **windy** *adj.*

wind *v.* To wrap around and around something; to turn, to crank. *n.* A turning or twisting.

wind-mill *n.* A machine operated or powered by the wind.

win-dow *n.* An opening built into a wall for light and air; a pane of glass.

win-dow--shop *v.* To look at merchandise in store windows without going inside to buy. **window-shopper** *n.*

wind-pipe *n.* The passage in the neck used for breathing; the trachea.

wine *n.* A drink containing 10-15% alcohol by volume, made by fermenting grapes.

wink *v.* To shut one eye as a signal or message; to blink rapidly. *n.* The act of winking; a short period of rest; a nap.

win-ning *adj.* Defeating others; captivating. *n.* Victory.

win-some *adj.* Very pleasant; charming.

win-ter *n.* The coldest season, coming between autumn and spring. *adj.* Relating to or typically of winter.

wipe *v.* To clean by rubbing; to take off by rubbing. *n.* The act or instance of wiping.

wis-dom *n.* The ability to understand what is right, true, or enduring; good judgment; knowledge.

wise *adj.* Having superior intelligence; having great learning; having a capacity for sound judgment marked by deep understanding. **wisely** *adv.*

wise-crack *n.*, *Slang* A witty remark or joke usually showing a lack of respect.

wish *v.* To desire or long for something; to command or request. *n.* A longing or desire.

wish-bone *n.* The bone of a bird, which, according to the superstition, when broken brings good luck to the person who has the longer end.

wish-ful *adj.* Having or expressing a wish; hopeful. **wishfully** *adv.*

wisp *n.* A tuft or small bundle of hay, straw, or hair; a thin piece. **wispy** *adj.*

wit *n.* The ability to use words in a clever way; a sense of humor.

with *prep.* In the company of; near or alongside; having, wearing or bearing; in the judgment or opinion of; containing; in the possession or care of; supporting; among; occurring at the same time. *v.* To take away or back; to retreat.

with-draw *v.* To take away; to take back; to remove; to retreat.

whither *v.* To dry up or wilt from a lack of moisture; to lose freshness and vigor.

with-hold *n.* To hold back or keep.

withholding tax *n.* The tax on income held back by an employer in payment of one's income tax.

with-in *adv.* Inside the inner part; inside the limits; inside the limits of time, distance, or degree. *n.* An inside area.

with-out *adv.* On the outside; not in possession of. *prep.* Something or someone lacking.

with-stand *v.* To endure.

wit-ness *n.* A person who has seen, experienced, or heard something; something serving as proof or evidence. *v.* To see or hear something; to give proof or evidence of; to give testimony.

wit-ty *adj.* Amusing or cleverly humorous.

wiz-ard *n.* A very clever person; a person thought to have magical powers. *Slang* One with amazing skill.

wob-ble *v.* To move unsteadily from side to side, as a rocking motion.

woe *n.* Great sorrow or grief; misfortune.

wok *n.* A convex metal cooker for stir-frying food.

woke *v.* Past tense of wake.

wolf *n.* A carnivorous animal found in northern areas; a fierce person. *v.* To eat quickly and with greed. **wolfish** *adj.*, **wolfishly** *adv.*

woman *n.* The mature adult human female; a person who has feminine qualities.

womanhood *n.* The state of being a woman.

womb *n.* The uterus; the place where development occurs.

won *v.* Past tense of win.

won-der n. A feeling of amazement or admiration. v. To feel admiration; to feel uncertainty. **wonderful** adj.

won-der-ment n. A feeling or state of amazement.

won-drous adj. Wonderful; marvelous.

won't contr. Will not.

won-ton n. A noodle dumpling filled with minced pork and served in soup.

wood n. The hard substance which makes up the main part of trees. adj. Made of wood. **woods** n. A growth of trees smaller than a forest.

wood-chuck n.

A rodent having short legs and a heavyset body, which lives in a burrow.

wood-en adj. Made of wood; resembling wood; stiff; lifeless; lacking flexibility.

wood-peck-er n. A bird which uses its bill for drilling holes in trees looking for insects to eat.

wood-wind n. A group of musical instruments which produce sounds when air is blown through the mouthpiece, as the clarinet, flute, and oboe.

wool n. The soft, thick hair of sheep and other such mammals; a fabric made from such hair.

word n. A meaningful sound which stands for an idea; a comment; a brief talk; an order or command. v. To express orally. **wording** n.

word proc-ess-ing n. A system which produces typewritten documents with automated type and editing equipment.

work n. The action or labor required to accomplish something; employment; a job; a project or assignment; something requiring physical or mental effort. v. To engage in mental or physical exertion; to labor to have a job; to arrange. **worker** n.

work-out n. A period of strenuous exercise.

world n. The planet Earth; the universe; the human race; a field of human interest or effort.

worldly adj. Interested in pleasure rather than religious or spiritual matters.

worm n.

A small, thin animal having a long, flexible, rounded or flattened body. Slang A crude person.

worn adj. Made weak or thin from use; exhausted.

wor-ry v. To be concerned or troubled; to tug at repeatedly; to annoy; to irritate. n. Distress or mental anxiety.

wor-ship n. Reverence for a sacred object; high esteem or devotion for a person. v. To revere; attend a religious service. **worshiper** n.

worst adj. Bad; most inferior; most disagreeable adv. In the worst degree.

worth n. The quality or value of something; personal merit; the quantity that can be purchased for a certain amount of money.

wor-thy adj. Valuable or useful; deserving admiration or honor.

would-n't contr. Would not.

wound n. A laceration of the skin. v. To injure by tearing, cutting, or piercing the skin.

wow interj. An expression of amazement, surprise, or excitement.

wran-gle v. To quarrel noisily. -ler n.

wrath n. Violent anger or fury.

wreak v. To inflict punishment upon another person.

wreath n. A decorative ring-like form of intertwined flowers, bows, and other articles.

wreck v. To ruin or damage by accident or deliberately; to spoil. n. Destruction; the remains of something wrecked or ruined; someone in poor condition.

wren n. A small brown songbird having a slender beak, short tail, and rounded wings.

wrench n.

A tool used to grip, turn, or twist an object as a bolt or nut.

v. To turn or twist violently; to give emotional pain.

wrest v. To twist or pull away in a violent way. n. A forcible twist.

wres-tle v. To struggle with an opponent in order to pin him down. n. The instance of wrestling. **wrestler** n.

wretch n. An extremely unhappy person; a miserable person. **wretched** adj.

wrig-gle v. To squirm; to move by turning and twisting.

wring v. To squeeze and twist by hand or machine; to press together.

wrin-kle n. A small crease on the skin or on fabric. v. To have or make wrinkles.

wrist n., Anat. The joint of the body between the hand and forearm; the part of a sleeve which encircles the wrist.

writ n., Law A written court document directed to a public official or individual ordering a specific action.

write v. To form symbols or letters; to form words on a surface.

writhe v. To twist, as in pain; to suffer greatly with pain.

writ-ing n. A book or other written work; handwriting; the process of forming letters into words; the occupation of a writer.

wrong adj. Incorrect; against moral standards; not suitable; immoral; unsuitable; inappropriate. n. An act which is wicked or immoral. v. To do wrong; to injure or hurt. **wrongly** adv.

wrote v. Past tense of write.

wrought adj. Fashioned; formed; beaten or hammered into shape.

wrung v. Past tense of wring.

X, x The twenty-fourth letter of the English alphabet.

Xan-a-du *n.* A place having idyllic beauty.

xan-thate *n.* Ester or slat of a xanthic acid.

xan-thic *adj.* The color yellow or all colors that tend toward the color yellow when relating to flowers.

xan-thin *n.* A carotenoid pigment that is soluble in alcohol.

xan-thine *n.* A crystalline nitrogen compound, closely related to uric acid, found in blood, urine and certain plant and animal tissues.

xan-tho-chroid *adj.* Pertaining to the light-complexioned caucasoid race.

xan-tho-ma *n.* A skin condition of the eyelids marked by small, yellow, raised nodules or plates.

X chro-mo-some *n.* The sex female chromosome, associated with female characteristics; occurs paired in the female and single in the male chromosome pair.

xe-bec *n.* A small vessel with three-masts having both leteen and square sails.

xe-nic *adj.* Relating to, or employing a culture medium that contains one or more unidentified organisms.

xe-non *n.* The colorless, odorless gaseous element found in small quantities in the air, symbolized by Xe.

xe-no-phile *n.* One attracted to foreign people, styles, manners, etc.

xen-o-phobe *n.* A person who dislikes, fears, and mistrusts foreigners or anything strange. **xenophobia** *n.*

xe-rarch *adj.* Originating or developing in a dry place.

xe-ric *adj.* Relating to or requiring only a small amount of moisture. **-ally** *adv.*

xe-roph-i-lous *adj.* Tolerant or characteristic of xeric environments. **xerophily** *n.*

xe-roph-thal-mi-a *n.* A itching soreness of the eyes that is caused by an insufficient amount of vitamin A. **-ic** *adj.*

xe-ro-phyte *n.* A plant that can live in a surrounding of extreme heat and drought. **xerophytic** *adj.*, **xerophytically** *adv.*, **xerophytism** *n.*

X--ra-di-a-tion *n.* Treatment with X-rays.

X ray *n.* Energy that is radiated with a short wavelength and high penetrating power; a black and white negative image or picture of the interior of the body.

x--sec-tion *n.* Cross section of something. **x-sectional** *adj.*

xy-lo-phone *n.*

A musical instrument consisting of mounted wooden bars which produce a ringing musical sound when struck with two small wooden hammers.

xy-lose *n.* A crystalline aldose sugar.

xy-lot-o-mous *adj.* Capable of cutting or boring wood. **xylotomic** *adj.*

Y, y The twenty-fifth letter of the English alphabet.

yacht *n.* A small sailing vessel powdered by wind or motor, used for pleasure cruises. **yacht** *v.*

yacht-ing *n.* The sport of sailing in a yacht.

yachts-man *n.* A person who sails a yacht. **yachtmanship** *n.*

yak *n.* A longhaired ox of Tibet and the mountains of central Asia.

yam *n.*

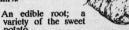

An edible root; a variety of the sweet potato.

Yan-kee *n.* A native of the northern United States. **Yankee** *adj.*

yap *v.* To bark in a high pitched, sharp way. *Slang* To talk in a relentess, loud, or stupid manner.

yard *n.* A unit of measure that equals 36 inches or 3 feet; the ground around or near a house or building.

yard goods *n.* Fabric that is sold by the yard.

yard-man *n.* A person employed as a worker in a railroad yard.

yard-mas-ter *n.* A person in charge of a railroad yard.

yard-stick *n.* A graduated measuring stick that equals 1 yard or 36 inches; standard of measurement.

yarn *n.* Twisted fibers, as of wool, used in knitting or weaving. *Slang* An involved tale or story.

yawn *v.* To inhale a deep breath with the mouth open wide. **yawn, yawner** *n.*

yawn-ing *adj.* Expressing tiredness by a yawn.

Y-Chro-mo-some *n.* The sex chromosome associated with male characteristics.

ye *pron.* You, used especially in religious contexts, as hymns.

yea *adv.* Yes; indeed; truly.

yeah *adv.*, *Slang* Yes.

year *n.* A period of time starting on January 1st and continuing through December 31st, consisting of 365 days or 366 days in a leap year.

year-book *n.* A book printed each year giving facts about the year; a book printed each year for a high school, college, etc.

year-ling *n.* An animal that is one year old.

year-ly *adj.* Pertaining to something that happens, appears, or comes once a year, every year.

yearn *v.* To feel a strong craving; deep desire; a wistful feeling. **yearner, yearning** *n.*

year--round *adj.* Lasting or continuing for an entire year.

yeast *n.* Fungi or plant cells used to make baked goods rise or fruit juices ferment.

yell *v.* To cry out loudly. *n.* A loud cry; a cheer to show support for an athletic team.

yel·low *n.* The bright color of a lemon; the yolk of an egg. *v.* To make or become yellow. *adj.* Of the color yellow. *Slang* Cowardly.

yel·low fev·er *n.* An acute infectious disease of the tropics, spread by the bite of a mosquito.

yel·low-jack·et *n.* A small wasp, having bright yellow markings, and usually makes its nest below ground level.

yelp *n.* A quick, sharp, shrill cry, as from pain.

yen *n.* An intense craving or longing.

yeo·man *n.* The owner of a small farm; a petty officer who acts as a clerk.

yes *adv.* To express agreement.

yes·ter·day *n.* The day before today; a former or recent time. *adv.* On the day before the present day.

yet *adv.* Up to now; at this time; even now; more so. *conj.* Nevertheless; but.

yew *n.* An evergreen tree having poisonous flat, dark-green needles and poisonous red berries.

Yid·dish *n.* A language spoken by Jews combining German and Hebrew; spoken by Jews. Yiddish *adj.*

yield *v.* To bear or bring forward; to give up the possession of something; to give way to. *n.* An amount that is produced.

yield·ing *adj.* Ready to yield, comply, or submit; unresisting. yieldingly *adv.*

YMCA *abbr., n.* Young Men's Christian Association.

yo·del *v.* To sing in a way so that the voice changes from normal to a high shrill sound and then back again. yodeler *n.*

yo·ga *n.* A system of exercises which helps the mind and the body in order to achieve tranquillity and spiritual insight.

yo·gurt *n.* A thick custard-like food made from curdled milk and often mixed with fruit.

yoke *n.* A wooden bar used to join together two oxen or other animals working together; the section of a garment fitting closely around the shoulders. *v.* To join with a yoke.

yo·del *n.* A very unsophisticated country person; a bumpkin.

yolk *n.* The yellow nutritive part of an egg.

Yom Kip·pur *n.* The Jewish holiday observed with fasting and prayer for the forgiveness of sins.

you *pron.* The person or persons addressed.

you all *pron., Slang* y'all A southern variation used for two or more people in direct address.

you'd *contr.* You had; you would.

you'll *contr.* You will; you shall.

young *adj.* Of or relating to the early stage of life; not old. *n.* The offspring of an animal. youngster *n.*

your *adj.* Belonging to you or yourself or the person spoken to.

yuc·ca *n.* A tropical plant having large, white flowers and long, pointed leaves.

Z, z The twenty-sixth letter of the English alphabet.

za·ny *n., pl* -nies A clown; a person who acts silly or foolish. *adj.* Typical of being clownish.

zaniness *n.*, zannily *adv.*

zap *v., Slang* To destroy; to do away with.

zeal *n.* Great interest or eagerness.

zeal·ot *n.* A fanatical person; a fanatic.

zeal·ous *adj.* Full of interest; eager; passionate. -ly *adv.*, zealousness *n.*

ze·bra *n.*

An African mammal of the horse family having black or brown stripes on a white body.

zeph·yr *n.* A gentle breeze.

ze·ro *n., pl.* -ros, -roes The number or symbol "0"; nothing; the point from which degrees or measurements on a scale begin; the lowest point. *v.* To aim, point at, or close in on. *adj.* Pertaining to zero; nonexisting.

zest *n.* Enthusiasm; a keen quality.

zestful *adj.*, zestfully, *adv.*, zesty *adj.*

zig·zag *n.* A pattern with sharp turns in alternating directions. *adv.* To move in a zigzag course or path. zigzag *v.*

zilch *n., Slang* Nothing; zero.

zil·lion *n., Slang* An extremely large number.

zinc *n.* A bluish-white crystalline metallic element, used as a protective coating for steel and iron, symbolized by Zn.

Zi·on *n.* The Jewish homeland, symbolic of Judaism; the Jewish people.

zip *v.* To act or move with vigor or speed. *v.* To move with energy, speed, or facility; to open or close with a zipper. *Slang* Energy; zero; nothing.

zip code *n.* The system to speed the delivery of mail by assigning a five digit number, plus four to each postal delivery location in the United States.

zip·per *n.* A fastener consisting of two rows of plastic or metal teeth that are interlocked by means of sliding a tab. zippered *adj.*

zir·co·ni·um *n.* A metallic element symbolized by Zr.

zit *n., Slang* A pimple.

zo·di·ac *n.* The celestial sphere; the unseen path followed through the heavens by the moon, sun, and most planets; this area divided into twelve parts or twelve astrological signs, each bearing the name of a constellation. zodiacal *adj.*

zo·ol·o·gy *n.* The science that deals with animals, animal life, and the animal kingdom. zoologist *n.*

zoom *v.* To move with a continuous, loud, buzzing sound; to move upward sharply; to move toward a subject with great speed.

zy·mo·scope *n.* An instrument that measures yeast's fermenting power.